Piety and the People

St Andrews Studies in Reformation History

Editorial Board:

Andrew Pettegree, Bruce Gordon and John Guy

Piety and the People

Religious Printing in French

1511-1551

FRANCIS M. HIGMAN

SCOLAR
PRESS

Published by
SCOLAR PRESS
Gower House
Croft Road
Aldershot
Hants GU11 3HR
England

Ashgate Publishing Company
Old Post Road
Brookfield
Vermont 05036-9704
USA

British Library Cataloguing in Publication Data

Higman, Francis M.
    Piety and the People: Religious Printing in French, 1511-1551.
    (St Andrews Studies in Reformation History)
    1. French literature — 16th century — Bibliography. 2. Christian literature, French — 16th century — Bibliography. 3. Printing — France — History — 16th century.
    I. Title.
    016.8'483'08'0382

    ISBN 1-85928-350-0

Library of Congress Cataloging-in-Publication Data

Higman, Francis M.
    Piety and the people: religious printing in French, 1511-1551/ Francis Higman.
        p. cm.
    (St Andrews Studies in Reformation History)
    Includes bibliographical references and index.
    ISBN 1-85928-350-0 (cloth)
    1. France — Church history — 16th century — Bibliography. 2. Reformation — France. 3. Counter-Reformation — France. 4. Christian literature, French — Bibliography. I. Title. II. Series
    Z286.R4H54 1996
    [BR370]
    016.2744'06—dc 20   96-26140
                                                                          CIP

    ISBN 1 85928 350 0

Printed in Great Britain by Ipswich Book Co. Ltd., Ipswich, Suffolk.

Contents

Foreword   vii

Introduction   1

List of works consulted   35

1   Alphabetical list   45

2   Finding list of anonymous titles   401

3   Chronological list   405

4   List of printers by city   457

5   Printers: alphabetical   525

Index of proper names   529

In memory of Gilbert Gadoffre

Foreword

This book has been too long in gestation. It began, nearly a quarter of a century ago, as a preliminary investigation for a linguistic study. My intention was to define the influence of the Reformation on the evolution of the French language. It was my late, dear friend Gilbert Gadoffre who pointed out that, unlike the case of Germany, the French Reformation had never been the object of a thorough bibliographical investigation, and that such an investigation was a necessary starting point for all the rest.

What began as a list of Reformation printing evolved over the years, thanks in particular to Jean-François Gilmont, who suggested that the investigation should not be limited to Reformation printing (the limits of which proved impossible to define), but extended to include all religious printing in French of whatever nature. He also suggested the chronological limits (explained in the Introduction) of the survey. For his advice, and for innumerable other acts of guidance and of friendship, I am deeply grateful.

An exploration of this nature is open-ended, in that there are always more libraries to be explored, more catalogues to read, more editions to identify. After years of gradual accumulation of material, I was finally pushed into publication by Andrew Pettegree, who kindly invited me to publish the results in the St Andrews Reformation Studies series. Without his warm encouragement, the work might have remained for ever in limbo.

I present this study with a lively sense of its inadequacies. The artisanal nature of my bibliographical descriptions, especially those done twenty years ago, is matched by my tenuous hold on the rapidly evolving mysteries of word-processing. There are certain to be errors, for which I plead indulgence. I can only hope that the positive information conveyed outweighs the blemishes.

I owe thanks to more people than can be named for help in the preparation of this work. Nicole Bingen, Jennifer Britnell, Bettye Chambers, Geneviève Guilleminot-Chrétien, Frank Hieronymus, Hélène Piccard, Stephen Rawles, Michael Screech, David Shaw and Jeanne Veyrin-Forrer have all generously shared their learning and their wise counsel at one time or another, and they have my deepest gratitude. A special word of thanks and of commemoration is due to two dear colleagues no longer with us: Brigitte Moreau and Rodolphe Peter. Each of them was a shining example of the *république des lettres* at its best, and I, among many others, was privileged to benefit from their learning and their generosity. The patient library staffs of many libraries have coped with my enquiries and requests over the years; I would mention in particular the staffs of Trinity College, Dublin, the University Libraries of Nottingham, Lausanne and Geneva; the British Library; the Paris libraries, especially the Bibliothèque Nationale, Arsenal, Mazarine, Sainte Geneviève, École des Beaux Arts, and the Société de l'Histoire du protestantisme français; the Herzog-August-Bibliothek, Wolfenbüttel, the Bayerische Staatsbibliothek, Munich, and the Österreichische Nationalbibliothek, Vienna.

The basis of this work has depended on numerous visits to libraries, and these do not come cheap. For financial support in this venture I am grateful to the authorities of Trinity College, Dublin, the University of Nottingham, the British Academy, the Cultural Services of the French government, the Institut francophone de Paris, the Centre d'Études sur la Renaissance, University of Sherbrooke, and the University of Geneva.

Finally, I am grateful to the staff of Scolar Press, and in particular to Caroline Cornish and Elizabeth Teague, for their meticulous work in advising on the preparation of camera-ready copy. And above all, I am profoundly indebted to Marlène Jaouich, Secretary of the Institut d'histoire de la Réformation, Geneva, who has patiently, courageously, and cheerfully performed the immense task of putting the whole work into its final shape.

Francis Higman
Institut d'histoire de la Réformation
University of Geneva

Introduction

Preliminary considerations

The close relationship between printing and the Protestant Reformation of the sixteenth century has long been a scholarly commonplace. By his translation of the Bible, Luther contributed massively to the unification of the German language, we are told. In English, the rich poetry of the Authorized Version has for centuries left an indelible mark on the literature of the English-speaking world. The Protestant stress on the Book as central to religious life implied an emphasis on education, and led to an accelerated growth in literacy rates in Protestant countries.[1]

In countries such as Italy and Spain, where the Reformation never achieved any deep penetration, much less attention has been paid to the possible combined effects of printing and religious change. That the Counter-Reformation created a great surge in educational provision, notably by the Jesuits, is obvious; but the education provided did not touch more than a minority of the population, and mass literacy was much later in coming.

The case of France is more ambiguous. On the one hand there are marked changes discernible in religious printing as a result of the Reformation, and these have been long commented on; on the other, the Reformation ultimately did not take root in France, and French historiography sometimes gives the impression that its impact in France was marginal.[2]

Curiously, however, statements about printing and the French Reformation are based on generalities and approximations, for one simple reason: there has never been a thorough investigation of what actually was produced by printing presses for consumption in France as a result of the Reformation. Yes, there was much printing of works of piety, saints' lives, the works of Jean Gerson, before the Reformation — but how much? Did it disappear? By what stages did an evolution take place?

---

[1] Recent discussions of these points are to be found in Philippe Ariès and Georges Duby (eds), *Histoire de la vie privée 3: De la Renaissance aux Lumières* (Paris, Seuil, 1986), in particular the chapter by Roger Chartier on 'Les pratiques de l'écrit'; Jean-François Gilmont (ed.), *La Réforme et le livre. L'Europe de l'imprimé (1517–c. 1570)* (Paris, Cerf, 1990).

[2] An exhibition in the Bibliothèque nationale, Paris, in 1991, entitled 'Dieu en son Royaume: la Bible en France sous l'Ancien Régime', gave the impression that the Reformation played no part in the evolution of the Bible in French.

What works were available in the early Reformation, where did they come from, and by whom were they written?

The present study is an attempt to provide a solid factual basis for answers to these questions. The bulk of this work is simply a list of all editions of religious works printed in the French language during a given time span (1511-1551). It is necessarily only very provisional. The field is vast, and does not lend itself to convenient questionnaires sent to libraries. Every scholar in the field will doubtless have additional titles and editions to add to those given here. But the objective of this work is to give a basis for further research in the field of the religious, and more widely cultural, impact of the Reformation in the French-speaking world. The centre of interest is not so much the Reformation of the theologians, as the Reformation of the people: what was available to the public at large, what forms of piety were promoted, what mental processes are invoked?

One obvious objection must immediately be addressed: why limit the study to works in French? It is of course true that a considerable proportion of religious literature, both from the Roman Catholic Church and from the Protestants, was in Latin. There is a sense in which the Reformation does not represent the swing from Latin to the vernacular which is often presented: theologians of all persuasions continued to write their major theological works in Latin, as before. But the centre of focus in the present study is the element of change which intervenes, not the continuity. To concentrate on works in French brings out more clearly the growth of a new culture alongside the old, an evolution which would have been submerged had the whole production of religious books been included.

It is of course also true that printing is only one aspect of 'popular piety'. R.W. Scribner's *For the Sake of Simple Folk*[3] draws attention to the central importance, at least in the German Reformation, of visual images, and refuses to concentrate 'more narrowly on printed propaganda alone'. But one of the curious differences between the German and the French Reformations is the relative absence of illustration in works in French. Visual images are rare in works produced in France; and when they are found, they are rarely for 'propaganda' reasons, being decorative and meditative (I have in mind for example the innumerable crucifixions on title pages of devotional

---

[3] R.W. Scribner, *For the Sake of Simple Folk. Popular Propaganda for the German Reformation* (Cambridge, C.U.P., 1981, revised edition 1994). As does Scribner, I use the word 'popular' to mean 'of the people at large', not 'widely acclaimed', 'much sought after'.

works) rather than argumentative. In Reformation printing in strict
terms images are almost entirely lacking.

Another major component of popular piety is of course the sermon, and
devotional and liturgical practices in general. The subject is an important one, and cannot be forgotten. However, the means for investigation
are fragmentary, and usually indirect: most sermons have not survived,
and if they have they are already at one remove from the original spoken
word. One can see the importance of the sermon in, for example, the
registers of the Paris Faculty of Theology,[4] where debates about the
orthodoxy of one preacher or another are frequent. But it is only the
dubious sermons which are mentioned; we learn little from the registers
about sermons which do not step out of line in one sense or another. An
investigation of devotional and liturgical practices would involve an
entirely different approach, based presumably on observations culled
from correspondence and from references in journals and the like. At
best the results would be fragmentary.

I have preferred to keep to a corpus which, if incomplete, is at least de-
finable, coherent, and accessible. If we can draw up a list of religious
works printed in French during the first decades of the Reformation
movement, we should have a sound basis on which to attempt answers to
some of our questions about the impact of the Reformation in France.

Why the seemingly arbitrary dates 1511 and 1551 for the limits of our
list? Why not go back to 1470 (the earliest printing in France); why stop
at 1551? The reason is that by the middle of the century forms of religious writing in French had taken on the qualities which would continue
to predominate for the rest of the century (with the one major exception
of the flowering of pamphlet literature of religio-political nature during
the Wars of Religion, from 1562 onwards). The period prior to mid-century
is the time of most significant, and rapid, change. The Edict of Château-
briant, dated 26 June 1551, provides a convenient symbolic date for the
terminus ad quem of our survey, since that edict consolidates all the
existing regulations concerning the book trade in France up to that date.
Article XI of the Edict lays down that no books on religious subjects
composed in the previous forty years may be printed without prior inspection by the Paris Faculty of Theology. In the perception of the legis-
lators themselves, the critical period is 'what has happened since 1511'.

---

[4] See *Registres des conclusions de la Faculté de Théologie de l'Université de
Paris*, Tome II: *du 26 novembre 1533 au 1er mars 1550*, ed. J.K. Farge (Paris,
Klincksieck, 1994). Preachers are criticized for simply reading passages from St
Paul, instead of preaching according to the accustomed fashion: e.g. p. 124,
para. 138 C, 6 February 1538. The 'accustomed fashion' is there described as
'the correction of sins and the teaching of morals', based on the Epistles and
Gospels of the liturgical calendar.

In fact, as we shall see, the Edict got it pretty well right: the vast majority of French religious works printed in and just after 1511 were re-editions of earlier writings (and are therefore representative of the preceding decades), and the few new compositions already show signs of a new contentiousness.

What lessons can be learned from this database? The following notes are intentionally no more than a sketch, picking out only the most obvious characteristics. There is plenty of scope for further study, for example of translations into French of the Church Fathers, or more generally on the relation between works composed in French and translations from other languages. It is hoped that the list will serve as a springboard for such further investigations.

Authors, titles and genres

Authors and titles

Our list contains some 1,300 editions. A convenient starting point is a glance at what we might call the popularity ratings: what authors, and what titles, received the largest number of editions?

A preliminary point needs to be made, concerning multiple editions. It will be noticed that, in several cases, the same title appears several times over in a single year. This sometimes represents completely independent editions in different cities (Lemaire de Belges in 1524 and 1528, for example). Sometimes, however, it represents two or more editions by the same printer in the same year (Lemaire de Belges in 1511 and 1512, for example; the most striking case is Branteghem's *Vie de Jesus Christ*, which received seven editions in 1540, four of them by Conrad Neobar in Paris). The reason is that the labour for typesetting an edition was cheap, but the cost of paper was high. It was standard practice at the time to print a small edition (say 750 copies), involving a relatively small investment in materials, and to recompose the whole edition if sales went well.[5] At least this indicates a marked demand for the work in question.

---

[5] See Jean-François Gilmont, 'Printers by the rules', *The Library*, 6th series, 2 (1980), pp. 143-8 for a discussion of size of editions. Printers' contracts suggest that print runs went in multiples of 700-750 copies; Gilmont concludes that the average number of copies produced in an edition was of the order of 1,000-1,350. For an even more spectacular case of multiple editions of the same work, see J.-P. Barbier, *Bibliographie des Discours politiques de Ronsard* (Geneva, Droz, 1984): Barbier counts eight editions of the *Discours* within a year of its composition, all by the same printer.

We shall therefore bear in mind both the number of editions and the number of different titles represented.

Top of the list is quite clearly John Calvin, with 77 editions involving 46 different titles. His position as the leading writer of the French-language Reformation has never been in doubt; but his position is amply confirmed here. Some works are relatively lightweight: short treatises on relics, or on the Lord's Supper, polemics against the Paris theologians, and several extracts from his *Institution*. Others, however, in particular towards 1550, are substantial texts like commentaries on books of the New Testament (his Old Testament commentaries will follow during the 1550s). The range of his work is also noteworthy, from solid theology to entertaining polemics, from catechisms to liturgies. His mark is indelible — and is seen as such by the Roman Catholics in the second half of the century, during which a whole genre grows up of replies to Calvin.[6]

It would have been difficult to guess the second most frequently edited writer in the period: Pierre Doré, Dominican and Paris Doctor of Theology, with 56 editions involving 24 titles. From 1537 on, while frequently affirming that he has done with writing in French and is turning back to more serious works in Latin, he continues to compose works of edification and of refutation of the 'heretics' in the vernacular. On purely statistical grounds, his place in the history of the Reformation conflict has clearly been seriously undervalued.[7]

Third most popular writer, and one more expected: Martin Luther, with 45 editions involving 20 titles. But these figures are somewhat misleading, since 16 of these editions are of the *Livre de vraye et parfaicte oraison*, including (edulcorated) Luther alongside numerous other devotional tracts by more traditionalist authors. For the rest, it is noteworthy that the more violently polemical works of Luther (*Adversus execrabilem Antichristi bullam, De captivitate Babylonica*, for example) are not translated into French. The Luther that is heard in France (though readers of French were not to know that it was Luther they were reading, since he is never named) is a teacher (*Betbüchlein, De libertate christiana*), scriptural expositor (*Declaration d'aucuns motz dont use S. Paul...*, *Exposition sur ... S. Pierre et S. Jude*), and above all spiritual counsellor and comforter (*Tessaradecas consolatoria*, appearing in at least four different translations, and twice edited by Paris doctors of

---

[6] The subject is touched on in my article 'Theology in French: Religious Pamphlets from the Counter-Reformation', in *Renaissance and Modern Studies* 23 (1979), pp. 128-46.

[7] The only recent study of Doré is the entry in J.K. Farge, *Biographical Register of Paris Doctors of Theology, 1500-1536* (Toronto, Pontifical Institute of Mediaeval Studies, 1980). His literary significance has never been examined.

theology).[8] While Luther is clearly an important player on the Reformation stage in France, it is rarely as an openly Protestant writer, more often as a spiritual leader (and, as such, acceptable to a variety of religious susceptibilities).

Alongside Luther, and in a sense more prized, is Erasmus, with 42 editions involving some 18 titles (approximately, since in some cases the same text, with modifications, appears under a new title). Most popular are the *Enchidirion militis christiani* (seven editions) and the *De praeparatione ad mortem* (11 editions in three different translations). It is an impressive performance for a writer who was considered by the traditionalists of the Paris Faculty to be as dangerous as Luther; and, unlike Luther, almost all editions of Erasmus carry the name of the author on the title page.

Rabelais is a somewhat eccentric presence in this list of religious writings; but he was clearly seen as a religious writer by the compilers of the *Catalogue des livres censurez*, and therefore must be included here. He ranks fifth, with 36 editions of his four titles (not to mention the spurious *Cinquiesme livre* attributed to him in 1549).[9]

These five authors constitute what must be called the first division. It is noteworthy that four of them are among the most admired *writers* of their age, with an aesthetic sense of language which sets them apart. In fact the fifth, Pierre Doré, is also a brilliant stylist, but in a manner alien to modern taste (see the titles of his books). His highly florid and metaphor-filled style was clearly more appreciated by contemporaries than it is today.

Calvin's closest collaborators, Guillaume Farel and Pierre Viret, come rather surprisingly, but clearly, in a second division, Farel with 26 editions (16 titles) and Viret with 23 editions (16 titles). It needs to be added that by 1550 Farel was close to the end of his career as a writer, while Viret continued to be productive throughout the 1550s and into the 1560s.

---

[8] W.G. Moore, *La Réforme allemande et la littérature française: recherches sur la notoriété de Luther en France* (Strasbourg, 1930) continues to offer the fullest study available of the penetration of Luther's writings in France. Complemented by my article 'Les traductions françaises de Luther, 1524-1550', in J.-F. Gilmont (ed.), *Palaestra typographica: Aspects de la production du livre humaniste et religieux au XVIe siècle* (Aubel, Gason, 1984), pp. 11-56.

[9] The information in the bibliography on Rabelais editions is based mainly on S. Rawles and M.A. Screech, *A New Rabelais Bibliography: Editions of Rabelais before 1626* (Geneva, Droz, 1987). I am deeply grateful to the authors and to the Librairie Droz for their permission to incorporate their findings in the present study.

Alongside them in terms of editions is the Flemish Carthusian Guillaume van Branteghem, with 23 editions also. But here we need to take serious account of the point made earlier about multiple editions. Branteghem is credited with only three titles, one of them, the *Vie de Jesus Christ*, achieving 17 editions. We shall return shortly to the question of the popularity of specific texts. The strongly anti-Protestant poet Pierre Gringore achieves 19 editions (four titles).

A number of authors achieve between ten and 15 editions, including Philippe Melanchthon (ten editions, six titles), Antoine Marcourt (13 editions but only four titles), Artus Désiré (a latecomer to the lists, but already marking up 14 editions (of six titles) by 1551. Translations from Saint Augustine and Saint Jerome account for ten and 11 editions respectively (including some, like Augustine's *Cité de Dieu*, of massive proportions). Guillaume Petit, Doctor of the Sorbonne and confessor to Francis I, provides ten editions of his three titles; but Juan-Luis Vivès has 12 editions, nearly all of the same work. Which brings us back to the question of particularly popular works.

Pride of place (almost) here goes to the *Internelle consolation* and other part translations of the *Imitatio Christi*, fundamental text of the Brethren of the Common Life, dating from the early fifteenth century and one of the most successful devotional texts ever: 31 editions are known in our period. Not far behind, however, is a text of energetically polemical nature, Jean Lemaire de Belges's *Traité de la difference des scismes et des concilles de l'eglise*, with 28 editions in 40 years. Its impeccably Gallican origins, written at royal command by the official historiographer of Louis XII, long enabled its violently anti-papal propaganda to pass uncensored (it was finally condemned in 1549). These, with the *Livre de vraye et parfaicte oraison* and the *Vie de Jesus Christ* (16 and 17 editions respectively) already mentioned constitute the most popular titles in our survey. It will be noted that none of the four can be considered as Reformation propaganda. On the other hand, the most popular text of all, though still ambiguous, does have a clearly Reformed connection: the versified Psalms of Clément Marot. Counting all its manifestations from the individual publication of Psalm VI in 1531 or thereabouts to the various Calvinist hymn books and to their incorporation in Marot's *Oeuvres*, Marot's psalms are set in 52 different editions by 1551 (and that despite Parisian condemnations of the text from 1543 on). Marot's enterprise also stimulates numerous other poets to complete his work or to compete with him: Gilles d'Aurigny, Théodore de Bèze, Bonaventure Des Periers, Guillaume Guéroult, Claude Le Maistre, Jean Poitevin, Maurice Scève all contribute at least a few, sometimes the complete run of one hundred psalms untouched by Marot, or even new versions of the total hundred and fifty psalms. Add the involvement of musical composers attracted by the melodies printed with the text in many Genevan editions (Loys Bourgeois, Pierre Certon, Antoine de Mornable within our period), and the unique place occupied by Marot's *Pseaumes de David* in the literature of the period is already clear. And that is only the beginning: the high point of the Psalms in French is reached with the completion (in 1562) of the Geneva *Psalter* by Théodore de Bèze, and subsequently with the massive output of musical settings and harmonizations (Claude Goudimel and Claude Le Jeune being only the most famous of the forty-odd composers who tried their hand at the genre).[10]

Genres

Marot's Psalms, both by virtue of drawing attention to the particular vogue of poetry and also as being a text of biblical origin, introduce us to a second approach to the analysis of our list. What range of genres is represented in religious printing in the period?[11]

We may start, like many early library classifications, with the absolutely fundamental text, the Bible. Up to the middle of the sixteenth century, the so-called *Bible abrégée* (the Old Testament as far as the book of Job) and the *Bible historiée* (Jean de Rély's translation from the Vulgate, first printed *c.* 1495) continued to appear: a total of 22 editions. By comparison, Lefèvre's translation received only four editions, and Olivétan's Reformed version ten (in the following 30 years, Lefèvre's version more or less disappeared, while Olivétan's, revised by Calvin and others, went from strength to strength).[12]

Quite different is the reception of the *Nouveau Testament*: Lefèvre's translation received 34 editions in the period 1523-1551, and Olivétan's 23 editions (1536-1551): a total of 57 editions. It will be remembered that from 1525 on, translations of the Bible or parts of it into French were illegal in France. (In fact, for 'France' one should say 'Paris': Lyon

[10] On the details of this success story see Pierre Pidoux, *Le Psautier huguenot du XVI° siècle. Mélodies et documents* (2 vols, Basle, Baerenreiter, 1962).

[11] On the Protestant side of this subject, see my article on 'Les genres de la littérature polémique calviniste au XVI° siècle', in *Prose et prosateurs de la Renaissance. Mélanges offerts à M. le professeur Robert Aulotte* (Paris, SEDES, 1988), pp. 123-34.

[12] The information on Bibles and New Testaments in the bibliography is based in large part on the admirable *Bibliography of French Bibles: Fifteenth- and Sixteenth-Century French-Language Editions of the Scriptures* by Bettye Chambers. I am profoundly grateful to Dr Chambers and to the Librairie Droz for permission to incorporate this material in the present study.

printers seemed to have few problems in producing translations of scripture.)

Other parts of scripture received relatively few editions, with the exception of the Psalms: 13 prose translations of the whole book, and eight editions (with or without commentary) of the seven penitential psalms. But by the end of the period, these versions had been almost entirely ousted by the tidal wave of Marot's versifications.

After the text of the Bible, the next category concerns biblical commentaries. These come in two main groups: homilies on the liturgical Epistles and Gospels in the Mass (*Postilles*), and commentaries on books of the Bible. Postils, in a text assembled by Pierre Desrey from various commentators, were already established in French at the beginning of the sixteenth century; despite their size (five bulky volumes), they were edited seven times during our period (including provincial editions as late as 1546); Jacques Lefèvre d'Étaples's more evangelical *Epistres et evangiles* also appeared in seven editions (including two 1544 Lyon editions here reported for the first time). By definition, these texts are situated in a Roman Catholic liturgical context, however evangelical the spirit may be.

The practice of commenting on a whole book (or series of books) of the Bible was, prior to the sixteenth century, a genre exclusively for professionals: in Latin, often with such a concentration of erudition that the text is difficult to decipher.[13] A major change is introduced by the Reformers when they abandon the accumulated marginal glosses and multiple senses of medieval commentary, and adopt the principles of humanist exegesis, providing the text of scripture, followed, section by section, by comments intended to bring out the direct sense of the original. Initially, however, commentary is a learned genre for specialists, and therefore in Latin.

A second change intervenes in our period: the provision in the vernacular of biblical commentaries. This is almost exclusively a Protestant speciality — but not quite: a first, rather plodding, verbal commentary on all St Paul's letters had already appeared in 1507, and was re-edited in 1521 and 1544 (the latter as a devious way of making available in Paris the Olivétan text of the epistles). Otherwise, the commentaries made available to a French-speaking public come from Luther, Bucer, Oecolampadius, Bullinger, and, above all, Calvin (in almost every case the French is translated from Latin). Given the bulk of the average commentary, and the uncompromisingly doctrinal content, these commen-

---

[13] A famous example is the edition of Nicholas of Lyra's commentary on the whole Bible (Basle, Froben, 1520).

taries are on the edge of what can be called 'popular', whatever language they may be in.

Far more accessible (both intellectually and to the purse) are the numerous *expositions* on the basic texts of the faith: the Lord's Prayer, the Apostles' Creed, the Ten Commandments (and, in a Roman Catholic context, the Five Commandments of the Church and the *Ave Maria*).[14] The earliest printings (found also in *ABC*s and in the so-called *Croix de par Dieu*) tend only to produce the plain text of the fundamentals; but, after Luther's lead in publishing commentaries on each text, then bringing them together in the *Betbüchlein* (1523), the same expository form is introduced in French by Farel and in translations from Erasmus and from Luther. Responses from the traditional Church were not slow in coming, and the genre rapidly became a major vehicle for teaching one or other of the competing versions of the faith.

Another form of teaching text pioneered by Luther (in 1529) but imported into French is the catechism, with Reformed texts from Gaspard Megander, Calvin and Farel, Christophe Fabri (and several anonymous *Confessions de foi*); responses come from Guillaume Petit and Pierre Doré (but are not established in Roman Catholicism until the second half of the century). The Reformed catechism is primarily aimed at the young; and several other Reformed and evangelical publications also illustrate the concern for right education: Olivétan's *Instruction des enfans*, the anonymous *Introduction pour les enfans*, the *ABC françois*. The level of teaching aimed at by the Roman Catholics seems markedly lower (the *ABC des chrestiens*, Noël Béda's *Doctrine et instruction des chrestiens*).

Two major categories of writing illustrate a significant change in mentality wrought by the Reformation: the devotional, meditational text and the doctrinal statement. At the start of our period, meditations, contemplations, *Miroirs*, encourage an intensity of pious emotion based on, for example, a precise evocation of each of Christ's wounds, or each detail of the Nativity, or of the life of the Virgin Mary. The doctrinal content is limited, and it is taken more or less for granted. This form of literature has almost no counterpart in Reformation writing. Conversely, from the mid 1520s on, brief statements of faith appear (the anonymous *Brief recueil*, c. 1525; Farel's *Summaire* and Lambert's *Somme chrestienne*, both c. 1529). This genre would be raised to an altogether higher plane when the second edition of Calvin's *Institutio* was translated into French (1541). The Roman answer (at least in the first half of the century) is not

---

[14] I have counted over 20 such expositions: see my article 'Theology for the Layman in the French Reformation, 1520-1550', *The Library*, 6th series, 9 (1987), pp. 105-27.

on the whole to provide an overview of the faith (though both Guillaume Petit and Pierre Doré come close to doing so), but to concentrate on two particularly sensitive points: confession, and the Eucharist. Numerous tracts appear advising the reader on how to prepare for confession, and how to prepare oneself to receive the Sacrament of the Altar. But these, like the Reformed tracts, are also appealing to the understanding rather than to the heart. The early meditations have all but disappeared by mid-century.

Even more than the doctrinal summaries, what has ousted the meditation is the polemical slanging-match; and in this all sides participate fully. From the early 1530s on, Antoine Marcourt, Matthieu Malingre and (probably) Guillaume Farel were producing fiery denunciations of the 'papists', and in particular of the Mass; they are followed ten years later by Calvin (*Treatise on relics*, 1543; pamphlets on the Paris *Articles of faith* and on the Sorbonne index of prohibited books, 1544), Viret (*De la difference...*, 1542; *Disputations chrestiennes*, 1544), and others (Joachim de Coignac, Henry Scrimgeour). The Roman Catholics were in fact already active in this area in the 1520s, with writers like Pierre Gringore, Nicolas Volcyr de Serouville and Jean Gacy; after something of a lull in the 1530s, polemics are again taken up by writers like Artus Désiré towards the end of our period. Again, the casualty in all this is the devotional spirituality characteristic of the beginning of the century.

We have so far explored genres directly appropriate to religious literature, whether commentaries, expositions or doctrinal summaries. But we should not overlook the exploitation for religious purposes of what we might call 'extraneous' genres: songs, dramas, educational manuals, histories and so on. The *Balade des leutheriens*, the *Te Deum des lutheriens*, appear in the 1520s; in the 1530s Matthieu Malingre and others produced several collections of *chansons*, some *spirituelles* (often re-working popular love songs to give them a religious bent, to be sung to the tune of the original), some polemical, ridiculing priests, prelates, and the Pope.

In the theatre, of course, the medieval tradition of religious drama survived into the sixteenth century, with mystery plays on the life of Christ, on the Virgin Mary, on the Old Testament, and so on. At least 24 editions of these earlier texts were printed in our period. While the Reformers regarded the theatre with some suspicion (though not the outright rejection sometimes attributed to them), they had recourse on occasion to dramatic form: traditional genres like the *Farce des theologastres* attributed to Louis de Berquin, the *Moralité de la chrestienté* by Malingre, the anonymous *Verité cachée devant cent ans*; on the other hand, and most momentously, Bèze's *Abraham sacrifiant* (1550), the first *tragédie* composed in French.

We have already mentioned school primers, in relation to catechisms
and other teaching texts. In the field of apparently educational material
exploited for propaganda purposes we may add a mention of historical
works: Dolet's *Faits et gestes de François Ier* (1540, six re-editions or
summaries), condemned by the Sorbonne more, it seems, because it was
by Dolet than for any reprehensible content, and an early work by Jean
Sleidan (later to make a major name for himself as Reformation histo-
rian).

In summary, then, the range of genres, of different manners of treating
the subject of religion, offered to the public during the early Reformation
period is considerable, and becomes markedly more variegated during
the course of our chosen time span. By 1550 a number of new genres
(Bible commentaries, doctrinal and polemical treatises, the metrical
Psalms, drama which distances itself from the medieval) were in place,
and would thereafter continue to develop into the literary flowering of
subsequent centuries.

The evolving picture

In the preceding survey we have had cause constantly to refer to the
evolution of book production in the period, since the story we are following is one of change. The question 'what was produced' has to be over-
laid with the question 'when was it produced'.

The main list contains descriptions of over 1,300 editions. Of these, a
date has not been assigned to 45, and one 'late' edition (of 1553) is included only because a misbound copy of that work in the Paris BEBA
library contains half of a 1550 printing. The undated editions are not all
of the same type; some are clearly early (Lacu, *La Quenouille spirituelle*,
editions of some mystery plays); others, like the undated editions of Rabelais's novels, or works by Pierre Doré, are by definition from the 1530s
or 1540s. Probably the undated editions are spread fairly evenly across
our time span.[15]

To take the editions year by year shows considerable fluctuations, especially in the earliest years: 12 editions in 1511, 13 in 1512, but only four

---

[15] It is during the period which concerns us that the printed book acquired a
'modern' appearance, with a proper title page, with the name and address of the
printer or editor, and with a date. Earlier, many books were only dated in the
colophon, and quite as many bear no date at all. And towards the end of our
period, censorship led to many religious texts being produced without address
and/or without date.

in 1513, for example. But if we look at five-year groups of printings, the evolution becomes much clearer:

1511-1515:	43
1516-1520:	68
1521-1525:	79
1526-1530:	111
1531-1535:	165
1536-1540:	189
1541-1545:	331
1546-1550:	242

The year 1551, left out of this table, was relatively prolific, with 64 editions.

Until 1545, there is a steady increase, seeming to accelerate markedly in the early 1540s. Thereafter a steadier rhythm sets in, with some 50 editions each year; that represents a decrease from the preceding five years.

The years 1511 and 1512 give a valid sample of religious printing as it had existed at least since the beginning of the sixteenth century. The writings of several saints (Ambrose, Bernard, [pseudo-] Dionysius, Jerome); the popular *Postilles*, already well established in fifteenth-century editions; short edificatory pamphlets by Noël Béda, already published a few years earlier; a mystery play dating from 1486. Among newly composed works are devotional manuals (François Le Roy, Laurent Desmoulins); and there are signs of things to come in two trend-setters: Lemaire de Belges's *De la difference des scismes*, and the *Exposition sur le sermon ... en la montaigne* atrributed to Jean Vitrier. The first of these, as mentioned earlier, was commissioned by Louis XII, as a political pamphlet directed against Pope Julius II; it was to take on a new significance a few decades later, when anti-papal polemics became the staple fare of Wittenberg and Geneva. Jean Vitrier was a disciple of Erasmus, and the *Exposition* attributed to him was criticized in 1515 by the Paris Faculty of Theology for a number of Erasmian propositions. Both these texts were to go through numerous editions before 1550.

Other texts from the early years fill out the picture of what was being made available to a public capable of reading French (or, quite as importantly, capable of having French read to them):[16] translations of the

---

[16] I have not addressed the question of literacy rates in sixteenth-century France. There is little hard evidence on the subject; but the very existence of this early religious printing in the French language demonstrates that there must have been a market somewhere. The significant expression 'to read, or have

Psalms, the *Légende dorée*, and works like *L'Ordinaire des chrestiens* or the *Instruction des curez* attributed to Gerson. The *Bible historiale* of Jean de Rély and the *Bible abrégée* receive several editions (and will continue to appear until 1545). The first known edition in French of the *Internelle consolation* is from 1520. It was to receive two editions in the 1520s, and then, from 1529 to 1544, it appeared in at least one, some-times two or more, editions every year.

It is evident that, well before the Reformation, religious literature in French was not in short supply. On the other hand, new compositions were relatively rare. The same texts (sometimes going back to the thir-teenth or fourteenth century) were re-edited at frequent intervals. And a major concentration of these early works is the provision of devotional aids (see for example the titles printed in or around 1516: the *Jardin spirituel*, the *Oraison tresdevote*, the *Jardin de contemplation*, and so on). Those aids are often primarily directed at a female audience (for example Jean Henry, *Le Livre de reformation ... pour toutes religieuses*, *Petite instruction et maniere de vivre pour une femme seculiere*, both 1516). Devotional and instructive material in French for nuns (who were not expected to be able to read Latin) was one of the early channels for the introduction of French into a religious context.

As is well known, a new impulsion to religious printing appears after 1520; in French, in fact, not until *c*. 1523. Prior to that, Erasmus's *Encomium Moriae* (1520) is the only hint of changes to come — except for two polemical pamphlets on ecclesiastical abuses (but also hostile to Luther) printed in Geneva in 1522. The Reformers were not first off the mark as is always assumed! And in the years up to 1525 (the first high point in printing, with 35 titles), there are not only the well-known first editions of Lefèvre's *Nouveau Testament* and *Psaultier*, translations of Erasmus by Louis de Berquin and Claude Chansonnette, Farel's first, and least militant, work, and (*c*. 1525) the first outburst of translations from Luther, but also Volcyr de Serouville's first anti-Lutheran composition (1523), Frère Jean Gacy's *Trialogue [sur] les erreurs de Martin Luther*, Pierre Gringore's *Blazon des heretiques* (both 1524), the *Balade des leutheriens* and anti-Lutheran pamphlets by Thomas Illyricus (1525).

All of these publications are new works (though many, of course, were destined to go through many editions subsequently). They introduce a quite new tone in religious writings. On the one hand, the works by Farel and Erasmus seek to renew and deepen the already existing devotional themes of earlier piety; on the other, the writings by Roman Catholics

read to them' is often encountered in texts of the time (e.g. G. Petit, *Le Viat de salut*). For further discussion on the matter, see the works mentioned in note 1.

are violent in their hostility to the 'new' doctrines and their purveyors. And it is important to note that these new texts, and new kinds of texts, are superimposed on a continued and sustained production of the works of the previous decade (mystery plays, lives of the saints and of Christ...).

In August 1525, and again in February 1526, the Paris Faculty of Theology and the Paris *parlement* condemned translations of the scriptures into French and several other works. The relative lull in publication in 1526 and 1527 (14 editions in each year) is perhaps not unconnected with these first edicts by the *parlement*. But during the years up to 1530, where the impetus again builds up, further new genres appear. The first summaries of Reformed teachings are found (*Brief Recueil de la substance ... de la doctrine evangelique*, c. 1526; Farel's *Summaire et briefve declaration*, c. 1529; Lambert's *Somme Chrestienne* of the same year). Partly to compensate for the forbidden Bible texts, extracts from the Bible such as Otto Brunfels's *Prieres et oraisons de la Bible* (1529), and admonitions (by Luther and others) to read the scriptures are published anonymously (1529). But, again, the Reformers do not have it all their own way: Guillaume Petit produced *Le Viat de salut*, c. 1526, Jean de Gaigny wrote on the Seven Words from the cross (1528). Numerous expositions on the fundamental texts of piety — the Lord's Prayer, the Creed, the Ten Commandments — appeared, representing all parts of the religious spectrum. It is in 1528 that one particularly significant representative of this genre appeared: the *Livre de vraye et parfaicte oraison* (with 13 further editions up to 1545). This collection of commentaries on the Lord's Prayer, Creed and Ten Commandments, together with prayers and the penitential psalms, draws on a variety of sources, none of whom is named, but including Farel and Luther (tidied up to avoid too forceful a Reformation message).[17] The publication is significant as representing an attempt (and there were later to be others) to find the common ground of religious attitudes and practice among the competing confessions.

If the printing of the text of Scripture was forbidden in Paris, the unfulfilled need was supplied from other sources, in particular Antwerp (Lefèvre's *Ancien Testament* in instalments from 1528 to 1532, the complete *Bible* in 1530 and 1534). Antwerp printers also provided the majority of translations of Luther into French at this period. Basle and Strasbourg were also centres of printing for material too dangerous to print in France; but both these centres became inactive before 1530.

The five years from 1531 to 1535 are marked by the increasingly confrontational nature of Reformed religious printing. From Neuchâtel in

---

[17] See my article 'Luther et la piété de l'Église gallicane: *Le Livre de vraye et parfaicte oraison*', *RHPR* 63 (1983), pp. 91-111.

particular come the violent pamphlets, and satirical songs, of Antoine
Marcourt, Matthieu Malingre and Guillaume Farel (as well as the notorious *placards* of 1534, and the first edition of the Olivétan *Bible*,
1535). In reply, the Roman Catholics do not on the whole join in the
polemics (except for Jérôme de Hangest's replies to the *placards* in
1535),[18] but rather redouble their output of traditional devotion, and add
new works in the same vein (Jean Clerici on penitence, 1533; Jean de
Gaigny on Psalm 50(51), Jean van Campen with his Psalm paraphrases):
works of edification, but bypassing the denominational debates.

The year 1536 marks a curious hiatus in the evolution of religious
printing in French. All the major printers so far involved in Reformed or
evangelical texts disappear almost simultaneously: Martin Lempereur in
Antwerp, Simon Du Bois and Antoine Augereau in Paris, Pierre de
Vingle in Neuchâtel. It is possible that the Paris decree forbidding any
printing whatsoever (January 1535), continued to have reverberations in
the French capital. In any case, only ten editions have been identified
from that year, one from Antwerp, three from Geneva (including the first
production, a *Nouveau Testament*, from the press of Jean Girard, a
printer destined to play a major role in the following 15 years), four from
Paris and one (possibly a ghost, at that) from Orleans.

Thereafter, a new course is irrevocably set; by 1540 (when 66 editions
are recorded) almost all the features of a new style of printing (with the
major exception of Calvin, Farel and Viret!) are in place. The *mystères*
are still appearing, the *Internelle consolation* is more frequently printed
than ever before, as is the *Livre de vraye et parfaicte oraison*; Branteghem's *Vie de Jesus Christ* receives multiple editions in Paris, after beginning its career in Antwerp. Gringore's anti-Lutheran poems continue
to appear, and a major new defender of tradition appears in the form of
Pierre Doré (prolific from 1537 on). Multiple editions of the *Nouveau
Testament* are printed, in Lefèvre's translation mainly in Antwerp (four
in 1538), in Olivétan's in Geneva, as well as the *Psalms*, including
(1539) the first application of Marot's psalm versifications to Reformed
liturgy. An important feature is the rising frequency of translations into
French of works by German-language Reformers (Bucer, Bullinger, Megander, Oecolampadius, Zwingli, alongside re-editions, and new translations, from Luther); these are added to re-editions of earlier transla-

---

[18] This is a point at which an eye needs to be kept on productions in Latin. The
Registres des conclusions record permissions granted to Robert Ceneau to pub-
lish his *Appendix ad coenam dominicam* (January 1535, para. 44C of the Farge
edition), to Claude Viexmont for his *Cathechismus seu Christiana institutio*
(October 1536, para. 103A), and to Guillaume Petit for his *Hortus fidei*
(December 1537, para. 106A).

tions from Sebald Heyden and 'Hermann Bodius' (Bucer by another name?). It is now that the new genre of biblical commentary makes its appearance.

The period from 1541 to 1545 is the climax of the story, both in terms of numbers of editions recorded and in terms of the nature of the texts produced. All the genres seen so far are still present (saints' lives, traditional devotional manuals, the *mystères*). But they are being swamped in a flood of new forms: the Paris theologians, followed by Louvain, produce *Articles of faith*, and the Paris Faculty publishes the first *Catalogue des livres censurez* (1544). Pierre Doré is at his most prolific, and is joined (in 1545) by that other indefatigable writer Artus Désiré, as also by lesser-known figures like Matthieu de Lalande. Their works are unambiguously polemical. Numerous editions of translations from Erasmus are still appearing, as are editions of Jean van Campen. But Calvin is now in full spate: from the first French edition of the *Institution* in 1541, to the numerous polemical treatises against Rome, against the Anabaptists, against the compromisers, and to his first, timid, ventures into biblical commentaries in French (a brief commentary on *Jude*, and summaries of his commentary on *Romans*): by 1545 he has established his position as a leader of the Reformation, whose views carry great weight (cf. the Nicodemite controversy). He is not alone: Farel and Viret also join in with didactic or polemical treatises and pamphlets. This is the period in which the Lyon printer Étienne Dolet produced a flood of *évangélique* editions (1542), was arrested, and burnt at the stake (1546). This is also the period in which Clément Marot's versifications of the *Psalms* became established as the basis of Reformed worship, and also as one of the most popular forms of poetry of the century. It is all there.

Perhaps the most striking feature of the period 1546-1550 is what is absent. Branteghem's *Vie de Jesus Christ*, the *Internelle consolation*, the *Livre de vraye et parfaicte oraison*, had consistently appeared in multiple editions each year up to 1544; only slightly less eminent were writers like the Paris doctor Jean de Gaigny. Quite suddenly, the tap is turned off, and these authors and texts disappear entirely, as do the mystery plays and the *Bible historiée*. Only rarely does Erasmus appear in this last period, and then with his non-religious *Apophthegmes*. The focus of publication has become confessional. Pierre Doré and Artus Désiré are now joined by the Doctor Claude d'Espence and the Franciscan Nicole Grenier, seconded by Gabriel Dupuyherbault, Gilles Corrozet, or Martial Mazurier (though the last-named, Doctor of the Paris Faculty as he was, was condemned by his colleagues for his pains). The 'holy triumvirate' (Bucer's phrase) of Calvin, Farel and Viret continue to compose prolifically; in the case of Calvin, however, the polemical treatises become much less frequent among new compositions, and more significant is the systematic appearance of French translations of his commentaries on the New Testament. But they are not alone as Reformed writers: Valérand Poullain, Joachim de Coignac, Jean Garnier, Benoît Textor, Henry Scrimgeour all contribute, and a new name appears in 1550: Théodore de Bèze. The contribution of Italian writers (vociferously polemical) is also notable: Bernardino Ochino, Celio Secondo Curione, Pietro Paulo Vergerio. It is in this final five-year segment of our period that Marot's *Psaumes* achieve the outstanding status we have already noted.

It needs only a glance at the beginning and the end of our story to see the size of the change that takes place in this period. The number of editions on the market has increased about sixfold. The beginning of the period was marked by stability — there is little change in the fare on offer — and by the priority implicitly given to prayer, to devotion, to meditation. Faith was seen as unquestioning, in a properly hierarchical world. Guillaume Petit sums it up when, in 1526, he advises any reader who doubts, is tempted, or does not understand some point of the faith to say: 'I believe in God, I believe in the Church, and I ask no more questions'. It is not the job of the simple believer to delve deeply into theology; that is the responsibility of prelates and priests, of doctors and 'supérieurs'. For the people at large, what is important is an emotional intensity of spiritual uplift.

By the middle of the century, there is little trace in the publications either of the stability or of the simple spirituality. With very few exceptions (one last edition of the *Internelle consolation*, some *Devotes oraisons*, Theodoret's *Sermons*) we have works appealing to the understanding rather than to the heart: in 1550, 14 editions of the *Bible*, *Nouveau Testament* or *Psautier* (including Marot's verse), three commentaries and a major treatise by Calvin, five editions of Artus Désiré (all polemical) and four of Pierre Doré (instructional — and including, probably without realizing it, a translation from Luther), Nicole Grenier's *Bouclier de la foy*, and Farel's answer *Le Glaive de la parolle*; Coignac's attack on monks, a parody of a court sentence and one of a papal pardon, Vergerio's violent denunciation of the 1550 pardon in Rome... Verse (Beaulieu, Désiré), drama (Bèze, Musculus), history (Sleidan) are all practised with a view to persuading the reader, to putting over a point of view, to convincing. In terms of reading matter, religion has become unstable, open to debate, and more intellectual than spiritual. 'Spirituality' is represented by the editions of the Genevan liturgy (*La Forme des prieres*) and by the 'hymn-book' editions of Marot.

Places of printing

The book trade in the sixteenth century was not without danger.[19] The printers Antoine Augereau and Étienne Dolet, the bookseller Jean de La Garde all perished at the stake; Pierre de Vingle, Robert Estienne and many others were forced into exile. Printing of material which conflicted with the views of 'the authorities' could take place either in a safe haven beyond the reach of the religious or secular powers, or in conditions of clandestinity or disguise.

In Germany (in particular the south), many printers were active in numerous centres by the end of the fifteenth century.[20] The political fragmentation of the region enabled Luther to spread his message widely and rapidly. Thus, in the short period 1517-25, writings by Luther had been published by 112 printers in 48 cities.[21] The contrast with France, under much more centralized control and with fewer centres of printing, is complete. Almost all printing was concentrated on Paris and Lyon, with a few printers in Poitiers, Avignon and Toulouse. The centralized government of France enabled a far more coherent and efficacious grip to be maintained on the book trade.

That control, however, was far from complete. There were seven *parlements* in France, and a royal decree, for example, had to be registered in each of them before it was (even theoretically) fully effective. The relative freedom of the press in Lyon, with no *parlement* and no Faculty of Theology, has often been noted. Moreover, while the control of the printing presses was fairly easy, control of the book trade was not. We shall see the implications in terms of centres of printing outside French jurisdiction, but conveniently placed on the French borders.

Of our list of over 1,300 editions, it has not been possible to identify the geographical origin of some 35 items. For the rest, about 1,290 editions, we find 40 towns or cities involved in one way or another in the production of French-language religious printing, sometimes only marginally, when for example a local bookseller had a text printed for him else-

---

[19] On the following paragraphs, see my *Censorship and the Sorbonne. A bibliographical study of books in French censured by the Faculty of Theology of the University of Paris, 1520-1551* (Geneva, Droz, 1979).

[20] See Lucien Febvre and Henri-Jean Martin, *L'Apparition du livre* (Paris, Albin Michel, 1958, many reprints; English translation by D.E. Gerard: *The Coming of the Book: the Impact of Printing, 1450-1800*, London, NLB, 1976), in particular chapter 6, 'Géographie du livre'.

[21] Figures derived from J. Benzing, *Lutherbibliographie. Verzeichnis der gedruckten Schriften Martin Luthers bis zu dessen Tod* (Baden-Baden, Heitz, 1966).

where, or because (in the case of Longeville) the local priest set up a printing press in his own house. A consideration of the major concentrations of religious printing activity, however, gives some surprising results. The highest scores[22] are recorded as follows:

Paris	586 editions
Geneva	243
Lyon	238
Antwerp	79
Rouen	23
Neuchâtel	18
Alençon	17
Strasbourg	17
Basle	16

Not surprisingly, Paris emerges as the most active centre, partly because it had the largest number of members of the book trade in the French-speaking world, and partly because of its sustained activity throughout the period.

Geneva and Lyon vie almost equally for second place, which is quite remarkable for Geneva, with its minute printing industry by comparison with that of the second largest city in France.

The only other centre of any significance at all is Antwerp; and of its 79 editions, 28 were produced by one printer, Martin Lempereur, and seven by his widow.

It is surprising to find Rouen, with 23 editions, ahead of Neuchâtel, Alençon, Strasbourg and Basle, known centres of Reformation printing. But a glance at the list of printers shows that with the one exception of the Du Gort brothers (who started printing in 1548) the involvement of Rouen is on the basis of fleeting individual cases, by printers or booksellers who were involved in only one or two productions.

Conversely, the cases of Neuchâtel and Alençon illustrate the effects of single-minded concentration. All 18 editions in Neuchâtel come from the press of Pierre de Vingle (who also printed 9 editions in Lyon and 4 in Geneva, giving a total of 31). The 17 Alençon printings are all by Simon Du Bois (who also printed 17 editions in Paris, giving a total of 34). In both cases there is a conscious, and courageous, commitment to the spreading of a message, quite different from the commercial considera-

---

[22] In the figures which follow, numbers should be taken as giving an order of magnitude, not as statistically precise statements. Thus the brothers de Marnef printed in both Paris and Poitiers, and it is not always possible to locate individual productions. Similarly, it is arbitrary to ascribe to Paris or to Bourges editions of a mystery play printed in Paris but sold in both cities.

tions which may lead a printer to dabble in a few editions on the edges of respectability.

Strasbourg and Basle are included in this listing because of their known role in the early diffusion of the Reformation message.[23] Together with Antwerp, these independent cities just outside the French border provided the best channel for the preparation of Reformed literature in the first years of the movement. Yet numerically their contribution is surprisingly slight. They illustrate just how minority a phenomenon the printing activity of the early Reformation was. The specificity of their message gives them a more than statistical importance; but quantitatively they are both surpassed by the activities of the jobbing printers of Rouen!

To return, however, to the top of our list for a closer look. In the table of printers and booksellers[24] later in this study, references are given for each named individual, resulting in well over the 586 Parisian editions mentioned above. The problem is caused by the widespread practice of the shared edition, with four or more booksellers distributing an edition identical except for the name and address on the title page or in the colophon; the name of the actual printer may appear nowhere at all. For the purposes of the present analysis of editions, therefore, I have arbitrarily ascribed each edition to one or another of the known participants, which allows at least account to be taken of all the actors involved. If we note the year of first printing or selling of religious books in French in each case, we obtain a rough indication of the evolution of the trade:

Years:	1511-20	1521-30	1531-40	1541-51	Total
Paris:	30	19	36	39	124
Lyon:	6	8	16	16	46
Geneva:		2	4	5	11

The number of Parisian printers and booksellers involved, and the relatively constant level of entries to the profession, suggests the diversity of the production. The printers of mystery plays, postils, and devotional tracts of the first decade of our period are already numerous; they are

---

[23] See J.-F. Gilmont (ed.), *La Réforme et le livre* (see note 1).

[24] The rather clumsy expression 'printers and booksellers' is unavoidable. The key figure in the book trade is the 'bookseller' or, in modern parlance, the 'commercial editor' who determines what texts shall be printed. He may contract out the actual printing to a jobbing or artisanal printer who simply carries out a commercial contract, and who may not be named in the book. But some 'booksellers' were themselves also printers (Robert Estienne, 'royal printer', being a major example). It is not always possible to differentiate between printer and bookseller; so I adopt the double terminology.

followed later, despite the censorship which limited the range of permissible printing, by purveyors of sermons, tracts and treatises of the nascent Counter-Reformation. While certain individuals (like Jean André) print exclusively anti-Reformation material, others (the Langelier brothers for example) tend to test the limits of the allowable. For the most part, however, it would seem that printers and booksellers were swayed more by commercial considerations than by conviction: they venture occasionally into a devotional publication, but their main focus of publication remains elsewhere, in non-religious printing.

Lyon, on a smaller scale, shows a similar pattern, with a sustained rate of entry to the profession, and a wide spread of genres produced. In certain cases, however, a stronger specialism in religious works becomes clear: the Arnoullets, father and son, have a sustained concentration on religious titles, in the case of Olivier devotional and traditional, in the case of Balthasar more adventurous (even though usually producing cheap editions of existing works). Most notable are the cases of Étienne Dolet (25 editions) and Jean de Tournes (39 editions), both involving considerable risks: Dolet was burnt at the stake in 1546, and de Tournes perhaps should have been, since he reprinted a fair proportion of Dolet's editions shortly after the arrest of the latter. With a total of 46 printers, Lyon seems to represent a larger proportion of printers with real interest in religious questions than the capital city.

But these figures serve most of all to set in stark relief the extraordinary position of Geneva. With no printers at all in the first decade, with a minute production in the second decade, with four printers established in the 1530s (of whom three disappeared rapidly), and five newcomers, all in 1550 or 1551, Geneva manages to rival the output of French religious printing in Lyon. Even more spectacular is the fact that, of the 243 editions counted, no less than 165 come from the presses of Jean Girard, who thereby stands out as by far and away the most prolific printer/bookseller in our survey.[25]

Reception

Even if we assume the relatively modest average figure of 750 copies per edition (see note 5), we may postulate that almost one million copies of religious texts in French were made available during our forty-year period (the population of France then being something like 20 million). Our bibliographical listing does not of itself say anything about the ac-

---

[25] The only serious study of Jean Girard is Stephen Brandt, *Jean Girard, Genevan publisher (1516-1557)*, to be published by Droz (Geneva), 1996.

tual readership, and I can do little here apart from drawing attention to
the question: who read all these works?

Two remarks may however be made, one based on external evidence,
the other based on the bibliography. On the one hand, it is well known
that the Reformation was an urban rather than a rural phenomenon.
Given that well under half the population lived in towns in the sixteenth
century, the potential target to be considered is effectively less than half
the total population. And, within towns, the literacy rates were markedly
higher than outside, higher among the 'middle classes' than among
workers, higher among males than females.[26] Bearing in mind our earlier
remarks about group reading, we may suggest that religious texts in
French, of whatever sort, could be accessible to the majority of the urban
population.

The second remark is based on information to be derived from the texts
themselves, in particular from prefatory epistles, dedications and the
like. Many texts (most of Calvin's polemical treatises, for example) carry
no dedication or preface; however, Calvin makes frequent reference to
'les simples, pour lesquels principalement je travaillais', which suggests
that he had a certain public, and a broad public, in mind. On the other
hand, Roman Catholic writers frequently do offer their texts to a named
person or community; and the proportion of female dedicatees is high:
high-born ladies like Queen Eleanor of France or the Queen of Scotland
or the Dowager Duchess of Lorraine, individual relatives of the writer
(often a widow to whom spiritual guidance is offered), and perhaps most
frequently of all communities of nuns.

A gradual movement towards a wider reading public on the part of
Roman Catholic writers is illustrated neatly by Pierre Doré's first works,
first printed between 1537 and 1539. He dedicates the *Allumettes de feu
divin* to a nun, the *College de sapience* to a widow from his home town,
and the *Voyes de paradis* to the countess of Montfort. But he dedicates
his *Dialogue de la foy* 'en général à tous', and in particular to young
people, to whom he offers 'le laict de catholique doctrine qu'ilz puissent
succer en croissant en eage'.[27] By the middle of the century, Roman
Catholic writers are directing their compositions, quite as much as the
Reformers, to the 'simple people', the uneducated (often with more than
a whiff of condescension).[28]

---

[26] See, in *La Réforme et le livre* (note 1), a brief discussion of these matters,
pp. 143-50.

[27] This particular choice of public is conditioned by the fact that Doré is refuting the catechism of Gaspard Megander in the *Dialogue de la foy*.

[28] For a more detailed treatment of the choice of reading public by Roman
Catholic writers, see my article '"Il seroit trop plus decent respondre en latin":

Impact and influence

In 1538 Cardinal Jacopo Sadoleto, Bishop of Carpentras, sent a letter (in Latin) to the people and government of Geneva, inviting them to return to the fold of the Roman Church. In the course of that letter Sadoleto imagines a simple member of Christ's flock standing before God on the Day of Judgement; he pleads that he has respected and humbly obeyed the doctrines and teachings of Holy Mother Church, handed down from antiquity, since it is not his job to judge others.

In the reply which Calvin wrote on behalf of the Genevans, he rejects this 'foolish and lazy' teaching. It is the task of every individual believer to fight off the attacks of Satan. Each individual must be equipped with the arms with which to fight; and those weapons are the Word of God. Each individual, Calvin insists: not just 'the average man' (*un homme du moyen peuple*), but even 'a stupid, uneducated keeper of pigs' (*le plus sot et rude porcher*).

It seems to me that the evolution represented in our survey of religious printing in French from 1511 to 1551 is symbolically expressed in this confrontation. From the respect for traditional authority to the prior claims of 'the truth', from the collective status of the member of Mother Church to the responsibility of the individual believer, from devotional, spiritual, often emotional uplift to the need to 'answer to every man that asketh you a reason of the hope that is in you' (I Pet. iii. 15): a profound shift in mentality is in process here.[29]

This movement towards doctrinal rather than devotional preoccupations is of course reflected elsewhere than in the history of printing. In this 'Age of Confessionalization', credal statements take on a new importance:[30] the Lutheran and Reformed catechisms and confessions of faith, the Roman Catholic 'articles of faith' as defined by the Paris Doctors (1543), or as affirmed by the Council of Trent (1545-1563).

These are intellectual statements, requiring lucidity, coherence, structure, definition; poetic metaphors, and exclamations of awe or praise, appropriate to a pious meditation, have no place in a credal statement. At the beginning of our period, there is a simple problem: the French language, whatever its riches in other directions, was not equipped to

---

les controversistes catholiques du XVIᵉ siècle face aux écrits réformés', in *Langues et nations au temps de la Renaissance*, ed. Marie-Thérèse Jones-Davies (Paris, Klincksieck, 1991), pp. 189-210.

[29] See my *Style of John Calvin*, p. 77, for Calvin's use of words like *devotion* and *zele*: there is almost always an implication of *misguided* devotion.

[30] See A.H.T. Levi, *Pagan virtue and the humanism of the Northern Renaissance* (London, Society for Renaissance Studies, 1974).

provide those requirements of clarity, coherence, structure or defini-tion.[31] So long as Latin was the universal language of debate and of thought, there was no problem. But in our period, through the new need to appeal to 'public opinion' (and this is the first time that such an appeal is being made), the French language has to assume new burdens for which, at the time, it was not suited.

To give only the most extreme illustrations of this,[32] I take a sample of each from Jérôme de Hangest, Doctor of Theology, Guillaume Farel, pioneer Reformer, Jean Calvin, and Antoine Du Val, Doctor of Theology in the second half of the century.

Jérôme de Hangest's *Contre les tenebrions lumiere evangelicque* ap-peared in January 1535 as a point by point answer to Antoine Marcourt's notorious *placards* of October 1534. To the claim in the *placards* that Christ's perfect sacrifice on the Cross makes redundant any further sac-rifice (in the Mass), Hangest replies:

> Honte debvrois avoir faire tant inepte argument. Je te respond, parfaict estoit, et de toute nature humaine redemptif et recon-ciliatif; par lequel les pechez des viateurs ont esté faictz remis-sibles, et leurs oeuvres à beatitude acceptables et d'aultres biens capables; mais non ainsi parfaict que par ledict sacrifice soit na-ture humaine de tous commandementz exempte: et que nulz pechez soient à elle imputez. Je te dis donc que ne se reitere le-dict sacrifice redemptif de nature humaine, mais trop bien le sa-cramental, et ce pour plusieurs choses impetrables. En oultre je te demande: l'amour parfaict de Dieu ou de ton prochain ne se doibt il reiterer? Oraison vers Dieu parfaicte ou adoration ou con-templation ou aultre chose vertueuse ne se doibt elle reiterer? Item increpe Jesuchrist, car dudict sainct sacrement par luy est ordonnee reiteration; increpe les apostres, lesquelz l'ont aussi re-iteré. Est doncq ton argument (comme tu dis) inevitable, povre aveugle, et pour lequel si presumptueusement avecq opprobres debvois dire: 'Mettez vous en avant sacrificateurs, et si avez puissance, respondez': certe à toy irrevinciblement respond la trespuissante verité evangelicque et apostolicque cy devant

---

[31] For a more detailed discussion, with sample passages, see my article 'The Reformation and the French Language', in *L'Esprit Créateur* 16/4 (1976), pp. 20-36.

[32] A more developed version in my 'De Calvin à Descartes: la création de la langue classique', in *Les Rapports entre les langues au XVIe siècle: Actes du colloque de Sommières, 14-17 septembre 1981* in *Bulletin de l'Association d'Études sur l'Humanisme, la Réforme et la Renaissance* 15/2 (1982), pp. 5-18.

> alleguee, et aussi n'est requise grande puissance à tant puerile,
> tant frivole et debile argument.[33]

Hangest is translating from Latin, and this shows most evidently in the
word order, and presence of Latin constructions ('Honte debvrois avoir
faire tant inepte argument') and the Latinized vocabulary ('reconciliatif',
'increper', 'irrevinciblement'). It is quite clearly a foreign idiom that he
is handling (even though he is a native French speaker).

Unlike Hangest, Guillaume Farel composed most of his works directly
in French. He is not an 'écorcheur de latin' like Hangest, and keeps to a
vocabulary with few, if any, obscurities for the contemporary reader. But
his syntax can be catastrophic. It is worth trying to follow the line of
thought in the following extract from his 1542, revised, edition of the
Sommaire, c'est une briefve declaration...; he is explaining that the idea
for his book, as originally his calling to preach, came from the Basle
Reformer Johann Oecolampadius:

> Il est certain, treschers en nostre Seigneur Jesus, que desja il y a
> environ treze ou quatorze ans, que le bon et fidele serviteur de
> Dieu docteur et pasteur de l'Eglise Jehan Oecolampade, à la re-
> queste d'aucuns bons personnaiges, m'admonesta d'estre en
> langue vulgaire pour donner quelque instruction à ceux qui ne
> sçavent en latin, en touchant briefvement aucuns poinctz, sur
> lesquelz le monde n'estoit bien enseigné, afin que tous ceux de la
> langue Françoyse peussent avoir plus droicte intelligence et
> congnoissance de Jesus, qui de si peu est purement congneu et
> servy, et qu'ilz fussent retirez et sortissent des tresgrandes tene-
> bres d'erreurs, esquelles tant de gens sont detenues, et qu'on
> peust avoir quelque ayde pour mieux entendre ce qu'on lit en la
> saincte Escriture. Combien que regardant ma petitesse, je n'eusse
> tasché ne proposé de rien escrire: comme aussi je n'eusse osé
> prescher, attendant que nostre Seigneur de sa grace envoyast par-
> sonnages plus propres et plus suffisans que ne suis: toutesfois
> comme en la predication à laquelle ce sainct personnage ordonné
> de Dieu, et legitimement entré en l'Eglise de Dieu, m'incita avec
> l'invocation du Nom de Dieu, je ne pensay qu'il me fust licite de
> resister: mais selon Dieu j'obeis estant requis et demandé du
> peuple et du consentement du Prince qui avoit congnoissance de
> l'Evangile, et prins la charge de prescher: aussi par luy admon-
> esté d'escrire, je ne peu refuser, que je ne misse peine et

---

[33] *Contre les tenebrions*, fol. e 2r-v.

diligence de faire comme j'estoye enhorté d'un si grand
Pasteur.[34]

Farel is not as eccentric as may appear to modern eyes. Examples of
similar syntactic structures can be found in the pages of every writer of
the time who sets his mind to expound an abstract argument or to argue
a case (here is a selection of names from the bibliography; any of their
works will make the point: Jean Lemaire de Belges, François Lambert,
Pierre Doré, Jean Gacy, Jean de Gaigny, Jacques Lefèvre d'Étaples,
Guillaume Petit). In fact a study of contemporary grammars, both of
Latin and of French, shows that grammarians of the time simply made
no mention of the sentence, and that the fundamental analytical tool of
co-ordination and subordination had not been invented.[35] The first
grammarians to consider questions about the sentence date from the
early seventeenth century.

In this welter of literary work wrestling with an unrewarding linguistic
medium (and it should be noted that it is only in the field of religious
controversy that the French language is being solicited in this way; the
only rival candidate is the few political pamphlets of the period, but they
are far from being as numerous as the religious production), one writer
stands out as qualitatively different: John Calvin. Here is not the place to
describe the qualities of Calvin's style: clarity and definition of vocabulary, the use of 'connectives' to provide an unbreakable chain of argument, the stark contrasts created by his use of antithesis, vulgar images
set against biblical language, and so on.[36] In the present context the
important point is the (relative) shortness of the sentences:

> Chascun confesse que ce qui a esmeu nostre Seigneur à cacher le
> corps de Moyse a esté de peur que le peuple d'Israel n'en abbu-
> sast en l'adorant. Or il convient estendre ce qui a esté faict en un
> sainct à tous les autres, veu que c'est une mesme raison. Mais
> encore que nous laissions là les sainctz, advisons que dit sainct
> Paul de Jesus Christ mesmes. Car il proteste de ne le congnoistre
> plus selon la chair, apres sa resurrection; admonestant par ces
> motz, que tout ce qui est charnel en Jesus Christ se doit oublier
> et mettre en arriere, afin d'emploier et mettre toute nostre affec-
> tion à le cercher et posseder selon l'Esprit. Maintenant donc, de

---

[34] *Sommaire* (1542), fol. S 2r-v.

[35] See 'De Calvin à Descartes', p. 6.

[36] See *The Style of John Calvin*. See also Olivier Millet, *Calvin et la dynamique
de la parole: Étude de rhétorique réformée* (Paris, Champion, 1992).

> pretendre que c'est une belle chose d'avoir quelque memorial,
> tant de luy que des sainctz, pour nous inciter à devotion: qu'est-
> ce sinon une faulse couverture pour farder nostre folle cupidité,
> qui n'est fondée en nulle raison? Et mesmes quand il sembleroit
> advis que ceste raison feust suffisante: puis qu'elle repugne aper-
> tement à ce que le S. Esprit a prononcé par la bouche de sainct
> Paul, que voulons nous plus? Combien qu'il n'est ja mestier de
> faire longue dispute sus ce poinct, assavoir s'il est bon ou mau-
> vais d'avoir des reliques, pour les garder seulement comme
> choses pretieuses sans les adorer. Car ainsi que nous avons dict,
> l'experience monstre que l'un n'est presques jamais sans
> l'autre.[37]

It can be said that Calvin invented the short sentence in French. Each sentence represents no more than two or three subordinate clauses, often joined into a structure like 'Since we see such and such, therefore it follows that...' Every sentence (except the first) is linked by a conjunction or adverb to the preceding sentence, and the reader is thus guided step by step through the argument. The result is what I have called a linear structure in Calvin's writing,[38] which sets him apart from his contemporaries, while anticipating the way in which French would evolve in the seventeenth century.

To stray briefly outside the limits of the present study, I would add that the similarity between Calvin's language and that of, say, Pascal is not by chance. I have mentioned that a whole genre of replies to John Calvin grew up in the second half of the sixteenth century. Many of the Paris theologians who replied, in French, to publications in French by Calvin, acquired some of his linguistic habits while refuting his thought. Just one example is Antoine Du Val, Doctor of the Paris Faculty of Theology, who wrote on *Les Contrarietez et contredictz qui se trouvent en la doctrine de Jean Calvin* (Paris, Nicholas Chesneau, 1561). Du Val's manner of writing shows how far French has come as a vehicle for intellectual thought and argument since the days of Jérôme de Hangest:

> Apres avoir examiné les propos susdicts, se contrarians du tout
> les uns aux autres, il n'y a homme de si bon cerveau ou jugement
> qui me peust persuader qu'il faille croire à tel Apostre ou Evan-

---

[37] Calvin, *Advertissement tresutile du grand proffit que reviendroit à la chrestienté s'il se faisoit inventoire de tous les corps sainctz, et reliques...* (1543), p. 3.

[38] See my article 'Linearity in Calvin's thought', *Calvin Theological Journal* 26 (1991), pp. 100-110.

geliste nouveau, et que sa doctrine soit evangelique, enseignée par les Apostres de Jesus Christ: car qu'on lise tant qu'on voudra, on ne me sçauroit monstrer que la doctrine et escrits des Apostres soyent contraires les uns aux autres, comme est celle de M. Jean Calvin. Or à fin qu'un chascun l'entende clairement, conferons je vous prie les propos susdicts les uns aux autres, et voyons donc si l'evangile selon M. Jean Calvin (ainsi fault il dire) se contredict point. L'evangile donc, selon Calvin, dit en un chapitre que, si ne voulons nous plonger en une fosse dont nous ne puissions sortir, qu'il nous fault laisser gouverner et enseigner à Dieu et nous contenter de sa simple parole. Or bien, cela est bien dit. Mais cecy gaste tout, et vous desmantez vous mesmes M. Jean Calvin, quand vous dictes en autre lieu, que Dieu a determiné et ordonné que l'homme trebuchast. Il me semble qu'on ne pourroit bien accorder tel propos. Car si, comme vous dictes, Dieu avoit ordonné et determiné que l'homme trebuchast, il ne nous faudroit donc laisser gouverner et enseigner à Dieu, comme estant celuy qui ne demanderoit sinon la damnation et perdition de l'homme. Conclusion: Or en la pure parole de Dieu, on ne trouve point que Dieu ayt voulu, determiné, decreté et arresté en son conseil estroit et admirable la cheute du premier homme, mais tout le contraire, c'est à sçavoir la defense, salut, etc. Il s'ensuit doncques que Calvin est menteur apert.

It is my contention[39] that via the repeated employment of Calvin's stylistic techniques by writers like Du Val, Christophe de Cheffontaines, Jacques Davy Du Perron, the evolution perceptible in our bibliographical listings was destined to become a standard element of the French language as it has been practised up to the present day. Despite the fact that the Reformation did not 'catch on' in France, its contribution to the evolution of French culture is profound.

That contribution is significant in terms of the language. It is also profoundly important in terms of poetry and of music. We have noted the outstanding popularity of Marot's metrical psalms, and mentioned the beginnings of the musical enthusiasm based on the psalm settings in the Genevan psalter which swept France in the second half of the century. Here again, the literary and aesthetic forms first developed in the Calvinist Reformation are later taken over in France by other persuasions (the Académie de Baïf, for example), and finally achieve official status when

---

[39] I hope to develop a fuller study of the afterlife of Calvin's style and its extension to become the basis of standard modern French.

'enfin Malherbe vint' — presented to King Henri IV by Jacques Davy Du Perron, who had himself had a Calvinist upbringing and education.[40]

These are areas for further exploration, since the present survey stops at 1551. Enough has, I hope, been said to show that this period of forty years up to 1551 is particularly significant in its formative nature. As was said at the beginning, a study of works in the French language is necessarily partial; but that does not prevent it from being extremely revealing.

The organization of the bibliography

Our corpus of material is presented in three main forms: an alphabetical list, a chronological list, and a list by places of printing (and within that by printers/booksellers). There is also a finding list of anonymous titles, an alphabetical finding list of printers, and an index of names mentioned in the text. Each of these elements will be explained in more detail below.

I have chosen to give the main notices in the alphabetical section rather than in the chronological list, for two reasons. Far too many of the dates given are not explicitly stated in the editions, but are deductions or approximations: not a good basis for the central formulation. Second, I should anticipate that the major use of this work will be as a finding list, as an aid for identifying unfamiliar or unknown editions; for that purpose the most common starting point will be the name of the author, or the title. The main burden of information is therefore carried in the alphabetical list; the other formats give cross-references to the main list.

The amount and quality of the information available varies considerably. To the best of my ability, descriptions are based on the inspection of at least one copy. In some cases, however, that has not been possible, and I have had to rely on library catalogue entries, descriptions in sale catalogues, references gleaned from the manuscripts of Philippe Renouard and the like. It is therefore possible that the list includes a number of 'ghosts', or of double descriptions of a single edition. I regret this; but, given the nature of a finding list, it seemed preferable to include even uncertain evidence, in the hopes that it may guide other researchers towards further discoveries.

---

[40] See my article 'Du Psautier de Genève à l'Académie de Baïf: fortune d'une esthétique calvinienne', in *Psaume* 10/11 (1995), 21-6.

The alphabetical list: the main entries

The list is arranged in alphabetical order by author, or, in the case of
anonymous works, by a brief generic title (*Postilles*, for example), or
short title (*Fontaine de vie*). Each author's works are given in alphabetical order of the first noun in the title, the editions arranged in chronological order (if more than one edition in the same year, places of printing in alphabetical order are taken into account). In cases where the
same text appears with more than one title, like Erasmus, *Preparatif à la
mort* or *Preparation à la mort*, or the same author's *Enchiridion* or
Chevalier chrestien, all editions are treated in one chronological se-
quence.

Rather than load the main list with numerous cross-references from
anonymous titles to authors who are known but not named in editions,
these cross-references have been brought together in an appendix to the
alphabetical list. Not included in that appendix are titles for which no
author at all has been proposed; such works will be found directly in the
main list, by short or generic title.

Each main notice takes the following form:

1. **Reference number**: I have followed H.M. Adams's practice in his
   Cambridge bibliography, attributing the first letter of the alphabetical entry followed by a number, each letter having a new number series.

2. **Name of author** in modern, French form (thus Jérôme, not Hieronymus nor Hierosme nor Jerome), in bold print. If the author is
   identifiable, but not named, the name is placed in brackets [ ]. An
   anonymous work for which no author can be identified is given a
   brief French title (**Fontaine de vie**) or a generic title (**Postilles,
   Imitation de Jésus-Christ**).

3. If called for, the author's name is followed, on the same line, by a
   secondary author, name of **translator**, or **source**.

4. The **title** of the work is given in italics, on a new line. The title is
   given in as complete a form as possible (some very long titles have
   been abbreviated), except for indications in the title of the name of
   the author, which have been replaced by <>.[41] In the transcriptions of titles, I have modernized the distinction between i and j, u
   and v, and I have resolved all contractions and abbreviations, but

---

[41] Those familiar with the *Inventaire chronologique des éditions parisiennes* of
Brigitte Moreau will recognize that my notices are in many ways modelled on
hers.

otherwise the spelling of the original has been retained. I have
rigorously respected punctuation and capitalization, since varia-
tions here frequently permit differentiation between otherwise very
similar editions.[42]

5. The title is followed by the **place of printing**, the **name of the printer
and/or bookseller**, and the **date**. Names of place and/or printer/
bookseller are printed in standardized form ('Jean', not 'Jehan'),
and are given in [ ] if they are not explicitly stated in the text. As
mentioned earlier (see note 24), it is not always possible to differentiate between printer and bookseller or commercial editor. The
date is given as on title page or colophon; if these are different,
the title page version is preferred. The normal practice in France
(but not in Geneva) in this period was to date the New Year from
Easter; but I have retained dates as given ('ancien style' or 'a.s.'),
not modernized. A '?' after a date may indicate various levels of
uncertainty: it may refer to a date inferred from a preface, dedication or *privilège*; or it may indicate a period: most of Simon Du
Bois's editions in Alençon (where he was active 1529-34) are undated, for example, and I have followed Mlle Moreau's practice of
attributing a (somewhat arbitrary) date within the period.

6. Certain **technical details** follow on the next line:

   (a) *format* (2° = folio, 4° = in-quarto, 8° = in-octavo, etc.)

   (b) *Pagination* (pp.) or *foliotation* (ff.), in [ ] if unnumbered.
   Pagination has not been systematically noted, and the
   pagination printed in works of this period is frequently
   erroneous.

   (c) *Signatures* (a far more reliable guide to the actual make-up
   of a book in the period). In gatherings signed with symbols other than letters, it has not been possible always to
   represent the original symbol (ivy-leaf, hand, Maltese
   cross...), and these symbols should not be used for purposes of identification of editions.[43]

---

[42] Some titles begin with a decorated capital, followed by a normal capital. In
these cases I have departed from my rule, and print 'Larmeure de patience', not
'LArmeure de patience', 'Sensuyt' not 'SEnsuyt'.

[43] Purist Anglo-Saxon bibliographers will doubtless denounce me for failing to
adhere slavishly to the rules for the indication of signatures laid down by Fred-
son Bowers. I am quite impenitent on this: there are cases in continental printing not covered by Bowers's rules; I have preferred to give a fuller transcription

(d) *Typeface*: a minimal indication is provided, distinguishing between all varieties of gothic, including the French 'lettres bâtardes' ('goth.'), roman ('rom.') and italic ('ital.'), as found in the bulk of the text. Naturally, some words, even whole sections, may be in some other typeface.

(e) *Colophon* (if present): the signature of the page where the colophon appears is given, and names of place and printer/bookseller are transcribed exactly. Any date is given in modernized form ('24.02.1524', not 'le xxiv. jour de febvrier l'An mil cinq cens vingt et quatre').

7. The following line gives **library locations**, if possible including shelf-mark. A mention preceded by an asterisk means that I have personally examined the copy. Up to five locations are given; if there are more copies known, the fifth location is followed by (+).

8. **References**: mentions in other bibliographical sources or studies of a text are noted in succinct form; the abbreviations are resolved in the bibliography at the end of this introduction.

9. **Notes**: this rubric allows for various types of information: an indication of contents, dedications, prefaces, problems of identification or dating...

Chronological list

Editions are listed alphabetically by author or (for anonyma) short title within each year, with the reference number in the main list. It should be noted that the question marks concerning dates have been omitted from this list; the omission does not imply any greater security of dating!

List of printers by city

All cities in which a printer or bookseller was involved in religious works in French are listed in alphabetical order (the names being anglicized); within each city, each printer/bookseller is listed in alphabetical order, and for each printer/bookseller the date, author and short title of each edition is given, together with the reference number in the main list. Editions are given in chronological order. It should be noted that in

---

than prescribed by Bowers, in the interest of the golden rule of bibliography, which is clarity.

this list the square brackets have been removed as well as the queries concerning dates. It is in the main list that the full information appears.

Finding list of printers

This simply lists all printers and booksellers in one alphabetical series, adding the city or cities where they were active; for information about the editions in which they were concerned, the reader will consult the preceding list by cities.

Index of proper names

Finally, names of persons mentioned as *secondary authors* or in the *Notes* section of the main notices are listed, with reference numbers to the relevant notices.

List of Works Consulted

Abélard: J. Abélard, *Les Illustrations de Gaule et singularitez de Troye de Jean Lemaire de Belges. Étude des éditions — Genèse de l'oeuvre* (Geneva, Droz, 1976).

Adams: H.M. Adams, *Catalogue of books printed on the continent of Europe, 1501-1600, in Cambridge libraries* (Cambridge, Cambridge University Press, 1967).

E. Armstrong *BHR* 1969: Elizabeth Armstrong, 'Notes on the works of Guillaume Michel, dit de Tours', *BHR* 31 (1969), pp. 257-81.

Babelon: J. Babelon, *La Bibliothèque française de Fernand Colomb* (Paris, Champion, 1912).

Baddeley: S. Baddeley, *L'Orthographe française au temps de la réforme* (Geneva, Droz, 1993).

Barnaud: J. Barnaud, *Pierre Viret, sa vie et son oeuvre (1511-1571)* (Saint-Amans, 1911).

Baudrier: H.-L. et J. Baudrier, *Bibliographie lyonnaise. Recherches sur les imprimeurs, libraires, relieurs et fondeurs de lettres de Lyon au XVIe siècle*, 12 vols (Lyon, 1895-1921).

Baudrier *Suppl.*: *Supplément provisoire à la Bibliographie lyonnaise du Président Baudrier*, fasc. 1 by Y. de la Perrière (Paris, Bibliothèque nationale, 1967).

Bense *Béda*: W.F. Bense, *Noël Béda and the Humanist Reformation at Paris, 1504-1534* (Ph.D. dissertation, Harvard, 1967, 3 vols).

Benzing *Luther*: J. Benzing, *Lutherbibliographie. Verzeichnis der gedruckten Schriften Martin Luthers bis zu dessen Tod* (Baden-Baden, Heitz, 1966). See also Claus.

Berthoud *APR*: G. Berthoud, 'Livres pseudo-catholiques de contenu protestant', in *Aspects de la propagande religieuse* (THR 28, Geneva, Droz, 1957, pp. 143-54).

Berthoud *BHR* 1947: G. Berthoud, 'L'Édition d'Avignon du *Miroir de l'âme pécheresse*', *BHR* 9 (1947), pp. 151-3.

Berthoud *BHR* 1967: G. Berthoud, 'La *Confession* de maître Noël Béda et le problème de son auteur', in *Bibliothèque d'Humanisme et Renaissance* 29 (1967), pp. 373-97.

Berthoud 'Michel': G. Berthoud, 'Les Impressions genevoises de Jean Michel (1538-1544)', in *Cinq siècles d'imprimerie genevoise* (Geneva, S.H.A.G., 1980), Vol. I, pp. 55-88.

Berthoud *Marcourt*: G. Berthoud, *Antoine Marcourt, réformateur et pamphlétaire du* Livre des marchans *aux* Placards de 1534 (THR 129, Geneva, Droz, 1973).

BG: J.-F. Gilmont, 'Bibliotheca Gebennensis. Les livres imprimés à Genève de 1535 à 1549', in *Genava* 28 (1980), pp. 229-51.

BHR: *Bibliothèque d'Humanisme et Renaissance*.

Biblio.belg.: F. Vander Haeghen, re-ed. under the direction of Marie-Thérèse Lenger, *Bibliotheca belgica. Bibliographie générale des Pays-Bas*, 7 vols (Bruxelles, Culture et Civilisation, 1964-75).

Bietenholz: P.G. Bietenholz, *Basle and France in the sixteenth century. The Basle humanists and printers in their contacts with Francophone culture* (*THR* 112, Geneva, Droz, 1971).

Bodenmann: Reinhard Bodenmann, 'Bibliotheca Lambertiana', in *Pour retrouver François Lambert. Bio-bibliographie et études*, ed. P. Fraenkel (Baden-Baden, Koerner, 1987), pp. 9-213.

Bordier *Chans. hug.*: H.-L. Bordier, *Le Chansonnier huguenot du XVIe siècle* (Paris, 1870).

Briquet: C.M. Briquet, *Les Filigranes. Dictionnaire historique des marques de papier dès leur apparition vers 1282 jusqu'en 1600*, 4 vols, 1907; revised edition, Amsterdam, The Paper Publications Society, 1968.

Britnell *Bouchet*: J. Britnell, *Jean Bouchet* (Edinburgh University Press, 1986).

Brun: R. Brun, *Le Livre français illustré de la Renaissance. Étude suivie du catalogue des principaux livres à figures du XVIe siècle* (Paris, A. & J. Picard, 1969).

Brunet: J.-C. Brunet, *Manuel du libraire et de l'amateur de livres...* 5th ed., 6 vols (Paris, Firmin-Didot, 1860-65).

Brunet *Suppl.*: *Supplément du Manuel* by P. Deschamps and G. Brunet, 2 vols (Paris, Firmin-Didot, 1877-80).

Calvin *OC*: J. Calvin, *Opera quae supersunt omnia*, ed. by G. Baum, E. Cunitz and E. Reuss, 59 vols (Brunswick and Berlin, 1863-1900).

Cartier *Arrêts*: A. Cartier, *Arrêts du Conseil de Genève sur le fait de l'imprimerie et de la librairie de 1541 à 1550* (extract from *Mémoires et documents publiés par la Société d'histoire et d'archéologie de Genève* vol. 23, 1888-1894: Geneva, Georg, 1893).

Cartier *De Tournes*: A. Cartier, *Bibliographie des éditions des de Tournes, imprimeurs lyonnais*, 2 vols (Paris, Bibl. nationales de France, 1937-38).

Cartier *Mélanges Picot*: A. Cartier, 'Les Dixains catholiques et Jacques Estauge imprimeur à Bâle', in *Mélanges offerts à M. Émile Picot* (Paris, Morgand, 1913), Vol. I, pp. 307-13.

Cat. Drilhon: F. Higman, 'A Heretic's Library: the Drilhon Inventory, 1545', in *Book production and letters in the western European Renaissance*, ed. A.L. Lepscky et al. (London, M.H.R.A., 1986), pp. 184-209.

CDM: P. Chaix, A. Dufour, G. Moeckli, *Les Livres imprimés à Genève de 1550 à 1600* (*THR* 86, Geneva, Droz, 1966).

Chaix, 'Pamphlet genevois': P. Chaix, 'Un Pamphlet genevois du XVIe siècle: l'*Antithèse* de S. Du Rosier', in *Mélanges offerts à M. Paul-É. Martin* (Geneva, 1961), pp. 467-82.

Chambers: B.T. Chambers, *Bibliography of French Bibles. Fifteenth- and sixteenth-century French-language editions of the Scriptures* (*THR* 192, Geneva, Droz, 1983).

Christie: R.C. Christie, *Étienne Dolet: the Martyr of the Renaissance, 1508-1546* (London, Macmillan, 1899).

Claudin *Agen*: A. Claudin, 'Le premier livre imprimé à Agen. Recherches sur la vie et les travaux du premier imprimeur agenais' (Paris, Claudin, 1894: extract from *Revue de l'Agenais*, 1894).

Claus/Pegg: H. Claus and M.A. Pegg, *Ergänzungen zur Bibliographie der zeitgenössischen Lutherdrucke* (Gotha, 1982).

Clive: H.P. Clive, *Marguerite de Navarre: an Annotated Bibliography* (London, Grant and Cutler, 1983).

Clutton: G. Clutton, 'Simon Du Bois of Paris and Alençon', in *Gutenberg Jahrbuch* 1937, pp. 124-30.

Coll.Eras.Tur.: *Colloquia Erasmiana Turonensia*, ed. J.-C. Margolin, 2 vols (Univ. of Toronto Press and Paris, Vrin, 1972).

Courvoisier *Cahiers RHPR* 1933: J. Courvoisier, 'Une traduction française du commentaire de Bucer de l'évangile selon saint Matthieu', *Cahiers de la Revue d'histoire et de philosophie religieuses* (Paris, 1933).

Dagens: J. Dagens, *Bibliographie chronologique de la littérature de spiritualité et de ses sources (1501-1610)* (Paris, Desclée de Brouwer, 1952).

Delarue *BHR* 1946: H. Delarue, 'Olivétan et Pierre de Vingle à Genève, 1532-1533', in *Bibliothèque d'Humanisme et Renaissance* 8 (1946), pp. 105-18.

Denis, *Églises*: *Les Églises d'étrangers en pays rhénans (1538-1564)* (Paris, Soc. Les Belles Lettres, 1984).

Donckel *AFH* 1933: E. Donckel, 'Studien über die Prophezeiung des Fr. Telesforus von Cosenza, O.F.M. (1365-1386)', in *Archivum Franciscanum Historicum* 26 (1933), pp. 29-104 and 282-314.

Droz *APR*: E. Droz, 'Pierre de Vingle, l'imprimeur de Farel', in *Aspects de la propagande religieuse* (THR 28, Geneva, Droz, 1957), pp. 38-78.

Droz *BHR* 1958: E. Droz, 'Une impression inconnue de Pierre de Vingle', in *BHR* 20 (1958), pp. 158-69.

Droz *BHR* 1960: E. Droz, 'Note sur les impressions genevoises transportées par Hernandez', in *BHR* 22 (1960), pp. 119-32.

Droz *Chemins*: E. Droz, *Chemins de l'hérésie. Textes et documents*, 4 vols (Geneva, Slatkine, 1970-76).

Th.Dufour *Ms fr.*: Th. Dufour, notes manuscrites sur l'imprimerie genevoise au XVIe siècle, Genève BPU Ms.fr. 3803-3808, 3811, 3818 and 3821.

Th.Dufour *Not.cat.*: Th. Dufour, *Notice bibliographique sur le catéchisme et la confession de foi de Calvin (1537) et sur les autres livres imprimés à Genève et à Neuchâtel dans les premiers temps de la Réforme (1533-1540)* (Geneva, Georg, 1878).

Du Verdier: A. Du Verdier, *La Bibliothèque d'Antoine Du Verdier, Seigneur de Vauprivas* (Lyon, Honorat, 1585).

Fairfax Murray: *Catalogue of a collection of early French books in the library of C. Fairfax Murray*, ed. H.W. Davies, 2 vols (London, Holland Press, 1961).

Farge *Bio.reg.*: J.K. Farge, *Biographical register of Paris doctors of theology, 1500-1536* (Toronto, Pontifical Institute of Mediaeval Studies, 1980).

Farge *Parti conservateur*: J.K. Farge, *Le Parti conservateur au XVIe siècle. Université et Parlement de Paris à l'époque de la Renaissance et de la Réforme* (Paris, Collège de France, 1992).

Farge *Registre*: J.K. Farge (ed.), *Registre des procès-verbaux de la Faculté de Théologie de l'Université de Paris*. Tome I: *de janvier 1524 à novembre 1533* (Paris, Amateurs de livres, 1990). *Registre des conclusions de la faculté de théologie de l'université de Paris*. Tome II: *du 26 novembre 1533 au 1er mars 1550* (Paris, Klincksieck, 1994).

Febvre *BHR* VI: L. Febvre, 'Dolet propagateur de l'évangile', in *BHR* 6 (1945), pp. 98-170.

Febvre *BSHPF* 1911: L. Febvre, 'Une édition de 1529 du *Sommaire* de Farel', in *BSHPF* 60 (1911), pp. 184-5.

Febvre/Martin: L. Febvre, H.-J. Martin, *L'Apparition du livre* (Paris, Albin Michel, 1958).

Fraenkel, 'Version française': Pierre Fraenkel, 'La version française d'un célèbre manuel de controverse: les *Lieux communs* de Jean Eckius', in *Mélanges d'histoire du XVIe siècle offerts à Henri Meylan* (*THR* 110, Geneva, Droz, 1970), pp. 49-61.

Frankfurt cat. 1610: *Bibliotheca exotica, sive Catalogus officinalis... La Bibliothèque universelle, contenant le catalogue de tous les livres qui ont esté imprimés ce siecle passé, aux langues Françoise, Italienne, Espaignole, et autres, qui sont aujourdhuy plus communes, despuis l'an 1500 jusques à l'an present 1610...* (Frankfurt, Pierre Kopf, 1610).

Franz: G. Franz, *Huberinus — Rhegius — Holbein. Bibliographische und druckgeschichtliche Untersuchung der verbreitesten Trost- und Erbauungsschriften des 16. Jahrhunderts* (Nieuwkoop, de Graaf, 1973).

Gardy: F. Gardy, *Bibliographie des oeuvres théologiques, littéraires, historiques et juridiques de Théodore de Bèze* (*THR* 41, Geneva, Droz, 1960).

Giese: F.S. Giese, *Artus Désiré, priest and pamphleteer of the sixteenth century* (Chapel Hill, U.N.C., 1973).

Gilmont *Calvin*: R. Peter, J.-F. Gilmont, *Bibliotheca Calviniana. Les oeuvres de Jean Calvin publiés au XVIe siècle.* Vol. I: *Écrits théologiques, littéraires et juridiques, 1532-1554* (*THR* 255, Geneva, Droz, 1991); Vol. II: *Écrits théologiques, littéraires et juridiques, 1555-1564* (*THR* 281, Geneva, Droz, 1994).

Gilmont *Crespin*: J.-F. Gilmont, *Bibliographie des éditions de Jean Crespin, 1550-1572*, 2 vols (Verviers, Gason, 1981).

Gilmont *Farel*: 'L'Oeuvre imprimé de Guillaume Farel', in *Actes du Colloque Guillaume Farel* (*Cahiers de la Revue de Théologie et de Philosophie*), 2 vols (Geneva, 1983), Vol. II, pp. 105-45.

Gilmont 'Sommaire': 'Le *Sommaire des livres du vieil et nouveau testament* de Robert Estienne ou l'étrange périple d'une confession de foi', in *Revue de l'Histoire des Religions* 212 (1995), pp. 175-218.

Ginzburg *Nicod.*: C Ginzburg, *Il Nicodemismo. Simulazione e dissimulazione religiosa nell'Europa del '500* (Turin, Einaudi, 1970).

Graesse: J.G. Graesse, *Trésor de livres rares et précieux ou Nouveau diction-naire bibliographique*, 7 vols (Dresden, Kuntze, 1859-69).

Guy, *Le Sermon d'A.M.*: H. Guy, 'Le Sermon d'Aimé Maigret', in *Annales de l'Université de Grenoble*, nouvelle série, Lettres-Droit, 5 (1928), pp. 181-222.

Haag, *Fr. Prot.*: E. and É. Haag, *La France protestante*, 2nd ed. directed by H. Bordier, 6 vols (Paris, Sandoz and Fischbacher, 1877-88).

Hari *APR*: R. Hari, 'Les placards de 1534', in *Aspects de la propagande reli-gieuse* (*THR* 28, Geneva, Droz, 1957), pp. 79-142.

Herm. *Corresp.*: A.-L. Herminjard, *Correspondance des réformateurs dans les pays de langue française*, 9 vols (Geneva, Georg, 1866-97).

Het Boek 1929: C.P. Burger, 'De *Introduction pour les enfants*', in *Het Boek* 18 (1929), pp. 161-8.

Higman *BHR* 1992: F. Higman, 'Calvin, le polar et la propagande: l'*Histoire d'un meurtre*', in *BHR* 54 (1992), pp. 111-23.

Higman *Censorship*: F. Higman, *Censorship and the Sorbonne. A bibliogra-phical study of books in French censured by the Faculty of Theology of the University of Paris, 1520-1551* (*THR* 172, Geneva, Droz, 1979).

Higman 'Dates-clé': F. Higman, 'Dates-clé de la réforme française: le *Som-maire de Guillaume Farel et La Somme de l'escripture saincte*', in *BHR* 38 (1976), pp. 237-47.

Higman 'Débuts': F. Higman, 'Les débuts de la polémique contre la messe: *De la tressaincte cene de nostre seigneur et de la messe qu'on chante com-munement*', in *Le Livre et la Réforme*, ed. R. Peter and B. Roussel (Bordeaux, Société des bibliophiles de Guyenne, 1987), pp. 35-92.

Higman 'Dolet': F. Higman, 'Étienne Dolet et Gaspard Megander: le problème du *Cato Christianus*', in *Études sur Étienne Dolet, le théâtre au XVIe siècle, le Forez, le Lyonnais et l'histoire du livre, publiées à la mémoire de Claude Longeon*, ed. G.-A. Pérouse (Geneva, Droz, 1993), pp. 75-84.

Higman 'Doré': F. Higman, 'La réfutation par Pierre Doré du catéchisme de Megander', in *Aux origines du catéchisme en France*, ed. P. Colin et al. (Paris, Desclée, 1989), pp. 55-66.

Higman 'Genres': F. Higman, 'Les genres de la littérature polémique calviniste au XVIe siècle', in *Prose et prosateurs de la Renaissance. Mélanges offerts à M. le professeur Robert Aulotte* (Paris, S.E.D.E.S., 1988), pp. 123-34.

Higman *Palaestra*: F. Higman, 'Les traductions françaises de Luther', in *Palaestra typographica*, ed. J.-F. Gilmont (Aubel, Gason, 1984), pp. 11-56.

Higman 'Prem. rép.': F. Higman, 'Premières réponses catholiques aux écrits de la Réforme en France, 1525-1540', in *Le Livre dans l'Europe de la Renaissance*, ed. P. Aquilon et H.-J. Martin (Paris, Promodis, 1988), pp. 361-77.

Higman *RHPR* 1980: F. Higman, 'Un pamphlet de Calvin restitué à son auteur', in *Revue d'histoire et de philosophie religieuses* 60 (1980), pp. 167-80 et 327-37.

Higman *RHPR* 1983: F. Higman, 'Luther et la piété de l'Église gallicane: le *Livre de vraye et parfaicte oraison*', in *Revue d'histoire et de philosophie religieuses* 63 (1983), pp. 91-111.

Higman 'Simon Du Bois': F. Higman, 'Simon Du Bois à Paris en 1534?', in *BHR* 42 (1980), pp. 413-19.

Higman 'Spiritualité': F. Higman, 'Farel, Calvin et Olivétan, sources de la spiritualité gallicane', in *Actes du Colloque Guillaume Farel (Cahiers de la Revue de Théologie et de Philosophie)*, 2 vols (Geneva, Lausanne, Neuchâtel, 1983), Vol. I, pp. 45-61.

Higman 'Theology': F. Higman, 'Theology for the Layman in the French Reformation, 1520-1550', in *The Library*, 6th series, Vol. 9 (1987), pp. 105-27.

Imbart de La Tour: P. Imbart de La Tour, *Les Origines de la réforme*, 4 vols (Paris, Hachette, 1905-35).

Index I: J.-M de Bujanda, J.K. Farge et F. Higman, *Index des livres interdits*, I: *Index de l'Université de Paris* (Sherbrooke, Centre d'Études de la Renaissance, 1985).

Index II: J.-M. de Bujanda et L.-E. Halkin, *Index des livres interdits*, II: *Index de l'Université de Louvain* (Sherbrooke, Centre d'Études de la Renaissance, 1986).

Index aurel.: *Index aureliensis. Catalogus librorum sedecimo saeculo impressorum*, 11 vols to date (Baden-Baden, 1965-).

Jodogne: O. Jodogne, *Le Mystère de la Passion de Jean Michel* (Gembloux, Duculot, 1959).

Johns *BHR* 1975: F.A. Johns, 'Clément Marot, Mathurin Cordier and the *Quatre epistres chrestiennes*', in *BHR* 37 (1975), pp. 445-6.

Jourda: P. Jourda, 'Tableau chronologique des oeuvres de Marguerite de Navarre', in *Revue du XVIᵉ siècle* 12 (1925), pp. 209-55.

Kemp: W. Kemp, 'Les petits livres français illustrés de Romain Morin (1530-1532) et leurs dérivés immédiats', in *Il Rinascimento a Lione, Atti del Congresso internazionale (Macerata, 6-11 maggio 1985)*, ed. A. Possenti and G. Mastrangelo (Rome, Ateneo, 1988), pp. 465-526.

E. Kronenberg, *Het Boek* 1938-39: E. Kronenberg, 'Een druk van Pierre de Vingle te Genève met een antwerpsch schijnadres, 1533', in *Het Boek* 25 (1938-39), pp. 257-65.

Labarre *HÉF* I: A. Labarre, 'Les incunables: la présentation du livre', in *Histoire de l'édition française*, I: *Le Livre conquérant*, ed. R. Chartier et H.-J. Martin (Paris, Promodis, 1982), pp. 195-215.

Labarthe: O. Labarthe, *La relation entre le premier catéchisme de Calvin et la première confession de foi de Genève* (typescript thesis, Geneva, 1967).

Labarthe *BHR* 1973: O. Labarthe, 'Jean Gérard, l'imprimeur des "Cinquante Pseaumes" de Marot', *BHR* 35 (1973), pp. 547-61.

La Croix: F. La Croix Du Maine et A. Du Verdier, *Les bibliothèques françoises... Nouvelle édition ... revue par M. Rigoley de Juvigny*, 6 vols (Paris, Saillant et Nyon, 1772-73).

Longeon *Dolet*: C. Longeon, *Bibliographie des oeuvres d'Étienne Dolet, écrivain, éditeur et imprimeur* (*THR* 174, Geneva, Droz, 1980).

Longeon *Hommes*: C. Longeon, *Hommes et livres de la Renaissance* (Saint-Étienne, Institut Claude Longeon, 1990).

Longeon *Préfaces*: Étienne Dolet, *Préfaces françaises*, ed. C. Longeon (TLF 272, Geneva, Droz, 1979).

Machiels: J. Machiels, *Catalogus van de boeken gedrukt voor 1600 aanwezig op de Centrale bibliotheek van de Rijksuniversiteit Gent*, 2 vols (Gand, 1979).

Mason *BHR* 1988: S. Mason, 'Viret adapted by Viret: the re-use of *De la différence* in Viret's later works', *BHR* 50 (1988), pp. 623-35.

Massaut *Clichtove*: J.-P. Massaut, *Josse Clichtove, l'humanisme et la réforme du clergé*, 2 vols (Paris, Belles Lettres, 1968).

Massaut 'Théologie universitaire': J.-P. Massaut, 'Théologie universitaire et requêtes spirituelles à la veille de la Réforme', in *La Controverse religieuse (XVIᵉ-XIXᵉ siècles)*, ed. M. Péronnet (Montpellier, 1980), pp. 7-18.

Mauriac *AFH* 1925: R. Mauriac, 'Nomenclature et description sommaire des oeuvres de fr. Thomas Illyricus, OFM', in *Archivum Franciscanum Historicum* 18 (1925).

Mayer *BHR* 1955: C.A. Mayer, 'The problem of Dolet's evangelical publications', in *BHR* 17 (1955), pp. 405-14.

Mayer *Marot*: C.A. Mayer, *Bibliographie des oeuvres de Clément Marot publiées au XVIᵉ siècle* (Paris, Nizet, 1975).

Mégret *BHR* (1944): J. Mégret, 'Deux impressions retrouvées d'Étienne Dolet', in *BHR* 4 (1944), pp. 123-37.

Meylan *Mélanges Martin*: H. Meylan, 'Une page oubliée du refuge genevois: le serment du 27 novembre 1547', in *Mélanges offerts à M. Paul-É. Martin* (Geneva, 1961), pp. 437-46.

Moore: W.G. Moore, *La Réforme allemande et la littérature française. Recherches sur la notoriété de Luther en France* (Strasbourg, 1930).

Moreau II: B. Moreau, *Inventaire chronologique des éditions parisiennes du XVIᵉ siècle, d'après les manuscrits de Philippe Renouard*, II: *1511-1520* (Paris, Service des travaux historiques, 1977).

Moreau III: B. Moreau, *Inventaire chronologique des éditions parisiennes du XVIᵉ siècle ...*, III: *1521-1530* (Abbeville, Paillart, 1985).

Moreau IV: B. Moreau, *Inventaire chronologique des éditions parisiennes du XVIᵉ siècle ...*, IV: *1531-1535* (Abbeville, Paillart, 1992).

Mortimer: R. Mortimer, *Harvard College Library, Department of Printing and Graphic arts. Catalogue of books and manuscripts*, I: *French 16th-century books*, 2 vols (Harvard U.P., 1964).

Naef *Origines*: H. Naef, *Les Origines de la réforme à Genève*, 2 vols (THR 100, Geneva, Droz, 1968).

NK: W. Nijhoff et M.E. Kronenberg, *Nederlandsche Bibliographie van 1500 tot 1540*, 3 vols (The Hague, 1923-71).

NRB: S. Rawles and M.A. Screech, *A new Rabelais bibliography. Editions of Rabelais before 1626* (THR 219, Geneva, Droz, 1987).

NUC: *National Union Catalog: pre-1956 Imprints. A cumulative author list representing Library of Congress printed cards and titles reported by other American libraries*, 685 vols with *Supplement* of 69 vols (London and Chicago, Mansell, 1968-81).

Oulmont: C. Oulmont, *Pierre Gringore* (Paris, Champion, 1911).

Peach/Brunel: T. Peach et J. Brunel, *Le Fonds Goujet de la Bibliothèque de Versailles. Catalogue alphabétique* (Geneva, Slatkine, 1992).

Peter *Du Bois*: R. Peter, 'Un imprimeur de Calvin: Michel Du Bois', extract from *Bulletin de la Société d'histoire et d'archéologie de Geneva* 16 (1978), pp. 285-335.

Peter, *Prem.ouvr.*: R. Peter, 'Les premiers ouvrages français imprimés à Strasbourg', in *L'Annuaire des amis du vieux-Strasbourg* 1974, pp. 73-108; 1979, pp. 11-75; 1980, pp. 35-46; 1984, pp. 17-28.

Peter, *RHPR* 1965: R. Peter, 'L'abécédaire genevois ou catéchisme élémentaire de Calvin', in *Revue d'histoire et de philosophie religieuses* 45 (1965), pp. 11-45.

Peter *RHPR* 1983: R. Peter, 'La réception de Luther en France au XVIᵉ siècle', in *Revue d'histoire et de philosophie religieuses* 63 (1983), pp. 67-89.

R. Peters, *Studies in Church hist.*: R. Peters, 'Who compiled the sixteenth-century patristic handbook *Unio dissidentium*?', in *Studies in Church History*, ed. G.J. Cuming, Vol. II (London, 1965), pp. 237-50.

Pidoux: P. Pidoux, *Le Psautier huguenot du XVIᵉ siècle. Mélodies et documents*, 2 vols (Basle, Baerenreiter, 1962).

Rawles: S.J. Rawles, *Denis Janot, Parisian printer and bookseller (fl. 1529-1546): a Bibliographical study* (thesis, University of Warwick, 1976).

Rawles *BHR* 1976: S.J. Rawles, 'An unrecorded edition of the works of Clément Marot printed by Denis Janot', *BHR* 38 (1976), pp. 485-8.

Renouard MSS: Fichier manuscrit des éditions parisiennes du XVIᵉ siècle, Bibliothèque nationale, Paris.

Rép.bib.: *Répertoire bibliographique des livres imprimés en France au seizième siècle*, 32 livr. (Baden-Baden, 1968-80).

Rice *Préf. Epist.*: E.F. Rice, *The prefatory Epistles of Jacques Lefèvre d'Étaples and Related Texts* (New York, 1972).

Ritter: F. Ritter, *Répertoire bibliographique des livres imprimés en Alsace aux XVᵉ et XVIᵉ siècles*, 7 vols (Strasbourg, Heitz, 1938-60).

Rothschild: *Catalogue des livres composant la bibliothèque de feu M. le Baron James de Rothschild*, ed. É. Picot, 5 vols (Paris, D. Morgand, 1884-1920).

Rouen: *Répertoire automatisé des livres du XVIᵉ siècle conservés à la bibliothèque municipale de Rouen (1501-1550)*, ed. Edith Bayle, Marie-Joseph Beaud et al. (Paris, K. Saur, 1983).

Roussel *BTT5*: *Bible de tous les temps*, V: *le temps des Réformes et la Bible*, directed by G. Bedouelle and B. Roussel (Paris, Beauchesne, 1989).

Roussel *Mélanges Jacob*: B. Roussel, 'Simon Du Bois, Pierre Olivétan, Étienne Dolet, auteurs ou éditeurs de traductions françaises de textes de Martin Bucer (1529-1542): l'exemple du Psaume 1', in *Prophètes, poètes et sages d'Israël: hommages à Edmond Jacob à l'occasion de son 70ᵉ anni-*

versaire par ses amis, ses collègues et ses élèves (Paris P.U.F., 1979: *RHPR* 59/3-4).

Runnalls: G. A. Runnalls, 'La circulation des textes des mystères à la fin du Moyen Age: les éditions de la *Passion* de Jean Michel', in *BHR* 58 (1996), pp. 7-33.

Schlaepfer *APR*: H.-L. Schlaepfer, 'Laurent de Normandie', in *Aspects de la propagande religieuse* (*THR* 28, Geneva, Droz, 1957), pp. 176-230.

Smith *BHR* 1991: M.C. Smith, 'A sixteenth-century anti-theist (on the *Cymbalum mundi*)', *BHR* 53 (1991), pp. 593-618.

STC: A.W. Pollard and G.R. Redgrave, completed by K.F. Pantzer, *A short-title catalogue of books printed in England, Scotland and Ireland and of English books printed abroad 1475-1640*, 2nd ed., 3 vols (London, 1976-86).

THR: *Travaux d'Humanisme et Renaissance*.

TLF: *Textes littéraires français*.

Trapman 1978: J. Trapman, *De Summa der godliker scrifturen (1523)* (Leiden, New Rhine Publishers, 1978).

Trapman *NAKG* 1983: J. Trapman, 'Le rôle des « sacramentaires » des origines de la Réforme jusqu'en 1530 aux Pays-Bas', *Nederlands Archief voor Kerkgeschiedenis* 63 (1983), pp. 1-24.

Tricard *APR*: A. Tricard, 'La propagande évangélique en France. L'imprimeur Simon Du Bois', in *Aspects de la propagande religieuse* (*THR* 28, Geneva, Droz, 1957), pp. 1-37.

Veyrin-Forrer: J. Veyrin-Forrer, 'Antoine Augereau, graveur de lettres, imprimeur et libraire parisien (mort en 1534)', in *La Lettre et le texte. Trente années de recherches sur l'histoire du livre* (Paris, Coll. de l'ENS de jeunes filles, 1987), pp. 3-50.

Vial *GJ*: J. Vial, 'De quelques exemplaires de l'*Internelle consolation*', in *Gutenberg Jahrbuch* 1964, pp. 171-4.

Vinay: V. Vinay, 'Die Schrift *Il Beneficio di Giesu Christo* nach der neuesten Forschung', in *Archiv für Reformationsgeschichte* 65 (1974), pp. 307-12.

Walsh *Harvard*: J.E. Walsh, 'The *Querela Pacis* of Erasmus: the "lost" French translation', *Harvard Library Bulletin* 17 (1969), pp. 374-84.

Weiss *BSHPF* 1902: N. Weiss and T. Dufour, 'Livres et reliures', in the report on the Jubilee exhibition of the Société de l'Histoire du Protestantisme français, *Bulletin de la Société de l'histoire du protestantisme français* 51 (1902), pp. 431-50.

Weiss *BSHPF* 1919: N. Weiss, 'Le premier traité protestant en langue française: *La Summe de l'escriture saincte*, 1523', *Bulletin de la Société d'histoire du protestantisme français* 68 (1919), pp. 63-79.

Weiss *BSHPF* 1926: N. Weiss, 'François Lambert, d'Avignon', in *Bulletin de la Société d'histoire du protestantisme français* 75 (1926), pp. 477-86.

46 Ps.: L. Guillo et al., 'Quarante-six psautiers antérieurs à 1562', in *Psaume* 2 (1988), pp. 27-34.

1 Alphabetical List

A

A 1.   **ABC.**

Le ABC des Chrestiens. — [Paris], 1550?
8°: 8 ff., §⁸, goth.
*Paris BEBA Masson 508.
Notes: Latin and French texts of the Lord's Prayer, Ave, Creed, Ten Commandments and Commandments of the Church (the last three in verse).

A 2.   **ABC.**

L'abc des chrestiens et chrestiennes. — [Paris], ?, Bertram Boulet, Lille, ?
8°: 16 ff., § §§⁸, goth. §§ 8r: Impr. à Paris pr. Bertram Boulet libr. à Lisle.
*Paris BEBA Masson 29.
Notes: Rhyming couplets, each beginning with a succeeding letter of the alphabet: 'Amour ayons en dieu le benoist createur: qui de loyer condigne est remunerateur ...'. Lord's Prayer in French, Creed (with the rhyming quatrains of BEBA Masson 508, 10 cdts. (rhymes different from those of Masson 508), several prayers, some by Béda and Warnet, *Doctrine et instruction.*

A 3.   **ABC français.**

L'ABC françois. — [Geneva], [J. Crespin], 1551.
8°: A-B⁸ C⁴, rom.
*London BL 3504.dg.15(1).
References: Peter, *RHPR* 45, 11-45 (with text). Gilmont, *Crespin* 51/1. *Index* I #370.
Notes: Later editions in Geneva, 1553, *c.* 1562, 1568...

A 4.   **Abouchement.**

L'Abouchement de nostre sainct pere le Pape, Lempereur et le Roy, faicte a Nice, avec les Articles de la trefve. — Lyon, François Juste, 1538.
8°: A-D⁴, rom.
*Paris BN Rotschild IV.3.181.

References: Rothschild #2674.
Notes: Non-religious, political text. Followed by 'La Chrestienté parlant à Charles Empereur et à Francoys ...' attrib. to Marot. 'Aproche toy Charles, tant loing tu soys ...'(D 1r).

A 5.   **Almanach spirituel.**

Almanach spirituel et perpetuel, necessaire a tout homme sensuel et temporel. — [Alençon], [Simon Du Bois], *c.* 1530.
8°: [16] ff., A-B⁸, goth.
*London BL C.37.b.43. *Paris SHP R.13452(2). Paris BN Rothschild IV.8.75.
References: Ginzburg, *Nicod.* 40. Moore #97. Clutton #216. Tricard, *APR* 33-7. Rothschild #3157.
Notes: Trans. of German *Eyn geistlich Almanach* (pr. in Hagenau, *c.* 1525). Evangelical and anti-astrological text: 'Jesuchrist est nostre veritable astrologue, lequel seul il fault craindre, regarder, servir et croire' (A 2v).

A 6.   **Ambroise, Saint,** trans. Jean Voirier.

Le traicte <> du bien de la mort nouvellement translate de latin en francoys. — Paris, François Regnault, 1511.
8°: a-e⁸, goth. e 7v: Impr. à Paris pr. francoys regnault. 20.01.1511.
*London BL 3832.aaa.20(2).
References: Moreau II #6.

A 7.   **Ambroise, Saint,** trans. Jean Voirier.

Sensuit le traictie <> du bien de la mort. — Paris, Simon Vostre, ?
8°: A-C⁸ D⁴, goth.
*Paris BN Rés. R 2047.
Notes: S. Vostre active 1486-1521.

A 8.   **Ambroise, Saint,** trans. Jean Voirier.

Le Traicte du bien et de la mort. — Paris, Jean de La Porte, François Regnault, Pierre Vidoue, 1517.
8°.
References: Moreau II #1510 (sale Yemeniz (1867)).

A 9. **Aneau, Barthélemy.**

Chant natal contenant sept noelz, ung chant Pastou-ral, et ung chant Royal, avec ung Mystere de la Nati-vité. — Lyon, S. Gryphe, 1539.
4°: a-d⁴, rom.
*Paris BN Rés. Ye 782.
Notes: Non-controversial piety.

A 10. **Apologie pour la foi.**

Apolologie pour la foy chrestienne contre les erreurs de ... George Halevin. — Paris, Geoffroy Tory, 1532.
8°: 72 pp., A-D⁸ E⁴, rom. E 4v: Impr. par Maistre Geofroy Tory de Bourges. 22.03.1531 (a.s.).
*Paris BM. Rés.25543(1). Aix Méj. Rés. D. 185.
References: Higman, 'Prem. rép.', 366-70. Moreau IV #326.
Notes: Georges seigneur de Hallewijn, correspondent of Erasmus and translator of the *Éloge de la folie*, had written a book (now lost) on 'les erreurs de Luther'. Josse Clichtove replied in an *Improbatio* (1533). The anonymous author of the *Apologie* seems also to have been a doctor of the Faculty of Theology of Paris.

A 11. **Arétin, Pierre,** trans. Jean de Vauzelles.

La Genese de M. Pierre Aretin, avec la vision de Noë, en laquelle il veit les mysteres du Vieil et Nou-veau testament. — Lyon, S. Gryphe, 1542.
8°: a-q⁸, rom.
*London BL 844.g.12. *Paris BA Rés.8 T.3861. *Paris SHP A 855. Aix Méj.
References: Dagens.
Notes: The Italian original dated from Venice, 1538. Para-phrastic narrative of Genesis up to Joseph's arrival in Egypt. The translator, who signs with his motto 'un vray zele', dedi-cated his work to Francis I.

A 12. **Arétin, Pierre,** trans. Jean de Vauzelles.

Trois livres De l'Humanite de Jesuchrist: divinement descripte, et au vif representée. — Lyon, M. & G. Trechsel, 1539.
8°: [8 ff.]+358 p.+[1 f.], *⁸ a-y⁸ z⁴, rom. z 3v: Lyon, Melchior et Gaspar Trechsel. 01.03.1539.

*Wolfenbüttel HAB 1229.19 Theol. Paris BN D 11892. *Paris BA
8° T.3899 (gathering * misbound).
References: Baudrier XII, 249. Brun.
Notes: Priv. (* 1v) for three years. Letter from the author to
count Maximian Stampe (* 2r). Dedic. (* 5r) by Jean de Vauzelles to the queen of Navarre.

A 13.   Arétin, Pierre, trans. Jean de Vauzelles.

La Passion de Jesus Christ. — Lyon, M. & G. Trechsel,
1539.
References: Baudrier XII, 249.

=>   *Armure de patience*: see *Imitation de Jésus-Christ,*
Paris, Langelier, 1542.

A 14.   Armure de patience.

Ung petit Traicte appelle L'armure de patience en
adversite tresconsolatif pour ceulx qui sont en tribu-
lation. — Paris, Yolande Bonhomme, 1530.
8°: 44 ff., A-E⁸ F⁴, goth.
Séville Colombine. Berlin DSB.
References: Babelon # 9. Brunet V, 914. Dagens. Moreau III,
#1982.

A 15.   Armure de patience.

Petit traicte appelle Larmeure de pacience en adver-
site, tresconsolatif pour ceulx qui sont en tribulation.
— Paris, [Nicolas Couteau], 1537.
8°: A-E⁸ F⁴, goth. F 3v:Imprimé a Paris. 04.01.1537.
*Rouen BM Leber 329(6). London BL C. 97.aa.17.

A 16.   Armure de patience.

Ung petit traicte appelle larmeure de patience tres-
consolatif pour ceulx qui sont en tribulation. —
Paris, Yolande Bonhomme, 1539.
8°: A-E⁸ F⁴, goth. F 4r: Paris, Yoland Bonhomme, 1539.
*London BL 4402.1.25(3). *Paris BN Rés. D 23738. Paris BSG D
55650 Rés.
Notes: BL copy bound with *Internelle consolation.* BN with
Preparation pour recevoir le s. sacrement de l'autel.

A 17. Armure de patience.

Larmeure de patience en adversité. — Paris, Denis Janot, 1541.
16°: A-H⁸, rom.
*Paris BN Rés. D 16304.
References: Rawles # 134.
Notes: *L'Armeure de patience* is followed (G 3r) by 'Aulcunes instructions et oraisons tressalutaires à tous Chrestiens et Chrestiennes'.

A 18. Armure de patience.

L'armeure de patience en adversité. — Lyon, Jean de Tournes, 1543.
16°: a-g⁸, rom.
*Paris SHP A 1169.
References: Cartier, *De Tournes* #4. Th.Dufour Ms.fr. 3821#649.
Notes: *L'Armeure de patience* is followed (f 8v) by 'Aucunes Instructions et Oraisons tressalutaires à tous Chrestiens et Chrestiennes'.

A 19. Arrêts et ordonnances.

Les Arrestz et ordonnances de la court contre Luther: les lutheriens et leurs livres: et aultres livres deffendus. — [Paris], 1526?
8°: 4 ff.
*Paris SHP A 1186. Ghent BU.
References: Moore #100. Moreau III #1073.
Notes: Extracts from Reg. Pt, 5 Feb. 1525 and 12 August 1526.

A 20. Arrêts et ordonnances.

Arrest notable donné le 4e jour d'Octobre, l'an 1546, par la Chambre ordonnée par le Roy... contre grand nombre d'Heretiques et blasphemateurs, du grand marché de Meaulx. — Paris, Jean André, 1546?
8°: A-C⁴, rom.
*Versailles BM Goujet 8° 92(2).
References: Peach/Brunel #602.
Notes: Bound with Désiré, *Miroer*.

A 21.   Arrêts et ordonnances.

Arrestz et ordonnances royaux de la supreme, tres-haute et souveraine Court du Royaume des Cieux. Avec la Generale Croisade, jadis donnée, et maintenant confirmée par nostre sainct Pere Dieu. — [Geneva], [Jean Girard], 1550.
4°: A-C⁴ D⁶, rom.
*Cambridge Emma. 330.1.31(8). *London BL 475.a.29 (- cah. D).
*Vienna ÖNB 78.G.52.
References: Moore #101. Adams A2007. *Index* I #365.
Notes: A similar title already censured in MS, June 1541 (Higman *Censorship*, p. 86). J. Girard asked permission to print this title in August 1542. In a style parodying parliamentary edicts, the *Arrests* recommend evangelical truths and Bible study. *La Generale croisade* (C 4r ss.) borrowed from Beaulieu, *Chrestienne resjouissance* (1546).

A 22.   Articles.

Les Articles de la faculté de Theologie de Paris, touchant et concernant nostre Foy et Religion Chrestienne. — [Paris], [J. André], 1543?
4°: 3 ff.
*Paris BN Rés. pD 53.
References: Renouard MSS.
Notes: Resolution of the Faculty dated 10 March 1542 (a.s.). Ed. J. Farge, *Le Parti conservateur* 141-9. See also *Édit*.

A 23.   Articles.

Articles tres utiles et necessaires composees par les venerables et scientificques doyen et docteurs de la tressacree faculte de theologie de Louvain. — Cambrai, Bonaventure Brassart, Baudouin Dacquin, Arras, 1545.
4°: 7 ff.
Lille BM Rés. 41576.
References: *Rép.bib.* #6.

A 24.   Articles.

Articles concernans la vraye religion et saincte foy catholicque ... de Louvain. — Paris, Chrestien Wechel, 1545.
4°: A-B⁴ A-B⁴, rom./ital.

*Bibl. Egl. réf. de France AP 36.715.

Notes: 32 articles approved by the Louvain theologians, 6.12.1544, authorized by Charles V on 14.3.1544 (a.s.). Cf. *Articles* of Paris.

A 25.   Assomption de la vierge.

Sensuyt lassumption de la glorieuse vierge Marie. A xxxviij. personnages Dont les noms sensuivent cy apres. — Paris, [Alain Lotrian],1530?
8°: A-K^8, goth. K 8v: Impr. à Paris, rue neufve n. Dame, ens. escu de France.
*Paris BN Rothschild IV.9.76.

References: Rothschild #3011.

Notes: Octosyllabic verse in various rhyme scheme. The instruction 'Orgues' appears several times: text for performance in church. The sign named in the colophon belonged in 1530 to Alain Lotrian.

A 26.   Augustin, Saint, trans. Raoul de Presles.

Le premier Volume <> de la Cite de Dieu. — Paris, Nicolas Savetier, Galliot Du Pré, Poncet Le Preux, 1531.
2°: [6] + 277 + [1] ff., *^{6} a-z A-K^8 L^6, goth. L 5v: Paris, Nic. Savetier. 20.04.1530.
*Canterbury cath. L.8.2. Paris BN vél.303. *Paris BA fol. T 1113. London BL 474.f.8. Paris BN Rés. C 557 (+).

References: Moreau IV #31.

Notes: The date of the colophon is probably wrong.

A 27.   Augustin, Saint, trans. Raoul de Presles.

Le second volume et acomplissement des .xxii. livres <> de la Cite de Dieu. — Paris, Nicolas Savetier, Galliot Du Pré, Jean Petit, Poncet Le Preux, 1531.
2°: [8] + 259 + [1] ff., *+^{8} aa-zz AA-HH^8 II-KK^6, goth. KK 5v: Ach. d'impr. à Paris par Nicolas Savetier. 12.06.1531.
*Canterbury cath. L.8.2. Paris BN vél.304. *Paris BA fol. T 1113. London BL 474.f.8. Paris BN Rés. C 557 (+).

References: Moreau IV #31.

A 28.   Augustin, Saint, trans. Valentin Du Caurroy.

Opuscule <> de l'Esprit et de la lettre. — Paris, Michel de Vascosan, 1551.

4°: 42 ff., A-I⁴ K⁶, rom.
*Paris BA 4° T 1265. *Paris BN Rés. Z. Payen. 608(2).
Notes: Dedication by Valentin Du Caurroy, lawyer in the
Parlement, to Charles de Pisseleu Bishop of Condom.

A 29.   Augustin, Saint.

*Sensuyt la saincte et sacree exposition <> sur la
premiere quinquagene du psaultier de David.* —
Paris, Gilles Couteau, Jean de la Porte & Jean Mullet,
Lille, 1519.
2°: 320 ff., a-z & A-X aa-hh⁶, goth. hh 6r: Impr. à Paris, Gilles
cousteau pour Jehan de la Porte, 22.01.1519.
Lille BM 43820. *London BL 3090.g.2 (de la Porte).
References: *Rép.bib.* Moreau II #1984.
Notes: No title page, the text begins a 1r.

A 30.   Augustin, Saint, Bernard, Saint, N. Béda, T. Warnet.

Le Mirouer des vanitez et pompes du monde. —
Paris, [Pierre Vidoue], pr. Galliot Du Pré, 1522?
4°: A-P⁸, goth.
*Paris BA Rés. C. 5969.
References: Moreau III #367.
Notes: Extracts from sermons by St Augustine and St Ber-
nard, denouncing excessive luxury in clothing. P 3r-4r: Béda
and Warnet, *La Doctrine et instruction.*

A 31.   Augustin, Saint.

*La Seule parole de Lame a Dieu <> Quy est ung
livre tresproufittable pour induyre la personne a la
vraye cognoissance, et dilection de Dieu.* — Ghent,
Godefroy de Rode, 1535.
8°: 80 ff., A-K⁸, goth. 80r: Impr. à Gandt par Godefroy de Rode.
23.06.1535.
Hamburg SB.
References: NK #156.

A 32.   Augustin, Saint, trans. Adrien Gémeau.

*Trois opuscules <> de lestat de veuvage, de la mani-
ere de prier Dieu, et de la vie de saincte Monique.*
— Paris, Jean Petit, 1517.
4°.

References: Moreau II #1528 < Brunet suppl. I.76 and Du Verdier III.21.

A 33. **Augustin, Saint,** trans. Joseph Gauchier.

De la Vanité de ce siecle et monde inferieur. — Paris, Vivant Gaultherot, 1542.
8°: a-c^8, rom.
*Paris BN Rés. C 5973.
Notes: Dedic. by Joseph Gauchier to Jeanne de La Fin, abbess of Port Royal, dated from Paris, 26.01.1542.

A 34. **Augustin, Saint,** trans. Joseph Gauchier.

De la vie Chrestienne, avec les Traictez de Charite, de la Vanite de ce Siecle et monde inferieur, Dobedience et Humilite, et Leschelle de Paradis. — Paris, Vivant Gaultherot, 1542.
8°: A-H^8, rom.
*Paris BN Rés. C 5972.
Notes: Dedic. by Joseph Gauchier to Catherine de La Charité du couvent du lys, dated from Paris, 20.02.1542.

A 35. **Augustin, Saint,** trans. Joseph Gauchier.

Les livres <> de la vie chrestienne, de Charite, de la Vanite de ce Siecle et monde inferieur, Dobedience et Humilite, et Leschelle de Paradis. — Paris, Vivant Gaultherot, 1546.
8°: A-C^8 D^4, rom.
*Paris BN Rés. C 5971.
Notes: Dedic. to Charlotte de La Tremoille of Fontevrault, dated from Paris, 15.08.1541. Despite the title it is a translation of the *Scalae paradisi* only. A letter to the reader pleads the authenticity of the text, which was denied by Erasmus.

A 36. **[Aumen, Gervais].**

La consolation des desolez, et les douze utilitez qui sont es tribulations paciemment pour lamour de dieu porteez. — Paris, Josse Badius, 1531.
4°: a^6 b-h^8 i^6, rom. i 5v: Impr. à Paris en la maison de Badius. 15.02.1530.
*Paris BSG D4° 2313(3) Rés. Inv 2489 (-i6).
References: Dagens. Moreau III #2041.

Notes: *Ép. Prohemiale* by 'tout vostre petit filz en religion et clerc regulier de lordre sainct Augustin', in the Abbey of St Victor, to his abbot.

A 37.   **Aurigny, Gilles d'.**

Contemplation sur la mort de Jesus-Christ. — Paris, J. Bogard, 1547.

8°.

References: Renouard MSS < Brunet suppl.

Notes: See also *Psaumes*, Paris, 1549.

B

B 1.   **Ballade des luthériens.**

La Balade des leutheriens avec la chanson. — [Lyon], [Jacques Moderne], 1525?

8°: 4 ff.

*Paris SHP R 15939.

References: Moore # 102.

Notes: Celebrates, in poor verse, the victory of the duke of Lorraine over the peasants at Saverne, 17 May 1525, and a mention of the Meaux group, in particular Martial Mazurier: 'A Meaulx les escardeurs de frise/Avec leur grant provincial/Le bon prophete marcial/I preschent Dieu sçait de quel guise.'

=>   Baptista Mantuanus: see Spagnuoli, Baptista.

B 2.   **Bâton pour chasser les loups.**

Le Baston pour chasser les loups. — [Geneva], [Jacques Vivian], 1522?

4°: 4 ff., a⁴, goth.

*Paris SHP R 2054.

References: Berthoud, *Marcourt* p. 151. Naef, *Origines* I.419.

Notes: First text on the subject of Church abuses ('quiteurs et prescheurs de pardons') published in French-speaking Switzerland.

B 3.   **Beaulieu, Eustorg de,** liminary poem by Guillaume
Gueroult.

Chrestienne resjouyssance. — [Geneva], [Jean Girard],
1546.
8°: π⁸ a-p⁸, rom.
*Chantilly Condé IV.D.36. *Vienna ÖNB 80.M.74.
References: *BG* 46/2. *Bull. du Bibliophile* (1867) 456-62.
Notes: 160 'belles et honnestes chansons', followed (o 5r) by
'La generalle Croisade' reprinted in *Arrestz et ordonnances*
(1550). Eustorg (or Hector) de Beaulieu was pastor at Thier-
rens, 1540-47. He later went to Basle. Cf. *Chansons.*

B 4.   **Beaulieu, Eustorg de.**

L'Espinglier des filles. — Basle, 1548.
8°: 8 ff., A⁸.
Basle.
References: Haag *Fr. prot.*
Notes: Dedic. to 'Claude Damas, damoyselle de Mareul en
Berry'. Very practical advice on how to serve the Lord by each
member of the body, by hairstyle, and by clothing.

B 5.   **Beaulieu, Eustorg de.**

*L'Espinglier des filles... Reveu et augmente par luy
mesme (despuis sa premiere impression).* — Basle,
[Robert Winter], 1550.
8°: A⁸, ital. A 8r: De Basle, ce 8. d'Avril 1550.
*Paris BN Rés. D² 12796.
Notes: Dedic. to Magdaleine de Beaulieu, niece of the author.
A curious note (A 1v) says he is withdrawing the dedication to
a girl named in previous editions: 'combien qu'il n'y ait plus
aulcuns Pilates ou Nicodemes sur la terre en personne: ... toutes-
fois il y a plusieurs heritiers et successeurs de leur craincte
servile.'

B 6.   **Beaulieu, Eustorg de.**

*Le souverain Blason dhonneur, à la louange du
tresdigne corps de Jesus Christ.* — [Basle], [Jacques
Estauge], 1548?
8°: A-B⁸, ital.
*Munich BSB Rar.107(3). *Vienna ÖNB 79.Ee.174 (incom.).
*Zurich ZB VI.263(6).

References: Bietenholz # 110. Cartier, *Mélanges Picot*.
Notes: An extract from *Chrestienne resjouissance*, 'reveu et augmenté' (t. p.).

B 7.   **Béda, Noël,** Warnet, Thomas.

La doctrine et instruction necessaire aux crestiens et crestiennes. — Paris, Jean Trepperel, 1511?
8°: 3 ff. 3r: Jehan Trepperel.
*Paris BN Rés. D 54034.
References: Bense, *Béda*, pp. 141-3.
Notes: Text, without commentary of the Lord's Prayer, Creed, Ten Commandments (in rhyme) and five commandments of the Church, with three prayers 'fondées en lescripture saincte'. Thomas Warnet was curé of S. Nicolas des Champs, Béda principal of the Collège de Montaigu. Farge, *Bio.reg.* suggests *c.* 1509 for this ed.

B 8.   **Béda, Noël,** Warnet, Thomas.

La doctrine et instruction necessaire aux crestiens et crestiennes. — Paris, Alain Lotrian, 1525?
8°: 3 ff. fol. 3r: Paris, Alain Lotrian.
*Paris BN Rés. D 17407(2).
Notes: Re-ed. of the preceding n°. See also St Augustin, *Mirouer des vanitez*.

B 9.   **Béda, Noël,** Warnet, Thomas, adapted from St Bernardino of Siena.

La petite Dyablerie dont lucifer est le chef, et les membres sont tous les joueurs iniques et pecheurs reprouvez intitule Leglise des mauvais. — Paris, Vve Jean Trepperel, Jean Jehannot, 1512?
8°: A-F⁸ G⁴, goth. G 4r: Impr. à Paris par la vefve feu jehan trepperel et Jehan Jehannot.
*London BL C.53.h.9(1).
Notes: Extract from S. Bernardinus Senensis, *Quadragesimale de Christiana religione.* G 2r sqq: 'La doctrine et instruction necessaire oux crestiens et crestiennes'.

B 10.   **Béda, Noël,** Warnet, Thomas, adapted from St Bernardino of Siena.

La petite diablerie dont lucifer est le chef et les membres sont tous les joueurs iniques et pecheurs reprouvez intitule leglise des mauvais. — [Paris], [Alain Lotrian], 1528?
8°: A-F⁸ G², goth.
*Paris BN Rés. D 17407.
References: Bense, *Béda*, pp. 126-40. Moreau III #1372.

B 11.   **Béda, Noël,** Warnet, Thomas.

La petite Dyablerie. Aultrement apellee Lesglise des mauvais, dont lucifer est le Chef. Et les membres sont les joueurs inicques et Pecheurs reprouvez. — Paris, Alain Lotrian, Denis Janot, 1534?
8°: A-F⁸, goth. F 8r: Alain Loctrian et Denys Janot.
*Paris BN Rothschild VI.3(bis).39.
References: Rothschild # 2542. Rawles # 242. Moreau IV #874.
Notes: Incorporates *La Doctrine et instruction* (F 6r-8r). The colophon says that 'venerables docteurs en theologie Maistre Thomas Varnet ... et maistre Noel Beda' had the work printed.

B 12.   **Béda, Noël,** Warnet, Thomas.

La petite dyablerie dont Lucifer est le chef, et les membres sont tous les joueurs iniques et pecheurs reprouvez, intitule leglise des mauvais. — Lyon, Olivier Arnoullet, 1541.
References: Baudrier X, 76 < Du Verdier I.474.

B 13.   **Bellemere, François.**

Directoire de la vie humaine contenant Quatre Traictez Le premier est du Regime de la personne. Le second est la forme et maniere de soy confesser. Le tiers est du Remede contre scrupule de conscience. Le quart est la forme de soy preparer a recepvoir le createur. — Bordeaux, Jean Guyant, 1521-42.
References: *Rép.bib.* #28.
Notes: Fr. Bellemere was a 'religieux de l'ordre des freres minimes de sainct Françoys de Paule' (t.p.). Very traditional-

ist text. E.g., among the seven 'signes d'un bon catholique': 'Je croy saincte eglise catholique, estre la congregation des chrestiens, militans soubz l'obeissance du sainct siege apostolique: auquel nostre sainct pere le pape est chef, vicaire de Dieu en terre...'(E 2v-3r).

B 14.   Bellemere, François.

Directoire de la vie humaine Contenant quatre traictez. Le premier est du regime de la personne. Le second est la forme et maniere de soy confesser. Le tiers est du remede contre scrupule de conscience. Le quart est la forme de soy preparer a recepvoir le createur. — Troyes, Jean Le Coq, 1525?
8°: A-E⁸, goth. E 6v: Impr. à Troyes chez Jehan Le Coq.
*Paris BN Rés. D 80206. *Troyes BM Rés. 57.
References: *Rép.bib.* #23.

B 15.   Bellemere, François.

Directoire de la vie humaine contenant quatre traictez. Le premier est du regime de la personne. Le second est la forme et maniere de soy confesser. Le tiers est du remede contre scrupule de conscience. Le quart est la forme de soy preparer a recepvoir le Createur. — Paris, [Nicolas Savetier], [Poncet le Preux], 1532.
8°: A-F⁸, goth.
*London BL 4408.a.24.
References: Dagens. Moreau IV #340.
Notes: The address ('rue S. Jacques, ens. du Loup') is that of Poncet Le Preux, the material is that of Nic. Savetier.

B 16.   Bellemere, François.

Examen de conscience. Sensuyt la maniere de bien soy confesser: tres utile et necessaire de scavoir a chacune personne: tant pour les confesseurs que pour les penitens. — [Troyes], [Jean Le Coq], ?
12°: 12 pp.
Coll. privée.
References: *Rép.bib.* #73.

B 17. **Bellemere, François.**
Instruction salutaire a toute personne de lestat seculier. — [Paris], [Poncet Le Preux], 1537?
8°: a-e⁸ f⁴, goth.
*Paris BM Rés. 51594 (- a1). Ghent UB Res. 1221.
References: Machiels #216.
Notes: Running title: 'Directoire de la vie humaine'.

B 18. **[Benedetto da Mantova],** [Marcantonio Flaminio], trans. Claude Le Maistre.
Traité du benefice de Jesus Christ crucifié envers les chrestiens, traduit de l'italien. Ensemble la 16. homelie de S. Jean Chrysostome. — Lyon, Jean de Tournes, 1545.
16°.
Munich BSB (destroyed).
References: Cartier *De Tournes* # 41. Droz, *Chemins*, III.111-83. Vinay. *Index* I #375 specifies this ed.
Notes: The most famous text produced by the circle around Juan de Valdès. *Il beneficio* incorporates extracts from Calvin's *Institution*. See Vinay for a summary of the debates about authorship of this text.

B 19. **[Benedetto da Mantova],** [Marcantonio Flaminio], trans. Claude Le Maistre.
Du Benefice de Jesuchrist crucifié, envers les Chrestiens. Traduict de vulgaire Italien... Avec une traduction de la XVI. Homilie de sainct Jean Chrysostome, de la femme Cananée. — Paris, Antoine Jurie, 1548.
8°: A-I⁸ K⁴, rom.
*Geneva MHR H.Pal.1(548).
References: Droz, *Chemins*, III. (facs. reprod.).
Notes: First surviving ed. of the *Bénéfice*.

B 20. **Bernard, Saint,** trans. A. Verard.
De la maniere d'aimer Dieu. — Paris, Nicolas Barbou, Jean André, 1542.
References: Renouard MS.

B 21.   Bernard, Saint (pseud.).

Le traitie ... envoye a sa seur contenant la maniere de vivre en la religion chrestienne. — Paris, Jean Petit, 1511?
8°: a-v⁸, goth. v 8v: Impr. à Paris pr. Jehan petit.
*Paris BN Rés. C 3332.
References: Moreau II #17.
Notes: Already an ed. in 1500 (Paris, BN). Seventy-three brief 'sermons' composed, as it says in the prologue, of 'certaines bonnes miettes' collected 'soubz la table des bons peres'.

B 22.   [Berquin, Louis de?].

La farce des theologastres a six personnages. — [Lyon], [Jean Cantarel], [Vve Barnabé Chaussard], 1533?
4°: A-B⁴, goth.
*Geneva MHR D 9. *Paris BN Rés. Yf 63.
References: Baudrier XI.55-6.
Notes: Crit. ed., *TLF*, 1989, by Cl. Longeon, who suggests the attribution to Berquin.

B 23.   Bèze, Théodore de.

Abraham sacrifiant. Tragedie françoise. — [Geneva], [Jean Crespin], [Conrad Badius], 1550.
8°: A-C⁸ D⁴, rom.
*Geneva MHR B 07(50). *Neuchâtel past. 100.2.
References: Gardy #23. CDM p. 15. Gilmont *Crespin* 50/1. Ed. Cameron, Hall, Higman, *TLF*, 1967.

B 24.   Bèze, Théodore de.

Abraham sacrifiant. Tragedie françoise. — [Geneva], [Jean Crespin], 1551.
8°: A-D⁸, rom.
Vienna ÖNB *36.M.106.
References: Gilmont *Crespin* 51/2.
Notes: Trans. of Ps. 31 by Bèze added.

B 25.   Bible, trans. Jean de Rely.

Le premier/second volume de la bible en francoiz. — Paris, Barthelemy Verard, 1514?

2°: a^6 b^4 a-l^6 m^4 n-z aa-vv A^6 B^4 A-X^6 yC^4 zC^4 AA-RR^6, goth. RR6r: Impr. à Paris pr. Barthelemy verard.
Liège BU 1823C. Paris BA f° T.142. Paris BN Rés. A 274. Vienna ÖNB 2.D.2.
References: Chambers #20.
Notes: *Bible historiale.* First edition 1495-96 (Chambers #13).

B 26.   **Bible,** trans. Julien Macho, Pierre Farget.
La bible en francois. — Rouen, hér. Richard Auzoult, François Regnault, 1516?
4°: A-F$^{8/4}$ G-I$^{4/8}$ K-M$^{4/8}$ N-P$^{4/8}$ Q-V$^{4/8}$ X^4 AA^8 BB-DD^4 EE^6 FF-II^4 KK^6 #^{4}, goth.
Geneva BPU Bb 92 Rés. Paris BN Rés. A 2399.
References: Chambers #21.
Notes: *Bible abrégée* (summary of Genesis-Job, with 'Les Sept ages du monde'). First known ed. *c.* 1473 (Chambers #1).

B 27.   **Bible,** trans. Julien Macho, Pierre Farget.
La bible en francoys. — Rouen, hér. Richard Auzoult, Michel Angier de Caen, 1516?
4°: A-F$^{8/4}$ G-I$^{4/8}$ K-M$^{4/8}$ N-P$^{4/8}$ Q-V$^{4/8}$ X^4 AA^8 BB-DD^4 EE^6 FF-II^4 KK^6 LL^4, goth.
Paris BA 4° T.2595 Rés.
References: Chambers #22.
Notes: *Bible abrégée.* Follows the 1516? ed., Chambers #21.

B 28.   **Bible,** trans. Jean de Rely.
Le premier/second volume de la bible en francoiz. — Paris, Barthelemy Verard, François Regnault, 1517.
2°: ã^6 ê^4 A-T aa-oo p-z^6 &^{6} 2^6 aaa-bbb^6 ccc^4 ãA^6 êB^4 AA-XX AAA-XXX yyy^6, goth. ccc 3v: Antoine Verard. 24.10.1517.
Bruxelles BR Inc. B 522 LP. London BFBS 207 B17. Paris BA f° T.509(1) (Vol. I). Carpentras BM A 481 (Vol. II: Regnault). Manchester UL 19512 (Vol. II: Regnault) (+).
References: Chambers #23, 24. Moreau II #1542.
Notes: *Bible historiale.*

B 29.   **Bible,** trans. Jean de Rely.
Le premier/second volume de la bible en francoys. — Lyon, Jacques Sacon, 1518.
2°: A a-z &^{8} 2^4 AA aa-xx^8 yy^6, goth. yy 5v: Impr. à Lyon, Jaques Sacon. 20.05.1518.

Cambridge UL Sel.2.66. Oxford Queen's 69.C.16. Strasbourg BNU
E 10618. Troyes BM B.3.132.
References: Chambers #25. Baudrier XII,346.
Notes: *Bible historiale.*

B 30.   Bible, trans. Jean de Rely.
Le premier/second volume de la bible en francoiz.
— Paris, François Regnault, Jean Petit, 1520.
2°: ã⁶ ê⁴ A-T aa-zz⁶ &&⁶ 22⁶ aaa-bbb⁶ ccc⁴ ãA⁶ êB⁴ AA-XX AAA-
XXX yyy⁶, goth.   ccc 3v: Impr. à Paris, Francois regnault.
24.10.1520.
Lyon BV 100042 (incomp.). Stuttgart LB. Paris BN Rés. g.A.11
(Petit). Stockholm KB Teol.Bibel.Övers.Fr.1520.
References: Chambers #27, 28. Moreau II #2259.
Notes: *Bible historiale.*

B 31.   Bible, trans. Julien Macho, Pierre Farget.
Sensuyt la Bible en francoys. — [Paris], [Vve Jean
Trepperel], 1520?
4°: a⁸ b-e⁴ f⁸ g-h⁴ i⁸ k-n⁴ o⁸ p-z⁴ v⁸ x-z⁴ &⁴ A⁸ B-E⁴ F⁸ G-K⁴ ã⁴, goth.
ã 4v: Impr. à Paris.
Edinburgh NLS D.N.S. 573 (- a 1). Ghent UB R 770.
References: Chambers #29.
Notes: *Bible abrégée.*

B 32.   Bible, trans. Jean de Rely.
Le premier/second volume de la bible en francoys.
— Lyon, [Jacques Sacon], pr. Pierre Bailly, 1521.
2°: A a-z &⁸ 2⁴ AA aa-xx⁸ yy⁶, goth.   yy 5v: Impr. à Lyon, Pierre
Bailly. 14.12.1521.
Aix Méj. F° 328. Cambridge Trinity A.11.10. Geneva BPU Bb 91.
London BL 466.d.6. Paris BN Rés. A 276 (+).
References: Chambers #30. Adams B 1125.
Notes: *Bible historiale,* copied from the Sacon ed., 1518.

B 33.   Bible, trans. Julien Macho, Pierre Farget.
Sensuit la bible en francois. — Paris, Philippe le
Noir, 1526?
4°: a-f⁸/⁴ g-k⁴ l⁸ m-p⁴ q⁸ r-x⁴ y⁸ z⁴ &⁴ A-E⁴ F⁸ G-I⁴ K⁶, goth.   K 6v:
Impr. à Paris par Philippe le Noir.
La Haye KB 232.E 41.

References: Chambers #37.
Notes: *Bible abrégée*, copied from the 1520? ed.

B 34. **Bible,** trans. Jean de Rely.

Le premier/second volume de la bible en francoiz.
— Paris, François Regnault, Jean Petit, 1529.
2°: ã⁶ ê⁴ A-L⁶ M⁴ N-T⁶ aa-zz⁶ &&⁶ 22⁶ aaa-bbb⁶ ccc⁴ ãA⁶ êB⁴ AA-XX
AAA-XXX yyy⁶, goth.   ccc 3v, yyy 5v: Paris, Francois Reg-
nault/Jean Petit. 29.06.'1539'. 03.08.1529.
Carpentras Ing A 482 (Vol. II). Fribourg BCU Gb 15. Paris BN Rés.
A 277. Copenhagen KB 1-94 fol (Petit). Toulouse BM Rés.
B.XVI.257 (Petit) (+).
References: Chambers #45, 46.
Notes: *Bible historiale.*

B 35. **Bible,** trans. J. Lefèvre d'Étaples.

*La saincte Bible. en Francoys, translatee selon la
pure et entiere traduction de sainct Hierome, con-
feree et entierement revisitee ... sus ung chascun
Chapitre est mis brief argument.* — Antwerp, Martin
Lempereur, 1530.
2°: [a]⁴ a-c A-Z a-d⁸ e-f⁶ g-i⁸ k-m⁶ n² o-z AA-FF⁸ GG¹⁰ π⁸ A-H⁸ I¹⁰
K-L⁸ M¹⁰, goth. M 9v: Anvers, Martin Lempereur. 10.12.1530.
Amsterdam VU Ned.Inc. 366. Geneva BPU Bb 528. *London BL
C.18.c.12. Paris BN Rés. A 283. Wolfenbüttel HAB Bibel-S.4° 89a
(+).
References: NK #417. Adams B 1126. Chambers #51.
Notes: First complete ed. of Lefèvre's trans.

B 36. **Bible,** trans. Julien Macho, Pierre Farget.

Sensuyt la bible translatee de Latin en francoys. —
Rouen, [Etienne Dasne?], Raulin Gaultier, 1530?
4°: A⁸ B-F⁴ G⁸ H-M⁴ N⁸ O-S⁴ T⁸ V-X AA-CC⁴ DD⁸ EE-KK⁴ LL⁸
MM⁴ NN⁸, goth. NN 8v: Impr. à Rouen pr. Raulin Gaultier.
Paris BSG A 4° 340 inv. 348 rés.
References: Chambers #52.
Notes: *Bible abrégée.* On the basis of typographical material
P. Aquilon attributes the ed. to the Rouen printer Etienne
Dasne.

B 37.   **Bible,** trans. Jean de Rely.

Le premier/second volume de la Bible en francoys.
— Lyon, Pierre Bailly, 1531.

2°: A a-z &^{8} 2^4 AA aa-xx^8 yy^6, goth. yy 5v: Lyon, Pierre Bailly.
1531.

London BL L.14.b.9. Lyon BV 20074 (-A 1). Oxford AS p.12.6.
Lyon BV 20073 (s.l., s.n.). Paris BN Rés. A 2277 (s.l., s.n.).

References: Baudrier II, 2-3. Chambers #54, 55.

Notes: *Bible historiale.*

B 38.   **Bible,** trans. Julien Macho, Pierre Farget.

*La Bible en Francoys. Sensuyt la Bible diligemment
translatee de latin en francoys. Au plus pres du vray
texte. Pour les gens qui point nentendent latin. Avec
les sept Aages.* — Lyon, Olivier Arnoullet, 1531?

4°: a-y^8 z^4, goth. z 4v: Impr. à Lyon par Olivier Arnoullet.

Lyon BV Inc. 317.

References: Baudrier X, 34-5. Chambers #56.

Notes: *Bible abrégée.*

B 39.   **Bible,** trans. J. Lefèvre d'Étaples.

*La saincte Bible en Francoys, translatee selon la
pure et entiere traduction de Sainct Hierome, dere-
chief conferee et entierement revisitee ... sus ung
chascun Chapitre est mis brief argument...* — Antwerp, Martin Lempereur, 1534.

2°: π^6 ℯ^8 *^{8} A-Z a-i^8 k^{10} l-z Aa-Bb^8 Cc^{10} ℯ^8 AA-MM^8 NN^6, goth.
NN 6r: Impr. en Anvers, Martin Lempereur. 06.04.1534.

Aix Méj. F° 326 no. 4530. Bruxelles BR VB 143a C Rés. Geneva
BPU Bb 529 Rés. Paris BA f° T.135. *Wolfenbüttel HAB Bibel-S.
2° 120 (+).

References: NK #419. Chambers #62.

Notes: Revision of the 1530 ed., possibly by Robert Estienne.
Censured by Louvain in 1546 (*Index* II, 1546/25).

B 40.   **Bible,** trans. Olivétan, prefatory material by Calvin, B.
Des Périers.

*La Bible Qui est toute la Saincte escripture. En
laquelle sont contenus, le Vieil Testament et le Nouveau, translatez en Francoys. Le Vieil, de Lebrieu: et
le Nouveau, du Grec.* — Neuchâtel, Pierre de Vingle,
1535.

2°: *8 a-z A-H AA-LL AAA-KKK aa-pp⁶ qq⁴ rr-ss⁶, goth. qq 4v and ss 6r: Neuchâtel, Pierre de Vingle dict Pirot Picard. 04.06 1535.
Aix Méj. F° 325 no 24671. Berne StUB Mut.3 et E 32. Geneva BPU Bb 542 Rés. *Paris BN Rés. A 310. Rouen BM A 36 Rés. (+).
References: Chambers #66.
Notes: Chambers lists over 100 copies of this ed.

B 41. **Bible,** trans. Julien Macho, Pierre Farget.

La Bible translatee de latin en francoys au vroy sens pour les simples gens qui nentendent pas latin corrigee et imprimee nouvellement. — [Caen], [Hér. Laurent Hostingue], 1535?
4°: A⁸ B-F⁴ G⁸ H-M⁴ N⁸ O-S⁴ T⁸ V-X⁴ AA-CC⁴ DD⁸ EE-KK⁴ LL⁸ MM-NN⁴ *⁴, goth.
Paris BN Rés. A.2398.
References: Chambers #67.
Notes: *Bible abrégée.*

B 42. **Bible,** trans. Jean de Rely.

Le premier/second volume de la bible en francoiz. — Paris, Antoine Bonnemere, 1537.
2°: ã⁶ ê⁴ A-L⁶ M⁴ N-T aa-zz⁶ &&⁶ 22⁶ aaa-bbb⁶ ccc⁴ ãA⁶ êB⁴ AA-XX AAA-XXX yyy⁶, goth. ccc 3v: 24.10.1537. yyy 5v: Paris, Anthoyne bonnemere. 1538.
Cambridge UL Young 45. London BL C.51.g.4. Lyon BV 100026. Paris BN Rés. A 280. Paris BM 657E Rés.
References: Chambers #71. Adams B 1129.
Notes: *Bible historiale.*

B 43. **Bible,** trans. Olivétan, tables by M. Malingre.

La Bible en laquelle sont contenus tous les livres canoniques, de la saincte escriture, tant du vieil que du nouveau Testament: et pareillement lés Apocryphes. — [Geneva], [Jean Girard], 1540.
4°: *⁶ a-z A-V⁸ X⁶ aa-kk⁸ ll⁴ AA-NN⁸ OO⁴ A-B⁸, rom.
Glasgow UL Eadie 46 (-* 1). London BL 3022.dd.9. Lyon BV Rés. 357210. *Paris SHP A 129. *Vienna ÖNB BE.1.Q.28 (+).
References: Chambers #82. *BG* 40/2. Th. Dufour *Not.Cat.* 181-6.
Notes: The 'Bible à l'épée'.

B 44.   **Bible,** trans. J. Lefèvre d'Étaples.

La saincte Bible en Francois. — Antwerp, Antoine Des Gois, Antoine de la Haye, 1541.
2°: π^6 $\mathfrak{e}^6$ $*^6$ A-Z a-i^8 k^{10} l-z Aa-Bb^8 Cc^{10} $\mathfrak{r}^6$ AA-MM^8 NN^6, goth.
NN 6r: Anvers, Antoine des Gois. 12.01.1541.
Amsterdam VU 1995 A 10. Berne StUB D.20. Geneva BPU Bb 530.
London BL 689.h.1. *Paris SHP R 388 (-π 1) (+).
References: Chambers #85. Adams B 1130.
Notes: Several copies of this ed. are bound with the t.p. of the Lempereur 1534 ed. Censured by Louvain in 1546 (*Index* II, 1546/26).

B 45.   **Bible,** trans. Jean de Rely.

Le premier/second Volume de la Bible en francois. — Paris, Nicolas Couteau pr. Oudin Petit, Vve François Regnault, Ambroise Girault, 1541.
2°: ã^6 ê^4 A-L^6 M^4 N-T^6 aa-zz^6 &&^{6} 22^6 aaa-bbb^6 ccc^4 ãA^6 êB^4 AA-XX^6 AAA-XXX^6 yyy^6, goth. yyy 5r: Paris, Nicolas Couteau pr. Oudin Petit. 23.11.1541.
Orléans BM A 124 (-ã 1) (Petit). Paris SHP A 36 (Petit). Paris BN Rés. A 279 (Regnault). Alençon BM Cab.1.2(Rés.XVI.C.11) (Girault). Paris BSG A.fol.173.inv.180.Rés. (Girault).
References: Chambers #87, 88, 89.
Notes: *Bible historiale.*

B 46.   **Bible,** trans. Julien Macho, Pierre Farget.

La Bible translatee de latin en francois au vray sens pour les simples gens qui nentendent pas latin. — Paris, Pierre Regnault, 1543.
8°: A-Z AA-KK^8 LL^4 ã^8, rom.
Glasgow UL Euing Coll. Dd-g.5. London BL 3025.b.1. Versailles BM Fonds A in-8° 045a.
References: Chambers #98.
Notes: *Bible abrégée.*

B 47.   **Bible,** trans. Jean de Rely.

Le premier/second Volume de la Bible en francois. — Paris, Jean Bignon, pr. Pierre Regnault, 1543.
8°: ã ê a-z aa-zz^8 &&^{8} aaa-uuu^8 xxx^4 ã ê AA-ZZ^8 &&^{8} Aaa-Kkk^8 a-z^8 &^{8} aa-cc^8 dd^6, rom. xxx 3v et dd 6r: Paris, Jean Bignon pr. Pierre Regnault. 11 and 15.05.1543.
Paris BN Rés. A 5835.

References: Chambers #99.
Notes: *Bible historiale.*

B 48. **Bible,** trans. Jean de Rely.

Le Premier/second Volume de la Bible en Francoys.
— Paris, Vve François Regnault, 1544.
8°: a-b⁸ a-z⁸ &⁸ aa-zz aaa-ttt aA-bB AA-ZZ Aa-Zz aa-tt⁸, rom.   ttt
8r: 20.10.1544. tt 8r: Impr. à Paris.
Manchester JRL Christie 14.e.8-9. Paris BN Rés. A 5833 (Vol. I, -a
1). St Andrews UL Bib BS 230.B43 (Vol. II).
References: Chambers #100.
Notes: *Bible historiale.*

B 49. **Bible,** trans. Olivétan.

La Bible en Francoys. — Lyon, Sulpice Sabon,
Antoine Constantin, 1544.
4°: @⁴ a-z A-S⁸ T¹⁰ aa-kk aaa-nnn⁸ ooo⁴ *⁸ **⁸, rom.
Autun BM S R m.30. Chaumont BM 5837 3G2 d. Orléans BM A
146. Paris BN A 2404.
References: Chambers #109.
Notes: First 'Protestant' Bible printed in Lyon.

B 50. **Bible,** trans. Jean de Rely.

Le premier/second Volume de la Bible en francois.
— Paris, Pierre Regnault, 1544.
2°: a⁶ b⁴ A-Z AA-VV⁶ ã⁶ ê⁴ A-Y AA-RR⁶ SS⁴, rom.   VV 5v:
17.06.1544. SS 3v: Impr. à Paris. 1546.
Bordeaux BM T 128. London BL 4.c.1. Paris BSG A.fol.174.inv.181.rés.
Stuttgart LB.
References: Chambers #110.
Notes: *Bible historiale.* Vol. II, dated 1546, is the last ed. of
the *Bible historiale.*

B 51. **Bible,** trans. Olivétan.

*La Bible en francois, En laquelle sont contenus tous
les Livres Canoniques, de la saincte Escriture, tant
du vieil, que du nouveau Testament, ensemble tous
les Livres dicts Apocryphes.* — Lyon, Godefroy et
Marcelin Beringen, 1545.
4°: a-z A-M⁸ N¹⁰ aa-hh⁸ ii⁶ Aa-Kk⁸ Ll¹⁰ aa-ee⁴, rom.

Colmar BV VIII/221. Villiers-le-Bel SBF 14. Paris BN A 2405
('1546'). Stuttgart LB ('1546').
References: Chambers #114, 130.

B 52.   **Bible,** trans. Julien Macho, Pierre Farget.

*La Bible translatee de Latin en Francoys, au vray
sens, pour les simples gens qui n'entendent pas latin.*
— Paris, Pierre Regnault, Nicolas Buffet, 1545?
8°: A-Z AA-KK⁸ LL⁴ MM⁸, rom.
London BL 3025.b.13 (Regnault). Villiers-le-Bel SBF 102(Regnault).
Paris BN Rés. A 8152 (Buffet).
References: Chambers #117, 118.
Notes: *Bible abrégée.*

B 53.   **Bible,** trans. Jean de Rely.

Le premier/second volume de la bible en francoiz.
— Paris, Nicolas Couteau, Oudin Petit, Guillaume Le
Bret, Thielman Kerver, Rémy Boyset, Pierre Sergent,
1545.
2°: ã⁶ ê⁴ A-Z AA-XX⁶ ãA⁸ a-x aa-rr⁶ ss⁸, goth. ss 8v: Paris, Nicolas
Couteau. 09.04.1545.
Bordeaux BM T 129 (Petit). Paris BN Rés. A 282 (Le Bret). Paris
BM (Kerver). Rouen BM A 37 (Boyset). Paris BM 657F (Sergent)
(+).
References: Chambers #119, 120, 121, 122, 123, 124.

B 54.   **Bible,** trans. Olivétan, revised by Calvin.

*La Bible, Qui est toute la saincte escriture, En
laquelle sont contenuz, le vieil Testament et le nouveau.* — Geneva, Jean Girard, 1546.
4°: a-z A-R⁸ S⁴ aa-tt⁴ vv² AA-MM⁸ NN⁴ A-D⁴, rom.   vv 2r
(Apocryphes): 10.07.1546.
*Lausanne BCU AB 437. *London BL 217.k.11. *Paris SHP R
1785. Geneva BPU Bb 2248 Rés. (s.l. s.n.). *Strasbourg BNU D
103414 (+).
References: Chambers #128, 129. *BG* 46/3.
Notes: A new preface by Calvin and a new *Advertissement sur
les Apocryphes.*

B 55.   **Bible,** trans. Olivétan.

*La Bible en Francoys, Qui est toute la saincte Escri-
ture, en laquelle sont contenuz le vieil et Nouveau*

Testament, Recentement reveuz. — Lyon, Jean Pidier, Nicolas Bacquenois, Guillaume Rouillé, Thibaud Payen, 1547.

2°: *6 **6 a-z A-T⁶ V⁸ aa-gg⁶ hh⁴ AA-NN⁶, rom. NN 5v: Lyon, Jehan Pidier et Nicolas Bacquenois.

Darmstadt LB V 508 (Pidier/Bacquenois). Neuburg SB Bibl.153 (Pidier/Bacquenois). Bourg-en-Bresse BM 20.011 (Rouillé/Payen). Lyon BV 20076 (Rouillé/Payen). Lausanne BCU AB 2070 (Rouillé/Payen 1548) (+).

References: Chambers #134, 135, 138.

B 56. **Bible,** trans. J. Lefèvre d'Étaples.

La saincte Bible en Francoys, translatee selon la pure et entiere traduction de Sainct Hierosme, de rechief conferee et entierement revisitee selon les plus anciens et plus correctz exemplaires. — Antwerp, Jean Loe, 1548.

2°: ☞⁶ ₴⁸ *⁸ A-Z a-i⁸ k¹⁰ l-z Aa-Bb⁸ Cc¹⁰ ☞⁸ AA-MM⁸ NN⁶, goth.

Cambridge UL Sel.1.14,15 (- NN6). Paris BN Rés. Vélins 90-91 (- NN6).

References: Chambers #136. Adams B 1131.

B 57. **Bible,** trans. Nicolas de Leuze.

La Saincte Bible Nouvellement translatée de Latin en Francois, selon l'edition Latine, dernierement imprimée à Louvain: reveuë, corrigée, et approuvée par gens sçavants. — Louvain, Bartholomy de Grave, Anthoine Marie Bergagne, Jean de Waen, 1550.

2°: *⁶ a-z Aa-Zz Aaa-Sss⁶ Ttt⁴ AA-OO⁶ PP⁴ QQ⁶, rom.

Bruxelles BR VH 24 C Rés. Lausanne BCU AC 375. London BL C.80.h.1. Paris BSG A fol.176.inv.183.rés. Stuttgart LB (+).

References: Chambers #145.

Notes: The first Louvain French Bible.

B 58. **Bible,** trans. Olivétan.

La Sainte Bible. Contenant les Saintes escritures, tant du Vieil, que du Nouveau Testament, avec aucunes des plus singulieres Figures, et Pourtraitz. — Lyon, Balthazar Arnoullet, 1550.

2°: A¹⁰ a-z A-G Aa-Yy aa-mm⁶ nn⁴ AA-QQ⁶, rom.

Bruxelles BR VB 144 C LP Rés. Geneva BPU Bb 2216. London BL 1605/716. Lyon BV 20075. *Vienna ÖNB 4.N.17 (+).

References: Chambers #146.

B 59.   **Bible,** trans. Olivétan.

La Bible, Qui est toute la saincte Escriture, En laquelle sont contenuz, le vieil Testament, et le nouveau, translatez en François, et reveuz. — Geneva, Jean Crespin, 1551.

4°: *[4] a-z A-N aa-hh[8] ii[6] AA-LL[8] A-D[4], rom.

Glasgow UL Euing Coll. Dw-e.16. Oxford Bodl. AA.171.Th.Seld. Stuttgart LB. Zurich ZB III.A.500. Paris BSG A 4° 357inv.385 (s.l.) (+).

References: Chambers #150, 151. Gilmont *Crespin* 51/3.

Notes: Some copies give the address 'Avignon, Jehan Daniel'.

B 60.   **Bible,** trans. Olivétan.

La Bible en Francoys, Qui est toute la saincte Escriture, en laquelle sont contenuz le Vieil et Nouveau Testament, Recentement reveuz et fidelement corrigez selon l'Ebrieu, grec et Latin. — Lyon, Philibert Rollet, 1551.

2°: *[8] **[8] a-z A-H[6] I-Z Aa-Gg[8] Hh-Ii[6] AA-LL[8] MM[10], rom.

Cambridge UL 1.28.14. Villiers-le-Bel SBF 201. Paris BM 657H (- *1). Rouen BM A 38. St Andrews UL Bib BS230.B51 (+).

References: Chambers #152. Adams B 1132. Baudrier X, 443, 445bis.

B 61.   **Bible,** trans. Olivétan.

La Sainte Bible. Avec les figures et Pourtraits du Tabernacle de Moyse, et du Temple de Salomon, et maison du Liban. — Lyon, Jean De Tournes, 1551.

2°: A[10] a-z A-R[6] S[4] A-Z Aa-Qq[6] Rr[4] a-v[6] x[4], rom.

Autun BM E 45. Geneva BPU Bb 2282. London BL L.10.d.6. Lyon BV 20079. Paris BM 657G (+).

References: Chambers #153. Cartier *De Tournes* #186.

B 62.   **Bible. A.T.,** trans. J. Lefèvre d'Étaples.

Le premier volume de lanchien testament contenant les chinq livres de Moyse: ascavoir Genese: Exode: Levitique: les Nombres: & Deuteronome translatez en fransois selon la pure et entiere translation de sainct Hierosme. — Antwerp, M. Lempereur, 1528.

8°: a-z Aa-Pp[8], goth. Pp 7r: Anvers Martin Lempereur, 30.04.1528.

London BL C.36.b.1. *Paris SHP A 105. Turin.

References: NK #2504. Chambers #43.

Notes: Earliest appearance of Lefèvre's Old Testament, brought out in five parts, over five years, and overtaken by the complete Bible in 1530.

B 63.   **Bible. A.T.,** trans. J. Lefèvre d'Étaples.

Le second volume de lanchien Testament contenant pour sa premiere partie le Livre de Josue, le Livre des Juges, et le Livre de Ruth. — Antwerp, M. Lempereur, 1532.

8°: A-I⁸ k⁶, goth. k 6r: Anvers, Martin Lempereur, 1531.

*Paris SHP A 106. Turin BNU Ris. 19.12.

References: NK #2504. Chambers #43.

Notes: The t.p. gives the date 1532.

B 64.   **Bible. A.T.,** trans. J. Lefèvre d'Étaples.

Le second volume de lancien Testament, contenant pour sa seconde partie les quattre livres des Roix, les deux livres de Paralipomenon, et les quattre livres de Esdras. — Antwerp, M. Lempereur, 1532.

8°: a¹⁰ b-z Aa-Zz⁸, goth.   Zz 7v: Anvers, Martin Lempereur. 01.07.1532.

*Paris SHP A 106. Turin BNU Ris. 19.13.

References: NK #2504. Chambers #43.

B 65.   **Bible. A.T.,** trans. J. Lefèvre d'Étaples.

Le troisiesme volume de lancien testament contenant le livre de Tobie, de Judith, de Hester, de Job: et les trois livres de Salomon, ascavoir les Paraboles, Ecclesiaste, et les Cantiques des cantiques avec le livre de Sapience et Ecclesiastique et pareillement les deux livres des Maccabees. — Antwerp, M. Lempereur, 1529.

8°: A-Z AA-PP⁸ QQ⁴, goth.   QQ 3v: 12.08.1530.

*Paris SHP A 107. Turin BNU Ris. 19.14.

References: NK #2504. Chambers #43.

Notes: The t.p. gives the date 1529.

B 66.   **Bible. A.T.,** trans. J. Lefèvre d'Étaples.

Le dernier volume de lanchien testament contenant les prophetes: ascavoir, Esaias: Jeremias: Hezechiel: Daniel: Oseas: Joel: Amos: Abdias: Jonas: Micheas:

*Naum: Habacuc: Saphonias: Aggeus: Zacharias: et
Malachias.* — Antwerp, M. Lempereur, 1528.
8°: A-Z AA-VV⁸ XX⁴, goth. XX 3r: Anvers, Martin Lempereur.
19.09.1528.
London BL C.36.b.1. *Paris SHP A 108. Turin BNU Ris. 19.15.
*Oxford Bodl. Mason FF.83. Geneva BPU Bb 2195 Rés. (+).
References: NK #2504. Chambers #43.

B 67.   Bible. A.T., Cantique.

*Les cantiques salomon translatez de latin en fran-
coys.* — Paris, [Denis Janot?], [Alain Lotrian?], ?
8°: a-k⁸, goth. k 8ᵛ: On les vent a Paris en la rue neufve Nostre
Dame a lenseigne de l'escu de France.
*Paris BN Rés. A 17900.

B 68.   Bible. A.T. Ecclesiaste, trans. J. Lefèvre d'Étaples,
comm. J. Brenz.

*Lecclesiaste Preschant que toutes choses sans dieu
sont vanite.* — [Alençon], [Simon Du Bois], 1531?
8°: 168 ff., A-X⁸, goth.
*London BL 1016.a.5.
References: Clutton #30. B. Roussel, *BTT*5, p. 165.
Notes: The commentary on *Ecclesiaste* (D 1r sqq.) is taken
from Johannes Brenz (German 1528, Latin 1529). See B.
Roussel.

B 69.   Bible. A.T. Job, comm. 'Le Viateur'.

*Texte de Hiob, translate selon la verite hebraique. Et
bref commentaire du Viateur, sur icelluy.* — [Paris?],
[Simon Du Bois], 1534?
4°: 134 ff., a-v⁸/⁴ x⁸ y⁶, goth.
*London BL 1005.a.13. Paris BM 23396.
References: Clutton #27. Moreau IV #878.

B 70.   Bible. A.T., Psaumes.

*Icy commence le Psaultier de David contenant cent
et cinquante pseaulmes avecq leurs titres leallement
translate de latin en franchois.* — Paris, Thomas
Kees, 1513.
8°: A-M⁸ N⁴, goth. N 4v: Impr. à Paris par Thomas Kees. En vente à
Tournai. 30.07.1513.
Bruxelles BR. *London BL C.64.a.2.

References: NK #2502. Moreau II #505.
Notes: Plain text of the Psalms. Northern forms of spelling:
chanchons, franchois, lowes (= louez).

B 71. **Bible. A.T., Psaumes,** trans. Lefèvre d'Étaples.

*Le psaultier de David... Argument brief sur chascun
Pseaulme.* — Paris, Simon de Colines, 1524.
8°: A⁴ a-r⁸ s¹⁰, goth. s 10r: Impr. Simon de Colines. 16.02.1523
(a.s.).
*Paris SHP A 1185. *Paris BSG A 8° 738 Rés. Paris BA.
References: Moreau III #427.
Notes: The translation of the Psalms into French was forbid-
den, together with other biblical translations, on 5 Feb. 1526
(Higman *Censorship*, pp. 80-81).

B 72. **Bible. A.T. Psaumes,** trans. Lefèvre d'Étaples.

*Le psaultier de David. Argument brief sur chascun
Pseaulme.* — Antwerp, Martin Lempereur, 1525.
8°: A-X⁸, goth. Col: Anvers, Martin Lempereur. 20.06.1525.
Ghent UB Res. 935.
References: Machiels #541. NK #416.
Notes: Probably the first evangelical printing by Martin Lem-
pereur.

B 73. **Bible. A.T. Psaumes,** comment. Pierre d'Ailly.

*Les sept pseaulmes du royal prophete David, expo-
sees: puis nagueres divulguees.* — [Paris], [Simon
Du Bois], 1525?
8°: a-k⁸ l², goth.
*Paris BN Rés. A 17958.
References: Moreau III #896 bis. Clutton #29. *Index* I #469.
Notes: Adaptation, in a distinctly evangelical sense, of *Devo-
tae Meditationes circa septem Psalmos poenitentiales* by cardinal Pierre d'Ailly. N. Weiss (*BSHPF*, 1902, p. 436) attributes the work to Pierre Caroli. The text, without its preface,
was incorporated in the *Livre de vraye et parfaicte oraison* by
[Farel et Luther].

B 74. **Bible. A.T. Psaumes,** trans. J. Lefèvre d'Étaples.

*Le psaultier de David. Argument brief sur chascun
pseaulme.* — Paris, Simon de Colines, 1526.
8°: A-T⁸ V⁴, goth. V 4r: Impr. Simon de Colines. 17.02.1525 (a.s.).

*Paris BA 8° T 300. *Paris SHP R 13294.
References: Moreau III #766.
Notes: The date of completion of the edition is less than 15 days after the Paris Parlement forbade any translation of the Bible into French.

B 75.   Bible. A.T. Psaumes, Felix Pratensis.

Le livre des Pseaulmes de David, traduictes selon la pure verite Hebraique ensuyvant ... linterpretation de Felix. — Antwerp, Martin Lempereur, 1531.
8°: π⁸ A-T⁸, goth.   T 8v: Impr. en Anvers par Martin Lempereur. 1531.
*Amsterdam VU Ned.Inc. 548.
References: NK #4504.
Notes: Felix de Prato, a converted Jew, had supervised an ed. of the Hebrew Bible in 1516-17.

B 76.   Bible. A.T. Psaumes.

Les sept pseaulmes en francoys. — Paris, Guillaume de Bossozel, Jean Saint Denys, 1531?
8°: [12] ff., A⁸ B⁴, goth.   B 4r: Impr. à Paris.
Villiers-le-Bel SBF B II/76.
References: Moreau IV #282.
Notes: Thanks to D. Fougeras, librarian of the SBF, for providing a description of the edition. Trans. (with Latin incipit for each sentence) of the seven penitential psalms, Lord's Prayer, Ave Maria and a litany.

B 77.   Bible. A.T. Psaumes, Clément Marot.

Le .VI. Pseaulme de David qui est le premier Pseaulme des sept Pseaulmes translate en françoys. — Lyon?, ?, 1531?
8°: 4 ff.
Séville Colombine.
References: Babelon #128.
Notes: First versified trans. of a psalm by Clément Marot. It was later (1533) incorporated into Marguerite de Navarre, *Miroir de l'ame pecheresse.* Date suggested by G. Defaux, ed. of Marot, *Cinquante Pseaumes.*

B 78. **Bible. A.T. Psaumes,** pref. by Martin Luther (gathering B).

Le Livre des Psalmes. — [Alençon], [Simon Du Bois], 1532?

8°: A-B¹⁰ a-z A-D⁸ ¶⁴, goth.

*London BL 1110.a.28 (-B 1-10). *Paris BM 34974 Rés. (-B 1-10, ¶ 1-4). *Paris SHP R 16046.

References: Moore pp. 144-6. Clutton #28.

Notes: Luther's preface to his 1531 *Psalter* is added in certain copies. The text is a revision of Lefèvre d'Étaples. The arguments trans. from M. Bucer (B. Roussel in *Mélanges Jacob*).

B 79. **Bible. A.T. Psaumes,** Olivétan.

Les Psalmes de David. Translatez d'Ebrieu en Françoys. — Geneva, [Jean Girard], 1537.

8°: a-n⁸ o⁴, rom. o 3r: Impr. à Geneve.

*Geneva BPU Rés. Bb 581. Paris BU R. XVI. 1176. *Wolfenbüttel HAB Bibel.S 580.

References: *BG* 37/1. Th. Dufour *Not.cat.* pp. 142-4. *Index* I #515.

Notes: Extract from Olivétan's Bible (1535). In the colophon the translator gives his name as 'Belisem de Belimakon' (= 'no name, no place' in Hebrew).

B 80. **Bible. A.T. Psaumes.**

Les sept pseaulmes penitenciaulx et la letanie en françoys. — ?, ?, 1537?

4°: a-c⁶, goth.

*Paris BN Rés. B 27790.

Notes: The BN copy belonged to Fernand Columbus, who died in 1539. Probably printed in the south of France (watermark of a bull's head, cf. Briquet #14340). The text consists of a quatrain in French on each key word of the penitential psalms, quoted in Latin.

B 81. **Bible. A.T. Psaumes,** trans. Olivétan.

Les Psalmes de David translatez d'Ebrieu en langue françoyse. — [Geneva], [Jean Girard], 1539.

8°: a-o⁸, rom.

Edinburgh NLS Newb 1636(2).

References: *BG* 39/2. Mayer *Marot* #74.

B 82.   **Bible. A.T. Psaumes,** Cl. Marot, Jean Calvin.

Aulcuns pseaulmes et cantiques mys en chant. — Strasbourg, [Johann Knobloch Jr.], 1539.
8°: A-D⁸, goth.
*Munich BSB Rar.107.1.
References: Peter 'Prem.ouvr.' #6. Mayer *Marot* #82. Pidoux 39/I. *Index* I #519. Facs. repr. Geneva 1919.
Notes: First use of Marot's Psalms in a reformed liturgy. Thirteen psalms by Marot, five by Calvin, with the 'Nunc dimittis', Ten Commandments, and Creed, versified by the latter. Each text accompanied by its melody.

B 83.   **Bible. A.T. Psaumes,** comm. Pierre Arétin, trans. Jean de Vauzelles.

Les sept Pseaulmes de la penitence de David. — Lyon, Sebastien Gryphe, 1540.
8°: a-g⁸, rom.
Harvard CL. *Paris BA 8° T 6124.
References: Baudrier VIII, 138.

B 84.   **Bible. A.T. Psaumes,** Felix Pratensis.

Le livre des Pseaulmes de David, traduictes selon la pure verite Hebraique: ensuyvant ... linterpretation de Felix. — Antwerp, Antoine des Gois, 1541.
16°: A-Z Aa-Bb⁸, goth. Bb 8v: Impr. en Anvers par Antoine des Gois. 1541.
*London BL 842.aa.49. *Paris SHP R 15932 bis. *Wolfenbüttel HAB A 70 Helmst. 12°.

B 85.   **Bible. A.T. Psaumes,** Clément Marot.

Psalmes de David, Translatez de plusieurs Autheurs, et principallement de Cle. Marot. Veu ... et corrigé par lés theologiens. — Antwerp, Antoine Des Gois, 1541.
8°: A-F⁸, ital. F 8v: Impr. en Anvers par Antoine des Gois. 1541.
*Paris SHP 15855.
References: Mayer *Marot* #93. Pidoux 41/I. Higman *Censorship* A8. See *Index* I #516.
Notes: The t.p. specifies that the text has been 'veu, recongneu et corrigé par M.F. Pierre Alexandre, Concionateur ordinaire de la Royne de Hongrie.'

B 86. **Bible. A.T. Psaumes,** Clément Marot.

Psalmes de David, Translatez de plusieurs Autheurs, et principallement de Cle. Marot... Sermon du bon et mauvais pasteur. — Antwerp, Antoine Des Gois, 1541.

8°: *⁴ A-F⁸, ital. F 8v: Impr. en Anvers par Antoine des Gois. 1541.
*Paris BN Rothschild VI.3.58.

References: Mayer *Marot* #94. Pidoux 41/I bis. Higman *Censorship* A8.

Notes: A separate issue of the previous notice, with a preliminary gathering containing the *Sermon du bon et mauvais pasteur*, 'extraict du x. chap. de S. Jean, nouvellement translaté par ledit Clement Marot'. This issue describes the text as 'veu, recongneu et corrigé dés theologiens'. The *Sermon* was condemned separately in 1543 (Higman *Censorship* A9).

B 87. **Bible. A.T. Psaumes,** Pierre Gringore.

Paraphrase et devote exposition sur les sept tres-precieux et notables Pseaulmes. — Paris, Charles Langelier, 1541.

16°: A-E⁸, rom.
*Paris BN Rés. A 6804.

References: Renouard MSS.

Notes: Versification by Pierre Gringore of the seven penitential psalms.

B 88. **Bible. A.T. Psaumes,** comm. Pierre Arétin, trans. Jean de Vauzelles.

Les sept pseaulmes de la penitence de David. — Paris, Denis Janot, 1541.

8°: A-L⁸, rom.
La Haye KB 488 K3.

References: Rawles #132.

B 89. **Bible. A.T. Psaumes.**

Les sept psalmes du pecheur converty à Dieu. — [Geneva?], [Jean Girard?], 1541.

Notes: Th. Dufour, *Not.cat.* p. 180: Jean Girard received permission to print this title on 10 Dec. 1540. No known copy.

B 90.   **Bible. A.T. Psaumes,** Cl. Marot.

Trente Pseaulmes de David mis en françoys par Clement Marot. — Paris, Estienne Roffet, 1541?
8°: a-g⁸, rom.
*Paris BN Rés. A 6165.
References: Mayer *Marot* #101. Pidoux 41/II.
Notes: The priv. (a 1v), dated 30 Nov. 1541, states that three Doctors of Theology have certified the orthodoxy of the text. It was nonetheless condemned in 1543 (Higman *Censorship* A2).

B 91.   **Bible. A.T. Psaumes,** comm Pierre d'Ailly, trans. A. Belard.

Traité tres utile des sept degres de l'echelle de penitence, figurez au vray sur les sept Pseaumes penitentiels. — Lyon, Denis de Harsy, 1542.
16°.
References: Frankfurt cat. 1610.

B 92.   **Bible. A.T. Psaumes,** Clément Marot, Maurice Scève.

[*Psaumes de Clement Marot. Sermon du bon et mauvais pasteur*]. — Lyon, Estienne Dolet, 1542.
32°: A-I⁸, rom.
Rome BV ris. spec. VI.26 (-A 1.8).
References: Longeon *Dolet* #155. Mayer *Marot* #112.
Notes: To Marot's versifications (taken from the 1541 Antwerp ed.) are added translations of psalms 26 and 83 by Maurice Scève.

B 93.   **Bible. A.T. Psaumes,** Olivétan, arguments by Bucer, treatise by Athanasius.

Psalmes du royal Prophete David. Fidelement traduicts de Latin en Françoys. Auxquelz est adjouxté son argument. — Lyon, Estienne Dolet, 1542.
16°: A-Z aa⁸, rom.
*London BL 1409.a.8. Paris BN Rothschild IV.5.83. *Paris SHP R 9590 (incom.).
References: Longeon *Dolet* #154. Rothschild #5.
Notes: Olivétan's prose version, as in Girard's 1537 ed. A 2r-3v: preface by Dolet, drawing attention to his 'arguments' on each psalm. Z 4r sqq: 'Opuscule de S. Athanase sur les Psalmes', trans. by Dolet.

B 94. **Bible. A.T. Psaumes,** Olivétan.

Les Psalmes de David, Fidelement traduicts de Latin en Françoys. Avec argument et sommaire à chascun Psalme. — Lyon, Jean de Tournes, 1543.
16°: a-t^8 v^4, rom.
*Paris SHP A 145.
References: Cartier *De Tournes* #13.
Notes: Follows Dolet's prose ed. of 1542, but without the preface.

B 95. **Bible. A.T. Psaumes,** Clément Marot.

Cinquante Pseaumes en françois par Clem. Marot. Item une Epistre par luy. — [Geneva], [Jean Girard], 1543.
4°: π^6 A-S^4 T^2, rom. L 1v: De Geneve le 15e de mars, 1543.
*Paris BEBA Les 552. *Paris SHP A 273.
References: Mayer *Marot* #116. Cartier *Arrêts* p. 401. *BG* 43/2. O. Labarthe, *BHR* 1973. See *Index* I #516.
Notes: No musical notation. Crit. ed. by G. Defaux (Paris, Champion, 1995), who sees this as the most authoritative ed. of Marot's psalms.

B 96. **Bible. A.T. Psaumes,** Clément Marot, preface by Jean Calvin.

Cinquante Pseaumes. — [Geneva], [Jean Girard], 1543.
References: *BG* 43/1.
Notes: This ed. of the psalms, with music, mentioned in the Geneva City Council, 09.06.1543. No known copy.

B 97. **Bible. A.T. Psaumes,** Clément Marot.

Trente-deux Pseaulmes de David ... Plus vingt autres Pseaumes. — Paris, Estienne Roffet, 1543?
16°: 53 + 36 ff., A-F^8 G^4 (32 pss.), a-d^8 e^4 (20 pss.)., rom.
*Troyes BM Y.16.3321.
References: Mayer *Marot* #119. *Index* I #516.
Notes: The ed. is undated, but the privilege (A 2r-v) is dated 31 Oct. 1543.

B 98.   **Bible. A.T. Psaumes,** Clément Marot.

Les psalmes du royal prophete David, traduictz par Clement Marot. Avec autres petits Ouvrages par luy mesme. — Lyon, Estienne Dolet, 1544.
16°: 172 + 46 pp.
Berlin SB (lost).
References: Longeon *Dolet* #156. Mayer *Marot* #130.

B 99.   **Bible. A.T. Psaumes,** Clément Marot.

Les Oeuvres de Clement Marot. — Lyon, [S. Sabon], A. Constantin, 1544.
8°: a-z A-H⁸ aa-qq⁸ rr⁴, rom. rr 4v: Impr. à Lyon.
*London BL C.57.k.11. Paris BN Rothschild III.5.40. Ly. of Congress (dated 1545). Harvard CL (dated 1545).
References: Baudrier II, 35-6.
Notes: *Les Psaumes* on fols. aa1 sqq. According to Baudrier, the 50 psalms are here incorporated for the first time in Marot's *Oeuvres*.

B 100.   **Bible. A.T. Psaumes,** Clément Marot.

Cinquante Pseaumes en Françoys. — Lyon, Balthazar Arnoullet, 1545.
12°: 96 ff., a-m⁸, rom. m 8v: Impr. par Balthazar Arnoullet.
*Versailles BM Goujet 12° 273.
References: Mayer *Marot* #134. Peach/Brunel #402.
Notes: The psalms are followed (1 6r sqq.) by the *Sermon ... du bon pasteur et du mauvais.*

B 101.   **Bible. A.T. Psaumes,** Clément Marot.

Cinquante Pseaumes. — Paris, Ambroise Girault, 1545.
16°.
References: Mayer *Marot* #136 < Brunet III, 1462.

B 102.   **Bible. A.T. Psaumes,** Clément Marot and others.

Cinquante deux Pseaumes de David, Traduictz en rithme Françoyse selon la verité Hebraique, par Clement Marot. — Paris, Jacques Bogard, Jean Ruelle, 1545.
16°: A-L⁸, ital.

*Geneva BPU Rés. Bb 2367 (Bogard). *Wolfenbüttel HAB Lm Sammelbd 131 (Ruelle).

Notes: K 5r sqq., some new accretions: psalms 33 and 41, trans. by Claude Le Maistre, ps. 61 by Estienne Pasquier, the *Song of Moses* by B. Des Périers.

B 103. Bible. A.T. Psaumes, Clément Marot.

Cinquante Pseaumes. — Paris, Jacques Bogard, Jean Ruelle, Nicolas Du Chemin, 1545.

16°: AA-II⁸, ital.

*Stuttgart LB HB 1304 (Bogard). *Paris BN Rés. Ye 1488 (Ruelle). Harvard CL WKR 25.5.9 (Ruelle). *Paris BN Rés. Ye 1486 (Du Chemin).

References: Mayer *Marot* #133.

Notes: Part of Marot's *Oeuvres*, but with independent t.p.

B 104. Bible. A.T. Psaumes, Clément Marot.

Cinquante Pseaumes de David. — Paris, Jeanne de Marnef, 1545.

16°: A-I⁸, rom.

*Paris BEBA Masson 292.

References: Rawles *BHR* 1976 p. 488.

B 105. Bible. A.T. Psaumes, Clément Marot.

Cinquante deux Pseaumes de David. — Paris, Guillaume Le Bret, 1546.

16°: a-l⁸, rom.

*Lincoln cath. Oo 7.14.

Notes: Does not correspond to any other known ed.

B 106. Bible. A.T. Psaumes, Clément Marot.

Cinquante deux Pseaumes de David. — Paris, Guillaume Thibout, 1546.

16°: A-L⁸, ital.

*Paris BN Rothschild II.5.54.

References: Mayer *Marot* #148.

Notes: Despite Mayer's statement, this is a different ed. from that of Bogard and Du Chemin.

B 107. Bible. A.T. Psaumes, Clément Marot.

Cinquante Deux Pseaumes de David. — Paris, Nicolas Du Chemin, Jacques Bogard, 1546.

16°: A-K⁸, ital.

*Paris BN Rés. Ye 1490 (Du Chemin). *Paris BN Rothschild IV.5.82 (Bogard). *Paris BN Rés. Ye 1501 (Bogard). *Lausanne BCU AZ 4322 (Bogard).

References: Pidoux 46/I.

Notes: In the Du Chemin issue there are two extra gatherings, a² et m², with an 'Eclogue sur la naissance du dauphin', a 'Chant royal', and 'Petis devis chrestiens'.

B 108. **Bible. A.T. Psaumes,** Clément Marot, music by Antoine de Mornable.

Livre premier/second contenant XVII. pseaulmes de David. — Paris, Pierre Attaignant, 1546.
4°: long: 2 vols, a-d⁸, e-h⁸, rom.
Lausanne Cortot.

References: Pidoux 46/IVbis.

Notes: This, and the following item, are the first published harmonizations of the music of Marot's *Psalter*.

B 109. **Bible. A.T. Psaumes,** Clément Marot, music by Pierre Certon.

Recueil de trente et un Psaumes à quatre voix. — Paris, [Pierre Attaignant?], 1546.
Munich BSB (lost in XIXth century).

References: Mayer *Marot* #153. Pidoux 46/III.

B 110. **Bible. A.T. Psaumes,** Clément Marot.

Cinquante deux Pseaumes de David. — Paris, [Pierre Sergent], 1546.
16°: A-L⁸, rom.
*Paris BN Rés. Ye 1513.

References: Mayer *Marot* #149.

Notes: On the t.p. the editor gives his address as 'rue neufve nostre Dame, à l'ens. sainct Nicolas'.

B 111. **Bible. A.T. Psaumes,** Clément Marot.

Cinquante deux Pseaumes. — [Lyon?], [J. et F. Frellon?], 1546.
16°: 104 ff.
Rutgers State UL BS 1443 F8 M33. Sacramento City L.

References: Mayer *Marot* #152. *NUC* NBi 0029966.

Notes: Same border on t.p. as in the *Bergerie* attrib. to Marot and which seems to have belonged to the Frellon brothers (Droz, *Chemins*, II, 223 n.).

B 112. **Bible. A.T. Psaumes,** Clément Marot.

Les Pseaumes de David, mis en rithme Françoyse par Clement Marot. — Geneva, Jean Girard, 1547.
16°: a-k⁸, rom.
*Strasbourg BNU R 103076.
References: Mayer *Marot* #159. *BG* 47/1.
Notes: The table of contents lists 49 psalms, plus the Nunc Dimittis, Creed, Lord's Prayer, Ten Commandments, and some prayers.

B 113. **Bible. A.T. Psaumes,** Clément Marot, music by Loys Bourgeois.

Le Premier Livre des Pseaulmes de David contenant xxiiii pseaulmes. Composé par Loys Bourgeois en diversité de Musique. — Lyon, Godefroy et Marcelin Beringen, 1547.
4°: long: 2 vols, A-E⁴ F² A-E⁴ F², rom. F 2v: ach. d'impr. 23.09.1547.
*Geneva BPU Rés. Bb 2187 (s.t.). *Munich BSB 4° Mus.Pr. 100/1 (s.a.t.b.). Orléans BM (a.b.).
References: Mayer *Marot* #158. Pidoux 47/II. Baudrier III, 44.
Notes: Priv. dated 04.04.1547. The 'diversité de Musique': 'à sçavoir, familiere, ou vaudeville, aultres plus musicales et aultres à voix pareilles, bien convenable aux instrumentz'. The melodies are not related to those of the Genevan psalter.

B 114. **Bible. A.T. Psaumes,** Clément Marot, music by Loys Bourgeois.

Pseaulmes cinquante de David ... mis en Musique par Loys Bourgeois à quatre parties. — Lyon, Godefroy et Marcelin Beringen, 1547.
4°: long: 2 vols, A-O⁴ (s.t.) A-O⁴ (a.b.), rom.
*Munich BSB 4° Mus Pr. 100. Amsterdam VU Muziek Bibl.
*Vienna ÖNB SA 76.D.31.
References: Mayer *Marot* #157. Pidoux 47/I. Baudrier III, 43.

Notes: The harmonizations of the Genevan melodies are 'à quatre parties, à voix de contrepoinct egal consonante au verbe'. A 2r: dizain by 'Guillaume Gueroult, natif de Rouen'.

B 115. **Bible. A.T. Psaumes,** Clément Marot.

Cinquante deux Pseaumes de David, Traduictz en rithme Françoyse selon la verité Hebraique, par Clement Marot. — Paris, Charles Langelier, 1547.
16°: A-L⁸, ital.
Munich BSB P.O.gall.3340/1. Wolfenbüttel HAB Lm Sammelbd 131(1). *Wrocław BU 372123. *Rome BV Rossiana 7636 (int 1).
Notes: I 7r sqq: additions: Ps. 33 et 41 trans. by Claude Le Maistre, Ps. 62 by Estienne Pasquier, *Song of Moses* by B. Des Périers. K 8r: eight-line poem by M[athurin] C[ordier]: 'Que gaignes tu, dy moy Chrestien'.

B 116. **Bible. A.T. Psaumes,** Clément Marot.

Cinquante deux Pseaumes. — Paris, Guillaume Le Bret, Guillaume Thibout, 1547.
16°: A-L⁸, rom.
*Zurich ZB XVIII.2025.2 (Le Bret). *Bruxelles BR LP FS IX.51.A (Thibout).

B 117. **Bible. A.T. Psaumes,** Clément Marot.

Cinquante deux Pseaumes de David traduictz en rithme Françoise selon la verité Hebraique <> Avec plusieurs autres compositions dudict Autheur, que d'autres, non jamais encore imprimees. — Paris, Pierre Gaultier, 1547?
16°: A-I⁴, rom.
Saint-Etienne 22163 Rés.
Notes: The ed. is not dated, and may be much later (bound with Marot's *Oeuvres*, Paris, Barbe Regnault, 1559). Gaultier began printing at the address 'rue sainct Jacques, enseigne de la Vigne' (t.p.) in 1547, but continued until 1562. Thanks to J.-G. Girardet of the St-Étienne BM for a description of the edition.

B 118. **Bible. A.T. Psaumes,** Clément Marot.

Cinquante deux Pseaumes. — Angers, 1548.
References: Mayer *Marot* #165.

B 119. Bible. A.T. Psaumes, Clément Marot.

Pseaulmes cinquante de David mis en vers françois.
— Lyon, Godefroy et Marcelin Beringen, 1548.
8°: A-K⁸, rom.
*Wrocław BU 372124.
References: Pidoux 48/II.
Notes: With melodies. The Wrocław copy bound with *La Forme des prieres*, 1548, and the *Catechisme de Geneve*.

B 120. Bible. A.T. Psaumes, Clément Marot.

Cinquante deux Pseaumes de David. — Paris, Guillaume Le Bret, 1548.
16°: A-K⁸, rom/ital.
*Geneva MHR O⁶e (548).
References: Mayer *Marot* #161.

B 121. Bible. A.T. Psaumes, Clément Marot and others.

Pseaumes de David traduictz en rithme françoise. —
[Strasbourg], [Rémy Guédon], 1548.
16°: [16] + 191 pp., a A-M⁸, rom.
*Wolfenbüttel HAB Tc 250(1).
References: Pidoux 48/I. Peter 'Prem.ouvr.' #14.
Notes: Contains 40 psalms by Marot, with six psalm versifications, Nunc Dimittis, Creed and Ten Commandments versified by Calvin (who is not named). Ps. 124 and the Te Deum versified by Guillaume Guéroult. With melodies, but neither preface nor prayers.

B 122. Bible. A.T. Psaumes, Clément Marot.

Pseaulmes cinquante de David, mis en vers françois.
— Lyon, Godefroy et Marcelin Beringen, 1549.
8°: A-K⁸ L⁴, rom.
*Geneva MHR O⁶e (549). *Paris SHP A 147 et R 5779.
References: Mayer *Marot* #173. Pidoux 49/I.
Notes: With melodies. The copies in Geneva and in Paris SHP R 5779 are both bound with *La Forme des prieres* [Geneva, Jean Girard], 1549, and the *Catechisme*, Geneva, J. Girard, 1549.

B 123. **Bible. A.T. Psaumes,** Gilles d'Aurigny, music by D. Lupi Second.

Psalmes trente du royal Prophete David, traduictz en vers francois <>. — Lyon, Godefroy et Marcelin Beringen, 1549.
4°: long: 2 vols, A-H⁴ A-H⁴, rom.
*Munich BSB 4° Mus.Pr. 100/2 (satb).
Notes: A 1v: priv. for five years, dated 04.08.1547. A 2r: dedic. by D. Lupi Second to Nicolas Baillivi, dated 15.02.1549.

B 124. **Bible. A.T. Psaumes,** Clément Marot.

Cinquante Pseaumes de David. Traduictz en rithme Françoyse selon la verité Hebraique <> Avec le latin en marge. A iceulx sont adjoustez autres Pseaumes et Cantiques. — Paris, Gilles Corrozet, 1549.
128 ff.
Cat. Libr. de la Seine, 1995.
Notes: Contains prefatory material as in Dolet's 1542 ed., and a Song of Zachariah unknown elsewhere.

B 125. **Bible. A.T. Psaumes,** Clément Marot.

Cinquante deux Psalmes de David. — Paris, Estienne Groulleau, 1549.
16°: A-K⁸, rom.
*Paris SHP R 6443.

B 126. **Bible. A.T. Psaumes,** trans. Gilles d'Aurigny.

Trente Psalmes du royal Prophete David, Traduictz de Latin (selon le vray texte et phrase Hebraique) en rithme françoyse. — Paris, Guillaume Thibout, 1549.
16°: A-G⁸ a-d⁸, ital.
*Paris BN Rés. Ye 1505(3).
Notes: The 30 psalms versified by Gilles d'Aurigny are followed (fol. a 1r, but no new t.p.) by 'Vingt et deux octonaires du Psalme 119. Treize psalmes traduictz par divers autheurs. Avec plusieurs cantiques, lesquelz n'ont esté imprimez jusques à maintenant.' Cf. the ed. above, Lyon, Beringen, 1549. New ed. in 1551.

B 127. Bible. A.T. Psaumes, Clément Marot, music by Clément Jannequin.

Premier livre contenant xxviii Pseaulmes de David ... mis en Musique par Clement Janequin. — Paris, Nicolas Du Chemin, 1549.
4°: long: 32 pp.
Lausanne Cortot. Orléans BM Rés. 8° C 3459(d).
References: Mayer *Marot* #171. Pidoux 49/II.

B 128. Bible. A.T. Psaumes, Clément Marot.

Les Pseaumes de David. — Geneva, Jean Girard, 1550.
8°: A-I⁸, rom.
*Geneva MHR O⁶e (550). Strasbourg Sém. prot.
References: CDM p. 15. Mayer *Marot* #180.
Notes: The table of contents lists 48 psalms, with the Lord's Prayer, Creed, Ten Commandments, Nunc Dimittis, and some prayers.

B 129. Bible. A.T. Psaumes, Clément Marot.

Pseaumes de David trad. et mis en vers françois selon la verité hebraique <> avec le latin qui est en marge. — Lyon, Claude Marchant, 1550.
16°.
Le Mans BM TH 8° 274 (missing). Frankfurt am M. (missing).
References: Mayer *Marot* #178.

B 130. Bible. A.T. Psaumes, Clément Marot.

Cinquante deux Pseaumes de David. — Paris, Estienne Groulleau, 1550.
8°: 128 ff., A-Q⁸, rom/ital.   Q 8v: Impr. à Paris par Estienne Groulleau. 1550.
Harvard CL Typ 515 50.210. *La Haye KB 488.K.32.
References: Mayer *Marot* #177. Mortimer #77.

B 131. Bible. A.T. Psaumes, Clément Marot.

Cinquante deux Pseaumes. — Paris, Guillaume Thibout, 1550.
16°: 104 ff.
References: Mayer *Marot* #182 < Cat. Stroehlin #891.

B 132.   **Bible. A.T. Psaumes,** Clément Marot, music by Pierre
Colin.

*Les cinquante pseaulmes de David <> Compris le
Cantique de Simeon. Plus L'oraison Dominicale. La
Salutation Angelique. Prieres devant, et apres le re-
pas. Le tout mis en Musique <> à quatre parties en
quatre volumes, en chant non vulgaire: mais plus
convenable aux instrumens, que Les aultres par cy
devant imprimez.* — Paris, Nicolas Du Chemin, 1550.
4°: 4 vols 16 ff.
Paris BN (Superius) (not found).
References: Mayer *Marot* #179. Pidoux 50/I.
Notes: The music is independent of the Genevan psalter.

B 133.   **Bible. A.T. Psaumes,** Clément Marot, poem by
Mathurin Cordier.

Cinquante deux Pseaumes de david. — Paris, pr.
Guillaume Merlin, 1550.
16°: 88 ff., A-L⁸, rom.
*Paris BN Rothschild V.7.85.
References: Mayer *Marot* #181. Rothschild #619.

B 134.   **Bible. A.T. Psaumes,** Clément Marot.

Cinquante deux Psalmes. — Paris, Vve Maurice de
La Porte, 1550.
16°.
References: Mayer *Marot* #183.

B 135.   **Bible. A.T. Psaumes,** Jean Poitevin.

Les Cent Psalmes de David, qui restoient à traduire.
— Poitiers, Nicolas Peletier, 1550.
8°: *⁶ a-t⁸ u⁶, ital. u 5r: ach. d'impr. à Poictiers chez Nicolas Pele-
tier. 15.11.1550.
*Geneva MHR O⁶e (550)a. *Paris BM 23654 (-u 2-6). *Paris BA 8°
T 932 (t.p. '1551').
Notes: Jean Poitevin: 'chantre de Saincte Radegonde de Poic-
tiers' (t.p.).

B 136. **Bible. A.T. Psaumes,** Clément Marot, Gilles d'Aurigny.

Cent Psalmes de David Traduictz ... selon la verité Hebraique, par Clement Marot, Gilles Aurigny, Et autres. — Rouen, Robert et Jean Du Gort, 1550.
16°: A-Z Aa-Cc⁸, ital.
*Paris BEBA Masson 1098.
Notes: Fifty psalms by Marot, 30 by Gilles d'Aurigny ('traduictz de latin selon le vray texte et phrase Hebraique'), the 'Octonaires du Ps. 119', and some prayers.

B 137. **Bible. A.T. Psaumes,** Clément Marot.

Cinquante Psalmes de David. — Rouen, Robert et Jean Du Gort, Jean Mallard, 1550.
16°: A-I⁸ K⁴, rom.
*Paris BEBA Masson 1096 (incomp.).
Notes: Paris BEBA: gatherings H-K are bound in Jean Poitevin, *Cent Psalmes*, 1553.

B 138. **Bible. A.T. Psaumes,** Clément Marot, Théodore de Bèze.

Pseaumes octantetrois de David, mis en rime Françoise. A savoir, quarante neuf Par Clement Marot... Et trentequatre par Theodore de Besze. — Geneva, Jean Crespin, 1551.
8°: A-V⁸, rom.
Rutgers UL X BS 1443. F8 M332.
References: Gilmont *Crespin* 51/6. *Index* I #333. Facs. reprod. ed. F.A. Johns, New Brunswick, 1973.
Notes: First ed. of Bèze's additions to the Psalter, and of his prefatory epistle. With melodies.

B 139. **Bible. A.T. Psaumes,** Théodore de Bèze.

Trente-quatre psaumes. — Geneva, Jean Crespin, 1551.
References: Gilmont *Crespin* 51/5.

B 140.   Bible. A.T. Psaumes, trans. Louis Budé, preface by Jean Calvin.

Les Pseaumes de David traduicts selon la verité Hebraique, avec annotations tresutiles. — Geneva, Jean Crespin, 1551.

8°: *⁸ A-Z⁸, rom./ital.

*Geneva BPU Rés. Bb 582 (a). *Geneva BPU Rés. S 91 (b).

References: Gilmont *Crespin* 51/4. Text in T. de Bèze, *Psaumes,* ed. P. Pidoux (Droz, 1984).

Notes: Gilmont: (a) mentions 'Geneva' and names Calvin as author of the preface, (b) suppresses the two references.

B 141.   Bible. A.T. Psaumes, trans. Gilles d'Aurigny.

Trente Psalmes du royal Prophete David. Traduictz de Latin (selon le vray texte et phrase Hebraïque) en rithme Françoyse. — Paris, Oudin Petit, 1551.

16°: A-G⁸ a-d⁸, ital.

*Versailles BM Goujet 12° 28.

References: Peach/Brunel #23.

Notes: Re-ed. of the 1549 text.

B 142.   Bible. A.T. Psaumes, Clément Marot and others.

Les Cent cinquante Psalmes du Prophete Royal David. — Paris, Estienne Mesviere, 1551.

32°: A-Z AA-OO⁸, rom.   OO 8r: Impr. à Paris par Estienne Mesviere.

*Geneva BPU Rés. Bb 660.

Notes: OO 8v: The authors are named: Clement Marot, Gilles d'Aurigny, Robert Brincel, C.R. et Cl. B.

B 143.   Bible. A.T. Psaumes, Clément Marot.

Cinquante deux Pseaumes de David. — Paris, Guillaume Thibout, Jean Bonfons, 1551.

16°: A-L⁸, ital.

*Paris BN Rés. Ye 1505 (Thibout). *Paris BN Rés. Ye 1506 (Bonfons).

B 144.   Bible. A.T. Psaumes, trans. Jean Poitevin.

Les Cent Psalmes de David qui restoient à traduire en rithme Françoyse. — Rouen, Jean Mallard, Robert et Jean Du Gort, 1553.

16°: A-V⁸ X⁴, rom.
*Paris BEBA Masson 1096 (incomp.).
Notes: Paris BEBA: gatherings H-X bound in *Cinquante Pseaumes*, Marot, 1550.

B 145. **Bible. A.T. Salomon,** trans. Lefèvre d'Étaples.

Les Sentences de Solomon, doctrine tressalutaire a tous vrais enfans de Dieu, desirans estre instruitz en toutes bonnes meurs: selon la verite Hebraique. — Antwerp, Martin Lempereur, 1530?
16°: A-L⁸, goth. L 8v: marque de M. Lempereur, devise 'SOLA FIDES SUFFICIT. M.K. 1525'.
*Rouen BM A 1065.
Notes: Plain text, without commentary. Extract from Lefèvre's Bible, of which this part first appeared in 1529.

B 146. **Bible. A.T. Salomon,** trans. P.-R. Olivétan.

Les Livres de Salomoh. Lés Proverbes, LEcclesiaste, le Cantique dés cantiques. Translatez d'Ebrieu en Francoys. — Geneva, Jean Girard, 1538.
8°: a-g⁸, rom. g 8r: impr. à Geneva par Jehan Gerard imprimeur.
Edinburgh NLS Newb.1636(1). *Geneva BPU Rés. Bb 581. *Wolfenbüttel HAB 1282.15 Theol. *Vienna ÖNB *43.Z.143.
References: *BG* 38/2.
Notes: g 8r: 'translatez et reveux par Belisem de Belimakon' (Hebrew for 'no name, no place'). Censured on 25.05.1542 (Higman *Censorship*, p. 90).

B 147. **Bible. A.T. Salomon,** trans. Lefèvre d'Étaples.

Les sentences de Solomon, doctrine tres salutaire a tous vrays enfans de Dieu, desyrans estre instruictz en toutes bonnes meurs: translatez selon la verite Hebraicque. — Antwerp, Vve Martin Lempereur, 1539.
16°: A-L⁸, goth.
*La Haye KB 150 F 46.
References: NK #2512.

B 148. **Bible. A.T. Salomon.**

Les Livres de Salomon. — Lyon, 1541.
Munich BSB (destroyed).
Notes: Only mention: BSB catalogue.

B 149.   Bible. A.T. Salomon, trans. P.-R. Olivétan.

*Les   Livres   de   Salomon.   Les   Proverbes,
L'Ecclesiaste, Le Cantique des Cantiques. Fidelle-
ment traduicts de Latin en Francoys.* — Lyon,
Estienne Dolet, 1542.
16°: A-I^8, rom.
*Paris SHP R. 15914.
References: Longeon *Dolet* #224. See *Index* I #318.

B 150.   Bible. A.T. Salomon, trans. J. Lefèvre d'Étaples.

*Salomon. Les Proverbes. Ecclesiastes. Les Can-
tiques. Sapience. Ecclesiastique.* — Antwerp, Jean
Loe, 1544.
16°: A-Z & Aa-Bb^8, goth.
*Bruxelles BR LP 8326A. *Wolfenbüttel HAB A 24 Helmst.12°.

B 151.   Bible. N.T.

*Le tressainct et sacres texte du nouniaulx testament
translates du latin en franhois.* — Antwerp, Adriaen
van Berghen, Jean Brocquart (Tournai), 1523.
8°: A-Z^8 §^{4} §§^{8} Aa-Ss^8, goth. Ss 6v: Impr. en anvers pour Jehan
Brocquart par Adrieu de Mons. 1523.
Utrecht UB Coll. Thomaase Rar.kast 4/74.
References: Chambers #30a. NK #415.
Notes: Lutheran version?

B 152.   Bible. N.T., trans. J. Lefèvre d'Étaples.

*Les choses contenues en ce present livre. La S.
Evangile selon S. Matthieu/Marc/Luc/Jehan.* [II]:
... *Epistres/Actes/Lapocalypse S. Jehan.* — Paris,
Simon de Colines, 1523.
8°: a-z & A-B^8 C^4. A^8 a-b^4 c-y aa-hh^8 aaa-ccc^8 ddd^6 #^{2} eee-hhh^8,
goth. B 7v, y 8v, hh 7v, ddd 5v: Impr. à Paris, Simon de Colines.
08.06.1523. 17.10.1523. 31.10.1523. 06.11.1523.
*London BL C.111.c.13 (Vol. I). Oxford Bodl. 8° Z 454 Th. Paris
BA 8° T.596 (Vol. I). *Paris BN Rés. A 6414 (incompl.). Rouen BM
A 1075 (+).
References: Chambers #31. Facs. reprod. ed. M.A. Screech,
1970.
Notes: First ed. of Lefèvre's trans. Two 'epistres exhorta-
toires' of 'Lutheran' flavour.

B 153. **Bible. N.T.,** trans. J. Lefèvre d'Étaples.

Les choses contenues en ce present livre. La S. Evangile selon S. Matthieu/Marc/Luc/Jehan. [II]*: Epistres/Actes/Apocalypse.* — Paris, Simon de Colines, 1524.

8°: a-z & A-C⁸ A b-y aa-ll⁸ mm⁴, goth. C 7v, mm 4r: Impr. à Paris, Simon de Colines. 12.04.1525. 10.01.1524 [1525].

*Lausanne BCU AZ 4352 (Vol. II). *London BL 2015.b.18 (without prefaces). *Paris BN Rés. A 6415. *Paris SHP A 101-102 and R 11437. Vienna ÖNB 1.K.25 (+).

References: Chambers #34.

Notes: Copies often bound as a mixture with 1523 ed. or with that of Antoine Couteau, 1524.

B 154. **Bible. N.T.,** trans. J. Lefèvre d'Étaples.

Les choses contenues en ce present livre. La S. Evangile selon S. Matthieu/Marc/Luc/Jehan. [II]*: Epistres/Actes/Apocalypse.* — [Paris], [Antoine Couteau], 1524.

8°: a-z & aa-cc⁶ A⁸ A-B⁴ C-X⁸ yC⁸ AA-HH aaa-ccc⁸ ddd⁶ A⁸ B¹⁰, goth. cc 7v: 12.10.1524.

*Lausanne BCU AZ 4352. *Paris SHP A 103-104. *Basle UB FG IX2 45. Besançon BM 234 964.

References: Chambers #35.

Notes: Contains prefatory epistles, does not name the printer.

B 155. **Bible. N.T.,** trans. J. Lefèvre d'Étaples.

Les choses contenues en ce present livre. La S. Evangile selon S. Matthieu/Marc/Luc/Jehan. [II]*: Epistres/Actes/Apocalypse.* — Paris, [Antoine Couteau], pr. Simon de Colines, 1524.

8°: π² b-z & aa-cc⁸ π² B⁴ C-X⁸ yC⁸ AA-HH aaa-ccc⁸ ddd⁶ A⁸ B¹⁰, goth. cc 7v: 12.10.1524.

*London BL G.12171.

References: Chambers #36.

Notes: Only gatherings π differ from the previous ed. S. de Colines named, but prefatory epistles are omitted.

B 156. **Bible. N.T.,** trans. J. Lefèvre d'Étaples.

Les choses contenues en ce present Livre. La S. Evangile selon S. Matthieu/Marc/Luc/Jehan. [II]*:*

Epistres / Actes / Apocalypse. — Antwerp, Guillaume Vorsterman, 1525.

8°: a-s⁸ t⁴ v⁸ aaa⁸ bbb⁴ A-Q⁸ AA-HH⁸ II⁴, goth. v 7r, Q 8v, II 3v: Anvers, Guillame Vosterman. 22.11.1524. 14.12.1524. 04.01.1525.
*London BL C.36.b.16. Oxford SJC LL 2/Ac.7.13. Villiers-le-Bel SBF 165.
References: Chambers #38. NK #2503.
Notes: Copied from the S. de Colines 1524 ed. (Chambers #34).

B 157.   **Bible. N.T.,** trans. J. Lefèvre d'Étaples.

Les choses contenues en ceste partie du nouveau testament. — Basle, [Andreas Cratander], [pr. Johann Schabler], 1525.

8°: a-z & A-T⁸ V⁴ AA-GG aaa-ddd⁸ eee⁴ fff-ggg⁸, goth.
Basle UB F.G. VI.91. Cambridge UL Young 169. London BL 217.d.12. Paris BN Rés. A 6416 (-a 1). Vienna ÖNB 4.M.44 (+).
References: Chambers #39.
Notes: Copied from Chambers #35.

B 158.   **Bible. N.T.,** trans. J. Lefèvre d'Étaples.

Les choses contenues en ce present Livre. La S. Evangile selon S. Matthieu/Marc/Luc/Jehan. [II]: *Epistres/Actes/Apocalypse.* — Paris, Simon Du Bois, 1525.

8°: a-z A-S AA-II⁸ KK⁴, goth. z 8r, S 8r, KK 3r: Impr. à Paris, Simon du boys. 14.10.1525. 06.10.1525. 19.10.1525.
*Geneva BPU Bb 806 Rés. Paris BN Rés. A 12153. Versailles BM Rés. in-8° 0103a (-a 1).
References: Chambers #40.
Notes: Last ed. of NT printed in Paris until 1565. The Parlement had forbidden editions of the Bible in French by edict of 28.08.1525 (Higman *Censorship*, p. 78).

B 159.   **Bible. N.T.,** trans. J. Lefèvre d'Étaples.

Le nouveau testament contenant ce qui est declare en la page subsequente. — 'Turin' [Lyon?], 'François Cavillon' [Claude Nourry?], [François Carcan?], 1525?

16°: a-z⁸ &⁸ 2⁸ 4⁴ A-V aa-gg⁸ hh⁴ AA-EE⁸, goth.
*Munich UB 8° Bibl.1007. Nice BM Rés. 2701. *Paris SHP R 15975 (lacks all before B1).

References: Chambers #41. Baudrier III, 88. Droz, *APR* 50-5 (reprod. t.p.).

Notes: Follows 1524 ed. Chambers #34. Fr. Carcan was a relative of Claude Nourry, and therefore also of P. de Vingle.

B 160.   Bible. N.T., trans. J. Lefèvre d'Étaples.

Les choses contenues en ce present livre... Une breve instruction, poür deuement lire lescripture saincte. — [Alençon], [Simon Du Bois], 1529.

8°: +[8] a-z[8] &[4] aa[4] bb-hh[8] *[4] A-X[8] yy[4], goth.

*London BL C.69.bb.12 (Vol. II). New York NN *KB 1529. Orléans BM A 293. Villiers-le-Bel SBF 80.

References: Chambers #47. Clutton #31.

Notes: Revision of S. de Colines, 1524 ed., possibly done by Pierre Caroli. The Villiers-le-Bel copy has a preliminary gathering A[8] containing 'La Maniere de lire levangile' trans. from Luther.

B 161.   Bible. N.T., trans. J. Lefèvre d'Étaples.

Le nouveau Testament, contenant les quattre Evangelistes... avec les faitz des Apostres et les Epistres de Saint Paul, de Saint Jaques... et avec Lapocalipse... — Antwerp, Martin Lempereur, Guillaume Vorsterman, 1529.

8°: A[8] A-Z AA-ZZ AAA-BBB[8], goth. BBB 6v: Anvers Martin Lempreur/Guilame Vorsterman. 18.01.1529.

Bruxelles BR LP 4483 A. London BL G.12172. New York NN Spencer Coll. Neth. 1529. London BL C.36.d.19 (Vorsterman). Villiers-le-Bel SBF 88 (Vorsterman) (+).

References: NK #2505, 2506. Chambers #48, 49.

Notes: No prefatory epistles.

B 162.   Bible. N.T., trans. J. Lefèvre d'Étaples.

La premiere/seconde partie du nouveau testament. — [Lyon], [Pierre de Vingle], 1529?

16°: a-z A-D[8] aa-yy[8], goth.

*Geneva MHR O[4]e(533?) (Vol. I, incompl.). *London BL 3025.b.10 and 1016.a.6. Villiers-le-Bel SBF 121. Stuttgart LB.

References: Droz *APR* 44-6 (reprods.) Chambers #50.

Notes: The date 1529? suggested by Mlle Droz on the basis of the 'Cor contritum' mark of Vingle/Nourry. A new exhortatory epistle, attrib. to Pierre de Vingle.

B 163. **Bible. N.T.,** trans. J. Lefèvre d'Étaples.

La premiere/seconde partie du nouveau Testament.
— [Lyon], [Pierre de Vingle], 1530?
8°: a-t⁸ v¹⁰ aa-pp⁸ qq⁶, goth.
Oxford Bodl. Mason D 23. Augsburg SB Th.B.8° VIII, 28(1). Paris
BN Rés. Z Don 594(214). Paris BM 48837. *Stuttgart LB (+).
References: Chambers #53.
Notes: Attrib. to Vingle by Mlle Droz. The ed. closely follows
that of 1529 (Chambers #50).

B 164. **Bible. N.T.,** trans. J. Lefèvre d'Étaples.

*Le nouveau Testament, auquel est demonstre Jesu
Christ sauveur du monde estre venu: annonce de
Dieu a noz Peres anciens des le commencement du
monde, et en plusieurs lieux predict par les Pro-
phetes.* — Antwerp, Martin Lempereur, 1531.
8°: π⁸ a-z A-Z⁸ *⁸ **⁸ ***⁴, goth. Z 8r: 01.07.1531.
London BL 3025.c.13. Paris BN Rés. A 6417. Paris SHP R 23430.
*Paris BM 34872 Rés. Boston MB G.288.34 (+).
References: Chambers #57. NK #2507.

B 165. **Bible. N.T.,** trans. J. Lefèvre d'Étaples.

*Le nouveau Testament de nostre saulveur Jesu Christ
translate selon le vray text en franchois.* — Antwerp,
Jean Graphaeus, 1532.
12°: A-Z Aa-Hh¹², goth.
*Geneva BPU Bb 2188 Rés. (-Hh 11-12). London BL 3025.c.15 (-
Hh 11-12). Manchester UL 225.54/B 10 (-Hh 12). Villiers-le-Bel
SBF 158 (-Hh 11). *Wolfenbüttel HAB A.84.12° Helmst. (+).
References: NK #2508. Chambers #58.

B 166. **Bible. N.T.,** trans. J. Lefèvre d'Étaples.

*Le nouveau Testament, contenant les quattre Evan-
gelistes... avec les faictz des Apostres: et les Epistres
sainct Paul, les Epistres Canoniques, et Lapocalipse: auquel est demonstre JesuChrist...* — Antwerp, Martin Lempereur, 1532.
16°: *⁸ A-Z a-t⁸ *⁸ **⁸, goth. t 4v: 10.04.1532.
Cologne USB GB.IV.3869 (-t.p.). *Munich BSB 8° B.lat.f.17. Stuttgart LB. Utrecht UB Doct. 212 (rariora).
References: NK #418. Chambers #59.

B 167.   Bible. N.T., trans. J. Lefèvre d'Étaples.

Le nouveau testament de nostre seigneur et seul sauveur Jesus Christ... Ce nouveau testament a este de nouveau imprime en telle grosse lettre que vous voyez, pour plus aysement et facilement lire. — Neuchâtel, Pierre de Vingle, 1534.

2°: AA⁴ A-K⁸ L-N⁶, goth.   N 5v: Neuchâtel, Pierre de Vingle. 27.03.1534.

Berne LB SL Sq 2.8 Rés. *Geneva MHR O⁴e(534). *Neuchâtel BV C 41 Rés. New York NN *KB +1534.

References: Chambers #64. Dufour *Not.cat.* 120-2.

Notes: Dufour attributes the *Table* to Matthieu Malingre. Some changes to the text anticipate the Olivétan 1535 Bible.

B 168.   Bible. N.T., trans. J. Lefèvre d'Étaples.

Le nouveau Testament, auquel est demonstre Jesu Christ sauveur du monde, estre venu annonce de Dieu a noz Peres anciens des le commencement du monde, et en plusieurs lieulx predict par les Prophetes. — Antwerp, Martin Lempereur, 1535.

8°: π⁸ A-Z a-z⁸ *⁸ **⁸ ***⁴, goth.

Antwerp MPM R.61.1. London BL 1110.a.42. Villiers-le-Bel SBF 176. Manchester JRL 13734.

References: Chambers #68. NK #2509.

B 169.   Bible. N.T., trans. Olivétan.

Le nouveau Testament, de nostre Seigneur et seul sauveur Jesus Christ. — [Geneva], [J. Girard], 1536.

8°: *⁸ a-z A-Q⁸ R⁴ A-B⁸ C⁴, rom.   C 4r: Impr. à Geneve.

Cambridge Trinity A.24.36. *Geneva BPU Bb 823 Rés. (-* 2). *Munich UB 8°Bibl.1008. Villiers-le-Bel SBF 113. *Wolfenbüttel HAB Td 37.

References: Chambers #70. Adams B 1760. Dufour *Not.Cat.* 140-2. *BG* 36/1a.

Notes: First ed. of scripture in roman type, possibly Jean Girard's first work. The last three gatherings (A-C) give the *Table dés plus communs passages du nouveau Testament,* dated (A 1r) 1536.

B 170.   Bible. N.T., trans. J. Lefèvre d'Étaples.

Le nouveau Testament, de nostre Seigneur Jesu Christ. — Antwerp, Matthieu Crom, 1538.

8°: A-Z a-p⁸ p-r⁸ s⁴ *⁸ **⁴, goth.   ** 4r: Anvers, Matthieu Crom.
1548.
London BL 3022.bb.8. Paris SHP A 112. Stuttgart LB. *London St
Paul's 38.c.31.
References: Chambers #72. NK #4470.
Notes: The date in the colophon, 'M.D.xxxxviii', has an 'x'
too many (C. Clair, *The Library*, 5e Série, 17 (1962), 155-6).

B 171.   Bible. N.T., trans. J. Lefèvre d'Étaples.
*Le Nouveau testament de nostre Seigneur Jesuchrist,
seul sauveur du monde.* — Antwerp, Vve Martin
Lempereur, 1538.
16°: π⁸ A-Z a-z aa-dd⁸ <⁸ *⁸ A-F⁸ G⁶, rom.
*Amsterdam VU Ned.Inc.369. Xanten StB 93.
References: Chambers #73. NK #421.

B 172.   Bible. N.T., trans. J. Lefèvre d'Étaples.
*Le Nouveau Testament. de nostre Seigneur Jesu
Christ seul sauveur du monde ... avec lés figures dés
Actes dés apostres et de l'Apocalypse. Item ... lés
Epistres du vieil testament.* — Antwerp, Guillaume
Du Mont, 1538.
16°: *⁸ A-Z a-z Aa⁸ ☞⁸ **⁸ ππ⁸ ()⁸ &⁸ ct⁸ Bb-Dd⁸, rom.   Dd 8r:
Anvers, Guiliaume du mont. 1538.
Antwerp MPM R.61.2(I-II).
References: Chambers #74. NK #420.

B 173.   Bible. N.T., trans. J. Lefèvre d'Étaples.
*Le nouveau Testament, auquel est demonstre Jesu
Christ sauveur du monde estre venu annonce de Dieu
a noz Peres anciens des le commencement du
monde... Avec la declaration des oeuvers par les-
quelles lhome peult estre congneu.* — Antwerp, Jean
Steelsius, 1538.
16°: π⁸ A-Z Aa-Zz Aaa-Hhh a-g⁸, rom.
Manchester JRL R 9056. Villiers-le-Bel SBF 120.
References: Chambers #75. NK #2510.

B 174.   Bible. N.T., trans. Olivétan.
*Le Nouveau Testament, Cest a dire, La nouvelle Alli-
ance. De nostre Seigneur et seul sauveur Jesus
Christ.* — Geneva, Jean Michel, 1538.

8°: *a⁸ *b⁴ a-z A-X⁸ y⁴ A-C⁸, goth. C 8r: Impr. par Jehan Michel. 1538.
*Geneva BPU Bb 1879 Rés. *London BL 1110.b.6 (s.l.). Oxford Bodl. Mason M 15 (-C 7-8). Paris BA 8° T.496 et 497. Stuttgart LB (+).
References: Chambers #76. *BG* 38/3a,b. Th. Dufour, *Not.Cat.*, 149-52, 187-8.

B 175.   Bible. N.T., trans. J. Lefèvre d'Étaples.

Le nouveau Testament auquel est demonstre Jhesu Christ nostre Sauveur, et en plusieurs lieu predict par les prophetes, avec la declaration des oeuvres et myracles quil a fait. — Antwerp, Jean de Liesvelt, 1539.
16°: π⁸ A-Z a-z aa-oo⁸, goth.   oo 8v: Anvers, Jean de Liesvelt. 13.11.1539.
Cambridge UL Young 170. *Oxford Bodl. Douce BB 11. Villiers-le-Bel SBF 82.
References: Chambers #77. Adams B 1761. NK #2511.

B 176.   Bible. N.T., trans. Olivétan.

Le Nouveau Testament, C'est à dire, La Nouvelle Alliance, de nostre Seigneur et seul Sauveur Jesus Christ. — [Basle], [J. Walder], 1539.
8°: *⁸ a-z A-T⁸, rom.
*London BL C.36.d.8. *Paris BSG A 8° 824 inv. 1003 Rés. *Wolfenbüttel HAB Bibel-S.918. *Geneva MHR O⁴e (539a).
References: Chambers #78. Bietenholz #781. Th.Dufour, *Not.Cat.* 169-73.

B 177.   Bible. N.T., trans. Olivétan.

Le Nouveau Testament, C'est à dire, La nouvelle Alliance, de nostre Seigneur et seul Sauveur Jesus Christ. — [Geneva], [Jean Girard], 1539.
8°: *⁸ a-y A-Q S-T⁸, rom.
*Geneva MHR O⁴e(539). Lausanne BCU AZ 4282. *London BL 218.a.9. *Montpellier FTP 1651.
References: Chambers #79. *BG* 39/3. Th. Dufour, *Not.Cat.* 167-9.

B 178. **Bible. N.T.,** trans. J. Lefèvre d'Étaples.

Le nouveau Testament de nostre Seigneur Jesu Christ, seul sauveur du monde ... avec lés figures dés Evangiles, et dés Actes et de L'apocalypse. Item ... les Epistres du vieil Testament. — Antwerp, Guillaume Du Mont, 1540.

12°: A-S^{12} a-r^{12}, rom. S 12r and r 12v: Anvers, Guiliaume du Mont. 1540.

Glasgow UL Euing Coll. Dc-c.1. London BL 3025.c.24. Villiers-le-Bel SBF 56. *Wolfenbüttel HAB Bibel-S.919. Warsaw BN XVI.O.2978.

References: Chambers #83. NK #2513.

B 179. **Bible. N.T.,** trans. J. Lefèvre d'Étaples.

La premiere/seconde partie du Nouveau Testament. — Lyon, Nicolas Petit, 1540.

8°: a-t^8 v^{10} A-Q^8, rom.

*Geneva BPU Bb 807. Villiers-le-Bel SBF 83.

References: Chambers #84.

B 180. **Bible. N.T.,** trans. J. Lefèvre d'Étaples.

La premiere/seconde partie du Nouveau Testament de Jesu Christ, extraicte de mot a mot de la Saincte Bible. — Antwerp, Vve Martin Lempereur, 1541.

8°: π^8 A-Z AA-GG^8 HH^4 Aa-Yy a-f^8 g^4 *^{8} **^{6} ☞^{6}, goth.

*London BL C.69.ff.13. Stuttgart LB.

References: Chambers #91.

Notes: M. Lempereur's widow gives her name on the t.p.: Françoise la Rouge.

B 181. **Bible. N.T.,** trans. J. Lefèvre d'Étaples.

La premiere/seconde partie du Nouveau Testament de Jesu Christ, extraicte de mot a mot de la Saincte Bible. — Antwerp, Vve Martin Lempereur, 1541.

8°: π^8 A-Z a-z aa-pp^8, goth.

Paris BN Rés. 8°Don 594(223) (-π 1). Paris SHP A 111.

References: Chambers #92.

B 182. **Bible. N.T.,** trans. J. Lefèvre d'Étaples.

La Premiere/seconde partie du Nouveau Testament. — Lyon, Thibaud Payen, 1541.

16°: a-z A-H⁸ I⁴ aa-zz Aa-Bb⁸, rom. Bb 7r: Lyon, Thibault Payen.
Stuttgart LB.
References: Chambers #93.

B 183. Bible. N.T., trans. Olivétan.

Le Nouveau Testament de nostre seigneur Jesus Christ. — Lyon, Jean Barbou, 1542?
16°: a-z A-G⁸ A-Z Aa⁸, rom. Aa 8r: Lyon, Jehan Barbou.
*Munich UB 8° Bibl.1197.
References: Chambers #94. Baudrier V,7.

B 184. Bible. N.T., trans. Olivétan.

Le Nouveau Testament de nostre seigneur Jesus Christ. — Lyon, Balthasar Arnoullet, 1542.
16°: a-z A-I⁸ aa-zz Aa-Cc⁸, rom. Cc 7r: Lyon, Balthasard Arnoullet.
Ghent UB A 3946.
References: Chambers #95.
Notes: B. Arnoullet inherited the equipment of his father-in-law Jean Barbou, who died in 1542 or 1543.

B 185. Bible. N.T., trans. Olivétan.

Le Nouveau Testament. — Lyon, Etienne Dolet, 1542.
References: Chambers #96. Longeon *Dolet* #214.
Notes: While well attested in Calvin's correspondence and in Dolet's prefaces, this ed. seems to have disappeared entirely after its condemnation in Paris (Higman *Censorship*, p. 99).

B 186. Bible. N.T., trans. J. Lefèvre d'Étaples.

La Premiere/seconde partie du Nouveau Testament. — Lyon, Thibaud Payen, 1542.
16°: a-z A-H⁸ I⁴ aa-zz Aa-Bb⁸, rom. I 4v, Bb 7v: Lyon, Thibault Payen. 1542.
Villiers-le-Bel SBF 117.
References: Chambers #97.

B 187. Bible. N.T., trans. J. Lefèvre d'Étaples.

Le Nouveau Testament de nostre Seigneur Jesu Christ, seul sauveur du monde ... avec lés Figures

*dés Evangiles, et dés Actes et de L'apocalypse. Item
... lés Epistres du vieil testament.* — Antwerp, Guillaume Du Mont, 1543.
16°: A-Z Aa-Zz AA-KK⁸, rom. KK 5v: Anvers, Guiliame du Mont.
31.03.1543.
Bruxelles, BR VB 158(2)A Rés. La Hague KB 1707 F 33.
References: Chambers #102.

B 188.   **Bible. N.T.,** trans. J. Lefèvre d'Étaples.

*Le Nouveau Testament de nostre Seigneur Jesu
Christ, seul sauveur du monde ... avec lés figures dés
Evangiles, et de L'apocalypse. Item ... lés Epistres
du vieil Testament.* — Antwerp, Henry Pierre, 1543.
16°: A-Z a-z aa-gg⁸, rom. gg 8r: Anvers, Henry Pierre de Middel-
burch. 1543.
London BL 3025.a.9.
References: Chambers #103.

B 189.   **Bible. N.T.,** trans. J. Lefèvre d'Étaples.

*Le Nouveau Testament de nostre Seigneur Jesu
Christ, seul sauveur du monde ... avec les figures des
Evangiles et des Actes, et de l'apocalypse. Item ...
les Epistres du vieil Testament.* — Antwerp, Jean
Richard, 1543.
12°: A-Z Aa-Tt¹², rom. Tt 12r: Anvers, Jehan Richard. 1543.
London BL 3025.c.1. Villiers-le-Bel SBF 89. Stuttgart LB.
References: Chambers #104.

B 190.   **Bible. N.T.,** trans. Olivétan, rev. J. Calvin.

*Le Nouveau Testament, C'est à dire, La nouvelle
Alliance de nostre Seigneur et seul Sauveur Jesus
Christ.* — Geneva, Jean Girard, 1543.
16°: *⁸ a-z A-Z Aa-Ee⁸ Aaa-Ddd⁸, rom.
Edinburgh UL TR/D6. *Vienna ÖNB 1.J.47 (anon.).
References: Chambers #105, 106. *BG* 43/3.
Notes: First appearance of Calvin's 'Recueil d'aucuns mots'.
The anonymous issue omits Calvin's name, and the name and
address of the printer.

B 191.   **Bible. N.T.,** trans. J. Lefèvre d'Étaples.

La premiere/seconde Partie du Nouveau Testament.
— Lyon, Jacques Crozet, 1543.

16°: a-z A-Q^8 Aa-Zz AA-HH^8, goth. HH 7v: Lyon, Jacques crozet.
Lyon BV800102.
References: Chambers #107.
Notes: The second part is dated 1544.

B 192. **Bible. N.T.,** trans. J. Lefèvre d'Étaples.

La Premiere/seconde Partie du Nouveau Testament.
— [Lyon], [Thibaud Payen], 1543.
16°: [a]b-z A-L^8 m^4 aa-rr^8 ss^6..., rom.
Villiers-le-Bel SBF 74 (fragment).
References: Chambers #108.

B 193. **Bible. N.T.,** trans. J. Lefèvre d'Étaples.

Le nouveau Testament auquel est demonstre Jesu Crist nostre Sauveur, et en plusieurs lieux predict par les Prophetes avec la declaration des oeuvres et myracles quil a faict. — Antwerp, Jacques de Liesvelt, 1544.
16°: π^8 A-Z a-z aa-qq^8 rr^{10}, goth. rr 10r: Jacques de Liesveldt. 1544.
*Paris BN Rés. A 6418 (-π 1). Villiers-le-Bel SBF 111. Xanten StB 85 (-π 1).
References: Chambers #111.

B 194. **Bible. N.T.,** trans. Olivétan.

Le Nouveau Testament, Cest a dire: La nouvelle Alliance De nostre Seigneur et seul Sauveur Jesus Christ. — [Geneva], [Jean Michel], 1544.
8°: *a^8 *b^4 a-z A-Z Aa-Cc^8 Dd^4 Ee^8, goth.
*Geneva BPU Bb 2265 Rés. (-*a 1). *Geneva MHR O^{4}e(544). London BL C.23.a.14.
References: Chambers #112. *BG* 44/2.

B 195. **Bible. N.T.,** trans. Olivétan.

La Premiere/seconde partie du Nouveau Testament. — Lyon, Thibaud Payen, 1544.
16°: a-z A-O aa-zz AA-DD^8, rom.
Villiers-le-Bel SBF 52.
References: Chambers #113.

B 196.   Bible. N.T., trans. Olivétan.

Le Nouveau Testament de nostre seigneur Jesus Christ. — Lyon, Balthazar Arnoullet, Guillaume Rouillé, 1545.

16°: a-z A-L⁸ M⁴ aa-yy⁸ zz⁴ aa⁸ bb⁴, rom. aa 3v: Lyon, Balthazar Arnoullet.

Lyon BV Rés. 808251. Stuttgart LB. *Wolfenbüttel HAB A 86.12°Helmst. London BFBS 207 B45b (Rouillé).

References: Chambers #125, 126. Baudrier X, 114.

B 197.   Bible. N.T., trans. Olivétan.

Le Nouveau Testament de nostre Seigneur Jesus Christ. — Lyon, Jean de Tournes, 1545.

16°: A-C a-z A-F aa-xx⁸, rom.

Avignon Cal 8° 22.375. London BL 3025.a.16.

References: Chambers #127. Cartier *De Tournes* #28.

B 198.   Bible. N.T., trans. Olivétan, rev. J. Calvin.

Le Nouveau Testament, C'est à dire, La nouvelle Alliance, de nostre Seigneur et seul Sauveur Jesus Christ. — Geneva, Jean Girard, 1546.

16°: *⁸ a-z A-Z Aa-Ee Aaa-Ddd⁸, rom.

Bourg-en-Bresse BM 101.862. *St Andrews UL Bib BS 2130.B46.

References: Chambers #132. *BG* 46/4.

B 199.   Bible. N.T., trans. Olivétan.

Le Nouveau Testament de nostre Seigneur Jesus Christ. — Lyon, 1546.

16°: a-z A-X⁸ Y¹², rom.

Rome BV Rossiana 7731.

References: Chambers #133.

B 200.   Bible. N.T., trans. Olivétan.

Le Nouveau Testament de nostre Seigneur Jesus Christ. — Lyon, Jean Frellon, 1548.

16°: a-z A-I⁸ K⁴ aa-zz⁸ A⁴, rom. A 4r: Impr. à Lyon, chez Jehan Frellon.

*Geneva MHR O⁴e(548). Gotha FB Theol.47/1. Paris BN Rés. A 17957. *Strasbourg BNU E 103415.

References: Chambers #140. Baudrier V, 212-13.

B 201. **Bible. N.T.,** trans. Olivétan.

Le Nouveau Testament de nostre Seigneur Jesus Christ. — Lyon, Philibert Rollet, Barthelemy Frein, pr. Thibaud Payen, Guillaume Rouillé, 1548.
16°: a-z aa-ll A-Y^8 Z^4 *^{8} **^{4}, rom. Z 4r: Impr. à Lyon par Philibert Rollet et Barthelemy Frein pr. Thibault Payen/Guillaume Rouillé et Antoine Constantin.
*Lausanne BCU AZ 5144 (Payen). Mainz SB XIV.b.79 (Rouillé). Stuttgart LB (Rouillé).
References: Chambers #141, 142.

B 202. **Bible. N.T.,** trans. Olivétan.

Le Nouveau Testament De nostre Seigneur Jesus Christ. — Lyon, Jean Frellon, 1550.
16°: a-z A-L aa-zz Aa-Bb^8, rom. Bb 6v: Impr. à Lyon chez Jehan Frellon. 1550.
*Munich UB 8° Bibl.1199 (-a 1). Villiers-le-Bel SBF 78.
References: Chambers #148.

B 203. **Bible. N.T.** trans. Olivétan.

Le Nouveau Testament de nostre Seigneur Jesus Christ. — Lyon, Guillaume Rouillé, 1550.
16°: a-z aa-ll^8 mm^4 A-Z ..., rom.
Le Havre BM R.880 (-Z 7 sqq.).
References: Chambers #149. Baudrier IX, 49, 179.

B 204. **Bible. N.T.,** trans. Olivétan.

Le Nouveau Testament, C'est à dire, La Nouvelle Alliance de nostre Seigneur et seul Sauveur Jesus Christ. Translaté de Grec en François, et reveu, par M. Jean Calvin. — Geneva, Jean Girard, 1551.
8°: A-Z Aa-Yy Aaa-Eee a-c^8, rom.
Basle UB F.G.IX(2) 72. Strasbourg BNU E 103416. Cambridge King's M.80.8. Geneva BPU Bb 2242 Rés. (with the extra gatherings).
References: Chambers #155, 156.
Notes: Two extra gatherings *^{8} and **^{8} at the beginning, giving the *Deux Epistres* of Calvin and Viret, first publ. 1543.

B 205. **Bible. N.T.,** trans. Olivétan.

Le Nouveau Testament, C'est à dire, La Nouvelle Alliance de nostre Seigneur et seul Sauveur Jesus

Christ. Translaté et reveu de Grec en Francois, Par
M. Jean Calvin. — [Geneva], [Jean Girard], 1551.
8°: *⁸ **⁴ a-z A-Y aa-cc⁸, rom.
*Geneva BPU Bb 2243 Rés. London BL C.51.a.4. Villiers-le-Bel
SBF 114.
References: Chambers #157.
Notes: In the Geneva BPU copy the words 'Par M. Jean Cal-
vin' have been erased on the t.p. But the prefatory epistle
(* 2r) still names the author.

B 206.   Bible. N.T., trans. Olivétan.

Le Nouveau Testament: C'est à dire, La Nouvelle
Alliance de nostre Seigneur, et seul Sauveur Jesus
Christ. Translaté et reveu de Grec en François, Par
M. Jean Calvin. — Geneva, Adam et Jean Rivery,
1551.
16°: a-z A-Z Aa-Rr aa-dd⁸, rom.
*Geneva BPU Bb 2306. Augsburg BS Th.B.16° VIII.28(5).
References: Chambers #158.

B 207.   Bible. N.T., trans. Olivétan.

Le Nouveau Testament, c'est à dire, La nouvelle
Alliance de nostre Seigneur et seul Sauveur Jesus
Christ, Translaté de Grec en Francoys. Reveu par M.
Jean Calvin. — London, Thomas Gaultier, Edward
Whitchurch, 1551.
8°: *⁸ **⁴ A-Z⁸ Aa-Ff⁸ ci⁸ c*⁸ cc⁸, ital.
Atlanta GEU (Gaultier). London BL C.106.a.2 (s.l. s.n.). Villiers-le-
Bel SBF 159 (s.l. s.n.). Caen BV Rés. A 1549 (Whitchurch).
References: Chambers #159, 160, 161.

B 208.   Bible. N.T., trans. Olivétan.

Le Nouveau Testament de nostre Seigneur Jesu
Christ. — Lyon, Jean de Tournes, 1551.
16°: a-z A-Z aa-gg⁸ hh⁶ *⁸, rom.
Gotha FB Theol. 47/2. Mainz SB 551/6.
References: Chambers #162.

B 209.   Bodius, Hermann.

L'Union de toutes discordes: qui est ung livre tres
utile a tous amateurs de paix et de verite: extraict
des principaulx docteurs de leglise chrestienne: par

le venerable docteur Herman Bodium. — [Antwerp],
Martin Lempereur, 1527.
8°: A-Z AA-CC^8 DD^4, goth.
*La Haye KB 230 G 16.
References: NK #430. Moore p. 159.
Notes: A work often attrib. to Martin Bucer. See R. Peters,
Stud. in Church Hist. 2 (1965), and J. Trapman in *NAKG*
63(1983). The original Latin ed. printed 'à Cologne' [= Ant-
werp] by [M. Lempereur], 1527.

B 210. Bodius, Hermann.

*La seconde partie de Lunion de toutes discordes:
livre tres utile a tous amateurs de verite, extrait des
principaulx docteurs de leglise de la foy Catholique.*
— Antwerp, Martin Lempereur, 1528.
8°: A-S^8 T^4, goth. T 4v: Anvers, Martin Lempereur, 1528.
*Paris SHP A 1165(2).
References: Moore #42. NK #2524.

B 211. Bodius, Hermann.

*La Premiere (-seconde) partie de Lunion de toute
discorde: qui est ung livre tres utile a tous amateurs
de paix et de unite: extraict des principaulx docteurs
de leglise Catholique <> revisite.* — Antwerp, Martin Lempereur, 1532.
8°: A-V a-k^8 I^4 (Pt. I) A-Y^8 (Pt. II), goth.
*Lausanne BCU AZ 4430 (incompl.). *Paris SHP A 1165(1).
*London BL 849.e.4.
References: Moore p. 154. NK #2525.
Notes: Only the BL has the second part.

B 212. Bodius, Hermann.

*La premiere partie de lunion de plusieurs passaiges
de lescripture saincte. Livre tresutile a tous amateurs de paix: Extraict des autenticques docteurs de
leglise chrestienne... reveu et corrige.* — [Geneva],
[Pierre de Vingle], 1533.
8°: A-Z AA-CC^8, goth. CC 8r: Anvers, Pierre du Pont, à l'enseigne
du pigeon blanc. 10.06.1533.
*Geneva MHR K Buc 6.
References: NK #4127. M.E. Kronenberg in *Het Boek* (1938-
9), 257-65.

Notes: H. Delarue in *BHR* 1946, 114: the Geneva Council forbade this ed. on 13.03.1533: hence the false address in the colophon.

B 213. Bodius, Hermann, dedic. by Antoine Saunier.

La seconde partie de Lunion de plusieurs passages de lescripture saincte: Livre tresutile a tous amateurs de verite, extraict des principaulx docteurs de leglise de la foy Catholicque ... reveu et corrige. — [Geneva], [Pierre de Vingle], 1533.
8°: Aa-Zz⁸, goth. Zz 8r: Anvers, Pierre du Pont, à l'enseigne du pigeon blanc. 12.06.1533.
*Geneva MHR K Buc 6.
Notes: Fol. Xx 3v: epistle by 'A. Sonnier aux lecteurs fideles'.

B 214. Bodius, Hermann.

La premiere Partie de Lunion de plusieurs passaiges de lescripture saincte. Livre tresutile a tous amateurs de paix: Extraict des autenticques docteurs de leglise Chrestienne ... reveu et corrige. — [Geneva], [Jean Michel], 1539.
8°: a-z⁸ &⁸ §⁸ +⁸, goth.
*Geneva BPU Bc 3325 Rés. Cambridge UL. *Vienna ÖNB 79.Ee.9.
References: Moore p. 159. Adams B 2254. Th. Dufour, *Not.cat.* p. 159. Berthoud 'Michel' #5. Cat. Drilhon #13 (this ed.). Higman *Censorship* A 27.

B 215. Bodius, Hermann, dedic. by Antoine Saunier.

La seconde partie de Lunion de plusieurs passaiges de lescripture saincte: Livre tresutile a tous amateurs de verite, extraict des principaux docteurs de leglise de la foy Catholique. — [Geneva], [Jean Michel], 1539.
8°: A-X Aa-Cc⁸, goth. Cc 8r: Ach. d'impr. 31.07.1539.
*Geneva BPU Bc 3325 Rés. Cambridge UL. *Vienna ÖNB 79.Ee.9.

B 216. Bodius, Hermann.

La premiere (-seconde) partie de l'Union de plusieurs passages de l'Escriture sainte: Extraite des Docteurs autentiques de l'Eglise Chrestienne ... reveue et corrigée. — [Geneva], [Philibert Hamelin], 1551.

8°: [3]+777 pp.+[24 ff.], a-z A-Z aA-cC⁸ *a-*c⁸, rom.
*Geneva BPU Bc 782. *Paris BN D² 4233.
References: *Index* I #510. CDM p. 17. *Index Aurel.* #120.888.
Notes: Saunier's epistle disappears, but is replaced by a new,
more violent, message 'au lecteur fidele' (a 2r): 'Ce livre te
monstrera comment ceux qui se veulent emparer de l'autorité
des Docteurs anciens, pour soustenir les abuz et erreurs qui
regnent aujourd'huy, sont bien loing de leur conte.' Fol E 3r:
new t.p. for beginning of Pt. II.

B 217.   **Bonaventure, Saint (attrib.),** trans. Jean Gerson.

Cy commence le prologue de laguillon damour divi-
ne fait par le docteur seraphic sainct Bonaventure.
et translate de latin en francois par ... jehan jerson.
— [Paris], [Philippe le Noir?], Denis Janot, Alain Lotrian, 1529?
4°: a-p⁸ q⁶, goth.
London BL 3805.aa.7. *Paris BA 4° T.2147 (- q6).
References: Moreau III #1658.
Notes: The attribution of the text to St Bonaventure and of the
translation to Gerson are given at the start of the text. J.-
P. Massaut, *Clichtove*, I, 195 gives the author of the *Stimulus
divini amoris* as Jacques de Milan (end of XIIIth century).
Another ed., by the same printers/booksellers, Paris BN Rés.
pD38.

B 217a.   **Bonaventure, Saint (attrib.),** trans. Jean Gerson.

Sensuyt lesguillon damour divin contenant quatre
parties ausquelles sont comprinses plusieurs devotes
meditations et oraisons tant sur la benoiste passion
de nostre seigneur Jesucrist que a lhonneur de la
benoiste vierge marie. — Paris, Philippe Le Noir,
Denis Janot, Alain Lotrian, 1529?
4°: 93 + [1] ff., A-C⁴ D⁸ F-N⁴ O⁸ P-V⁴ X⁶, goth. X 6v: Impr. à Paris par
Alain lotrian et Denys janot.
*Paris BN Rés. pD 38.
Notes: Prologue by Gerson dedicating the work to his 'seur ou de
sa fille de confession'.

B 218.   **Bonaventure, Saint (attrib.),** trans. Jean Gerson.

Le libvre tressalutaire nomme Lesguillon damour
divin: translate de latin en francois: par Maistre Je-

han Gerson. — Paris, [Pierre Ratoire], Pierre Sergent, 1541.

4°: A-T⁴ V⁸ X², goth. X 2v: Impr. à Paris pr. Pierre Sergent libraire, rue neufve nostre Dame, enseigne sainct Nicolas, 07.07.1541.

*Paris BU R.r.34 in-12°. *Nantes Dobrée 117.

References: Renouard MSS.

Notes: Same printer as for *La Marchandise spirituelle* with which it is bound in the Nantes copy.

B 219.   Bonaventure, Saint (attrib.).

Le Mirouer de discipline compose Par Sainct Bonadventure docteur seraphique. — Paris, Jean Petit, 1514.

8°: 109 + [7] ff., a-o⁸ p⁴, goth. p 4v: Impr. à Paris pour Jehan petit. 14.10.1514.

Poitiers BM D 598.

References: Moreau II #775 (naming the author as 'Bernardus a Bessa').

Notes: Thanks to Régis Rech of the Poitiers BM for this description.

B 220.   Bouchet, Jean.

La deploration de leglise militante sur ses persecutions interiores et exteriores et imploration de aide en ses adversitez par elle sonstenues en lan mil cinq cens dix: et cinq cens unze. — Paris, [Raoul Cousturier], pr. Guillaume Eustace, 1512.

8°: A-C⁸ D⁴, goth. D 2r: Impr. à Paris, rue Judas pres les carmes, pr. Guillaume Eustace. 15.05.1512.

*Paris BN Rés. Ye 1635. *Paris BEBA Masson 428(2) (- A 1,8). Manchester JRL. Paris BN Rothschild.

References: Moreau II #255.

Notes: Lamentation on ecclesiastical abuses in 1510-11: simony, sale of benefices, unworthy prelates, ambition, avarice, a military pope (Julius II). The author is identified on the t.p. by his pseudonym 'Le traverseur des voies perilleuses'. D 2v: priv. by Pt. de Paris to Guillaume Eustache for two years, dated 15.05.1512.

B 221.   Bouchet, Jean.

Les Triumphes de la noble et amoureuse dame, Et lart de honnestement aymer. — Poitiers, Jacques Bouchet, 1530.
2°: [10] + 166 ff., a⁴ +⁶ A-Z AA-DD⁶ EE⁴, goth.   EE 4r: Impr. à Poictiers par Jacques Bouchet. 20.06.1530.
*Paris BSG Rés. Y fol.141 inv. 201. Poitiers BM.
References: *Rép. bib.* 115. *Index aurel.* 122.870. Britnell *Bouchet* 14/1.
Notes: Royal priv. (a 1v) on request of Jean Bouchet, granted to Jacques Bouchet for four years, dated fr. Paris, 20.02.1530 (a.s.). Approval by two Poitiers Professors (+ 1r), dated 22 and 27 Nov. 1530. Dedic. by Bouchet to Queen Eleanor of France. Liminary poem to 'Loys rousart' (Louis Ronsard, father of Pierre). Despite the title, it is a 'recueil de la doctrine necessaire pour batailler contre les vices', and intended to turn women and girls away from reading the New Testament and heretical tracts from the Germans translated into French (fol. + 2v, Britnell, *Bouchet*, p. 222). Extracts from scripture and religious authors, in particular Gerson.

B 222.   Bouchet, Jean.

Les Triumphes de la noble et amoureuse dame, Et l'art de honnestement aymer. — Poitiers, J. et E. de Marnef, 1532.
2° Col: 27.03.1532.
London BL C.107.f.1.
References: *Index aurel.* 122.873. Britnell *Bouchet* 14/2.

B 223.   Bouchet, Jean.

Les Triumphes de la Noble et amoureuse dame Et lart de honnestement aymer. — Poitiers, Jacques Bouchet, pr.Jean et Enguilbert de Marnef, 1533.
2°: [8] + 166 ff., A-B⁴ C-Z AA-FF⁶ GG⁴, goth.   GG 4r: Impr. à Poictiers par Jacques Bouchet. 15.09.1533.
*Paris BA 4° BL 2862.
References: *Index aurel.* 122.874. Britnell *Bouchet* 14/3.

B 224.   Bouchet, Jean.

Les Triumphes de La Noble et amoureuse Dame: Et lart de honnestement aymer. — Paris, Nicolas Couteau, pr. Galliot Du Pré, Jacques Kerver, 1535.

2°: [6] + 154 + [2] ff., A⁶ C-Z AA-EE⁶, goth. EE 5r: Impr. à Paris par Nicolas couteau. 05.08.1535.
*Paris BN Vélins 585 (Du Pré). Paris BN Rothschild (Kerver). Grenoble BM. Vienna ÖNB. The Hague KB.
References: *Index aurel.* 122.875. Britnell *Bouchet* 14/5. Moreau IV #1216. Rothschild #509.

B 225.   Bouchet, Jean.

Les Triumphes de La Noble et amoureuse Dame: Et lart de honnestement aymer. — Paris, pr. Ambroise Girault, 1536.
2°: [6] + 154 + [2] ff., A-Z AA-DD⁶, goth. DD 5r: Impr. à Paris pr. Ambroise girault. 21.06.1536.
London BL C.7.b.2. *Paris BA 4° BL 2863 Rés. Poitiers BM.
References: *Index aurel.* 122.882. Britnell *Bouchet* 14/6.

B 226.   Bouchet, Jean.

Les Triumphes De la Noble et amoureuse dame. Et lart de honnestement aymer. — Paris, Guillaume de Bossozel, Pierre Sergent, 1536.
2°: [8] + '169' ff. (gathering F misnumbered, no fol. 27), A-Z AA-DD⁶ EE⁴, goth. EE 4v: Impr. à Paris par Guillaume de Bossozel. 1536.
*Paris BN Rés. Y² 187. Paris BM 3.681.
References: *Index aurel.* 122.881. Britnell *Bouchet* 14/7.

B 227.   Bouchet, Jean.

Les triumphes de la Noble et amoureuse Dame, et lart de honnestement aymer. — Paris, Jean Macé, Les Langeliers, Jean Longis, 1537.
8°: [12] + 390 ff., +¹² A-Z AA-ZZ⁸ &&⁸ 99⁸ KK⁸, goth. KK 8v: Impr. à Paris. 06.10.1537.
London BL 1073.c.2 (Macé). *Paris BA 8° BL 8738 Rés. (Macé). Paris BM Rés. 45.366 (Langeliers). Munich BSB (Longis).
References: *Index aurel.* 122.891. Britnell *Bouchet* 14/9.

B 228.   Bouchet, Jean.

Les triumphes de la Noble et amoureuse Dame, et lart de honnestement aymer. — Paris, Estienne Caveiller, Guillaume Le Bret, Henry Paquot, Jean André, Simon de Colines, 1539.
8°: [12] + 390 ff., ã¹² A-Z AA-ZZ⁸ &&⁸ 99⁸ aa⁸, goth. aa 8v: Impr. à Paris par Estienne caveiller. 06.06.1539.

London BL C.38.b.3 (Lebret). Cambridge (Pacquot). Oxford Bodl.
Douce B 570 (André). *Paris BA 8° BL 8739 Rés. (Colines).
References: Adams B 2583. Britnell *Bouchet* 14/10. *Index aurel.* 122.897.

B 229.   Bouchet, Jean.

Les triumphes de la noble et amoureuse dame, Et l'art de honnestement aymer. — Rennes, Jean Georget, 1541.

2°: [9] + 5-124 ff., [A 5,6] B-V^6 X^4, goth. X 4v: Impr. à Rennes, Jehan georget.

*Paris BN Vélins 586 (incomplete).

References: *Index aurel.* 122.905. Britnell *Bouchet* 14/11.

Notes: In the only known copy, 9 ff. in MS copy prior to A 5, and G 4 MS. Numerous ms. illustrations added.

B 230.   Bouchet, Jean.

Les triumphes de la Noble et amoureuse Dame, et lart de honnestement aymer. — Paris, Jean Réal, Philippe Le Noir, François Regnault, Oudin Petit, 1541.

8°: [12] + '390' (= 392) ff. (nos. 143 and 144 appear twice), *^{12} A-Z AA-ZZ^8 &&^{8} 99^8 KK^8, goth. KK 8v: Impr. à Paris. 20.02.1541.

*Paris BA 8° BL 8740 (Petit). *Paris BA 8° BL 8741 (Le Noir). *Paris BN Rés. Y^2 2074 (Réal). Poitiers BM DP.117 (Regnault).

References: *Index aurel.* 122.904. Britnell *Bouchet* 14/12.

Notes: The Paris BN copy claims it is 'imprimé par Jean Real', the others giving the address of the respective bookshops.

B 231.   Bouchet, Jean.

Les Triumphes de la noble et amoureuse dame, et lart de honnestement aymer. — Paris, Jean André, Galliot Du Pré, Jacques Tyson. Nicolas Du Chemin, 1545.

8°: [12] + '390' (=392) ff., ã^{12} A-Z AA-ZZ^8 &&^{8} 99^8 aa^8, rom. aa 8v: Impr. à Paris. 1545.

Paris BM 21.805 (André). *Paris BN Rés. Y^2 2076 (Tyson). Vienna ÖNB (Du Chemin).

References: *Index aurel.* 122.907. Britnell *Bouchet* 14/13.

Notes: Page-for-page copy of the 1541 Réal ed. (although the characters are different), including misnumbering of pages. Several ornamented caps. identical with the Réal ed.

B 232.   [Bougain, Michel].

Le jardin amoureux de lame devote compose par tresexcellant docteur maistre Pierre dally. — Lyon, Barnabé Chaussard, 1520?
8°: a-b⁸, goth.
Séville Colombine.
References: Babelon #96.

B 233.   Bougain, Michel.

Le Jardin spirituel de lame devote. — Paris, [Jean Jehannot], 1516?
8°: A-E⁸ F⁴, goth. F 3r: Impr. à Paris.
*Paris BN D 17400(1). *London BL 1360.a.6(2).
Notes: Dedic. to Mme la contesse de Dampmartin, signed 'Michel Bougain' but undated, and naming Jean Jehannot as printer. Text begins: 'En ce mondain desert est le jardin de vertus et consolations qui est devote religion' (A 2v). Jean Jehannot printed at 'rue N. Dame, écu de France', 1512-17. According to the colophon, Bougain was a Carthusian from the Paris convent.

B 234.   Bougain, Michel.

Le Jardin spirituel de lame devote. — Paris, Alain Lotrian, 1528.
8°: A-E⁸ F⁴, goth.
*Paris BN Rés. D 26902.
References: Moreau III # 1381. Brunet I, 1167.
Notes: The author named in the explicit. Dedic. (A 2r) to Madame la comtesse de Dampmartin, dated 16.08.1528.

B 235.   Bougain, Michel.

Le Jardin spirituel de lame devote. — Paris, Alain Lotrian, Denis Janot, 1531?
8°: A-E⁸ F⁴, goth. F 4v: impr. à Paris par Alain lotrian et Denis janot impr. et libr.
Séville Colombine 15.2.2.
References: Babelon #18. Rawles #246. Brunet I, 1167.

B 236.   [Bougain, Michel].

Le Jardin de paradis. — Lyon, Barnabé Chaussard, 1520?

8°: A-B⁸, goth.
Séville Colombine.
References: Babelon #97.

B 237. **[Branteghem, Guillaume de].**

Enchyridion ou Manuel contenant plusieurs matieres traictees es livres de Lancien Testament, exprimees par figures, avec le texte appertenant a icelles. — Antwerp, Martin Lempereur, Simon Coc, 1535.

8°: A-R⁸ S⁴, goth. S 4r: Impr. à Anvers par Martin Lempeureur et Simon Coc. 1535.

Antwerp MPM R 11.18 (incompl.). *London BL C 107.c.17. Oxford Bodl. (fragment). Paris BEBA Masson 1208.

References: NK #2839.

Notes: Guillaume de Branteghem was a Carthusian from Ghent.

B 238. **[Branteghem, Guillaume de].**

Enchyridion ou Manuel contenant plusieurs matieres traictees es livres de Lancien testament, exprimees par figures, avec le texte appertenant a icelles. — Antwerp, Henry Pierre, 1536.

8°: A-R⁸ S⁴, goth. S 4r: impr. à Anvers par Henry Pierre, rue de la Chambre au Fouan. 1536.

*Cambridge Emma. S1.5.38.

References: Adams B 1968. NK #4332.

B 239. **[Branteghem, Guillaume de].**

Enchyridion, ou Manuel contenant plusieurs matieres traictees es livres de Lancien Testament, exprimees par figures, avec le texte appartenant a icelles. — Antwerp, Jacques de Liesvelt, 1539.

16°: π⁸ A-Z Aa-Bb⁸, goth. Impr. en Anvers sus le pont de Chambre à lescu Dartoys, par Jaques de Liesvelt. 29.04.1539.

Cambridge UL.

References: Adams B 1256. NK #4222.

B 240. **Branteghem, Guillaume de.**

Vergier spirituel et mistique remply tant de nouveaux que de anciens fruictz de lame fidele, distingue par aucunes figures monstrant les commencementz de la

creation du monde. — Antwerp, Guillaume Vorsterman, 1535.

8°: A-H aa-dd⁸ ee4, goth. ee 4v: Impr. par Guillaume Vorsterman en
Anvers, enseigne de la licorne d'or. 1535.

Ghent UB Res. 769. London BL 4402.o.13. *Paris BA 8° T.6952.
*Paris BM Rés. 35458.

References: NK #489. Machiels #926.

Notes: Gatherings aa-ee contain 'Aucunes images de sainctz
et de sainctes', already mentioned on the t.p. The prefatory
letter (dated from Antwerp, 30.09.1534) cautiously justifies
the invocation of the saints.

B 241.   Branteghem, Guillaume de.

*Le vergier spirituel et mystique, rempli tant de nou-
veaux que anciens fruits de lame fidele avec figures
ou images et oraisons appartenantes à la matiere.* —
Lyon, Jean et François Frellon, 1542.
16°.

References: Dagens. Du Verdier. Brunet I, 1211.

Notes: Brunet mentions an ed., Lyon, Trechsel, 1542, in 16°:
probably the same ed.

B 242.   Branteghem, Guillaume de.

*Vergier Spirituel et mystique, remply tant de nou-
veaulx que d'anciens enseignementz doctrines pour
L'ame fidele. Avec Figures et Oraisons fidelement
appartenantes à la matiere.* — Paris, Arnoul Langelier, 1542.
16°: A-P⁸, rom.
*Paris BSG D 8°6467(4) Rés.

References: Droz, *Chemins* I, 322-4.

B 243.   Branteghem, Guillaume de.

*La Vie de Nostre Seigneur JesuChrist par figures,
selon le Texte des quattre Evangelistes, avec toutes
les Evangiles Epistres et Propheties de toute lannee,
chantee en loffice de la Messe.* — Antwerp, Adrien
Kempe, Matthieu Crom, 1539.
8°: +⁸ A-Z a-g⁸, goth. g 8r: Anvers, par Adrien Kempe et Matthieu
Crome. 1539.

*Bruxelles BR LP II 64579. *London BL C.51.b.1. *London St
Paul's 38 E 18. *Paris BA 8° T.1267.

References: NK #490. Dagens.

Notes: Adams B1829 describes an ed. in Cambridge UL with the same address and date, but with collation aa⁸ A-X a-o⁸: a separate ed.? First ed. of the French translation of Branteghem's *Vita Christi* (Antwerp, Kempe and Crom, 1537). To the Latin text have been added prayers after each extract from the Bible, but the French translation continues to mention the certificate of pure doctrine granted to the Latin text. See notes to the ed. dated 3 May 1540.

B 244.   Branteghem, Guillaume de.

La Vie de nostre Seigneur Jesu Christ par figures, selon le Texte des quattre Evangelistes, avec toutes les Evangiles Epistres et Propheties de toute lannee, chantees en loffice de la Messe. — Antwerp, Matthieu Crom, 1540.

8°: +⁸ A-I k L-Z a-g⁸, goth.   g 8r: Anvers, par Matthieu Crome. 1540.

Antwerp. Cambridge UL. *Oxford Bodl. Douce CC80. Oxford Keble. *Paris BA 8° T.1269 (incompl.).

References: Adams B1830. NK #2559. Dagens.

B 245.   Branteghem, Guillaume de.

La Vie de Jesus Christ. — Lyon, François Juste, 1540.

References: Brunet I, 1210.

B 246.   Branteghem, Guillaume de.

La Vie de Nostre Seigneur Jesus Christ par figures selon le texte des quatre Evangelistes, et les Evangiles, Epistres et Propheties de toute l'année, chantées en la Messe. — Paris, Conrad Neobar, 1540.

8°: aa⁶ A-X a-o⁸ ã⁸ ẽ⁸, rom.   ẽ 8r: Paris, Conrad Neobar. 03.05.1540.

*Basle UB XE.x.13.

References: *Index* I #509.

Notes: On 5 Oct. 1543 the Paris Faculty of Theology condemned this text, quoting several prayers. The pagination shows that the quotations are taken from one of the four eds by Neobar or by Pierre Regnault in 1540-41. These prayers were already in the 1539 ed.

B 247.   Branteghem, Guillaume de.

La Vie de Nostre Seigneur Jesus Christ par figures,
selon le texte des quatre Evangelistes, et les Evan-
giles, Epistres et Propheties de toute l'année,
chantées en la Messe. — Paris, Conrad Neobar, 1540.
8°: aa⁸ A-X a-o⁸ a⁸ ẽ⁸, rom.   ẽ 8r: Impr. à Paris, Conrad Neobar
imprimeur du Roy. 03.07.1540.
*Rouen BM A 1563.

B 248.   Branteghem, Guillaume de.

La Vie de Nostre Seigneur Jesus Christ par figures,
selon le texte des quatre Evangelistes, et les Evan-
giles, Epistres et Propheties de toute l'année,
chantées en la Messe. — Paris, Conrad Neobar, 1540.
8°: aa⁸ A-X a-o⁸ a⁸ ẽ⁸, rom.   ẽ 8r: Impr. à Paris, Conrad Neobar
imprimeur du Roy. 19.08.1540.
*London BL C.36.b.31 (- aa 1-8). *Paris BA 8° T.1268. *Paris BN
Rés. D 80436.

B 249.   Branteghem, Guillaume de.

La Vie de Nostre Seigneur Jesus Christ par figures,
selon le texte des quatre Evangelistes, et les Evan-
giles, Epistres et Propheties de toute lannée,
chantées en la Messe. — Paris, Conrad Neobar, 1540.
8°: aa⁸ A-X a-o⁸ ã⁸ ẽ⁸, rom. Impr. à Paris, 1541.
*Paris BU Rés. XVI. #1218.
Notes: The printer Conrad Neobar died at the end of 1540.
The t.p. gives '1540', but the colophon '1541'.

B 250.   Branteghem, Guillaume de.

La Vie de Nostre Seigneur Jesus Christ par figures
selon le texte des quatre Evangelistes, et les Evan-
giles, Epistres et Propheties de toute l'année,
chantées en la Messe. — Paris, Pierre Regnault, 1540.
8°: aa⁸ A-X a-o⁸ ã⁸ ẽ⁸, rom.   ẽ 8r: Impr. à Paris, 1541.
*Stuttgart LB Bibl.gall. 8° 1540 Paris.

B 251.   [Branteghem, Guillaume de].

La vie de nostre Seigneur, selon les quattres Evan-
gelistes. — Antwerp, Matthieu Crom, 1541.
8°: A-M⁸, goth.

*Bruxelles BR LP 653A. *Stuttgart LB Biblia K 8° 37. *Aix Méj. C. 2992.

Notes: A simplified, and versified, version of Branteghem's *Vie de Jesuchrist*, with engravings on almost every page.

B 252.   Branteghem, Guillaume de.

La vie de nostre Seigneur Jesuchrist, selon le texte des quatre Evangelistes, et les Evangiles, Epistres et Propheties de toute l'Année, chantées en la Messe. — Lyon, François Juste, 1541.

8°: a-s A-O⁸ P⁴, goth. P 3v: Impr. à Lyon par Françoys Juste.

Bordeaux BM. *Cambridge UL A*.7a.48(G). *Paris BEBA Masson 683. Terrebasse.

References: Adams B1831. Baudrier *Suppl.* #103.

B 253.   Branteghem, Guillaume de.

La Vie de Nostre Seigneur Jesus Christ par figures, selon le texte des quatre Evangelistes, et les Evangiles, Epistres et Propheties de toute lannée, chantées en la Messe. — Paris, Pierre Regnault, 1541.

8°: aa⁸ A-X a-o⁸ ã⁸ ẽ⁸, rom.

*Oxford Bodl. Mason B.20.

References: Renouard MSS.

B 254.   Branteghem, Guillaume de.

La Vie de nostre Seigneur Jesus Christ par figures, selon le texte des quatre Evangelistes, et les Evangiles, Epistres et Propheties de toute l'année, chantées en la Messe. — Antwerp, Jean Richard, 1542.

8°: aa⁸ A-X a-o⁸ ã⁸ ẽ⁸, rom. ẽ 8r: Impr. en Anvers. 1542.

Cambridge UL Rel.e.54.21 (incompl.). *Paris BEBA Masson 1210.

References: Sale Heber (1824) #7006.

Notes: Careful copy of the 1540-41 Parisian eds.

B 255.   Branteghem, Guillaume de.

La Vie de nostre Seigneur Jesus Christ, selon le texte des quatre Evangelistes, contenant les Evangiles, Epistres, et propheties de toute l'année qu'on list à la messe. — Paris, Jean Ruelle, Guillaume Le Bret, 1542.

16°: A-Z⁸ &⁸ Aa-Oo⁸, rom. Oo 8r: Impr. par Jehan Ruelle libr., rue S. Jacques, Paris.

*Wolfenbüttel HAB 1325 Theol.

B 256.   Branteghem, Guillaume de.

La vie de nostre seigneur Jesu Christ selon le texte des quatre Evangelistes, et les Evangiles. Epistres et Propheties de toute lannee, chantees en la messe. — 1543.

16°: ã⁸ a-r A-P⁸, rom.

References: Sales Renard (1881) #32, Stroehlin (1912) #481.

B 257.   Branteghem, Guillaume de.

La Vie de Nostre Seigneur Jesus Christ, Selon le texte des quatre Evangelistes, et les Evangiles, Epistres et Propheties de toute l'Année, chantées en la Messe. — Lyon, Balthasar Arnoullet, 1543.

16°: [8]+254+[10] ff., a-z A-L⁸, rom. L 8r: Par Baltazard Arnoullet, avec les Heritiers Jehan Barbou. 1543.

*Lyon BV Rés. 808183.

References: Baudrier X, 112-13. Brunet I, 1210.

Notes: Arnoullet adds a word to the reader (a 8r-v) referring to additions to the text, and affirms the orthodoxy of the work, 'quoy que pourroient dire les ennemys de verité'. It was in October 1543 that the work was censured by the Sorbonne. The condemned expressions are all present (see Higman *Censorship*, pp. 94-5).

B 258.   Branteghem, Guillaume de.

La Vie de Jesus Christ. — Paris, Estienne Caveiller, Arnoul et Charles Langelier, 1543.

16°.

References: Renouard MSS < Brunet I, 1210 and III.1717. Droz, *Chemins* I, 325 sqq. Méon cat. (1803).

B 259.   Branteghem, Guillaume de.

La Vie de nostre Seigneur Jesus Christ par figures, selon le texte des quatre Evangelistes, et les Evangiles, Epistres et Propheties de toute lannee, chantees en la Messe. — Antwerp, Jean de Grave, Jean Richard, 1544.

8°: A-Z a-p⁸, rom. p 8r: Impr. par Jehan de Grave. 1544.

Oxford Bodl. Mar 334. *Paris SHP A 1031.

B 260. **Branteghem, Guillaume de.**

La Vie de Jesuchrist. — ?, ?, ?
References: Sale C.L. Fiere (1933) #140.

B 261. **Bref Discours.**

Brief Discours de la Republique françoyse desirant la lecture des livres de la saincte Escripture luy estre loisible en sa langue vulgaire. — Lyon, Estienne Dolet, 1542.
16°.
References: Christie #51. Longeon *Dolet* #225 < Du Verdier (who gives '1544').
Notes: Among the books printed by Dolet condemned on 2 March 1543. The condemnation specifies of this text: 'il semble de Dolet, à cause qu'il a fait l'épistre preliminaire.' See *Index* I #316.

B 262. **Bref Discours.**

Brief Discours de la Republique Francoyse, desirant la lecture des Livres de la saincte Escripture (et iceulx approuvés par les Docteurs de l'Eglise) luy estre loysible en sa langue vulgaire. — Caen, Martin & Pierre Philippe, 1550+.
8°: a-c^8, ital., rom. c 8v: 'De l'imprimerie de Martin et Pierre Philippe.'
*Vienna ÖNB 79.V.56.
References: Longeon *Dolet* #225.
Notes: C. Longeon, in *Hommes et livres de la Renaissance*, pp. 269 sqq., prints the text. The printers Martin and Pierre Philippe were active 1550-69. Only known ed. of this text.

B 263. **Brigitta, Sainte (pseud.).**

Sensuyvent les Quinze oraisons <> en Francoys. Avec les sept principalles peines des dampnez. Et les sept joyes des Saulvez. — [Paris], [Guillaume de Bossozel], 1531?
8°: A^8, goth.
*Chantilly Condé IV D 66(3).
References: Moreau IV #50.
Notes: The 15 prayers of St Brigitte. One must daily recite 15 Pater, 15 Ave, the 15 prayers of St Brigitte. For whoever

does so, 'de ses parens seront delivrées quinze ames de purgatoyre.' 'Elle estant a romme en grand devotion avoit acoustumez a dire tous les jours devant un imaige du crucifix estant en leglise de sainct Pol.'

B 264.   Brigitta, Sainte (pseud.).

Les oraisons <> en francoys. Avec une moult devote orayson a nostre seigneur Jesuchrist. — Lyon, hér. de Barnabé Chaussard, 1537.

16°: A-B⁴, goth.   B 4v: Impr. à Lyon en la maison de feu Barnabe Chaussard. 08.06.1537.

*Aix Méj. Rés. S. 128(4).

References: Baudrier XI.63.

Notes: A different translation from the Parisian one. A 1v: the introduction says 'royne de Suesse quant elle estoit a Rome pres de sainct Pol'.

B 265.   Bris, Nicolas de.

Institution a porter les adversitez du monde patiemment, avec paix d'esperit, joye, et liberté interieure. — Paris, Jean Loys, 1542.

4°: A⁸ B-Z aa-zz aaa-bbb⁴, rom.   bbb 3v: '... le 23 ... 1542' (damaged page, BSG, missing in BM).

*Paris BM 14405 (incompl.). *Paris BSG R 4° 511(3) Rés. inv 556.

References: Higman 'Prem. rép.' pp. 363-4.

Notes: Nicolas de Bris, Doctor of the Faculty of Theology of Paris, was in the service of Marie de Lorraine, Queen of Scotland, for whom he composed this treatise to console her on the death of her two sons. De Bris obtained the permission of the Faculty of Theology on 18 Sept. 1542 to print a 'librum gallice scriptum', presumably this text (Farge, *Registre* n° 248 I, p. 207).

B 266.   Brodeau, Victor.

Les Louanges De Jesus Nostre Saulveur Oeuvre tresexcellent Divin. et elegant. <> Avecques Les Louenges de la glorieuse Vierge Marie. — ?, ?, 1540.

8°: A-E⁴ F², goth.

*Paris BM Rés. 21652(2).

References: Christie p. 551.

B 267. Brodeau, Victor.

Les Louanges de JesuChrist nostre Saulveur. Oeuvre treselegant et Divin. — Lyon, Sulpice Sabon, pr. Antoine Constantin, 1540.

8°: a-b⁸, rom.

*Aix Méj. C. 3082.

References: Ed. Tomlinson *TLF* (1982). Baudrier II.31. Du Verdier p. 1188.

Notes: Victor Brodeau, secretary to Marguerite de Navarre, died in September 1540 (note at the end of the text). Poem in decasyllabic couplets.

B 268. Brodeau, Victor, with sermons trans. by Jean de Gaigny.

Les Louanges Du sainct nom de Jesus, avec la correspondence des figures à la verité <> Six sermons des six parolles de nostre Seigneur en croix. — Paris, Estienne Roffet, 1542.

8°: a⁴ A-G⁸, rom.

*Wolfenbüttel HAB 1240.6 Theol.

References: Ed. Tomlinson.

Notes: Priv. to Estienne Roffet dated 27 March 1541 'avant pasques'. The sermons on the 'six words' were reprinted by Jean de Tournes in 1543.

B 269. Brodeau, Victor.

Les Louanges du sainct nom de Jesus... plus Une epistre d'ung pecheur à JesuChrist. — Lyon, Estienne Dolet, 1543?

16°: A-D⁸, rom.

*London BL C.107.a.22 (- A 1).

References: Christie #82. Longeon *Dolet* #226. *Index* I #279.

Notes: The Sorbonne condemnation in the 1544 *Catalogue* specified 'l'Epistre d'ung pecheur imprimée par Dolet'. The text does not seem explicitly heterodox.

B 270. Brodeau, Victor.

Les Louanges du sainct nom de Jesus. Avec la correspondence des Figures, a la verite <> Plus une Epistre dung pecheur a Jesus Christ. — Lyon, Olivier Arnoullet, 1543.

8°: 32 ff., A-D⁸, goth. D 8r: Impr. à Lyon, par Olivier Arnoullet. 20.10.1543.

*Aix Méj. Rés. S. 81.

References: Brunet I, 1273. Baudrier X, 78-9.

Notes: Contains (C 3v sqq.) the *Epistre dung pecheur* censured in the preceding notice.

B 271.   [Brunfels, Otto].

Les Prieres et oraisons de la Bible, faictes par les sainctz peres, et par les hommes et femmes illustres: tant de lancien que du nouveau testament. — Antwerp, Guillaume Vorsterman, Martin Lempereur, 1529.

16°: A-X⁸, goth. X 8r: ach. d'impr. 18.08.1529.

*Vienna ÖNB 19.Aa.138. *Paris BEBA Masson 21 (-A 1, X 1-8).

References: Moore #45. NK #2577. Ginzburg, *Nicod.* pp. 98 sqq.

Notes: The Latin original of this collection of biblical prayers, Strasbourg, Johann Schott, 1528.

B 272.   [Brunfels, Otto].

Les oracions de la Bible faictes par les Peres et Femmes fideles, tant de l'Ancien comme du Nouveau Testament, avec plusieurs introductions. — Antwerp, Martin Lempereur, 1530.

Oxford Wadham (missing).

Notes: A copy featured in a Paris exhibition in 1902 (see *BSHPF* 51 (1902), p. 438).

B 273.   [Brunfels, Otto], preface by Antoine Marcourt?

Les Prieres et Oraisons de la Bible, faictes par les Sainctz Peres, et par les hommes et femmes illustres: tant de Lancien que du Nouveau Testament. — [Lyon], [Pierre de Vingle], 1530.

12°: +¹² A-H¹², goth. H 12v: ach. d'impr. 19.08.1530.

*Geneva MHR K Bru 2. *Paris BN Rés. A 17884 (- +1-12).

References: Baudrier XII. Berthoud, *Marcourt.* Droz *BHR* 1958, 158-69, with ed. of the text.

Notes: Mlle Berthoud suggests A. Marcourt as author of the *Prologue preparatif pour veritable et salutaire oraison* (absent from the BN copy).

B 274. **[Brunfels, Otto]**, [M. Luther, D. Erasmus, J. Brenz].

Les Oraisons de la Bible Faictes par les Peres et femmes fideles, tant de Lancien comme du Nouveau Testament: avec plusieurs Introductions. — Antwerp, Martin Lempereur, 1533.

16°: a-z A-G⁸, goth. G 7v: ach. d'impr. 09.01.1533, par Martin Lempereur.

*Strasbourg Gd. Sém. *Wolfenbüttel HAB 1326.7 Theol 12°.

References: NK #2578. Febvre *BHR* VI, 110.

Notes: Several additions, texts by Luther, Brenz and Erasmus, appear at the end. See Higman *RHPR* (1983), p. 106.

B 275. **[Brunfels, Otto]**.

Les Prieres et oraisons de la Bible, faictes par les Sainctz peres, et par les hommes, et femmes illustres: tant de l'Ancien, que du nouveau Testament. — Lyon, Estienne Dolet, 1542.

16°: A-S⁸, rom.

Harvard CL.

References: Christie #52. Longeon *Dolet* #223. Febvre *BHR* VI, 110. Droz *BHR* 1958, p. 160. *Index* I #462. Cat. Drilhon #12.

Notes: Dolet follows the 1530 Vingle ed., but suppresses the prologue, replacing it by his own preface (reprod. Longeon, *Préfaces fr.*, 153-4). The 1544 *Catalogue* condemns the text in the eds by Dolet and De Tournes (1544).

B 276. **[Brunfels, Otto]**.

Les Prieres et oraisons de la Bible, Faictes par les Sainctz Peres, tant du Vieil, que du Nouveau Testament. — Lyon, Jean de Tournes, 1543.

16°: a-m⁸, rom.

*Paris SHP A 1168. *Paris SHP A 1210(3). *Wrocław BU 454323.

References: Cartier *De Tournes* #12.

Notes: De Tournes follows Dolet's ed., but omits the preface.

B 277. **[Brunfels, Otto]**.

Les Prieres et oraisons de la Bible. — Lyon, Jean de Tournes, 1544.

References: Ginzburg *Nicod.* p. 100n. *Index* I #462.

Notes: No trace of this ed. apart from the Paris censure.

B 278.   [Bucer, Martin].

Exposition de Levangile de nostre seigneur Jesus Christ, selon S. Matthieu. — [Geneva], [Jean Michel], 1540.

8°: *[4] a-z A-P[8] Q[4], goth. Q 3v: ach. d'impr. 05.06 1540.

La Rochelle BM Rés. 72C. *Paris BM Rés. 49730 (- Q 1,4).

References: Moore #46. Berthoud 'Michel' #9. *BG* 40/3. Courvoisier, *Cahiers RHPR* 1933 (ed. of the text). *Index* I #414. Cat. Drilhon #8.

Notes: A summary of part of Bucer's *In sacra quatuor evangelia Enarrationes perpetuae* (Basle, Herwagen, 1536).

B 279.   Bucer, Martin.

Exposition sur l'evangile selon sainct Matthieu. Recueillie et prinse des commentaires de M.M. Bucer. Depuis reveue, augmentée et enrichie de plusieurs sentences, exhortations et declarations. — Geneva, Jean Girard, 1544.

8°: π[8] a-z A-Z aa-oo[8] pp[4], rom.

La Rochelle BM Rés. 29C (s.l.s.n.). *Lausanne BCU AZ 4910.

References: Berthoud 'Michel' pp. 81-2. *BG* 44/2. *Index* I #280.

B 280.   [Bullinger, Heinrich], adapt. Antoine Du Pinet?

Exposition sur les deux epistres de Sainct Paul, envoiées aux Thessaloniciens. — Geneva, Michel Du Bois, 1540.

8°: a-h[8], rom.   h 8v: Impr. à Geneva par Michel Du Bois, 01.05.1540.

*Lausanne BCU 1 U 451. *Vienna ÖNB 77.Aa.102.

References: Peter *Du Bois* #3. *BG* 40/4. *Index* I #405.

Notes: Trans. and adapted, in a more polemical sense, from Bullinger's commentary publ. in Latin in 1535.

B 281.   [Bullinger, Heinrich], adapt. Antoine Du Pinet?

Exposition sur les deux epistres de Sainct Paul aux Thessaloniciens. — Geneva, Jean Girard, 1545.

8°: A-G[8] H[4], rom.

*Paris SHP A 588.

References: *BG* 45/2.

B 282. Bullinger, Heinrich.

La Source d'erreur: redigé en deux livres. — Geneva, Jean Girard, 1549.

8°: a-z A-V⁸, rom.

*Lausanne BCU AZ 5065. *Munich BSB Polem 425. Paris SHP R 15831. *Zurich ZB Zw 271. Paris BU Rés.XVI TR p 67(12°) (+).

References: *BG* 49/3. Cartier *Arrêts* pp. 142-4.

Notes: *Index* I #46: the 1544 *Catalogue* condemned the Latin *De origine erroris*, probably referring to the Latin original ed. of this text, Zurich, Froschauer, 1539.

C

C 1. Cabosse, Jean.

Le mirouer de prudence. — Paris, Denis Janot, 1541.

8°: A-B⁸, ital.

*Paris BN Rés. pYe 303.

References: Rawles #137.

Notes: Text in verse, dedic. to Jean Destournel, escuyer de M. le Dauphin.

C 2. Cabosse, Jean. poem by François Habert.

Traicte du treshault et excellent mistere de l'incarnation du verbe divin, extraict du viel et nouveau testament, demonstrant le chemin de laeternelle foelicité. — Paris, Denis Janot, 1541.

8°: A-E⁸, ital.

*Paris BN Rés. pYe 304. Tournai BM.

References: Rawles #138.

Notes: Sort of catechism in dialogue form. Becomes absorbed into the *Livre de vraye et parfaicte oraison*, Paris, Les Angeliers, 1545.

C 3. Cabosse, Jean.

Traité et dialogue d'entre le precepteur et le disciple du treshault et tresexcellent mystere de l'Incarnation du Verbe divin. — Paris, Charles Langelier, ?

16°.

References: Renouard MS < Du Verdier.

C 4.   [Cailleau, Gilles].

Paraphrase sur les Heures de nostre Dame, scelon l'usaige de Rome: traduictes de Latin en Francoys <> avec aultres choses concernans la forme de vivre des Chrestiens, en tous estatz. — Poitiers, Jean et Enguilbert de Marnef, 1543.

8°: A¹⁰ B-Z AA⁸ BB⁶, rom/ital.   BB 6r: Impr. à Poictiers par Jehan et Enguilbert de Marnef. 1543.

Bordeaux BM T 3769 Rés. *Paris BEBA Masson 1027 (-BB 6). *Paris BSG BB 8° 1493 Rés. Rouen BM A 1175. Saumur BM.

References: *Rép.bib.* #38. Cat. Drilhon #4.

Notes: Text in French of the *Heures* (G 2v sqq.) in rom., embroidered by a paraphrase in ital. Preceded by an *Almanach perpetuel* and a list of feast days with, on facing page, copious biblical quotations. Dedic. to Anne de Poulignac comtesse de La Rochefoucault.

C 5.   [Cailleau, Gilles].

Paraphrase sur les Heures de nostre Dame, selon l'usage de Rome, traduit du latin en francoys. — Poitiers, Jean et Enguilbert de Marnef, 1547.

16°.

References: *Rép.bib.* #64.

C 6.   Calvin, Jean, Heinrich Bullinger.

L'Accord passé et conclud touchant la matiere des sacremens, entre les Ministres de l'Eglise de Zurich, et Maistre Jehan Calvin Ministre de l'Eglise de Geneve. — Geneva, Jean Crespin, 1551.

8°: A-B⁸, rom.

*Geneva BPU Rés. Bc 1436. Lunel BM u 6,1317. Vienna ÖNB 79.Ee.170. Zurich ZB SM 71.2.

References: Gilmont *Crespin* 51/13. CDM p. 17. *Index* I #369.

Notes: The agreement between the Zurich and Geneva Churches, reached in 1549, was published in Zurich by Rudolf Wyssenbach in 1551. Crespin published an ed. of the Latin in 1551 as well as this first ed. of the French translation.

C 7.   [Calvin, Jean].

Les Actes de la journee imperiale, tenue en la cité de Regespourg, aultrement dicte Ratispone ... sur les

differens qui sont aujourdhuy en la Religion. —
[Geneva], [Jean Girard], 1541.
8°: a-z A-C⁸, rom.
*Cambridge UL Syn.8.54.213(1). *Geneva BPU Rés. Ba 3028.
*Neuchâtel past. 106.5. *Paris SHP 15930. *Zurich ZB
XVIII.363 (+).
References: Adams R 170. *BG* 41/2. Cartier *Arrêts* p. 369.
Gilmont *Calvin* 41/1.

C 8.   [Calvin, Jean].

*Les Actes de la journee imperiale, tenue en la çité de
Reguespourg, aultrement dicte Ratispone ... sur ᶜles
differens qui sont aujourdhuy en la Religion.* —
[Geneva], [Jean Girard], 1542.
8°: a-z A-C⁸, rom.
*London BL 701.a.7. *Rouen BM Leber 3357. Strasbourg BNU D
144737. *Vienna ÖNB 36.M.47.
References: *BG* 42/2. Cartier *Arrêts* p. 369. Gilmont *Calvin*
42/2.

**C 9.   Calvin, Jean, poems by Guillaume Gueroult, R. de
Bienassis.**

*Les Actes du Concile de Trente, avec le remede con-
tre la poison.* — [Geneva], [Jean Girard], 1548.
8°: a-y⁸, rom.
*Geneva BPU Rés. Bc 848(3). *Munich BSB Rar. 107.4. *Paris
SHP R 14015(1). *Vienna ÖNB 79.J.59. *Zurich ZB C 260 and FF
1163 (+).
References: *BG* 48/1. Gilmont *Calvin* 48/3.
Notes: The Latin original appeared in 1547 (Gilmont 47/3).
Calvin reproduces, and criticizes, the decrees of the first seven
sessions of the Council.

C 10.   Calvin, Jean.

*Advertissement contre l'astrologie, qu'on appelle
judiciaire: et autres curiositez qui regnent aujour-
d'huy au monde.* — Geneva, Jean Girard, 1549.
4°: A-G⁴, rom.
*Paris BN Rés. D² 15978. *Vienna ÖNB 72.X.96. Paris BA 8° S
14401. Wolfenbüttel HAB 287.12 Qu.4°.
References: *BG* 49/5. Gilmont *Calvin* 49/2. Ed. O. Millet,
TLF 1985.

C 11.   [Calvin, Jean].

Advertissement sur la censure qu'ont faicte les Bestes de Sorbonne, touchant les livres qu'ilz appellent heretiques. — [Geneva], [Jean Girard], 1544.
8°: A-B⁸, rom.
*Geneva BPU Rés. Bc 2543. *Lincoln cath. Nn 7.12(6). *Zurich ZB XVIII.2002.3.
References: Moore #96. *BG* 44/4. Gilmont *Calvin* 44/3. Ed. Higman, *RHPR* 1980.

C 12.   [Calvin, Jean].

Advertissement sur la censure qu'ont faicte les Bestes de Sorbonne, touchant les livres qu'ilz appellent heretiques. — [Geneva], [Jean Girard], 1547.
8°: A-B⁸, rom.
*Paris BN Rés. D² 13785. *Vienna ÖNB *48.K.30(4).
References: *BG* 47/3. Gilmont *Calvin* 47/4.

C 13.   Calvin, Jean.

Advertissement tresutile ... s'il se faisoit inventoire de tous les corps sainctz, et reliques, qui sont tant en Italie, qu'en France, Allemaigne, Hespaigne, et autres Royaumes et pays. — Geneva, Jean Girard, 1543.
8°: 110 pp.+[1 f.], A-G⁸, rom.
*Strasbourg BNU R 100524. *Vienna ÖNB 70.Bb.249. *Zurich ZB XVIII.2002.4. *Aix Méj. Rés. S. 93.
References: *BG* 43/5. Gilmont *Calvin* 43/2. *Index* I #287. Ed. Higman, Athlone Pr., 1970.

C 14.   Calvin, Jean.

Advertissement tresutile ... sil se faisoit inventoire de tous les corps sainctz, et reliques, qui sont tant en Italie, qu'en France, Allemaigne, Hespaigne, et autres Royaumes et pays. — Geneva, Jean Girard, 1544.
8°: A-G⁸, rom.
*Geneva BPU Rés. Bc 3421. Gotha FB Theol. 61/1 Rara.
References: *BG* 44/3. Gilmont *Calvin* 44/2.

C 15.   Calvin, Jean.

Advertissement tresutile ... sil se faisoit inventoire de tous les corps sainctz, et reliques, qui sont tant en Italie, qu'en France, Allemaigne, Hespaigne, et autres Royaumes et pais. — Geneva, Jean Girard, 1545.

8°: A-G^8, rom.

*Cambridge St Johns Ferrari O 29(1). *Geneva BPU Bc 3422 Rés. (- B1,8).

References: *BG* 45/3. Gilmont *Calvin* 45/1. Adams C 267.

C 16.   Calvin, Jean.

Advertissement tresutile ... s'il se faisoit inventoire de tous les corps sainctz, et reliques, qui sont tant en Italie, qu'en France, Allemaigne, Hespaigne, et autres Royaumes et pais. — Geneva, Jean Girard, 1551.

16°: A-H^8, rom.

*Wolfenbüttel HAB 1338.8° Theol (1).

References: Gilmont *Calvin* 51/1.

C 17.   Calvin, Jean.

Argument et sommaire de l'epistre sainct Paul aux Romains, pour donner intelligence à toute l'epistre en peu de parolles. — [Geneva], [Jean Girard], 1545.

8°: A-B^8, rom.

*Geneva BPU Rés. Bc 2701bis.

References: *BG* 45/4. Gilmont *Calvin* 45/2. *Index* I #294.

Notes: French trans. of the 'argument' prefacing the *Commentarii in Epistolam Pauli ad Romanos* (Strasbourg, Rihel, 1540), a revision of the 'argument' published in the *Exposition sur l'Epistre aux Romains* of 1543.

C 18.   [Calvin, Jean].

Les Articles de la sacree Faculté de Theologie de Paris, concernans nostre Foy, et religion Chrestienne, et forme de prescher. Avec le Remede contre la Poison. — [Basle?], ?, 1544.

8°: a-f^8 g^4, rom.

*Geneva BPU Rés. Bc 3429.

References: Gilmont *Calvin* 44/5.

C 19.   **[Calvin, Jean].**

*Les Articles de la sacree faculte de theologie de
Paris concernans nostre foy et religion Chrestienne,
et forme de prescher. Avec le remede contre la poi-
son.* — [Geneva], [Jean Girard], 1544.
8°: a-f⁸ g⁴, rom.
*Geneva BPU Rés. Bc 848(4).
References: *BG* 44/5. Gilmont *Calvin* 44/4. *Index* I #523.
Modern ed. by J. de Senarclens, Geneva, 1941.
Notes: French trans. (probably by Calvin) of the Latin original
published the same year.

C 20.   **Calvin, Jean.**

Le catechisme de l'Eglise de Geneve. — Geneva?,
Jean Girard?, 1542.
References: *BG* 42/3. *Index* I #286.
Notes: It is known that Calvin had completed his *Catechisme*
by January 1542. No copies are known to survive, but the ed.
must have existed, since it was censured in Paris in March
1543 (Higman *Censorship* A 25).

C 21.   **Calvin, Jean.**

*Le catechisme de l'Eglise de Geneve: c'est à dire, le
Formulaire d'instruire les enfans en la Chrestienté:
faict en maniere de dialogue, ou le Ministre inter-
rogue, et l'enfant respond.* — [Geneva], [Jean
Girard], 1545.
8°: A-I⁸, rom.
Gotha FB Theol 61/1 Rara.
References: *BG* 45/6. Ed. Pfisterer, Munich, 1937.
Notes: Earliest surviving ed. of the Genevan catechism.

C 22.   **Calvin, Jean.**

*Le Catechisme De Geneve: c'est a dire, le Formu-
laire d'instruire les enfans en la Chrestiente fait en
maniere de dialogue, ou le Ministre interrogue, et
l'enfant respond.* — Geneva, Jean Girard, 1548.
8°: A-I⁸, rom.
*Strasbourg BNU R 100574. *Wrocław BU 372124(b) (- A 1).
References: *BG* 48/4.

Notes: In this ed. the text is divided for the first time into 'Dimanches'.

C 23. Calvin, Jean.

Le Catechisme de Geneve: C'est à dire le formulaire d'instruire les enfans en la Chrestienté, fait en maniere de dialogue, où le ministre interrogue, et l'enfant respond. — Geneva, Jean Girard, 1549.
8°: A-I⁸, rom.
*Geneva MHR O⁶e (549). *London BL C.53.aa.5. *Munich BSB Catech 46 (variant t.p.). *Paris SHP R 5779(3).
References: *BG* 49/6.
Notes: The t.p. of the Munich copy gives 'où ... Ministre ... Enfant'. The content seems unchanged.

C 24. Calvin, Jean.

Commentaires <> sur les Canoniques. — Geneva, Jean Girard, [René de Bienassis], 1551.
8°: π⁸ 2π⁴, rom.
Cambridge UL. *Geneva BPU Rés. Bb 2301. *Paris BN Rés. D² 15973. *Paris SHP A 456. *Montpellier ITP 1557 (fragment) (+).
References: Gilmont *Calvin* 51/2. CDM p. 17.
Notes: Latin original in 1551. See the commentaries on Jacques, Pierre, Jude, Jean (listed immediately after this notice). Described here are the two preliminary gatherings giving the general title and the dedic. to Edward VI King of England (dated 23.1.1551) intended to precede the commentaries themselves. The individual sections could each, with their own t.p., be sold separately or together.

C 25. Calvin, Jean.

Commentaire <> sur l'epistre de sainct Jaques. — Geneva, Jean Girard, [René de Bienassis], 1550.
8°: A-I⁸ K⁴, rom. K 4r: 'Assez tost, si assez bien'.
*Geneva BPU Rés. Bb 2301(2). *La Haye KB 1175.C.20(1). *London BL C.65.f.15(2). *Paris SHP A 456(2). *Paris BM Rés. 23607(2) (+).
References: Gilmont *Calvin* 50/2.
Notes: Harbinger of the collected volume of *Commentaires sur les canoniques*, 1551. In some copies this ed. is bound with the 1551 commentaries (Geneva BPU, Paris SHP). The motto 'Assez tost, si assez bien' signifies a participation in the edi-

tion of René de Bienassis, a French refugee who worked in Geneva in the book trade. See Gilmont, *Calvin*, pp. 244-6.

C 26.   Calvin, Jean.

Commentaire <> sur l'epistre de S. Jaques. — Geneva, Jean Girard, [René de Bienassis], 1551.
8°: A-I⁸ K⁴, rom. K 4r: 'Assez tost, si assez bien'.
*Paris BN Rés. D² 15973(2). *Montpellier IPT 1595.
References: Gilmont *Calvin* 51/2.1. CDM p. 17.

C 27.   Calvin, Jean.

Commentaire sur la premiere et seconde Epistre de sainct Pierre Apostre. — Geneva, Jean Girard, [René de Bienassis], 1551.
8°: a-y⁸, rom. p 8v and y 7r: 'Assez tost, si assez bien'.
*Geneva BPU Rés. Bb 2301(3). *Paris BN Rés. D² 15973(3). *Paris SHP A 456(3). *Montpellier ITP 1558.
References: Gilmont *Calvin* 51/2.2. CDM p. 17.

C 28.   Calvin, Jean.

Commentaire <> sur l'Epistre Canonique de sainct Jude. Reveu et augmenté par luymesme. — Geneva, Jean Girard, [René de Bienassis], 1551.
8°: a-c⁸, rom. c 6v: 'Assez tost, si assez bien'.
*Geneva BPU Rés. Bb 2301(4). *Paris BN Rés. D² 15973(4). *Paris SHP A 456(4). *Montpellier ITP 1560.
References: Gilmont *Calvin* 51/2.3. CDM p. 17.
Notes: Radically revised version by comparison with the *Exposition sur l'epistre de sainct Judas apostre* of 1542.

C 29.   Calvin, Jean.

Commentaire <> sur l'Epistre Canonique de sainct Jean. — Geneva, Jean Girard, [René de Bienassis], 1551.
8°: a-o⁸, rom. o 6r: 'Assez tost, si assez bien'.
*Geneva BPU Rés. Bb 2301(4). *Paris BN Rés. D² 15973(5). *Paris SHP A 456(5). *Montpellier ITP 1557 (- o 1-2).
References: Gilmont *Calvin* 51/2.4. CDM p. 17.

C 30. **Calvin, Jean,** prefatory poem by Jacques Bienvenu (?).

Commentaire <> sur la premiere epistre aux Corinthiens, traduit de Latin en François. — [Geneva], Jean Girard, [René de Bienassis], 1547.

8°: a-z A-O^8 P^4, rom. P 3r: 'Assez tost, si assez bien'.

*Geneva BPU Bb 2204. *Glasgow Trin. Coll. Stuttgart LB Theol 8° 2703. *Wolfenbüttel HAB 917.8 Theol. *Strasbourg CW, don Peter (+).

References: *BG* 47/4. Gilmont *Calvin* 47/5.

Notes: French translation by an unknown hand (not Calvin) of the Latin original printed in Strasbourg by Rihel in 1546.

C 31. **Calvin, Jean.**

Commentaire <> sur la seconde Epistre aux Corinthiens traduit de Latin en François. — Geneva, Jean Girard, [René de Bienassis], 1547.

8°: a-x^8, rom. x 5v: 'Assez tost si assez bien'.

*Munich UB 8° Bibl. 1319. *Oxford Magd. Q 2.2. Stuttgart LB Theol 8° 2704. *Wolfenbüttel HAB 917.8 Theol. Beaune BM Rés. A 232 (+).

References: *BG* 47/5. Gilmont *Calvin* 47/6.

Notes: Although printed before the Latin text (1548), this is a translation from the latter.

C 32. **Calvin, Jean.**

Commentaire <> sur quatre Epistres de sainct Paul: Assavoir aux Galatiens, Ephesiens, Philippiens, Colossiens. — Geneva, Jean Girard, [René de Bienassis], 1548.

8°: A^8 B^4 a-z A-T^8 V^4, rom. V 3r: 'Assez tost, si assez bien'.

Amsterdam VU XC 05753. *Geneva BPU Bb 1990. Lausanne BCU AZ 4776. *Paris SHP R 20925. Stuttgart LB Theol 8° 2702 (+).

References: *BG* 48/6. Gilmont *Calvin* 48/6. *Index* I #300.

Notes: The Latin original appeared the same year.

C 33. **Calvin, Jean.**

Commentaire <> sur l'epistre aux Ebrieux, traduite du Latin. — Geneva, Jean Girard, [René de Bienassis], 1549.

8°: Aa-Bb a-z A-F^8, rom. F 8v: 'Assez tost, si assez bien'.

*Geneva BPU Bb 1901. *Geneva MHR A 127,1(49). Lyon BV 336227. *Strasbourg BNU E 100664. *Wolfenbüttel HAB 1164.85 Theol (+).

References: *BG* 49/7. Gilmont *Calvin* 49/3. Cartier *Arrêts* pp. 119-21. *Index* I #305.

Notes: The Latin original appeared the same year.

C 34.   Calvin, Jean.

Commentaire sur l'epistre de sainct Paul a Philemon. — Geneva, Jean Girard, [René de Bienassis], 1551.

8°: A⁸ B⁴, rom. B 2r: 'Assez tost, si assez bien'.

Beaune BM Rés. A 233(3). *Cambridge Emma. 321.6.38(4).

References: Gilmont *Calvin* 51/3. CDM p. 17. Adams C 335. *Index* I #302.

Notes: The Latin original appeared the same year.

C 35.   Calvin, Jean.

Commentaire <> sur l'epistre aux Romains. — Geneva, Jean Girard, [René de Bienassis], 1550.

8°: α-ß a-z A-M⁸, rom. M 5r: 'Assez tost, si assez bien'.

*Geneva BPU Bb 2313. *Lausanne BCU AZ 4521. *Paris SHP A 455. *Strasbourg BNU E 112991. Wrocław BU 451300 (+).

References: Gilmont *Calvin* 50/4. CDM p. 15.

Notes: Trans. of the revised ed. (publ. in 1551) of the 1540 *Commentarii* (cf. *Argument*, 1545, and *Exposition*, 1543).

C 36.   Calvin, Jean.

Commentaire sur les deux epistres de sainct Paul aux Thessaloniciens. — Geneva, Jean Girard, [René de Bienassis], 1551.

8°: a-m⁸ n⁴, rom. h 1r and n 2v: 'Assez tost, si assez bien'.

Beaune BM Rés. A 233(1). Cambridge Emma.

References: Gilmont *Calvin* 51/4. CDM p. 17. Adams C 331.

Notes: The Latin original printed in 1550.

C 37.   Calvin, Jean.

Commentaire <> sur les deux Epistres de sainct Paul à Timothée: traduites du Latin. — Geneva, Jean Girard, [René de Bienassis], 1548.

8°: a-v⁸, rom. v 7r: 'Assez tost, si assez bien'.

*Cambridge Emma. 321.6.38(2). *Lausanne BCU AZ 4350.
*Munich BSB Catech. 641(2). Stuttgart LB Theol 8° 2706.
*Montpellier ITP 1706 (+).
References: *BG* 48/5. Gilmont *Calvin* 48/5. Adams C 333.
Notes: Dedic. epistle to Edward Duke of Somerset dated from
Geneva, 24 June 1548 (error for 25 July, date given in the
Latin ed.).

C 38.   Calvin, Jean.

Commentaire <> sur l'epistre à Tite. — Geneva,
Jean Girard, [René de Bienassis], 1550.
8°: A-F⁸ G⁴, rom. G 2v: 'Assez tost, si assez bien'.
*Cambridge Emma. 321.6.38(3). *Geneva BPU Rés. Bb 2300.
*Lausanne BCU AZ 4350. Beaune BM Rés. A 233(2). Dresden SLB
Exeg.C.861 (+).
References: Gilmont *Calvin* 50/3. Adams C334. *Index* I #301.
Notes: The Latin original printed the same year.

C 39.   Calvin, Jean, Pierre Viret.

*Deux Epistres, l'une demonstre comment nostre Sei-
gneur Jesus Christ est la fin de la Loy... L'autre
pour consoler les fideles qui souffrent pour le Nom
de Jesus.* — [Geneva], [Jean Girard], 1543.
8°: A-H⁸ I⁴, rom.
*Lausanne BCU IU 451.1. *Zurich ZB Gall XVIII.2002(6).
References: *BG* 43/11. Gilmont *Calvin* 43/8. *Index* I #295, 410.
Notes: The first letter, by Calvin, is his preface to the NT in
the 1535 Olivétan Bible. The second, by Viret, is a revision of
his *Epistre consolatoire* first publ. in 1541.

C 40.   Calvin, Jean, Pierre Viret.

*Deux Epistres. L'une demonstre comment nostre Sei-
gneur Jesus Christ est la fin de la Loy... L'autre,
pour consoler les fideles qui souffrent pour le Nom
de Jesus.* — [Geneva], [Jean Girard], 1545.
8°: A-H⁸ I⁴, rom.
*Geneva BPU Rés. Bd 1898. *Lyon BV 802983.
References: *BG* 45/14. Gilmont *Calvin* 45/12.
Notes: Re-ed. of the 1543 text. See also B 204.

C 41.   Calvin, Jean.

Epistre au treschrestien roy de France Françoys premier de ce nom: en laquelle sont demonstrées les causes dont procedent les troubles qui sont aujour-d'huy en l'Église. — [Geneva], [Michel Du Bois], 1541.

4°: [22 ff.], A-D⁴ E⁶, rom.   E 5v: letter dated from Basle, 23.08.1535.

*Paris BN Ld¹⁷⁶.1041 (-E 3,4). *Vienna ÖNB 78.G.50 (anon.). *Zurich ZB Gall. XVIII.450(2). Grenoble BM D 7678.

References: Peter, *Du Bois* #8. *BG* 41/3. Gilmont *Calvin* 41/2. *Index* I #290. Ed. J. Pannier, Paris, 1927.

Notes: Separate ed. of the preliminary epistle of the *Institution* (Latin original 1536, first French trans. 1541).

C 42.   Calvin, Jean, Sadolet, Jacques.

Epistre de Jaques Sadolet Cardinal envoyée au Senat et Peuple de Geneve:... Avec la Response de Jehan Calvin: translatées de Latin en Françoys. — Geneva, Michel Du Bois, 1540.

8°: a-i⁸ k¹⁰, rom.   k 9v: Impr. à Geneve par Michel Du Bois. 06.03.1540.

*Geneva MHR A 17,1(40). *Geneva BPU Rés. Bc 1989. *Lausanne BCU AZ 4354. Paris BN Rés. Z.2206. *Strasbourg BNU R 1022525 (+).

References: Peter, *Du Bois* #1. *BG* 40/10. Gilmont *Calvin* 40/7. Berthoud, *Marcourt* p. 57. *Index* I #282. Ed. Fick, 1860.

Notes: The Latin orig. published in Strasbourg, 1539. The translation is not by Calvin.

C 43.   Calvin, Jean.

Excuse <> à Messieurs les Nicodemites, sur la complaincte qu'ilz font de sa trop grand'rigueur. — [Geneva], [Jean Girard], 1544.

8°: A-D⁸, rom.

Berlin SB Libri impr. rari. oct. 205(3). *Lincoln cath. Nn 7.12(4). *Vienna ÖNB 79.W.40. *Zurich ZB XVIII.2002.2.

References: *BG* 44/9. Gilmont *Calvin* 44/9. Droz *Chemins* I, 131-67. *Index* I #292. Ed. Higman, Athlone Press, 1970.

Notes: The *Excuse* is a sequel to the 1543 *Petit Traité monstrant...*, and in all subsequent eds the two texts are printed together.

C 44.   [Calvin, Jean].

Excuse de noble seigneur Jaques de Bourgoigne, S. de Fallez et Bredam: pour se purger vers la M. Imperiale, des calomnies à luy imposées, en matiere de sa Foy, dont il rend confession. — [Geneva], [Jean Girard], 1547.

4°: A-E⁴ F⁶, rom.

*Geneva BPU Rés. Bc 3511.

References: *BG* 48/10. Gilmont *Calvin* 47/1. Ed. A. Cartier, 1896.

Notes: The only surviving copy includes a letter dated 1 March 1548. But the first and last gatherings of the original ed., printed in Dec. 1547, had to be recomposed to eliminate the fictitious address 'Strasbourg, Wendelin Rihel' (see Gilmont, *Calvin*).

C 45.   [Calvin, Jean], [Philippe Melanchthon].

Exposition des dix commandemens du Seigneur, en laquelle est traicte quel doit estre le vray service de Dieu. — Geneva, Jean Crespin, 1551.

8°: A-K⁸ L⁴, rom.

*Vienna ÖNB 77.K.58.

References: Gilmont *Calvin* 51/14.

Notes: Extracts from Calvin's *Institution*, ch. III (1545 ed.) and from Melanchthon's *Somme de théologie* (1546), trans. of his *Loci communes*.

C 46.   Calvin, Jean.

Exposition sur l'epistre de sainct Paul aux Romains, Extraicte des Commentaires de M. J. Calvin. — Geneva, Jean Girard, 1543.

8°: α⁸ β⁴ a-z A⁸ B⁴, rom.

Bordeaux BM T 3421. *Geneva MHR A 117,1(43) (-B 2-4).

References: *BG* 43/7. Gilmont *Calvin* 43/4. Cartier *Arrêts* p. 375. *Index* I #291, 404.

Notes: 'Extraicte des Commentaires de M. Jean Calvin' (t.p.): an abridged form of the 1540 *Commentarii*. This ed. was censured by the Sorbonne in 1543 itself (Higman *Censorship*, A 1 and 28).

C 47.   Calvin, Jean.

Exposition sur l'epistre de sainct Judas apostre de nostre Seigneur Jesus Christ. — [Geneva], [Jean Girard], 1542.
8°: A-B⁸, rom.
*Geneva MHR A 132,1(42). La Haye KB 1175.C.20(4). *Paris BM Rés. 23607(1).
References: *BG* 42/4. Gilmont *Calvin* 42/3.
Notes: Unique among Calvin's commentaries: this *Exposition* seems to have been composed directly in French. Profoundly revised and enlarged in the 1551 *Commentaire sur ... Jude.*

C 48.   Calvin, Jean.

Exposition sur l'oraison de nostre Seigneur Jesus Christ. — [Geneva], [Jean Crespin], 1551.
8°: A-B⁸, rom.
*Vienna ÖNB 79.V.87. *Vienna ÖNB 79.Ee.173 (anon.). Strasbourg BNU E 100672 (anon.).
References: Gilmont *Calvin* 51/9. Gilmont *Crespin* 51/12. CDM p. 17.
Notes: Extract from ch. XV of the 1545 *Institution.*

C 49.   [Calvin, Jean], [Clément Marot].

La Forme des prieres et chantz ecclesiastiques, avec la maniere d'administrer les Sacremens, et consacrer le Mariage: selon la coustume de l'Eglise ancienne. — [Geneva], [Jean Girard], 1542.
8°: a-l⁸ m⁴, rom.
*Stuttgart LB R 16 Cal 1.
References: Pidoux 42/II. Mayer *Marot* #104. *BG* 42/5. *Index* I #382. Facs. reprod. Pidoux, Kassel, 1959.
Notes: First ed. of the Genevan liturgy, with 30 Psalms and their melodies.

C 50.   [Calvin, Jean], [Clément Marot].

La Forme des prieres et chantz ecclesiastiques, avec la maniere d'administrer les sacremens, de celebrer le mariage et la visitation des malades. — [Geneva], 1543.
References: *BG* 43/8.
Notes: No known copies. Mentioned in the Council Reg., 09.06.1543, and in the catalogue Drilhon #17, which gives the

title including the 'visitation des malades', absent from the first ed.

C 51.   **[Calvin, Jean]**, [Clément Marot].

La Forme des Prieres et Chants ecclesiastiques. Avec la maniere d'administrer les Sacremens, et consacrer le Mariage: selon la coustume de L'eglise ancienne. — Strasbourg, Johann Knobloch Jr., 1545.
8°: A-B a-n AA-CC⁸, rom.   CC 8: Strasbourg, Jehan Knobloch. 1545.
Strasbourg BNU (destroyed in 1870).
References: Peter 'Prem. ouvr.' #12. Mayer *Marot* #131. Pidoux 45/I.
Notes: Revision of the 1542 *Maniere de faire prieres*, incorporating elements of the Genevan 1542 *Forme des prieres*.

C 52.   **[Calvin, Jean]**.

La Forme des prieres Ecclesiastiques, avec la maniere d'administrer les Sacremens, et celebrer le Mariage, et la visitation des malades. — [Geneva], [Jean Girard], 1547.
8°: A-D⁸, rom.
*Strasbourg BNU R 102512.
References: *BG* 47/7.
Notes: First surviving ed. to mention 'la visitation des malades' on the t.p. The Psalms no longer printed in the liturgy.

C 53.   **[Calvin, Jean]**.

La forme des Prieres Ecclesiastiques, Avec la maniere d'Administrer les Sacremens, et celebrer le Mariage, et la visitation des malades. — [Geneva], [Jean Girard], 1548.
8°: A-D⁸, rom.
*Wrocław BU 372124(a).
References: *BG* 48/11.
Notes: Re-ed. of the 1547 text.

C 54.   **[Calvin, Jean]**.

La forme des Prieres Ecclesiastiques: Avec la maniere d'administrer les Sacremens, et celebrer le Mariage, et la visitation des malades. — [Geneva], [Jean Girard], 1549.

8°: A-D^8, rom.
*Geneva MHR O^{6}e(549). *London BL C.53.aa.5. *Paris SHP R 5779(2).
References: *BG* 49/10.
Notes: Re-ed. of the 1548 text. The London and Paris copies have variants on the t.p. by comparison with the Genevan copy.

C 55.   [Calvin, Jean].

La forme des Prieres Ecclesiastiques: avec la maniere d'administrer les Sacremens, et celebrer le Mariage, et la visitation des Malades. — [Geneva], [Jean Girard], 1550?
8°: A-D^8, rom.
*Geneva BPU Rés. Bc 1979. *Vienna ÖNB 80.X.37.

C 56.   [Calvin, Jean].

La forme des prieres ecclesiastiques, Avec la maniere d'administrer les Sacremens, celebrer le Mariage, et la visitation des Malades. — ?, ?, 1550.
16°: A-C^8 D^6, rom.
*Vienna ÖNB 80.V.99.
Notes: This very anonymous ed. not reported in any bibliography to date. The printer is not Jean Girard.

C 57.   [Calvin, Jean].

Histoire d'un meurtre execrable: commis par un Hespagnol, nommé Alphonse Dias, Chambellan du Pape, en la personne de Jehan Dias son frere... Qui est un bel exemple du zele des Papistes. — [Geneva], [Jean Girard], 1546.
8°: A^8, rom.
*Geneva BPU Rés. Ba 4689. *Vienna ÖNB *48.K.30(5).
References: Gilmont *Calvin* 46/5. Higman *BHR* 1992 with ed. of the text.

C 58.   Calvin, Jean.

Institution de la religion chrestienne: en laquelle est comprinse une somme de pieté, et quasi tout ce qui est necessaire a congnoistre en la doctrine de salut. — [Geneva], [Michel Du Bois], 1541.
4°: A-D^4 E^6 a-z A-Z Aa-Zz AAa-ZZz AAAa-LLLl^4, rom.

Bordeaux BM. *Geneva BPU Rés. Bc 2485. Paris BN Rés. D² 35010. *Paris SHP A 407. Lausanne BCU AA 9182 (+).

References: Peter *Du Bois* #7. *BG* 41/4. Gilmont *Calvin* 41/3. *Index* I #283, 284, 439, 443.

Notes: First French ed. translated mainly from the second (1539) Latin ed. There are 17 chapters.

C 59. **Calvin, Jean,** preface by Johann Sturm.

Institution de la religion chrestienne: composee en latin <> et translatée en Francoys... : en laquelle est comprise une somme de toute la Chrestienté. — Geneva, Jean Girard, 1545.

4°: A-B⁸ C² a-z A-Z aa-ss⁸ tt² vv-yy⁴, rom. tt 2r: ach. d'impr. 10.02.1545.

*Edinburgh NLS H.26.a.37. *Geneva BPU Rés. Bc 2486. *Lausanne BCU AZ 4741. *Paris SHP A 408. *Strasbourg BNU R 102688 (+).

References: *BG* 45/9. Gilmont *Calvin* 45/6.

Notes: Second French ed., incorporating the modifications of the third Latin ed. (1543). There are 21 chapters.

C 60. **Calvin, Jean,** preface by Johann Sturm.

Institution de la religion Chrestienne: composee en latin <> et translatée en Françoys ... depuis de nouveau reveuë et augmentée: en laquelle est comprinse une somme de toute la Chrestienté. — Geneva, Jean Girard, [Laurent de Normandie], 1551.

2°: a-z A-Z aa-ii⁶ kk-pp⁴ qq⁶, rom. ll 4v: ach. d'impr. 20.10.1551.

*Geneva BPU Rés. Bc 62. Lausanne BCU AB 1972. Strasbourg BNU R 10721. Avignon BM in-fol. 3816. Poitiers BM B 329 (+).

References: Gilmont *Calvin* 51/11. CDM p. 18.

Notes: Third French ed., incorporating the modifications in the Latin 1545 and 1550 eds, in particular the division of chapters into numbered paragraphs.

C 61. **Calvin, Jean.**

Brieve Instruction, pour armer tous bons fideles contre les erreurs de la secte commune des Anabaptistes. — Geneva, Jean Girard, 1544.

8°: A-M⁸, rom.

*Geneva BPU Rés. Bc 3320. Lausanne BCU AZ 5002. *Paris SHP A 424. Paris BA 8° T 9473. *Vienna ÖNB 79.J.57 (+).

References: *BG* 44/7. Gilmont *Calvin* 44/7. *Index* I #298.

Notes: Calvin's reply to a French trans. of Balthazar Hubmaier, *Von dem Christenlichen Tauff der Gläubigen*, which Farel had sent him.

C 62.   **Calvin, Jean.**

Brieve Instruction, pour armer tous bons fideles contre les erreurs de la secte commune des Anabaptistes. — Geneva, Jean Girard, 1545.

8°: A-L⁸, rom.

*Basle UB F.O.IX.10. *Geneva BPU Rés. Bc 3113. *Paris SHP A 425(2). London BL 1352.a.17(2). *Munich BSB Polem. 2529(2) (+).

References: *BG* 45/5. Gilmont *Calvin* 45/3.

C 63.   **[Calvin, Jean].**

Instruction et confession de Foy, dont on use en Leglise de Geneve. — [Geneva], [Wigand Koeln], 1537?

8°: a-f⁸, goth.

*Paris BN MSS Dupuy 940.

References: Dufour *Not.cat. BG* 37/2. *Index* I #447.

Notes: The *Instruction* is normally attributed to Calvin and the *Confession de la foy* published at the same time to Farel. The *Instruction* includes passages translated from the 1536 *Institutio*.

C 64.   **Calvin, Jean,** prefatory poem by Jaques Bienvenu(?).

L'Interim. C'est à dire, Provision faicte sur les differens de la religion, en quelques villes et pais d'Allemaigne... Avec la vraye façon de reformer l'Eglise Chrestienne. — [Geneva], [Jean Girard], 1549.

8°: a-p⁸ q⁴, rom.

*Geneva BPU Rés. Bc 848(1). *Lincoln cath. Oo.7.5. *Paris SHP R 14015(2). Neuchâtel past. 106.3. *Vienna ÖNB 79.J.58 (+).

References: *BG* 49/13. Gilmont *Calvin* 49/9. Cartier *Arrêts* 110-15. *Index* I #304.

Notes: The text of the *Interim* imposed in Germany in 1548 by Charles V, a 2r-f 4v. This is followed by Calvin's 'La vraye façon de reformer l'Eglise' (f 5r-q 4v).

C 65.   **[Calvin, Jean]**, [Clément Marot].

La Manyere de faire prieres aux eglises Françoyses. tant devant la predication comme apres, ensemble pseaulmes et canticques francoys quon chante aus dictes eglises. — [Strasbourg], [Johann Knobloch Jr.], 1542.

8°: A-K⁸, goth. K 7r: 'Imprimé à Rome par le commandement du Pape. par Theodore Brüß son imprimeur ordinaire. Le 15. de febvrier'.
*Geneva MHR A 27,1(42).

References: Moore #180. Peter 'Prem. ouvr.' #9. Ritter #1267. Mayer *Marot* #103. Pidoux 42/I.

Notes: Re-ed. supervised by Calvin's successor in Strasbourg, Pierre de Brully, of a text already printed in 1540 (no known copy).

C 66.   **Calvin, Jean,** prefatory poem by Conrad Badius.

Des scandales qui empeschent aujourdhuy beaucoup de gens de venir à la pure doctrine de l'Evangile, et en desbauchent d'autres. — Geneva, Jean Crespin, 1550.

4°: A-T⁴, rom. T 3v: Geneva, imprimerie de Jean Crespin. 10.12.1550. Paris BN D² 1759. *Paris SHP A 437. *Paris BU Rés.XVI. b.20 4°. Gotha FB Theol 4° 193/2. Washington DC Folger 182111 (+).

References: Gilmont *Calvin* 50/12. Gilmont *Crespin* 50/6. Cartier *Arrêts* 165-6. *Index* I #494. CDM p. 15. Ed O. Fatio *TLF*, 1984.

Notes: Dedic. to Laurent de Normandie, formerly royal lieutenant in Noyon and, from 1549 on, at the hub of the Genevan book trade. See H. Schlaepfer, *APR*. The original Latin (from which the French varies significantly) appeared the same year.

C 67.   **Calvin, Jean.**

Des scandales qui empeschent aujourdhuy beaucoup de gens de venir à la pure doctrine de l'Evangile, et en desbauchent d'autres. — Geneva, Jean Crespin, 1551.

8°: *⁸ A-M⁸, rom.   M 8r: Geneva, imprimerie de Jean Crespin. 24.03.1551.
Cambridge Emma. *Paris SHP A 438 and 439. Wolfenbüttel HAB 1241.50 Theol (2). Vienna ÖNB 79.W.44.

References: Gilmont *Calvin* 51/8. Gilmont *Crespin* 51/11. CDM p. 17. Adams C381.
Notes: Re-ed. of the 1550 treatise.

C 68.   Calvin, Jean.

Contre la secte phantastique et furieuse des Libertins. Qui se nomment spirituelz. — Geneva, Jean Girard, 1545.

8°: A-O⁸ P¹⁰, rom.

*Dublin TCD Fag. RR.1.77. *Geneva BPU Rés. Bc 3426. *Paris BSG D 8° 7009(1) Rés. (-A 1). *Wolfenbüttel HAB 1131 Theol (-P 5,6). *Zurich ZB D 247.1 (+).

References: *BG* 45/8. Gilmont *Calvin* 45/4. *Index* I #289.

Notes: Calvin was asked by Valérand Poullain and evangelicals in the Tournai region to reply to two 'Libertine' pamphlets: *Instruction et salutaire admonition pour parfaitement vivre en ce monde,* 'seulement d'une feuille', and to 'un autre plus gros, d'environ 14 quayers', *La Lunette des Chrestiens.*

C 69.   Calvin, Jean.

Contre la secte phantastique et furieuse des Libertins, qui se nomment spirituelz. Avec une epistre de la mesme matiere, contre un certain Cordelier suppost de la secte: lequel est prisonnier à Roan. — [Geneva], [Jean Girard], 1547.

8°: A-O⁸ P⁴, rom. P 3v: epistle dated from Geneva, 20.08.1547.

Amsterdam VU XI 06021. *Munich BSB Polem 2529(1). *Paris SHP A 425(1). *S. Gallen SBV Misc E 154.1. *Geneva BPU Rés. Bc 3425 (+).

References: *BG* 47/6. Gilmont *Calvin* 47/7.

Notes: Re-ed. of the 1545 treatise, adding a letter denouncing a Franciscan from Rouen. See Higman *Censorship,* pp. 101-2.

C 70.   Calvin, Jean, noted by Jean Cousin, Ps. 124 by G. Gueroult.

Deux sermons <> ... l'un le mercredy 4e de Novembre 1545... le second, le mercredy prochainement suyvant. — Geneva, Jean Girard, 1546.

8°: A-D⁸, rom.

*Geneva BPU Rés. Bd 2096. London BL 3902.a.6. *Neuchâtel past. 100.2. *Paris BM Rés. 23607(3).

References: *BG* 46/6. Gilmont *Calvin* 46/3. Pidoux 46/II. *Index* I #297.

Notes: First sermons of Calvin to be printed, taken from notes made by Jean Cousin. On 20 Oct. 1545 Philip of Hesse had defeated duke Henry of Brunswick. The first sermon treats of the impending danger, the second was preached 'apres que nouvelles furent venues que Dieu avoit donné victoire aux siens' (t.p.).

C 71.   **[Calvin, Jean].**

Supplication et remonstrance, sur le faict de la Chrestienté, et de la reformation de l'Eglise, faicte au nom de tous amateurs du Regne de Jesu Christ, a l'Empereur, et aux Princes et estatz. — [Geneva], [Jean Girard], 1544.

4°: a-x⁴, rom.

Cambridge Clare D.1.25. *London BL 476.a.6(1). *Munich UB 4° Hist.eccl. 2594. Paris BSG D 4° 2571 inv. 2768 rés.

References: *BG* 44/11. Gilmont *Calvin* 44/12. Adams S 2090. *Index* I #493. Cat. Drilhon #31.

Notes: Trans. of the Latin original, 1543.

C 72.   **[Calvin, Jean].**

Supplication et remonstrance, sur le faict de la Chrestienté, et de la reformation de l'Eglise, faicte au nom de tous amateurs du Regne de Jesu Christ, à l'Empereur, et aux Princes et estatz. — [Geneva], [Jean Girard], 1544.

8°: a-n⁸, rom.

*Dublin TCD Fag. RR.1.24. Ghent UB Res. 538. *Geneva BPU Rés. Bc 848(1). *Paris SHP A 423. *Vienna ÖNB 36.M.53 (+).

References: *BG* 44/12. Gilmont *Calvin* 44/13. Machiels #C53.

C 73.   **Calvin, Jean,** ten-line poem by Michel Du Bois.

Petit Traicté de la saincte cene de nostre Seigneur Jesus Christ. Auquel est demonstré la vraye institution, proffit et utilité d'icelle. — Geneva, Michel Du Bois, 1541.

8°: a-d⁸ e⁶, rom. e 5v: Inprimé[!] à Geneve par Michel Du Bois. 1541.

Berlin SB Libri impr. rari Oct. 205(2). *Vienna ÖNB 79.V.91.

References: Peter *Du Bois* #9. *BG* 41/5. Gilmont *Calvin* 41/4. *Index* I #285. Ed. Higman, Athlone, 1970.
Notes: The first treatise composed by Calvin directly in French. Written either during his stay in Strasbourg, or before leaving Geneva in 1538.

C 74.   **Calvin, Jean,** ten-line poem by Michel Du Bois.

Petit Traicté de la saincte cene de nostre Seigneur Jesus Christ. Auquel est demonstré la vraye institution, profit et utilité d'icelle. — [Geneva], [Jean Girard], 1542.
8°: a-d^8 e^4, rom.
Gotha FB Theol. 61/1 Rara.
References: *BG* 42/6. Gilmont *Calvin* 42/4. Cat. Drilhon #19 (specifies an otherwise unknown 1544 ed.).
Notes: Stylistic retouches by comparison with the previous ed. clarify the structure of the treatise.

C 75.   **Calvin, Jean,** ten-line poem by Michel Du Bois.

Petit Traicté de la saincte cene de nostre Seigneur Jesus Christ. Auquel est demonstrée la vraye institution, profit et utilité d'icelle. — [Geneva], [Jean Girard], 1545.
8°: A-D^8 E^4, rom.
*Geneva BPU Rés. Bc 2703. *Lincoln cath. Nn.7.12(3). *London BL 701.b.33.
References: *BG* 45/11. Gilmont *Calvin* 45/8. *Index* I #500.

C 76.   **Calvin, Jean,** ten-line poem by Michel Du Bois.

Petit Traicté de la saincte cene de nostre Seigneur Jesus Christ. Auquel est demonstrée la vraye institution profit et utilité d'icelle. — [Geneva], [Jean Girard], 1549.
8°: A-D^8 E^4, rom.
*Wolfenbüttel HAB 1241.50 Theol (5).
References: *BG* 49/14. Gilmont *Calvin* 49/12.

C 77.   **Calvin, Jean.**

Petit traicté, monstrant que c'est que doit faire un homme fidele congnoissant la verité de l'evangile: quand il est entre les papistes, Avec une Epistre du mesme argument. — [Geneva], [Jean Girard], 1543.

8°: A-F⁸ G¹⁰, rom.   G 10r: '2e épître' dated from Strasbourg, 12.09.1540.
*Lausanne BCU IU 451.
References: *BG* 43/9. Gilmont *Calvin* 43/6. Droz *Chemins* I, 131-67. *Index* I #497.
Notes: Already censured in Paris by March 1543 (Higman *Censorship* A 30).

C 78.   Calvin, Jean.

Petit traicté, monstrant que c'est que doit faire un homme fidele congnoissant la verité de l'Evangile: quand il est entre les papistes, Avec une Epistre du mesme argument. — [Geneva], [Jean Girard], 1544.
8°: A-G⁸, rom.
*Lausanne BCU AZ 4207. *Paris SHP A 422. *Vienna ÖNB 80.X.42.
References: *BG* 44/10. Gilmont *Calvin* 44/11.

C 79.   Calvin, Jean, judgements of Melanchthon, Bucer, Martyr.

Petit traicté monstrant que doit faire un homme fidele... Ensemble l'Excuse faicte sur cela aux Nicodemites. — [Geneva], [Jean Girard], [René de Bienassis], 1545.
8°: A-N⁸ O⁴, rom.   O 4v: letter from Calvin to [V. Poullain] dated 14.07. or 18.06.1546. 'Assez tost, si assez bien'.
*Geneva BPU Rés. Bc 2703bis (A-K only). *Geneva BPU Rés. Bd 1432.
References: *BG* 45/12. Gilmont *Calvin* 45/9. *Index* I #292.
Notes: Gatherings A-K simply repeat the 1543 *Petit Traité* and the 1544 *Excuse*. Gatherings L-O print the judgements of Melanchthon, Bucer and Martyr, with two letters from Calvin, one dated 1546.

C 80.   Calvin, Jean, judgements of Melanchthon, Bucer, Martyr.

Petit Traicté mostrant que doit faire un homme fidele... Ensemble l'Excuse faicte sur cela aux Nicodemites. — [Geneva], [Jean Girard], [René de Bienassis], 1551.
8°: A-I⁸ k⁴ L-N⁸ O⁴, rom.   O 4v: 'Assez tost, si assez bien'.

*Wolfenbüttel HAB 1241.50 Theol (1).
References: Gilmont *Calvin* 51/13. CDM p. 18.

C 81. **Calvin, Jean,** pref. by [Jean Crespin].

Traicté tresexcellent de la vie Chrestienne. Qui est comme une Instruction et Formulaire, à tous ceulx qui font profession de Chrestienté, pour reigler leur vie. — Geneva, Conrad Badius, Jean Crespin, 1550.
8°: A-E⁸, rom. E 8v: Geneve, imprimerie de Jean Crespin, par Conrad Badius. 1550.
*Munich BSB H.ref. 400(28). *Paris SHP A 1222. *Vienna ÖNB 79.V.88.
References: Gilmont *Calvin* 50/18. Gilmont *Crespin* 50/8. CDM p. 16. *Index* I #306.
Notes: 'Offprint' of chap. XXI of the 1545 *Institution*.

C 82. **Calvin, Jean.**

Traicté tresexcellent de la vie Chrestienne. Qui est comme une Instruction et Formulaire, à tous ceux qui font profession de Chrestienté, pour reigler leur vie. — Geneva, Jean Crespin, 1552.
8°: A-F⁸, rom. F 7v: 1551.
*London BL 3504.dg.15(3) (- A1). Munich BSB Asc. 4945.1. Vienna ÖNB 80.Y.114.
References: Gilmont *Crespin* 52/13. Gilmont *Calvin* 52/10. CDM p. 19.
Notes: Re-ed. of the 1550 ed. Although the t.p. says '1552', the colophon reads '1551'.

C 83. **Campen, Jean van,** pref. adapted from Bucer and Zwingli.

Paraphrase, cest à dire, Claire translation faicte jouxte la sentence non pas jouxte la Lettre, sur tous les Psalmes, selon la verité Hebraique. — [Paris], [Simon Du Bois], 1534.
8°: 234 ff., A-Z AA-EE⁸ FF¹⁰, goth. FF 10v: 1534. xv.Calendes de Juillet (= 17.06).
*Lyon BV 800131. *Paris BN Rés. A 6141.
References: Moreau IV #907. Cartier *Arrêts* p. 377n. Higman 'Simon Du Bois'.
Notes: Trans. of the Latin original printed in Antwerp by Martin Lempereur, 1532. Van Campen, Hebrew scholar in

Louvain, used Bucer's 1529 commentary on the Psalms in his introduction (B. Roussel, 'Les nouveaux Jérôme').

C 84.   **Campen, Jean van,** pref. adapted from Bucer, text by Athanasius.

Paraphrase, cest a dire, Claire et succincte Interpretation juxte la sentence, non pas juxte la lettre, sur tous les Psalmes, selon la verite Hebraique... Traictie du sainct Athanase. — Antwerp, Vve de Martin Lempereur, 1537.

16°: 210 ff., [A]⁸ B-Z Aa-Cc⁸ Dd², goth. Dd 2v: Anvers, Vve de Martin Lempereur. 1537.

*Paris BN Rés. 8° Z.Don 594(294) (-Y6-8).

References: NK #3260.

Notes: To the 1534 ed. have been added the treatise on the Psalms by Athanasius, and Van Campen's *Interpretation paraphrastique sur l'Ecclesiaste.*

C 85.   **Campen, Jean van.**

Paraphrase. C'est adire, claire, et briefve interpretation sur les Psalmes de David. Item, Aultre interpretation Paraphrastique sur l'Ecclesiaste de Salomon. — Lyon, Estienne Dolet, 1542.

16°: 446 pp., A-Z aa-ee⁸, rom.

*Paris BN Rés. A 6142.

References: Longeon *Dolet* #230. Cartier, *Arrêts* p. 377n.

C 86.   **Campen, Jean van.**

Paraphrase. C'est à dire, claire, et briefve interpretation sur les Psalmes de David. Aultre interpretation Paraphrastique sur l'Ecclesiaste de Salomon. — Lyon, Estienne Dolet, 1542.

16°: a-z A-E⁸, rom.

*Lyon BV Rés. 811577. *London BL C.27.a.25. Stuttgart LB Biblia gall. oct.Lyon 1542.

References: Longeon *Dolet* #229. Mayer *BHR* 1955 p. 406.

Notes: The preface 'Est. Dolet au lecteur Chrestien' printed in both Dolet's 1542 eds is in fact from the 1534 Du Bois ed. (see Longeon, *Préfaces*, 160-63).

C 87.   **Campen, Jean van.**

Paraphrase, c'est à dire claire et briefve interpreta-
tion sur les psalmes ... et sur l'Ecclesiaste. —
Geneva, Jean Girard, 1542?
References: *BG* 42/7. Cartier *Arrêts* 377-8.
Notes: Cartier indicates that permission to print this title was
requested on 29.09.1542. No known copy.

C 88.   **Campen, Jean van,** with treatise by Athanasius.

Paraphrase sur les Psalmes par le tres savant M.
Jean Campensis. Saint Athanase sur le livre des
Pseaulmes. L'interpretation sur Lecclesiaste. Orai-
sons pour le temps daffliction. — Antwerp, Jean
Steelsius, 1543.
16°.
References: Cartier *Arrêts* 378n < Brunet IV, 928.
Notes: To the 1537 ed. are added 'Oraisons pour le temps
d'affliction'. No known copy.

C 89.   **Campen, Jean van.**

Paraphrase ou briefve interpretation sur les Psalmes
de David. Plus, Autre interpretation Paraphrastique
sur l'Ecclesiaste de Salomon. — Lyon, Balthazar
Arnoullet, 1545.
16°: a-z A-D⁸, rom.
*Geneva BPU Bb 1731.
References: Cartier *Arrêts* 378n. Baudrier X.
Notes: The BPU copy lacks the paraphrase on Ecclesiastes
announced on the t.p.

C 90.   **Caracciolo, Antoine.**

Le mirouer de vraye religion. — Paris, Simon de
Colines, Regnault Chaudiere, 1544.
8°: A-C⁸ D¹⁰, ital.
*Paris BN Rés. pD 28.
Notes: The priv. to Regnault Chaudiere dated 5 Jan. 1543
(a.s.). Censured on 27 May 1544, when a corrected version
was demanded. On 15 July the theologians agreed to wait for
the new version before deciding whether the text should be
included in the *Catalogue des livres censurés*. In fact the title
does not appear in the *Catalogue*. It is not known whether

either this ed. or the following represents the corrected version, antedated.

C 91. Caracciolo, Antoine.

Le mirouer de vraye religion. — Paris, Simon de Colines, Regnault Chaudiere, 1544.
16°: A-D⁸, rom.
*Paris BSG D8° 6197(3) inv 7892 bis Rés.
Notes: The priv. to Regnault Chaudiere is here dated to 4 Jan. 1543 (a.s.)

C 92. Castellion, Sébastien.

Dialogi sacri, latino-gallici, ad linguas, morésque puerorum formandos. Liber primus. — [Geneva], [Jean Girard], 1543.
8°: A-I⁸, rom.
*Wrocław BU 458132.
References: *BG* 42/8. See *Index* I #72.
Notes: T.p. wrongly dated '1553'. French and Latin on facing pages. Later eds of Castellio's *Dialogues* omit the French text. The work is dedic. to Mathurin Cordier.

C 93. Caupain, Henri.

Le desert de devotion qui est ung traicte plaisant, utile et proffitable a toutes manieres de gens devotz ou curieulx, seculiers ou reguliers. Nouvellement compose. — [Paris], [Alain Lotrian], 1528?
8°: A-I⁸, goth. I 8r: Impr. à Paris.
*London BL 695.a.2. Paris BN Rés. D 17403.
References: Moreau III #1442.
Notes: Henri Caupain is described in the colophon as a 'frere mineur du couvent d'Abbeville'.

C 94. Caupain, Henri.

Le sepulchre spirituel pour donner a congnoistre comment on doibt dignement recepvoir et garder le precieulx corps de nostre seigneur au sainct sacrement de Lautel. — Paris, 1525?
8°: A-C⁸ D², goth. D 2v: Impr. à Paris.
*Paris BN Rés. D 80289.
Notes: Author's name given in the colophon. In his prologue Caupain refers to his previous work *Le desert de devotion*.

C 95.   Chansons, ed. Matthieu Malingre?

Chanson spirituelle sur la saincte Cene de nostre Seigneur ... avec le Deviz consolatif d'un Chrestien affligé, et un D'eglogue rustic d'un Pastoureau Chrestien. Et la Confession d'un chascun fidelle. — Lyon?, ?, 1545.

8°: A-E^8 F^4, rom.

*Geneva BPU Bd 1915.

Notes: Bordier, *Chans.hug.* II, 428, notes this title, but knew of no copies. The 'chanson spirituelle' (A 6r-C 2r) is interspersed with extracts from Calvin's *Institution.* A MS note attributes the *Eglogue rustic* to Marot, as does Defaux, ed. of Marot, *Oeuvres poetiques* II, 683 (text) and notes. The *Deviz consolatif* was attrib. to Marot in a 1558 plaquette ed., under the title 'Le Riche en pauvreté, joyeux en affliction et content en souffrance', but Defaux doubts this (*Oeuvres* II, 691 (text) and notes). Matthieu Malingre was probably author of the text, adding Marot's *Complainte.*

C 96.   Chansons.

Chansons spirituelles sur la saincte Cene de nostre Seigneur Jesus Christ. — ?, ?, 1546.

8°.

References: Bordier, *Chans. hug.* p. xxix < Brunet I, 1791.

C 97.   Chansons.

Chanson nouvelle contre la secte Lutheriane, sur le chant de la chanson, Les Bourguignons ont mis le camp, devant la ville de Peronne. — Paris, Jean André, 1545.

8°: A^4, rom. A 4r: Impr. à Paris. 06.10.1545.

*Paris BSG D 8° 4285(3) Rés.

Notes: Could be by Artus Désiré? The BSG copy bound with several Désiré texts.

C 98.   Chansons, ed. Matthieu Malingre?

Chansons nouvelles demonstrantz plusieurs erreurs et faulsetez: desquelles le paovre monde est remply par les ministres de Satan. — [Neuchâtel], [Pierre de Vingle], 1534?

8°: AA^8, goth.

*Zurich ZB Res. 1327.

References: Moore #111. Higman *Censorship* #C 186. Th. Dufour *Not.cat.* pp. 104-5.

Notes: The title censured in the 1547 *Catalogue*, but omitted from later eds five polemical songs.

C 99.   Chansons, ed. Matthieu Malingre?

Chansons Nouvelles demonstrantz plusieurs erreurs et faulsetez, desquelles le paovre monde est remply par les ministres de Satan. — [Geneva], [Wigand Koeln], 1535?

8°: π⁸, goth.

*Zurich ZB Res. 1328.

References: Th Dufour *Not. cat.* p. 131. *BG* 35/3.

Notes: Copied from the P. de Vingle ed.

C 100.   Chansons, ed. Nicolas Du Val.

Chansons demonstrant les erreurs et abuz du temps present, lesquelles le fidele pourra chanter au lieu des chansons vaines et pleines de mensonges. — [Geneva], [Jean Girard], 1542.

8°: a-d⁸, ital.

*Vienna ÖNB 80.X.38.

References: *BG* 42/10. Drilhon cat. #15: 1544 ed. of this title.

Notes: The name Nicolas Du Val is given in an acrostic, a 1v. There are 30 poems, some taken from the 'belles et bonnes chansons' of 1533 and from the *Chansons nouvelles* of [1534]. The new items consist mainly of polemical poems.

C 101.   Chansons, ed. Matthieu Malingre.

Sensuivent plusieurs belles et bonnes chansons, que les chrestiens peuvent chanter en grande affection de cueur: pour et affin de soulager leurs esperitz et de leur donner repos en dieu. — [Neuchâtel], [Pierre de Vingle], 1533.

8°: A-C⁸, goth.

*Geneva BPU Rés. Bd 1475. *Zurich ZB Res. 1329.

References: Moore #110. Th. Dufour *Not.cat.* pp. 108-10.

Notes: 19 songs. Malingre's name is given in an acrostic and in an anagram, 'Y me vint mal a gre', fol. A 1v.

C 102.   Chansons, ed. Matthieu Malingre.

Chansons spirituelles, pleines de louenges à Dieu: de saincte doctrine et exhortations, pour edifier le prochain, tant vieilles que nouvelles. — [Geneva], [Jean Girard], 1545.

8°: A-H⁸, rom.

*Vienna ÖNB 80.X.39.

References: Cat. Drilhon #7 and 20 (the latter dated 1544). *Index* I #379. *BG* 45/22.

Notes: 64 poems, the last by Mathurin Cordier. Includes most of the 'belles et bonnes chansons' of 1533, and two of the [1534] *Chansons nouvelles*, but not the poems first found in the Nicolas Du Val collection. Malingre's name in an acrostic, fol. A 1v.

C 103.   Chapeau des Luthériens.

Le Chappeau des lutheriens Avec la revocation de Luther lapparition Lexemplaire aux bons chrestiens. — ?, ?, 1530?

8°: a-b⁸, goth.

Séville Colombine.

References: Moore #112. Babelon #22 (text on pp. 260 sqq.).

C 104.   Charles Quint.

Edit et mandement ... Ordonne et fait a la journee imperiale celebree en la cite de Vvormes. Lan de grace Mil cinq cens.xxi. Contre Frere Martin luther. — [Paris], [Pierre Gromors], 1521?

4°: A-B⁴ C², goth.

*Paris BSG C 8° 548 inv. 113 Rés. (4) (- A 2,3).

References: Moreau III #57.

Notes: List of Luther's 'errors', command not to spread his doctrines or to publish books on scripture or on its interpretation without permission of the local ecclesiastical authorities. Dated from Worms, 8 May 1521.

C 105.   Chevalet.

Sensuyt la vie de sainct Christofle elegamment composee en rime francoise et par personnages. — Grenoble, pr. Anemond Amalberti, 1530.

4°: A-M⁴ N² O-Z AA-BB⁴ CC⁶ DD-MM⁴ NN⁶ OO-ZZ AAA-CCC⁴,
rom.   CCC 3v: Impr. à Grenoble, pr Anemond amalberti.
28.01.1530.
*Chantilly Condé VIII G 11.
Notes: Divided into four 'journées', with new gathering
beginning each journée. Each t.p. gives '1537'. The author
described as 'maistre Chevalet jadis souverain maistre en telle
compositure'. N 2r (colophon of the first part): the *mystère*
was performed at Grenoble on 9 June 1527.

C 106.   Chocquet, Louis.

*Lapocalypse Sainct Jehan Zebedee ... ensemble les
cruaultez de Domicien Cesar.* — Paris, [Nicolas
Couteau], pr. A. et C. Langelier, 1541.
2°: AA-GG⁶ HH⁴, goth.   HH 4v: ach. d'impr. 27.05.1541. Pour
Arnoul et Charles Langelier.
*Bruxelles BR LP VH 12355 C (-A1). *Nantes Dobrée 13/3. Aix
Méj. Rés. Q. 11. Chantilly Condé V H 6(3).
References: *Rép. bib. suppl. Bourges*: Alabat 3.
Notes: AA1v: dedic. in Latin by Louis Choquet to Antoine Le
Coq docteur en médecine.

C 107.   Chrysostome, St Jean, trans. and versif. Pierre Rivrain.

*Exhortation à prier Dieu <> Avecq'la louange de
parfaite oraison, et autres petitz oeuvres spirituelz.*
— Paris, Estienne Groulleau, 1547.
8°: A-G⁸ H⁴, ital.   H 2r: Impr. à Paris par Estienne Groulleau.
20.02.1547.
*La Haye KB 1123.J.56. *Paris BN Rés. Ye 1398. *Paris BEBA
Masson 232 (- H4).
Notes: Priv. dated 22.01.1546. Approbation by two Doctors,
T. Du Mont et A. Aubert, 24.11.1546. Dedic. (in verse) by
Pierre Rivrain to 'Loys cardinal de Bourbon, archevêque de
Sens'. The whole text in verse.

C 108.   Chrysostome, St Jean, trans. Pierre Pesseliere.

*Traicté <> Que nul n'est offensé sinon par soy-
mesme.* — Lyon, Jean de Tournes, 1543.
16°: a-e⁸, rom.
*Coll. G. Berthoud.
References: Cartier *De Tournes* #11.

C 109.   Chrysostome, St Jean, trans. Pierre Pesseliere.

Traicté <> que nul n'est offensé, sinon par soy-mesmes. — Paris, Adam Saulnier, 1543.

8°: a-i⁴, rom.

*Paris BA 8° T 3045.

Notes: Dedic. by Pierre Pesseliere to Antoinette de Bourbon, duchesse de Guise, dated from Paris, 20.12.1542.

C 110.   Clément VII.

La translation en francoys de la bulle decernee <>, a la requeste du roy treschrestien pour extirper lheresie Lutherienne et autres sectes pullulans en ce royaulme. — Paris, [Antoine Couteau], Vve Pierre Roffet, André Roffet, 1533?

8°: A⁸, goth.

*Paris BN Rothschild IV.3.206.

References: Moreau IV #627. Rothschild #2049.

Notes: A 1v: priv. to Vve Pierre Roffet ('Le Faulcheur') and her son André for three months, dated 21.12.1533. The bull dated (A 8r) from Rome, 30.08.1533.

C 111.   Clerici, Jean.

Sensuit ung traicte des fondemens du temple spirituel de dieu ... presche en forme de sermon. — Paris, Nicolas Savetier, Antoine Bonnemere, Jean Le Bailli, 1531?

8°: A-N⁸, goth.   N 8r: Impr. a Paris pr Jehan le bailli messagier demourant a Bethune.

*Paris BN Rés. D 30339. Amiens. Ghent BU Res. 465.

References: Machiels #479. Moreau IV #99.

Notes: In his prologue the author mentions his 'manuel des chrestiens' explaining the Creed. Here he intends to 'principalement parler des nobles et vertueulx effectz fruictz et prouffictz de foy et des douzes articles dicelle contenus ou simbole des Apostres et figures par les douze fondemens de la cite dont il est mention faicte en lapocalipse ou xxi. chapitre.' The text was 'presche en forme de sermon ... en la ville dathelan', 1527.

C 112. Clerici, Jean.

Le manuel des chrestiens, traictant, de foy de espe-
rance et de charite. — Paris, [Gérard Morrhy],
Ambroise Girault, 1532?
8°: [8]+274 ff., A⁸ a-z A-L⁸, goth.
*Paris BN Rés. D 80400.
References: Moreau IV #384.
Notes: Priv. (A 1v) to Ambroise Girault for two years dated
07.02.1531, signed 'Pie de fer'. The text explains the Creed,
Lord's Prayer, and Ten Commandments. m 7v: prayers to the
Virgin Mary and to saints, against the modern heretics. Jean
Clerici, 'profes en lordre de sainct Francoys au convent du
Biez en Arthois' (a 1v) is writing in order that 'les simples
chretiens estre grossement et simplement informes et ensei-
gnes des choses principalles apartenantes au salut'.

C 113. Clerici, Jean.

Le Manuel des chrestiens traictant de Foy, de Espe-
rance et de Charite. — [Paris], [Nicolas Savetier],
1533?
8°.
Paris B. du Saulchoir.
References: Moreau IV #628.

C 114. Clerici, Jean.

Le Manuel des chrestiens. — Paris, Ambroise Girault, 1535+.
References: Ref. in Moreau IV #384.

C 115. Clerici, Jean.

Le Traicte de Exemplaire penitence. — Paris,
[Nicolas Savetier], Ambroise Girault, 1533?
8°: A-P⁸ Q⁴, goth.
*Paris BN Rés. D 80042. Paris BEBA Masson 150. Ghent BU Res.
761.
References: Machiels #478. Moreau IV #629.
Notes: Dedic. to 'Jehanne de Hornes, vefve de ... Hugues de
Melun, vicomte de Ghent'. The author of the dedication,
chaplain to Mme de Hornes, has put in order this posthumous
work by Clerici. He mentions the *Manuel des chrestiens*,
which Mme de Hornes had had printed. Clerici is described as

a Franciscan in the convent of Biez en Artois, and confessor to the Sisters of the Annunciade in Béthune. The treatise summarizes his Lent sermons preached in Béthune.

C 116.   Coignac, Joachim de.

Deux Satyres, l'une du Pape, l'autre de la Papauté. — [Geneva], [Adam et Jean Rivery], 1551.
8°: A^8 B^4, rom.
*Paris BN Rothschild V.4.76.
References: CDM p. 18. *Index* I #485.
Notes: Joachim de Coignac (*c.* 1520-80) was pastor in Thonon until 1553. He translated several works from Italian.

C 117.   Coignac, Joachim de.

Huict Satyres de l'estat et vie des moines. — [Geneva], [Adam et Jean Rivery], 1550.
8°: A-D^8, rom.
*Cambridge Emma. 324.7.82(4).
References: Adams C 2318.
Notes: A 2r: prefatory epistle addressed to Jacques de Bourgogne.

C 118.   Coignac, Joachim de.

La desconfiture de Goliath, Tragedie. — Geneva, Adam et Jean Rivery, 1551.
8°: 71 pp., A-D^8 E^4, rom.
*London BL C.65.c.11.
References: CDM p. 18.
Notes: A 1v: ten-line poem by Jacques Bourgeois on the analogy between David/Goliath et Gospel/Pope. Dedic. to Edward VI of England (A 2r-6v). Praise of Reformed cities in Switzerland and Germany. A mixture of octosyllabics and decasyllabics.

C 119.   Columbi, Jean.

Confession generale avec certaines rigles au commencement tres utiles tant a confesseurs que a penitens... et une oraison tresdevote a dire devant que on recepve le corps d'nostre seigneur et une apres. — Avignon, Jean de Channey, 1517.
16°: A-E^8, goth.
Coll. Baudrier.

References: Baudrier X.299.

Notes: Columbi was Bishop of Troyes and 'penitencier de nostre sainct pere le Pape en Avignon'. First ed. of this work: Avignon, Pierre Rohault, 1499.

C 120. Columbi, Jean.

Confession generale avec certaines regles au commencement tresutile: tant a confesseurs que a penitens... Et une oraison tresdevote a dire devant que on recepve le corps de nostre seigneur... — Lyon, Claude Nourry, 1516?

8°: A-D⁸, goth. D 7v: Impr. à Lyon par Claude nourry alias le Prince.

Carpentras BM.

References: Baudrier XII.81-2.

Notes: Baudrier describes four eds by Nourry, almost identical but separate, all s.d.

C 121. Columbi, Jean.

Confession generale avec certaines reigles au commencement tresutile: tant a confesseurs que a penitens:... Et une oraison tresdevote a dire devant que on recepve le corps de nostre seigneur... — Avignon?, Jean de Channey?, 1520?

8°: a-d⁸, goth.

*London BL 845.a.30 (- d8).

Notes: Attrib. to Jean de Channey on the basis of typographical material.

C 122. Columbi, Jean.

Confession generale, avec certaines reigles au commencement, tresutiles tant a confesseurs que a penitens... Et une oraison tresdevote a dire devant que on recoyve le corps de nostre seigneur. — Lyon, Jacques Moderne, ?

16°: A-F⁸, goth. F 8r: Impr. à Lyon par Jaques Moderne dit grand Jaques.

*Aix Méj. Rés. S. 125(3).

Notes: E 7r-F 2r, prayers before and after receiving the Eucharist. F 2v sqq: 'Directoire de ceulx qui sont en larticle de la mort: extraict de la bonne doctrine de maistre Jehan Gerson'.

C 123.   Columbi, Jean.

Confession generale, avec certainez reigles utiles, tant a confesseurs que a penitens... avec deux oraysons tres devotes. — Lyon, hér. Barnabé Chaussard, 1548.

8°: A-D⁸, goth. D 8r: Impr. en la maison de feu Barnabe Chaussard. 15.07.1548.

*Paris BN Rés. D 80220.

References: Baudrier XI.69-70.

Notes: How to prepare for confession, with a list of sins. Then (D 2r), Columbi adds a treatise and several poems by Gerson on preparing for death.

C 124.   Combat chrétien.

Le combat chrestien. — [Alençon], [Simon Du Bois], 1530?

8°: a-e⁸, goth.

*Paris BN Rés. D² 15951 (fragment). *Paris SHP A 1160.

References: Clutton #35. Tricard *APR* 24-9.

C 124a.   Commandements de l'église, Jean Gerson.

Les commandemens de saincte eglise et la confession generale du jour de pasques par les paroisses. Le petit traicte de maistre Jehan gerson qui aprent a bien mourir. — Paris, Vve Jean Trepperel, Jean Jehannot, 1516?

4°: A⁸ B⁴, goth.

*Paris BN Rés. D 80336.

Notes: Cf. *Prières et commandements.*

C 124b.   Complainte de l'église.

La complainte de nostre mere sainte eglise. — Paris?, 1516?

4°: π⁴, goth.

*Paris BN Rés. D 80336(2).

Notes: Bound with *Commandements de l'église* printed by Vve Jean Trepperel and Jean Jehannot, but not the same characters. The text laments immoral behaviour but not heresy.

C 125. Concile. Pise.

Censuivent Les faitz institutions et ordonnances par messigneurs les cardinaulx, archevesques evesques, prelatz, abez, et docteurs ... faitz dedans la ville de Pise, pour commencer le concile. — Paris, Guillaume Nyverd, 1512?

8°: 4 ff.

*Paris BN Rés. B 16859.

References: Moreau II #47.

Notes: Jules II had denied access to Pisa cathedral to the prelates. In Nov. 1511 the latter ignored the interdiction and rejected the authority of the Pope. A considerable number of French Bishops in the lists.

C 126. Confession de Béda.

La confession et raison de la foy de maistre Noel Beda Docteur en theologie et Sindique de la sacree universite a Paris: envoyee au treschrestien Roy de france, Francoys premier de ce nom. — [Neuchâtel], [Pierre de Vingle], 1533.

8°: A-H^8 I^4, goth. I 4r: Ach. d'impr. 01.12.1533.

*Lucerne ZB S.45.4. *Paris SHP R 1000(4).

References: Moore #116. Th. Dufour *Not.cat.* pp. 118-20. Berthoud *BHR* 1967 pp. 373 sqq.

Notes: The t.p. reads: 'Imprime a Paris par Pierre de Vignolle, demourant en la rue de la Sorbonne. Avec privilege.' Text often attrib. to Antoine Marcourt; but Mlle Berthoud has demonstrated the fragility of this hypothesis.

C 127. Confession de Béda.

La confession et raison de la foy de Maistre Noel Beda, Docteur en theologie et Sindique de la sacree Universite a Paris: envoyee au treschrestien Roy de France, Francoys premier de ce Nom. — [Geneva], [Jean Michel], 1540?

8°: A-I^8, goth.

*Geneva MHR D Marc 3 et 3a. *London BL C.53.a.29. *Paris BM 25412. Paris BN D^2 15957 Rés. *Vienna ÖNB 79.K.60 (+).

References: *BG* 42/9. Berthoud *BHR* 1967 p. 397. Berthoud 'Michel' p. 60 and #24.

C 128.   Confession de foi.

La confession de Foy faicte par le Chrestien joyeux en Christ: laquelle il tient pour son testament et ordonnance de derniere volunte. — [Geneva], [Jean Michel], 1539.
8°: A-B⁸, goth.
*Bruxelles BR LP VH 2021(3).
References: Berthoud 'Michel' #6 and p. 74.

C 129.   Confrérie du Rosaire.

La declaration de lestat et ordonnance de la tressaincte et profitable confrarie du psaultier: rosier: et chappelet de la tresglorieuse vierge Marie. — Paris, Jean Petit, 1520?
4°: [12] + 117 + [1] ff., Aa8 Bb⁴ A-V⁸ᐟ⁴, goth.
*Paris BN Rés. E 2652.
References: Moreau II #2293.
Notes: Most people, says the Prologue (Aa 2v), have copies of the psalms, rosary and prayers, but do not know how to recite them properly, or the fruit to be obtained thereby. This book, 'recuilly et extraicte des livres qui en sont escriptz et composez par plusieurs notables docteurs', fills the gap. Mainly based on the works of Alain de la Roche and of 'Michel Françoys des iles' (le P. Michel François de Lille)(both 15th-cent.). Written in French 'pour le profit et salut du commun peuple lequel est, et de piecza en merveilleuses tribulacions et adversitez'.

C 130.   Conrard, Olivier.

Le mirouer des pecheurs. — Paris, François Regnault, Galliot Du Pré, 1527?
8°: [4]+134+[2] ff., A¹² B-R⁸, goth.
*Paris BN Rés. Ye 3755. Chantilly Condé. *Aix Méj. C. 2746.
References: Moreau III #1174.
Notes: Letter by frère Olivier Conrard, Franciscan, to the Parlement dated (A 5v) 15.12.1526. A violent attack, in verse, on Luther, Hus, Wycliffe, and their doctrines. Praise for Henry VIII, John Fisher, Clichtove, defenders of the faith. A no less violent attack on clerical and monastic abuses.

C 131. Conrard, Olivier.

La Vie, faictz et louanges de sainct Paul. — Paris, R. Avril, Jean Ruelle, 1546.
16°.
References: Renouard MSS.

C 132. Contemplation.

Devote contemplation: sur le mistere de nostre redemption. — Hesdin, Vauldrain Jacquin, 1518.
8°: 143 ff. Impr. à Hesdin par Vauldrain Jacquin. 18.12.1518.
Chantilly Condé VI G 1.

C 133. Conversion des Luthériens.

La conversion et revocation des Lutheriens faicte en Alemaigne presens les ambassadeurs du pape de lempereur et du roy de Hongrie avec une oraison du sainct sacrement de laustel. — Rouen, Guillaume de La Motte, 1538.
8°: [4] ff., π^4, goth.
Paris BN Rothschild IV.3.233.
References: Rothschild #2050.
Notes: π 4v: 'Escript a Besancon le xx. jour de Juillet 1538.'

C 134. Cordier, Mathurin.

Quatre epistres chrestiennes en ryme Françoise <> Lisez hardiment, car il n'y a rien qui soit contre l'Eglise catholique. — Strasbourg, [Rémy Guédon], 1547.
8°: A-C^8 D^4, rom.
*Wolfenbüttel HAB Tc 250(2).
References: Peter 'Prem. ouvr.' #XIIIa. Johns *BHR* 1975, 445-6.

C 135. [Corrozet, Gilles].

La Tapisserie de l'église chrestienne et catholique: en laquelle sont depainctes la Nativité, Vie, Passion, Mort, et Resurrection de nostre Sauveur et Redempteur Jesus Christ. — Paris, Estienne Groulleau, 1549?
16°: A-N^8, ital.

*Paris BEBA Masson 231 (- A 1-8, N 1,3). *Paris BN Rés. A 7636 (-A8).
Notes: The BEBA copy has lost its t.p. Small engravings based on the Gospels on each page, each accompanied by an octet 'pour l'intelligence d'icelle'. L 1r: a new t.p. for *La Passion.* M 5r: id. for *La Resurrection.* A later ed. with the title *La Nativité, vie, passion, mort et Resurrection de nostre Sauveur...,* Paris, Jean Ruelle, 1556+, BEBA Masson 590. Identical text, similar but different engravings.

C 136.   [Curione, Celio Secondo].

Les Visions de Pasquille. Le jugement d'iceluy, ou Pasquille prisonnier. Avec le Dialogue de Probus. — [Geneva], [Jean Girard], [René de Bienassis], 1547.
8°: a-x⁸ y⁴, rom. y 4v: 'Assez tost, si assez bien'.
Edinburgh NLS Newb 154. *Geneva BPU Bc 2930 Rés. *Lincoln cath. Nn 7.12(1) and Oo 7.12(1). *Neuchâtel past. 106.5. *Vienna ÖNB BE.8.S.39 (+).
References: *BG* 47/8.
Notes: Trans. of *Pasquillus ecstaticus* which Girard had printed in 1544 (see *Index* I #271).

C 137.   Cymbalum mundi.

Cymbalum mundi en françoys contenant quatre Dialogues Poetiques, fort antiques, joeux, et facetieux. — Lyon, Benoist Bonnyn, 1538.
8°: A-C⁸ D⁴, goth. D 4r: Impr. à Lyon par Benoist Bonnyn impr., rue du Paradis. 1538.
*Chantilly Musée Condé VI.E.36. *Paris BN Rés. Z 2442.
Notes: See notes on next number.

C 138.   Cymbalum mundi.

Cymbalum mundi en françoys, contenant quatre Dialogues Poetiques, fort antiques, joyeux, et facetieux. — Paris, Jean Morin, 1538.
8°: A-H⁴, rom. H 4r: impr. à Paris pour Jehan Morin libr., rue S. Jacques, ens. du croissant. 1537.
Versailles BM Goujet 12° 241.
References: Peach/Brunel #182. *Index* I #386. Facs. reprod. 1914. Modern ed. P. Nurse, *TLF*, 1983.
Notes: Attrib. to Bonaventure Des Périers. This attribution is questioned by M.A. Screech, preface to the Nurse ed., but reaffirmed by M.C. Smith, *BHR* 1991, pp. 593-618.

D

D 1. **Défensoire de la conception.**

Le defensoire de la conception de la glorieuse vierge Marie. — Rouen, Martin Morin, 1515?

4°: A-K⁸ L⁶ M⁴, goth. M 4v: Maistre martin morin.

*Paris BEBA Masson 1110 (-A1,8).

Notes: M 4r: Priv. by the lt.-gen. of the bailli de Rouen to Martin Morin dated 24.11.1514, giving the title. Theological mixture on Creation and on the Immaculate Conception, with numerous quotations from the Fathers, popes and councils. See also F 2.

D 2. **Définition d'amour.**

Diffinition et perfection d'amour. Sophologe d'amour. — Paris, Gilles Corrozet, 1542.

8°.

References: Dagens.

Notes: According to Dagens, a partial trans. of Ficino's commentary on the *Banquet*.

D 3. **Demontrance des abus.**

Demonstrance des abuz de l'eglise, des constitutions humaines, de l'Eglise de Christ, et de l'Antechrist, des voeux des Moines, et si en les rompant on offense Dieu. — [Geneva], [Jean Girard], 1545.

8°: A-D⁸ []², rom. D 7v: 'De Paris, en Sorbonne, ces Calendes Grecques. Finis legis Christus'.

*Paris BN Rés. 8° Z Don 594(218.VI)(-[]2).

References: *BG* 45/15. *Index* I #368.

Notes: Takes the form of a letter addressed to a monk, encouraging him to leave his monastery.

D 4. **Dentière, Marie.**

Epistre tresutile <> Envoyée à la Royne de Navarre seur du Roy de France. Contre les Turcz, Juifz, Infideles, Faulx chrestiens, Anabaptistes, et Lutheriens. — [Geneva], [Jean Girard], 1539.

8°: a-d⁸, ital.

*Geneva MHR D Den 1 (anon.). *Paris BM Rés. 25543(4)(author named a 2r).

References: Moore #131. Th. Dufour *Not.cat.* pp. 155-9. *BG* 39/8.

Notes: T.p.: 'Anvers, Martin Lempereur'. J. Girard had a lawsuit because of the false address. Marie Dentière, former nun from Tournai, was married to the pastor Antoine Froment. She here attacks the Genevan pastors appointed to replace Calvin and Farel.

D 5.   [Dentière, Marie].

La Guerre et deslivrance de la ville de Geneve. — [Geneva], [Wigand Koeln?], 1536?
4°: 23 pp.

References: Th. Dufour *Not.cat.* pp. 134-6. *BG* 36/4. Re-ed. Fick, 1863.

Notes: Fick re-edited a printed work, now lost. Summary of the passage of Geneva to the Reform, 1532-36. Attrib. to Marie Dentière on the basis of similarity of thought to Dentière's *Epistre*.

D 6.   Denys, Saint.

La contemplation spirituelle Extraicte des Livres de Sainct Denys, et de plusieurs passage de la Saincte Escriture. Utile et profitable à toute personne tendant à perfection, soit seculier ou regulier. — Paris, Jean Bonfons, ?
8°: A-D⁸, rom.
*Paris BN Rés. D 80285.

Notes: Bonfons was active 1543-66.

D 7.   Désiré, Artus.

Les combatz du fidelle Papiste pelerin Romain, contre l'apostat Antipapiste tirant à la synagogue de Geneve. — Rouen, Robert et Jean Du Gort, 1550.
16°: A-S⁸, rom.
*Paris BA 8° BL 10838.

References: Giese #17.

Notes: The t.p. of the only known copy, giving the date '1550', is handwritten. It could well be a copy of the 1552 ed. which mentions 'l'Apostat Antipapiste', absent from the known 1550 ed.

D 8. **Désiré, Artus.**

Les combatz du fidelle papiste pelerin Romain, contre l'apostat Priapiste, tirant à la synagogue de Geneve, maison babilonicque des Lutheriens. Ensemble la description de la cité de Dieu. — Rouen, Robert et Jean Du Gort, 1550.

16°: A-S⁸, rom.

*Paris BEBA Masson 1097. *Paris BN Rés. p Ye 228(1).

References: Giese #15.

Notes: Dialogue in octosyllabics between 'le fidele papiste' and 'l'antipapiste'. Geneva here presented (for the first time?) as major target for anti-Reform propaganda.

D 9. **Désiré, Artus.**

Les Combatz du Fidelle Chrestien, dit Papiste, contre l'Infidelle apostat antipapiste, reveu et corrigé... Ensemble la description de la Cité de Dieu assiegee des heretiques. — Lyon, Jean Pullon, 1551.

16°: 165 ff., A-X⁸, rom.

*London BL C.70.a.10.

References: Giese #18.

D 10. **Désiré, Artus.**

Le deffensoire de la foi Chrestienne, Sur les Contradictions des Francs Taulpins, autrement nommez Lutheriens. — Paris, René Avril, Jean André, 1547.

16°: A-M⁸, rom. M 8r: Impr. à Paris par René Avril pr. Jehan André. 1547.

*Aix Méj. Rés. S. 74.

References: Renouard MSS. Giese #5.

Notes: General survey, in octosyllabics, of points of controversy between Roman Catholics and 'luthériens'.

D 11. **Désiré, Artus.**

Le deffensoire de la foy Chrestiene, contenant en soy le Miroer des Francs Taupins autrement nommez Lutheriens. — Paris, Jean André, 1548.

8°: A-M⁸, rom.

*Nantes Dobrée 146.

References: Giese #6.

Notes: M7v: Priv. to Jean André for two years, dated 29.07.1547. A 2r-8r: dedic. by Désiré to Me Durand à Serta, second president of the Toulouse parlement.

D 12.   Désiré, Artus.

Le Deffensoire de la foi chrestienne, contenant le Miroer des Francs Taupins. — Rouen, Robert et Jean Du Gort, 1550.
16°: [A]⁸ B-L⁸ [M]⁶, rom. M 6v: se vendent à Rouen, par Robert et Jehan Dugort freres.
*Paris BA Rés. 8° BL 10837.
References: Giese #9.

D 13.   Désiré, Artus.

Le Defensoire de la foy chrestienne, contenant en soy le Miroër des Francs Taulpins, autrement nommez Lutheriens. — Paris, Jean Ruelle, Estienne Groulleau, 1551.
16°: A-M⁸, rom. M 7v: Se vendent à Paris par Estienne Groulleau.
*Rouen BM O 1698.
Notes: 'Pour Jean Ruelle' on t.p. Numerous engravings.

D 14.   Désiré, Artus.

La Description de la cité de Dieu ... ensemble aussi la Complaincte. — Rouen, Robert et Jean Du Gort, 1550.
16°: T-X⁸, rom.
*Paris BN Rés. 8° Z Don 594(5). *Paris BN Rés. pYe 228(2).
References: Giese #20.
Notes: As the collation implies, the ed. was intended to be bound with the *Combatz...* But there is a separate t.p.

D 15.   Désiré, Artus.

Les grands jours du Parlement de Dieu, publiez par monsieur sainct Mathieu. — Rouen, Robert et Jean Du Gort, 1551.
Paris BA Rés. 8° BL 10839 (missing, 1993).
References: Giese #41.

D 16.   Désiré, Artus.

Lamentation de nostre mere saincte Eglise, sur les contradictions des heretiques. — Paris, Vve de Pierre Vidoue, 1545.
8°.
References: Renouard MSS < Du Verdier. Giese #1 < Brunet.

D 17.   Désiré, Artus.

Le Miroer des francz Taulpins, Autrement ditz Antichristiens, et de la nouvelle alliance du tresmiserable et reprouvé Luther, precurseur du filz de perdition. — Paris, Jean André, 1546.
8°: [48] ff., A-F⁸, rom. F 8v: marque de Jean André. 1546.
*Aix Méj. C. 3138. Paris BN Rothschild IV.7.46.
References: Giese #2 < Brunet. Rothschild #3253.
Notes: Priv. (F 8r) to Jean André for two years dated 22.03.1546 (a.s.). Poem in octosyllabics, comparable (in content) but contrasted (in style) with Ronsard's *Discours.*

D 18.   Désiré, Artus.

Le Miroer des Francs Taulpins, autrement dictz Antechristz, et de la nouvelle alliance du tresmiserable et reprouvé Luther. — Paris, Jean André, 1546.
8°: A-F⁸, rom.
*Paris BSG D 8° 4285(1) Rés.
References: Giese #3.
Notes: T.p. says: 'Nouvellement reveu et corrigé'.

D 19.   Désiré, Artus.

Le Miroer des Francs Taulpins, autrement dictz Antechristz, et de la nouvelle alliance du tresmiserable et reprouvé Luther. — Paris, Jean André, 1547.
8°: A-F⁸, rom.
*Versailles BM Goujet 8° 92.
References: Peach/Brunel #171.
Notes: Same priv. as in 1546 ed.

D 20.   Désiré, Artus.

Le Miroir Des francs taupins, autrement dictz Antechrists. Auquel est contenu le deffensoire de la foy Chrestienne. — Rouen, Robert et Jean Du Gort, 1550?

16°: A-E⁸, rom.
*Paris BN Rés. p Ye 387.
References: Giese #8.

D 21.   Desmoulins, Laurent.

Le cymetiere des Malheureux. — Paris, pr. Jean Petit,
Michel Le Noir, 1511.
8°: A-N⁸ O⁴, goth. O 4r: Impr. à Paris pr. jehan petit et Michel le
noir. 31.07.1511.
*Paris BN Rés. Ye 1353. *Aix Méj. C. 2929.
References: E. Armstrong *BHR* 1969 p. 261. Moreau II #70.
Notes: The author's name given in acrostic (O 3v) and in the
privilege. It is a *memento mori* in verse, reviewing heroes,
biblical (David) and classical (Hercules, Hannibal), who let
themselves be tempted by women ('Peu de femmes sont
plaines de vertus').

D 22.   Desmoulins, Laurent.

Le cymetiere Des Malheureux. — Paris, Vve Jean
Trepperel, Jean Jehannot, 1512?
8°: A-P⁸ Q⁴, goth.
*Paris BN Rés. Ye 1354.
Notes: The date suggested because this ed. follows the 1511
ed., not that of 1513. Address on t.p.: 'Paris, rue neufve nostre
dame, ens. de l'escu de France'.

D 23.   Desmoulins, Laurent.

*Le catholicon des mal advisez autrement dit le Cy-
metiere des malheureux.* — Paris, Jean Petit, Michel
Le Noir, 1513.
8°: A-N⁸ O⁴, goth. O 4r: Impr. à Paris pr. Jehan petit et Michel le
noir. 02.08.1513.
*Paris BN Rés. Ye 1355.
References: Moreau II #560.
Notes: The *Cymetiere* of 1511, with some additions, incl. (A
1v-2r) an epistle by the author to 'Me. Milles d'Illiers, grand
doyen de Chartres.'

D 24.   Desmoulins, Laurent.

Le cymetiere des malheureux. — Lyon, Olivier
Arnoullet, 1534.
8°: a-p⁸ q⁴, goth. q 4r: Impr. à Lyon par Olivier Arnoullet. 28.03.1534.

Versailles BM Goujet 8° 44.
References: Baudrier X, 67. Peach/Brunel #180.

D 25. **Dialogue de la passion.**

Le dialogue spirituel de la Passion. Lequel se doit lire en forme de oraison et contemplation en solitude. — Paris, Jean Du Pré, Regnault Chaudiere, 1520.
8°: A-D⁸ E⁴, goth. E 4v: Impr à Paris par Jehan dupre pr Regnault chauldiere. 05.07.1520.
*Paris BN Rothschild IV.3.114. Séville Colomb.
References: Moreau II #2313. Rothschild #548.
Notes: Priv. (E 3v-4v) for three years to Regnault Chaudiere dated 24.02.1519. Dialogue between the soul and Jesus.

D 26. **Dialogue de la passion.**

Dialogue spirituel de la passion. — Paris?, ?, ?
8°: A-B⁸ C⁶, goth.
*London BL C.107.a.12(2)(-A 1,8).

D 27. **Dialogue et parlement.**

Dyalogue et ung merveilleux parlement faict pas loing de Trient sur le cheming de Romme, d'ung Abbe, Curtisan et du Dyable, allencontre le bon pape Adrian. — [Geneva], [Wigand Koeln], 1522.
4°: 4 ff.
*London BL 3901.ee.11.
References: Moore #55 and pp. 221-2.
Notes: Celebrates the new Pope Hadrian VI, denounces the debauchery of previous popes, demands reform of ecclesiastical administration. Appreciates Luther's teaching, but condemns his violence. The attrib. to Wigand Koeln on the basis of the typographical material.

D 28. **Directoire des âmes.**

Le directoire de la salut des Ames: tant pour les Pasteurs d'icelles que aussi pour le commun peuple. — Agen, Antoine Reboul, 1526.
8°: [32] ff., A-D⁸, goth. D 7v: Impr. à Gen par Anthoine Rebol imprimeur. 07.11.1526.
Toulouse BM Rés. D XVI.550 (- gathering B).
References: *Rép.bib.* #2. Claudin *Agen* pp. 7-8.

Notes: A 1v: dedic. by Petrus de Mundavilla to Jean Bartou, Bishop of Lectoure. My thanks to Mme S. Bernillon for providing details of the description.

D 29.   Discipline d'amour.

Le livre de la discipline damour divine: contenant La repeticion de la disciple. — Paris, [Pierre Vidoue], pr. Regnault Chaudiere, 1519.

8°: [8]+175+[1] ff., π^8 a-k^8 'm'^{8} m-y^8, goth. y 7r: Fait à paris pr. regnault chaudiere. 28.11.1519.

Harvard CL (incompl.). Troyes BM K 13.6931. *Paris BN Rés. D 42239. *Aix Méj. C. 7871. Séville Colomb.

References: Moreau II #2131.

Notes: According to the table of contents, the work was composed in the 'monastere des celestins de nostre dame dambert es forestz dorleans' in 1470. In the prologue the author offers 'aulcuns exercices et considerations qui pourront valoir et ayder a dieu aymer seurement, et a le querir et trouver fructueusement et salutairement.' y 7v-8r: Priv. from Francis I to Regnault Chaudière for three years, dated 3 May 1519.

D 30.   Discipline d'amour.

Le Livre de la Discipline d'amour divine: contenant La repeticion de la disciple. — Paris, Regnault Chaudiere, 1537.

8°: A^8 A-Y^8, goth. Y 7r: Pour Regnault Chauldiere. 01.03 1537.

*Paris BA 8° T 7365 and 7364.

D 31.   Discipline d'amour.

Le livre de la Discipline et amour divin. — Lyon, Jean de Tournes, 1538.

16°.

References: Dagens.

Notes: Unknown apart from ref. in Dagens. J. de Tournes had not begun printing in 1538. A ghost? Or by another printer?

D 32.   Discipline d'amour.

Le livre de la Discipline Damour divine, contenant .x. chapitres: Ensemble la Repetition de la Disciple. — Paris, [Estienne Caveiller], [Henry Paquot], Jean Longis, 1538.

8°: A^8 A-T^8, goth. T 8r: Fait à Paris. 22.01.1538.

*Paris BA 8° T 7366. *Paris BSG D 6080 Rés. inv 7733. *Aix Méj. Rés. D. 110 (Longis).
References: Dagens. Du Verdier.
Notes: The t.p. gives address of editor as 'à l'enseigne de la Rose rouge, rue neufve nostre Dame' (i.e. Henri Paquot, acc. to Renouard, *Répertoire*). Typographical material identical to that of Doré, *Allumettes...*, Caveiller pour J. Ruelle (whose address was 'rue s. Jacques, queue de regnard'), 1539.

=>   *Discours*: see *Bref Discours*.

D 33.   Dolet, Estienne.

Les Gestes de Françoys de Valois Roy de France. Dedans lequel oeuvre on peult congnoistre tout ce qui a esté faict par les Francoys depuis 1513 jusques en 1539. — Lyon, Estienne Dolet, 1540.
4°: A-K⁴, rom.
*Dublin TCD QQ.kk.24. *Geneva BPU Rés. Gg 200. *Paris BN Rés. Lb³⁰.1. *Paris SHP A 1064. *Wolfenbüttel HAB 70.45 Hist (+).
References: Longeon *Dolet* #119.
Notes: The Latin original condemned in 1544 (*Index* I #84), and featured among the books by Dolet burnt by edict of Parlement in 1543 (Higman *Censorship*, pp. 96-7).

D 34.   Dolet, Estienne.

Les Gestes de Françoys de Valois Roy de France ... depuis l'An Mil cinq cens treize, jusques en l'An Mil cinq cents quarante, et troys. — Lyon, Estienne Dolet, 1543.
8°: 94 p. + [1 f.], A-F⁸, rom.
Cambridge Clare. *London BL 285.e.42. *Munich BSB P.O.Gall. 1392(4). *Paris BN Rés. Lb³⁰.1A and Rothschild. *Vienna ÖNB 58.X.20 (+).
References: Longeon *Dolet* #120. Adams D 767. Rothschild #2116.
Notes: An addition extends the narrative to 1541. But Dolet's epistle to the king still dated (A 4r) from Lyon, 12 August 1539.

D 35.   Dolet, Estienne.

Les faictz et gestes du Roy Françoys premier de ce nom, tant contre L'empereur que ses subjectz, et aultres nations estranges ... depuis 1513 jusques à present. — Paris, Alain Lotrian, 1543.

8°: A-M⁴, rom.   M 4r: Impr. à Paris par Alain lotrian, escu de France.

*Paris BM Rés. 53486. *Stuttgart LB Franz.G. 8° 582.

References: Longeon *Dolet* #122.

D 36.   Dolet, Estienne.

Les Faitz et gestes du Roy Françoys: premier de ce nom tant contre Lempereur que ses subjectz et aultres nations estranges ... depuis 1513 jusques a present. — [Paris?], [Alain Lotrian?], 1544?

8°: A⁶ B⁸ C-D⁴ E⁸ F-G⁴ H⁸ I-K⁴ L⁸ M-N⁴ O⁸ P⁶, goth.

*Paris BN Rés. Lb³⁰.3 (-P 3-6).

References: Longeon *Dolet* #124. Moore #124.

Notes: An addition presents events from 1542 and 1543, ending with a mention of a monstrous birth on 19 Jan. 1544.

D 37.   [Dolet, Estienne], extracts from Jean Carion.

Des faictz et gestes du Roy Françoys premier de ce nom. — [Paris], [Charles Langelier], 1546?

8°: A⁴ B-H⁸, rom.

*Paris BN Rés. pG 24.

Notes: Adaptation and extension of Dolet's text.

D 38.   Dolet, Estienne.

Sommaire et recueil des faictz et gestes, du Roy Françoys premier de ce nom, tant contre L'empereur que ses subjectz, et autres nations estranges ... depuis 1513 jusques à present. — Paris, Alain Lotrian, 1543.

8°: A-M⁴, rom.   M 4r: Impr. à Paris par Alain lotrian, escu de France.

*Berne StU w.92. *Paris BN Rés. Lb³⁰.2. Rouen BM Leber 3879(1).

References: Longeon *Dolet* #121. Rothschild #2117.

D 39.   Dolet, Estienne.

Sommaire et recueil des faictz et gestes, du Roy Françoys premier de ce non, tant contre L'empereur que ses subjectz, et aultre nations Estranges ... de puis 1513 Jusques a present. — Rouen, Jean Petit, Nicolas de Burges, 1543.

8°: A-K⁴, rom.   K 4v: De l'imprimerie de Jehan Petit.

Dijon 16188. Stuttgart Franz.geschich 8° 582.
References: Longeon *Dolet* #123.

D 40.   **Doré, Pierre.**

L'adresse du pecheur. — Paris, Jean Ruelle, 1549.
References: Frankfurt cat. 1610. Brunet (ref. to 1548).

D 41.   **Doré, Pierre.**

Les Allumettes du feu divin, pour faire ardre les cueurs humains en lamour de dieu... Avec les Voyes de paradis. — Paris, Estienne Caveiller, pr. François Regnault et Jean Ruelle, 1538.
8°: a-s^8 t^4 A-F^8, goth. t 2v: Impr. à Paris par Estienne Caveiller imprimeur.
*Bruxelles BR LP 481 A. *Paris BSG D 8° 6199/2 Rés. inv. 7898.
Notes: Brussels copy: 'enseigne de Lelephant' (Regnault). BSG copy: 'enseigne de la queue de regnard' (Ruelle). Dedic. to 'une devote seur, religieuse au royal monastere de Poyssi'. *Les Voyes de Paradis* announced on the t.p., but given an independent collation (A-F^8).

D 42.   **Doré, Pierre.**

Les Allumettes du feu divin pour faire ardre les cueurs humains en lamour de dieu... Avec les Voyes de Paradis. — Paris, Jean Petit, Fr. Regnault, 1538.
8°: a-s^8 t^4 A-F^8 (*Voyes*), goth. t 2v: Impr. à Paris.
*Paris BA T 7367 8°. *Troyes BM G 16.4525(1) (- A1,8). *Aix Méj. Rés. D. 89.
Notes: May be another issue ('ens. S. Nicolas') of the preceding ed.

D 43.   **Doré, Pierre.**

Les Allumettes du feu divin pour faire ardre les cueurs humains en lamour de dieu: Ou sont declairez les principaulx articles et mysteres de la passion ... Avec les Voyes de Paradis. — Paris, [Estienne Caveiller], [Alain Lotrian], 1538.
8°: 146 + [2] ff., a-s^8 t^4 A-F^8 (*Voyes*), goth. t 2v: Impr. à Paris.
*London BL 1360.b.7 (- F8).
References: Britnell, *Bouchet.*

Notes: The t.p. address is 'rue neufve n. Dame, à l'enseigne de lescu de France' (= Alain Lotrian in 1538). Another issue of the preceding two entries?

D 44.   Doré, Pierre.

Les Allumettes du feu divin, pour faire ardre les cueurs humains en lamour de dieu... Avec les Voyes de paradis. — Paris, Estienne Caveiller, Jean Ruelle, 1539.
8°: a-s⁸ t⁴ A-F⁸, goth. t 2v: Impr. à Paris par Estienne Caveiller.
*Paris BSG D 8° 6199(2) Rés. Inv 7898.
Notes: T.p.: 'Rue s. Jacques, à l'enseigne de la queue de regnard'. *Les Allumettes* dedic. to 'une devote seur, religieuse au royal monastere de Poyssi.' *Les Voyes to* Françoyse de Bouchet, Comtesse de Montfort.

D 45.   Doré, Pierre.

Les Allumettes du feu divin, pour faire ardre les cueurs humains en lamour de Dieu... Avec les Voyes de paradis. — Paris, Antoine Bonnemere, G. Le Bret, 1540.
8°: A-Z AA-FF⁸ GG⁴, rom. X 2r & GG 4v: Impr. a Paris par Anthoine bonnemere [GG 4v adds 'et Guillaume le bret']. 1540.
Ghent UB Rés. 994. *Paris BN Rés. D 32762. Paris BM 49269. Lyon BV 321726.
References: Machiels #D 305. Farge *Bio.reg.* p. 139.
Notes: Guillaume Le Bret's initials in the t.p. border. A separate 't.p.', X 4v, for the *Voyes de paradis*, with the initials NS in the border.

D 46.   Doré, Pierre.

Les Allumettes du feu divin pour faire ardre les cueurs humains en l'amour de Dieu... Avecques les Voyes de Paradis. — Paris, Guillaume Thibout, 1548.
16°: a-z A-G⁸, rom. y 1v et G 8v: Impr. à Paris par Guillaume Thibout. 1548.
*Rouen BM Dieusy p 594.
Notes: *Les Voyes de Paradis* have a separate 't.p.', y 4r. But the collation is continuous.

D 47.   Doré, Pierre.

Les Allumettes du feu divin. — Paris, Jean Ruelle, 1548.

References: Farge *Bio.reg.* p. 139.

D 48. **Doré, Pierre.**

Les allumettes du feu divin. — Lyon?, 1550?
References: Farge *Bio.reg.* p. 139 <Baudrier XII,164-5.
Notes: According to Baudrier, 200 copies of this ed. were seized from the printer on 16 March 1551.

D 49. **Doré, Pierre.**

Anti-Calvin, contenant deux defenses catholiques de la verité du sainct Sacrement. — Paris, 1551.
References: Farge *Bio.reg.* p. 142.

D 50. **Doré, Pierre.**

L'arbre de vie, appuyant les beaux lys de France, ou sont mis en lumiere les haults titres d'honneur de la croix de nostre redempteur Jesus. — Paris, Vivant Gaultherot, 1540.
8°.
References: Dagens.

D 51. **Doré, Pierre.**

L'arbre de vie, appuyant les beaux lys de France, ou sont mis en lumiere les haults tiltres d'honneur de la croix de nostre redempteur Jesus. — Paris, Guillaume de Bossozel, Vivant Gaultherot et Jean Foucher, 1542.
8°: 175 + [1] ff., A-Y⁸, rom. Y 8r: Impr. à Paris par Guillaume Bossozel pr. Vivant Gaulterot et Jehan Foucher. 1542.
*London BL 4400.ff.53. *Paris BA 8° T 7415. *Paris BN Rés. D 80253. *Munich BSB P.O. gall. 340/1.
References: Frankfurt cat. 1610. Farge *Bio.reg.* p. 140.
Notes: Priv. (Y 8r) to V. Gaultherot for three years, dated 12 Jan. 1541. The work is dedic. to Francis I. The 'arbre de vie' is the cross.

D 52. **Doré, Pierre.**

L'arche de l'alliance nouvelle, et testament de nostre Saulveur Jesus Christ, contenant la manne de son precieux corps, contre tous sacramentaires heretiques. — Paris, Benoist Prevost, Jean Ruelle, 1549.

8°: [18]+233+[1] ff., ã ẽ⁸ ĩ² A-Z Aa-Ff⁸ Gg², rom. Gg 1v: Impr. à Paris par Benoist Prevost, rue Frementel, ens. Estoille d'or. 1549. Ghent UB Theol 1697. *Paris BN D 21877. Marseille. Douai.
References: Machiels #D 306. Frankfurt cat. 1610. Farge *Bio.reg.* p. 141.
Notes: Priv. (ã 1v) to J. Ruelle for four years, but undated. Dedic. to Henri II. Three-quarters of chap. 1 (27 pp.) is direct quotation from Calvin, *Inst.* (1541), chap. 7.

D 53.   Doré, Pierre.

Le cerf spirituel, exprimant le sainct desir de l'Ame, d'estre avec son Dieu, Selon qu'il est insinué au Psalme de David, 41... Avec L'adresse de l'esgaré pecheur. — Paris, Jean Ruelle, 1544.
16°: ã⁸ ẽ⁸ A-Y AA-QQ⁸, rom. QQ 8v: Impr. à Paris, pour Jehan Ruelle. *Wolfenbüttel HAB Yv 1492.8° Helmst.
References: Farge *Bio.reg.* p. 141.
Notes: The priv. (ã 1v) dated 9 June 1544 to Jean Ruelle and Jean de Brouilly: prob. a shared ed. Dedic. to 'Renée de Lorraine, abbesse de S. Pierre de Reims'.

D 54.   Doré, Pierre.

Le Cerf Spirituel, exprimant le sainct desir de l'Ame, d'estre avec son Dieu, Selon qu'il est insinue au Psalme de David, 41. — Paris, Jean Ruelle, ?
16°: A-M⁸, rom. M 7v: Impr. à Paris.
*Paris BA 8° T 6943 and 8° T 6959(4). *Rouen BM Leber 334.
Notes: Probably later than 1551 (BA 6959 copy bound with several later texts, *c.* 1554).

D 55.   Doré, Pierre.

La premiere partie des Collations royales, contenant l'exposition de deux Psalmes Davidiques ... 24 et 26... Le Chevallier errant ... le Chevalier hardy... — Paris, René Avril, Jean André et Jean Ruelle, 1546.
8°: 428 pp. + [1 f.], a-z A-D⁸, rom. D 8r: Impr. à Paris par René Apvril pour Jehan André et Jehan Ruelle. 1546.
*Troyes BM K.15.7287 (André). *Paris BA 8° T 869 (Ruelle). *Paris BN A 6838.
References: Frankfurt cat. 1610. Farge *Bio.reg.* p. 141.

Notes: Two issues of t.p. Originally sermons preached in Lent 1545 by Doré before Claude de Lorraine duc de Guise, to whom Doré dedicates his work.

D 56.   Doré, Pierre.

La seconde partie, des collations royalles, contenant le trespas du Roy des Chevaliers Chrestiens, mort au lict d'honneur, en la Croix: selon que David l'enseigne, au Psalme 21. Avec ung nouvel office. — Paris, René Avril, Jean André, Jean Ruelle, 1546.

8°: 308 pp., a-r^8 s^4 t-v^8, rom. s 4r: Impr. à Paris, par René Apvril, pour Jehan André et Jehan Ruelle.
*Paris BN A 6838(2).
Notes: t-v^8: *Officium in festo desponsationis beatae Mariae*, dated 1546 (cf. *Image*, 1547). Dedic. by Doré to Antoinette de Bourbon duchesse de Guise. Priv. (a 1v) for both parts to André and Ruelle for three years, dated 09.03.1545 (a.s.).

D 57.   Doré, Pierre.

Le College de sapience, fondé en Luniversité de Vertu, auquel cest rendue escolliere Magdelaine disciple et Apostole de JESUS. Avec le Dialogue de la Foy, adjousté et recongneu. — Paris, Antoine Bonnemere, 1539.

8°: 168 + [7] ff., A-Z a-m^8 n^4, rom.
*Paris BA 8° T 6955 (erreur de reliure). *Paris BN Rés. R 2044 (- A 4,5). *Wolfenbüttel HAB 1028.19 Theol. London BL 1360.f.8. *Paris BM 49405 (+).
References: Dagens. Frankfurt cat. 1610. Farge *Bio.ref.* p. 139. Britnell *Bouchet.*
Notes: Y 8r sqq.: incorporates the *Dialogue instructoire*, with separate t.p. Certified by Doctors Deauratus, Thierry, Divolle, Corrigie and de Bolo (n 4v) in the priv. dated 17.11.1539.

D 58.   Doré, Pierre.

Le College de sapience. — Paris, Jean de Brouilly, 1546.
References: Farge *Bio.ref.* p. 139.

D 59.   Doré, Pierre.

Le College de sapience, fonde en l'universite de Vertu. — Paris, Pierre Sergent, 1546.

16°: A-Z Aa-Bb⁸, rom.
*Troyes BM G.17.4625. *Paris BA 8° T 6956 (- A1).
Notes: Dedic. to 'une bien humble servante de Jesus, en Bloix'. Does not contain the *Dialogue instructoire*.

D 60.   Doré, Pierre.

La Conserve de grace. — Paris, Guillaume Cavellat, 1548.
References: Frankfurt cat. 1610. Brunet. Farge *Bio.ref.* p. 141.

D 61.   Doré, Pierre.

La croix de penitence, enseignant la forme de se confesser, avec le cri du penitent, contenu au psalme penitentiel De profundis clamavi. — Paris, Mathurin Du Puys, 1545.
8°.
Paris BA. Troyes BM.
References: Dagens. Farge *Bio.reg.* p. 141 ('Jean Ruelle').

D 62.   Doré, Pierre.

La croix de penitence. — Paris, Jean Ruelle, 1548.
References: Frankfurt cat. 1610.

D 63.   Doré, Pierre.

La Deploration de la vie humaine, avec la disposition a dignement recepvoir le Sainct Sacrement, et mourir en bon catholicque. — Paris, Nicolas Barbou, pr. Jean de Brouilly, 1541.
16°: A-Y Aa-Hh⁸, rom. Hh 8v: Impr. à Paris par Nicolas Barbou impr. pour Jehan de Brully libr. 1541.
*Paris BSG D 8° 6428(2) Rés.
Notes: Dedic. to Loyse de Bourbon, abbesse de Fontevrault.

D 64.   Doré, Pierre.

La deploration de la vie humaine, avec la disposition a dignement recepvoir le Sainct Sacrement, et mourir en bon catholicque. Avec le sermon funebre ... de feu messire Philippes chabot. — Paris, Jean de Brouilly, 1543.
16°: A-Y Aa-Ll⁸, rom. Ll 8r: Impr. à Paris pour Jehan de Broully libr., ens. S. Genevieve. 1543.

*Wolfenbüttel HAB 1325.2 Theol.
References: Farge *Bio.reg.* p. 140.

D 65.   Doré, Pierre.

*La deploration de la vie humaine, avec la disposition
à dignement recepvoir le S. Sacrement, et mourir en
bon catholique. Avec le sermon funebre ... de feu
messire Philippes Chabot.* — Paris, Guillaume Thibout, 1548.
16°: a-v⁸, rom. v 8r: Impr. à Paris par Guillaume Thibout, ens. du Paon.
*Wolfenbüttel HAB 1329.19 Theol.
References: Farge *Bio.reg.* p. 140.

D 66.   Doré, Pierre.

*Dialogue instructoire, des Chrestiens en la foy, espe-
rance, et amour de Dieu.* — Lyon, Pierre de Sainte-
Lucie, 1538.
8°: A-P⁴ Q², rom.
Terrebasse.
References: Baudrier XII, 172. Farge *Bio.reg.* p. 139.
Notes: A refutation of Gaspard Megander's catechism. See
Higman 'Doré'.

D 67.   Doré, Pierre.

*Dyalogue Instructoire des Chrestiens en la Foy, espe-
rance, et amour en Dieu.* — Paris, Jean Réal, Vincent
Sertenas, 1538.
8°: A-O⁸, rom. O 7r: Impr. à Paris par Jehan Real, ens. des Corbillons.
*Paris BN Rés. D 32766.
References: Farge *Bio.reg.* p. 139.

D 68.   Doré, Pierre.

*Dialogue. Instructoire, des Chrestiens en la foy, Espe-
rance, et Amour en Dieu.* — Paris, Antoine Bonnemere, 1539.
8°: [1] + 106 + [2] ff., Z⁸ a-m⁸ n⁴, rom.
London BL 1360.b.7. *Paris BN Rés. R 2045 (-g4,5).
References: Farge *Bio.reg.* p. 139.
Notes: In fact printed as a continuation (Y 8r sqq.) of the *College de Sapience*, q.v.

D 69.   **Doré, Pierre.**
Dyalogue Instructoire des Chrestiens, en la Foy, Espe-rance, et Amour en Dieu. — Paris, Denis Janot, 1542.
16°: A-Y⁸, goth.
*Paris BN Rés. D 13571.
References: Rawles #168. Farge *Bio.reg.* p. 139.

D 70.   **Doré, Pierre.**
Dyalogue instructoire. — Paris, Denis Janot, 1544.
References: Farge *Bio.reg.* p. 139.

D 71.   **Doré, Pierre.**
Dialogue Instructoire, des Chrestiens en la foy, Espe-rance, et Amour en dieu. Nouvellement adjousté et recongneu. — Paris, René Avril, pr. Jean Ruelle, 1544.
16°: a-s⁸, rom. s 8v: Impr. par René Apvril impr., pour Jehan Real libr., Paris. 1544.
*Paris BSG D8° 6197(2) inv 7892 bis Rés.

D 72.   **Doré, Pierre.**
Dialogue Instructoire, des chrestiens en la foy, espe-rance, et Amour en Dieu: Nouvellement adjousté et recongneu. — Paris, Guillaume Thibout, Jean de Brouilly, 1545.
16°: a-s⁸, rom. s 8v: Impr. à Paris par Guillaume Thihout [!].
*Versailles BM Pérate A 42.
References: Farge *Bio.reg.* p. 139. *NUC* ND 0338626.

D 73.   **Doré, Pierre.**
Limage de vertu demonstrant la perfection et saincte vie de la bienheuree vierge Marie, par les escriptures. — Paris, Pierre Vidoue, Jérôme de Gourmont, 1540.
8°: #⁴ +⁸ a-z A-Z Aa-Ff⁸ Gg⁴, rom. Ff 8v: 1540. Gg 4r: Impr. à Paris par P. Vidoue.
*Versailles BM Pérate B 34.
References: Renouard MSS: 'Vidoue, 14 nov. 1540. Versailles' Same ed.?
Notes: 50 chapters, presenting the Virgin Mary as the eighth wonder of the world, plus 'Office de la desponsation de la vierge.' Each chap. introduced by a quotation from the Song of Songs.

D 74. **Doré, Pierre.**

L'image de vertu demonstrant la perfection et saincte vie de la bienheuree vierge Marie mere de dieu, par les escriptures. — Paris, Nicolas Bonfons?, Jérôme de Gourmont, Jean de Brouilly, 1540.
8°: [8] + 416 ff., +⁸ a-z A-Z Aa-Ff⁸, rom.
*Aix Méj. 8° 8448.
References: Dagens. Farge *Bio.reg.* p. 140: 'Jérôme de Gourmont'. Same ed.?
Notes: Aix copy: priv. to J. de Gourmont and J. de Brouilly for three years, dated 14.11.1540. The Aix copy has part of a gathering Gg bound at the beginning ('Epistre au lecteur', table).

D 75. **Doré, Pierre.**

L'image de vertu, demonstrant la perfection et saincte vie de la bien heuree vierge Marie, mere de Dieu par les Escritures. — Paris, Nicolas Bonfons, 1547?
8°: [8] + 408 ff., ã⁸ A-Z Aa-Zz AA-EE⁸, rom.
*Paris BN D 32767.
Notes: O 6v: letter from P. Doré to Pope Paul III dated 31 March 1546. The BN copy has t.p. damage making the date illegible. The initial gathering contains a 'Prologue de l'auteur' (but without dedication), followed by a table.

D 76. **Doré, Pierre.**

L'image de Vertu, demonstrant la perfection et saincte vie de la bienheurée vierge Marie, mere de Dieu, par les escriptures... La seconde edition nouvellement reveue, additionnée, & quotée sur la marge. — Paris, René Avril, Jean de Brouilly, 1549.
8°: [12]+333+[1] ff., aa⁸ bb⁴ a-z A-T⁸, rom. T 8v: Impr. à Paris, par René Avril. 1549.
Cambrai. Valognes. *London BL C.46.b.1.
References: Farge *Bio.reg.* p. 140.
Notes: Priv. to J. de Brouilly for four years, dated 18 March 1548. Epistle by Doré to Catherine de Sarrebruche, Contesse de Roussy. Fifty-five chapters on the life of Mary in the form of a rosary.

D 77.   Doré, Pierre.

L'image de vertu, demonstrant La perfection et saincte vie de la bienheurée vierge Marie, mere de Dieu, par les escriptures... La tierce edition, nouvellement reveue et corrigée. — Paris, Jean Ruelle, ?
8°: aa⁸ bb⁴ a-z A-T⁸, rom.
*Troyes BM D.13.6917 (- aa1). *Rome Casanatense x.xx.4. * Aix Méj. 8° 8276.
Notes: Address on t.p.: 'Jean Ruelle, r. S. Jacques, ens. queue de Regnard' (address which he left in 1556). The text is 'déclaratif de la tressaincte vie de nostre Dame' (aa 7r), and seems to follow exactly the second ed. Dedic. (aa 2r) to 'Catherine de Sarrebruche, comtesse de Roussy et Dame de Muret'. Doré's message to Pope Paul III on fol. 1 6v, with the date 31 March 1546.

D 78.   Doré, Pierre.

Le Livre des divins benefices, enseignant la maniere de les recongnoistre. Avec Linformation de bien vivre, et la consolation des affligez ... Ps. 33. Avec la consolation evangelique. — Paris, Benoist Prevost, Jean Ruelle, 1544.
8°: [8] + 151 ff., ã⁸ A-T⁸, rom.
Le Mans. *Paris BN D 86037 (- T8).
References: Dagens. Frankfurt cat. 1610. Farge *Bio.reg.* p. 140. Droz *Chemins* I, 346-51.
Notes: The *Table* of the first three books printed before Bk 4. The priv. (ã 1v) to J. Ruelle for three years, dated 03.03.43. Dedic. to 'une bien devote dame parisienne'. The title imitated from Seneca.

D 79.   Doré, Pierre.

Le livre des divins benefices, enseignant la maniere de les recongnoistre. Avec l'information de bien vivre, et la consolation des affligez ... Psalme 33. — Paris, Jean Ruelle, ?
16°: A⁸ A-Z & AA-EE⁸ FF⁶, rom.
*Aix Méj. 16° 292.

D 80.   Doré, Pierre.

La meditation devote du bon Chrestien sus le sainct sacrifice de la Messe. — Paris, Jean Ruelle, 1544.

16°: A-Q⁸, rom.
*Paris BSG D 8° 6197(1) Inv 7892 bis Rés.
References: Dagens. Farge *Bio.reg.* p. 140.

D 81.   Doré, Pierre.

Oraison Panegyrique ... pour hault et puissant prince, Claude de Lorraine, Duc de Guyse, Per de France, decedé ceste presente année, 1550. <> Avec la doulce Musique Davidique, ouye au Cantique .125 ...Item un Remede salutaire contre les Scrupules de conscience. — Paris, Jean de Brouilly, 1550.
8°: 128 ff., ãã⁸ A-P⁸, ital.
*Paris BA 8° BL 3258. *Paris BN Rés. 8° Ln²⁷.9400.
References: Farge *Bio.reg.* p. 142.
Notes: Claude de Lorraine died in 1550. Doré had been his confessor. His 'oraison' is a 'lamentation consolable, ou consolation lamentable, entremeslée du vieil et nouveau testament, au nouveau consolation, au viel lamentation, que j'ay faicte selon l'ordre de l'alphabet Hebraique' (A 7v).

D 82.   Doré, Pierre. sermon by St Cyprian.

La Passe-solitaire à tous amateurs de Dieu. — Paris, Jean de Brouilly, 1547.
16°: A-S⁸, rom.
Amiens. *Paris BA 8° T 6957.
References: Farge *Bio.reg.* p. 141.
Notes: Includes a commentary on Ps. 123(124), and a sermon by St Cyprian *De Mortalitate.*

D 83.   Doré. Pierre.

La Passe-solitaire. — Paris, 1549.
References: Farge *Bio.reg.* p. 141.

D 84.   Doré, Pierre.

Le Pasturage de la brebis humaine, selon que lenseigne le Royal prophete David au vingtdeuxiesme Psalme. Avec lanatomie et mystique description des membres et parties du nostre Saulveur Jesus Christ. — Paris, Jean de Brouilly, 1546.
16°: A-Z a⁸ b⁴, rom. b 3v: Impr. à Paris.
*Aix Méj. C. 8976.
References: Renouard MSS. Farge *Bio.reg.* p. 141.

Notes: Dedic. (A 1v) to 'ma bonne fille spirituelle et escolliere Parisienne'. The 'anatomie ... de Jesuchrist' (begins N 5r) is very up to date: just as doctors cut up executed criminals in order to understand the functioning of the human body, Doré intends to do the same with the body of Christ crucified for the edification of the faithful.

D 85.   Doré, Pierre.

La celeste pensée, des graces divines arrousée. — Paris, Jean Ruelle, 1543.
8°.
Epernay.
References: Dagens. Renouard MSS. Farge *Bio.reg.* p. 140.

D 86.   Doré, Pierre.

La caeleste pensée de graces divines arrousée, ou sont declairez les sept dons du sainct esprit, et la maniere de les demander à Dieu. — Paris, Adam Saulnier, pr. Jean André, 1543.
8°: a-y^8 z^4. Impr. à Paris par Adam Saulnier pour Jehan André. 17.09.43.
Bordeaux BM T 7106.
Notes: My thanks to Mme H. de Bellaigue of the Bordeaux BM for this description.

D 87.   Doré, Pierre.

La celeste pensée, des graces divines arrousée. — Paris, Adam Saulnier, pr. Jean André, 1546.
References: Farge *Bio.reg.* p. 140.

D 88.   Doré, Pierre, [Martin Luther].

La Piscine de patience ... avec le Miroir de Patience, veu et corrigé. — Paris, Benoist Prevost, Jean Ruelle, 1550.
16°: A-K^8, ital.
*Paris BA 8° T 6959(1).
References: Farge *Bio.reg.* p. 142.
Notes: Dedic. to Anthoinette de Bourbon duchesse douairière de Guise. A printer having shown Doré a printed text *Le Miroir de patience*, Doré has corrected it and 'lavé à la piscine de patience'. The *Miroir* is an unknown, and archaic,

translation of Luther's *Tessaradecas Consolatoria.* See Luther, *Consolation.*

D 89.   Doré, Pierre.

Le Nouveau Testament d'amour, de nostre Pere Jesus Christ, signé de son sang. Autrement, son dernier sermon, faict apres la Cene, avec sa passion, ou sont confutées plusieurs heresies. — Paris, Benoist Prevost, pr. Jean Ruelle, 1550.

8°: ã⁸ a-z A-S⁸, rom. S 8v: Impr. à Paris par Benoist Prevost. 1550.
*Munich BSB Asc. 1488.
References: Farge *Bio.reg.* pp. 141-2.
Notes: Priv. to Jean Ruelle for six years, but undated. Dedic. (ã 2r-5v) to Queen of France: discussion on the utility of making plain text of scripture available to the laity.

D 90.   Doré, Pierre.

Les Triomphes du Roy sans pair, avec l'excellence de l'Eglise, son espouse, et leur noble lignage. — Paris, Jean de Brouilly, 1548.
Arras (destroyed).
References: Frankfurt cat. 1610. Farge *Bio.reg.* p. 141.
Notes: Commentary on Ps. 44(45).

D 91.   Doré, Pierre.

Les Voyes du Paradis que a enseignees nostre benoist Saulveur Jesus pour la reduction du povre pecheur. — Lyon, François Juste, 1537.
16°.
References: Baudrier *suppl.* #66. Du Verdier III, 263. Farge *Bio.reg.* p. 139.
Notes: The eight 'voyes' are the Beatitudes.

D 92.   Doré, Pierre.

Les Voyes de Paradis que a enseignees nostre benoist saulveur Jesus en son evangile, pour la reduction du povre pecheur. — [Paris], [E. Caveiller], [François Regnault], [Alain Lotrian], 1538.
8°: A-F⁸, goth.
*Bruxelles BR LP 481A. *London BL 1360.b.7 (- F8). *Paris BA 8° T 7367(2) (- F8). *Troyes BM G 16.4515(2). *Aix Méj. Rés. D. 89 (+).
References: Farge *Bio.reg.* p. 139.

Notes: Same typographical material as *Les Allumettes du feu divin* of the same year (with which it is bound in BL copy). Dedic. to Françoyse du Bouchet, Contesse de Montfort.

D 93.   Doré, Pierre.

Les Voyes du Paradis. — Lyon, 1540.
References: Farge *Bio.reg.* p. 139.

D 94.   Doré, Pierre.

Les Voyes de Paradis. — Paris, Antoine Bonnemere, 1540.
References: Farge *Bio.reg.* p. 139.

D 95.   Du Boullay, Emond.

Le combat de la chair, et l'esprit ... Auquel combat la chair sera premierement vaincue en un camp clos de la saincte escripture. Et finablement subjugué, en un autre camp ouvert. — Paris, Jean Longis, 1549.
8°: '72' ff., A-F^8 G^4 H-I^8, rom.
*Aix Méj. C. 3858.
Notes: Priv. (A 1v) to Gilles Corrozet for three years, dated 6 Feb. 1548. Text dedic. to Leonor, Archiduchesse d'Autriche, reine douairière de France. Decasyllabics.

D 96.   Du Buc, Richard.

Devot Traité de la genese. — Paris, Pierre Sergent, Jean Bignon, ?
8°.
References: Renouard MSS < Sale cat.

D 97.   [Dumolin, Guillaume].

Le traicte de lutilite et honneste de mariage. Et sil est licite aux prestres de soy marier. — Strasbourg, Johann Pruss, 1527.
8°: A-E^8, goth. E 5v: Impr. en Argentine par Jehan prüß. 04.04.1527.
*Amsterdam VU XC 05993(4). *London BL 3901.a.3(4).
References: Peter 'Prem. ouvr.' #4. Moore p. 79, ref. to Brunet II,878. Ritter #1528.

D 98.   Dumolin, Guillaume, adapted from Johann Bugenhagen.

Tresutile traicte, du vray regne de antechrist maintenant revele et cogneu, a treshault et trespuissant seigneur, Philippe Marquis Darrescot. — Strasbourg, Johann Pruss, [Johann Knobloch sen.], 1527.
8°: A-C⁸, goth. C 7r: Impr. à Argentine par Jehan Preus. 06.01.1527.
*Amsterdam VU XC 05993(2). *London BL 3901.a.3(3).
References: Peter 'Prem. ouvr.' #2. Moore #127. Ritter #1527.
Notes: Commentary on 2 Thess. 2, taken from Johann Bugenhagen (as Dumolin says, C 6v-7r).

D 99.   Dumolin, Guillaume, adapted from Sebald Heyden.

Notable et utile traicte Du zele et grant desir que doibt avoit ung vray christien pour garder a Jesuchrist son honneur entier. — Strasbourg, Johann Pruss, 1527.
8°: A-D⁸, goth. d 8r: Impr. à Argentine par Jehan Preys impr. 28.01.1527.
*London BL C.37.a.22(1) et 3901.a.3(2).
References: Peter 'Prem. ouvr.' #3. Moore #126. Ritter #1526.
Notes: Dedic. to Madame Bone gouvernante de Tournay et du Tournesis. Moore: adapt. from S. Heyden, *Unum Christum mediatorem esse* (1525).

D 100.   [Du Pinet, Antoine], adapted from François Lambert, Seb. Meyer.

Familiere et briefve exposition sur l'apocalypse De Sainct Jehan l'apostre. — Geneva, Jean Girard, 1539.
8°: a-q⁸, rom.
*Geneva BPU Rés. Bb 1592. *Geneva MHR A 132,1(39). *Zurich ZB D 361. *Zurich ZB D 658 (s.l. s.n.).
References: Moore #172. *BG* 39/9. Bodenmann #17bis a et b. Droz *Chemins* II, 56-60.
Notes: Text based essentially on Fr. Lambert, *Commentariorum ... in S. Ioannis Apocalypsim* (Marburg, 1526), but it is a summary rather than a translation. Mlle Droz suggests the attribution to Antoine Du Pinet, pastor of Ville la Grande (Chablais), who also did a translation of the exchange of letters between Sadolet and Calvin. Censured on 1 Sept. 1543 (Higman *Censorship*, p. 93).

D 101.   **[Du Pinet, Antoine],** adapted from François Lambert, Seb. Meyer.

Exposition sur l'Apocalypse de Sainct Jehan l'Apostre, extraicte de plusieurs docteurs tant anciens que modernes: reveuë, et augmentée de nouveau. — Geneva, Jean Girard, 1543.

8°: α^8 *^{4} a-z A-B^8 C^4 aa-cc^8, rom.

*Geneva BPU Rés. Bb 2364. *Paris BA 8° T 1347.

References: Cat. Drilhon #2. *BG* 43/15. Bodenmann 17bis c. *Index* I, #363.

Notes: Revision, considerably 'reveuë et augmentée', of the *Familiere et briefve exposition* of 1539. Prefatory letter from Antoine Pignet (Du Pinet) to 'Simon Sylvius mon amy', dated from Ville La Grand, 1 Apr. 1543.

D 102.   **[Du Pinet, Antoine],** adapted from François Lambert, Seb. Meyer.

Exposition sur l'apocalypse de sainct Jehan l'apostre, extraicte de plusieurs Docteurs, tant anciens que modernes: reveue, et augmentée de nouveau. — [Geneva], [Jean Girard], 1545.

8°: a^8 b^4 c-z A-D^8 E^4 aa-bb^8, rom.

*Geneva MHR D.Dup.1. *Paris BM 23616. *Paris BN Rés. A 7262. *Wolfenbüttel HAB 1057 Theol. Zurich ZB.

References: *BG* 45/16. Bodenmann 17bis d. *Index* I, #420.

Notes: Page-for-page re-ed. of the 1543 ed. The epistle now dated 1 Apr. 1545.

D 103.   **Dupuyherbault, Gabriel.**

Regle et maniere de prier Dieu purement, deuement et avec efficace: et de s'addresser à luy en tous articles et necessitez, contenant quatre livres. — Paris, Jean de Roigny, 1548.

16°: a-z A-Z Aa-Cc^8, rom.

*Wolfenbüttel HAB Ti 135.

Notes: Priv. (a 2r-v) for five years dated 4 May 1548.

E

E 1.   Échelles de la passion.

Sensuyt ung devot traicte appelle les Eschelles de la passion: par le moyen desquelles on pourra a chascun jour de la sepmaine soy spirituellement occuper a penser a la douloureuse mort et passion de Jesucrist. — Paris, pr. Jean Saint Denys, 1530?

4°: [82] ff., A-D^4 E^8 F-P^4 Q^6 R-T^4, goth. T 4v: Impr. à Paris pour Jehan sainct denys.

*Paris BN Rés. D 80188.

Notes: Dedic. (A 1v) to 'Mgr. le prieur de sainct Martin des champs en paris' (Etienne Gentils, from 1508 to 1536), signed 'le tout vostre petit chapelain et orateur. N.N.' (cf. *Marchandise spirituelle* and J. Mauburne, *Le Beneficiaire divin*). 'N.N.' seems to lay particular stress on daily devotion: the three works signed by him all refer to the days of the week. Devotional meditation on the Passion, with 11 rungs on the ladder, from 'preparation' to 'inseparable union', followed, at end, by 'trois devotz chappeletz: dont les deux premiers sont de la passion de Jesucrist: Et lautre faict mention des douleurs de la vierge marie.'

E 2.   Eck, Johann.

Les Lieux communs de Jean Ekius, contre Luther. — Lyon, Jean Marnax, 1551.

16°: 624 pp., a-z A-Q^8, rom.

*Lyon BV 800633. Strasbourg BNU.

References: Baudrier III, 194. Fraenkel, 'Version française'.

Notes: The printer's address may be false. Another issue of part of the text, s.l.n.d., in Avignon BM. Eck's dedic. to Conrad évêque de Kungen (Albanie) is dated 1539.

E 3.   Édit sur les articles.

Edict sur les articles faictz par la faculte de theologie. — Paris, Denis Janot, pr. Ponce Roffet, 1543.

16°: A-C^8 D^4, goth.

*Paris BEBA Masson 288.

References: Rawles #197.

Notes: The 26 articles of faith of the Paris Theology Faculty were approved on 6 March 1543. On 12 March the king ratified them and sent them to the parlement. After remonstrances by the parlement, the articles were imposed by edict on 23 July and published on 31 July 1543. See *Articles*.

E 4.   **Édit sur les articles.**

Edict du Roy Sur les articles faictz par la faculte de Theologie de luniversite de Paris concernans nostre foy. — Lyon, 1543?
8°: a-b⁴, rom.
*Lincoln cath. RR.6.25(6).
Notes: On the t.p. the address is given 'à Lyon pres Nostre Dame de confort'. Text of the edict in French, but of the articles in Latin.

=>   *Effusions*: see *Quinze effusions*.

E 5.   **Enfant prodigue.**

Lenfant Prodigue par personnaiges. Nouvellement Translate de latin en francoys Selon le texte de levangille. — Paris, [Alain Lotrian], 1530?
4°: A⁸ B-D⁴, goth. D 4r: Impr. à Paris.
*Paris BN Rés. Ye 1596. Aix Méj.
References: Moreau III #2068.
Notes: The explicit, D 4r, says: 'En ceste presente hystoire sont plusieurs parsonnaiges Mais troys principaulx Le pere et ses deux filz desquelz le plus jeune est dit enfant prodigue. Et morallement celuy pere est Dieu et ses deux enfans sont manieres de gens au monde, les ungs bons les autres pecheurs...'

E 6.   **Enseignement trèsutile.**

Ung breif enseignement tire hors de la saincte escripture Pour amener la personne a volentier morir et point craindre la mort. — [Antwerp?], [M. Crom?], 1533?
16°: A-E⁸ F⁴, goth.
*London BL 4405.aa.37.
References: *Index* I, #403.
Notes: French version of *Een cort onderwijs wt der heilighen schrift...*, censured by Louvain, 1546 (*Index* II, 1546/159). The French version already existed in 1541, when it was con-

demned (1 June) by the Faculty of Theology (Higman *Censorship*, pp. 87-8).

E 7.   Enseignement trèsutile.

Enseignement tresutile tiré de la saincte Escriture, pour fortifier la personne à voulentiers mourir, et ne craindre point la mort. — [Geneva], [Jean Girard], 1545.
8°: A-D⁸ E¹⁰, rom.
*Cambridge Emma. 324.7.82(6). *Geneva BPU Rés. Bc 2705. *Lincoln cath. Nn 7.12(2). *London St Pauls 38.E.26(1). Vienna ÖNB 79.Ee.7 (missing).
References: Moore #129. *BG* 45/17.
Notes: Re-ed. of *Un breif enseignement* (previous item). This title already on the 1544 *Index*, so the present item is a re-ed. of it.

E 8.   Enseignement trèsutile.

Enseignement tresutile tiré de la saincte Escriture, pour fortifier la personne à volontiers mourir, et ne craindre point la mort. — [Geneva], [Jean Girard], 1551.
8°: A-D⁸, rom.
*London BL 3103.a.30.

E 9.   Épître consolatoire.

Epistre consolatoire à une soeur soufrant persecution. — [Geneva?], 1544.
References: *BG* 44/15. *Index* I, #421 (1547). Th. Dufour MS.fr. 3807#124: < sale cat., 1725.
Notes: In the Du Fay sale cat. this text is described as bound with four Genevan eds of 1543-45. A later ed., [Geneva], A. Cercia, 1555, in Vienna ÖNB, 17.J.82.

E 10.   Épître d'un gentilhomme.

Epistre d'un gentilhomme à un sien ami contenant la perfection Chrestienne, traduite de l'Italien. — Toulouse, Guyon Boudeville, pr. Thomas Du Fert, 1546.
References: *Rép.bib.* Toulouse: Du Fert #2. Frankfurt cat. 1610. Du Verdier I, 553.

E 11.   Épître d'un gentilhomme.

Epistre d'un gentilhomme à un sien ami contenant la perfection Chrestienne, traduite de l'italien. — Lyon, Thibaud Payen, 1549.
References: Baudrier IV, 242. *Index* I, #418.

E 12.   Épître de s. Jacques.

L'Epistre Catholique de Sainct Jaques Apostre. Avec une exposition breve, et bien facile. — Geneva, Jean Girard, 1541.
8°: A-L⁸ M⁴, rom/ital.
*Geneva BPU Rés. Bb 2363 (s.l. s.n.). *Paris BM Rés. 49186(2) (s.l. s.n.). *Stuttgart LB Bibl.gall 8° 1541.
References: *BG* 41/6. *Index* I #406, 407.

E 13.   Épîtres de s. Paul.

Les Epistres sainct Pol glosees. — Paris, Michel Le Noir, 1521.
Paris BN?
Notes: This first biblical commentary in French first appeared in 1507, Paris, Antoine Verard (copies in London BL and Paris BN). The author of the gloss is described as a Doctor of Theology and Augustinian.

E 14.   Épîtres de s. Paul.

Les Epistres de monseigneur Sainct Paul glosées, par un venerable Docteur en la faculté de Theologie. — Paris, Charles Langelier, 1544.
8°: A-Z Aa-Bb⁸, rom. Bb 8r: 'nouvellement imprimées à Paris. 1544'.
*Paris BN A 10870.
References: Droz *Chemins* I, 340.
Notes: As explained in a note from the printer, t.p. verso, the 'gloses' are the same as in the previous eds (1507, 1521). But (and this is not explained) the text of St Paul is based on the New Testament printed in Geneva by Jean Girard in 1539 (identification made by B. Roussel). The Louvain theologians criticized their Parisian colleagues for not censuring this text in 1544.

E 15. **Erasme, Desiderius,** trans. Louis de Berquin, extracts from Farel.

Brefve admonition de la maniere de prier ... avec une brefve explanation du Pater noster. Extraict des paraphrases de Erasme. — [Paris], [Simon Du Bois], 1525?

8°: A⁸, goth.

Geneva BPU Rés. Bc 651 and Bb 806(4).

References: Moore #134. Clutton #37. *Index* I #321. Moreau III #813. Facs. reprod. Telle, *TLF*, 1979.

Notes: The text is based on Erasmus's paraphrases on Matthew and Luke. Certain 'additions', including the 'Breve admonition', are taken from [Farel et Luther], *L'Oraison de Jesuchrist* (*c.* 1525). Censured on 20 May 1525 (Higman *Censorship*, pp. 75-6).

E 16. **Erasme, Desiderius,** trans. Antoine Macault.

Les Apophthegmes. Cest à dire promptz subtilz et sententieulx ditz de plusieurs Royz: chefz darmee: philosophes et autres grans personnaiges tant Grecz que Latins. — Paris, Charlotte Guillard, 1539.

8°: a-z A-N⁸, rom.

*Paris SHP A 1189.

E 17. **Erasme, Desiderius,** trans. Antoine Macault.

Les Apophthegmes, c'est à dire prompt, subtilz, et sententieux dictz de plusieurs roys, chefz d'armées, Philosophes et autres grans personnaiges, tant Grecz que Latins. — Paris, Charles Langelier, 1547.

16°: a-z A-Z⁸, rom.

*Bruxelles BR LP 6991A.

Notes: a 1v and Z 8r: poems by Clément Marot.

E 18. **Erasme, Desiderius,** trans. Antoine Macault.

Les Apophthegmes, cueilliz par Didier Erasme de Roterdam. — Lyon, Balthazar Arnoullet, pr. Thibaud Payen, 1549.

16°: a-z A-X⁸, rom. X 7v: impr. à Lyon par Balthazar Arnoullet.

*Bruxelles BR LP VI.32240A.

E 19.   Erasme, Desiderius, trans. Pierre Saliat.

La Civilité puerile. — Lyon, Jean de Tournes, 1544.
16°: A-D⁸, rom.
*Paris BN Rés. pR 376.
References: Cartier *De Tournes* #33.

E 20.   Erasme, Desiderius, trans. Clément Marot.

Colloque d'Erasme ... intitulé Abbatis et Eruditae.
— ?, ?, 1548?
16°: a-d⁸, rom.
*Paris BN Rés. Ye 1573.
References: Mayer *Marot* #166.
Notes: The colloquy 'De l'abbé et de la femme sçavante' (a 2r-b
5r) is followed by 'de la vierge mesprisant mariage'. General
condemnation of the *Colloquia* (in Latin) in 1544 (*Index* I #94).
This is probably a Parisian ed., but very anonymous.

E 21.   Erasme, Desiderius, trans. Clément Marot.

Deux colloques d'Erasme ... Abbatis et Eruditae,
l'autre Virgo Misogamos. — Lyon, Jean Le Converd,
1549.
16°: 40 ff.
References: Mayer *Marot* #168. Baudrier I, 103.

E 22.   Erasme, Desiderius, trans. Clément Marot.

Deux colloques d'Erasme plus le Balladin du mesme
Marot. — Paris, Guillaume Thibout, 1549.
16°: 40 ff.
References: Mayer *Marot* #167.

E 23.   Erasme, Desiderius, trans. B. Aneau.

Comedie ou dialogue matrimonial, exemplaire de
paix en mariage, extraict du devis <> Uxor memphi-
gamos, C'est à dire: La femme mary plaignant. —
Paris, Denis Janot, Jean Longis et Vincent Sertenas,
1541.
8°: A-C⁸ D⁴, ital.
*Paris BN Rés. Yf 4354.
References: Rawles #143. Renouard MSS.

E 24. **Erasme, Desiderius,** trans. Louis de Berquin?

La complainte de la Paix. — [Lyon], [Pierre de Vingle], 1531?
8°: a-b cc-gg⁸, goth.
*Bruxelles BR LP II 64573A. Harvard CL.
References: Walsh *Harvard Ly Bull* 17(1969). Facs. ed. Telle, *TLF*, 1978.
Notes: The French trans. of the *Querela pacis* was condemned in MS, under the title *Declamation de la paix*, in June 1525 (Higman *Censorship*, pp. 75-7).

E 25. **[Erasme, Desiderius],** trans. Pierre Saliat.

Declamation contenant la maniere de bien instruire les enfans ... avec ung petit traicté de la civilité puerile. — Paris, Simon de Colines, 1537.
8°: a-k⁸, rom. k 7v: impr. à Paris par Simon de Colines. 02.08.1537.
Bordeaux BM. *London BL 8306.aaa.3. *Paris BM Rés. 28029(3). *Paris BN Rés. R 2365. *Wolfenbüttel HAB Lg 1814.2(2) (+).
References: Moore #137.

E 26. **Erasme, Desiderius,** trans. [Georges d'Halewijn].

De la declamation des louenges de follie, stille facessieux et profitable pour congnoistre les erreurs et abuz du monde. — Paris, Pierre Vidoue, pr. Galliot Du Pré, 1520.
4°: [4] + 68 ff., π⁴ A-L⁸/⁴, goth. L 8r: Impr. à Paris par Pierre vidoue pour Galliot du pre. 02.08.1520.
*London BL 90.h.15 (gathering π misbound). *Paris BN Rés. Y² 949. *Paris BSG Z 4° 395 inv 271 Rés. (-π 1-4, L 6-8). *Rouen BM Leber 2650. Harvard CL (+).
References: Moreau II, #2324.
Notes: Priv. to Du Pré for three years, dated 24.07.1520. Numerous engravings. The translator is identified, *Erasmi Op.Epis.* III, 4 and 63. The Latin original was condemned by the Sorbonne in the 1543 list, and *Index* I #91.

E 27. **Erasme, Desiderius,** trans. Louis de Berquin.

Declamation des louenges de mariage. — [Paris], [Simon Du Bois], 1525?
8°: a-c⁸ d⁴, goth.
*Geneva BPU Rés. Bb 806(3).

References: Moore #134. Moreau III #816. Clutton #38. Facs. ed. Telle, *TLF*, 1976.
Notes: Condamned in MS by the Sorbonne, May 1525 (Higman *Censorship*, pp. 75-6).

E 28.   Erasme, Desiderius, trans. Louis de Berquin?

Enchidirion (ou Manuel) du chevalier Chrestien: aorne de commandemens tressalutaires ... avec un prologue merveilleusement utile et de nouveau adjouste. — [Antwerp], Martin Lempereur, 1529.
8°: A-R⁸, goth.
Ghent UB Res. 820. *Munich UB 8° Theol 4437.
References: NK #880. Machiels #E 419. Marcel *Coll. Eras. Tur.* II, 634 sqq.
Notes: The Latin text condemned by the Sorbonne on 31 Jan. 1540. *Index* I #89 (1544) condemns the Latin original without specifying an edition. The French translation condemned in Dolet's ed.

E 29.   Erasme, Desiderius, trans. Louis de Berquin?

Enchiridion (ou Manuel) du Chevalier Chrestien: aorne de commandemens tressalutaires ... avec ung prologue merveilleusement utile et de nouveau adjouste. — [Lyon], [Pierre de Vingle], 1532?
8°: A-X⁸, goth.
Edinburgh NLS Newb 740. *London BL 697.b.4. Paris SHP R 16072 (missing). *Paris BN Rés. D 67969 et Rés. D 80083. *Chantilly Condé III.F.68.
References: Droz *APR* 61-4. Moore #133.

E 30.   Erasme, Desiderius, trans. Louis de Berquin?

Le Chevalier Chrestien. Premierement composé en Latin par Erasme: et depuis traduict en Francoys. — Lyon, Estienne Dolet, 1542.
16°: a-x⁸ y⁶, rom. y 6r: impr. à Lyon chés Estienne Dolet. 1542.
Dresden SLB Theol.cath. B663. Manchester JRL Christie 3.c.23.
References: Christie #48. Longeon *Dolet* #215. *Index* I, #323.
Notes: This is the ed. of the *Enchidirion* condemned by the Sorbonne in 1543 (Higman *Censorship*, p. 98). See Dolet's preface (Longeon, *Préfaces*, p. 141): Dolet attacks the 'vicieux' who condemn Erasmus's book (as the Paris theologians had done for the Latin in 1540).

E 31. **Erasme, Desiderius,** trans. Louis de Berquin?

Le Chevalier Chrestien. Premierement composé en Latin par Erasme: et depuis traduict en Françoys. — Lyon, Estienne Dolet, 1542.
16°: a-x⁸ y⁶, rom. y 6r: Impr. à Lyon chés Estienne Dolet. 1542.
*Aix Méj. C. 8974.
References: Longeon *Dolet* #216.
Notes: Description identical with that of the preceding number, but the text is entirely recomposed.

E 32. **Erasme, Desiderius,** trans. Louis de Berquin?

Le Chevalier Chrestien, Composé en Latin par Erasme, et puis traduict en langue Françoyse. — Lyon, Jean de Tournes, 1542.
1 ⸱ : a-v⁸, rom.
*Paris BN Rothschild IV.7.55.
References: Cartier *De Tournes* #3. Rothschild #2748.
Notes: De Tournes follows Dolet's ed., but omits the latter's preface.

E 33. **Erasme, Desiderius,** trans. Louis de Berquin?

Enchiridion, ou manuel du chevalier chrestien, avec des commandemens tressalutaires ... avec ung prologue merveilleusement utile et de nouveau adjousté. — Antwerp, Antoine Des Gois, 1543.
16°.
References: Cartier *De Tournes*, I, p. 159. *Bull. du bibliophile* 1845.

E 34. **Erasme, Desiderius,** trans. Louis de Berquin?

Le Chevalier Chrestien. Composé en Latin par Erasme, et puis traduit en langue Françoise. — Lyon, Jean de Tournes, 1544.
16°: a-v⁸, rom.
*Paris SHP A 1210(2). *Strasbourg BNU R100570.
References: Cartier *De Tournes* #22.

E 35. **Erasme, Desiderius.**

Exhortation au peuple. — [Antwerp], [Martin Lempereur], 1525?
8°: A⁸ B⁴, goth.

*Geneva BPU Rés. Bd 1994. *London BL C.37.a.22(3) and 848.a.2(1).
References: Moore #136. NK #2984.
Notes: Translation of Erasmus's *Paraclesis*.

E 36. **Erasme, Desiderius,** trans. Claude Chansonnette.

Maniere de se confesser. — Basle, [Andreas Cratander], 1524.

8°: A-D^8 E^{10}, goth.

Paris SHP R 16072 (missing). *Paris BM Rés. 22540(5).

References: Moore #135. Bietenholz #241. Condemned in the Paris *Index* I #88 (Latin), 92 (Latin and French), 259 (Latin, anonymous), 322 (Fr.), 390 (Fr., anonymous). Droz *Chemins* I 6-41, with text.

Notes: Trans. of the *Modus Confitendi*. The attribution to the printer Andreas Cratander rather than to Johann Froben (as in most authorites) is based on the printing materials.

E 37. **Erasme, Desiderius,** trans. Claude Chansonnette.

Maniere de se confesser. — 1530.

References: Mégret, *BHR* IV, p. 124.

E 38. **Erasme, Desiderius,** trans. Claude Chansonnette.

Le vray moyen de bien et catholiquement se confesser. — Lyon, Estienne Dolet, 1542.

16°: A-H^8, rom.

Toulouse BM Rés. D.xvi.175.

References: Christie #49. Longeon *Dolet* #217. Mégret *BHR* IV, 129-37. *Index* I #390, title as in this ed.

Notes: The Dolet ed. was censured in 1543 (Higman *Censorship*, p. 98).

E 39. **Erasme, Desiderius.**

Paraphrase, ou briefve exposition sur toutes les Epistres Canoniques. — Lyon, Claude La Ville, 1543.

8°: A-M^8 N^4, rom. N 3v: 'Assez tost, si assez bien'.

*Basle UB DJ V 103. Ghent UB Acc 9080. La Rochelle BM. London BL.

References: Machiels #E 634. Baudrier I, 237 < Du Verdier I, 461.

Notes: The motto 'Assez tost, si assez bien' is associated with the Genevan bookseller and financier René de Bienassis, known to be active in Geneva from 1545 on.

E 40.   Erasme, Desiderius.

Paraphrase sur le troisieme pseaulme de David, faicte en maniere d'oraison. — 1543.

References: *Index* I #324.

Notes: The Sorbonne condemnation is the only trace of this French translation of *In psalmum tertium paraphrasis* (1524).

E 41.   Erasme, Desiderius, trans. anon.

Preparation a la Mort. — Lyon, François Juste, 1537.

16°: A-H^8, rom. H 8v: Lyon, François Juste, 1537.

*Paris BSG D 8°Sup 29 Rés.

References: Dagens.

E 42.   Erasme, Desiderius, trans. Guy Morin.

Le Preparatif à la mort Livre tres utille et necessaire a chascun Chrestien. — Paris, Olivier Mallard, pr. Galliot Du Pré, 1537.

16°: a-n^8, rom. n 8v: ach. d'impr. à Paris par Olivier Mallart pour Galiot Du Pré. 31.12.1537.

*Paris BA 8°BL 10686.

Notes: After the text of Erasmus, a 'Discours [in verse] de la vie et mort accidentelle de ... Guy Morin, traducteur de ce present Preparatif' (k 8r sqq.) by 'François de Sagon'. Morin died on 3 Aug. 1536. The translation is different from that of the Lyon series.

E 43.   Erasme, Desiderius, trans. anon.

Preparation à la mort. — Lyon, Jean Barbou, pr. Guillaume de Guelques, 1538.

16°: A-H^8, rom. H 7v: impr. à Lyon par Jehan Barbou.

*Paris BN Rés. D 80460(2).

References: Baudrier V, 293 < Brunet II, 1044.

E 44.   Erasme, Desiderius, trans. Guy Morin.

Le Preparatif à la mort... Adjoustee une instruction chrestienne pour bien vivre, et soy preparer a mourir. — Paris, Galliot Du Pré, 1539.

16°: A-M^8, rom. M 8r: ach d'impr. à Paris pour Galiot Du Pré. 18.02.1539.

*Paris BM 49656(2). *Versailles BM Goujet 16° 27 (incompl.).

References: Peach/Brunel #524.

Notes: The Versailles copy only contains gatherings I-M: 'Discours..., plus une Instruction chrestienne, pour soy disposer à bien vivre...: Toute creature raisonnable sur toutes choses doibt aymer Dieu de tout son cueur...'

E 45.   **Erasme, Desiderius,** trans. Guy Morin.

Le Preparatif à la mort... Adjoustée une instruction chrestienne pour bien vivre, et soy preparer à mourir. — Paris, Vincent Sertenas, Jean Longis, 1539. 16°: A-Q⁸, rom.
*Paris BM 25348 (Sertenas). *Cambridge Emma. 321.6.54 (Longis). *Paris BN Rés. D 80206 bis (Longis).
References: Adams E 614. Renouard MSS.

E 46.   **Erasme, Desiderius,** trans. Guy Morin.

Le Preparatif à la mort. — Paris, Denis Janot, 1541. 16°.
Munich BSB (missing). Göttingen (missing).
References: Rawles #144. Brunet II, 1044. *Biblio. belg.* 2ᵉ série XN. E 1203 #47.

E 47.   **Erasme, Desiderius.**

Preparation à la mort. — Lyon, Estienne Dolet, 1542.
References: Longeon *Dolet* #233.
Notes: No known copy. In his preface to Erasmus, *Vray moyen de se confesser* (Longeon, *Préfaces*, p. 137), Dolet states that he had already printed 'la préparation à la mort'.

E 48.   **Erasme, Desiderius.**

La Preparation à la mort. — Lyon, Jean de Tournes, 1543.
16°: a-g⁸, rom.
*Wrocław BU 457564.
References: Cartier *De Tournes* #5.

E 49.   **Erasme, Desiderius,** trans. anon.

Preparation à la mort... Avecques aulcunes Prieres et Pseaulmes de la Saincte escripture moult prouffictables a tous Christiens. — [Antwerp?], ?, 1543.
16°: A-L⁸, goth.
*Paris BN Rés. D 80105.

Notes: Translation independent of the two preceding 'families'.

E 50.   **Erasme, Desiderius,** trans. anon.

De la preparation à la mort. — Lyon, François Juste, 1544.
16°.
References: Baudrier suppl. #112 < Brunet II, 1045, Du Verdier II, 160.

E 51.   **Erasme, Desiderius,** trans. Guy Morin?

Preparation à la mort. — Paris, 1544.
References: Renouard MSS < Brunet Suppl. II, 549.

E 52.   **Erasme, Desiderius.**

Brief recueil du livre de l'enseignement du prince Chrestien. — Paris, Oudin Petit, 1549.
16°: I 5-8 K-L⁸ M², rom.
*Rouen BM Leber 888.
Notes: Actually part of Gilles d'Aurigny, *Livre de police humaine.*

E 53.   **Erasme, Desiderius.**

Brief recueil du livre <> de l'enseignement du prince Chrestien. — Paris, Charles Langelier, 1549.
16°: R-T⁸, rom.
*Rouen BM Montbret p 9311.
Notes: Part of Gilles d'Aurigny, *Livre de Police humaine,* in 2 vols. Vol. 1, signed Ch. l'Angelié, dated 1550 at the end. But both t.ps are dated 1549.

E 54.   **Erasme, Desiderius,** trans. Philibert de Vienne.

Le sermon de Jesus enfant. — Paris, Galliot Du Pré, 1542.
References: Dagens. Du Verdier.

E 55.   **Erasme, Desiderius,** trans. Philibert de Vienne.

Le Sermon de Jesus enfant... Avec le songe du combat entre le corps et l'esprit. — Lyon, Jean de Tournes, 1543.
16°: 62 ff.
References: Cartier *De Tournes* #6. Sale Behagne (1880) #67.

Notes: According to the t.p., Philibert de Vienne (who calls himself 'L'Amoureux de Vertu, champenois') is the author of the *Songe*...

E 56.   Erasme, Desiderius, trans. Philibert de Vienne.

Le sermon de Jesus enfant. — Lyon, Thibaud Payen, 1543.

References: Frankfurt cat. 1610.

E 57.   Erasme, Desiderius, trans. [Louis de Berquin].

Le symbole des apostres ... par maniere de dialogue: par demande et par response. — [Paris], [Simon Du Bois], 1525?

8°: a-b⁸, goth.

*Geneva BPU Rés. Bb 806(5).

References: Moore #134. Clutton #39. Moreau III #819. Facs. reprod. Telle, *TLF*, 1979.

Notes: Censured by the Sorbonne in May 1525 (Higman *Censorship*, pp. 75-7). Translation of the *Inquisitio de fide* (1524), but with 'additions' (indicated in the margin) copied from the *Oraison de Jesuchrist* of [Farel and Luther], in particular from the part of Luther's *Betbüchlein* incorporated into Farel's text.

=>   Espence, Claude d': see [Luther], *Consolation*.

E 58.   Espence, Claude d'.

Homelies sur la Parabole de l'enfant prodigue. — Lyon, Jean de Tournes, 1547.

16°: A-I⁸, rom.

*Geneva BPU Rés. Bd 1887. *Paris BN D 88506(1).

References: Cartier *De Tournes* #83.

Notes: There are four sermons.

E 59.   Espence, Claude d'.

Homelies sur la parabole de l'enfant prodigue. — Paris, Jean Ruelle, ?

16°: A-E⁸, rom.

*Paris BSG D 8° 6502(2) Rés.

E 60.   Espence, Claude d'.

Institution d'un Prince chrestien. — Lyon, Jean de Tournes, 1548.
8°: A-E⁸, ital.
*Geneva BPU Rés. Se 6333(1). Paris BN Vélins 1841. *Paris BM 41993(3).
References: Cartier *De Tournes* #112.
Notes: Dedic. to Henri II, from Bologna, first day of Advent 1547 (d'Espence was representing the French king at the Council). The author encourages the new king to protect the true faith and to punish its enemies, but also to proceed with discretion.

E 61.   Espence, Claude d'.

Institution d'un Prince chrestien. — [Paris], [Estienne Groulleau], 1548.
16°: A-C⁸ D⁴, rom.
*Vienna ÖNB 19.Aa.130(2).

E 62.   Espence, Claude d', extracts from Gabriel Biel.

Paraphrase, ou Meditation, sur l'oraison dominicale. — Lyon, Jean de Tournes, 1547.
16°: a-f⁸ []², rom.
*Geneva BPU Rés. Bd 1890. *Paris BN D 88506(4).
References: Cartier *De Tournes* #84. *Index* I #527.
Notes: Commentary on the Lord's Prayer 'entièrement extraicte des leçons de G. Biel'. The work was censured in 1553 and placed on the *Index* of 1556. But d'Espence obtained an order from the parlement to have the mention suppressed.

E 63.   Espence, Claude d', extracts from Gabriel Biel.

Paraphrase, ou meditation, sur l'oraison Dominicale. Et autres opuscules. — Paris, René Avril, 1548.
16°: A-Z AA-BB⁸, rom.
*Vienna ÖNB 19.Aa.133.
Notes: The 'autres opuscules' are the *Consolation en adversité*, the *Sermons de Theodoret*, the *Homelies sur la Parabole de l'enfant prodigue*, and the *Institution d'un Prince chrestien*.

E 64.   Espence, Claude d', extracts from Gabriel Biel.

Paraphrase, ou, Meditation, sur l'oraison Dominicale. Et autres opuscules. — Paris, Estienne Groulleau, 1548.

16°: A-V⁸ X⁴, rom.
*Vienna ÖNB 19.Aa.130.
Notes: Same contents as the René Avril ed., 1548. But the *Institution d'un Prince chrestien*, bound in the same vol., is a separate bibliographical unit.

E 65.   Espence, Claude d', extracts from Gabriel Biel.

Paraphrase, ou Meditation, sur l'oraison dominicale, Avec autres opuscules ... de nouveau reveuz, corrigez et augmentez. — Lyon, Jean de Tournes, 1550.
16°: A-T⁸ V⁶, rom.
*Paris BA 8° T 7656. *Vienna ÖNB 18.Aa.135.
Notes: The 'autres opuscules' as in the Parisian 1548 eds, except that the *Consolation en adversité* has disappeared.

E 66.   Espence, Claude d'.

Traicté Contre l'erreur vieil et renouvellé des predestinez. — Lyon, Jean de Tournes, 1548.
8°: A⁴B-O⁸, ital.
*Geneva BPU Rés. Bc 2933 and Se 6333(2). *Munich BSB Polem 914.1. *Paris BA 8° T 4105. *Strasbourg BNU E 143639. *Vienna ÖNB 11.K.22 (+).
References: Cartier *De Tournes* #113. *NUC* NE 0169724.

E 67.   Eusèbe de Césarée (pseud.).

Le testament du tresglorieux sainct et amy de dieu <>. — Paris, Guichard Soquand, Jean de la Porte, 1518?
8°: A-C⁸ D⁴, goth. Impr. à Paris par Guichard soquand pr. Jehan de la porte.
*Paris BN Rés. D 80284.
Notes: J. de La Porte ceased his activity in 1520, Soquand only began in 1516. Hence the suggested date.

E 68.   Exercice d'une religieuse.

Lexcercice pour jeunes gens lesquelz veullent parvenir en bien et perfection de leur estat. Speciallement pour les religieuses de lordre de saincte Clere, et pour toutes autres. — Paris, Jean Bonfons, 1543?
8°: A-F⁸, goth. F 8v: Impr. à Paris pour Jehan bonfons.
*Paris BN Rés. D 80288.

Notes: In the colophon the title is given as 'La journee d'une jeune religieuse'. The author was herself a nun. J. Bonfons was active 1543-66. The printing material used here is fatigued.

E 69. **Exhortation à la lecture.**

Exhortation à la lecture des sainctes lettres. Avec suffisante probation des Docteurs de l'Eglise, qu'il est licite, et necessaire, icelles estre translatées en langue vulgaire. — Lyon, Estienne Dolet, 1542.

8°: A-H⁸ I⁴, rom. I 3r: Impr. à Lyon par Estienne Dolet, ens. de la Doloire. 1542.

*Paris SHP R 15913. *Vienna ÖNB *43.Y.28.

References: Christie #50. Longeon *Dolet* #218. *Index* I #315.

Notes: In his preface Dolet explains that he is publishing this work following his eds of scripture.

E 70. **Exhortation à la lecture.**

Exhortation à la lecture des Sainctes Lettres. Avec suffisante probation des Docteurs de l'Eglise, qu'il est licite et necessaire, icelles estre translatées en Langue vulgaire. — Lyon, Balthazar Arnoullet, 1544.

16°: A-F⁸, rom.

*Paris BM Rés. 23254. *Vienna ÖNB 10.M.25.

References: Baudrier X, 113. Dagens.

Notes: A 1562 ed. with the title 'Le Moyen de parvenir à la cognoissance de Dieu', Lyon, R. Granjon: London BL. This latter title was censured in 1549 (*Index* I #456), but no ed. is known to survive from that period.

E 71. **Exhortation sur ces paroles.**

Exhortation sur ces sainctes parolles de nostre Segneur Jesus. Retournes vous, et croyes a Levangile, prinse sur la saincte escripture, en laquelle est declaire lefficace de Levangile. — [Basle], [Andreas Cratander], 1525?

4°: A⁴ B⁶, goth.

*Vienna ÖNB 78.G.60.

Notes: Identification of the printer, by means of the typographical material, provided by Frank Hieronymus.

E 72.   Exhortation sur ces paroles.

*Exhortation sur ces sainctes parolles de nostre Sei-
gneur Jesu. Retournez vous et croyez a levangile:
Prinse sur la saincte escripture, en laquelle est
declaire lefficace de Levangile.* — [Neuchâtel?],
[Pierre de Vingle], 1534?
8°: 16 ff.
References: Brunet III, 1367. Droz *APR* p. 71. Berthoud *APR*
p. 143. Sales La Vallière (1784), Du Fay (1725) et Gaignet
(1769). Th. Dufour *Not.cat.* pp. 127-8.

E 73.   Exhortation sur ces paroles.

*Exhortation tresutile sur les sainctes parolles de nostre
Seigneur Jesus, Retournez vous et croyez à l'Evan-
gile. Aussi comment on doit faire les bonnes oeuvres,
et quelles sont les bonnes oeuvres.* — [Geneva],
[Jean Girard], 1541.
8°: a-b⁸ c⁴, rom.
*Vienna ÖNB 80.W.99.
References: *Index* I #416 et 468. *BG* 41/7.

E 74.   Exposition de l'oraison.

*Brefve exposition sur la treschrestienne et trespar-
faicte oraison du Pater noster.* — [Alençon], [Simon
Du Bois], 1530?
8°: A¹⁰, goth.
*Geneva MHR K Lut 5(4).
References: Moore #140. Clutton #43. Tricard *APR* pp. 22-4.
Higman 'Theology' p. 113 and #8.

E 75.   Exposition de l'oraison.

*Brefve et devote exposition par maniere dexhortation
et doraison, faicte sur le Pater noster: et autres
parolles de nostre Seigneur Jesuchrist recitees au
.vi. chapitre de sainct Matthieu.* — [Lyon], [Pierre
de Vingle], 1530?
8°: A⁸ B⁴ C⁸, goth.
*London BL G.6492(3).
References: Higman 'Theology' p. 113 and #9.
Notes: Identification of the printer by ornamental capitals also
found in Erasmus, *Complainte de la paix, c.* 1531. See *Exposition*, 1539.

E 76.   **Exposition de l'oraison,** 2nd part M. Luther.

Breve exposition faicte par maniere d'exhortation et d'oraison prinse sur le Pater noster, et aultres parolles de nostre Seigneur Jesus Christ, recitées au 6. chapitre de sainct Matthieu. — [Geneva], [Jean Girard], 1539.
8°: a-c⁸, ital.
*Geneva BPU Rés. Bb 2290.
References: Moore #19. Benzing *Luther* #1441. *BG* 39/5. *Index* I #415.
Notes: First part is a re-ed. of the *Briefve et devote exposition*, [P. de Vingle], *c.* 1530. Second part (B 6r sqq.): *Exposition sur ces parolles de Jesus Christ: Faictes vous dés amis dés richesses d'iniquité*, trans. from Luther, *Sermon de mammone iniquitatis* (1522, Lat. 1525). See S. Heyden, *Dung seul mediateur, c.* 1526.

E 77.   **Exposition de l'oraison,** extracts from Calvin.

Exposition De l'Oraison de nostre Seigneur Jesus,... Avec l'exposition du Symbole Apostolique ... et aussi une exposition sur les dix Commandemens de la Loy. — [Paris], ?, 1549?
8°: A-D⁸ E⁴, rom.
*Paris BSG C 8° 600(2) inv 193 Rés.
References: Higman 'Theology' #13.
Notes: A MS note in the only known copy notes a baptism in 1549, hence the proposed date. Incorporates large extracts from Calvin, *Instruction et confession de foi* (1537). See Higman 'Spiritualité'.

E 78.   **Exposition de l'oraison dominicale.**

Cy commence ung devot et nouveau Traicte contenant plusieurs expositions utilles sur l'oraison dominicale, aultrement dicte la Patinostre. — Paris, Vve Jean Saint Denys?, 1533.
4°: A-E⁴ F⁸ G-I⁴ K⁶, goth. K 6v: Impr. à Paris, se vend rue neufve N.D., ens. s. Nicolas. 1533.
*Aix Méj. Inc. D. 61(2).
References: Renouard MSS. Brunet.
Notes: Four expositions of the *Pater*, in different styles, for 'les ignorans, les devotz, les indignes, les parfaictz', in the form respectively of lesson, meditation, prayer and contemplation. Jean S. Denys's mark on t.p. No connection with the

Livre de vraye et parfaicte oraison. Cf. *Exposition sur la salutation.*

E 79.   **Exposition de l'oraison dominicale.**

Traicte contenant plusieurs expositions utiles et salutaires sur loraison dominicale aultrement dicte la Patinostre. — [Lyon], [Olivier Arnoullet], 1542?
8°: a-g⁸, goth.
References: Baudrier X, 50.

E 80.   **Exposition des articles.**

Exposition Sur les Articles de la Foy et Religion chrestienne, qu'on appelle communement le Symbole des Apostres. Contenant le sommaire de la doctrine apostolique. — [Geneva], [Jean Girard], 1541.
8°: A-G⁸ H⁴, rom.
*Paris BN Rés. D² 3980(1).
References: Moore #141. Higman 'Theology' #15. *BG* 41/8.

E 81.   **Exposition des articles.**

Exposition des articles de la Foy et Religion Chrestienne, qu'on appelle communement le Symbole des Apostres: contenant le sommaire de la doctrine Apostolique. — [Geneva], [Jean Girard], 1543.
8°: A-H⁸, rom.
*Geneva BPU Rés. Bc 3374. Montauban.
References: *BG* 43/16.

E 82.   **Exposition sur la salutation.**

Brefve et salutaire exposition sur la salutation angelique. — Paris, [Guillaume de Bossozel], Pierre Sergent, 1533.
4°: A-G⁴ H⁶, goth. H 6v: Impr. à Paris pr. Pierre Sergent, ens. S. Nicolas. 1533.
*Paris BA 8° T 5555(3).
References: Moreau IV #680.
Notes: The author says he had already sent 'ung petit et nouveau traicté contenant plusieurs et devotes expositions dessus la patinostre' to the lady to whom he offers this treatise. Cf. *Exposition de l'oraison dominicale*, Vve Jean Saint Denys, 1533.

E 83. **Exposition sur la salutation.**

*Traicte devot contenant une briefve et salutaire expo-
sition sur la salutation angelique. vulgairement dicte
Lave Maria. — Lyon, Olivier Arnoullet, 1535.*
8°: a-f⁸, goth. f 7r: I[...]8.11.1535.
Toulouse BM 523.
References: Baudr[...]

[handwritten note: 1543:15 ? 14]

E 84. **Exposition sur l[...]**

Exposition sur [...] Yolande
Bonhomme, 153[...]
8°.
Douai.
References: Renouard MSS.

E 85. **Extraits de plusieurs docteurs.**

*Extraits de plusieurs saincts Docteurs propositions
dicts et sentences, contenans les graces fruicts,
proffitz, utilitez et louenges du tressacre et digne sacrement de lautel. — Limoges, Claude Garnier, ?*
8°: 24 ff., A-C⁸, goth. C 8v: Impr. à Lymoges par Claude Garnier.
*Paris BA Rés. 8° T 1560.
References: *Rép. bib.* Limoges/Garnier #25.
Notes: Collection of quotations and biblical examples, with
extracts from Gerson, Bonaventura, and Church Fathers. Very
traditionalist.

E 86. **Extraits de plusieurs docteurs.**

*Extraict de plusieurs sainctz Docteurs, Propositions,
dictz et Sentences contenans les graces, fruicts,
profits, utilitez et louanges du sainct et digne Sacrement de Lautel. — Troyes, Jean Le Coq II, ?*
8°: A-L⁸ M⁴, goth. M 4v: Impr. à Troyes chez Jean Lecoq.
*Paris BEBA Masson1135 (-cahs A-G, H 1-4).
Notes: The 'colophon' may be false, since it is glued on to a
blank page. Fol. H 5r has the form of a t.p. (which is copied here).
But the entire vol. probably had some other title. See I 56.

F

F 1. Fabri, Christophe.

Familiere instruction des petis enfans selon la forme qu'on tient en l'Eglise de Neufchastel. — Geneva, Jean Crespin, 1551.
8°: A-G⁸, rom.
Coll. privée.
References: Gilmont *Crespin* 51/16. Droz *Chemins* II, 147-226, with reprod. of the text.

F 2. Fabri, Pierre.

Le defensoir de la conception en deux personnages, lamy et le sodal. — Rouen, Martin Morin, 1514.
4°: 89 + [1] ff., π² A-K⁸ L⁶ M⁴, goth.
*Aix Méj. C. 8649.
References: Priv. v° of the t.p. to Martin Morin for one year, dated 24.11.1514.
Notes: Defence of the doctrine of the Immaculate Conception. See also D 1.

F 3. Fagot de myrrhe.

Le Fagot de myerre, presche en ... la cite Dangiers. 1525. — Paris, [Guillaume de Bossozel], pr. Yolande Bonhomme, 1525?
8°: A-M⁸ N², goth. N 2r: Impr. à Paris pour Yoland Bonhomme.
*Paris BN Rés. C 3293(7). Paris BEBA Masson 309.
References: Moreau III #822.
Notes: Based on the Lent sermons preached in Angers by a 'religieux de l'ordre des cordeliers du couvent de la Balmete pres Angiers'.

F 4. Fagot de myrrhe.

Le livre intitule le Fagot de Myerre. — Paris, Jean Réal, Ambroise Girault, 1540?
8°: A-L⁸, goth. L 8r: Impr. à Paris par Jehan Real.
*Paris BA 8° T 6962.
Notes: Jean Réal began his career in 1538, Ambroise Girault died in 1547. The ed. was therefore produced somewhere between those dates.

F 5. **[Farel, Guillaume?], [Pierre Viret?].**

De La Tressaincte Cene de nostre Seigneur Jesus: Et De la Messe quon chante communement. — [Basle], [Thomas Wolff], 1532?
16°: A-M⁸, goth.
*Vienna ÖNB 79.V.31. Florence BN Guicciardini (missing).
References: *Index* I #383. Higman 'Débuts' with ed. of the text.

F 6. **[Farel, Guillaume].**

Confession de la Foy, laquelle tous Bourgeois et habitans de Geneve et subjectz du pays doivent jurer de garder et tenir, extraicte de Linstruction dont on use en Leglise de ladicte Ville. — [Geneva], [Wigand Koeln], 1536?
8°: A⁸, goth.
*Geneva BPU Rés. Bc 3356.
References: O. Labarthe, thèse Fac. de Théologie de Genève. Dufour, *Not.cat. BG* 36/3. Gilmont 'Farel' 7-1.
Notes: There may have been a second ed. in 1537 (permission from Geneva City Council), but there is no known copy.

F 7. **[Farel, Guillaume?].**

Epistre chrestienne. — Basle, 1524.
References: Tricard *APR* pp. 4-12. Droz *Chemins* I, 45n. Gilmont 'Farel' 21-1.
Notes: According to Mlle Droz an *Epistre* by Farel printed in Basle in 1524 may be the same text as the *Epistre chrestienne* printed by Simon Du Bois *c.* 1525. But Gilmont doubts the attribution: the Basle text must have been markedly longer than that edited by Du Bois.

F 8. **[Farel, Guillaume?].**

Epistre Chrestienne tresutile a ceulx qui commencent lire la saincte escripture, affin que en lysant la saincte parolle de dieu, ilz soient edifiez, congnoissant la consummation de toute lescripture. — [Paris], [Simon Du Bois], 1525?
8°: 20 ff., a-b⁸ c⁴, goth.
*Geneva MHR K Lut 5(2).

References: Moore #130. Tricard *APR* 4-12. Gilmont 'Farel'
21-1 (dubious attrib.). *Index* I #419. Moreau II #811.
Notes: Censured in 1531 (Higman *Censorship*, p. 83).

F 9.   **Farel, Guillaume,** Caroli, Pierre.

*Une Epistre de Maistre Pierre Caroly docteur de la
Sorbone de Paris ... envoiée à Maistre Guillaume Farel
... avec la response.* — Geneva, Jean Girard, 1543.
8°: A^8 B^4, rom.
Berne StB. *Geneva BPU Rés. Bc 3357. *Zurich ZB XVIII.2002.9.
References: Gilmont 'Farel' 10-1. *BG* 43/12. *Index* I, #325.
Notes: Preface by Calvin (A 1v) certifying the authenticity of
the text. Letter from Caroli (A 2r-4v) dated 14 May 1543.
Farel's reply (A 5r-B 4r) dated 21 May 1543.

F 10.   **Farel, Guillaume.**

La Seconde Epistre envoyée au Docteur Pierre Caroly.
— Geneva, Jean Girard, 1543.
8°: A-B^8, rom.
Berlin SB Libri impr. rari oct. 205(4). Berne StUB M.108. *Geneva
BPU Rés. Bc 3382. *Vienna ÖNB 70.Bb.276. *Zurich ZB
XVIII.2002.10.
References: Gilmont 'Farel' 11-1. *BG* 43/18. *Index* I, #325.
Notes: The letter is dated from Strasbourg, 25 June 1543.

F 11.   **Farel, Guillaume.**

*Epistre exhortatoire, à tous ceux qui ont congnoissance
de l'Evangile, les admonestant de cheminer purement
et vivre selon iceluy, glorifiant Dieu et edifiant le
prochain par parolles, et par oeuvres.* — [Geneva],
[Jean Girard], 1544.
8°: A-D^8, rom.   D 8r: the letter dated from Neuchâtel, 11 August 1542.
*Lincoln cath Nn 7.12(5). *Paris BA 8° T 9727. *Vienna ÖNB
79.Ee.10.
References: Gilmont 'Farel' 13-1. *BG* 44/18.
Notes: A warning of the dangers of 'nicodemism'.

F 12.   **Farel, Guillaume.**

Epistre envoyee au duc de Lorraine. — Geneva, Jean
Girard, 1543.
8°: A-G^8 H^4, rom.   H 3v: the letter signed 'De Gocze, ce 11. de
Fevrier. 1543'.

Berlin SB Libri impr. rari oct. 205(5). Berne StUB M.108. *London
BL 1085.c.10. *Geneva BPU Rés. Bc 3381. *Vienna ÖNB 36.M.45 (+).
References: Gilmont 'Farel' 9-1. *BG* 43/17. *Index* I, #326.
Notes: Farel rejects the accusation that his preaching in Lorraine
was seditious.

F 13.   **Farel, Guillaume.**

Epistre envoyee au duc de Lorraine. — Geneva, Jean
Girard, 1545.
8°: A-G⁸ H⁴, rom.
*Cambridge St Johns Ferrari O 29(2).
References: Gilmont 'Farel' 9-2. *BG* 45/18. Adams F 155.

F 14.   **Farel, Guillaume.**

*Epistre envoyee aux reliques de la dissipation horrible
de l'Antechrist.* — [Geneva], [Jean Girard], 1544.
8°: A⁸, rom. A 8v: letter signed 'de Strasbourg, le 1er août 1543'.
Florence BNC. *Lincoln cath Nn 7.12(7). *Paris BN Rés. D² 7640.
*Vienna ÖNB 77.Cc.263.
References: Gilmont 'Farel' 14-1. *BG* 44/17.

F 15.   **Farel, Guillaume.**

*Forme d'oraison pour demander à Dieu la saincte
predication de l'Evangile, et le vray et droit usage
des Sacremens: avec confession des pechez, qui sont
cause de la ruine de l'Eglise.* — Geneva, Jean
Girard, 1545.
8°: A-K⁸, rom. C 1r: the dedic. dated from Neuchâtel, 11 Jan. 1545.
*Lausanne BCU AZ 4519. *Munich BSB Polem 963(2). *Neuchâtel
past. 100.2. *Vienna ÖNB 79.V.86.
References: Gilmont 'Farel' 12-2. *BG* 45/19. *Index* I, #461.
Notes: Re-ed. of the *Oraison tresdevote* of *c.* 1543.

F 16.   **Farel, Guillaume.**

*Le Glaive de la parolle veritable, tiré contre le
Bouclier de defense, duquel un Cordelier libertin
s'est voulu servir, pour approuver ses fausses et
damnables opinions.* — Geneva, Jean Girard, 1550.
8°: π⁸ a-z A-G⁸ H⁴, rom.
*Glasgow UL Beb.g.9. *Geneva BPU Rés. Bc 1200. *Munich BSB
Polem 963(1). *Vienna ÖNB 79.J.71. *Wolfenbüttel HAB 1034.25
Theol (+).

References: Gilmont 'Farel' 15-1. Moore #146. CDM p. 16. Rothschild #87. *Index* I #327.

Notes: The 'cordelier libertin' of Rouen attacked by Calvin in *Contre les Libertins*, 1547, replied with a *Bouclier de defense* (lost). Farel wrote this response.

F 17.   [Farel, Guillaume].

Letres certaines daucuns grandz troubles et tumultes advenuz a Geneve, avec la disputation faicte lan 1534. — [Neuchâtel], [Pierre de Vingle], 1535.
16°: A-F⁸, goth. F 8r: 'De Geneve ce premier Davril. 1534'.
*London BL 1193.a.20. *Munich BSB Polem 1608. *Vienna ÖNB *48.K.30(1).

References: Gilmont 'Farel' 5-1. Berthoud *APR* pp. 146-9.

Notes: The narrative is presented as being written by 'un notaire demourant à Geneve'. Describes the disputation held in Jan. 1534 between Guy Furbiti, Dominican and Doctor of the Sorbonne, and Farel and Viret.

F 18.   [Farel, Guillaume].

Letres certaines daucuns grandz troubles et tumultes advenuz a Geneve, avec la disputation faicte lan 1534. — [Geneva], [Jean Michel], 1540?
8°: A-F⁸, goth.
*Geneva BPU Rés. Ba 1588 and 1588W.

References: Th. Dufour, *Not.cat.*, pp. 128-9. Gilmont 'Farel' 5-2. *BG* 44/20. Berthoud 'Michel' #26.

F 19.   [Farel, Guillaume].

La maniere et fasson quon tient en baillant le sainct baptesme ... et en espousant ... et a la saincte Cene de nostre seigneur, es lieux lesquelz dieu de sa grace a visite. — Neuchâtel, Pierre de Vingle, 1533.
8°: A-E⁸ F⁴, goth. F 3r: Impr. par Pierre de Vingle à Neufchastel. 29.08.1533.
*Geneva BPU Rés. Bd 1474. *Zurich ZB Res. 1333.

References: Moore #140. Gilmont 'Farel' 4-1. Th. Dufour *Not.cat.* pp. 107-8.

Notes: First Reformed liturgy in French. There may well have been an earlier ed., *c.* 1528 (no known copy). The work was revised in 1538, with new title *Lordre et maniere...*

F 20.   [Farel, Guillaume].

Lordre et maniere quon tient en administrant les sainctz sacremens: assavoir, le Baptesme, et la Cene de nostre Seigneur. Item, en la celebration du Mariage, et en la Visitation des malades. — [Geneva], Jean Michel, 1538.

8°: A-D⁸, goth. D 8r: Impr. par Jehan Michel demourant en la place S. Pierre. 1538.

*Bruxelles BR LP VH 2021(2). *Geneva BPU Rés. Bd 1473. *Neuchâtel BV Rés. C 31. *Paris BN Rés. D² 3980(2).

References: Gilmont 'Farel' 4-2. Moore #145. *BG* 38/5. Berthoud 'Michel' #1. *Index* I #491.

Notes: Re-ed. with minor modifications of *La Maniere et fasson* (1533).

F 21.   [Farel, Guillaume].

La tressainte oraison que Jesus Christ a baillé à ses Apostres. — Geneva, Jean Girard, 1541.

References: Gilmont 'Farel' 8-1. *BG* 41/9. *Index* I #459, 460.

Notes: Jean Girard was given permission by the Geneva Council on 22 Dec. 1540 to print an 'Exposition de l'orayson de N.S., composée par Farel'. On 25 May 1542 the Sorbonne censured the title given here (Higman *Censorship*, pp. 91-2).

F 22.   [Farel, Guillaume].

La tres sainte oraison que nostre Seigneur Jesus Christ a baillé à ses Apostres, les enseignant comme ils et tous bons chrestiens doivent estre, avec un Recueil d'aulcuns passages. — Geneva, 1543.

References: Gilmont 'Farel' 8-2. *BG* 43/19. Durel sale cat. (1894). *Index* I #460.

F 23.   Farel, Guillaume, poem by Jean Menard.

Oraison tresdevote en laquelle est faicte la confession des pechez, des fidelles qui ainsi crient apres Dieu. — [Strasbourg], [Johann Knobloch Jr], 1543?

8°: A-C⁸ D⁴, rom.

*Neuchâtel BV A de F C 32. *Paris SHP A 1173.

References: Gilmont 'Farel' 12-1. Peter 'Prem. ouvr.' #11. Pidoux 43/III.

Notes: Letter of consolation to the faithful in Metz. At the end, versification of Ps. 120 by Jean Menard, with melody. A second ed., with title *Forme d'oraison...*, 1545.

F 24.   **[Farel, Guillaume], [Luther, Martin].**

Le Pater noster, et le Credo en francoys, avec une tresbelle, et tresutile exposition, et declaration sur chascun, faicte en forme de contemplation et oraison fort proufitable pour enflamber le cueur. — [Basle], [Andreas Cratander], 1524.

8°: A-B⁸ C⁴, rom.

*Vienna ÖNB 80.X.40.

References: Gilmont 'Farel' 2-1. Ed Higman, *TLF*, 1982.

Notes: Commentary on the Lord's Prayer in the form of a prayer, composed by Farel, followed by a commentary on the Creed, also in prayer form, trans. from Luther's *Betbüchlein*.

F 25.   **[Farel, Guillaume], [Luther, Martin et al.].**

Loraison de Jesuchrist, qui est le Pater noster, et le Credo, avec la declaration diceulx. La salutation angelique. Les dix commandemens. Les sept pseaulmes: et autres choses tresutiles. — [Paris], [Simon de Colines], 1525?

16°: a-o⁸, goth.

Ghent UB Res. 935(1).

References: Machiels #O77. NK #1632. Gilmont 'Farel' 2-2. Higman, *Palaestra*.

Notes: Second ed., augmented, of [Farel], *Pater noster*, adding among other texts a *Declaration d'aucuns mots dont use S. Paul*, trans. of the *Praefatio methodica* (1523), Latin version by Justus Jonas of Luther's preface to the Epistle to the Romans, and *La Maniere de mediter et penser à la passion de Jesus Christ*, trans. of a Luther sermon. Censured in 1531 (Higman *Censorship*, p. 83).

F 26.   **[Farel, Guillaume].**

Summaire, et brieve declaration daucuns lieux fort necessaires a un chascun Chrestien. — [Lyon], [Pierre de Vingle], 1529.

References: Gilmont 'Farel' 3-1.

Notes: No known copy. On 14 May 1530 a sentence from the Dole parlement mentioned this title, said to be 'imprimé à

Venise par Pierre du Pont à l'enseigne du pigeon blanc, le 12e de nov., 1529' (Febvre, *BSHPF* 1911, pp. 184-5). This false address surely indicates Pierre de Vingle.

F 27.   **[Farel, Guillaume].**

Summaire et briefve declaration daulcuns lieux fort necessaires a ung chascun chrestien, pour mettre sa confiance en Dieu, et ayder son prochain. — 'Turin' [=Alençon], [Simon Du Bois], 1532?
8°: A-N⁸, goth.
*London BL C.37.a.21.
References: Gilmont 'Farel' 3-2. Moore #144. Facs. ed. Piaget, Paris, 1935.
Notes: The t.p. indicates 'impr. a Turin Lan de grace 1525'. But the characters and the paper are those of Simon Du Bois in Alençon, so the ed. must be dated between 1529 and 1534. See Higman, 'Dates-clé'.

F 28.   **[Farel, Guillaume].**

Summaire, et briefve declaration daucuns lieux fort necessaires a ung chascun Chrestien, pour mettre sa confiance en Dieu... Item, ung traicte du Purgatoire nouvellement adjouste sur la fin. — [Neuchâtel], [Pierre de Vingle], 1534.
8°: A-N⁸, goth. N 8v: ach. d'impr. 23.12.1534.
*Geneva BPU Rés. Bc 3379. *Neuchâtel Coll. Henriod. *Zurich ZB Res. 1335.
References: Gilmont 'Farel' 3-3. Facs. ed. Geneva, 1867.
Notes: A more accurate text of the *Sommaire* than in the Du Bois ed. The *Traité de purgatoire* here printed for the first time. Because of its incorporation into this ed. of the *Sommaire*, the *Traité* has long been ascribed to Farel. But the hypothesis is fragile. See *Purgatoire*.

F 29.   **[Farel, Guillaume].**

Summaire, et briefve declaration daucuns lieux fort necessaires a ung chascun Chrestien, pour mettre sa confiance en Dieu... Item, ung traicte du Purgatoire nouvellement adjouste sur la fin. — [Geneva], [Jean Michel], 1542.
8°: A-L⁸, goth. L 8v: Ach. d'impr. 25.07.1542.
*Vienna ÖNB 17.G.59.

References: Gilmont 'Farel' 3-4. Berthoud 'Michel' #15. *BG*
42/12. *Index* I #492.
Notes: Follows the 1534 ed. Censured on 1 Sept. 1543 (Higman
Censorship, pp. 93-4).

F 30. **Farel, Guillaume.**

*Summaire. C'est, une brieve declaration d'aucuns lieux
fort necessaires à un chascun Chrestien ... corrigé,
reveu, et augmenté par Guillaume Farel auteur
d'iceluy.* — [Geneva], [Jean Girard], 1542.
8°: A-T⁸, rom.
*London St Pauls 38 E 26(4) (anon.). *Neuchâtel past. 100.3.
References: Gilmont 'Farel' 3-5. *BG* 42/11.
Notes: The St Paul's copy has on the t.p. '...augmenté par son
auteur'. Added in this ed., 'La Raison pour quoy ceste oeuvre
a esté faicte, et tant differée d'estre reveuë, et pourquoy a esté
augmentée par Guillaume Farel' (S 2r sqq.).

F 31. **Figures de l'Apocalypse,** poem by 'le petit Angevin'
(=Jean Maugin).

*Les Figures de l'Apocalipse ... exposées en Latin et
vers François.* — Paris, Estienne Groulleau, 1547.
8°: A-F⁸, ital. A 2v: ach. d'impr. 13.08.1547. F 8r: Impr. à Paris,
Estienne Groulleau. 1547.
Ghent UB Res. 960(1). Harvard CL Typ.515.47.210. Chicago Newberry. *Wolfenbüttel HAB 196.2 Poet. *Montpellier BM C 345.
References: Machiels #677. Mortimer #75. *NUC* NBi 0065915.
Notes: Royal priv. for six years, dated 14 Aug. 1546. Each
engraving has a border, often with the motto 'Nul ne s'y
frote'. Ten 'Histoires du Nouveau Testament' (E 1r - F 4v),
presenting Judas, the martyrdom of St Stephen, the conversion
of St Paul..., and St James's doctrine of works. A 'cantique
Crestien' (F 5r) by Jean Maugin invites poets to stop singing
'une Venus paillarde', and to praise the mercy 'du puissant
Dieu des Dieux'.

F 32. **Figures de l'Apocalypse,** poem by 'le petit Angevin'
(=Jean Maugin).

*Les Figures de l'Apocalypse ... exposées en Latin et
vers Françoys.* — Paris, Estienne Groulleau, 1551?
8°: A-F⁸, ital. A 2v: ach. d'impr. 13.08.1547. F 8r: Impr. à Paris par
Estienne Groulleau. 1551.

*London BL 554.a.5. *Paris SHP A 247. *Paris BN Rothschild IV.8.70. *Paris BEBA Masson 233. Versailles BM Goujet 12° 298 (+).
References: *NUC* NBi 0065918. Rothschild #2739. Peach/ Brunel #414.
Notes: The t.p. and 'achevé d'impr.' both read '1547' as in the previous ed. But the ed. is entirely reset, and '1551' appears at the end of the text.

F 33. Figures et visions.

Les Figures et Visions de L'apocalypse ... Extraictes de la Bible. — Paris, Nicolas Buffet, 1548.
16°: A-H⁸, rom.
*Paris BN Rés. 8° Z don 594(375)(3).
Notes: Text of Revelation with a few comments and 23 woodcuts. Antichrist = the heretics.

F 34. Fleur de dévotion.

Sensuyt le prologue de ce present livre intitule la fleur de devotion ... Auquel sont contenus les abismes ... et martyre spirituel du filz de Dieu avec lhystoire ... de sa ... passion. — Paris, Denis Janot, Alain Lotrian, 1535?
4°: A-C⁴ D⁸ E-O⁴ P⁸ Q-X AA-CC⁴, goth. CC 3v: Impr. à Paris par Alain lotrian et Denys janot.
*Paris BN Rés. D 80035 (E 1-8 bound before D).
References: Moreau IV #1304. Rawles III, #275.
Notes: Meditation on the Passion in the context of monastic Hours. Some engravings. The colophon says the work is 'extraict de plusieurs beaulx livres'.

F 35. Fleur des commandements.

La fleur des commandemens de dieu avec plusieurs exemples et auctoritez, extraictes tant de sainctes escriptures que dautres docteurs et bons anciens peres. — Paris, Michel Travers, pr. François Regnault, 1512.
2°: a-b⁶ c⁴ a-z & ¶ A-F⁶ G⁴, goth. G 3v: Impr. à Paris par Michel travers. 07.11.1512.
*Avignon BM in-4° 323. Cambridge UL. Séville Colomb.
References: Moreau II #315. Babelon #66.
Notes: The text already existed in the 15th cent., with eds known from 1496, 1499, 1500, 1510... Based on the Ten

Commandments, the text presents examples of obedience, then
of disobedience.

F 36.   Fleur des commandements.

*La fleur des commandemens de dieu. Avec plusieurs
exemples et auctoritez extraictes tant des sainctes
escriptures que dautres docteurs et bons anciens
peres.* — Paris, Guillaume Nyverd, pr. Hémon Le
Fèvre, 1516.

2°: A^8 B-C^6 a-z & ¶ aa^8 bb^6, goth. bb 6r: Impr. à Paris par Guil-
laume Nyverd pr. Aymon le fevre. 12.03.1516.
*Paris BA fol. T 1511.
References: Moreau II #1350.

F 37.   Fleur des commandements.

*La fleur des Commandemens de Dieu Avec plusieurs
exemples et auctoritez: extraictes tant de sainctes
escriptures que daultres docteurs et bons anciens
peres.* — Paris, Bernard Aubry, Antoine Bonnemere,
Philippe Le Noir, 1525.

2°: [14]+168 ff., A^6 B-C^4 a-z & ¶ []^6 aa-bb^4 cc^6, goth. cc 6v: Impr. à
Paris par Anthoyne bonne Mere. 1525.
*Paris BN Rothschild II.4.7. Yale UL Me 34 F 63 1525.
References: Brunet II, 1288. Moreau III #824. Rothschild
#2538.

F 38.   Fleur des commandements.

*La fleur des commandemens de Dieu, avec plusieurs
exemples et auctoritez, extraictes tant de sainctes
escriptures que dautres docteurs et bons anciens
peres.* — Paris, [Nicolas Couteau], 1536.

2°: a^6 b-c^4 A-Z & 9 AA-EE^6 FF^4 GG^6, goth. GG 6r: Impr. à Paris, 1536.
*London BL 1216.k.16. *Paris BA fol T 1512.
References: Renouard MSS.

F 39.   Fleur des commandements.

*La fleur des commandemens de Dieu, avec plusieurs
Exemples et Auctoritez, Extraictes tant des sainctes
escriptures que dautres Docteurs et bons anciens
peres.* — Paris, Nicolas Couteau, 1539.

2°: ã^6 ẽ^8 A-Z AA-DD^6 EE^4, goth. EE 4v: Impr. à Paris par Nicolas
couteau. 30.06.1539.

Amiens BM Les 1257 D. *Avignon BM in-fol. 4002. *Paris BA fol
T 1732.

F 40.   Fleur des commandements.

*La fleur des commandemens de Dieu, avec plusieurs
Exemples et Auctoritez Extraictes tant des sainctes
escriptures que dautres Docteurs bons anciens peres.*
— Paris, Jean Réal, Guillaume Le Bret, Poncet Le
Preux, 1548.
2°: ã⁶ ẽ⁸ a-h, I-X, y-z, AA-DD⁶ EE⁴, goth. EE 4v: Impr. à Paris par
Jehan Real. 24.03.1548.
*Paris BN Rés. D 1614 (Le Bret). *Rouen BM A 448 (P. Le Preux).
*Avignon BM in-fol. 4003 (P. Le Preux).
References: Renouard MSS.
Notes: Seemingly intentional antiquarian presentation, incl.
some woodcuts used by A. Verard in 1507.

F 41.   Fleurs de la somme angélique.

*Les Fleurs de la somme angelique des branches des
sept pechez mortelz.* — Paris, Michel Le Noir, 1519.
8°.
Séville Colomb.
References: Moreau II #2058: 'extraits d'Angelo Carletti,
Summa angelica.'

F 42.   Florimond, Clément Marot.

*Epistre familiere de prier Dieu. Aultre Epistre familiere
d'aymer   chrestiennement.*   —   Paris,   [Antoine
Augereau], 1533.
8°: a-e⁴, rom. e 2r: 1533.
Paris BN Vélins 2265(2).
References: Veyrin-Forrer #20. Moreau IV #685.
Notes: With the *Briefve doctrine pour deuement escripre
selon la propriete du langaige francoys*, and the *Instruction et
foy d'ung chrestien* attrib. to Marot. Jourda identifies 'Florimond' with Jean Salomon (p. 214).

F 43.   Florimond, Clément Marot.

*Epistre familiere de prier Dieu. Aultre epistre familiere
d'aymer Chrestiennement.* — [Paris], [Antoine Auge-
reau], 1533.
8°: a-d⁴, rom.

*Paris BN Rés. Ye 1409. *Paris SHP R 11742(2).

References: Veyrin-Forrer #18. Mayer *Marot* #241. Moreau IV #683.

Notes: Fol. c 3v: *Briefve doctrine pour deuement escripre selon la proprieté du langaige françoys.* d 2r: *Instruction et foy d'un Chrestien mise en Françoys par Clement Marot.*

F 44.   Florimond, Clément Marot.

Epistre familiere de prier Dieu. Aultre Epistre familiere d'aimer chrestiennement. — Paris, [Antoine Augereau], 1533.

8°: a-e⁴, rom. e 4r: Mense Decembri. 1533.

*Chantilly Condé III.B.51. *Paris BN Rés. Ye 1632.

References: Veyrin-Forrer #19. Moreau IV #684.

Notes: With the *Briefve doctrine pour deuement escripre selon la proprieté du langaige françoys* and the *Instruction et foy d'ung chrestien.* See Marguerite de Navarre, *Miroir*, Augereau, 1533.

F 45.   Fontaine de vie.

La Fontaine de vie. — Lyon, Estienne Dolet, 1542.

References: Longeon *Dolet* #219. Christie #54.

Notes: No known copy.

F 46.   Fontaine de vie.

La Fontaine de Vie. De laquelle resourdent tresdoulces consolations, singulierement necessaires aux cueurs affligez. Plus y est adjouste linstruction pour les enfans. — Paris, Estienne Caveiller, pr. Arnoul Langelier, 1542.

16°: a-i⁸, rom. i 7v: Impr. à Paris par Estienne Caveiller pr. Arnoul Langeliet libr.

*Paris SHP A 1167(3).

References: Moore #151. *Index* I #361. Droz *Chemins* I, 298-319 avec texte.

Notes: The censure of this ed., 25 May 1542 (Higman *Censorship*, pp. 89-90), referred to the *Introduction pour les enfans* (h 4r sqq.), and not to the *Fontaine. La Fontaine...* is a collection of biblical quotations, followed by some examples of consolation.

F 47.   Fontaine de vie.

La Fontaine de vie. — Lyon, Jean de Tournes, 1543.
16°.
References: Cartier *De Tournes* #7. Brunet II, 1325.
Notes: No known copy.

F 48.   Fontaine de vie.

La Fontaine de vie, de laquelle resourdent tresdoulces consolations, singulierement necessaires aux coeurs affligez. — Paris, Jean Ruelle, 1547.
16°: A-F⁸, ital.
*Paris BSG D 8° 6193(3) inv 7888 Rés.

F 49.   Fontaine de vie.

La Fontaine de vie: De laquelle distillent tresdoulces consolations, singulierement necessaires aux coeurs affligez. Plus y est adjoustée l'instruction pour les enfans: le tout reveu, et augmenté tout de nouveau. — Lyon, Jacques Berion, 1549.
8°: A-G⁸ H⁴, rom.
*Munich BSB Asc 1918(1).
References: Du Verdier.
Notes: Follows the ed. of Charles Langelier, 1542.

F 50.   Fossetier, Julien.

Conseil de volentier morir. — Antwerp, Martin Lempereur, 1532.
8°: 24 ff., a-c⁸, goth.
*Paris BN Rothschild IV.3.250.
References: NK #3038. Rothschild #512.
Notes: Prologue (a 2r) dedicating the work to Charles V, by 'Julien Fossetier prebstre indigne,/ qui en Haynault ay en Dath origine,/ Anchien de quattre vingz ans et plus'. Dialogue between Soul and Body, in decasyllabics. Includes (c 4v sqq.) a 'Recordt de la passion, pour utilement rechepvoir le pain de lautel'.

G

G 1.   Gacy, Jean.

La deploration de la Cite de Genesve sur le faict des hereticques qui lont Tiranniquement opprimee. — [Lyon?], [Pierre de Sainte-Lucie?], 1535?
4°: A⁴, goth.
*Paris BN Rés. pYe 138. Séville Colombine.
References: Babelon #72.
Notes: The author's name given at the end of the text in anagram 'Jen feray Grace' (= 'Frere Jean Gacy'). Poem in decasyllabics denouncing the sermons of 'Pharel', Oecolampadius, Froment and Viret. Uses (first attestation?) the word 'anguenots'.

G 2.   Gacy, Jean.

Trialogue nouveau contenant lexpression des erreurs de Martin Luther. Les doleances de Ierarchie ecclesiastique Et les triumphes de verite invincible. — [Geneva], [Wigand Koeln], 1524.
4°: a-i⁴, goth. i 3v: 'Faict lan mil cinq cens et xxiiii.'
*Aix Méj. Rés. O. 30. London BL C.97.b.19. *Paris SHP A 1162. *Paris BM Rés. 10828.
References: Moore #153. Th. Dufour *Not.cat.* pp. 136-8.
Notes: i 2r-3r: epistle to Charles de Montbrun, discussing the use of vernacular languages among other things. Mixture of narrative (in prose) and speeches (in verse) from 'Zele divin', 'Ierarchie ecclesiastique', and 'Verité invincible'. The style of the text has been compared to that of the *écolier limousin* in Rabelais's *Pantagruel*.

G 3.   [Gaigny, Jean de].

Le Livre contenant devote exposition sur le cinquantiesme pseaulme ... avec aucunes contemplations extraictes de la saincte escriture et des ditz et sentences des docteurs autenticques et approuvees de saincte eglise. Nouvellement reveu et corrige. — Paris, Denis Janot, [Jean Longis], 1533?
8°: A-L⁸, goth. L 8v: Impr. à Paris par Denys Janot.
*London BL C.97.aa.14.
References: Rawles #283. Moreau IV #690.
Notes: The priv. (L 8r-v) to Jean Longis for two years dated 17 Feb. 1532, hence the suggested dating.

G 4.   **[Gaigny, Jean de].**

Le Livre contenant devote exposition sur le cinquantiesme pseaulme ... avec aucunes contemplations extraictes de la saincte escripture et des ditz et sentences des docteurs autenticques et approuvees de saincte eglise. Nouvellement reveu et corrige. — Paris, Denis Janot, [Jean Longis], 1538?

8°: A-L⁸, goth. L 8v: Impr. à Paris par Denys Janot.

*Paris BA 8° T 873.

References: Moreau IV #690.

Notes: Moreau treats this and the previous item as two copies of the same ed. But the t.p. is entirely recomposed, and the priv. to Jean Longis is dated 17 Feb. 1537.

G 5.   **[Gaigny, Jean de].**

Le livre contenant devote exposition sur le cinquantiesme Pseaulme ... avec aucunes contemplations extraictes de saincte escripture et des ditz et sentences des docteurs autentiques et approuvees de saincte eglise Nouvellement ... veu et corrige par lautheur diceluy livre chanoine de la saincte chapelle. — Paris, Nicolas Barbou, 1541.

8°: a-m⁸ n⁴, goth. n 4v: Impr. à Paris par Nicolas Barbou impr.

*Paris BN Rés. A 9995.

G 6.   **[Gaigny, Jean de].**

Le livre faisant mention des sept parolles que nostre benoist saulveur ... dit en larbre de la croix: avec aulcunes expositions et contemplations sur icelles: extraictes des dictz et sentences des docteurs autentiques et approuvez de saincte eglise. — Paris, Simon Du Bois, Chrestien Wechel, 1528.

4°: π⁴ a-z ã ẽ ĩ õ ũ A-L⁴ M⁶, goth. M 2v: Impr. à Paris par Simon Du Bois pour Chrestien Wechel. 1528.

*Bruxelles BR LP 566 A. *London BL C.97.b.33. *Paris BN Rés. pD 63 (-M 4-6). Avignon BM in-8° 23.103.

References: Clutton #16. Moreau III #1467. P. Renouard, 'Le Livre des sept parolles (1528)' in *Byblis* 8 (1929).

G 7.   **[Gaigny, Jean de].**

Le livre faisant mention des sept parolles. — Paris,
Estienne Caveiller, Jean Macé, 1533.
References: Cartier *De Tournes* p. 175.

G 8.   **[Gaigny, Jean de].**

*Le livre de nouvel reimprime faisant mention des
sept parolles que nostre saulveur ... dit en larbre de
la croix: avec aulcunes expositions et contemplations
sur icelles: extraictes des dictz et sentences des
docteurs autentiques et approuvez de saincte eglise,
avec aulcunes additions utiles et prouffitables concernans lesdictes parolles.* — Paris, Chrestien
Wechel, 1535.
4°: æ^4 a-z A-S^4, goth.
*London BL 1412.g.24. *Paris BM 35877. Avignon BM in-8° 23.102.
References: Moreau IV #1316.

G 9.   **[Gaigny, Jean de].**

*Le livre de nouvel imprime faisant mention des sept
parolles que nostre benoist saulveur ... dist en larbre
de la croix: avec aucunes expositions et contemplations sur icelles: extraictes des dictz et sentences des
docteurs autentiques et approuvez de saincte eglise
avec aulcunes additions utiles et prouffitables
concernans lesdictes parolles.* — Paris, Estienne
Caveiller, pr. Henri Paquot, Les Angeliers, 1538.
8°: a-z^8 &^{8} ¶^{4}, goth. ¶ 3v Impr. à Paris par Estienne caveiller.
*London BL 1360.e.7 (Angeliers). *Paris BN Rés. D 17409(2)
(Paquot). Cambridge UL.
References: Adams L 1369.

G 10.   **[Gaigny, Jean de].**

*Le livre de nouvel reimprime Faisant mention des
Sept parolles que nostre benoist Saulveur ... dist en
larbre de la croix: avec aucunes expositions et contemplations sur icelles: extraictes des dictz et sentences des docteurs authentiques et approuvez de
saincte eglise, avec aucunes additions utiles et
proffitables concernans lesdictes parolles. Veu et
corrige par lautheur de ce livre, Chanoine de la*

saincte chappelle. — Paris, Estienne Caveiller, pr. Maurice de La Porte, François Regnault, 1539.

8°: a-z &^{8} ¶^{4}, goth. ¶ 3r: Impr. à Paris par Estiene caveiller.
*Paris BN Rés. D 42244 (de la Porte). *Paris BM Rés. D 49521 (Regnault) (-a 6-8, ¶ 1-4).

G 11.   [Gaigny, Jean de].

Le livre de nouvel reimprime Faisant mention des Sept parolles que nostre benoist Saulveur ... dist en larbre de la croix: avec aucunes expositions et contemplations sur icelles: extraictes des dictz et sentences des docteurs authentiques et approuvez de saincte eglise, avec aucunes additions tres utiles et proffitables concernans lesdictes parolles. Veu et corrige par lautheur de ce livre. — Paris, Pierre Regnault, 1540.

8°: A-Z & Aa-Bb^8 Cc^4, rom.
*Vienna ÖNB 18.M.121.

G 12.   [Gaigny, Jean de].

Le livre de nouvel reimprime faisant mention de sept parolles que nostre benoist saulveur ... dit en larbre de la croix: avec aulcunes expositions et contemplations sur icelles: extraictes des dictz et sentences des docteurs autentiques et approuvez de saincte eglise, avec aulcunes additions utiles et prouffitables concernans lesdictes parolles. — Paris, Chrestien Wechel, 1545.

8°: A-N^8 O^4, goth. O 3r: 1546.
*London BL C.66.d.17. *Paris BN D 11912.
Notes: In the colophon, 'veu et corrige par laucteur diceluy livre, Chanoine de la saincte Chappelle. 1546'. But the t.p. reads '1545'.

G 13.   Garnier, Jean.

Briefve et claire confession de la foy Chrestienne, Contenant Cent articles, selon l'ordre du Symbole des Apostres, faicte et declairee l'an 1549. — [Basle], Jacques Estauge, 1551?

8°: A-I^8, rom. I 8r: 'Q. PARCI'.
*Paris SHP A 1171 (-A 1, I 8). *Vienna ÖNB 79.V.92. *Zurich ZB C 260(3).

References: Bietenholz #453.
Notes: Dedic. epistle dated from Strasbourg, 24 July 1549. The work was originally a sermon series. Garnier was pastor of the Strasbourg French church, 1545-55. The proposed date of the ed. suggested by a letter from Garnier to Calvin in 1552 saying the work had been printed the previous year (P. Denis, *Églises*).

G 14.   Gerson, Jean.

Sensuyt le Confessional, aultrement appelle le Directoire des confesseurs: livre tresfructueux et prouffitable et utille contre tous erreurs concernant la foy catholicque, a tous fidelles chrestiens pour scavoir et apprendre la maniere de soy confesser et examiner sa conscience. — Paris, Poncet Le Preux, 1537.
8°: A-K⁸ L⁴, goth. L 3r: Impr. à Paris.
*Paris BM Rés. 51594(3).
References: Renouard MSS.
Notes: Priv. (A 1v) to Poncet Le Preux for two years, dated 17 Feb. 1536, and applying to three works: the present, the *Doctrinal de la foy catholique*, and Bellemere's *Directoire de la vie humaine*. First ed.? See also O. Maillard, *Lexemplaire de confession*.

G 15.   Gerson, Jean.

Le Directoire des confesseurs. — Paris, Poncet Le Preux, 1538.

G 16.   Gerson, Jean.

Le Directoire des confesseurs. — Paris, Poncet Le Preux, 1539.

G 17.   Gerson, Jean.

Sensuyt le Confessional, aultrement appelle le Directoire des confesseurs, ... contre tous erreurs concernant la foy catholicque, ... pour scavoir et apprendre la maniere de soy confesser. — Paris, Poncet Le Preux, 1547.
16°: a-x⁸, goth. x 7v: Impr. à Paris.
*London BL 4412.e.8 (- x 8).
References: Renouard MSS < Brunet.

G 18. Gerson, Jean.

Le confessional appelle le directoire des confesseurs.
— Paris?, pr. Poncet Le Preux?, ?
8°: a-l⁸, goth.
*Paris BEBA Masson 8 (-a 1, l 8).
Notes: A MS note in the Paris BEBA copy suggests that this
very anonymous ed. was printed for Poncet Le Preux.

G 19. Gerson, Jean.

*Le doctrinal de la foy catholique: auquel est comprins
en brief le manipule des curez.* — Paris, Poncet Le
Preux, 1537.
8°: aa-cc⁸ dd⁴, goth.
*Paris BM 51594(1) (-aa 1).
References: Renouard MSS.

G 20. Gerson, Jean.

*La mendicité spirituelle. Les meditacions de lame: le
consolatif de tristesse.* — Paris, Michel Le Noir, 1519.
4°: a-d⁶ᐟ⁴ e-l⁸ᐟ⁴, goth. l 8r: Impr. à Paris par Michel Le Noir. 03.05.1519.
*London BL 1412.c.13. Nantes Dobrée 130.
References: Dagens. Frankfurt cat. 1610. Moreau II #2063.
Notes: The 'Meditacions de lame', c 5v sqq. 'Le Consolatif',
by 'ung venerable religieux de lordre des celestins', begins
h 1r, but without separate t.p.

G 21. Gouda, Gerard van der.

Linterpretation et signification de la Messe. — Antwerp, Guillaume Vorsterman, 1529.
8°: A-T⁸ V⁴, goth. V 3r: Impr. en Anvers par Guillamme Vorsterman. 1529.
Antwerp MPM. *Paris BN Rés. B 21307.
References: NK #3077.
Notes: Very traditionalist presentation of the Mass by a Franciscan 'de l'ordre des observans'.

G 22. Gouda, Gerard van der.

Linterpretation et signification de la Messe. — Antwerp, Guillaume Vorsterman, 1538.
8°: []⁸ B-T⁸ V⁴, goth. V 3r: Impr. en Anvers par Guillaume Vorsterman. 1538.

*London BL C.53.h.10.
References: NK #988.

G 23.   Greban, Simon.

Le premier (-second) volume du triumphant mystere des Actes des Apostres translate fidelement a la verite Historiale. — Paris, Nicolas Couteau, Guillaume Alabat, 1538.
2°: 2 vols, +^{4} a^6 A^4 B-X^8 Y^4. +^{8} AA-ZZ aa-cc^8 dd-ee^6, goth. ee4v: Impr. à Paris pour Guillaume Alabat de Bourges par Nicolas Couteau. 15.03.1537.
Edinburgh NLS H.23.a.3. Bourges BM By 30042. Chantilly Condé III H 23. *Paris BN Rés. Yf 19-20. London BL C.107.f.10 (+).
References: *Rép.bib.* #1. Rothschild #1074.
Notes: First ed., it seems, of a mystery play composed by a Doctor of Theology in the mid-15th cent.

G 24.   Greban, Simon.

Le premier (-second) volume du triumphant mystere des actes des Apostres. — Paris, [Nicolas Couteau], A. et C. Angelier, Guillaume Alabat (Bourges), 1540.
4°: 2 vols, ã^6 ẽ^4 a^4 b-z §^{8} aa^6 bb^4. ã^4 ẽ^4 a-z aa-zz aaa-rrr^4, goth. rrr 3v: Impr. à Paris pour Arnoul et Charles les Angeliers. 1540.
Chantilly Condé IX G 25-26. London BL C.51.1.1. *Paris BN Rés. Yf 111-112. Lyon BV Rés. 317067 (missing).
References: *Rép.bib. suppl.* Bourges Alabat 2.
Notes: Second ed.: ref. to the play 'dernierement joué à Bourges'. Guillaume Alabat, 'bourgeois et marchant de Bourges' seems to have financed the performance and the edition.

G 25.   Greban, Simon.

Les Catholiques oeuvres et Actes des Apostres redigez en escript par sainct Luc Evangeliste. — Paris, [Nicolas Couteau], A. et C. Angelier, Guillaume Alabat, 1541.
2°: 2 vols, *^{4} a-z aa-mm^6. §^{2} A-X Aa-Hh^6 Ii^8, goth. Ii 7v: Impr. ainsi que le mistere est joue a Paris. 1541.
Chantilly Condé V H 6. Paris BN Rés. Yf 21-22. La Haye KB 164 B2. *Paris SHP A 49. Edinburgh NLS Newb 4780 (+).
References: *Rép.bib. suppl.* Bourges Alabat 3.
Notes: Third ed. The gathering §^{2} at the beginning of Vol. 2 includes a poem in praise of the four 'entrepreneurs' (including the butcher Leonard Chobelet and the florist Jean Louvet) res-

ponsible for the Paris performance, and a prayer to Francis I
to build a theatre.

G 26. **Grégoire de Nazianze, Saint.**

De la cure, et nourrissement des Pauvres. Sermon.
— Lyon, Sebastien Gryphe, 1539.
4°: A-H⁴, rom.
*Geneva BPU Rés. Bd 1268.

G 27. **Grégoire, Jean.**

Devote exposition sus le Pater noster. — Avignon, Jean
de Channey, 1535?
8°: a-b⁸, goth.
Séville Colombine.
References: Babelon #78. Baudrier X, 296. *Rép.bib.* #39.
Notes: The text reappears in modified form in [Farel and
Luther], *Livre de vraye et parfaicte oraison.*

G 28. **[Grenier, Nicole].**

*Le Bouclier de la foy, en forme de Dialogue, extraict
de la Saincte escripture, et des Sainctz Peres et plus
anciens docteurs de l'Eglise.* — Paris, Vivant Gaultherot, 1547.
16°: ã⁸ a-z A-S⁸ T⁴, rom.
*Paris BSG D 8° 4408 Rés.
Notes: The author gives his name ('frere Nicole Grenier, chanoine regulier de S. Victor') in his dedic. to Henri II. The
priv. for the work dated 5 Apr. 1546, so the t.p. statement
'nouvellement Reveu et augmenté par l'Auteur' could be true.

G 29. **[Grenier, Nicole].**

*Le Bouclier de la foy, en forme de Dialogue extraict
de la saincte escripture, et des sainctz Peres et plus
anciens docteurs de l'Eglise ... nouvellement reveu et
augmenté par l'Autheur.* — Avignon, Imbert
Parmentier, 1548.
16°: [16]+654+[2] pp.
Terrebasse.
References: Baudrier X,384. *Rép.bib.* #1.

G 30.   Grenier, Nicole.

Le Bouclier de la foy, en forme de Dialogue, extraict de la saincte escripture, et des saincts peres, et plus anciens docteurs de l'Eglise ... Nouvellement reveu et augmenté par l'autheur. — Paris, 1548.
8°: a-z A-S⁸, rom.
*Paris BM 25392(1).

G 31.   Grenier, Nicole.

Le Bouclier de la foy, en forme de Dialogue, extraict de la Saincte escripture, et des Sainctz Peres et plus anciens docteurs de l'Eglise ... nouvellement reveu, et augmenté par l'Autheur. — Paris, Jean David, pr. Jean André, Vivant Gaultherot, 1548.
16°: ãã⁸ aa-zz AA-SS⁸ TT⁴, rom. TT 4v: Paris, par Jehan David pr. Jehan André & Vivant Gaulterot. 24.04.1548.
*Paris BN D 36696 (-TT 4). *Munich BSB Dog. 113 (-ãã 1,2,8).

G 32.   Grenier, Nicole.

Le Bouclier de la foy, en forme de Dialogue, extraict de la Saincte escripture, et des sainctz Peres et plus anciens docteurs de l'eglise ... nouvellement reveu et augmenté par l'Autheur. — Paris, Michel Fezandat, pr. Jean André, Vivant Gaultherot, 1548.
8°: ã⁸ ẽ⁸ a-z A-H⁸, rom. H 8v: Imp. à Paris par Michel Fezandat pour Jehan André & Vivant Gaultherot.
*Paris BN D 36695.

G 33.   Grenier, Nicole.

Le Bouclier de la foy, en forme de dialogue, extraict de la Saincte escripture, et des Sainctz Peres et plus anciens docteurs ... Reveu et augmenté. — Antwerp, Martin Nuyts, Jehan Rijckaerts, 1549.
16°: [16]+297+[1] ff., a-z Aa-Rr⁸, rom. Rr 8r: Impr. par Martin Nuyts.
*London BL 1018.b.10.
Notes: Rr 7v-8r: priv. for Brabant to Jehan Rijckaerts, libr. d'Anvers, for three years, dated 29 Mar. 1547.

G 34.   Grenier, Nicole.

Le Bouclier de la foy. — Paris, Vivant Gaultherot, 1549.

16°.
Charleville. Paris BN D 21837 (missing).
References: Renouard MSS.

G 35. **Grenier, Nicole.**

*Le Bouclier de la foy, en forme de Dialogue, extraict
de la saincte escripture, et des sainctz Peres et plus
anciens docteurs de l'eglise ... Reveu et augmenté par
l'Autheur outre les precedentes impressions.* — Paris,
Vivant Gaultherot, 1550.
16°: ã⁸ ẽ⁸ ĩ⁴ aaa-zzz AAA-ZZZ AAa-FFf⁸ GGg⁴, rom.   GGg 4r:
Impr. à Paris pour Vivant Gaultherot. 26.07.1550.
*Wolfenbüttel HAB 1291.15 Theol.

G 36. **Grenier, Nicole.**

*Tome second du Bouclier de la foy, contenant l'anti-
dote contre les adversaires de la pure Conception de
la mere de Dieu.* — Paris, Vivant Gaultherot, 1549.
16°: ã⁸ ẽ⁸ a-z A-F⁸, rom.
*Rouen BM Montbret p 16651. *Wolfenbüttel HAB 1291.15.1 Theol.
Notes: In the priv. (ã 1v-2v) Grenier is described as 'grand
vicaire et prieur de Sainct Victor lez Paris'.

G 37. **Grenier, Nicole.**

*L'espee de la foy, pour la defense de l'eglise chres-
tienne, contre les ennemis de verité, extraicte de la
saincte escripture, des saincts conciles, et des plus
anciens peres et docteurs de l'Eglise.* — Paris, Benoist
Prevost, Guillaume Cavellat, 1551.
8°: [12]+300 ff. aa⁸ ee⁴ a-z A-O⁸ P⁴, rom. P 4v: Impr. à Paris par
Benoist Prevost.
*London BL 850.d.2.
Notes: aa 1v: priv. for six years to Cavellat and Prévost, dated
27 Feb. 1550. Dedic. by Grenier to Anne de Montmorency,
dated 25 Apr. 1551. A continuation of his *Bouclier*, with
numerous mentions of Luther but none explicitly of Calvin
(acc. to the *table des matieres*). Several later eds, and translations
into Italian and Dutch.

G 38. **Gringore, Pierre.**

Le Blazon des heretiques. — Paris, Philippe Le Noir,
1524?

4°: a-d⁴, goth.
Chartres (destroyed).
References: Oulmont #21. Peter *RHPR* 1983. Reprod.
Chartres, 1832 (Paris BN Rés. Ye 4106). Moreau III #675.
Notes: According to R. Peter, this is the first satirical portrait
of Luther in France.

G 39.   Gringore, Pierre.

Le Blazon des heretiques. — S. Nicolas du Port,
Jérôme Jacobi, 1524.
References: *Rép.bib.* #1.

G 40.   Gringore, Pierre.

Le Blazon des heretiques. — ?, ?, 1530?
8°: A-C⁸, goth.
Séville Colombine.
References: Babelon #79.
Notes: F. Columbus bought the book in 1531.

G 41.   Gringore, Pierre.

*Chantz Royaulx, figurez morallement sur les misteres
miraculeux de Nostre saulveur ... et sur la Passion
avec plusieurs devotes Oraisons et Rondeaux contemplatifz.* — Paris, [Nicolas Higman], Jean Petit,
1528?
4°: a-h⁴, goth.
*Paris BA Rés. 8° T 2579. *Paris BA 4° T 954.
References: Moreau III #1490.
Notes: The two Paris BA copies bound with copies of *Heures
de nostre dame*, Paris, Jean Petit, 1528? The *Chantz Royaulx*
are mentioned on the t.p. of the *Heures*, but have an independent
t.p. and collation. Despite their apparent identity, the two
copies represent different eds. The text consists of a series of
images (hunter, doctor ...) for the life of Christ. Thoroughly
orthodox.

G 42.   Gringore, Pierre.

*Chantz royaulx figurez morallement sur les misteres
miraculeux de Nostre saulveur ... Jesuchrist et sur la
Passion.* — Paris, Guillaume de Bossozel, Jean Petit,
1532?
4°: [32 ff.], a-h⁴, goth.

Washington LC PQ 1625.G7 A78.
References: Moreau IV #434.
Notes: h 4r.: Priv. to Gringore for four years, dated 10 Oct. 1527.
The date of this edition suggested by Mlle Moreau. Thanks to
Bettye Chambers for information concerning this edition.

G 43.   Gringore, Pierre, Gilles de Redon.

Chantz Royaulx, Figurez morallement sur les mis-
teres miraculeux de Nostre saulveur et redempteur
Jesuchrist, et sur la passion avec plusieurs devotes
Oraisons ... La musique angelicque. — Paris, Denis
Janot, 1535.
8°: A-F⁸ G⁴, rom. G 4r: Impr. à Paris par Denys Janot.
*Versailles BM Goujet 8° 33.
References: Moreau IV #1329. Rawles #39. Peach/Brunel
#271.
Notes: See separate entry for G. de Redon, *Musique angelique.*

G 44.   Gringore, Pierre.

Chantz Royaulx figurez moralement sur les mysteres
miraculeux de nostre saulveur ... et sur la Passion
avec plusieurs devotes Oraisons et Rondeaulx con-
templatifz. — Paris, Pierre Regnault, 1540.
8°: a-d⁸, rom.
*Paris BA 8° T 2580(2).
Notes: Bound with *Heures de nostre Dame*, Paris, Pierre Regnault, s.d. The t.p. of the *Heures* mentions the *Chantz*
Royaulx, but these have independent t.p. and collation.

G 45.   Gringore, Pierre.

Chantz Royaulx, Figurez morallement sur les mysteres
miraculeux de nostre saulveur ... et sur la Passion
avec plusieurs devotes Oraisons et Rondeaulx con-
templatifz. — Paris, Oudin Petit, 1540?
4°: a-h⁴, goth.
*Paris BA 8° T 2578. *Paris BA 4° T 955. *Paris BN Rés. B 2913.
Notes: The copy in Paris BA 8° T 2578 is bound with a 1528
ed. of the *Heures de nostre dame*, and the ed. gives (h 4r) the
priv. to Gringore for four years, dated 10 Oct. 1527. But
Oudin Petit (named on t.p.) was not working until 1540.

G 46.   Gringore, Pierre.

Chantz Royaulx figurez moralement sur les mysteres miraculeux de nostre saulveur ... et sur la Passion avec plusieurs devotes Oraisons et Rondeaulx contemplatifz. — Paris, Pierre Regnault, 1542.
8°: a-d⁸, rom.
*Paris BEBA Les 406.

G 47.   Gringore, Pierre.

La complaincte de la cite crestienne faicte sur les lamentations Hieremie. — [Paris], [Jacques Ferrebouc], Pierre Bige, 1530?
8°: A-B⁴, goth. B 4v: On les vent cheulx Pierre Bige ... rue de Byevre a lhostel de Troye.
*Paris BN Rés. Ye 2947 (-B 1-4). *Chantilly Condé IV D 106.
References: Moreau III #2121.
Notes: Lamentation in decasyllabics on the devastation of Nancy by 'la foy Lhuter'. B 4v: GRINGORE named in an acrostic.

G 48.   Gringore, Pierre.

Heures de nostre dame translatees en Françoys et mises en rithme. — Paris, [Nicolas Higman], Jean Petit, 1525?
4°: A-B⁴ a-p⁴ᐟ⁸ q², goth.
*Paris BA Rés. 8° T 2577. *Paris BN Rothschild V.8.17. *London BL C.24.a.26. Vienna ÖNB.
References: Moreau III, #830.
Notes: The Paris Faculty of Theology banned the printing of Gringore's *Heures* on 26 Aug. 1525, decision confirmed by the Parlement on 28 Aug. (Higman *Censorship*, pp. 77-9). The royal privilege is dated from Lyon, 10 Oct. 1525.

G 49.   Gringore, Pierre.

Heures de nostre dame, translatees de latin en françoys et mises en ryme, additionnees de plusieurs chantz Royaulx figurez et moralisez. — Paris, Jean Petit, 1530?
4°: A-B⁴ a-p⁴ᐟ⁸ q² a-h⁴, goth.
*Paris BA Rés. 8° T 2578. Harvard CL. Séville Colomb.
References: Moreau III #2122. Mortimer #259. Babelon #81.

Notes: A new royal priv. (A 1v-2r) dated 15 Nov. 1527. *Almanach* for 1528-43. In the Paris BA copy the *Chantz royaulx* are present, a-h⁴, but in a later ed.

G 50.   Gringore, Pierre.

Heures de nostre dame, translatees de latin en françoys et mises en ryme, additionnees de plusieurs chantz royaulx figurez et moralisez. — Paris, [Guillaume de Bossozel], Jean Petit, 1532?
4°: A-B⁴ a-p⁴/⁸ q² a-h⁴, goth.
*Paris BA Rés. 4° T 954. Paris BN Rés. B 2913 and 2913 ter.
References: Moreau IV #436.
Notes: T.p. identical with prec. ed., but the text entirely recomposed. Fols. a-h⁴: the *Chantz royaulx*.

G 51.   Gringore, Pierre.

Heures de nostre dame, translatees de latin en francoys et mises en ryme, additionnees de plusieurs chantz Royaulx figurez et moralisez. — Paris, [Guillaume de Bossozel], Jean Petit, 1534?
4°: π⁴ B⁴ a-p⁴/⁸ q², goth.
Nantes. Manchester JRL. *Paris BA Rés. 8° T 2579. *Paris BM Rés. 11957. Harvard CL.
References: Mortimer #260. Moreau IV #1009.
Notes: At least the first gathering recomposed by comparison with the 1532? ed., with an almanac for 1534-49.

G 52.   Gringore, Pierre.

Heures de nostre Dame. — Paris, 1539.
References: Renouard MSS < Brunet.

G 53.   Gringore, Pierre.

Heures de nostre dame translatees de latin en françoys et mises en ryme, Additionnees de plusieurs chantz royaulx figurez et moralisez. — Paris, Jean Petit, 1540?
4°: π⁴ B⁴ a-o⁴/⁸ p⁶, goth.
*Chantilly Condé VIII.F.11. *Paris BA 4° T 955. *Paris BN Rés. B 2913. *Paris BSG OE XV 4° 371(2) Rés. *Rouen BM O 523.
Notes: Almanac for 1540-54. Bound, in the Paris BN and Paris BA copies, with the *Chantz royaulx* printed by Oudin Petit, *c*. 1540.

G 54.   Gringore, Pierre.

Heures de nostre dame translatées de latin en françoys et mises en rhyme, Additionnées de plusieurs chantz royaulx figurez et moralisez. — Paris, Pierre Regnault, 1540?

8°: a-n⁸, rom.

*Paris BEBA Les 406.

Notes: Almanac for 1540-54. Paris BEBA copy bound with 1542 ed. of *Chantz royaulx*.

G 55.   Gringore, Pierre.

Heures de nostre dame translatées de latin en françoys et mises en rhyme, Additionnées de plusieurs chantz royaulx figurez et moralisez. — Paris, Pierre Regnault, 1540?

8°: A⁸ b⁸ c⁶ d-h I-N⁸, rom.

*Paris BA 8° T 2580 (-A 7, b 7, d 1, e 7).

Notes: Bound with *Chantz Royaulx*, Paris, Pierre Regnault, 1540. Almanac for 1540-54.

G 56.   Gringore, Pierre.

Heures de Nostre Dame, à l'usage de Romme, translatées de latin en françoys et mises en rhythme, avec le dict latin en marge: nouvellement reveues et augmentees de tres belles declarations de chascun pseaulme par ung reverend docteur en theologie en l'universite de Paris, additionnees de plusieurs chants royaulx, figurez et moralisez. — Paris, Antoine Bonnemere, 1544.

8°: A-T⁸, rom.

References: Oulmont pp. 58-9.

Notes: Almanac for 1544-58.

G 57.   Gueroult, Guillaume, music by Didier Lupi.

Premier Livre de chansons spirituelles, Nouvellement composees. — Lyon, G. et M. Beringen, 1548.

8°: a-g⁸, ital.

*Chantilly Condé IV.F.8.

References: Baudrier III, 47. Brunet II, 1791. Pidoux 48/III.

Notes: Priv. (a 1v) for five years, dated 4 Aug. 1547. Contains 21 songs, most of them biblical paraphrases.

G 58. **Guerric,** trans. Jean de Gaigny.

Sermons. — Paris, Simon de Colines, Estienne Roffet, 1540?

8°: π⁴ A-Z AA-FF⁸ GG⁴, rom.

*Paris BN C 3347. *Paris BA 8° T 6240
(without Roffet).

References: Farge *Bio. reg*, Gaigny.

Notes: Jean de Gaigny edited the Latin original of the *Sermones* by the 'bienheureux Guerric, abbé d'Igny', in 1539. He says he undertook the French translation at the request of Francis I, in order to counter the heterodox books in French which were circulating.

G 59. **Guillaume d'Auvergne,** trans. Adrien Gémeau.

La rethoricque divine. — Paris, Jean Petit, 1514?

4°: [8] + '202' [= 188] ff. (1-8,17-72, 78-202), A⁸ a-e F-Z⁸ &⁴, goth.

& 4v: Impr. à Paris pour Jehan petit.

*Paris BN Rés. D 80456. Lille.

References: Moreau II #848.

Notes: Guillaume d'Auvergne was Bishop of Paris, 1228-49, and is named on t.p. as 'Guillaume de paris'. Dedic. (A 1v-3r) by 'Adrian Gemelli prestre, docteur en theologie, grand archidiacre de Laon' to Marie de Luxembourg, at whose demand he did the translation. A treatise on prayer, in two parts and 56 chapters. Text dated (a 1r) 1512.

G 60. **Guillaume d'Auvergne,** trans. Adrien Gémeau.

La Rhetorique divine. — Paris, Michel Le Noir, 1520.

8°.

References: Moreau II #2345 < La Croix - Du Verdier III, 21.

G 61. **Guillaume d'Auvergne,** trans. Nicolas Sellier.

Traite touchant la doctrine et enseignement de prier Dieu. — Paris, Antoine Verard, 1511.

8°.

References: Moreau II #104 < Brunet II, 1821. Du Verdier II, 193-4.

H

H 1.   **Hangest, Jérôme de.**

Contre les tenebrions lumiere evangelicque. — Paris, Guillaume de Bossozel, Jean Petit, 1535.
8°: a-g^8 h^4, rom. a 1v: ach. d'impr. 15.01.1534 (a.s.).
Edinburgh UL De S.93. *Paris BN Rés. D 80052. *Paris SHP A 641. Séville Colombine.
References: Moore #156. Babelon #86. Hari *APR* p. 113. Berthoud *Marcourt.* M.M. de La Garanderie, *Christianisme et lettres profanes* (Paris, 1976), I, 220-21. Higman, 'Prem. rép.', pp. 370-2. Moreau IV #1330.
Notes: Reply by a Doctor of Theology to the 1534 placards. The t.p. describes this as a 'secunde et ampliee edition', but no other ed. is known.

H 2.   **Hangest, Jérôme de.**

En controversie voye seure. — Paris, Jean Petit, 1537.
8°: a-d^8 e^4, rom. e 3r: ach. d'impr. 27.01.1536 (a.s.).
*Paris BM Rés. 25543(2).
References: Higman, 'Prem. rép.', pp. 371-2.
Notes: Laymen, says Hangest, should not delve too deeply into theology, but submit to the teachings of ecclesiastical superiors.

H 3.   **Henry, Jean.**

Le Jardin de contemplation. — Paris, Jean Petit, 1516.
8°: a-z & A-D^8, goth.   D 7r: Impr. a Paris pr. Jehan Petit. 25.10.1516.
*Paris BN Rés. D 37508 (-D 7,8). *Paris BEBA Masson 529. *Paris BSG D8° 5899(2) inv 7338 Rés. (-a 1).
References: Moreau II #1373.
Notes: a 2r: dedic. to the Abbess 'du College des seurs minorettes de Saincte Clere à Aigueperse' by Jean Henry, 'chantre de leglise de Paris, conseillier du Roy nostre Sire, et President en la chambre des enquestes de la court de parlement'.

H 4.   **[Henry, Jean].**

Le livre de la toute belle sans pair qui est la vierge Marie. — Paris, Jean Petit, 1516?
8°: aa-zz &&^{8}, goth. && 8v: Impr. à Paris pr. Jehan Petit.
*Paris BN Rés. D 18713. Séville Colomb.

References: Moreau II #1374.

H 5.   Henry, Jean.

Le livre de meditation sur la reparation de nature humaine. Ensemble le livre de consolation sur la joyeuse meditation de la nativite de Jesus. — Paris, Jean Petit, 1516?
8°: A-S⁸, goth. S 8v: Impr. à Paris pr. Jehan Petit.
*Paris BN Rés. D 37532(1). *Versailles BM Incunable P 74. Séville Colomb.
References: Moreau II #1375.
Notes: The *Livre de meditation* dedic. (A 2r) to Gabrielle de Bourbon, 'fille du comte de Montpensier'. *Le Livre de consolation* (I 2r) dedic. to the 'religieuses et devotes meres prieure et couvent de la Casedieu'.

H 6.   Henry, Jean.

Le livre de reformation utile et profitable pour toutes religieuses. — Paris, Jean Petit, 1516?
8°: a-k⁸ l¹⁰, goth. l 9v: Impr. à Paris pr. Jehan Petit.
*Paris BN Rés. D 37532(3). *Paris BSG D 8° 6325(1) inv 8018 Rés.
References: Moreau II #1376.
Notes: Dedic. (a 2r) to 'Marie de Bretaigne abbesse de Fontevrault'. Henry describes himself as 'archidiacre en leglise Devreux'.

H 7.   Henry, Jean.

Le livre dinstruction pour religieuses novices et professes. — Paris, Jean Petit, 1516.
8°: a-g⁸, goth. g 6r: Impr. à Paris pr. Jehan Petit. 31.10.1516.
*Paris BN Rés. D 37532(2). *Paris BSG D 8° 6325(2) inv 8018 Rés. *London BL 1360.a.6(1).
References: Moreau II #1377.
Notes: Dedic. (a 2r) to 'Marie Gastarde novice en lordre de Fontevrault au convent de Chaizedieu'. The t.p. mentions that the author died on 2 Feb. 1483.

H 8.   Henry, Jean.

Le pelerinage de nostre dame, et de joseph, de nazareth en Bethleem, La nativite de nostre seigneur, La venue des pastoureaulx. — Paris, Pierre Sergent, 1535?
8°: A-G⁸, goth. G 8v: Impr. pr. Pierre sergent.

*Paris BN Rés. D 80265.

Notes: Dedic. (A 2r) to 'Alis, espouse de Gilles Cornu, changeur du Tresor'. Earlier ed. in 1506 (Moreau I 1506 #75).

H 9.   Herp, Henry de, with J. Gerson, *Miroir de la cour,* trans. E.B.

Premiere partie du Directoire des contemplatifz <> laquelle traicte de la vie active, donnant singuliere instruction et briefve doctrine a tous chrestiens pour parvenir a la vie spirituelle et contemplative. — Paris, Jean Réal, pr. Poncet Le Preux, 1549.

16°: a-c² C-Z⁸ &², goth. & 2v: Impr. à Paris par Jehan Real pour Poncet le Preux. 1549.

London BL 1410.a.32. *Paris BA 8° T 6958. *Paris BN Rés. D 17236 and 80053.

Notes: a 2r-v: priv. to Poncet Le Preux for four years, dated 26 Sept. 1549. A second part of this work published in 1552. Henri van Erp, founder (in 1445) of the Gouda community of the Brethren of the Common Life, later became a Franciscan, and died in 1475.

H 10.   Hervet, Gentian.

Oraison ou Sermon de l'Ascension. — Orléans, Éloi Gibier, 1536.

8°.

References: *Rép.bib.* #1.

Notes: According to the t.p. this a translation by Hervet himself of his own Latin sermon (copy in BN).

H 11.   Heures de la compagnie.

Les Heures de la compagnie des penitents. — Lyon, Estienne Dolet, 1542.

16°.

References: Longeon *Dolet* #220 < Du Verdier.

Notes: Du Verdier (p. 1080) gives the title *Livre de la compagnie des penitens* (q.v.). The present title censured on 14 Feb. 1543 among Estienne Dolet's books (Higman *Censorship*, p. 98).

H 12. **[Heyden, Sebald], [Martin Luther].**

Dung seul mediateur entre dieu et les hommes, Jesu-
christ... Ung sermon de mammona iniquitatis. —
[Paris], [Simon Du Bois], 1526?
8°: A-E⁸, goth.
*Geneva MHR K Lut 5(5).
References: Moore #62. Benzing *Luther* #1441. Moreau III
#852. Clutton #45.
Notes: The first part translated from Sebald Heyden, *Unum*
Christum mediatorem esse (1525), the second, beginning
D 2r, from Luther's *Sermon von dem unrechten Mammon*
(1522, trans. into Latin, 1525).

H 13. **[Heyden, Sebald].**

D'ung seul mediateur et advocat entre Dieu et les
hommes nostre Seigneur Jesus Christ. — Geneva, Jean
Girard, 1538.
8°: A-D⁸, ital. D 8v: Impr. à Geneve par Jehan Gerard. 1538.
*Geneva BPU Rés. Bb 581. *Geneva MHR K.Hey.1 (without colophon).
References: Moore #62. *Index* I, #453. *BG* 38/6.
Notes: Censured on 25 May 1542 (Higman *Censorship*, p. 92).

H 14. **[Heyden, Sebald].**

D'un seul mediateur, advocat, et intercesseur entre
Dieu et les hommes, nostre Seigneur Jesus Christ.
Ou est aussi demonstré comment la Vierge Marie
doit estre honnorée. — [Geneva], [Jean Girard], 1544.
8°: A-C⁸ D⁴, rom.
*Geneva BPU Rés. Bc 2706. *Vienna ÖNB 79.Ee.8.
References: Moore #62. *BG* 44/19.

=> *Homélies*: see *Quatre homelies*.

H 15. **Hugues de Saint-Victor,** trans. Jean Potin.

Larre de lame Qui est du gaige de amour divin...
Ensemble le Cueur navre de amour divin ... par ...
Richard de sainct Victor. — Paris, [Nicolas Couteau],
Pierre Roffet, 1533?
8°: A-L⁸, goth.
*Paris BN Rés. D 80198.

References: Moreau IV #733.

Notes: Trans. of *Soliloquium De arrha animae* and *Tractatus de quattuor gradibus violente charitatis.* The date suggested by Mlle Moreau. Two dedications, one to the Abbot of St Victor and the other to 'Reverende et venerable mere N.N. et à ses devotes filles en Jesuchrist', the latter signed 'Jehan de sainct Victor clerc regulier', who also signs the dedic. of the *Cueur navré* (E 2r-3v).

H 16.   Hymnes communes, trans. N. Mauroy.

Les Hymnes communes de lannee. — Troyes, 1527.

References: I. de La Tour III, 354n.

I

I 1.   Illyricus, Thomas.

Devotes oraisons en françois avec une chanson d'amour divin. — Paris, 1528.

References: Brunet V, 832 < Du Verdier. Moore #161. Moreau III #1616.

Notes: Thomas Illyricus was appointed Inquisiteur général of Savoy in 1527. He died in 1529.

I 2.   Illyricus, Thomas.

Copie de la prophetie faicte par le pauvre frere thomas souverain exclamateur de la parolle de dieu nouvellement translatee de ytalien en francoys. — [Paris?], ?, 1530?

8°: [4] ff., []⁴, goth.

*Paris BN Rés. Ye 2952.

References: Naef, *Origines* II, 76n. Mauriac *AFH* 17(1925).

Notes: Paris BN copy bound with 11 pamphlets of the same period. Prophecies of the angelic Pope, imminent reform of the Church, and of disasters for those (and for Rome in particular) who do not heed the warnings.

I 3.   Illyricus, Thomas, trans. Nicolas Volcyr de Serouville.

Le Sermon de Charité, avec les probations des erreurs de Luther. — Paris, 1525.

References: Naef *Origines* II,73.

I 4.   Illyricus, Thomas, trans. Nicolas Volcyr de Serouville.

Le Sermon de Charité, avec les probations des erreurs de Luther. — Saint Nicolas du Port, Jérôme Jacobi, 1525.
4°: 40 pp.
References: Brunet V, 832. Moore #160. Naef, *Origines* II, 73. *Rép.bib.* #4.

I 5.   Images de la mort, Hans Holbein, Jean de Vauzelles.

Les simulachres et historiees faces de la mort, autant elegamment pourtraictes, que artificiellement imaginées. — Lyon, Melchior et Gaspar Trechsel, pr. Jean et François Frellon, 1538.
4°: A-N⁴, rom. N 4v: Excud. Lugduni Melchior et Gaspar Trechsel. 1538.
*Amsterdam UL 073-183. *Geneva BPU Rés. Ia 432. *London BL 1044.f.30. *Munich BSB Im.mort.11. *Rouen BM Leber 1362 (+).
References: Baudrier V, 175. Mortimer #284. Rothschild #237. G. Franz.
Notes: Engravings attrib. to Holbein on the omnipresence of death, accompanied by quatrains by Jean de Vauzelles ('d'un vray zele', A 2r), and various examples and biblical quotations on death. The work ends with a treatise 'De la necessité de la mort' (M 3v sqq.). Dedic. (A 2r) from Jean de Vauzelles to 'moult reverende Abbesse du religieux convent S. Pierre de Lyon, Madame Jehanne de Touszele'.

I 6.   Images de la mort, Hans Holbein, Jean de Vauzelles.

Les simulachres et faces hystoriées de la Mort. — Paris, Denis Janot, 1538?
16°: A-M⁸, rom.
*Paris BEBA Masson 278. Geneva Bodmer.
References: Rawles #343.
Notes: Same contents as the Lyon ed., with copies of the engravings. At the end (M 5r sqq.), an added 'Instruction chrestienne pour soy disposer à bien vivre'.

I 7.   Images de la mort, Holbein, J. de Vauzelles, U. Rhegius.

Les Simulachres et historiees faces de la mort, contenant La medecine de l'ame, utile et necessaire non seulement aux Malades, mais à tous qui sont en bonne disposition corporelle. D'avantage, La Forme et maniere de consoler les malades. Sermon de sainct Cecile Cyprian, intitulé, de Mortalite. Sermon de S. Jan Chrisostome, pour nous exhorter à Patience. — Lyon, Jean et François Frellon, 1542.

8°: A-N⁸ O⁴, rom. O 3v: Impr. à Lyon par Jan & françois frellon. 1542. *London BL C.37.a.32. *Munich BSB Im.mort. 20. Paris BA 8° T 7960. **References:** Baudrier V, 186. Franz #5.10. Cat. Drilhon #1. *Index* I #489.

Notes: The Paris censure in the 1544 *Index* must refer to this ed. including the *Medecine de l'ame* and other treatises. To Holbein's engravings and Vauzelles's quatrains have been added the *Medecine de l'ame*, trans. from Urbanus Rhegius, *Seelenertzney* (1519, Latin 1537), 'La forme et maniere de consoler les malades', and sermons by St Cyprian and St Jean Chrysostome.

I 8.   Images de la mort, Holbein, J. de Vauzelles, U. Rhegius.

Les Images de la mort, auxquelles sont adjoustées douze figures. Davantage, La Medecine de l'Ame. La Consolation des Malades. Un Sermon de Mortalité, par sainct Cyprian... Un Sermon de Patience, par sainct Jehan Chrysostome. — Lyon, Jean Frellon, 1547.

8°: A-N⁸, rom. N 8v: Impr. à Lyon par Jehan Frellon. 1547. Harvard UL. *Paris SHP A 265. *Wolfenbüttel HAB 1089.13 Theol(2). *Montpellier BM C 273. Paris BEBA Les 419.(+). **References:** Baudrier V, 210. Mortimer #289. Franz #5.11. **Notes:** Contents identical to the 1542 *Simulachres*, except that 12 new engravings have been added (C 7r - D 5r).

I 9.   Imitation de Jésus-Christ.

Le livre intitule Internelle consolacion. — Paris, Jean Du Pré, [pr. Pierre Viart], 1520.

8°: π⁶ A-T⁸ V⁶, goth. V 6r: Impr. à Paris par Jehan du pre. 18.09.1520. *Paris BM Rés. 24915. Troyes BM. **References:** Vial, *GJ* 1964. Moreau II #2377. **Notes:** The publisher identified by his address on the t.p.: 'en la rue sainct Jaques à l'enseigne du Lyon d'argent'. Translation of three parts of the *Imitatio Christi*, traditionally attrib. to Thomas à Kempis. Eds since 1490 at least (Paris BN, BM).

I 10.   **Imitation de Jésus-Christ.**

Le livre intitule Internelle consolation nouvellement corrige. — Paris, Jean Du Pré, Pierre Viart, 1522.
8°: a⁸ A-V⁸, goth. V 8r: Impr. à Paris par Jehan du pre pour Pierre Viart. 04.03.1522.
*Paris BM Rés. 24916. London BL 4401.a.50.
References: Moreau III #338.

I 11.   **Imitation de Jésus-Christ.**

Le Livre intitu Internelle consolation nouvellement corrige. — Paris, Ambroise Girault, Pierre Leber, 1529?
8°.
Paris BSG.
References: Moreau III #1803.

I 12.   **Imitation de Jésus-Christ.**

Le livre intitule Internelle consolation nouvellement corrige. — Paris, Nicolas Savetier, 1530.
8°: *⁸ A-S⁸, goth.   S 8r: Impr. à Paris par Nicolas Savetier. 13.05.1530.
*Paris BA 8° T 6949. *Paris BSG Rés. D 8° 5861(1).
References: Moreau III #2155.

I 13.   **Imitation de Jésus-Christ.**

Livre intitule Internelle consolation nouvellement corrige. — Paris, Yolande Bonhomme, 1530.
4°.
References: Moreau III #2154 < Libr. A. Fontaine (1872) #4033.
Notes: Dated 30 May 1530.

I 14.   **Imitation de Jésus-Christ.**

Le livre intitule Internelle consolation, tresutile et proffitable a tous Chrestiens qui desirent faire le salut de leurs ames, Nouvellement reveu et corrige. — Paris, Nicolas Savetier, 1531.
8°: [8]+144 ff., §⁸ A-S⁸, goth.   S 8r: Impr. à Paris par Nicolas Savetier. 10.06.1531.
*Paris BN Rés. D 80274. Paris BSG. *Lyon BV 390305.
References: Moreau IV #206.

Notes: The t.p. contradicts the colophon, reading 'Imprimé à Paris le septiesme jour de Juillet 1531'.

I 15.   **Imitation de Jésus-Christ.**

Sensuyt le livre tressalutaire de Limitation de nostre seigneur Jesuchrist: Et du parfaict contempnement de ce miserable monde. — Paris, Philippe Le Noir, 1531?

4°: A⁸ B-Q⁴ R⁶, goth. R 3v: Impr. à Paris par Philippe le Noir.
*Paris BSG D 4° 2300 inv 2482 Rés.

References: Moreau IV #205.

Notes: A different translation from the *Internelle consolation*, including all four parts of the original.

I 16.   **Imitation de Jésus-Christ.**

Le livre intitule Internelle consolation, tresutile et proffitable a tous Chrestiens qui desirent faire le salut de leurs ames, Nouvellement reveu et corrige. — Paris, Philippe Le Noir, 1532.

8°: ã⁸ a-t⁸, goth. t 8r: Impr. à Paris par Philippe le Noir.
*Paris BN Rés. D 16300.

References: Moreau IV #457.

I 17.   **Imitation de Jésus-Christ.**

Le livre intitu[le Internelle] consolation nouvellement corrigee, [avec plusieu]rs additions jouxte les aultres comm[e on p]ourra veoir au commencement. — Paris, Pierre Leber, 1533.

8°: A⁸ A-V⁸, goth. V 8r: Impr. à Paris par Pierre leber. 01.03.1533.
*Paris BN Rés. D 16301. *Paris BSG D 8° 5861(3) inv 7277 Rés.
(-A 1-8, V 1-8).

References: Moreau IV #735.

Notes: Includes an extract from the fourth part of the *Imitatio*. The Paris BM copy lacks its t.p., and the Paris BN t.p. is damaged. The missing text is tentatively presented here in square brackets.

I 18.   **Imitation de Jésus-Christ.**

Le livre intitule internelle consolation nouvellement corrige. — Paris, Nicolas Higman, pr. Ambroise Girault, 1534?

8°: a⁸ A-V⁸, goth. Par Nicolas Hygman pour Ambroise girault.

Séville Colombine. Vienna ÖNB. Paris Bibl. V. Cousin.
References: Babelon #92. Moreau IV #1040.
Notes: Girault took over 'l'enseigne du Pellican' (t.p.) in 1533, and the book was purchased in 1535. Hence the suggested date.

I 19. Imitation de Jésus-Christ.

Le livre intitule Internelle consolation nouvellement corrige. — Paris, [Antoine de la Barre], Jacques Kerver, 1535.
8°: [8] + 160 ff., a⁸ A-V⁸, goth. V 8r: Impr. à Paris.
*Paris BN Rés. D 80218.
References: Moreau IV #1345.

I 20. Imitation de Jésus-Christ.

Internelle consolation. — Paris, 1536.
16°.
References: Renouard MSS < Brunet.

I 21. Imitation de Jésus-Christ.

Le livre intitu Internelle consolation nouvellement corrige. — Paris, Ambroise Girault, 1537.
Harvard CL.
References: *NUC* NSi 0004862.

I 22. Imitation de Jésus-Christ.

Le livre de L'internelle consolation, nouvellement reveu, et diligemment corrige. — Lyon, Jean Barbou, Guillaume de Guelques, 1538.
16°: a-y⁸ z⁶, rom. Z 6v: Impr. à Lyon par Jehan Barbou.
*Paris BN Rés. D 80460(1).
References: Baudrier V, 293.

I 23. Imitation de Jésus-Christ.

Internelle consolation. — Paris, Denis Janot, 1539.
16°: A-Y⁸ Z⁶, rom.
Coll. privée.
References: Vial *GJ* 1964. Rawles #103.

I 24. **Imitation de Jésus-Christ.**

Le livre intitule Internelle consolation nouvellement corrige. — Paris, Yolande Bonhomme, 1539.
8°: +⁸ A-S⁸, goth. S 8r: Impr. à Paris par Ioland bonhomme. 08.02.1539.
*London BL 4402.i.25(1).
Notes: Bound in London BL with *Preparations pour recevoir le sainct sacrement* and *Larmeure de patience*, with separate collations but no t.p. All three texts printed by Yolande Bonhomme, 1539.

I 25. **Imitation de Jésus-Christ.**

Le livre intitule Internelle consolation Nouvellement corrige. — Paris, [Pierre Sergent], 1539.
8°: [6]+132+[56] ff., +⁶ A-Q⁸ R⁴ S-Z⁸ &⁸, goth. R 4v: Impr. à Paris. 04.05.1539.
*Paris BN Rés. D 16302. *Paris BSG Δ 55650 Rés. (-+ 1-6).
References: Vial *GJ* 1964.
Notes: S 1r sqq: 'Petit traicte appelle Larmeure de pacience'.

I 26. **Imitation de Jésus-Christ.**

Le livre de l'internelle consolation nouvellement reveu et diligemment corrige. — Lyon, François Juste, 1540.
16°.
References: Baudrier suppl. #97 < Cat. Yemeniz #261.

I 27. **Imitation de Jésus-Christ.**

Le livre de l'Internelle consolation, nouvellement reveu et diligemment corrigé. — Paris, Denis Janot, 1540.
16°: A-Y⁸ Z⁶, rom. Z 6r: Impr. à Paris par Denys Janot.
*Paris BN Rés. D 16304.
References: Vial *GJ* 1964. Rawles #122.

I 28. **Imitation de Jésus-Christ.**

Le livre de l'Internelle consolation nouvellement reveu, et diligemment corrigé. — Paris, Jean Ruelle, 1540.
8°: A-Z a-c⁸, rom. c 8v: Impr. à Paris par Iehan Ruelle. 1540.
*Bruxelles BR LP 448 A. Paris BN Rés. D 16303 (missing).

I 29.   **Imitation de Jésus-Christ.**

Le livre de l'Internelle consolation, nouvellement reveu, et diligemment corrigé. — Paris, Denis Janot, 1541.
16°: A-Z⁸, rom. Z 6v: Impr. à Paris par Denys Janot.
*Paris BSG Rés. Δ 55653.
References: Rawles #155.

I 30.   **Imitation de Jésus-Christ.**

Le livre de Linternelle Consolation tresutile au Chrestien, nouvellement reveu, et dilgemment corrige... Larmeure de Patience... Devote contemplation ... sur le Salve regina. — Lyon, Denis de Harsy, 1542.
16°: A-Z a-k⁸, goth. k 7v: Impr. à Lyon par Denys de harsy.
Paris BN Rés. D 16305 (-k 1-8). *Vienna ÖNB 17.J.73.
References: Vial *GJ* 1964. Cat. Drilhon #23.

I 31.   **Imitation de Jésus-Christ.**

L'Internelle consolation. oeuvre divisée en trois parties et necessaire à tout esprit Chrestien. — Lyon, Estienne Dolet, 1542.
16°: A-Z AA⁸, rom.   AA 7r: ach. d'impr. à Lyon, 'Chés Estienne Dolet, retenu pour lors aux prisons de Rouenne'. 1542.
*Paris BN Rés. D 16307 (-A 1).
References: Longeon *Dolet* #222. Vial *GJ* 1964.
Notes: The title is copied from Du Verdier. AA 7r-8r, two dizains by Dolet, who blames his imprisonment on 'l'envye et calumnie d'aulcuns maistres Imprimeurs (ou pour myeulx dire, barbouilleurs) et libraires dudict lieu.'

I 32.   **Imitation de Jésus-Christ.**

Le livre intitule Internelle consolation Nouvellement corrige. — Paris, Arnoul Langelier, 1542.
8°: ¶⁸ A-P⁸ Q¹⁰ R-Z⁸, goth. Q 10v: Impr. à Paris. 27.06.1542.
*Paris BN Rés. D 16306.
References: Vial *GJ* 1964.
Notes: R 1r sqq.: 'Larmeure de pacience en adversite.' Copied from the 1539 ed. by Pierre Sergent.

I 33.   **Imitation de Jésus-Christ.**

Le livre de l'Internelle consolation... Et y sont adjouxtées les Tentations du Diable, avec la defense du bon Ange. — Lyon, Jean de Tournes, 1543.
16°: a-x⁸, rom.
*Vienna ÖNB 17.J.70.
References: Cartier *De Tournes* #10.
Notes: Copied from Dolet's 1542 ed., but omitting Dolet's preface and poems.

I 34.   **Imitation de Jésus-Christ.**

De limitation de Jesu Christ selon la saincte Evangile, et contempnement de vanite de ce monde, translate de hault Alemant en langue Francoise. Avec ung dialogue du Seigneur et du Serviteur... Le tout diligemment et fidelement corrige et purge de faultes innumerables, comme lon poura veoir conferant ces exemplaires a tous autres. — Antwerp, Jean de Grave, 1544.
16°: A-X⁸, goth.
*Paris BSG ∆ 54989 Rés.
Notes: A 1v: preface from the 'translateur' to 'sa soeur Marguerite religieuse observante de lordre sainct Dominique, en la noble Cite de Metz', dated from 'Vienne en Austriche, le premier lundi de carême, 1538.' A different translation from previous items. Contains only three parts.

I 35.   **Imitation de Jésus-Christ.**

De limitation de Jesu Christ selon la saincte Evangile, et contempnement de vanite de ce monde, translate de hault Alemant en langue Françoise. Avec ung dialogue du Seigneur et du Serviteur... Le tout diligemment et fidelement corrige et purge de faultes innumerables, comme lon poura veoir conferant ces exemplaires a tous aultres. — Antwerp, Jean de Grave, 1544.
16°: A-X⁸, goth.
*Paris BSG Rés. D 8° 5862.
Notes: Entirely reset ed. by comparison with the preceding number.

I 36.   **Imitation de Jésus-Christ.**

L'Internelle Consolation. Oeuvre tresutile, et neces-saire a tout esprit Chrestien. — Lyon, François Juste, Pierre de Tours, 1544.
16°: 212 ff., A-Z AA-CC⁸ DD⁴, goth.   DD 4v: Impr. à Lyon par Françoys Juste. 04.05.1544.
*Carpentras BM C 263.
References: Baudrier *Suppl.* #113.

I 37.   **Imitation de Jésus-Christ.**

Internelle consolation. — Paris, Jean Ruelle, 1544.
References: Renouard MSS.

I 38.   **Imitation de Jésus-Christ.**

Le livre de l'Internelle Consolation, nouvellement reveu, et diligemment corrigé. Avec l'Armeure de patience en adversité. Un autre petit traicté ou sont contenues aucunes Instructions et Oraisons. — Paris, Jean Amazeur, pr. Jean Ruelle, 1550.
16°. Impr. à Paris par Jehan Amazeur.
Paris Univ Rés. XVI b. 27 nains (being restored).

I 39.   **Imitation de Jésus-Christ.**

Sensuit le livre salutaire de Limitation de Nostre Seigneur Jesuchrist et du parfaict contemnement de ce miserable monde. — Paris, Denis Janot, ?
4°: 78 ff.
References: Rawles #296 < Brunet III, 419.

I 40.   **Instruction des curés,** ed. Denis Briçonnet.

Linstruction des curez pour instruire le simple peuple ... par tout levesche de Sainct Malo. — Paris, Olivier Senant, 1515?
4°: a-m⁸, goth.
*Paris BSG C 4° 322 inv 320(2) Rés. Dinan.
References: Moreau II #1147: 'extraits de Gerson et Hugues de S. Cher', already printed before 1511.
Notes: Added are the decisions of a synod held on 31 May 1515 in the Abbey of St Jacques 'prope montem fortez'.

I 41.   **Instruction des curés.**

*Linstruction des curez pour instruire le simple peuple,
cest assavoir le livre des troys parties des commandemens de Dieu, de confession: et de lart de bien
mourir.* — Poitiers, Enguilbert de Marnef, 1516?
4°: A-F^8 G^6, goth.
References: *Rép.bib.* #1.
Notes: The *Opus tripartitum* attrib. on t.p. to Jean Gerson.

I 42.   **Instruction des curés.**

*Linstruction des curez pour instruire le simple peuple
... par tout levesche De Sainct Malo.* — Nantes, Jean
Baudouin, 1518.
4°: a-m^8, goth. A 1v: Nannetis per Johannem Baudouyn. 10.04.1518.
*Paris BSG BB 4° 239 inv 462 Rés.

I 43.   **Instruction des curés.**

Linstruction des curez pour instruire le simple peuple.
— Paris, Nicolas Higman, Nicolas de La Barre, Jean
Barbaram (Nevers), 1521.
4°.
References: Graesse VII, 391. Moreau III #143.

I 44.   **Instruction des curés.**

*Linstruction des curez Et vicaires pour instruire le
simple peuple avec la maniere de faire le prosne.* —
Lyon, Olivier Arnoullet, 1525.
4°: [34] ff., A-G^4 H^6, goth. H 6r: Impr. à Lyon par Olivier Arnoullet.
18.02.1525.
*Paris BN Rothschild II.3.33.
References: Rothschild #46.
Notes: A 1v-2r: letter in Latin from Stephanus Parisien. Epis.
[Étienne Poncher] to curates, vicars, etc., dated 1506. A 2r-4r:
same letter in French. Bilingual throughout.

I 45.   **Instruction des curés.**

*Linstruction des Curez pour instruyre le simple peuple,
Compose par maistre Jehan Gerson,... appelle en
latin Opus tripartitum.* — Paris, [Guillaume de
Bossozel], 1531.
4°: A-D^4 E^8 F-M^4, goth. M 4v: Impr. à Paris.

*Paris BSG E 4° 1896 inv 1140 Rés. *Paris BSG C 548 inv 113 Rés. (5) (-M 1,3,4). Paris BN Rés. B 2278(2).
References: Moreau IV #168.

I 46.   Instruction des curés.

Linstruction des curez pour instruire le simple peuple. — Paris, Olivier Senant, 1533.
4°.
Cambrai BM 10064 (destroyed).
References: Renouard MSS.
Notes: My thanks to Mme A. Fournier of the Cambrai BM for information on this edition, drawn from the outdated library inventory.

I 47.   Instruction des curés.

Linstruction des curez pour instruire le simple peuple. — Paris, Nicolas Higman, Simon Vostre, 1537?
4°: a-e^8, goth. e 5v: Impr. à Paris par Nicolas Higman pour Simon Vostre.
*Paris BEBA Masson 253.
Notes: Preliminary epistle signed 'Stephanus Parisiens. Epis.' (Étienne Poncher) and dated (a 3r) 1506. The text of the *Opus tripartitum* in Latin and in French.

I 47a.   Instruction des curés.

Linstruction des curez. — Paris, Antoine Bonnemere, Charles Dudé, 1541.
8°: 92 + [4] ff., A-M^8, rom. M 7v: impr. à Paris. 1541.
*Paris BN Vélins 2952 (-A 1.8, M 8).
Notes: The colophon states the edition was printed by command of 'Monseigneur le Reverendissime archevesque de Reims, pour instruire le simple peuple'. A 2r: command from Charles de Lorraine archevesque de Reims to Antoine Bonnemere and Charles Dudé to provide this ed. for the 'curez, vicaires et gens deglise du diocese dudict Reims', dated from Reims, 16 Feb. 1540. (Acc. to Renouard, Charles Dude or Dudé ceased activity in 1535.) Printed on vellum. Latin and French throughout, except a final *opusculum* on sacraments, in Latin only.

I 48.   Instruction des enfants.

Introduction pour les enfans. — Antwerp, Martin Lempereur, 1534?

8°: A-B⁴, goth. B 4v: Impr. en Anvers par Martin Lempereur.
*London BL C.37.b.43(3).
References: NK #1177. *Index* I #361.
Notes: See *Fontaine de vie* for a 1542 ed.

I 49.   Instruction des enfants, [Martin Luther, Guillaume Farel].

Introduction pour les enfans. Recogneue et corrigee a Lovain. — Antwerp, Vve Martin Lempereur, 1538.
8°: A-D⁸, goth.
*Chantilly Condé IV.B.73.
References: NK #3235. *Het Boek* 1929 p. 162.
Notes: To the 1534? ed. are added one of the 'expositions sur l'oraison dominicale', 'l'exposition de l'Ave Maria', and the expositions by Luther on the ten commandments and by Luther /Farel on the Creed, all these additions being taken from the *Livre de vraye et parfaicte oraison*, Antwerp, Lempereur, 1533.

I 50.   Instruction des enfants, [Luther, Farel], Alde Manuce, Cl. Marot.

Introduction pour les enfans, recongneue et corrige a Louvain: Lan M.CCCCC. et xxxviii. Ou sont adjoustees de nouveau, une tresutile maniere de scavoir bien lire, et orthographier, par Alde. Et la doctrine pour bien et deuement escripre selon la propriete du language francois, par Clement Marot. — Antwerp, Antoine Des Gois, 1540.
8°: 64 ff., A-H⁸, goth.
*Amsterdam VU Ned.Inc. 437.
References: NK #3236. *Het Boek* 1929 pp. 161-8.
Notes: All the elements of the 1538 ed., plus the new items as on t.p.

I 51.   Instruction des enfants.

Instruction pour les Chrestiens. — ?, ?, 1540?
16°: +⁸ ¶⁸, goth.
*Cambridge UL CCE.2.3(2).
References: Adams I 141.
Notes: Reproduces part of the *Introduction pour les enfans.* Undated. Cambridge copy bound with *Les Testamentz des douze patriarches*, 'Anvers, Martin Lempereur, 1540' — but Lempereur died in 1535.

I 52.   Instruction des enfants.

An Instruction for chyldren/Linstruction des enfans.
— London, John Roux, 1543.
8°: A-B⁸, goth. B 8v: London, John Roux. 1543.
St Mary's church, Finedon. *Cambridge UL (microfilm).
References: *STC* 14106.2.
Notes: Bilingual ed., text close to the 1542 ed. (see *Fontaine de vie*), but omitting some of the most theologically questionable expressions. The colophon claims that the work 'fyrst was set forthe in Frenche in Paris by certayne doctours in divinitie'.

I 53.   Instruction et admonition.

Instruction et salutaire admonition pour parfaictement vivre en ce monde, et comment en toute nostre adversité serons patiens. — ?, ?, ?
Notes: J. Calvin, *CO* VII, 242: title of one of the 'libertin' texts, 'seulement d'une fueille', refuted by Calvin in *Contre la secte...* (1545). No other trace apart from this mention by Calvin.

I 54.   Instruction et créance.

L'Instruction et creance des Chrestiens contenant l'oraison de Jesus Christ, les articles de la Foy, les dix commandemens: et plusieurs bonnes doctrines et oraisons extraictes de la saincte escripture. — [Strasbourg], [Rémy Guédon], 1546.
16°: 40 ff., A-E⁸, rom.
Gotha FB Theol 682a 2 Rara.
References: Peter 'Prem. ouvr.' XIIa. *Index* I #438.
Notes: The work was censured on 25 May 1542 (Higman *Censorship*, p. 91, with corrections in *Index* I #438). Guédon's ed. must be a re-ed. of a lost work. See Higman, 'Spiritualité', pp. 46-7.

I 55.   Instruction et manière.

Cy commence une petite instruction et maniere de vivre pour une femme seculiere, comment elle se doit conduire en pensees, parolles et oeuvres tout au long du jour. — [Paris], [Vve Jean Trepperel?], [Jean Jehannot?], 1516?
8°: A-D⁸, goth.
*Paris BN Rés. D 17400(3).

Notes: The Paris BN copy bound with J. Sauvage, *Eschelle*, printed with the same material. Hence the suggested printers and date. Dedic. (A 1v) to 'ma treschere seur' who is 'entre les dangiers de salut qui sont au monde'. The author is a woman (A 2r: 'me suis sentue pressee en esperit, et quasi contraincte...'). Probably a nun, and certainly sent to a woman living 'in the century' and married.

I 56.   Instruction et manière.

Cy commence une petite instruction et maniere de vivre pour une Femme seculiere: et comme elle se doibt conduire en pensees, en parolles, et en oeuvres. — Troyes, Jean Le Coq II, 1541?

8°: A-L⁸ M⁴, goth. M 4v: Impr. à Troyes chez Jean Lecoq.
*Paris BEBA Masson 1136.

Notes: Jean Le Coq II was active 1541-89. The ed. includes a *Meditation sur la mort...*, and an *Extraict de plusieurs sainctz Docteurs... sainct sacrement de Lautel* with their own t.ps. but without independent collation.

I 57.   Instruction pour se confesser.

Breve Instruction pour soy confesser en verite. — [Alençon], [Simon Du Bois], 1530?

8°: a-d⁸ e⁴, goth.
*Paris SHP A 1159.

References: Moore #165. Clutton #41. Tricard *APR* pp. 29-33. Droz *Chemins* I, 52-78 with text. *Index* I #445.

Notes: Mlle Droz suggests as author Jean Le Comte de la Croix, disciple of Lefèvre d'Étaples.

I 58.   Instruction pour se confesser.

Breve instruction faicte par maniere de Lettre missive: pour se confesser en verité. — [Geneva], [Jean Girard], 1539.

8°: a-b⁸ c⁴, rom.
*Geneva BPU Rés. Bc 3365.

References: Moore #164. Droz *Chemins* I, 56-8 et 77-8. *BG* 39/6. *Index* I #442.

Notes: Re-ed. of the *Breve Instruction*, c. 1530. But the 'Forme de soy confesser à ung homme' is replaced by scriptural quotations, entitled 'Confession du peuple'.

I 59.   **Irrision des Luthériens.**

*La grande Irrision des Lutheriens de Meaulx: Avec
la presumption de deux heretiques bruslez en leur
obstination. Et la punition faite a Lagni d'ung garson
heretique natif de Meaulx.* — ?, ?, 1528?
8°: 4 ff.
Séville Colombine.
References: Moore #168. Babelon #94.
Notes: A reply to placards put up in Meaux in 1528.

J

J 1.   **Jérôme, Saint,** trans. Jean Cailleau.

*Epistre à Paulin, l'induisant à l'estude des lettres, prin-
cipallement des sacrees.* — Lyon, Jean de Tournes,
1543.
References: Frankfurt cat. 1610.

J 2.   **Jérôme, Saint,** trans. Antoine Du Four.

*Les Epistres <> Translatees ... a la requeste de tres-
haulte, tresillustre, et excellente dame anne de bretaigne en son vivant royne de France.* — Paris, Jean
Trepperel, 1511?
8°: A-H⁸, goth. H 8r: Impr. à Paris.
*Paris BN Rés. D 80287.
Notes: The letters of St Jerome end on E 4v, and are followed
by 'Sensuyt le testament sainct jherosme'.

J 3.   **Jérôme, Saint,** trans. Antoine Du Four.

Les Epistres. — Paris, [Guillaume Le Rouge], pr. Jean
de La Garde, 1519?
8°: A-H⁸, goth. H 7r: Impr. à Paris pr Jehan de la garde.
*Paris BN Rés. C 5984.
References: Moreau II #1852.
Notes: Priv. (A 1v) to Jean de La Garde for two years dated 17
Jan. 1518.

J 4.   **Jérôme, Saint.**

Les epistres. — Paris, [Hémon Le Fèvre], pr. Guillaume
Eustace, 1521.

2°: +⁴ a-t A-D A-N⁸ O⁶, goth. + 4v: Impr. à Paris pour Guilaume eustace libr. a la fin du moys de Mars 1520 (a.s.).
*Paris BA fol T 1097. *Paris BM Rés. 1437F. Paris BN Rés. C 455-7. Harvard CL. *Troyes BM F.2.587 (+).
References: Moreau III #140.
Notes: The work is in three parts, with independent collation for each. But there is no new t.p. for either Pt. 2 (A-D⁸) or Pt. 3 (A-N⁸ O⁶).

J 5.   Jérôme, Saint, Basile, Saint, trans. G. Cailleau.

Les Epistres de s. Jérôme et de s. Basile. — Paris, Vincent Sertenas, 1538.
8°.
References: Renouard MSS < Du Verdier.

J 6.   Jérôme, Saint.

La Vie des peres nouvellement imprimee a paris. — Paris, François Regnault, 1512.
2°: 219 + [1] ff., a-z & A-M⁶ N-O⁴, goth. O 3v: Impr. à Paris. 1512.
*Paris BA 4° H 6457.
References: Moreau II #358.
Notes: In four parts, on the desert fathers (*degypte, thebaydes, mesopotamie, et aultres lieux solitaires*). Many woodcut illustrations.

J 7.   Jérôme, Saint.

La vie des peres renommee En plusieurs terres et pays. — Paris, Hémon Le Fèvre, 1517.
2°: a-z & A-K⁶ L⁴, goth. L 3v: Impr. à paris pr. Hemon le Fevre. 1517.
*Geneva BPU Ba 638. Paris BM.
References: Moreau II #1636.

J 8.   Jérôme, Saint.

La vie des peres tant degipte de sirie que dautre pays. — Paris, Jean et Enguilbert de Marnef, 1520.
2°: 202 + [4] ff., a-z A-K⁶ L-M⁴, goth. M 4r: Impr. à Paris. 1520.
*Paris BN Rés. H 206. *Paris BEBA Masson 156 (-a 1, M 4).
References: Moreau II #2373.

J 9.   Jérôme, Saint.

La Vie des Peres tant Degypte que de sirie et de plusieurs autres pays. — [Paris], [Antoine de La Barre], [Jean Petit], 1534?
2°: 222 + [5] ff., a-z & § A-N⁶, goth.
*Paris BA fol. H 3497.
References: Moreau IV #1033. Libr. Guérin, 1988.
Notes: T.p. has the motto 'Petit à Petit'. I take the Paris BA copy to be the same ed. as that described by Mlle Moreau from a sale cat.

J 10.   Jérôme, Saint.

La vie des Peres tant Degypte que de Sirie et de plusieurs autres pays. — Paris, Nicolas Couteau, 1540.
2°: [6]+197 ff., *⁶ A-Z AA-KK⁶, goth.   KK 5r: Impr. à Paris par Nicolas couteau. 02.01.1540.
*London BL 204.e.13(2) (- *1, KK6). *Paris BA fol. H 3493.
Notes: The London BL copy bound with the *Légende dorée*. T.p. border with initials E G (Estienne Groulleau? — but Groulleau only began his career in 1545). KK 5v: mark of Les Angeliers.

J 11.   Jordan, Raymond, dit Idiota, trans. Guillaume Briçonnet.

Les Contemplations faites à l'honneur et louange de la Tres sacree Vierge Marie... <> *14.08.1519.* — [Paris], [Simon de Colines], 1522?
8°.
Paris SHP (missing, 1993).
References: Dagens. Moreau III #341.
Notes: The *Contemplationes Idiotae* by Raymond Jordan (Augustinian, 15th cent.) were published in 1519 by J. Lefèvre d'Étaples and dedic. to Guillaume Briçonnet. The date on the t.p. seems to refer to that Latin ed.

J 12.   Jordan, Raymond, dit Idiota, trans. Matthieu de Lalande.

Les contemplations du simple devot. Damour divin. De vraye pacience. De la mort. De la vierge Marie. <> *En la fin est adjoinct ung sermon preparatoire a recepvoir le Sainct sacrement de lautel.* — Rouen, Louis Bouvet, 1532.

8°: [76 ff.], a-i^8 k^4, goth. Col: Impr. à Rouen pour Louis Bouvet. 18.05.1532.

Séville Colombine. Cambridge UL.

References: *Colombina* IV, 209-10.

Notes: The Sermon at the end is by Matthieu de Lalande (on this Carmelite, Doctor of Theology, see Farge *Bio.reg.*).

J 13.   **Jordan, Raymond, dit Idiota,** trans. Mathieu de Lalande.

Les Contemplations du Simple devot, lesquelles traictent de ce qui ensuyt: Cest assavoir, Damour divin. De vraye pacience. De la mort. De la vierge Marie. <> En la fin est adjoinct ung sermon preparatoire a recepvoir le sainct sacrement de lautel. — Paris, [Estienne Caveiller], Les Angeliers, Vivant Gaultherot, 1538.

8°: A-N^8 O^4, goth. O 4r: Impr. à Paris.

*Paris BN Rés. D 80139. *Paris BSG D 8° 6199/2(3) Rés. Inv 7898. Paris BA 8° T 6711.

References: Renouard MSS. Dagens.

L

L 1.   **La Boulaye, Guillaume de.**

La pronostication du Ciecle advenir, contenant troys petis traictez. Le premier determine comment la mort entra premierement au monde. Le second parle des Ames des trespassez, Et de la difference des Paradis. Le tiers de la derniere tribulation, Et de la resurrection des corps... — Paris, Pierre Leber, [Vve Jean de Saint Denys], 1532.

8°: A-I^8, goth. I 4r: Impr. à Paris par Pierre leber. 03.06.1532.

*Rouen BM Leber 223.

References: Moreau IV #439.

Notes: According to the t.p., Guillaume de La Boulaye, after being wounded in the wars, composed the text in 1478. A meditation on death and the life to come.

L 2. **Lactantius Firmianus,** trans. René Fame.

Des Divines institutions, contre les Gentilz et Idolatres.
— Paris, Galliot Du Pré, Estienne Roffet, 1543.
2°: *⁶ §⁶ a-z A-E⁶ F⁸, rom. F 8r: Impr. à Paris. 09.02.1542.
*Paris BA fol T 1073. *Paris BM Rés. 1402A. Paris BN Vélins 288.
*Munich BSB 2° P.lat. 924. *Rouen BM A 321.
Notes: The *Divinae Institutiones* date from the early 4th cent.
In his preliminary epistle to Francis I, René Fame ('notaire et
secretaire dudit Seigneur', t.p.) suggests a parallel between the
religious troubles of his era and those of the time of Constantine.

L 3. **Lactantius Firmianus.**

Des Divines institutions. — Paris, Estienne Roffet,
1546.
8°.
Chaumont.
References: Renouard MSS.

L 4. **Lactantius Firmianus,** trans. René Fame.

Des Divines institutions, contre les Gentilz et idolatres
<> de nouveau corrigé. — Paris, Pasquier Le Tellier,
Galliot Du Pré, 1546.
8°: a-b A-Z Aa-Ii⁸, rom. Ii 8r: ach d'impr. par Pasquier le Tellier
pour Galiot du pré. 15.03.1546.
*Paris BA 8° T 3226.

L 5. **Lactantius Firmianus,** trans. René Fame.

Des divines Institutions, contre les Gentilz et idolatres.
— Paris, Benoist Prevost, pr. Mathurin Du Puys, G.
Cavellat, 1547.
8°: a-b A-Z Aa-Ff⁸ Gg⁴, rom. Gg 3v: ach. d'impr. 18.07.1547, par
Benoist Prevost impr.
*Lausanne BCU AZ 4893. *Paris BN C 4151. *Paris BA 8° T 3227
(pr. G. Cavellat).

L 6. **Lactantius Firmianus,** trans. René Fame.

Des Divines Institutions, contre les Gentilz et Idolatres,
nouvellement imprimé avec histoires. — Paris, Jean
Ruelle, 1548.
16°: ++⁸ +⁸ a-y A-Z AA-CC⁸ DD⁴, rom.
*Paris BA 8° T 3228. *Paris BEBA Masson 582. *Montpellier BM
C 318.

References: Brun, *Livre fr. illustré.*

Notes: The 'histoires' are 179 engravings (actually 74, many used more than once) on biblical subjects (MS note in the Montpellier copy).

L 7.   **Lactantius Firmianus,** trans. René Fame.

Des Divines Institutions, contre les Gentilz et Idolatres, nouvellement recogneu aux premiers exemplaires et imprimé avec histoires. — Paris, Jean Ruelle, 1551?

16°: ++⁸ +⁸ a-y A-Z AA-CC⁸ DD⁴, rom.

*St Andrews UL Typ FP B48.RL. Lausanne BCU.

Notes: T.p. damage in St Andrews copy, so no date (in any case Ruelle frequently did not date his publs). May be post-1551.

L 8.   **Lactantius Firmianus,** trans. René Fame.

Des Divines Institutions, contre les Gentilz et Idolatres, nouvellement recogneu aux premiers exemplaires et imprimé avec histoires. — Paris, Estienne Groulleau, 1551.

16°: ++⁸ +⁸ a-y⁸ A-Z AA-CC⁸ DD⁴, rom.

*Paris BN Rés. C 4994. Paris BEBA Masson 236.

Notes: Shared ed. with Ruelle (previous number)?

L 9.   **Lacu, Jean.**

La quenouille spirituelle. — [Paris], ?, ?

8°: A-C⁸, goth.

*London BL C.107.a.12(1).

Notes: A 'devote contemplation ou meditation de la croix de nostre saulveur et redempteur Jhesucrist que chacune devote femme pourra spiculer en fillant sa quenoulle materielle, faicte et composee par Maistre Jehan de Lacu chanoyne de Lisle' (A 2r). In verse, with a variety of stanza forms.

L 10.   **Lalande, Matthieu de,** Martin Bucer.

Manuel des abus de lhomme ingrat <> Avec la copie des lettres de Martin Bucere de Strabourg: envoyées audit F. Mathieu (pour lors preschant à Metz) et la response d'icelles. — Metz, Jean Pallier, 1544.

4°: a-f⁸ g⁶, rom. g 6r: On les vend à Paris ... par Jehan Pallier. 1544.

*Strasbourg BNU R 100542.

References: Moore #169.

Notes: On Matthieu de Lalande, see Farge *Bio.reg*. *The Manuel des abuz* (in particular chap. 3) is an attack on Reformed doctrines. Bucer had written to Lalande demanding a disputation in Metz. Lalande publishes Bucer's letter and his own, negative, response.

=> Lalande, Matthieu de: see Jordan, Raymond, *Contemplations*, 1532 et 1538, and [Luther], *Livre de vraye...* eds of 1539 sqq.

L 11.   Lambert, François.

Somme Chrestienne a tresvictorieux empereur Charles. — Marburg, [Franciscus Rhode], 1529.
8°: A-E⁸, goth. E 7r: Impr. à Marpurg. 17.03.1529.
*Paris SHP A 1164.
References: Moore #174. Berthoud *Marcourt*. N. Weiss *BSHPF* 75 pp. 477-86. Bodenmann #18a.

L 12.   Lambert, François.

Traictie devot et tresutile a ceulx qui desirent a avoir en practique la vie de nostre seigneur appelle la Corone de nostre saulveur jesuschrist avec les commendemens de la loy. — Lyon, Jean de La Place, 1522?
4°: 48 ff., A-L⁸, goth. Lyon, Jehan de la place.
Séville Colombine.
References: Moore #170. Babelon #103. Bodenmann #1.
Notes: Lambert left the Franciscans, and France, in 1522. This publication must be dated before his conversion.

L 13.   [Landry, François].

La declaration De la Foy chrestienne, faicte par ung bachelier en theologie ... touchant aulcuns articles a luy imposez Lesquelles de point en point a confessees et confirmees en la presence de la faculte de theologie. — [Rouen], Jean Lhomme, 1544?
8°: 4 ff.
*Paris BN Rés. D 80395.
References: *Rép.bib*. #42.
Notes: The retractation of his 'erreurs' imposed on François Landry in 1544. See Droz, *Chemins* I.

L 14.   Lasseré, Louis.

La Vie de monseigneur sainct Hierosme. — Paris, Josse Badius, Jean Petit, 1529?
4°: a-q⁸ r¹⁰, rom. r 9v: Impr. à Paris par Josse Badius, pour luy et Jehan Petit.
*Paris BN Rés. H 2247 (- r 5,6). *Paris BSG H 4° 2080(2) inv 2146 Rés. *Paris BA 4° H 6650. London BL.
References: Moreau III #1816.
Notes: The author, 'chanoine et granger en l'eglise sainct Martin de Tours', is named in the privilege. First ed. of this work, in 42 chaps, including a chapter of praise of the Sorbonne and three chaps (38-40) of refutation of the 'luthériens'.

L 15.   Lasseré, Louis.

La Vie de monseigneur sainct Hierosme. Recongneue et augmentee au double, par lautheur. — Paris, Josse Badius, 1530?
4°: 370 + [6] ff., a-z A-Z⁸ ET¹⁰, rom. ET 9r: Impr. de rechief à Paris par M. Josse Badius.
*Aix Méj. (- a 8). *Paris BN Rés. H 1682 (- a 4,5, ET 9,10). Grenoble. Séville Colombine.
References: Moreau III #2174.
Notes: Augmented second ed. with 56 chaps. New priv. dated 30 Dec. 1530 to Josse Badius, and describes the work as 'extraict de plusieurs autheurs, et translaté ... par maistre Loys Lasseré'. Lasseré's prologue is dated (a 5r) 'le jour s. Luc' (18.10) 1528. Dedic. to Françoise de Tonnerre, prieure du convent reformé de N.D. de Relay, diocèse de Tours.

L 16.   Lasseré, Louis.

La Vie de monseigneur sainct Hierosme. Recongneue et augmentee du tiers, pour la troisiesme fois, par lautheur: ou sont inserees en brief, la vie de ma dame saincte Paule, et celle de mon seigneur sainct Loys, Roy de France ... est faicte addition specialle et adjoustee linterpretation des dix commandemens de la loy: de loraison dominicalle: de la salutation angelique: et des articles de la foy... Et aussy, y a este adjouste ung traicte ample du sainct sacrement de l'autel. — Paris, Charlotte Guillard, 1541.
4°: [10] + 398 + [2] ff., aa¹⁰ a-z A-Z Aa-Dd⁸, rom. Dd 7v: Impr. pour la troisiesme fois à Paris par Charlotte Guillard.

*Rouen BM U 1041. *Paris BN Rés. H 1683 (- Dd 7,8). Paris BEBA Masson 346. *Paris BSG H 4° 2081 inv 2147 Rés. (-aa 1). *Paris BA 4° H 6620.

Notes: Despite the augmentation announced on the t.p., there are still 56 chaps as in the preceding ed. In his dedic. to Loyse de Bourbon, Abbesse de Fontevrault, Lasseré says he has made three additions: the commentaries on the Lord's Prayer, Decalogue and Ave, the explanation of the Creed, and the 'traité du saint sacrement de l'autel', which is in fact added at the end of chap. 47. Lasseré obtained the approval of the Paris Faculty of Theology for this ed. on 4 Nov. 1541 (Farge, *Registre* n° 229 B, p. 191). A new priv. to Charlotte Guillard, dated 26 Nov. 1541, describes Lasseré as 'proviseur du College de Navarre'.

L 17.   Le Conte, Jean.

Les miracles de la benoite et glorieuse vierge marie.
— Lyon, Claude Nourry, 1524.
4°: a-l⁴, goth. l 4r: Impr. à Lyon par Claude nourry alias le Prince. 03.12.1524.
*Paris BEBA Masson 566(2).

Notes: a 1v: the work was composed 'par frere Jehan le conte frere mineur au commandement de monseigneur Pierre dalencon: et a la requeste de noble dame Marie sa femme'.

L 18.   Lefèvre d'Étaples, Jacques, trans. Jean Liege.

Contemplations salutaires d'Innocence perdue... avec une oraison à Dieu pour la paix et union de nostre Mere l'Eglise. — Lyon, François Juste, 1539.
References: Baudrier *Suppl.* #88. Frankfurt cat. 1610. Du Verdier II, p. 451.

L 19.   [Lefèvre d'Étaples, Jacques].

Les choses contenues en ce present livre Epistres et Evangiles pour les cinquante et deux sepmaines de lan: commenceans au premier dimenche de Ladvent... Apres chascune epistre et evangile briefve exhortation selon lintelligence dicelle. — [Paris], [Simon Du Bois], 1525?
8°: a-z A-M⁸ N⁴, goth.
*London BL 3025.a.6.

References: Moore #176. Clutton #32. *Index* I #401. Moreau
III #861. Facs. ed. by M.A. Screech, *THR* 1963.
Notes: Censured on 6 Nov. 1525 (Higman *Censorship*,
pp. 80-1). The pagination given in the censure does not
correspond to this ed.: either there was a previous ed., or the
censure referred to a MS version.

L 20. **[Lefèvre d'Étaples, Jacques]**, additions by Gérard
Roussel?

*Epistres et evangiles des cinquante et deux dimenches
de lan, avecques briefves et tresutiles expositions
dycelles, necessaires et consolables pour tous fideles
Chrestiens, nouvellement reveues et augmentees par
gens doctes en la saincte escripture.* — [Lyon],
[Pierre de Vingle], 1530?
16°: a-z A-P⁸, goth.
*Geneva BPU Bd 1570 (fragment). *Geneva MHR M Lef 3.
References: Ed. Bedouelle and Giacone, Brill, 1976.
Notes: The attribution to Gérard Roussel of the additions to
the text is proposed by Bedouelle and Giacone.

L 21. **[Lefèvre d'Étaples, Jacques].**

*Les choses contenues en ce present livre. Epistres et
evangiles pour les cinquante et deux sepmaines de lan,
commenceans au premier dimenche de Ladvent...
Apres chascune Epistre et Evangile, briefve
exhortation selon lintelligence dicelle.* — [Alençon],
[Simon Du Bois], 1532?
8°: a-z A-M⁸, goth.
*Geneva BPU Rés. Bd 1969. *London BL 1016.a.9. *Paris SHP R 8717.
References: Clutton #33.

L 22. **[Lefèvre d'Étaples, Jacques].**

*Les Epistres, et Evangiles des cinquante, et deux
Dimenches de l'An, Avecques briefves, et tresutiles
expositions d'ycelles.* — Lyon, Estienne Dolet, 1542.
16°: 655 pp., a-z A-S⁸, rom.
Manchester JRL Christie 3.e.22. *Paris BN Rés. B 21371 (-a 1, all
after P 1). *Aix Méj. Rés. S. 75.
References: Christie #44. Longeon *Dolet* #209. *Index* I #319.
Cat. Drilhon #22.

Notes: Reproduces the 1530 P. de Vingle ed., adding a preface dated 3 May 1542, which promises a Bible in three or four months, and another (large format) in eight months.

L 23. **[Lefèvre d'Étaples, Jacques].**

Epistres et Evangiles des cinquante et deux Dimenches de l'An, Avecques briefves, et tresutiles expositions d'ycelles. — Lyon, Balthazar Arnoullet, 1544.
16°: a-z A-V⁸, rom.
*Munich UB 8° Bibl 1013.
Notes: Follows the Dolet 1542 ed., but without Dolet's preface.

L 24. **[Lefèvre d'Étaples, Jacques].**

Epistres et evangiles des cinquantes et deux dimenches de L'An. Avecques briefves, et tresutiles expositions d'icelles. — Lyon, Jean de Tournes, 1544.
16°: a-z A-M⁸, rom.
*Munich UB 8° Bibl 1013a. *Wolfenbüttel HAB Tc 228.
Notes: The Munich copy omits the words 'Avecques briefves, tresutiles expositions d'icelles' from the title. Follows the Dolet 1542 ed., but without Dolet's preface.

L 25. **[Lefèvre d'Étaples, Jacques].**

Les Epistres et evangiles des cinquante, et deux Dimenches de L'an. Avecques breves et tresutiles expositions d'icelles. — [Lyon], ?, 1549.
16°: a-z A-K⁸, rom.
*Vienna ÖNB 2.W.19.
References: *Rép.bib.* livr. 22 p. 75.
Notes: *Rép.bib.*: the t.p. mention of 'Rouen, Claude Treszet' is probably a false address. The ed. does not seem to be Norman, and may have been printed in Lyon. Same contents as the De Tournes and Arnoullet eds.

L 26. **[Lefèvre d'Étaples, Jacques],** dedic. epistle by Martin Bucer.

Vocabulaire du pseautier exposé en François. — Paris, Simon de Colines, 1529.
8°: a-g⁸ h⁴, rom.
*Paris BM 23280. *Paris BSG A 8° 645 inv 743(2) Rés.
References: Moreau III #1818.

Notes: The Latin vocabulary found in each Psalm translated and explained in French. The work was composed for the children of the King and those of Marguerite de Navarre. The Paris BSG copy reduces the title to 'Vocabulaire du Psautier', and Bucer's preface is replaced by a table of conjugations.

L 26a.   Le Grand, Jacques.

Le livre de bonnes mœurs. — Paris, Vve Jean Trepperel, 1519.
References: Moreau II # 2118 < Brunet.

L 26b.   Le Grand, Jacques.

Le Tresor de Sapience et fleur de toute bonte, remply de plusieurs bonnes authoritez. — Lyon, Denis de Harsy, Romain Morin, 1530.
8°: A-K⁸, rom. K 7v: Impr. à Lyon par Denys de harsy pour Romain Morin.
Seville Colomb. Paris BEBA Masson 765.
References: Baudrier V, 370. Kemp.
Notes: Same as previous item, with change of title. Thanks to William Kemp for information on all these editions of Le Grand.

L 26c.   Le Grand, Jacques.

Le Tresor de sapience et fleur de toute bonte. — Paris, Jean Longis, Pierre Vidoue, 1531.
8°.
Aix-Méj. Charleville.
References: Moreau IV # 214. Kemp.

L 26d.   Le Grand, Jacques.

Le Tresor de sapience. — Paris, Alain Lotrian, 1539.
References: Kemp.

L 27.   Le Grand, Jacques.

Le Tresor de Sapience et fleur de toute bonte, remply de plusieurs bonnes authoritez des saiges Philosophes, et aultres: lequel enseigne la voye et le chemin que Lhomme doibt tenir en ce monde durant le temps de sa calamiteuse vie. — Lyon, Denis de Harsy, 1542.
16°: A-Q⁸, goth. Q 8v: Impr. à Lyon par Denys de Harsy.
*Paris Univ Rés. XVI R.ra.2(24°).

Notes: A 4r: Jacques Le Grand was a 'religieux de l'ordre sainct Augustin'.

L 28.   Lemaire de Belges, Jean.

Le traictie Intitule, de la difference des scismes et des concilles de leglise. Et de la preeminence et utilite des concilles, de la saincte eglise Gallicaine. — Lyon, Estienne Baland, 1511.
4°: a-i⁴ k⁶, goth. k 6r: Impr. à Lyon pour J. Lemaire de Belges 'expensis propriis', par Estienne Baland. 05.1511.
Göttingen 4° H. Gall. un. II, 91 Rara. Orléans BM E 2707.
Notes: First ed. of this diatribe composed for Louis XII, against Pope Julius II. The t.p. lists the additional items at the end of the text: 'La Vraye histoire ... du prince Syach Ysmail, dit Sophy. Le saufconduit, que le souldan baille aux Francois, pour frequenter en la terre saincte. Avec le Blason des armes des Venitiens.' The anti-papal polemics took on a new significance a few years later, witness the number of eds. Much information on all these eds provided by Dr J. Britnell (Durham University).

L 29.   Lemaire de Belges, Jean.

Le traictie Intitule, de la difference des scismes et des concilles de leglise. Et de la preeminence et utilite des concilles, de la saincte eglise Gallicaine. — Lyon, Estienne Baland, 1511.
4°: a-i⁴ k⁶, goth. k 6r: Impr. à Lyon pour J. Lemaire de Belges 'expensis propriis', par Estienne Baland. 05.1511.
London BL G 10248(5). *Paris BN Rés. La² 2. *Lyon BV R 104685. *Lyon BV R 317049 (-k 2-5). *Paris BSG C 4° 9 inv. 9 Rés.
Notes: Closely resembles the first ed., but entirely reset.

L 30.   Lemaire de Belges, Jean.

Le traictie Intitule, de la difference des scismes et des concilles de leglise. — Paris, Geoffroy de Marnef, 1512.
4°: a-k⁴, goth. k 4r: Impr. à Paris pr. Jan Lemaire par Geffroy de Marnef. 01.1512.
*Paris BN Rés. La² 3A(2). *Paris BSG L 4° 351 inv 7(2) Rés. Manchester JRL. *Versailles BM Incunable G 293.
References: Moreau II #394.
Notes: The t.p. still gives the date 1511.

L 31.   Lemaire de Belges, Jean.

Le traictie Intitule de la difference des scismes et des concilles de leglise. — Paris, Geoffroy de Marnef, 1512.

4°: a-k⁴, goth. k 4r: Impr. à Paris pour Jan Lemaire par Geffroy de Marnef. 01.1512.

London BL 492.i.1(1). *Paris BN Rés. La² 4(4). Bordeaux BM H 4379.

References: Moreau II #393. Rothschild #2008.

Notes: The t.p., copied from the first ed., still reads '1511'. Entirely reset from previous number.

L 32.   Lemaire de Belges, Jean.

Le traictie intitule de la difference des scismes et des Concilles de leglise. Et de la preeminence et utilite des concilles: de la saincte eglise Gallicaine. — Paris, Geoffroy de Marnef, 1514?

4°: a-k⁴, goth.

*London BL G 10249(4). Paris BA 4° H 3663. Oxford Bodl. Douce M.100.

Notes: The treatise *De la difference...*, *avec lhistoire de Syrach*, etc., fill the gatherings a-k. Followed (gatherings aa-cc⁴ dd⁶ A-C⁶ D⁴ E⁶) by *La Legende des venitiens, L'Epistre du Roy à Hector de Troye,* and various poems, with a colophon giving 'Impr. à Paris pr. Geoffroy de Marnef. Juillet 1516'. But the French royal coat of arms in the *Traité* includes Louis XII's porcupines, which leads Abélard and J. Britnell to date the ed. earlier than the death of Louis (1515).

L 33.   Lemaire de Belges, Jean.

Le traictie de la difference des scismes et des Concilles de leglise. Et de la preeminence et utilite des concilles: De la saincte eglise Gallicaine. — Paris, [Nicolas Higman] pr. Enguilbert et Jean de Marnef, Pierre Viart, 1517.

4°: a-i⁴ k², goth. k 2v: Impr. à Paris pr. Englebert & Jehan de Marnef et pr. Pierre Viart. 11.1517.

*Lyon BV Rés. 357253 bis. Oxford All Souls. Tours BM Rés. 2693.

References: Moreau II #1656. Mortimer #347.

Notes: Textual modifications, apparently by the printer, are here introduced, and are reproduced in all subsequent eds.

L 34. **Lemaire de Belges, Jean.**

Le Traictie de la difference des scismes et des concilles de leglise. — Paris, Enguilbert et Jean de Marnef, Pierre Viart, 1519.
4°: a-i⁴ k², goth. k 2v: Impr. à Paris pour Englebert et Jehan de Marnef et pr. pierre viart. 08.1519.
London BL 634.k.6(3). *Paris BN Rés. La² 5(4).
References: Moreau II #2123.
Notes: The t.p. still reads '1511'.

L 35. **Lemaire de Belges, Jean.**

Le traictie de la difference des scismes et des Concilles de leglise. — Paris, Enguilbert et Jean de Marnef, Pierre Viart, 1521.
4°: a-i⁴ k², goth. k 2r: Impr. à Paris pour Englebert et Jehan de Marnef et pr. Pierre Viart. 09.1521.
London BL C.39.g.4(4). Paris Univ (incompl.). *Paris BEBA Masson 349(4).
References: Moreau III #162.

L 36. **Lemaire de Belges, Jean.**

Le traicte de la difference des Scismes, et des Concilles de leglise. — Paris, Enguilbert de Marnef, Pierre Viart, Jean Petit, François Regnault, 1523.
4°: a-d⁸ e⁴, goth. e 4r: Impr. à Paris pour Françoys regnault. 09.1523.
Aix Méj. Paris BA. *Paris BN Rés. La² 6(5) (Regnault). Paris BU.
References: Moreau III #534.

L 37. **Lemaire de Belges, Jean.**

Le traicte de la difference des Scismes et Concilles de leglise. — Paris, Philippe Le Noir, 1524.
2°: AA-EE⁶, goth. EE 6r: Impr. à Paris par Philippe le Noir. 07.1524.
*Paris BN Rés. La² 8(5). Bourges BM E 756. Rennes.
References: Abélard ed. J. Moreau III #699.
Notes: From this ed. on, eds are collective publications of Lemaire's works.

L 38. **Lemaire de Belges, Jean.**

Le traictie de la difference des scismes et des Concilles de leglise. — Lyon, Jacques Mareschal, 1524.
4°: [30] ff., aA-cC⁸ dD⁶, goth. dD 6r: Impr. à Lyon par Jaques Mareschal. 01.06.1524.

Toulouse BM Rés. XVI 150. Cambridge Clare (- gathering dD).
References: Abélard ed. K. Adams L 404.
Notes: Lacks the *Blason des Venitiens.*

L 39.   Lemaire de Belges, Jean.

Le traicte de la difference des Scismes, et des Concilles de leglise et de preeminence et utilite des concilles de la saincte eglise Gallicane. — Paris, Philippe Le Noir, François Regnault, 1526?
2°: [30] ff., AA-EE⁶, goth.
Paris BHVP Rés. 110 001 (missing). London BL C.81.d.5. Oxford Bodl. Douce L subt 61.
References: Abélard ed. Z. Moreau IV #1050.
Notes: Mlle Moreau proposes the date 1534? But the text is based on the 1524 Le Noir ed., not on the improved 1528 ed. Abélard (p. 138-40) therefore suggests a date between 1524 and 1528.

L 40.   Lemaire de Belges, Jean.

Le traictie de la difference des scismes et des Concilles de leglise. Et la preeminence et utilite des concilles: de la saincte eglise Gallicane. — Lyon, Antoine Du Ry, 1528.
4°: [36] ff., Aa-Dd⁸ Ee⁴, goth. Ee 3v: Impr. à Lyon par Antoyne du Ry. 1528.
*Paris BN Rés. H 2158. London BL C.38.g.12. Nantes Dobrée #II.665. Munich BSB gall. g 158a. Chicago Newberry.
References: Abélard ed. L.
Notes: Omits the *Blason des Venitiens.*

L 41.   Lemaire de Belges, Jean.

Le traicte de la difference des Scismes et des Concilles de leglise. — Paris, François Regnault, 1528.
4°: [30] ff., AA-CC⁸ DD⁶, goth. DD 5v: Impr. à Paris par Françoys Regnault.
*Paris BN Rés. La² 8.A(5). Paris BM. Cambridge UL. Versailles BM Réserve G 59. Rouen BM (+).
References: Abélard ed. M. Moreau III #1538. Adams L 411.

L 42.   Lemaire de Belges, Jean.

Le traictie de la difference des scismes et des Concilles de leglise. Et de la preeminence et utilite des concilles: de la saincte eglise Gallicane. — Paris, [Julien Hubert], Ambroise Girault, 1529.

4°: [36] ff., A-I⁴, goth. I 4v: Impr. à Paris pr. Ambroise Girault. Grenoble BM Rés. E 14705. *Lyon BV Rés. 105183.

References: Moreau III #1822.

L 43. **Lemaire de Belges, Jean.**

Le traicte de la difference des Scismes et des Concilles de leglise. Et de la preeminence et utilite des concilles de la saincte eglise gallicane. — Paris, [Nicolas Higman], pr. Ambroise Girault, 1533.

4°: AA-CC⁸ DD⁶, goth. DD 5v: Impr. à Paris pour Ambroise Girault. *Munich BSB 4° Hist.Eccl. 466m. Harvard CL. *Paris BN Rés. La² 11. Paris BEBA Masson 350(3). Cambridge Trin (+).

References: Abélard ed. P. Mortimer #349. Moreau IV #751. Rothschild #2090.

L 44. **Lemaire de Belges, Jean.**

Le traicte de la difference des Scismes et des concilles de L'Eglise, et de la preeminence et utilité des concilles de la Saincte Eglise Gallicane. — Paris, [Pierre Vidoue], Jean Foucher, Charles Langelier, Ambroise Girault, 1540.

8°: [78] ff., aa-ii⁸ kk⁶, rom. kk 6r: Impr. à Paris. 1540. *Wolfenbüttel HAB 402.7 Hist (Vidoue). *Versailles BM Réserve B 227 (4) (Langelier). Paris BU Rés. XVI S. 1212 (J. Foucher). Bruxelles BR II 61 845 ALP (A. Girault) (+).

References: Abélard ed. Q.

Notes: First ed. in rom. print.

L 45. **Lemaire de Belges, Jean.**

Le traicte de la difference des scismes et des Conciles de l'Eglise. — Paris, Jean Réal, pr. Guillaume Le Bret, Jean Bonfons, Vivant Gaultherot, 1548.

4°: [54] ff., aaa-fff⁸ ggg⁶, rom. ggg 6r: Impr. à Paris, 1549. *Rouen BM U 1182. *Versailles BM Fonds A I-5-d (V. Sertenas). Bordeaux BM H 2624 (J. Ruelle). Lyon BV Rés. 348128. London BL 594.b.29 (Vve François Regnault) (+).

References: Abélard ed. R.

Notes: Part of the *Illustrations de Gaule*, signed (in the Rouen copy, not mentioned by Abélard) by Le Bret in Vol. I, and with his printer's mark (tree) and motto 'Spes mea Deus' in this vol., ggg 6v. But this ed. shared between numerous editors (see

Abélard p. 153). The *Traité de la difference* ends on fol. eee 6v.
eee 7r-ggg 6r: *Le Temple d'honneur.*

L 46.   Lemaire de Belges, Jean.

Le Traicté de la difference des Schismes et des Conciles de lEglise. — Lyon, Jean de Tournes, 1549.
2°: 80 pp., Aa-Ff⁴ Gg⁶ Hh⁴ Ii⁶, rom.
*Paris BN Rés. La² 13. Aix-Méj. D 3832. Lyon BV 108167. London BL 594 h.14. Geneva BPU Gg 115 (+).
References: Abélard ed. S. Cartier *De Tournes* I, pp. 280-84.
Notes: For the first time, the *Illustrations de Gaule*, the *Traité* and other items are treated as a single collection, with no new t.ps. The signatures and pagination begin afresh, however, for the *Traité* (up to p. 58, Gg 5v) followed after a blank sheet by the *Legende des Venitiens* (pp. 61-80, Hh 1r-Ii 6v). This is the last collected ed. However, a new family of the *Traité* begins to appear from 1532 on, under the title *Promptuaire...*

L 47.   Lemaire de Belges, Jean.

Le Promptuaire des Conciles de Leglise Catholique, avec les Scismes et la difference diceulx. — Lyon, [Denis de Harsy], Romain Morin, 1532.
8°: 72 ff., a-i⁸, rom.
Harvard CL. *London BL C.37.b.43(1). Paris BA 8° T 2868 Rés. Paris BEBA Masson 796. *Lyon BV Rés. 805690.
References: Mortimer #348. Baudrier V, p. 375.

L 48.   Lemaire de Belges, Jean.

Le Promptuaire des Conciles de Leglise Catholique, avec les Scismes et la difference diceulx. — Lyon, [Denis de Harsy], Romain Morin, 1533.
8°: 72 ff., a-i⁸, rom.
*Paris BN Rés. pB 24. *Lyon BV Rés. 808283.
References: Baudrier V, p. 376.
Notes: Identical with 1532 ed., only one number changed in date. Second issue?

L 49.   Lemaire de Belges, Jean.

Le Promptuaire des Conciles de l'Eglise catholique, avec les schismes et la difference d'iceulx. — Paris, Guillaume Le Bret, 1543.
References: *Index* I #472.

Notes: The 1551 censure specifies 'par Guillaume Le Bret, 1543. Et par autres semblables'. This ed. unknown apart from this condemnation.

L 50.   **Lemaire de Belges, Jean.**

Le Promptuaire des conciles de l'Eglise catholique, avec les Scismes et la difference d'iceulx. — Paris, Denis Janot, Galliot Du Pré, 1545.
16°: A-P⁸, rom.
*Chantilly Condé VI.F.57. *Munich BSB Conc.c 45.
References: Rawles #224.

L 51.   **Lemaire de Belges, Jean.**

Le Promptuaire des conciles de l'Eglise Catholicque, avec les Scismes et la difference diceulx. — [Paris], [Jean Longis], [Vincent Sertenas], 1545?
8°: 86 + [2] ff., A-L⁸, rom.
*Paris BA 8° T 2869 and 2870. *Paris BN B 5694. *Paris BSG C 8° 445 inv. 6 Rés. *Rouen BM Montbret p 10221. *Lyon BV 321715 (- A1).
Notes: The Paris BA T 2870 copy bound with a 1545 work printed for Longis and Sertenas, and the material is identical. Hence the attribution and dating. Two issues: Paris BA T 2870, BSG, Rouen copies have 'l'Eclise Cacholicque' on t.p. The other Paris BA copy is corrected.

L 52.   **Lemaire de Belges, Jean.**

Le Promptuaire des conciles de Leglise catholique, avec les scismes et la difference diceulx. — Lyon, Jean de Tournes, 1546.
16°: A-O⁸, rom.
*Geneva BPU Rés. Se 6382. *London BL 5016.a.24.
References: Cartier *De Tournes* #59.

L 53.   **Lemaire de Belges, Jean.**

Le Promptuaire des conciles de Leglise catholique, avec les Scismes et la difference diceulx. — Lyon, Jean de Tournes, 1547.
16°: 214 pp. + [5 ff.], A-O⁸, rom.
*Paris BSG C 8° 443 inv. 4 Rés. Munich BSB (destroyed). Terrebasse. Rome BV Racc.I.VI.112. *Lyon BV 800801.
References: Cartier *De Tournes* #98.

L 54.   Lemaire de Belges, Jean.

*Le Promptuaire des conciles de l'Eglise Catholique,
avec les Scismes et la difference d'iceulx.* — Paris,
Jean Ruelle, Guillaume Thibout, Guillaume Le Bret,
1547.

16°: 115 + [5] ff., A-P⁸, rom.

*Paris BSG C. 8° 444 inv. 5 Rés. (Ruelle). *Munich BSB Conc.c.47
(Ruelle). *Paris BN Rothschild V.7.71 (Ruelle). *Paris BN B 5696
(Thibout). Cambridge Kings (Le Bret).

References: Brunet III, 965. Adams L 410.

L 55.   [Le Moyne, Pasquier].

*Lardant miroir de grace Compose par le Riche de
povrete.* — Paris, Gilles Couteau, 1520.

8°: [48] ff., a-f⁸, goth. f 8v: Ach. d'impr. 20.09.1520.

*Paris BN Rés. Ye 1384.

References: Moreau II #2391.

Notes: a 1v: royal priv. to 'le moyne sans froc' for four years,
dated 03.08.1519. Mixture of prose and verse: spiritual itin-
erary in the form of a *roman de chevalerie.*

L 56.   [Le Roy, François].

Le Dialogue de consolation entre lame et raison. —
Paris, [Estienne Caveiller], pr. Denis Janot, Pierre
Sergent, 1537.

8°: A-V⁸, goth.

*Paris BA 8° T 6954 (s.l.). *Paris BN Rés. D 17397. *Vienna ÖNB
17.J.29. Chicago Newb. Case *696.5. Avignon BM in-8° 19.749.

References: Rawles #65.

Notes: François Le Roy was a 'religieux de la reformation de
lordre de Fontevrault' (t.p.), and active *c.* 1512 (see Le Roy,
Mirouer).

L 57.   Le Roy, François.

*Le livre de la femme forte Et vertueuse declaratif du
cantique de salomon es proverbes au chapitre qui
commence. Mulierem fortem quis inveniet.* — Paris,
Jean Petit, 1517?

8°: A-V x-z a-i⁸ k⁴, goth. i 8v: Impr. à Paris pr. Jean Petit libr.

*London BL C.36.b.32. Séville Colomb.

References: Moreau II #1657.

Notes: Moreau: 'suit l'éd. de 1501'. There was an intermediate ed. in [1508] (London BL C.36.b.33), not in Moreau.

L 58.   Le Roy, François.

Le Mirouer de penitence tresdevot et salutaire: tresutile et proffitable a toutes personnes et specialement a gens de religion. — Paris, Simon Vostre, 1512?
8°: 2 vols, a-z A-S⁸ (gatherings A and B signed a and b), goth.
London BL 1360.e.1 (?). *Paris BEBA Masson 632(Vol. II). *Paris BA 8° T 6947 et 6946 (-a 1). *Paris BN Rés. 13825. Beaune BM.
References: Moreau II #395.
Notes: According to the t.p., the work was 'fait et composé nouvellement en l'an 1512 par celuy qui autresfoys a compillé en françoys le Livre de la femme forte, et le dyalogue de consolation entre l'ame et raison'. It is an anthology of extracts from Church Fathers on the theme of penitence. Second part based on Ps. 50(51). At the end (R 8r sqq.), narrative by Le Roy of the death of Frère Jacques Daniel, dated 1 March 1511 (a.s.).

L 59.   Lescagne, Tristan de.

Le Lys treschrestian florissant en la foy chrestiane. — Paris, Denis Janot, 1540.
4°: A-O⁴, rom.
*Paris BN Rés. 4° L³⁵ 356.
References: Rawles #121.
Notes: The author is described on the t.p. as 'Official de sainct Julien du Sault, pres Sens'. The text is a long panegyric of faith, of France, of Francis I, violently hostile to the 'heretics'.

L 60.   Lescagne, Tristan de.

Livret intitule C'est Nostre Dame <> En l'honneur de la tressacrée vierge Marie ... et à la confusion de ces mal advisez et mauldictz lutheriens. — Paris, Jean André, 1548.
8°: 32 ff., a-d⁸, rom. Dd 8r: 'Fin du livre. 548'.
*Paris BN D 41519.
Notes: Dedic. to Henri II. Twelve short chapters showing that the Virgin Mary is 'nostre Dame: et qu'en elle, apres dieu, debvons figer nostre esperance' (Ch. 1). d 8v: priv. to Jean André for three years, dated 3 Nov. 1548.

L 61.   Lesnauderie, Pierre de.

*La Louenge de mariage et recueil des hystoires de
bonnes, vertueuses et illustres femmes.* — Paris,
[Gilles Couteau], François Regnault, 1523.
4°: a⁶ b⁴ c-t^{8/4} v⁶, goth. v 6v: Impr. à Paris pr. Francoys regnault ...
ens. sainct Claude. 09.05.1523.
*Paris BN Rés. Ye 1046 (- a 1,2, e 1). *Rouen BM Leber 2742.
References: Moreau III #535. *Index* II #1546.185.
Notes: Censured by Louvain theologians in 1546. The author
aligns classical and biblical examples to demonstrate the su-
periority of marriage over celibacy, with the intention of
encouraging his 'voisin familier et disciple Me Zacharie Le
Gouez' to marry rather than become a priest. P. de
Lesnauderie is described as 'scribe de l'université de Caen'.

L 62.   Lesnauderie, Pierre de.

*La Louenge de mariage et recueil des hystoires des
bonnes, vertueuses et illustres femmes.* — Paris,
Antoine Couteau, François Regnault, 1525.
8°: A-S⁸, goth. S 7v: Impr. à Paris par Anthoine couteau pr.
François Regnault. 25.10.1525.
*Paris BA 8° S 3329bis.
References: Moreau III #862.

L 63.   Lesnauderie, Pierre de.

*La Louange de mariage et recueil des hystoyres des
bonnes, vertueuses et illustres femmes.* — Paris,
Alain Lotrian, Denis Janot, 1532?
4°: 88 ff., A-G⁴ H⁸ I-P⁴ Q⁸ R-V⁴, goth. V 4v: Impr. à Paris par Alain
Lotrian et Denis Janot.
*Paris BA 4° SA 599. Oxford Bodl. Douce L 194.
References: *Index* II #1546.185. Rawles #307. Moreau IV #468.

L 64.   Livre de consolations.

Le Livret des consolations contre toutes tribulations.
— Paris, Alain Lotrian, 1528?
8°: A-H⁴, goth. H 4r: Impr. à Paris pour Alain lotrian.
*Paris BN Rés. H 2092(1).
References: Moreau III #1546.
Notes: Dialogue between the 'povre pecheur' and 'Jesus pendant
en la croix'.

L 65.   Livre de consolations.

Le livre de consolations contre toutes tribulations.
— Lyon, Vve Barnabé Chaussard, 1532.
8°: A-L⁴, goth. L 3r: Impr. à Lyon en la maison de feu Barnabe
Chaussard. 13.06.1532.
Séville Colombine. *Paris BEBA Masson 730.
References: Babelon #113. Baudrier XI, 61.

L 66.   Livre de la compagnie.

*Livre de la compagnie des Penitens contenant l'ordre
de recepvoir un Novice.* — Lyon, Estienne Dolet, 1542.
References: Christie #53. Longeon *Dolet* #220. Du Verdier
p. 1080.
Notes: See *Heures de la compagnie.*

L 67.   Livre de la loi.

Le livre de la loy et de l'Evangile avec la force d'iceux.
— ?, ?, ?
References: *Index* II #1546.189.
Notes: Censured on 2 March 1531 (Higman *Censorship*,
p. 83). No known copy. Probably the same as the *Petit livre de
la loy et de Levangile, sans auctuer* condemned by Louvain in
1546, equally untraced.

L 68.   Livre de paix.

Le livre de paix en Jesuchrist. — Lyon, Vve Barnabé
Chaussard, 1532.
8°: [20 ff.], a-b⁸ c⁴, goth. c 4r: 19.06.1532.
Séville Colombine.
References: Babelon #115.

L 69.   Livre merveilleux.

*Livre merveilleux, contenant en brief la fleur et sub-
stance de plusieurs traictiez, tant des Propheties et
revellations, que anciennes Croniques. faisans
mention de tous les faitz de leglise universelle,
comme des scismes discors et tribulations advenir en
leglise de Romme, Et dung temps ouquel on ostera et
tollira aulx gens deglise et clerge leurs biens temporelz, tellement quon ne leur laissera, que leur*

vivre et habit necessaire... — Paris, [Nicolas Buffet?], 1543?
8°: A-F⁸, rom.
*Paris BN Fb 20228. *Paris BSG V 8° 697 Rés. (-F 5-8).
References: *Index* I #470.
Notes: Censured in 1544, perhaps in this ed. The work thereafter had at least 12 eds in the second half of the century, from Paris or Lyon. Attrib. to Fr. Telesforo di Cosenza, 14th-cent. Franciscan (see E. Donkel, *AFH* 26 (1933)).

L 70.   Loys, Jean.

Le ravisement du pelerin de verite nomme Jehan Loys a qui il a este reveller par miracle divine de souverains remedes pour nature humaine. — [Paris], [Simon Vostre?], 1516?
8°: A⁸, goth.
*Paris BN Rés. D 49673.
References: Moreau II #1422.
Notes: The author claims to have been 'advisé et enluminé soudainement et miraculeusement de tant de fondemans de la foy et de la verité et de la raison et de la justice...' In peculiar French he calls on all to listen to him, but asks 'que de mes escriptures ne laissent imprimer a personne: car je leurs declairere plus amplement les raisons pour quoy: car il ny a personne du monde qui le sache ne les principes ne les fondemens ne les oeuvres ne les fins de riens'.

L 71.   Lucidaire.

Lucidaire ... diverses matieres subtilles et merveilleuses en maniere dinterrogation. — Lyon, Claude Nourry, 1516?
4°: a-f⁴, goth. f 4r: Impr. à Lyon par Claude nourry.
*Paris BN Rés. D 10673.
References: Baudrier XII, 93.
Notes: Nourry had already produced an earlier ed. of this text in 1506 (copy in Paris BA). A book of piety in dialogue form, trans. from the Latin *Lucidarius* (the Latin text ed. C.J. Brandt, Copenhague, 1849).

L 72.   Lucidaire.

Lucidaire en françoys. — Lyon, Vve Barnabé Chaussard, 1540.

4°: A-F⁴, goth.   F 4v: Impr. à Lyon pr. Vve Barnabé Chaussard.
27.03.1540.
References: Baudrier XI, 63 < Fairfax Murray.

L 73.   Lucidaire.

Lucidiaire en françoys. — Troyes, Jean Le Coq, ?
8°: A-D⁸, goth.   D 8r: Impr. à Troyes par Jehan Le coq.
*Paris BN Rés. D 80200.
References: *Rép. bib.* #83.

L 74.   Ludolphus de Saxe, trans. Guillaume Le Menand.

*Le premier (-second) volume du grant vita Christi en
françois.* — Paris, [Gilles Couteau], Jean Petit, François
Regnault, 1521.
2°: 2 vols, a-y A-X⁶ Y⁴ Z AA-QQ⁶ RR¹⁰ AAA-XXX AAAA-EEEE⁶
FFFF⁴, goth.   FFFF 3v: Impr. à Paris pr. Jehan Petit. 29.03.1521.
Amiens. Cambridge UL. *Paris BN Rés. D 667. *Paris BA fol. T 423
(lacks all after Z 2).
References: Moreau III #169bis.
Notes: The name of the translator given in the colophon, and
in his prologue.

L 75.   Ludolphus de Saxe, trans. Guillaume Le Menand.

Le grant Vita Christi ... en francoys. — Paris, Guillaume de Bossozel, Ambroise Girault, 1531?
2°: 4 parts.
Metz Inc. 173. New York PML.
References: Moreau IV #227.

L 76.   Ludolphus de Saxe, trans. Guillaume Le Menand.

*Le premier (-second) volume du grant vita Christi
translaté de latin en francoys.* — Paris, Guillaume de
Bossozel, [Didier Maheu], 1534?
2°: 4 pts, 2 vol., a-p⁸ q⁴ aa-qq A-K⁸ L¹⁰ M AA-TT⁸, goth.   TT 7r:
Impr. à Paris par Guillaume de bossozel.
*Paris BN Rés. D 2850.
References: Moreau IV #1066.
Notes: In the colophon Bossozel gives his address as 'rue
sainct Jacques au Chasteau rouge pres les Mathurins', address
which he kept until 1542.

L 77.   Ludolphus de Saxe, trans. Guillaume Le Menand.

Le grand vita Christi translate de Latin en Françoys, Et nouvellement reveu et diligentement corrige, et aussi reduict de quatre parties en deux. — Paris, Charles et Arnoul Langelier, 1544.

2°: 2 vols, a-z & § # aa-ii⁶ kk⁴ A-Z AA-LL⁶ MM⁸ NN², goth. NN 1r: Impr. à Paris.

*London BL 1217.k.8. *Paris BA fol. T 424.

Notes: The Paris BA copy is s.l.n.d., and reads 'corrigé' on the t.p. where the London copy had 'reveu'. But the collation is identical. Two issues, or two eds?

L 78.   Lunette des Chrétiens.

La Lunette des Chrestiens par laquelle ils pourront facilement voir les raisons pour ... moult miseres et calamitez. — ?, ?, ?

References: Du Verdier ('lutherique').

Notes: In *Contre les libertins* Calvin mentions a 'libertin' text, 'à environ 14 quayers', with the title *La Lunette des Chrestiens* (*CO* VII, 242). Same text?

L 79.   Luther, Martin.

Antithese de la vraye et faulse Eglise extraicte d'un livre envoyé au Duc de Brunsvic. — [Geneva], [Jean Girard], 1545.

8°: A-F⁸, rom.

*Geneva BPU Rés. Bc 2702. *Lausanne BCU NED 673. *Paris BN 8° Z Don 594(218.I). *Vienna ÖNB 36.M.44.

References: Moore #35. Benzing *Luther* #3374. *BG* 45/20. *Index* I #330.

Notes: Trans. of *Wider Hans Worst* (1541), or rather of the Latin version *Antithesis verae et falsae ecclesiae* (1543). See Chaix, 'Un pamphlet genevois...'

L 80.   Luther, Martin.

Antithese de la vraye et faulse Eglise extraite d'un livre envoyé au Duc de Brunsvic. — [Geneva], [Jean Girard], 1546?

8°: A-F⁸, rom.

*Geneva BPU Rés. Bc 3373.

References: Benzing *Luther* #3375. *BG* 46/9.

Notes: It is uncertain whether the undated ed. is earlier or later than the 1545 ed.

L 81.   [Luther, Martin].

Brief racueil des oeuvres des dix commandemens. —
[Antwerp], [Martin Lempereur], 1525?
8°: A⁸ B⁴, goth.
*London BL C.111.aa.8. *Paris SHP A 1158.
References: Moore #5. Benzing *Luther* #812. NK #3470.
Notes: Trans. of *Kurtze Form der zehen Gebote* (1520), different from that of the *Exposition sur les dix commandemens...*

L 82.   [Luther, Martin].

Consolation chrestienne, contre les afflictions de ce monde. — [Alençon], [Simon Du Bois], 1532?
8°: A-M⁸, goth.
*Geneva MHR K Lut 5. *Paris SHP R.13452(1).
References: Moore #3. Clutton #36. Benzing *Luther* #606.
Index I #385.
Notes: Censured on 1 June 1541 (Higman *Censorship*, p. 88), and entered in the 1544 *Index*. Trans. of *Tessaradecas Consolatoria* (1519).

L 83.   [Luther, Martin].

Les quatorze miroirs pour consoler la creature en Dieu. — [Geneva], 1543?
References: Cartier *Arrêts* p. 410. BG 43/21. *Index* I #329.
Notes: No known copy of this ed. Jean Girard obtained permission to print this title in 1543. The 1547 *Index* condemned *Le miroer de consolation pour ceux qui sont travaillez et chargez*, which may refer to the same. In 1552 Jean Crespin produced an ed. with the title *Quatorze miroirs de vraye et parfaite consolation*, a revision and modernization of the Du Bois *Consolation*.

L 84.   [Luther, Martin], trans. Claude d'Espence.

Consolation en adversité. — Lyon, Jean de Tournes, 1547.
16°: A-I⁸, rom.
*Geneva BPU Rés. Bd 1888. *Paris BN D 88506(3).
References: Cartier *De Tournes* #82. *Index* I #528.

Notes: Although the t.p. says 'faite par Claude d'Espense', this work, offered to Marguerite de France to console her on the death of her father Francis I, is a faithful translation of the *Tessaradecas Consolatoria*, different from that of Du Bois. The work should have featured in the 1556 *Index*, but Claude d'Espence obtained an order from the Parlement to have the mention removed (see *Index* I, p. 117). See also P. Doré, *La Piscine de patience*, 1550.

L 85.   [Luther, Martin].

Declaration d'aucuns motz desquelz use souvent sainct Pol en ses epistres.
Notes: See [Farel] et [Luther], *L'Oraison de Jesuchrist*. Trans. of the *Praefatio methodica*, Latin version (by Justus Jonas, 1523) of Luther's preface to his translation of the Epistle to the Romans (1522). The text reprod. in *Palaestra typographica*, pp. 47 sqq.

L 86.   [Luther, Martin].

Des bonnes oeuvres sus les commandemens de Dieu. — [Antwerp], [Martin Lempereur], 1525?
8°: A-O⁸, goth.
*London BL 848.a.2(4). Geneva BPU Rés. Bc 2554. *Paris BA 8° T 5160.
References: Moore #4. Benzing *Luther* #648. NK #3469.
Notes: Trans. of the *Sermon von den guten werken* (1520, Latin trans. 1521).

L 87.   [Luther, Martin], trans. Antoine Du Pinet from Bucer's Latin version.

Exposition de l'histoire des dix Lepreux, prinse du dixseptiesme de Sainct Luc. Ou est amplement traicté de la confession auriculaire: et comme on peut user d'allegories en la saincte Escripture. — [Geneva], [Jean Girard], 1539.
8°: a-i⁸ k⁴, ital.
*Geneva BPU Rés. Bb 2289. *Paris BN Rés. D² 15956.
References: Moore #10. Benzing *Luther* #995. *Index* I #430. Droz *Chemins* II, 55-144, with text.
Notes: Trans. of Bucer's Latin version of *Von den tzehen auszsetzigen vordeutscht und auszgelegtt* (1521).

L 88.   [Luther, Martin].

Une exposition sur le Magnificat. — [Antwerp], [Martin Lempereur?], 1525?
8°: A-G⁸, goth.
*Lyon BV 329946.
Notes: Translation of *Das Magnificat verdeutscht* (1521) or its 1525 Latin version. Ed. not before noted. The attrib. to Lempereur is very hypothetical.

L 89.   [Luther, Martin].

Une exposition sur le Magnificat. — [Paris], [Simon Du Bois], 1525?
8°: A-H⁸ I⁴, goth.
*Geneva MHR K Lut 5(3). *Vienna ÖNB *43.Z.185.
References: Moore #9. Benzing *Luther* #864. Clutton #44. Moreau III #863.
Notes: Text identical to the previous number. Censured on 1 March 1531 (Higman *Censorship*, p. 83).

L 90.   [Luther, Martin].

Exposition sur le cantique virginal, Magnificat, lequel nous apprent la maniere de bien louer et remercier Dieu de ses graces. — Agen, A. Villotte, 1546.
References: *Index* I #423.
Notes: This title censured on 20 Jan. 1546 (Higman *Censorship*, p. 103), details of the printer being added in the 1547 *Index*. No known copies.

L 91.   [Luther, Martin].

Exposition sur les dix commandemens de la loy. — [Paris], [Simon de Colines], 1525?
16°: a-c⁸ d⁴ e⁸, goth.
Ghent BU Res. 935(2). *Paris BEBA Masson 7.
References: Moreau III #821.
Notes: Censured on 2 March 1531, again on 1 June 1541 (Higman *Censorship*, p. 88). Trans. of part of the *Betbüchlein*, bound, in the Ghent copy, with the *Oraison de Jesuchrist* by [Farel and Luther]. The text is later incorporated in the *Livre de vraye et parfaicte oraison*.

L 92.   [Luther, Martin].

Exposition sur les deux Epistres de S. Pierre, et sur celle de S. Jude: en laquelle tout ce qui touche la doctrine Chrestienne est parfaictement compris. Avec un Sermon du vray usage de la loy, auquel la plus grande partie du premier chapitre de la premiere Epistre a Timothee est fidelement exposee. — [Geneva], [Jean Michel], 1540.
8°: a-z A-D⁸ A⁸, goth.
*Geneva BPU Rés. Bb 2288. *Geneva MHR K Lut 13 and 13a.
*London St Pauls 38 E 26(2). *Zurich ZB D 350.
References: Moore #24. Benzing *Luther* #1732. *BG* 40/5.
Berthoud 'Michel' #10. *Index* I #408.
Notes: Trans. of *Enarrationes ... in Epistolas D. Petri duas et Judae unam* (1524), with part of the *Sermon von der heubtsumma gottes gepots* (1526).

L 93.   [Luther, Martin].

Exposition sur les deux Epistres de S. Pierre, et sur celle de S. Jude: en laquelle tout ce qui touche la doctrine Chrestienne est parfaictement comprins. — Geneva, Jean Girard, 1545.
8°: a-z⁸, rom.
*London BL C.65.f.15(1) and 689.a.11(1).
References: *BG* 45/21. *Index* I #422.
Notes: The 1547 censure specifies this ed. The sermon included in the previous ed. is here omitted.

L 94.   [Luther, Martin], woodcuts copied from Lucas Cranach.

Les faictz de Jesus Christ et du Pape, par lesquelz chascun pourra facilement congnoistre la grande difference de entre eulx: nouvellement reveuz, corrigez, et augmentez, selon la verite de la saincte Escripture, et des droictz canons, par le lecteur du sainct Palais. — [Neuchâtel], [Pierre de Vingle], 1534?
2°: A-F⁴, goth. F 4v: Impr. à Rome par Clement de medicis au chasteau de sainct Ange.
*Paris SHP A 1001.
References: Berthoud 'Michel' pp. 64-7.

Notes: Trans. of *Passional Christi et Antichristi* (1521). The only illustrated book in the early francophone Reformation.

L 95.   [Luther, Martin], woodcuts copied from Lucas Cranach.

Les faitz de Jesus Christ et du Pape, par lesquelz chascun pourra facilement congnoistre la grande difference dentre eulx: nouvellement reveuz, corrigez, et augmentez selon la verite de la saincte Escripture, et des droictz canons, par le lecteur du sainct Palais. — [Geneva], [Jean Michel], 1540?
4°: A-M⁴, goth. M 4v: Impr. a Rome, au chasteau sainct Ange.
*Berne StU B 64.4. *Geneva MHR K Lut 8. *Strasbourg St Guillaume 16.4(10). *Vienna ÖNB 78.G.48.
References: Berthoud 'Michel' #25. *BG* 44/16. Higman *Censorship* A 32. *Index* I #426, 508. Cat. Drilhon #9.
Notes: The various censures do not specify which ed. is intended.

L 96.   [Luther, Martin].

La Fleur des Commandementz, et declaration des Bonnes Oeuvres. — [Alençon], [Simon Du Bois], 1530?
8°: a-x⁸, goth.
*London BL C.83.a.21.
References: Moore #4. Benzing *Luther* #649. Clutton #51.
Notes: A modified version of *Des bonnes oeuvres...*

L 97.   [Luther, Martin], [Guillaume Farel et al.].

Le livre de vraye et parfaicte oraison. — Paris, Simon Du Bois, pr. Chrestien Wechel, 1528.
8°: 166 ff., A¹⁰ a-b⁸ c² Aa⁸ A¹⁰ ¶⁸ b-c⁸ +² a-b⁸ a-i⁸ k⁶, goth. k 5r: Impr. à Paris par Simon du bois pr. Chrestien Wechel. 07.1528.
Harvard CL Typ 515 28.526.
References: Mortimer #352. Moreau III #1545.
Notes: A mixture of devotional texts including elements from the *Oraison de Jesuchrist* by [Farel and Luther], more traditionalist texts, and the penitential psalms. Each part forms a separate pamphlet of one or more gatherings, which explains the bizarre collation. But the components are all listed on the v° of the t.p.: 'Le Sermon de Jesuchrist en la montaigne (plain text). Deux homelies de sainct Jehan chrysostome des louen-

ges doraison. Trois brefves expositions sur le Pater noster.
Une exposition sur le Ave Maria. Une exposition sur le Credo.
Expositions sur les dix commandemens de la loy. Aulcunes
Benedictions de la table avec les actions de graces, louenges a
dieu, cantiques et prieres. Les sept Pseaulmes penitentiaulx
exposez par maniere doraison.' The contents of the book
evolve from one ed. to another. See Higman, *RHPR* (1983).

L 98.   **[Luther, Martin], [Guillaume Farel et al.].**
Le livre de vraye et parfaicte oraison. — Paris,
Simon Du Bois, pr. Chrestien Wechel, 1529.
8°: a[10] A-T[8], goth.   T 8r: Impr. à Paris par Simon du bois pr.
Christien Vvechel. 04.1529.
*Bruxelles BR LP II 61120 A. *Geneva MHR D 2 (1524).
*Lausanne BCU AA 8215. *London BL 1359.a.6. *Paris BN Rés.
D[2] 35024.
References: Moore #18. Clutton #17. Moreau III #1831.
Gilmont 'Farel' #18.1.
Notes: The priv. (T 7v-8r) is for five years, dated 17 June 1528.

L 99.   **[Luther, Martin], [Guillaume Farel et al.].**
Le livre de vraye et parfaicte oraison. — Paris, Jean
Kerbriant, pr. Chrestien Wechel, 1530.
8°: a[8] A-Q[8] R[4], goth.   R 3v: Impr. à Paris par Jehan Kerbriant impr.
pr. Chrestien Vvechel. 04.1530.
*Paris BEBA Les 414.
References: Moore #18. Moreau III #2187. Gilmont 'Farel'
#18.2.

L 100.   **[Luther, Martin], [Guillaume Farel et al.].**
Le livre de vraye et parfaicte oraison. — Antwerp,
Martin Lempereur, 1534.
8°: π[8] A-R[8], goth.   R 8r: Impr. en Anvers par Martin Lempereur.
07.1534.
*Bruxelles BR LP 4049A (-[] 1,2). *Lausanne BCU AZ 4329.
References: Moore #18. NK #3414. Benzing *Luther* #813.
Gilmont 'Farel' #18.3.
Notes: Eccentric ed.: several pieces added here which do not
appear in any other ed.

L 101.   [Luther, Martin], [Guillaume Farel et al.].

Le livre de vraye et parfaicte oraison. — Antwerp, Jean Steelsius, 1538.
16°: π⁸ A-S⁸, goth.
*Bruxelles BR LP II 33.221A.
References: Benzing *Luther* #814. NK #3415. Gilmont 'Farel' #18.4.

L 102.   [Luther, Martin], [Guillaume Farel et al.].

Le livre de vraye et parfaicte oraison. — Paris, Jean Foucher, Vivant Gaultherot, Nicolas Gilles, 1539.
16°: A-S⁸, rom.
*Wolfenbüttel HAB Th 1626.
References: Gilmont 'Farel' #18.5.
Notes: A 'Sermon du sainct sacrement de lhostel' by Matthieu de Lalande added here for the first time.

L 103.   [Luther, Martin], [Guillaume Farel et al.].

Le livre de vraye et parfaicte oraison. — Paris, Gilles Corrozet, 1540.
8°: A-S⁸, rom.
*Cambridge Emma. 321.6.3(1).
References: Gilmont 'Farel' #18.6. Adams O 228.

L 104.   [Luther, Martin], [Guillaume Farel et al.].

Le livre de vraye et parfaicte oraison. — Paris, Jean Foucher, 1540.
16°: A-S⁸, rom.
*Paris BSG D 8° 6479 inv 8208 bis Rés. Poitiers BU XVI.199(1) (s.l.).

L 105.   [Luther, Martin], [Guillaume Farel et al.].

Le livre de vraye et parfaicte oraison. — Paris, Vve Jean de Brie, 1540.
16°: A-R⁸, rom.
*Paris BN Rés. D² 35026.
References: Moore #18. Gilmont 'Farel' #18.7.

L 106.   [Luther, Martin], [Guillaume Farel et al.].

Le livre de vraye et parfaicte oraison. — Poitiers, Enguilbert et Jean de Marnef, 1542.
16°: A-S⁸, rom.

*Paris BU Rés. XVI b 18 nain.
References: Gilmont 'Farel' #18.9.

L 107. **[Luther, Martin], [Guillaume Farel et al.].**

Le livre de vraye et parfaicte oraison. — Lyon, Jean de Tournes, 1543.
16°: a-v⁸, rom.
Terrebasse. *Wrocław BU 454322. Yale UL.
References: Cartier *De Tournes* #16. Gilmont 'Farel' #18.11.

L 108. **[Luther, Martin], [Guillaume Farel et al.].**

Le livre de vraye et parfaicte oraison. — Paris, Nicolas Buffet, pr. Jacques Regnault et Antoine Foucault, 1543.
8°: A-S⁸, rom.
*Paris SHP R 16182 and A 1211(1) (-S 1,8). *Troyes BM H.12.4705(1).
References: Gilmont 'Farel' #18.10.
Notes: The Troyes copy, and Paris SHP A 1211, bound with [Jean Vitrier], *Sermon...*, 1544.

L 109. **[Luther, Martin], [Guillaume Farel et al.].**

Le livre de vraye et parfaicte oraison. — Lyon, Olivier Arnoullet, 1543?
8°: A-Q⁸ [R⁸?], goth.
*Paris SHP R 11368.
References: Moore #18. Cartier *De Tournes* I, 177. Gilmont 'Farel' #18.8.
Notes: The only known copy is incomplete, lacking probably one gathering at the end.

L 110. **[Luther, Martin], [Guillaume Farel et al.].**

Le livre de la vraye et parfaite Oraison avec le Sermon que nostre Seigneur feist en la montagne, et l'exposition contenant les huict beatitudes, deux Homelies de S. Jean Chrisostome pour apprendre la maniere de prier Dieu, Les Pseaumes penitentiaux exposez par maniere d'oraison. Et le mistere de l'incarnation du verbe divin. — Paris, Charles Langelier, 1544.
References: Du Verdier.

L 111. **[Luther, Martin]**, [Guillaume Farel et al.].

Le livre de vraye et parfaicte oraison. — Antwerp, Jean de Grave, Guillaume Vissenaken, 1545.
16°: π⁸ A-Z⁸, goth. Z 8v: Impr. par Jean de Grave. 1545.
*Paris SHP R 11369. *Vienna ÖNB 18.Aa.136.
References: Gilmont 'Farel' #18.13. *Index* II #1546.187.
Notes: Contents as in the earliest eds. The Louvain censure of 1546 may have been aimed at this ed.

L 112. **[Luther, Martin]**, [Guillaume Farel et al.].

Le livre de vraye et parfaicte oraison. Avec le Sermon que nostre Seigneur feist en la montaigne, et L'exposition contenant les huit beatitudes, prinses du .v. vi. et .vii. Chapitres de sainct Matthieu. Ensemble le Mystere de l'incarnation du Verbe divin, et plusieurs autres petitz traictez ... Le tout veu et corrigé oultre les precedentes impressions. — Paris, Charles Langelier, 1545.
16°: 260 ff., A-Z Aa-Ii⁸ Kk⁴, rom.
*Coll. R. Peter, Strasbourg.
References: Benzing *Luther* #814a. Droz *Chemins* I, 332-8. Gilmont 'Farel' #18.12.
Notes: Last known, and fullest, ed., incorporating the [Vitrier] sermon, previously a separate publication although frequently bound together.

L 113. **[Luther, Martin]**, trans. François Lambert?

Livre tresutile de la vraye et parfaite subjection des chrestiens, et ensemble de la sacree franchise et liberte, quilz ont en Saint Esprerit. — [Strasbourg], [Johann Schott], [Wolfgang Köpfel], 1525?
4°: A-I⁴, goth.
*Munich BSB Polem 3340(1).
References: Peter 'Prem. ouvr.' #0a. *Index* I #488. Bodenmann p. 162.
Notes: Trans. of *De libertate christiana* (1520). Censured on 2 March 1531 (Higman *Censorship*, p. 83). A new trans. appears in 1556 (Moore #8).

L 114.   [Luther, Martin].

La Maniere de lire levangile et quel profit on en doibt attendre. — [Antwerp], [Guillaume Vorsterman], [Martin Lempereur], 1529?
8°: a⁸, goth.
*London BL 848.a.2(2). Villiers-le-Bel SBF 1795.
References: Moore #12. Benzing *Luther* #2003. NK #3468. Chambers #47.
Notes: Trans. of *Eyn kleyn Unterricht was man in den Evangeliis suchen und erwarten soll* (1522). The SBF copy is bound at the beginning of Simon Du Bois's 1529 ed. of the *Nouveau Testament*.

L 115.   [Luther, Martin].

Breve Instruction pour deuement lire lescripture saincte. — [Alençon], [Simon Du Bois], 1529.
8°: +⁸, goth.
New York P.L. KB.1529. Orléans BM A 293.
References: Chambers #47. Rice, *Pref. Epist.* 502-11 with text.
Notes: Trans. of *Eyn kleyn Unterricht* different from *La Maniere de lire*. Bound in New York copy with Simon Du Bois's 1529 *Nouveau Testament*.

L 116.   [Luther, Martin].

La Maniere de lire levangile et quel proffit on en doibt attendre ... et aussi la maniere de mediter et penser a la passion de nostre saulveur Jesuchrist, fort consolatoire a toute personne qui a quelque tribulation. — [Lyon], [Pierre de Vingle], 1530?
8°: 23 ff.
References: Brunet III, 1366. Benzing *Luther* #2004. Th. Dufour *Not.cat.* p. 127.
Notes: The only known copy, in the recueil Gaignat-La Vallière, is untraceable, but certainly existed. In all probability the ed. assembles the preceding and following numbers.

L 117.   [Luther, Martin].

La Maniere de mediter et penser a la passion de nostre sauveur Jesuchrist.
Notes: see [Farel], *L'Oraison de Jesuchrist*.

L 118. **[Luther, Martin]**, trans. de François Lambert?

Prophetie de Iesaie de lenfant nouveau ne Jesu-christ. Avec les annotations du docteur De Clere-mont. — [Strasbourg], [Johann Pruss], 1527.
8°: A-E⁸ F⁴, goth.
*Amsterdam VU XC 05993/1. *London BL 3901.a.3(1) and C.37.a.22(4).
References: Moore #25. Benzing *Luther* #2266. Peter 'Prem. ouvr.' #5. Bodenmann p. 162.
Notes: Trans., perhaps by François Lambert, of Die *Epistel des Propheten Iesaia, so man in der Christmesse lieset* (1526, Latin in 1527).

L 119. **[Luther, Martin]**.

Quatre instructions fideles pour les simples, et les rudes. La premiere Lhomme fidele, visitant. La seconde. Lhomme fidele, catechisant. La tierce. Lhomme fidele, introduisant a Levangile. La quarte. Lhomme fidele psalmodiant. — [Alençon], [Simon Du Bois], 1532?
8°: A-E⁸ F⁴, goth.
*Geneva MHR K Lut 6. *London BL C.22.a.31. Paris BN Rés. D² 15952.
References: Moore #29. Benzing *Luther* #2665. Clutton #42. *Index* I #446.
Notes: The first two parts trans. from Luther, *Klein Catechis-mus* and *Enchiridion* (1529).

L 120. **[Luther, Martin]**.

Sermon au jour de l'ascension. — [Antwerp], [Martin Lempereur], 1527?
8°: A-B⁸ C⁴, goth.
*Geneva BPU Rés. Bd 1995. *London BL 848.a.2(3).
References: Moore #20. Benzing *Luther* #1356. NK #3471.
Notes: Trans. of the *Sermon von der Tröstung des hl. Geistes in der Verfolgung* (1522, Latin 1526).

L 121. **[Luther, Martin]**.

Ung sermon de mammone iniquitatis.
Notes: See [Heyden, S.] *Dung seul mediateur.*

L 122.   [Luther, Martin].

Sermon de la maniere de prier Dieu et comment on doibt faire processions et rogations. — [Antwerp], [Martin Lempereur], 1527?

8°: a⁸, goth.

*London BL C.37.a.22(2).

References: Moore #2. Benzing *Luther* #391. NK #3472.

Notes: Trans. of the *Sermon von der gepeet und procession yn der creutzwochen* (1519, Latin 1526).

M

M 1.   Maillard, Olivier.

Lexemplaire de confession nouvellement imprimee et corrigee avecques la confession de frere Olivier Maillart. — Lyon, Olivier Arnoullet, 1524.

4°: A-L⁴, goth. L 4v: Impr. à Lyon par Olivier Arnoullet. 23.07.1524.

*Paris BA 4° T 1893.

Notes: A 1v: 'En ce petit livret pourra trouver le confesseur la vraye voye et maniere d'estudier l'enseignement par lequel il pourra cognoistre la droite voye de confession et l'adressement des penitens qui à luy se viendront confesser.' A general, and systematic, confession: five senses, seven deadly sins... See Gerson, *Directoire des confesseurs* (same text).

M 2.   Maillard, Olivier.

La confession generalle de frere Olivier Maillard. — Lyon, Jacques Moderne, ?

16°: A-D⁴, goth.   D 3v: Impr. a Lyon cheulx le grand Jaques Moderne.

* Aix Méj. Rés. S. 128(2).

M 3.   Maillard, Olivier.

La confession generale de frere Olivier maillard. — [Lyon], [Claude Nourry], 1526?

8°: a-b⁸, goth.

*Paris BEBA Masson 681.

References: Baudrier XII.133 < Yemeniz Cat #326.

M 4.   Mailly, Nicolas de.

La divine cognoissance compilee et extraicte tant du viel que nouveau testament, ensemble les cantiques divins de l'ame regrettant, joinct l'exposition de l'oraison dominicalle. — Paris, Guillaume de Bossozel, pr. Galliot Du Pré, 1541.

8°: A⁴ B-M⁸, ital. M 8r: Impr. à Paris par Guillaume de bossozel pour Galiot du pre libr. 1541.

*Paris BA Rés. 8° BL 10303.

Notes: Theological summary in verse, recommending Bible reading in order to grasp its spiritual marrow.

M 5.   Malingre, Matthieu, Clément Marot.

L'Epistre <> envoyee à Clement Marot: en laquelle est demandee la cause de son departement de France. Avec la responce dudit Marot. — Basle, Jacques Estauge, 1546.

8°: A⁸ B⁴, rom.

Berne BNS A 4946. Neuchâtel past. *Paris BN Rothschild IV.6.135.

References: Mayer *Marot* #268. Rothschild #3248. Facs. ed. Paris, 1868.

Notes: Includes two poems by Marot dated from Geneva, 6 Jan. 1543 and 5 May 1546 [! for 1543], reprod. in Marot, *Oeuvres*, ed. Defaux, II, 337.

M 6.   Malingre, Matthieu.

Indice des principales matieres contenues en la Bible: ou les diligentz Lecteurs pourront trouver et practiquer plusieurs lieux communs, tant pour exhortations publiques que particulieres, Ainsi qu'a un chascun Dieu donnera grace. Nouvellement corrigé et augmenté. — Geneva, Jean Girard, 1543.

8°: A-G⁸, rom.

*Stuttgart LB Bibl.gall.8°1543. *Vienna ÖNB 79.Ee.4 (s.l. s.n.).

References: *BG* 43/22. *Index* I #434. Cat. Drilhon #14 specifying this ed.

Notes: G 5r names the author as 'N. Malingre prescheur du sainct Evangile, à Iverdun'. Malingre's *Indice* first appeared in the 1535 Vingle *Bible*. Here it is a separate publication, not accompanying an ed. of the *Bible*.

M 7.   Malingre, Matthieu.

Indice des principales matieres contenues en la Bible. Nouvellement corrigé et augmenté. — Geneva, Jean Girard, 1546.

4°: A-D⁴, rom.

*Hereford cath. A.6.ix (s.l. s.i.). *London BL 217.k.11. *Paris SHP R 1785. *Strasbourg BNU E 103414. Lausanne BCU AB 437 (+).

References: *BG* 46/3a. *Index* I #448.

Notes: Censured independently, and also with the 1546 *Bible* printed by Girard (*Index* I #281). The separate t.p. and collation enable the *Indice* to circulate independently of the *Bible*.

M 8.   [Malingre, Matthieu].

Moralite de la maladie de Chrestiente, a .xiij. personnages: en laquelle sont monstrez plusieurs abuz, advenuz au monde, par la poison de peche et lhypocrisie des hereticques. — [Neuchâtel], [Pierre de Vingle], 1533.

8°: A-F⁸, goth. F 8v: Impr. à Paris par Pierre de Vignolle, rue de la Sorbonne. 1533.

Neuchâtel Coll. Henriod. *Paris BN Rés. Yf 2917. *Paris SHP R 1000(2) (incom.). *Zurich ZB Res. 1331.

References: Moore #188. Th.Dufour *Not.cat.* p. 110. Berthoud *APR* pp. 143 sqq.

Notes: Malingre's name given in an acrostic, fol. F 8r, and in an anagram 'Y me vint mal a gre' on the t.p.

M 9.   [Malingre, Matthieu].

Moralite de la maladie de Chrestiente, a .xiij. personnages: en laquelle sont monstrez plusieurs abuz, advenuz au monde, par la poison de peche et lhypocrisie des hereticques. — [Geneva], [Jean Michel], 1540?

8°: A-F⁸, goth.

*Vienna ÖNB +48.V.87.

References: Berthoud 'Michel' #28. *BG* 44/21.

M 10.   [Malingre, Matthieu].

Noelz nouveaulx. — [Neuchâtel], [Pierre de Vingle], 1533?

8°: A-C⁸, goth.

*Geneva BPU Rés. Bd 1476 (gathering A only). *Zurich ZB Res. 1332.

References: Th. Dufour *Not.cat.* pp. 112-13. Berthoud *APR* 143 sqq.

Notes: Malingre's name is given in an acrostic, fol. A 2r, and in an anagram 'Y me vint mal a gre', fol. A 1v. 24 'noëls'.

M 11.   Mandement de Jésus-Christ.

Le Mandement de Jesus Christ a tous les Chrestiens et fideles. — [Geneva], [Jean Girard], 1544.
8°: A⁸ b⁸ C⁴, rom. C 4v: 1544.
*Vienna ÖNB 79.Ee.6.
References: Moore pp. 267-8. *Index* I #454. Cat. Drilhon #21 (specifies this ed.). *BG* 44/22.
Notes: Trans. of *Ein new Mandat* (1524). Parody of a government edict which recommends evangelical doctrines, ending (C 4v): 'Donné, à la dextre de Dieu mon Pere. L'an de mon incarnation, mil v. cens quarante quatre. Ainsi signé, Jesus Christ, Filz de Dieu vivant, et Sauveur du monde.'

M 12.   Mandement de Jésus-Christ.

Le mandement de Jesus Christ a tous les Chrestiens et fideles. — [Geneva], [Jean Girard], 1545.
8°: A-B⁸, rom.
*Geneva BPU Rés. Bc 2704.
References: Moore p. 268. *BG* 45/23.

M 13.   Manuel des Chrétiens.

Le manuel des Christians continant en soy les plus nobles et salutaires lieux de la saincte escripture touchant les commandemens et benefices du seigneur nostre Dieu: avecq plusieurs psalmes et cantiques et oraisons. — ?, ?, ?
References: *Index* II #1546.186.
Notes: Known only from this censure by Louvain.

M 14.   Marchandise spirituelle.

Cy commence ung devot et salutaire Traite intitule La Marchandise spirituelle laquelle est tresutille et necessaire a tous marchans et marchandes. Et generallement a tous bons crestiens et crestiennes Et est la dicte marchandise distinguee et divisee en Sept regions spirituelles. Avecques ce est applicquee et

ordonnee aux sept jours de la sepmaine. — Paris, [Julien Hubert], pr. Jean Saint Denys, 1529?
4°: A-D⁴ E⁸ F-K⁴ L⁸ M⁴ N⁶ O⁴, goth. O 4v: Impr. à Paris pr. Jehan sainct denys.
*Paris BA 4° T 2185 and 2186. Séville Colombine.
References: Moreau III #1840. Babelon #123.
Notes: The preface is signed, fol. A 2r, 'le tout vostre petit chapelain et orateur N.N.' (cf. *Échelles de la passion*, and J. Mauburne, *Beneficiaire divin*).

M 15.   **Marchandise spirituelle.**

Tressingulier devot et salutaire traicte, intitule La Marchandise spirituelle ordonnee et distinguee en sept regions spirituelles, selon les sept jours de la sepmaine. — Paris, [Antoine et Nicolas Couteau], pr. Jean Saint Denys, 1530?
4°: A-D⁴ E⁸ F-N⁴ O⁶ P⁴, goth. P 4v: Revisité et réimprimé pr. Jehan sainct Denys.
*Paris BN Rés. D 80034. *Aix Méj. Inc. D. 61 (- k 1-4).
References: Moreau III #2209.

M 16.   **Marchandise spirituelle.**

Tressingulier devot et salutaire traicte, intitule La marchandise spirituelle ordonnee et distinguee en sept regions spirituelles, selon les sept jours de la sepmaine Et est ladicte marchandise Tresutile et necessaire a tous marchans et marchandes Et generallement a tous bons Chrestiens et chrestiennes qui desirent de gaigner Paradis. — Paris, Pierre Ratoire, pr. Pierre Sergent, 1541?
4°: A-N⁴ O⁶, goth. O 5v: Revisité et reimpr. à Paris par Pierre Ratoyre pr. Pierre sergent.
*Nantes Dobrée 124. *Rouen BM Leber 328.

M 17.   **Marchepallu, Jacques.**

Les vertus et excellences des pseaulmes du roy David selon lordre du psaultier ... selon les sentences des docteurs de saincte Theologie. — Lyon, Jacques Moderne, ?
8°: a-d⁸, goth.
Séville Colombine.
References: Babelon #124. Du Verdier II, 288.

Notes: Du Verdier mentions a Toulouse ed.

M 18.   [Marcourt, Antoine].

Articles veritables sur les horribles, grandz et impor-
tables abuz de la Messe papalle: inventee direc-
tement contre la saincte Cene de Jesus Christ. —
[Neuchâtel], [Pierre de Vingle], 1534?
1°: 1 f., goth.
*Berne StU AD fol 62. Neuchâtel BV ZQ 143. *Geneva BPU.
References: Hari *APR.* Berthoud *Marcourt* pp. 157 sqq.
Notes: The placards of October 1534.

M 19.   [Marcourt, Antoine], [Pierre Viret].

Declaration de la Messe, Le fruict dicelle, La cause,
et le moyen, pourquoy et comment on la doibt main-
tenir. — [Neuchâtel], [Pierre de Vingle], 1534?
8°: A-F⁸, goth.
Neuchâtel Coll. Henriod. *Paris SHP R 1000(5) (-C 8, F 6-8).
References: Berthoud *Marcourt* #16. *Index* I #455. Th. Dufour
Not.cat. pp. 116-18.
Notes: Censured on 1 Sept. 1543 (Higman *Censorship*, p. 94).
Despite its title, a virulent attack on the Mass. The *Articles*
are a summary of the text. Viret is usually identified behind
the secondary author named as 'Cephas Geranius'.

M 20.   [Marcourt, Antoine], [Pierre Viret].

Declaration de la Messe, Le fruict dicelle, La cause, et
le moyen, pour quoy et comment on la doibt maintenir.
— [Geneva], [Jean Michel], 1542?
8°: A-F⁸, goth.
*Cambridge Emma. 321.7.6(1). *Geneva BPU Rés. Bc 3367.
References: Berthoud *Marcourt* #17. Berthoud 'Michel' #27.
BG 42/13.

M 21.   Marcourt, Antoine, [Pierre Viret].

Declaration de la Messe, Le fruict dicelle, La cause, et
le moyen, pour quoy et comment on la doibt maintenir.
Nouvellement reveu et augmente, par son premier
Autheur M. Anthoine Marcourt. — [Geneva], [Jean
Michel], 1544.
8°: A-F⁸ G⁴, goth.

Gotha FB Theol 61/1 Rara. *Paris SHP A 1170. *Vienna ÖNB
79.H.47. London BL 701.b.24 (anon.). *Paris BM 42788(4) (anon.).
References: Berthoud *Marcourt* #18. Berthoud 'Michel' #19.
BG 44/23.
Notes: First ed. to name the author (but a separate issue
remains anonymous: '... par son premier Autheur').

M 22.   **Marcourt, Antoine,** [Pierre Viret].

*Declaration de la Messe, Le fruict d'icelle, La cause, et
le moyen, pourquoy et comment on la doit maintenir.*
— [Geneva], [Jean Girard], 1551.
8°: A-F⁸, rom.
Wolfenbüttel HAB 1241.50 Theol (4).
Notes: The t.p. states 'Composée par M. Anthoine Marcourt'.
Description kindly supplied by Christian Hogrefe, Wolfen-
büttel HAB.

M 23.   **[Marcourt, Antoine].**

*Le livre des marchans, fort utile a toutes gens nouvel-
lement compose par le sire Pantopole, bien expert en
tel affaire, prochain voysin du seigneur Pantagruel.*
— [Neuchâtel], [Pierre de Vingle], 1533.
8°: A-C⁸, goth. C 7r: Impr. à Corinthe. 22.08.1533.
*Zurich ZB XVIII.2002.8 and Res. 1330.
References: Berthoud *Marcourt* #1. Th. Dufour *Not.cat.*
pp. 105-7. *Index* I #450.
Notes: The censure, in 1544, probably aimed at the 1541 ed.

M 24.   **[Marcourt, Antoine].**

*Le livre des marchans, fort utile a toutes gens, pour
congnoistre de quelles marchandises on se doit
garder destre trompe. Lequel a este nouvellement
reveu et fort augmente, par son premier autheur,
bien expert en tel affaire.* — [Neuchâtel], [Pierre de
Vingle], 1534.
16°: A-D⁸, goth. D 6r: ach. d'impr. 30.12.1534.
*Chantilly Condé XII.B.78. *Neuchâtel BV A de fer C 34. *Paris
SHP R 1000(3) and A 1166.
References: Berthoud *Marcourt* #2. Th. Dufour *Not.cat.*
pp. 125-7.

Notes: D 6r: 'Riche marchant ou paovre poullailler': Dufour suggests this is an anagram for 'Anthoi Marcour precheur a la ville poli'.

M 25. [Marcourt, Antoine].

Le livre des marchans, fort utile a toutes gens, pour cognoistre de quelles marchandises on se doit garder destre trompe. Lequel a este nouvellement reveu et fort augmente, par son premier autheur, bien expert en tel affaire. — [Geneva], [Jean Michel], 1541.
8°: A-D⁸, goth. D 6r: ach. d'impr. 30.12.1541.
*Oxford Bodl. Douce C 356(1). *Paris BN Rés. 8° Z Don 594(218.III).
References: Berthoud *Marcourt* #3. Berthoud 'Michel' #13. *BG* 41/11. Cat. Drilhon #16.
Notes: Copy of the 1534 ed.

M 26. Marcourt, Antoine.

Le livre des marchans, fort utile a toutes gens, pour cognoistre de quelles marchandises on se doit garder destre trompe. Nouvellement reveu et augmente, par son premier autheur M. Anthoine Marcourt, bien cognoissant telles affaires. — [Geneva], [Jean Michel], 1544.
8°: A-D⁸, goth.
*Geneva MHR D Marc 1. *Strasbourg BNU R 100612. *Munich BSB P.O.gall.1283 (anon.).
References: Berthoud *Marcourt* #4. Berthoud 'Michel' #20. *BG* 44/23.
Notes: For the first time the author is named on the t.p. But a separate issue omits the words 'M. Anthoine Marcourt'.

M 27. Marcourt, Antoine.

Le livre des marchans, fort utile à toutes gens, pour cognoistre de quelles marchandises on se doit garder d'estre trompé. Lequel a esté nouvellement reveu et fort augmenté, par son premier autheur, M. Anthoine Marcourt bien expert en tel affaire. — Strasbourg, Rémy Guédon, 1547.
16°: A-D⁸ E⁴, rom.
*Vienna ÖNB 44.Mm.502.
References: Peter 'Prem.ouvr.' #13b.

Notes: According to R. Peter, this ed. is an intermediary state
of the texts between the Genevan 1541 and 1544 eds.

M 28.   [Marcourt, Antoine].

*Le livre des Marchans, fort utile a toutes gens: pour
cognoistre de quelles marchandises on se doit garder
d'estre trompé. Nouvellement reveu, et augmenté par
son Auteur.* — [Geneva], [Jean Girard], 1548.
8°: A-C⁸ D⁴, rom.
*Cambridge Emma. 324.7.82(2). *Lincoln cath Oo 7.12(3).
*Neuchâtel BV A de fer C 33. *Paris BN Rés. D² 6446.
References: Berthoud *Marcourt* #5. *BG* 48/15.
Notes: A further six eds appeared between 1552 and 1588.

M 29.   [Marcourt, Antoine].

*Petit traicte tres utile, et salutaire de la saincte
eucharistie de nostre Seigneur Jesuchrist.* — [Neu-
châtel], [Pierre de Vingle], 1534.
8°: A-E⁸, goth. E 7v: ach. d'impr. 16.11.1534.
*Geneva BPU Rés. Bc 3368. Neuchâtel Coll. Henriod. *Zurich ZB
Res. 1334 (- A1).
References: Berthoud *Marcourt* #14.
Notes: Pamphlet distributed with the placards of Jan. 1535
(see Berthoud, *Marcourt*, pp. 187-8).

M 30.   [Marcourt, Antoine].

*Petit traicte tres utile, et salutaire de la saincte
eucharistie de nostre Seigneur Jesuchrist.* — [Geneva],
[Jean Michel], 1542.
8°: A-D⁸ E⁴, goth. E 4r: ach. d'impr. 26.07.1542.
*Geneva BPU Rés. Bc 3369. *Paris SHP A 1219.
References: Berthoud *Marcourt* #15. Berthoud 'Michel' #15.
BG 42/14. *Index* I #499.
Notes: Censured on 1 Sept. 1543 (Higman *Censorship*, p. 94),
probably in this ed.

M 31.   Marguerite de Navarre.

*Dialogue en forme de vision nocturne, entre tresnoble
et excellente princesse ma dame Marguerite de
France, soeur unique du Roy nostre sire ... Et Lame
saincte de defuncte ma dame Charlote de France,*

fille aysnee dudit sieur. — Alençon, Simon Du Bois, 1533.

4°: A-E⁴ F⁶, goth.

*Chantilly Condé VIII.F.21. *Paris BM Rés. 21661.

References: Clutton #22. Jourda pp. 212-13. Clive BE1.

Notes: The t.p. also mentions the *Miroir de l'ame pecheresse*, but that text has its own t.p. and independent collation.

M 32.   Marguerite de Navarre.

Marguerites de la Marguerite des princesses, tres-illustre Royne de Navarre. — Lyon, Jean de Tournes, 1547.

8°: 2 vols, a-z A-L a-y⁸, rom.

*Bruxelles BR LP FX.ix.50 (Vol 2:a-x⁸ y⁴). *Geneva BPU Hf 330 Rés. (Vol. 2: a-x⁸ y⁴). Paris BEBA Masson 914. *Wolfenbüttel HAB Lm 2377. Zurich ZB XXV.931 (+).

References: Cartier *De Tournes*. Jourda pp. 224-31. Clive BBa 1. Facs. ed. R. Thomas, New York, 1970.

Notes: The first collected ed. of Marguerite's works. Two issues: *Enigmes* added at the end of Vol. 2 in the copies other than Brussels and Geneva. Priv. (Vol. 1, a 1v) to 'Simon Sylvius dit De la Haye' for six years, dated 29 March 1546.

M 33.   Marguerite de Navarre.

Marguerites de la Marguerite des Princesses. — Lyon, Simon Du Bois dit de la Haye, Guillaume Rouillé, Pierre de Tours, Thibaud Payen, 1549.

16°: 2 vols, *⁸ a-y A-I AA-VV⁸, rom.

*Rouen BM Leber 1702. Aix Méj.

References: Jourda p. 231. Clive BBa2.

Notes: Copied from the 1547 ed. * 1r: t.p.: 'chez Guillaume Rouillé'. a 1r: t.p. of the *Miroir de l'ame pecheresse*: 'par Pierre de Tours'. AA 1r: t.p. of the 'Suyte': 'par Pierre de Tours'.

M 34.   [Marguerite de Navarre], [Sebald Heyden].

Le miroir de lame pecheresse. ouquel elle recongnoist ses faultes et pechez. aussi les graces et benefices a elle faictz par Jesuchrist son espoux. La Marguerite tresnoble et precieuse, sest preposee a ceulx qui de bon cueur la cerchoient. — Alençon, Simon Du Bois, 1531.

4°: A-I⁴, goth.

*London BL C.97.b.15. *Paris BN Rés. Ye 203.
References: Moore #183. Clutton #21. Jourda p. 211. Clive BI1.
Notes: First ed. Includes two prayers in prose trans. from Sebald Heyden.

M 35.   **[Marguerite de Navarre], [Sebald Heyden].**

Le miroir de lame pecheresse: ouquel elle recongnoist ses faultes et pechez. aussy les graces et benefices a elle faictz par Jesus Christ son espoux. La Marguerite tresnoble et precieuse, sest preposee a ceulx qui de bon cueur la cerchoyent. — Alençon, Simon Du Bois, 1533.
$4°$: A-I^4, goth.
*Chantilly Condé VIII.F.20. *Paris BM Rés. 21661(2).
References: Clutton #23. Jourda pp. 212-13. Clive BI2.
Notes: Printed with the *Dialogue en forme de vision nocturne*. Same contents as first ed.

M 36.   **[Marguerite de Navarre], [Sebald Heyden].**

Le miroir de lame pecheresse. Auquel elle recongnoist ses faultes et pechez. aussi les graces et benefices a elle faictz par Jesuchrist son espoux. — [Paris], [Antoine Augereau], 1533?
$8°$: a-i^4, rom.
*Paris BM Rés. 21712. *Paris SHP R 11742(1).
References: Veyrin-Forrer #22. Moreau IV #762. Jourda pp. 213-14. Clive BI4.
Notes: Same contents as the previous eds. It was probably this anonymous and anonymously printed ed. which caused a scandal in Oct. 1533.

M 37.   **Marguerite de Navarre, [Sebald Heyden], Cl. Marot: Ps. 6.**

Le miroir de treschrestienne princesse Marguerite de France ... auquel elle voit et son neant et son tout. — Paris, Antoine Augereau, 1533.
$8°$: a-i^4, rom.
References: Veyrin-Forrer #23. Moreau IV #763. Sales Pichon #997, Ruble #163. Jourda pp. 214-15. Clive BI3.
Notes: The versification of Ps. VI by Marot is added here for the first time.

M 38.   **Marguerite de Navarre,** [Sebald Heyden], Cl. Marot: Ps. 6.

Le miroir de treschrestienne princesse Marguerite de France ... auquel elle voit et son neant, et son tout. — Paris, Antoine Augereau, 1533.

8°: a-i⁴, rom.

*Chantilly Condé III.B.51. *Geneva BPU Rés. Hf 4604. *Paris BN Rés. Ye 1631. Paris BN velins 2265.

References: Veyrin-Forrer #24. Moreau IV #764. Jourda pp. 214-15. Clive BI5.

Notes: The Paris BN Rés. Ye 1631 and Geneva BPU copies have an extra leaf inserted after fol. a 1 with a poem by Marguerite to the reader, 'Si vous lisez ceste oeuvre...'. Paris BN velins 2265, copy bound with Florimond, *Epistre,* dated Dec. 1533.

M 39.   **Marguerite de Navarre,** [Sebald Heyden], Cl. Marot: Ps. 6.

Le miroir de treschrestienne princesse Marguerite. — [Paris], [Nicolas Buffet], 1535?

8°: a-d⁸ e⁴, rom.

*London BL C.97.aa.5. *Paris BM Rés. 21660.

References: Moreau IV #1367. Jourda p. 215. Clive BI6.

Notes: See Veyrin-Forrer p. 47. Copied from the previous ed.

M 40.   **Marguerite de Navarre,** [Sebald Heyden], Cl. Marot.

Le miroir de treschrestienne princesse Marguerite de France ... auquel elle voit et son neant, et son tout. — Lyon, Pierre de Sainte-Lucie, 1538.

8°: A-M⁴, rom. M 3v: Impr. à Lyon par Pierre de sainte Lucie.

*Munich UB 8° P.gall. 408. *Paris BA Rés. 8° BL 8756. *Wolfenbüttel HAB QuH 116(3).

References: Baudrier XII, 173. Jourda p. 220. Clive BI7.

Notes: Incorporates the *Briefve doctrine pour deuement escripre* and the *Instruction et foy d'un chrestien* by Marot.

M 41.   **Marguerite de Navarre,** [Sebald Heyden], Clément Marot.

Le miroir de treschrestienne princesse Marguerite de France ... auquel elle voit et son neant, et son tout. — Geneva, Jean Girard, 1539.

8°: a-e⁸ f⁴, ital.

*Paris BA Rés. 8° BL 8757 (a). *Paris BN Rothschild VI.3.58 (a).
*Cambridge Emma. 324.7.82(5)(b).
References: Rothschild #2860. Jourda p. 221. Clive BI8. *BG*
39/12. Adams M 570.
Notes: The copies labelled (b) above carry the address:
'Avignon, Honorat d'Arles', but it is simply an issue of Girard's
ed. (see G. Berthoud, *BHR* 1947). Includes the *Instruction et*
foy, but not the *Briefve doctrine*.

M 42. Marguerite de Navarre.

Le Triumphe de l'agneau de tresillustre Princesse Mar-
guerite de France Royne de Navarre. Plus une orai-
son de l'Ame fidele à son Seigneur Dieu. — Rouen,
Robert & Jean Dugort, 1548.
16°: A-K⁸, rom.
*Vienna ÖNB *38.K.180.
Notes: Ed. not apparently previously known. Extracts from
the *Marguerites*: 'Tous les esluz et souldats' (1547, I, p. 381),
'Seigneur duquel le siege sont les cieux' (1547, I, p. 77),
'Oraison à nostre seigneur Jesus Christ' (1547, I, 135), 'Voicy
nouvelle joye' (1547, I, 491), 'Las pas n'avois apperceu'
(1547, I, 494).

=> Marot, Clément: see *Bible. A.T. Psaumes.*

M 43. [Marot, Clément?].

La Bergerie du bon pasteur. — [Geneva], [Jean
Michel], 1539?
References: Mayer *Marot* #84. Moore p. 181. Berthoud
'Michel' #3. *BG* 39/1.
Notes: On 5 Sept. 1539 the Geneva Council granted permission to Jean Michel to print *Laz bergeyrie*, of which nothing is
known. *Index* I #374 ('La bergerie spirituelle, envoyée au
roy') may perhaps refer to it. Often attrib. to Marot (see the
following number), but nothing proves that it is the same text.

M 44. [Marot, Clément?].

Bergerie. Du bon pasteur et du mauvais. — [Lyon],
[J. & F. Frellon], 1545?
16°: A-B⁸, rom.
*Paris BN Rothschild IV.7.61.
References: Rothschild #3247. Mayer *Marot* #139. *Index* I #332.

Notes: *A Sermon du bon pasteur et du mauvais* was incorporated into one of the eds of Marot's *Psaumes*, Antwerp, A. Des Gois, 1541, and thence into Dolet's 1542 ed. of the same. There was also this 'offprint', probably by the Frellon brothers of Lyon (printing material). The attribution to Marot is doubtful, the author is more likely Almanque Papillon.

M 45.   Mauburne, Jean.

Cy commence ung devot et nouveau Traicte Intitule le Beneficiaire divin. Lequel est fort util et prouffitable a toutes gens: Pour recongnoistre a chascun jour de la sepmaine les benefices de Dieu le createur. Et pour luy en rendre graces et mercys selon la qualite et variete desdictz benefices de dieu. — Paris, [Julien Hubert], pr. Jean Saint Denys, 1529?
4°: A-Q⁴, goth. Q 4r: Impr. à Paris, pr Jehan sainct denys Librayre.
*Paris BA 8° T 5555(2).
References: Moreau III #1645.
Notes: Dedic to the Abbot of St Victor, 'de par le tout vostre petit Chappelain N.N.' (cf. *Échelles de la passion, Marchandise spirituelle*). Extract from J. a Mauburno, *Rosetum*.

M 46.   Mauburne, Jean.

Cy commence ung petit traicte bien devot contenant premierement une petite eschelle pour faire bonne et entiere confession, contenant apres plusieurs eschelles de communion pour bien recepvoir sacramentellement et spirituellement le sacrement de lautel, avecques aucunes spirituelles refections, devotes contemplations, et salutaires compunctions. — Paris, [Guillaume de Bossozel], pr. Pierre Ricouart, 1525?
4°: A-S⁴, goth. S 4v: Impr. à Paris pr. Pierre Ricouart.
*Paris BA 8° T 5555(1). Paris BN Rés. H 998(2). Paris BM.
References: Moreau III #810.
Notes: A 2r: the preface names the author, Jean Mauburne, abbé de Livry, and the title of the Latin original, *Rosetum*. Fol. a 1v: priv. to Pierre Ricouard dated 3 May 1525. The prologue condemns the 'heretics' who demand Communion in both kinds, and who refuse to confess themselves to a priest.

=>   Maugin, Jean: see *Figures de l'Apocalypse*.

M 47.   Maurice de Sully.

Les expositions des evangiles en francoys. — [Lyon],
[M. Harvard], 1515?
4°: a-q⁴, goth.
*Paris BEBA Masson 768 (- cahs. g et h).
Notes: Sermons by Maurice de Sully on the Gospel readings
for the liturgical year. Maurice de Sully (*c*. 1120-96) was
Bishop of Paris from 1160 to 1196.

M 48.   Maurice de Sully.

*Sensuyvent Les expositions des evangiles. Avec les
cinq festes nostre Dame. Et la dedicasse de leglise et
sermons des Confesseurs, et des vierges.* — Paris,
[Alain Lotrian], Denis Janot, 1535?
4°: A⁸ B-E⁴ F⁸ G-M⁴, goth.
References: Rawles #314 < Fairfax-Murray, 368. Moreau IV
#1371.

M 49.   Maurice de Sully.

Sensuyt les expositions des evangiles en françoys. —
Lyon, Olivier Arnoullet, ?
4°: A-K⁴, goth.
Séville Colombine.
References: Babelon #129.

M 50.   Mazurier, Martial.

*Instruction et doctrine a se bien confesser, et prier
Dieu pour ses pechez, extraicte des sainctes escriptures: tant du vieil que du nouveau testament.* —
[Paris], ?, 1550.
8°: a-e⁸ f⁴, rom.
*Paris BN D 43705.
References: *Index* I #334.
Notes: Censured on 15 Oct. 1550 (Higman *Censorship*,
pp. 105-6). Mazurier (described on the t.p. as 'docteur regent
en la faculté de Theologie, Chanoine et Penitencier de Paris')
writes about confession without ever mentioning auricular confession or priestly absolution. Hence the condemnation.

M 51.   Méditation sur la passion.

Meditation tresdevotte pour chascune heure du jour sur la passion douloureuse de nostre doulx saulveur Jhesus Avec les heures de la croix. — Paris, Vve Trepperel, Jean Jehannot, 1516?
8°: A-D⁸ E⁴, goth.   E 4r: Impr. à Paris par la veufve feu jehan trepperel et Jehan Jehannot.
*Paris BN Rés. D 17400(4). *Paris BN Rés. D 65774(1) (-A 1).
Notes: The author writes this work for 'mes devotes creatures de dieu amies et espouses du doulx jesus'.

M 52.   Méditation sur la passion.

Devote meditation sur la mort et passion de nostre saulveur et redempteur... — Antwerp, Guillaume Vorsterman, 1524.
8°: 32 ff., A-E⁸, goth.   32b: Anvers, Guillaume Vorsterman. 12.??.1524.
Ghent BU.
References: NK #2418 (details taken from here).

M 53.   Méditation sur la passion.

Sensuyt une devote meditation sur la mort et passion de nostre saulveur et redempteur jesuchrist avec les mesures mises de place en place ou nostre seigneur a souffert pour nous. — Paris, [Julien Hubert], pr. Jean Saint Denys, 1529?
8°: A-C⁸, goth. C 8r: Impr. à Paris pour Jehan sainct Denis.
*Paris BEBA Masson 474.
References: Moreau III #1843.
Notes: A 1v: 'Ung honnorable homme deglise nommé sire Bethleem, qui a demouré long temps en la terre de promission en la cité de Hierusalem, a descript ce livre devot...' Pious tourism. The ed. must be earlier than 1531 (date of Saint Denys's death).

M 54.   Méditation sur la passion.

Devote meditation sur la mort et passion de nostre saulveur et redempteur... Une meditation pour lespasse dune basse messe. — [Paris], [Simon de Colines?], [pr. Guillaume Merlin], 1540?
8°: a-c⁸, goth.
*Paris BEBA Masson 109 (-c 8)

M 55.   Méditation sur la passion.

Tresdevote meditation de la ... passion de nostre benoist sauveur et redempteur Jesuchrist... Et avec ce les rigles et enseignemens que ung chascun ... doit scavoir. — Paris, Jean Du Pré, Jaspard Bernard (Armentières), 1521?

8°: A-B⁸ C⁴, goth.   Impr. à Paris par Jehan du pre pour Jaspard bernard, Armentiere.

*Paris BN Rés. D 65774(2).

References: Moreau III #180.

Notes: A 1v: 'Ce present livre nous demonstre comment lame espouse du benoist Jesucrist doit mediter la mort et passion que souffrit son espoux: selon que nous representent les sept heures quon chante en saincte eglise'.

M 56.   [Megander, Gaspard].

Instruction observée par la ville, baillage et pais de Berne. — Geneva?, Jean Girard?, 1538?

References: Th. Dufour, *Not.cat. BG* 39/13. Higman 'Doré'.

Notes: This title is given in Pierre Doré's *Dyalogue instructoire* (1539), which is a refutation of Megander's work. Megander's catechism (German, 1536) was translated into Latin (prob. 1537: Dolet adapts it in his *Cato Christianus*, 1538, *Index* I #83), and into French in 1538 (Doré's ref.). In 1539 Jean Girard said he had printed 'les quatre missives de Berne pour les enfans'.

M 57.   [Megander, Gaspard].

Exposition chrestienne Dés dix commandemens, Dés articles de la Foy, De l'oraison de nostre Seigneur, Reiglée et moderée selon la capacité et entendement dés enfans. — [Geneva], [Jean Girard], 1540.

8°: A-E⁸, ital.

Berlin SB Libri impr. rari Oct. 205(1).

References: Moore #73. Th. Dufour *Not.cat.* 178-9. *BG* 40/6. Higman 'Dolet'. *Index* I #402.

Notes: First known ed. of the French translation of Megander's Berne catechism (see previous number).

M 58. Meigret, Aimé.

Epistre en latin <> à messeigneurs de Parlement de Grenoble. Plus un sermon en françois presché à Grenoble <> le jour S. Marc Évangeliste, l'an de grace mil cinq cens vingtquatre. — ?, ?, ?
16°: a-f⁸, rom.
*Paris BSG D 8°11148(5) Rés.
References: Moore #185. Guy, *Le Sermon d'A.M.* (1928). Farge *Bio.reg.* (Maigret).
Notes: Censured by the Paris Faculty of Theology in 1525 (Higman *Censorship*, p. 75). Meigret, Dominican and Doctor of the Faculty, published his sermon in 1524. The only surviving ed., however (described here), seems much later (see Farge's article).

M 59. Melanchthon, Philippe.

De l'authorité de l'Eglise, des docteurs d'icelle, et de l'authorité de la Parolle de Dieu. — [Geneva], [Jean Girard], 1542.
8°: A-I⁸, rom.
*Cambridge Emma. 321.7.6(2). *Cambridge UL 8.54.213(2). *Paris BA 8° T 5341(2).
References: Moore #75. Adams M 1115. *BG* 42/15. *Index* I #335.
Notes: Trans. of *De ecclesiae autoritate et de veterum scriptis libellus.*

M 60. Melanchthon, Philippe.

De la puissance et authorité de la saincte Eglise chrestienne, et comment elle peut estre congneuë par la Parolle de Dieu. — [Geneva], [Jean Girard], 1543.
8°: A-I⁸, rom.
*Geneva BPU Rés. Bc 2701. *Munich BSB Polem 1816. *Vienna ÖNB 79.W 42.
References: Moore #75. *Index* I #336. *BG* 43/24.
Notes: Second ed., unchanged except for the title, of *De l'autorité de l'Eglise* of 1542.

M 61. Melanchthon, Philippe.

De la puissance et authorité de l'Eglise, et comment sans la parolle de Dieu elle ne peut estre cogneue. — [Geneva], [Jean Girard], 1550.

8°: A-H⁸ I⁶, rom.
*Geneva BPU Rés. Bc 842.
References: CDM p. 16.

M 62.   **Melanchthon, Philippe,** trans. Jean Dalichamps.

Confession de la foy presentee a Tresinvictissime Empereur Charles V. a la journee d'Auspurg. — Strasbourg, [Johann Knobloch Jr.], 1543.
8°: A-I⁸, rom. I 8r: ach. d'impr. 09.01.1543. A Strasbourg.
*Geneva MHR K Mel 7. Nantes Dobrée 166. *Paris SHP A 176 and R 12832.
References: Moore #74. Peter 'Prem.Ouvr.' #10.
Notes: Trans. of the *variata* version (1540) of the *Augsburg Confession.* Dated on t.p. '1542', but we have followed the colophon.

M 63.   **Melanchthon, Philippe.**

Histoire de la vie et faitz de venerable homme M. Martin Luther, pur et entier Docteur de Theologie. — Geneva, Jean Girard, [René de Bienassis], 1549.
4°: A-M⁴, rom. M 4r: 'Assez tost, si assez bien'.
*Cambridge Emma. 30.6.14(3). *Lincoln cath Oo 2.14. *Munich BSB 4° Biogr. 154. Paris SHP A 566. *Vienna ÖNB 78.G.51.
References: Adams M 1157. *BG* 49/17.
Notes: Text condemned in Latin in 1551 and 1556 (*Index* I #172, 189), and in French in 1556 in a later ed. (*Index* I #432).

M 64.   **Melanchthon, Philippe,** trans. Jean de l'Archer.

De l'office des princes que Dieu leur commande touchant d'oster les abuz qui sont en l'Eglise. — [Geneva], [Jean Girard], 1544.
8°: A-D⁸ E⁴, rom.
Rouen BM (missing).
References: Moore #76. *BG* 44/26. Cat. Drilhon #18.
Notes: Trans. of *De officio principum, quod mandatum Dei praecipiat eis tollere abusus Ecclesiasticos* (Wittenberg, 1539). The Drilhon cat., usually accurate, specifies '1544'. But no known surviving copy.

M 65.   **Melanchthon, Philippe,** trans. Jean de l'Archer.

De l'office des princes, que Dieu leur commande, touchant d'oster les abuz qui sont en l'Eglise, Avec la maniere d'apprendre la Theologie. — [Geneva], [Jean Girard], 1545.

8°: A-D⁸ E⁴, rom.

*Geneva MHR K Mel 14. *Paris BN 8° Z Don 594(218.II). *Vienna ÖNB 36.M.43.

References: *BG* 45/24.

Notes: A 2r: dedic. by Jean de l'Archier to the magistrates of 'Noeuveville', dated 10 July 1544. Jean de L'Archer was pastor at La Neuveville.

M 66. **[Melanchthon, Philippe], [trans. Jean Calvin].**

La Responce donnee par les princes d'Allemaigne ... en matiere de la Religion Chrestienne: sur l'advertissement a eux envoyé a Smalcalt. — Geneva, Michel Du Bois, 1541.

8°: A-C⁸ D⁴, rom. D 4v: A Geneve par Michel Du Bois. 1541.

Aix Méj. D 3126(3). *Geneva BPU Rés. Ba 4619. *Vienna ÖNB 79.M.67.

References: Peter *Du Bois* #6. *BG* 41/12.

Notes: Trans. of Melanchthon's reply, on behalf of John Frederick of Saxony and Philip of Hesse, to approaches made in 1540 by Charles V. R. Peter (in *Mélanges Rott*) has established the identity of the translator.

M 67. **Melanchthon, Philippe,** pref. by Jean Calvin.

La Somme de theologie, ou lieux communs, reveuz et augmentez pour la derniere foys. — [Geneva], [Jean Girard], 1546.

8°: *⁸ a-z A-Z Aa-Hh⁸, rom.

*Geneva MHR K Mel 9,2. *Neuchâtel BV 3R694. Paris BN Rés. D² 9335. *Strasbourg coll. Peter. *Wolfenbüttel HAB G 9a 8° Helmst (+).

References: *BG* 46/10. *Index* I #486 (specifies this ed.).

Notes: First French trans. of Melanchthon, *Loci communes* (Latin ed. of 1545).

M 68. **Melanchthon, Philippe,** pref. by Jean Calvin.

La Somme de theologie, ou lieux communs reveuz et augmentés de nouveau. <> Ce qui estoit en la precedente edition improprement traduict, et mesmement obmis, a esté fidelement remis et conferé à l'original. — Geneva, Jean Crespin, 1551.

8°: *⁸ A-Z Aa-Zz AA-DD⁸, rom.

*Geneva BPU Rés. Bc 88. London BL 849.e.5. La Rochelle BM.
Paris BN D² 9336.
References: Moore #77. Gilmont *Crespin* 51/17. CDM p. 18.
Index I #338 (specifies this ed.).
Notes: Corrected ed. of the 1546 *Somme*.

M 69.   [Menard, Jean].

*Epistre Chrestienne, aux Freres Mineurs, de lordre
de S. Françoys. En laquelle est briefvement et
fidelement exposee la regle desdictz freres, par
quelcun jadis de leur estat: maintenant de
Jesuchrist.* — [Geneva], [Jean Michel], 1540.
8°: A-Q⁸, goth. Q 7v: ach. d'impr. 18.08.1540.
*Geneva BPU Rés. Bc 847. *Geneva MHR D Marc 3/2. *Lausanne
BCU G 1020 (incompl.). *Vienna ÖNB 31.X.41.
References: Moore #186. Berthoud 'Michel' #11. *BG* 40/7.
Notes: Jean Menard, former Franciscan, was pastor at Saint
Julien en Genevois. His name is given in an acrostic at the end
of the text (Q 5v).

M 70.   [Menard, Jean].

*Declaration de la reigle et estat des Cordeliers:
composee par ung jadiz de leur ordre, et maintenant
de Jesus Christ. En laquelle, il rend raison de son
yssue davec eulx, nouvellement par luy reveue: et en
plusieurs lieux augmentee, depuis la premiere
impression.* — [Geneva], [Jean Michel], 1542.
8°: A-R⁸, goth. R 8r: ach. d'impr. 04.08.1542.
*Cambridge St Johns Ferrari O 29(3). Aix Méj. *Geneva BPU Rés.
Bc 3376 and MHR D Men 1. Paris BN Rés. H 2098. *Vienna ÖNB
80.Y.113.
References: Moore #186. Berthoud 'Michel' #16. *BG* 42/16.
Index I #328. Adams F 916.
Notes: Second ed., with additions, of the 1540 *Epistre chrestienne*. The Paris *Index* attributes the *Declaration* to François
Lambert, but the name of Menard is given in acrostic, fol. R 6r.

M 71.   Merlin, Jacques.

*Lexposition de levangille Missus est ... contenant le
mystere de la reparation de nature humaine.* — Paris,
Yolande Bonhomme, pr. Jean Petit, 1539.

8°: AA⁸ A-X⁸ Y⁴, goth/rom.   Y 3r: Impr. a Paris par Ioland bonhomme pour Jehan petit libr. 17.01.1539.
*Paris BN Rés. D 15296. Poitiers BU. Paris BA 8° T 6124 (-AA 1,2,7,8, Y 3,4).
References: Farge *Bio.Reg.*
Notes: Dedic. (AA3r) by 'Jacques Merlin docteur en theologie, chanoine et penitencier de Paris', to 'tresdevotes religieuses, trescheres, et bien aymees filles, mere abbesse et convent du val de grace', dated (AA 6v) from Paris, 17 Jan. 1538.

M 72.   Michel, Guillaume.

La forest de conscience contenant la chasse des princes spirituelle. — Paris, Michel Le Noir, 1516.
8°: A-P⁸, goth. P 7v: Impr. par Michel le noir Libraire. 30.09.1516.
Oxford Bodl. Douce MM 319. *Paris BA 8° BL 19 376. *London BL 241.g.35.
References: E. Armstrong *BHR* 1969 p. 257. Moreau II #1436.
Notes: Moralizing poem illustrated with numerous biblical and allegorical scenes. Priv. (P 7r-v) granted to Guillaume Michel who financed the ed.

M 73.   Michel, Guillaume.

La forest de conscience contenant la chasse des princes spirituelle. — Paris, Michel Le Noir, Guillaume Michel, 1520.
8°: A-P⁸, goth. P 7v: Impr. par Michel le noir. 31.08.1520.
*Paris BN Rés. Ye 3214. *Paris BM 35445. *Aix Méj. C. 2916. *Chantilly Condé III F 61. *Versailles BM Goujet 8° 55.
References: Moreau II #2420. Peach/Brunel #422.
Notes: Follows the 1516 ed.

M 74.   Michel, Guillaume.

Le Penser de royal memoire ... les epistres envoyez par le royal prophete David au magnanime ... et treschrestien roy de France ... avecq aucuns mendemens et aultres choses convenables a lexortation du soulievement et entretiennement de la saincte foy catholicque. — Paris, Jean de La Garde, Pierre Le Brodeur, 1518?
4°: A⁴ a-m⁸/⁴ n⁴, goth. n 4v: Impr. à Paris pour Jehan de la garde et Pierre le brodeur libr.
*Paris BN Rés. Ye 376. Versailles BM Goujet 4° 16.

References: E. Armstrong *BHR* 1969 p. 264. Moreau II #1897. Peach/Brunel #421.

Notes: The priv. (A 1v) for two years, dated 2 July 1518.

M 75.   Michel, Guillaume.

Le siecle dore: contenant le temps de Paix, Amour, et Concorde. — Paris, Guillaume Fezendat, pr. Hémon Le Fèvre, 1521.

4°: A-B⁴ C⁸ D⁴ E-P⁸ Q⁴, goth.   Q 4r: Impr. par Guillaume Fesendad pr. Hemon le fevre. 20.02.1521.

Oxford Bodl. Douce M 709. *Paris BN Rés. Ye 375. *Paris BSG Y 4° 426(9) inv 573 Rés. Chantilly Condé. *London BL C.39.g.1.

References: E. Armstrong *BHR* 1969 p. 268. Moreau III #182.

Notes: Meditation in verse on seven deadly sins. The London BL copy has collation A-B⁴ C-P⁸ᐟ⁴ Q⁴, and there is no date in the colophon. Separate ed., but close in date to the 1521 ed. (Guillaume Fezendat active 1519-22, acc. to Renouard).

M 76.   Miroir d'or, trans. by the Doctors of the Sorbonne.

Le Mirouer dor de lame pecheresse. — Paris, Denis Janot, Alain Lotrian, 1532?

4°.

References: Moreau IV #526. Rawles #268.

Notes: Attrib. to Denis le Carthusien, but probably by Jacobus de Gruytrode or Jacobus de Jüterborg. The only known copy was sold (Drouot cat., #79) in 1991.

M 77.   Miroir de contemplation.

Le mirouer de contemplation fait sur la tressaincte vie, mort et passion de nostre seigneur JesuChrist. — Paris, pr. Guillaume Eustace, 1517.

8°: §⁴ a-o⁸, goth. o 8r: Impr. pr. guillaume eustace libr. 30.06.1517. *Paris BA 8° T 2155 (-§ 2).

References: Moreau II #1669.

Notes: An anthology of pious meditations by various writers assembled by the author at the request of his 'tres chiere et peculiere amye et cousine'.

M 78.   Miroir de l'humaine rédemption.

Miroir de lhumaine redemption contenant plusieurs belles matieres de lAncien Testament. — Paris, Philippe Le Noir, 1531.

2°.

References: Moreau IV #290 < Du Verdier.

Notes: Eight eds of a *Miroir de la redemption de l'humain lignage* in Lyon, trans. of a work in German, are known between 1478 and 1491 (A. Labarre, *HÉF*, I, p. 209).

M 79. Miroir du pénitent.

Le Miroir du penitent. — Lyon, Jean de Tournes, 1549.
16°: 136 pp., A-H⁸ I⁴, rom.
*Paris BN Rés. D 67940(4).
References: Cartier *Arrêts* p. 50. Cartier *De Tournes* #148.
Notes: See *Index* I #344, and see Ponisson, *Miroir*.

M 80. Missus est.

Missus est translate de latin en francois. — Paris, [Alain Lotrian], 1531?
8°: A⁸, goth.
*Chantilly Condé IV D 66(1).
References: Moreau IV #243.
Notes: Poem in octosyllabics, paraphrasing and developing the *Ave Maria*. With the prayer of 'N.D. de recouvrance', a ballade with the refrain 'Preserve mon corps et mon ame'.

M 81. Missus est.

Cy ensuyt loraison de Missus est, translate en francoys selon le latin Avec loraison de nostre dame de recouvrance. Et le testament de nostre sauveur jesuchrist. — 1531?
8°: A⁸, goth.
*Chantilly Condé IV D 66(2).
Notes: A more cramped typographical composition than the previous number, which allows the addition (A 7v-8v) of the *Testament de n.s. Jesucrist*.

M 82. Montfiquet, Raoul de.

Exposition de l'oraison dominicale. — Paris, Pierre Gaultier, 1545.
16°.
References: Renouard MSS < Du Verdier.

M 83. **Moyen de parvenir.**

Le Moyen de parvenir à la congnoissance de Dieu, et consequemment à salut. — ?, ?, ?

References: *Index* I #456.

Notes: The title only known by 1557 and 1562 eds, in *caractères de civilité*, by Robert Granjon, but it was included in the Paris *Index* in 1549. The text reproduces Dolet's *Exhortation à la lecture...* (q.v.).

M 84. **[Musculus, Wolfgang],** trans. Valérand Poullain.

Le Temporiseur. Par Eutichius Myonius: Avec plusieurs bons conseilz et advis sus la mesme matiere. Savoir est comment chascun fidele se doibt maintenir entre les Papistes. — London, Stephen Mierdman, 1550.

8°: A-R⁸, goth/rom. R 7v: Impr. à Londres par Estienne Mierdman. 1550.

London BL C.108.a.12. Oxford Bodl. *Paris BN D² 9631. *Paris SHP A 1191.

References: *STC* 18311. Droz *Chemins* I, 173-269 with text.

Notes: Dialogue translated from the *Proscaerus* by Musculus (Basle, J. Estauge, 1549). The 'bons conseils' (H 4v sqq.) are the various opinions on the subject of 'nicodemism' assembled by Calvin in *De vitandis superstitionibus* (1549), with several additions. A 3r-8v: preface signed by Valérand Poullain, dated 4 Oct. 1550.

M 85. **Mystère de la conception.**

Le mistere de la conception Nativite Mariage Et annonciation de la benoiste vierge marie Avec la nativite de Jesucrist et son enfance contenant plusieurs belles matieres. — Paris, Vve Jean Trepperel, Jean Jehannot, 1515?

4°: 94 ff., A⁸ B-D⁴ E⁸ F-H⁴ I⁸ K-M⁴ N⁸ O-Q⁴ R⁶ S-T⁴, goth. T 4r: Impr. à Paris par Vve Jehan trepperel et Jehan jehannot, ens. escu de France.

*Paris BN Rothschild IV.4.64.

References: Rothschild #2617.

Notes: The Rothschild catalogue suggests 'c. 1525' as date. But Vve Jean Trepperel and Jean Jehannot ceased their collaboration c. 1522 at the latest (Renouard).

M 86.   Mystère de la conception.

Le mistere de la conception Nativite Mariage Et annonciation de la benoiste vierge marie. Avec la nativite de Jesucrist et son enfance Contenant plusieurs belles matieres. — Paris, Vve Jean Trepperel, 1522?

4°: 94 ff., A⁸ B-D⁴ E⁸ F-H⁴ I⁸ K-M⁴ N⁸ O-Q⁴ R⁶ S-T⁴, goth.   T 4r: Impr. à Paris par Vve Jehan trepperel, ens. escu de France.
*Paris BN Rés. Yf 1604.

M 87.   Mystère de la conception.

Le mistere de la conception Nativite Mariage. Et annonciation de la benoiste vierge marie. Avec la nativite de Jesuchrist et son enfance. — Paris, Alain Lotrian, 1530?

4°: A-D⁴ E⁸ F-H⁴ I⁸ K-M⁴ N⁸ O-Q⁴ R⁶ S-T⁴, goth.   T 4r: Impr. à Paris par Alain lotrian, ens. escu de France.
*Aix Méj. Rés. D. 84(1).

M 88.   Mystère de la conception.

Le mistere de la conception, Nativite, mariage, et annonciation de la benoiste vierge Marie. Avec la nativite de Jesuchrist et son enfance. — Paris, Alain Lotrian, 1535?

4°: 93 + [1] ff., A⁸ B-X⁴ y⁶, goth.   y 6r: Impr. à Paris par Alain lotrian, ens. escu de France.
*Paris BEBA Masson 475(1) (-A 1). Nantes Dobrée 524. Chantilly Condé IX F 15(3). *Paris BN Rés. Yf 104 and Rés. Yf 105.
Notes: The Paris BEBA copy lacks t.p. It is bound with the *Mistere de la passion* printed by Lotrian in 1539. Prob. the same ed. as the other copies given here: the signatures are generally in the form $i-iii, same engraving on fol. A 2r, same characters for the colophon.

M 89.   Mystère de la conception.

Le mistere de la conception: nativite: mariage: et annonciation de la benoiste vierge Marie. — Paris, Alain Lotrian, 1540.

4°: A⁸ B-X⁴ Y⁶, goth.   Y 6r: Impr. à Paris par Alain lotrian, ens. escu de France.
*Paris BN Rés. Yf 1603.

References: The signatures of this ed: $ $.ii.-.iii. The engraving, fol. A 2r: annunciation.

M 90.   Mystère de la conception.

Le mistere de la conception, Nativite, mariage, et annonciation de la benoiste vierge Marie. — Paris, Alain Lotrian, ?

4°: A⁸ B-X⁴ Y⁶, goth. Y 6r: Impr. à Paris par Alain lotrian, ens. escu de France.

*Paris BN Rés. Yf 1601.

References: The signatures of this ed.: $i-iii. Characters for the colophon are taller than those in the text. The engraving, fol. A 2: Mary surrounded by angels.

M 91.   Mystère de la conception.

Le mistere de la conception, Nativite, mariage, et annonciation de la benoiste vierge Marie. — Paris, Alain Lotrian, ?

4°: 93 + [1] ff. A⁸ B-X⁴ y⁶, goth.   y 6r: Impr. à Paris par Alain lotrian, ens. escu de France.

*Paris BN Rés. Ye 1602(1) (- A 1,8).

Notes: The signatures are indicated $ $.ii.-.iii. A 2 signed A by mistake. The characters in the colophon are the same size as those of the text. Engraving on fol. A 2r: annunciation.

M 92.   Mystère de la passion, A. Greban, Jean Michel.

Le mistere de la Passion de nostre saulveur et redempteur jesuchrist avec les adictions et corrections <> joue a Angiers moult triumphamment Et dernierement a Paris Lan mil cinq cens et sept. — Paris, Michel Le Noir, 1512.

4°: 262 + [1] ff., A-H⁸ᐟ⁴ I-R⁴ᐟ⁸ S-X⁴ᐟ⁸ aa-gg⁴ᐟ⁸ hh⁴ ii⁸ (N 3-4 O 1-3) ll-ss⁸ᐟ⁴ tt-zz⁴ᐟ⁸ &&⁶, goth. && 6v: Par Michel le noir. 03.02.1512.

*Paris BN Rés. Yf 1600.

References: Moreau II #412. Jodogne G.

Notes: The *Mystère de la passion* by Arnoul Greban (mid-15th cent.), adapted by Jean Michel and performed in Angers in 1486. Editions already known in 15th cent. Greban's version was some 25 000 lines long, Michel's work took it to 65 000 lines. Several woodcuts. Between gatherings ii and ll the BN copy has ff. N 3-4 and O 1-3 of an ed. corresponding to those of Alain Lotrian, but not fitting the preceding or following text. Runnalls studies all known eds.

M 93. **Mystère de la passion, A. Greban, Jean Michel.**

Sensuyt le mistere de la passion nostre seigneur jhesucrist avec les adicions <> joue a angiers moult triumphantement et dernierement a Paris. — Paris, Vve Jean Trepperel, Jean Jehannot, 1515?
4°: a-h$^{8/4}$ i^4 k^6 l-n$^{4/8}$ o-r^4 s-x$^{8/4}$ y-z A-B^4 C^6 D-M$^{4/8}$ N-R$^{4/8}$ S-Y^4 AA-CC^4 DD^6, goth. DD 6v: Impr. à Paris par la veufve Jehan Trepperel et Jehan Jehannot.
*Paris BEBA Masson 621. *Paris BN Rothschild IV.4.65.
References: Rothschild #2618. Jodogne M.

M 94. **Mystère de la passion, A. Greban, Jean Michel.**

Sensuyt le mistere de la passion de nostre seigneur jhesucrist nouvellement corrigee Avec les additions <> jouee a Angiers moult triumphantement et derrenierement a Paris. — Paris, Philippe Le Noir, 1523?
4°: 263 + [1] ff., a^8 b-d^4 e^8 f-i^4 k^8 l-n^4 o^8 p-s^4 t^8 v-z^4 &^{8} #^{4} A-B^4 C^8 D-F^4 G^8 H-K^4 L^8 M-O^4 P^8 Q-S^4 T^8 V-X yy AA^4 BB^8 CC^4 DD^6, goth. DD 6v: Impr à Paris, rue s. Jacques, ens. de la rose blanche couronnee (Philippe Le Noir).
*Paris BN Rés. Yf 1597.
References: Moreau III #874. Jodogne F.

M 95. **Mystère de la passion, A. Greban, Jean Michel.**

Sensuyt le mistere de la passion nostre seigneur Jhesucrist nouvellement corrigee Avec les adicions <> joue a angiers moult triumphantement et dernierement a Paris. — Paris, Vve Jean Trepperel, 1524?
4°: 263 + [1] ff., a^8 b-d^4 e^8 f-i^4 k^8 l-n^4 o^8 p-s^4 t^8 v-z^4 &^{8} #^{4} A-B^4 C^8 D-F^4 G^8 H-K^4 L^8 M-O^4 P^8 Q-S^4 T^8 V-Y^4 AA^4 BB^8 CC^4 DD^6, goth. DD 6v: Impr. à Paris par la vefve feu jehan trepperel.
*Paris BN Rés. Yf 1599.
References: Jodogne H.
Notes: Page-for-page copy of preceding edition, except where different size of woodcut leads to a momentary discrepancy. The woodcuts in this ed. (some copied from Michel and Philippe Le Noir's set) pass to Alain Lotrian, who reuses them in his eds of the text.

M 96.   **Mystère de la passion,** A. Greban, Jean Michel.

Sensuit le mistere de la Passion de nostre seigneur Jesuchrist nouvellement corrigee Avec les adicions <> joue a Angiers moult triumphantement et dernierement a Paris. — Paris, Denis Janot, Alain Lotrian, 1532?

4°: 253 + [1] ff., a^8 b-d^4 e^8 f-i^4 k^8 l-t^4 v^8 x-z & # A-D^4 E^8 F-N^4 O^8 P-X AA^4 BB^8 CC-KK^4, goth. KK 6v: Impr. à Paris par Alain lotrian et Denys janot.
London BL 241.l.17. Vienna ÖNB 47.Ji.3.
References: Moreau IV #498. Rawles #315.

M 97.   **Mystère de la passion,** A. Greban, Jean Michel.

Sensuyt le mistere de la Passion notre seigneur Jesuscrist ... avec les additions... Lequel mistere fut joue a Angiers Et dernierement a Paris. — Paris, Philippe Le Noir, 1532.

4°: 254 ff., a^8 b-z & A-E^4 F^8 G-O^4 P^8 Q-X AA-LL^4 MM^6, goth. MM 6v: Impr. à Paris pour Phelippe le noir. 1532.
*Lyon BV Rés. 317228. Nantes Dobrée 525. Oxford Bodl.
References: Moreau IV #499. Runnalls P.

M 98.   **Mystère de la passion,** A. Greban, Jean Michel.

Sensuit le mistere de la Passion de nostre seigneur Jesuchrist nouvellement corrigee, Avec les aditions <> joue a Angiers moult triumphantement, et dernierement a Paris. — Paris, Alain Lotrian, 1535?

4°: a^8 b-d^4 e^8 f-i^4 k^8 l-t^4 v^8 x-z & # A-D^4 E^8 F-N^4 O^8 P-X AA^4 BB^8 CC-II^4 KK^6, goth. KK 6v: Impr. à Paris par Alain lotrian.
*Aix Méj. Rés. D. 84(2). *Paris BN Rés. Yf 104(2).
References: Jodogne I.
Notes: The printing material is less worn than in the two eds by Lotrian dated 1539.

M 99.   **Mystère de la passion,** A. Greban, Jean Michel.

Sensuit le mistere de la Passion de nostre seigneur Jesuchrist Nouvellement reveu et corrige ... Avec les additions <> joue a Angiers moult triumphamment, Et dernierement a Paris. Avec le nombre des personnages qui sont ... en nombre. Cxli. 1539. — Paris, Alain Lotrian, 1539.

4°: 253 + [1] ff., a⁸ b-d⁴ e⁸ f-i⁴ k⁸ l-t⁴ v⁸ x-z & # A-D⁴ E⁸ F-N⁴ O⁸ P-X⁴ AA⁴ BB⁸ CC-II⁴ KK⁶, goth. KK 6v: Nouvellement impr.
*Paris BN Rés. Yf 1598.
Notes: This and the next ed. both dated on t.p. '1539', but two entirely reset eds.

M 100. Mystère de la passion, A. Greban, Jean Michel.

Sensuit le mistere de la Passion de nostre seigneur Jesuchrist Nouvellement reveu et corrige ... Avec les additions <> joue a Angiers moult triumphamment, et dernierement a Paris. 1539. — Paris, Alain Lotrian, 1539.
4°: 253 + [1] ff., a⁸ b-d⁴ e⁸ f-i⁴ k⁸ l-t⁴ v⁸ x-z & # A-D⁴ E⁸ F-N⁴ O⁸ P-X AA⁴ BB⁸ CC-II⁴ KK⁶, goth. KK 6v: Impr. à Paris par Alain lotrian. 1539.
*Paris BEBA Masson 475(2). Chantilly Condé IX F 15. *Paris BN Rés. Yf 107.
References: Jodogne J.
Notes: Some textual improvements and page layout, and more worn material, suggest this ed. is later than the previous number.

M 101. Mystère de la passion, A. Greban, Jean Michel.

Sensuit le mistere de la Passion de nostre seigneur Jesuchrist Nouvellement reveu et corrige oultre les precedentes impressions. — Paris, Alain Lotrian, 1541.
4°: 253 + [1] ff. a⁸ b-d⁴ e⁸ f-i⁴ k⁸ l-t⁴ v⁸ x-z & § A-D⁴ E⁸ F-N⁴ O⁸ P-X AA⁴ BB⁸ CC-II⁴ KK⁶, goth. KK 6r: Impr. à Paris par Alain lotrian. 18.08.1542.
*Paris BN Rés. Yf 1602(2)(- E1-3, 6-8, AA 1).
References: Jodogne K.

M 102. Mystère de la résurrection.

La Resurrection de nostre seigneur jhesuchrist Par personnages Comment il sapparut a ses apostres et a plusieurs autres Et comment il monta es cieulx le jour de son assencion. — Paris, Vve Jean Trepperel, Jean Jehannot, 1515?
4°: 51 + [1] ff., A⁸ B-D⁴ E⁸ F-H⁴ I⁸ K⁴, goth. K 4v: Impr. à paris par Vve Jehan trepperel et Jehan jehannot.
*Paris BN Rés. Yf 109.

Notes: Text already known at the end of the 15th cent. Attributed either to Jean Michel or to Jean Du Périer (both late 15th cent.).

M 103. Mystère de la résurrection.

Sensuit la Resurrection de nostre Seigneur Jesuchrist par personnaiges Comment il sapparut a ses apostres et a plusieurs autres, et comment il monta es cieulx le jour de son assencion. — Paris, Vve Jean Trepperel, 1525?

4°: 51 + [1] ff., A⁸ B-D⁴ E⁸ F-H⁴ I⁸ K⁴, goth. K 3v: Impr. à Paris par la vve Jehan trepperel.

*Paris BN Rothschild IV.4.100.

References: Rothschild #2619.

M 104. Mystère de la résurrection.

Sensuit la Resurrection de nostre seigneur jesucrist par personnages. Comment il sapparut a ses apostres et a plusieurs aultres, et comment il monta es cieulx le jour de son assention. — Paris, Alain Lotrian, Denis Janot, 1530?

4°: A⁸ B-D⁴ E⁸ F-L⁴, goth. L 3v: Impr. à Paris par Alain loctrian et Denys janot.

*Aix Méj. Rés. D. 84(3).

Notes: A. Lotrian and D. Janot collaborated until 1530, hence the suggested date.

M 105. Mystère de la résurrection.

Sensuit la Resurrection de nostre seigneur Jesuchrist: Par personnages. Comment il sapparut a ses apostres, et a plusieurs aultres, et comment il monta es cieulx le jour de son Ascention. — Paris, Alain Lotrian, 1539?

4°: 51 + [1] ff., A⁸ B-M⁴, goth. M 3v: Impr. à Paris par Alain lotrian.

Paris BEBA Masson 475(3). Nantes Dobrée 526. Chantilly Condé IX F 15(2). *Paris BN Rés. Yf 105 and Rés. Yf 108.

Notes: Alain Lotrian's eds being almost identical, and undated, it is possible that not all these copies belong to the same ed.

M 106. Mystère de la résurrection.

Sensuyt la Resurrection de nostre seigneur Jesuchrist: Par personnages. — Paris, Alain Lotrian, 1541.

4°: 51 + [1] ff. A⁸ B-M⁴, goth. M3r: Impr. à Paris par Alain Lotrian.

*Paris BN Rés. Yf 1602(3) (- M 1,4)

M 106a. Mystère de la Sainte hostie.

Le mistere de la saincte hostie Lisez ce mistere grans et petis | Comment le traistre et mauldit juifz | Lapida moult cruellement | De lautel le sainct sacrement. — [Paris], [Vve Jean Trepperel], 1520?

8°: [36] ff., A-D⁸ E⁴, goth.

*Paris BN Rés. Yf 564.

Notes: Attrib. to Vve Jean Trepperel on the basis of typographical material.

M 107. Mystère de la Sainte hostie.

Le mistere de la saincte hostie nouvellement imprime A Paris. Lysez ce fait grans et petis/ Comment ung faulx et mauldit juifz/ Lapida moult cruellement/ De lautel le sainct sacrement. — Paris, [Alain Lotrian], 1531?

8°: A-I⁴, goth.

*Aix Méj. Rés. S. 60.

References: Moreau IV #248. Reprt. 1817 (Aix, A. Pontier).

Notes: Dramatization (in octosyllabics) of the 'miracle du saint canivet', according to which, in Paris, in 1290, a Jew attacked a consecrated host with a knife, and the host bled.

M 108. Mystère de la Sainte hostie.

Le Jeu, et Mystere de la Saincte Hostie, par personnages. — Paris, Jean Bonfons, 1546?

8°: A-D⁸ E⁴, goth.

*Chantilly Condé IV D 76.

Notes: Jean Bonfons was active 1543-66. This ed. is probably later than that of A. Lotrian.

M 108a. Mystère de ss. Pierre et Paul.

Sensuit le mistere de monseigneur sainct pierre et sainct paul Par personnages. Contenant plusieurs

*aultres vies Martires et conversions de sainctz
Comme de sainct estienne, sainct clement Sainct lin,
sainct clete, Avec plusieurs grans miracles faitz par
lintercession desditz sainctz, et la mort de Symon
magus: Avec la perverse vie et mauvaise de
lempereur Neron Comment il fist mourir sa mere Et
comment il mourut piteusement.* — Paris, Vve Jean
Trepperel, Jean Jehannot, 1518?

4°: A-D$^{8/4}$ E-I$^{4/8}$ K-O$^{4/8}$ P-T$^{4/8}$ V^4 X^8 y^4 z^6, goth. z 6v: Impr. à Paris par la
veufve feu Jehan trepperel et Jehan jehannot.
*Paris BN Rés. Yf 117.

M 108b. Mystère d'une fille.

*Sensuyt ung beau mystere de nostre Dame a la
louenge de sa tresdigne Nativite, dune jeune Fille
laquelle se voulut habandonner a peche pour nourrir
son Pere et sa mere en leur extreme pouvrete.* —
Lyon, Olivier Arnoullet, 1543.

8°: [48] ff., a-f^8, goth. f 8v: Impr. à Lyon par Olivier Arnoullet.
10.03.1543.
*Paris BN Rés. Yf 2909.
References: Baudrier X.79.
Notes: Play (with 18 characters) in verse. An earlier ed. by Jean
Saint Denis (*c.* 1528?) in Seville Colomb. Crit. ed. by L. and M.
Locey, *TLF*, 1976.

M 108c. Mystère du vieil Testament.

(a) Vol. 1: *Sensuit le mistere du viel Testament Par
personnaiges Hystorie, joue a paris Et imprime
Nouvellement audit lieu. Auquel sont contenus les
misteres Comment les enfans disrael partirent
degipte Et passerent par la mer Rouge et conquirent
la terre saincte Avec plusieurs autres belles
hystoires.* — Paris, Vve Jean Trepperel, Jean Jehannot,
1516?

4°: [2] + '2-304' ff., a-z$^{4/8}$ &^{8} 9^4 A-X$^{8/4}$ AA-CC$^{4/8}$ DD^4 goth. DD 4v:
Impr. à Paris par la veufve feu jehan trepperel Et jehan jehannot.
*Paris BN Rés. Yf 102 (-b 1.8).

(b) Vol. 2: *Sensuit le second volume du viel Testament
par Personnaiges Contenant huyt hystoires de la
bible, cestassavoir Lhystoire de job Lhystoire de
thobie Lhystoire de daniel Lhystoire de suzanne
Lhystoire de judich Lhystoire de hester Lhystoire de*

Octavien empereur Et la sibille thiburtine Et les prophecies des douze sibilles Et plusieurs aultres matieres. — Paris, Vve Jean Trepperel, Jean Jehannot, 1516?

4°: [1] + 117 ff., A-L⁴′⁸ M-Q⁴′⁸ R⁴ S⁸ T⁴ V⁶, goth.

*Paris BN Rés. Yf 103 (-O 1-4, V 1.6(?)).

Notes: Vol. 2 may have contained at least one further gathering.

M 109. Mystère du vieil Testament.

Le tresexcellent et sainct mystere du vieil testament par personnages, ouquel sont contenues les hystoires de la bible Reveu et corrige. — Paris, Jean Réal, Vincent Sertenas, Gilles Corrozet, 1542.

2°: 324 ff., a-z & A-P⁸ Q-R⁶, goth. R 6r: Impr. à Paris par Jean Real. 1542.

*Paris BEBA Masson 650 (-a1, R6). Aix Méj. Rés. Q. 22. *Lyon BV R 106133 (Corrozet). Paris BN Rés. Yf 66 and 67.

Notes: In the Paris BEBA copy, lacking t.p. and R 6, these have been replaced by MS transcriptions. Verse, two columns.

N

N 1. [Nachtigall, Ottomarus], trans. Jean de Vauzelles.

Hystoire evangelique des quatre evangelistes en ung, fidelement abregee, recitant par ordre sans obmettre ny adjouster Les notables faictz de nostre seigneur jesuchrist ... en ces petitz dixneuf chapitres redigee au soulaigement de la memoire de tous chrestiens. — Lyon, Gilbert de Villiers, 1526.

8°: a-e⁸ f⁴, goth. f 4r: Impr. à Lyon par Gilbert de villiers. 1526.

*London BL C.111.aa.11.

References: Moore #84.

Notes: The translator (who signs 'le chevalier de vray zele' and 'Crainte de Dieu vault zele') dedicates his work to Marguerite d'Alençon, with praise for her protection of the persecuted. He says he has translated the work from the Latin text of Otto-marus Luscinius, who himself had translated it from the Greek of Ammonius of Alexandria. See Moore p. 155.

O

O 1.   **Ochino, Bernardino.**

Epistre aux magnifiques Seigneurs de Siene <> auxquelz il rend raison de sa foy et doctrine. Avec une Epistre à Mutio Justinopolitain, par laquelle il rend aussi raison de son departement d'Italie, et du changement de son estat. — [Geneva], [Jean Girard], 1544.

8°: a-b^8 c^{10}, rom.

*Vienna ÖNB 39.Mm.87.

References: *BG* 44/27. *Index* I #342, 343.

Notes: The Italian originals of these letters by the former Vicar General of the Capuchins appeared separately in Geneva, printed by J. Girard, in 1543.

O 2.   **Ochino, Bernardino.**

L'Image de l'Antechrist. — [Geneva], [Jean Girard], 1544.

8°: A^8, rom.

*Zurich ZB XVIII.2002.7.

References: *BG* 44/28. Droz *BHR* 1960. *Index* I #520.

Notes: Translated from the Italian original printed in Vol. 2 of Ochino's *Prediche*, Geneva, J. Girard, 1544.

O 3.   **Ochino, Bernardino.**

L'image de l'Antechrist. — [Geneva], [Jean Girard], 1545.

8°: A^8, rom.

Florence BN An 481. *Paris BN 8° Z Don 594(218.IV). *Vienna ÖNB 21.Mm.221.

References: *BG* 45/26.

O 4.   **[Oecolampadius, Johann].**

Exposition sur la premiere Epistre de S. Jehan Apostre, divisee par Sermons tresutiles a tous amateurs de vraye et chrestienne predication. — [Geneva], [Jean Michel], 1540.

8°: a-z^8 *^{4}, goth.

*Geneva MHR K Lut 13a. *Paris BM Rés. 49186(1).

References: *BG* 40/8. Berthoud 'Michel' #12. Cat. Drilhon #11, 26. *Index* I #320.

Notes: The 1544 censure of this title included among Estienne Dolet's publications, but no Dolet ed. is known of it. The Latin original appeared in 1524.

O 5.   **[Olivétan, Pierre Robert].**

Linstruction des enfans, contenant la maniere de prononcer et escrire en françoys. Loraison de Jesu Christ. Les articles de la foy. Les dix commandemens. La salutation angelicque. Avec la declaration diceux, faicte en maniere de recueil des seulles sentences de lescripture saincte. Item les figures des chiphres, et leurs valeurs. — [Geneva], [Pierre de Vingle], 1533.
8°: A-H⁸, goth.
*Geneva BPU Rés. Bd 1477.
References: Moore #162. Berthoud *APR* pp. 143 sqq. Higman, 'Spiritualité'.
Notes: See Baddeley, *Orthographe*.

O 6.   **[Olivétan, Pierre Robert].**

L'Instruction dés enfants, contenant la maniere de prononcer et escrire en françoys. Lés dix commandemens. Lés articles de la Foy L'oraison de Jesus Christ. La salutation angelique. Avec la declaration d'iceux, faicte en maniere de recueil, dés seulles sentences de l'escriture saincte. Item, lés figures dés siphres, et leurs valeurs. — Geneva, Jean Girard, 1537.
8°: a-i⁸ k⁴, rom. k 4r: Impr. à Geneve par J. Gerard.
*Geneva BPU Rés. Bb 581.
References: Moore #162. *Index* I #435. *BG* 37/4. Th. Dufour *Not.cat.* pp. 144-5.
Notes: Censured on 1 June 1541 (Higman *Censorship*, p. 88). An augmented ed. of the 1533 ed., introducing accents which were lacking in the first ed. See Baddeley, *Orthographe*.

O 7.   **Oraison de notre seigneur.**

Lorayson de nostre seigneur Jesuchrist appellee le Paternoster Avec lave maria. Le credo contenant les articles de la foy. Les dix commandemens de la loy Avec les cinq de leglise. — ?, ?, 1527.
8°: 8 ff.

Séville Colombine 15.2.1.
References: Babelon #158.

O 8. Oraisons de notre dame.

Devotes oraisons. — ?, ?, 1550?
8°: A-D⁸ E⁴, goth.
*Paris BEBA Masson 509.
Notes: The date suggested by a MS note in the Paris BEBA copy. Various prayers in prose and in verse, followed (C 6v sqq.) by *Commendationes defunctorium* in Latin. No t.p. The running title at the beginning is 'Devotes oraisons de nostre Dame'. Cf. G. Petit, *Tres devotes oraisons*.

O 9. Ordinaire des Chrétiens.

Le grant Ordinaire des chrestiens. — Paris, Jean Jehannot, Vve Jean Trepperel, 1514.
4°.
London BL.
References: Moreau II #925.
Notes: The text, composed *c.* 1468, had already been printed several times before 1511.

O 10. Ordinaire des Chrétiens.

Lordinaire des crestiens. — Paris, Michel Le Noir, 1514.
4°: A-K⁸ᐟ⁴ L-N⁴ᐟ⁸ O-S⁴ᐟ⁸ T⁴ V⁸ X-Y⁴ Z⁸ AA-BB⁴ BB⁴ CC⁸ DD-EE⁴ FF⁶ GG⁴ HH⁶, goth. HH 6r: Impr. à Paris par Michel le noir. 25.07.1514.
*Paris BN Rés. D 5454.
References: Moreau II #926.
Notes: There are five sections: baptism and the creed, ten commandments, works of mercy, confession, and the sufferings of hell and joys of paradise.

O 11. Ordinaire des Chrétiens.

Sensuyt le grand ordinaire des chrestiens: qui enseigne a chascun bon chrestien et crestiene la voye et le chemin de aller en paradis: et declaire la joye et felicite des sauvez: Et pareillemenet la miserable peine et tourment perpetuel des dampnez. — Paris, Jean Trepperel II, 1532.
4°: A⁴ B⁸ C-D⁴ E⁸ F-G⁴ H⁸ I-O⁴ P⁸ Q-S⁴ T⁸ V-X AA-FF⁴ GG⁸ HH-II⁴ KK⁶ LL⁴, goth. Impr. à Paris par Jehan Trepperel.

Bordeaux BM T 6674.
References: Renouard MSS.
Notes: Description kindly supplied by Mme de Bellaigue of Bordeaux BM.

O 12.   Ordonnances ... luthériens.

Ordonnances nouvelles nagueres faictes ... contre les imitateurs de la secte lutherienne et recellateurs diceulx. Et aussi touchant les denonciateurs et accusateurs. — Paris, [Nicolas Couteau], Jean André, 1535.
4°: 4 ff., []⁴, goth. [] 3v: Impr. à Paris pr. Jehan andre. 05.02.1534 (a.s.).
*Chantilly Condé IV E 60. *Rouen BM Leber 3906(1).
References: Moreau IV #1308.
Notes: The same punishment for those who hide 'Lutherans' as for the heretics themselves, but pardon, and a quarter of the confiscated property, to denunciators.

O 13.   [Osiander, Andreas], [trans. Wigand Koeln].

Mandat et advertissement a ses Ecclesiastiques de recepvoir la parolle de Dieu, et delaisser toute faulse doctrine, quil nest point fonde en la saincte Escripture. — [Geneva], [Wigand Koeln], 1542.
4°: 4 ff., A⁴, goth.
Colmar BV V 12025(7).
References: *BG* 42/19. Droz *Chemins* II 43-52 with text.
Notes: Ordinance from Otto Heinrich Duke of Bavaria imposing the Reformation. Dated from Neuburg, 22 June 1542.

P

P 1.   Parceval, Jean.

Brieve Doctrine de l'amour divine. — Paris, Gaultier, ?
8°.
References: Renouard MSS < Du Verdier.

P 2.   **Pardon.**

Le grand pardon de pleniere remission, pour toutes personnes, durant à tousjours. — Geneva, Adam et Jean Rivery, 1550.
References: *Index* I #473. Texte dans *APR* pp. 163-6.
Notes: Title, address and date taken from the 1551 censure. No known copy (but the text is known from a later, 1561, ed., with copies in Paris BN, BA, BSG). A parody of Roman Catholic pardons.

P 3.   **Pardon.**

Les grans pardons et indulgences, le tresgrand Jubile de plainiere remission de peine et de coulpe a tous les confraires de la tressacree confrairie du sainct esperit. — [Geneva], [Pierre de Vingle], [1533].
8°: A-B⁸, goth.
*Neuchâtel BV Rés. C 30.
References: Droz *APR* pp. 155-66. See *Index* I, #476.
Notes: Censured on 1 June 1541 (Higman *Censorship*, p. 87). A reply to the Jubilee proclaimed by Clement VII in 1532. Address on the t.p.: 'imprimé a Ghent par Pieter van winghue'.

P 4.   **Parenti, Ch. de.**

Instructions et oraisons tres salutaires. — Paris, Vivant Gaultherot, 1539.
8°.
References: Renouard MSS < Brunet.

P 5.   **Parfaite foi pour être sauvé.**

Parfaite foy pour estre sauve cest croire tout ce que saincte eglise croit. — [Paris], ?, 1520?
8°: 4 ff.
*London BL C.107.a.12(10).
Notes: Contains the text of Lord's Prayer and Ten Commandments.

P 6.   **Paroles mémorables.**

Les paroles memorables entre Jesus Christ et le pecheur, qui est un Dialogue contemplatif, pour l'attirer à son amour, pleines d'instruction salutaire,

avec la maniere de savoir bien se confesser. — Lyon,
Romain Morin, 1532.
8°.
Séville Colomb.
References: Babelon.

P 7.   Paroles mémorables.

*Les Parolles memorables de Jesuchrist au pecheur
pour le attirer a son amour, plaine de instruction
salutaire. Avec la maniere de se scavoir bien confesser, utile et necessaire a tous vrays Chrestiens
desirans leur salut.* — Lyon, Olivier Arnoullet, 1541.
8°: a-h⁸, goth. h 8v: Impr. à Lyon par Olivier Arnoullet. 17.06.1541.
Terrebasse.
References: Baudrier X, 76.

P 8.   Pasquille d'Allemagne.

*Le Pasquille Dallemaigne. Auquel l'histoire de
levangile de nouveau retourne en lumiere, et la cause
de la guerre presente sont touchees, Aucuns Princes,
Estatz, et Citez, sont admonnestez de leur condition
et office. Aucuns aussi sont painctz au vif, par
aucunes belles et graves sentences tirees de la
Saincte Bible.* — [Basle?], [Jacques Estauge?], 1546.
4°: A-H⁴, rom. H 4r: ach. d'impr. 31.10.1546.
*Paris BM Rés. A 14959.
References: Moore #191.
Notes: To each city (particularly in Germany), to each leading
personality of the Reformation, is applied one or more biblical
quotations, either to praise their fidelity to the cause, or to
condemn their weakness. A remarkable snapshot of the situa-
tion at the end of 1546. See H. Meylan, 'Sur un pasquin de
Rome' in *Charles V et son temps* (CNRS, 1959).

P 8a.   Patience de Job.

*La pacience de job selon lhystoire de la bible.
Comment il perdit tous ses biens par guerre et par
fortune: et la grant povrete quil eust. Et comment
tout luy fut rendu par la grace de dieu.* — Lyon, Jean
Lambany, 1529.
4°: [42] ff., A-D⁸ E⁴ F⁶, goth. F 6v: impr. à Lyon par Jehan Lambany.
20.11.1529.

*Paris BN Rés. Yf 114.
References: Baudrier XI.41-2.
Notes: Jean Lambany was the second husband of the widow of Barnabé Chaussard (1528-29). After his death she continued the firm under the name 'Veuve de Barnabé Chaussard'.

P 9.   **Penser à la mort.**

Penser a la Mort cest chose proffitable. — ?, ?, ?
16°: 4 ff., a⁴, goth.
*Paris SHP A 1157.

P 10.   **Petit, Guillaume.**

La formation de lhomme et son excellence, et ce quil doibt acomplir pour avoir Paradis <> Avec plusieurs bonnes doctrines, et enseignemens utiles et necessaires a tous chrestiens. — Paris, Olivier Mallard, pr. Galliot Du Pré, 1538.
8°: *⁸ a-v⁸, rom. v 8r: Impr. à Paris par Olivier Mallard pour Galiot du Pre. 15.02.1538.
Harvard UL. *Paris BN Rés. D 17409(1) (-gathering *). *Paris BM 24839 (-gathering *). *Aix Méj. Rés. D. 90.
References: Mortimer #422.
Notes: Includes the *Viat de salut* and an *Instruction pour sçavoir soy confesser.* On G. Petit, see Farge, *Bio.reg.*

P 11.   **Petit, Guillaume.**

La formation de l'homme et son excellence et ce qu'il doibt accomplir pour avoir Paradis. — Paris, Pierre Regnault, 1540.
8°.
Cambrai BM 7651 (destroyed).
References: Renouard MSS. Du Verdier.
Notes: My thanks to Mme A. Fournier for providing the only surviving information on this text, drawn from the 'anciens registres thématiques' of the Cambrai BM.

P 12.   **Petit, Guillaume.**

Tres devotes oraisons a lhonneur de la tressacree et glorieuse Vierge Marie mere de dieu, avec plusieurs aultres devotes chansons. — Paris, Simon de Colines, 1534?
8°: a-c⁸, rom.

*Paris BN Rés. pYe 297.
References: Moreau IV #1109.

P 13.   Petit, Guillaume.

*Le viat de salut tresnecessaire et utile a tous chres-
tiens pour parvenir a la gloire eternelle. Imprime a
Troyes par lauctorite de Reverend pere en dieu
Monsieur Lesvesque dudit lieu. Lequel commanda a
son Senne dernier M.ccccc.xxvi. celebre le .xv. de
May. A tous curez, chappelains, vicaires, et maistres
descolle Avoir ce present Livre. Pour le lire ou faire
lire au Prosne, les dimenches et festes. Et aux escol-
les, aux enfans capables de lentendre.* — Troyes,
Jean Le Coq, 1526?
8°: A-F⁸, goth. F 6v: Impr. à Troyes chez Jehan Lecoq impr. et libr.
*Paris BN Rés. D 80374.
References: *Rép. bib.* #26.
Notes: Probably in response to [Farel and Luther], *Oraison de
JesuChrist.* See Higman, 'Prem.rép.' An explanation of the
Creed, Lord's Prayer and Ten Commandments.

P 14.   Petit, Guillaume.

*Le viat de salut tresnecessaire et utile a tous chres-
tiens pour parvenir a la gloire eternelle. Imprime a
longeville ... par lauctorite de Reverend pere en dieu
Hector dailly Evesque et conte de toul. Lequel a
commande a son Senne dernier M CCCCC.xxvii.
celebre le xxiiii. doctobre. A tous curez, chapellains,
vicaires, et maistres descolle Avoir ce present Livre.
Pour le lire ou faire lire, au Prosne: les dimenches
et festes. Et aux escolles, aux enfans capables de
lentendre.* — Longeville, Martin Mourot, 1527?
8°: a-l⁸, goth. l 6v: Impr. à Longevile en la maison de ... martin
mourot prestre.
*Paris BA Rés. 8° T 7322.
References: *Rép.bib.* #4.
Notes: See L. Loriot, 'Deux impressions de Longeville devant
Bar, 1525?-1527', *Rev. du livre ancien* 1 (1913), 200-203.

P 15.   Petit, Guillaume.

*Le Viat de Salut necessaire et utile a tous chrestiens
pour parvenir a la gloyre eternelle. Imprime a Lyon*

par la permission de tresreverend pere en dieu Monseigneur larchevesque de Lyon ou de ses vicaires. — Lyon, Antoine Blanchard, [Claude Veycellier], 1527?
8°: A-G⁸, goth. G 8r: Impr. à Lyon par Antoine Blanchard. On les vend ... à lenseigne S. Jehan Baptiste.
*Aix Méj. Rés. S. 128(1). *Glasgow UL BDI-1.51.
References: Baudrier V, 94-5 and XII, 426.

P 16.   Petit, Guillaume.

Le viat de salut necessaire et utile a tous chrestiens pour parvenir a la gloyre eternelle, imprime a Lyon par la permission de tresreverend pere en dieu Monseigneur larchevesque de Lyon ou de ses vicaires. — Lyon, Antoine Blanchard, Gilbert de Villiers, 1528?
8°: A-G⁸, goth. G 8r: Impr. à Lyon par Antoine Blanchard. On les vend ... Gilbert de Villiers.
*London BL 697.a.48.

P 17.   Petit, Guillaume.

Le viat de salut, Ouquel est comprins lexposition du simbole, des dix commandemens de la Loy, de la Patenostre et Ave Maria, Livre tressalutaire pour ung chascun chrestien. — Paris, Denis Janot, pr. Pierre Sergent, Jean Longis, 1535?
16°: A-H⁸ I⁴, rom. I 4r: Impr. à Paris par Denis Janot pour Pierre sergent et Jehan longis.
*Paris BSG D 8° 3335/5 inv. 3707 Rés.
References: Moreau IV #1402. Rawles #321.

P 18.   Petit, Guillaume.

Le viat de salut utile a tous chrestiens pour parvenir a la vie eternelle ou est comprins lexposition du Symbole, des dix commandemens du Pater et de Lave Maria: instruction pour soy confesser et plusieurs devotes chansons. — Lyon, Olivier Arnoullet, 1539.
8°.
References: Baudrier X, 74 < Du Verdier and Brunet IV,393.

P 19.   Petit, Guillaume.

Le Viat de salut. — Paris, Jean Réal, 1540.
8°.
References: Renouard MSS < Du Verdier and Brunet.

P 20.   Petit, Pierre.

La chanson de frere Pierre petit Religieux de lave Maria. — [Paris], [Alain Lotrian], 1531?
8°: A⁴, goth.
*Chantilly Condé IV D 135. Séville Colomb.
References: Moreau IV #263.
Notes: Meditation on the Passion, in verse: 'Resveille toy cueur endormy / En saincte meditation / Jesus ton espoux ton amy / Suppliras en devotion.'

P 21.   Picard, Jean, O.F.M.

Les trois mirouers du monde. — Paris, Jean Longis, 1524.
8°.
References: Moreau III #727 < Sale Méon #214.
Notes: The three 'miroirs' for knowing human nature are Scripture and the Ten Commandments, 'l'ame cree a l'image de Dieu', and 'Jesus en croix'. Picard is described on the t.p. as a Doctor of the Faculty of Theology, but he is not mentioned in Farge *Bio.reg.*

P 22.   Picard, Jean, O.F.M.

Les trois. Mirouers du monde. — Paris, [Antoine Couteau], pr. Jean Longis, 1530.
8°: A-Y⁴, goth. Y 4r: Impr. à Paris pr. Jehan Longis. 01.04.1530.
*Paris BA 8° T 6948. Paris BN Rés. D 65435. Paris BM. Saumur. Séville Colomb.
References: Moreau III #2242.

P 23.   Pinet, Guillaume.

Le Contemnement du monde ... la conversion de l'ame, ou sont Ballades et Rondeaux, avec un chant royal et deux narrations, une Oraison a la sainte croix, une epistre ou est compare la Chrestiente a un jardin. — Lyon, François Juste, 1540.
16°.
References: Baudrier suppl. # 95. Du Verdier II, 114.
Notes: According to the t.p. Guillaume Pinet is the translator of an anonymous Latin work.

P 24.   **Ponisson, François.**

Le miroir du pauvre pecheur penitent sur le pseaume de David L. — Toulouse, Jean Lemosin, 1545.
16°.
References: Du Verdier I, 668. Frankfurt cat. *Rép. bib.* Boudeville #149.
Notes: According to *Index* I #344, Frère François 'Poinson' was a Dominican from the Toulouse reformed monastery. This may be the same text as the anonymous *Miroir du penitent* edited by Jean de Tournes in 1549.

P 25.   **Postilles,** trans. and comm. Pierre Desrey.

Le Premier (-Second) volume des exposicions des Epistres et Evangilles de Karesme. — Paris, [Guillaume Le Rouge], Antoine Verard, 1511.
2°: 2 vols, ã⁴ a-e⁶ f⁴ g-z & A-K⁶ L⁸ M-R⁶ S-V⁴ X-Z⁶ & AA-BB⁴ CC-KK⁶ LL-MM⁴ NN-OO⁶, goth. OO 5v: Impr. à Paris pr. Anthoine verard. 26.04.1511.
*Paris BEBA Masson 172. *Paris BM 1994A. Carpentras. *Paris BN Vélins 118, 119. Dole.
References: Moreau II #187, 188.
Notes: Vol. 2 begins on fol. L 3r. Paris BN Vélins copy has a variant: Vol. I: f⁶. But the colophon is identical.

P 26.   **Postilles,** trans. and comm. Pierre Desrey.

Le Tiers volume des exposicions des Epistres et Evangiles de Toute lannee. — Paris, [Guillaume Le Rouge], pr. Antoine Verard, 1511.
2°: ẽ ẽ ẽ⁴ aaa-sss⁶ ttt⁴ vvv⁸ xxx-zzz §§§ AAA-DDD⁶ EEE-GGG⁴ HHH-XXX⁶ yyy⁴, goth. yyy. 4v: Impr. à Paris pr. Anthoine verard. 28.09.1511.
*Paris BN Vélins 120. *Paris BM 1994B.
References: Moreau II #189.
Notes: According to a prefatory note (aaa 1r), Pierre Desrey extracted his commentaries from four Doctors of the Church: Augustine, Jerome, Gregory and Ambrose.

P 27.   **Postilles,** trans. and comm. Pierre Desrey.

Le Quart (-Ve) volume des exposicions des Epistres et Evangilles de Toute lannee. — Paris, [Guillaume Le Rouge], pr. Antoine Verard, 1512.

2°: 4ã⁴ 4a-4m⁶ 4n-4o⁴ 4p-4r⁶ 4s-4t⁴ 4v-4z⁶ 4& 4§⁶ ....⁴ 9999⁴. Vol 5:
π⁴ 4A-4F⁶ 4G-4H⁴ 4I-4K⁶ 4L-4M⁴ 4N-4R⁶ 4S⁴ 4T-4X⁶ 4yC⁴ 4zC⁶
4&C⁶ 4#C², goth.   Vol. IV: 9999 4v: impr. à Paris pr. Anthoine
verard. 07.05.1512. Vol. V (4#C 2r): 13.08.1512.
*Paris BN Vélins 121, 122. *Paris BA fol T 429. *Paris BM 1994C.
References: Moreau II #431.

P 28.   **Postilles,** trans. and comm. Pierre Desrey.

*Le Tiers (-Ve) volume des exposicions des Epistres et
Evangilles de Toute lannee.* — Paris, Jean Petit, pr.
Antoine Verard, 1519.
2°: [4] + 268 ff., 3 ẽ⁴ 3a-3s⁶ 3t⁴ 3v⁸ 3x-3z 3& 3A-3D⁶ 3E⁴-3G⁴
3H-3X⁶ 3Y⁴, goth. III: YYY 4v: 03.09.1519. IV: 17.10 V: 02.12.1519.
Pr anthoine verard.
*Paris BN Rés. A 1267 (III). Paris BSG (IV, V).
References: Moreau II #2178.

P 29.   **Postilles,** trans. and comm. Pierre Desrey.

*Le premier (-second) volume des exposicions des
Epistres et Evangilles de Karesme.* — Paris, Jean
Petit, 1519?
2°: π² a-e⁶ f⁴ g-z & A-K⁶ L⁸ M-R⁶ S-V⁴ X-Z⁶ &⁴ AA-BB⁴ CC-KK⁶
LL-MM⁴, goth.
*Paris BN Rés. 16997 (- q 1,2, II 2, MM 1, 4). Valenciennes. Paris BM.
References: Moreau II #2177.

P 29a.   **Postilles,** trans. and comm. Pierre Desrey.

*Sensuivent les Postilles et expositions Des epistres Et
evangilles dominicalles.* — Paris, Vve Jean Trepperel,
Jean Jehannot, 1520?
4°: 211 + [1] ff., a-o⁸/⁴/⁴ p-z⁸/⁴/⁴ &⁸ A-M⁴/⁴/⁸ N-Q⁴, goth. Q 4v: Impr. par
la veufve feu jehan trepperel. Et Jehan jehannot.
*Paris BN Rés. A 3322.

P 30.   **Postilles,** trans. and comm. Pierre Desrey.

*Sensuyvent les Postilles et expositions des Epistres et
Evangiles dominicales.* — Lyon, Olivier Arnoullet,
1530.
References: Baudrier X, 62 < Brunet IV, 843.

P 31.   **Postilles,** trans. and comm. Pierre Desrey.

Le premier (-second) volume des grandes Postilles et expositions des epistres et Evangilles pour toute lannee. — Paris, Guillaume de Bossozel, Pierre Gaudoul, Ambroise Girault, François Regnault, 1531.
2°: 235 and 353 ff., a⁴ b⁶ c-z aa-gg⁸ hh⁶. A⁶ B-X y-z AA-VV xx⁸ yy¹⁰, goth. hh 5v: Impr. à Paris pour Francois regnault. 28.01.1531. yy 9v: Impr. à Paris pour francoys regnault. 25.10.1530.
Paris BSG B fol 278²-278³ inv. 355-356. Bourges. Versailles.
References: Moreau IV #141 and III #2073.

P 32.   **Postilles,** trans. and comm. Pierre Desrey.

Les Postilles et expositions des epistres et evangiles dominicalles. Aussi celles des festes solemnelles. — Poitiers, Jean et Enguilbert de Marnef, 1536.
4°: A-Z a-d⁸, goth. d 8r: Impr. à Poictiers par Jehan et Enguilbert de Marnef. 12.08.1536.
*Paris BEBA Masson 1026.
References: *Rép.bib.* #17.

P 33.   **Postilles,** trans. and comm. Pierre Desrey.

Sensuyvent les Postilles et expositions des Epistres et Evangilles dominicalles. Avec celles des festes. — Lyon, Olivier Arnoullet, 1546.
4°: a-y & A-E⁸, goth. E 8v: Impr. à Lyon par Olivier Arnoullet. 05.01.1546.
Vaganay.
References: Baudrier X, 81 (reprod. t.p.)

P 34.   **Postilles,** trans. and comm. Pierre Desrey.

Postilles et expositions des epistres: et evangilles dominicalles avecques celles des festes qui sont sollempnelles... aussi des cinq festes de la tressacree vierge marie. — [Rouen], ?, ?
4°: a-z ⁶/⁶/⁴ &⁴ aa-ss ⁶/⁶/⁴ tt³..., goth.
*Paris BEBA Masson 1028 (incompl.).
Notes: Attrib. to Rouen according to a MS note in the Paris BEBA copy, which lacks all after tt 3, and the bottom of the t.p.

P 35. [**Poullain, Valérand**], [poem by Martin Luther].

Oraison Chrestienne au Seigneur Dieu, faicte par maniere de complaincte: sur le temps present. — [Strasbourg], [Jacques Froelich], 1545?
8°: A⁴, goth.
*Vienna ÖNB 79.Ee.172.
References: Peter 'Prem.ouvr.' #11b.
Notes: The prayer seems to be a response to the execution of the Strasbourg pastor Pierre de Brully. Includes (A 4r) the first French trans. of a Luther hymn, 'Empesche Seigneur souverain...'

P 36. **Poullain, Valérand (a), 'Jean de Rochefort' (b).**

Traicte tresutile du S. Sacrement de la Cene. Avec response aux principaulx arguments des anciens et modernes contre ce s. Sacrement. — [Basle], [Robert Winter], 1547?
8°: A⁸ a-f⁸, ital.
*Vienna ÖNB 79.W.48 (a). *Vienna ÖNB 39.Mm.89 (b).
References: Peter 'Prem.ouvr.' (1984) pp. 17-18.
Notes: The prefatory epistle, to the Strasbourg French church, is dated from Strasbourg, 8 June 1547. Issue (b) is identical to (a) except for the name of the author on the t.p.

P 37. **Poyvreault, Simon.**

Douze devotes Contemplations. — ?, ?, ?
References: Brunet IV, 851. See Moreau IV #228.

P 38. **Préparations.**

Sensuyvent aucunes belles Preparations pour devotement recevoir le Sainct Sacrement de lautel. — Paris, Yolande Bonhomme, 1530.
8°.
Berlin SB.
References: Moreau III #2255.

P 39. **Préparations.**

Sensuyvent aucunes belles preparations pour devotement recepvoir le sainct sacrement de lautel. — Paris, Yolande Bonhomme, 1539.
8°: a⁸, goth. a 8v: Impr. à Paris par Ioland bonhomme. 1539.
*London BL 4402.i.25(2). *Paris BN Rés. D 23738(2).

Notes: In the two known copies bound with the *Armure de patience.*

P 40.   Prières et commandements.

Les prieres et commandemens de saincte eglise La confession generalle du jour de pasques par les paroisses. Et Le petit traicte maistre Jehan gerson qui aprent a bien mourir. — Paris, ?, Jean Garnier, 1519?

4°: a-d^4, goth.

*Paris BSG C 4° 302 inv 302 Rés.

References: Moreau II #2184 < sale Roger (1884).

Notes: Fol. d 4v: engraving of a shipwreck, with words below: 'IOANNES GARNERIUS'. Paris BSG: half of fol. d 3 missing: perhaps a colophon? The text contains liturgical prayers in French. Cf. *Commandements de l'église.*

P 41.   Primasius, trans. Jean de Gaigny.

Briefve et fructueuse exposition sus les Epistres Sainct Paul aux Romains et Hebreux. — Paris, Estienne Roffet, 1540.

8°: a-z A-H^8 I^4, rom.

La Rochelle BM. *Paris BN C 3140 and C 4273. *Troyes BM B 16 2935 (- I 3,4).

Notes: a 1v: priv. to Gaigny and Roffet for five years, dated 25 March 1539 (a.s.). In his dedic. to Francis I and his preface to the readers, Gaigny warns the latter against the apparent sola-fideism of Primasius, 'disciple d'Augustin': the author, he says, was refuting Pelagius. In fact Primasius lived in the 6th century, and this commentary is no longer attributed to him.

P 42.   Primasius, trans. Jean de Gaigny.

Exposition sur les Epistres S. Poul aux Romains et Hebrieux. — Paris, Estienne Roffet, 1549.

References: Frankfurt cat. 1610.

P 43.   Procession générale.

Procession generale faicte a Paris, Le Roy estant en personne. Le xxij. jourt de janvier. Mille. cinq centz, trente et cinq. — [Paris], 1535.

8°: 4 ff., a^4, goth.

*Paris SHP R 15938.

References: Berthoud *Marcourt* p. 190.
Notes: Narrative of the expiatory procession of 21 Jan. 1535, printed the following day.

P 44.   Procession générale.

L'Ordre de la procession generalle celebree a Paris, le .xxj. jour de Janvier Mil cincq cens trentequatre en lhonneur de Dieu et reverence du sainct sacrement. — Paris, Vve de Pierre Roffet, 1535.
8°: A^8 B^4, goth.
*Paris BN Rés. B 13873.
References: Moreau IV #1412.
Notes: Priv. (A 1v) to the widow of P. Roffet and to her son André for one year dated 12 Feb. 1534 (a.s.).

P 45.   Profession de foi.

Profession de foy accoustumee d'estre juree Par les Bourgeois et subjects de Messeigneurs de Frybourg de cinq ans en cinq et par ceux que ilz recoivent pour subjects et habitants de leur ville et pais. — ?, ?, ?
4°: A^4, rom.
*Lausanne BCU (formerly Past. Hist 1335).
References: Meylan *Mélanges Martin* 437-46.
Notes: This ed. is probably more recent, but the text existed in the 1540s.

P 46.   Profit de la messe.

Le proufit quon a douyr messe. — Lyon, Barnabé Chaussard, 1520?
8°: [8] ff. Fol. 7v: Impr. à Lyon par Barnabe chaussard.
Chantilly Condé IV.D.141.
References: Baudrier XI.33.

P 47.   Profit de la messe.

Le proufit quon a d'ouyr messe. — Lyon, Barnabé Chaussard, 1523?
8°: [8] ff. Fol. 7v: Impr. à Lyon par Barnabe Chaussard.
References: Baudrier XI.33-4.

P 48.   Profit de la messe.

Le profit quon a douyr messe. — Lyon, Barnabé
Chaussard, 1524?
8°: [8] ff. Fol. 7v: Impr. à Lyon cheux Barnabe chaussard.
Avignon Récollets.
References: Baudrier XI.34.

P 49.   Profit de la messe.

Le proufit quon a de ouyr messe. — Lyon, [Barnabé
Chaussard], 1525?
8°: [8] ff.
Paris BN Y Falconnet 7702.
References: Baudrier XI.34.
Notes: No colophon in this ed., but the material is that of
B. Chaussard.

P 50.   Psautier de notre Dame.

Le Psaultier nostre dame. — Paris, Vve Jean Trepperel,
Jean Jehannot, 1511?
8°: A-B⁸ C⁴, goth. C 4r: Impr. à paris par la veufve feu jehan trepperel
et Jehan jehannot.
*Paris BEBA Masson 618.
Notes: Presented as 'le livre et ordonnance de la devote confrairie du psaultier de la glorieuse vierge marie lequel est de Cent
cinquante Ave maria et quinze pater noster a dire chascun jour'.

P 51.   Purgatoire.

Traicté de purgatoire. — [Geneva], [Jean Girard],
1543.
8°: A-B⁸ C⁴, rom.
*Oxford Bodl. Douce C.356(2).
References: Gilmont 'Farel' 23-1. *BG* 43/33. *Index* I #471.
Notes: Frequently attributed to Farel, but this is very doubtful.
Text first printed as an appendix to Farel, *Sommaire*, 1534.

P 52.   Purgatoire.

Brief Traicté de Purgatoire. — [Geneva], [Jean
Girard], 1545.
8°: A-B⁸ C⁴, rom.
*Lincoln cath Oo 7.12(2). *Paris BN Rés. 8° Z Don 594(218.V).
*Vienna ÖNB +48.K.30(6).
References: *BG* 45/1.

P 53.   Purgatoire.

Brief Traité de Purgatoire. — [Geneva], [Jean Girard], 1551.

8°: A-B⁸, rom.

*Cambridge Emma. 324.7.82(3). *Paris BN Rothschild VI.3.62.

References: Adams P 2284. CDM p. 18. Rothschild #88.

Notes: Contains two polemical poems, A 1v, one being a 'Complainte des prestres', the other a 'Consolation des prestres'.

Q

Q 1.   Quatre homelies, trans. Guillaume Chrestien.

Quatre homelies de trois antiques et excellens Theologiens ... S. Gregoire Nazianzene, S. Jean Chrysostome, S. Basile. — Lyon, Jean de Tournes, 1544.

16°.

References: Cartier *De Tournes* #24.

Q 2.   Quatre voies spirituelles.

Quatre voyes spirituelles pour aller à Dieu. — Paris, [Pierre Vidoue], pr. Regnault Chaudiere, 1519.

4°: a⁶ B-P⁴, goth.

*Paris BA 4° T 2094.

References: Moreau II #2188.

Notes: The four 'voies' are 'purgative, illuminative, unitive et superlative' (t.p.). Priv. (a 1v) dated 3 May 1519.

Q 3.   Quentin, Jean.

Lorloge de devotion Compose en Francoys par Maistre Jehan Quentin Docteur en Theologie Et penitencier de Paris. — Paris, [Pierre Ratoire], Pierre Sergent, 1541?

4°: A-P⁴, goth. P 4r: Impr. à Paris pr. Pierre Sergent.

*Nantes Dobrée 125.

Notes: Same typographical material as in *La Marchandise spirituelle* with which it is bound in Nantes Dobrée copy.

Q 4.   Quinze effusions.

Les quinze effusions du sang de nostre Sauveur Jesuchrist. — Troyes, Jean Le Coq II, 1541?

8°: A⁸ B⁴, goth. B 4r: Impr. à Troyes chez Jean Lecoq.

*Paris BEBA Masson 1136(3).

Notes: Jean Le Coq II was active 1541-89. A prayer, accompanied by an engraving, on each shedding of Christ's blood. Reciting these prayers daily for a year will save 15 souls from Purgatory, convert 15 sinners, etc. A very 'antiquarian' ed., in gothic letters, in 1615 (Paris BN Rés. Ye 1385).

Q 5.   Quinze joies.

Les .xv. joyes de nostre dame moult devotes. Les sept requestes. Obsecro en francoys. Et deux belles et devotes oraisons en francoys. — Lyon, Vve Barnabé Chaussard, 1533.

8°: [8] ff., a⁸, goth.

Séville Colombine.

References: Baudrier XI.50. Babelon #188.

R

R 1.   [Rabelais, François].

Pantagruel. Les horribles et espoventables faictz et prouesses du tresrenomme Pantagruel Roy des Dipsodes, filz du grand geant Gargantua. — Lyon, Claude Nourry, 1532?

8°: A-Q⁴, goth.

*Paris BN Rés. Y² 2146.

References: *NRB* 1.

R 2.   [Rabelais, François].

Pantagruel. Les horribles et espoventables faictz et prouesses du tresrenomme Pantagruel roy des Dipsodes. — Paris, pr. Guillaume Bineaulx, 1533?

Vienna ÖNB (missing).

References: NRB 2. Moreau IV #806.

R 3. **[Rabelais, François].**

Pantagruel Les horribles et espoventables faitz et prouesses du tresrenomme Pantagruel Roy des Dipsodes filz du grant geant Gargantua. — [Paris?], [Jean et Enguilbert de Marnef], 1533.
8°: A-K^8 L^4, goth.
*Paris BN Rés. Y^2 2147 and Y^2 2148 (incompl.).
References: *NRB* 3.

R 4. **[Rabelais, François].**

Pantagruel Les horribles et espoventables faictz et prouesses du tresrenomme Pantagruel roy des Dipsodes, filz du grant geant Gargantua. — Paris, [Nicolas Couteau?], pr. Jean Longis, 1533?
8°: A-N^8, goth.
*Paris BN Rothschild II.5.38.
References: Rothschild #1508. *NRB* 4. Moreau IV #806.

R 5. **[Rabelais, François].**

Pantagruel Les horribles et espoventables faictz et prouesses du tresrenomme Pantagruel roy des Dipsodes, filz du grand geant Gargantua. — [Paris], [pr. Jean Longis?], 1534?
8°: A-N^8, goth.
Paris BN *Rés. Y^2 2143.
References: *NRB* 5. Moreau IV #807.

R 6. **[Rabelais, François].**

Pantagruel. Les horribles et espoventables faictz et prouesses du tresrenomme Pantagruel roy des Dipsodes, filz du grant geant Gargantua. — [Paris], [Pierre Leber], 1534?
8°: A-N^8, goth.
London BL G 10420.
References: *NRB* 6. Moreau IV #1125.

R 7. **[Rabelais, François].**

Pantagruel. Les horribles et espoventables faictz et prouesses du tresrenomme Pantagruel, Roy des Dipsodes, Filz du grant geant Gargantua ... Augmente et

Corrige fraichement, par maistre Jehan Lunel doc-teur en theologie. — Lyon, François Juste, 1533.
8°: 88 ff., A-L⁸, goth.
Dresden (destroyed).
References: *NRB* 7.

R 8. **[Rabelais, François].**

Pantagruel. Les horribles faictz et prouesses espoventables de Pantagruel roy des Dipsodes. — Lyon, François Juste, 1534.
8°: 92 ff., A-L⁸ M⁴, goth.
*Paris BN Rothschild VI.2.35. Chantilly Condé III.C.50. Glasgow UL Hunterian Cm.3.25. Geneva Bodmer.
References: *NRB* 8.

R 9. **[Rabelais, François].**

Pantagruel Les horribles faictz et prouesses espoventables de Pantagruel: Roy des Dipsodes. — Lyon, Pierre de Sainte-Lucie, 1535.
4°: a-s⁴, goth.
London BL 245.f.43.
References: *NRB* 9.

R 10. **[Rabelais, François].**

Pantagruel. — [Lyon], [Denis de Harsy], 1537.
16°: A⁸ b-p⁸, rom.
Paris BN Rés. Y² 2132. Paris BEBA Les 696. Munich BSB Rar 54 acc.
References: *NRB* 10.

R 11. **[Rabelais, François].**

Les horribles faictz et prouesses espoventables de Pantagruel, roy des Dipsodes. — Lyon, François Juste, 1537.
16°: A-O⁸, goth.
Paris BN Rés. pY² 164.
References: *NRB* 11.

R 12. **[Rabelais, François].**

Pantagruel, Roy des Dipsodes, restitue a son naturel, avec ses faictz et prouesses espoventables. — Lyon, François Juste, 1542.
16°: A-S⁸, goth.

Paris BN Rés. Y^2 2135. Paris BA 8° BL 19586. London BL G10322. Oxford Bodl. Douce R 230. Glasgow UL Hunt. Cm.3.19 (+).
References: *NRB* 12.

R 13. **[Rabelais, François].**

Pantagruel, Roy des Dipsodes, restitué à son naturel: avec ses faictz, et prouesses espouventables. — Lyon, Estienne Dolet, 1542.
16°: A-Y^8, rom.
Paris BN Rés. Y^2 2145. Paris BA 8° BL 19585 Rés. Grenoble BM F 25732 Rés. Lyon BV Rés. 389862. Manchester JRL Christie 3.c.2b (+).
References: *NRB* 13.

R 14. **[Rabelais, François].**

[Gargantua]. — [Lyon], [François Juste], 1535?
8°: A-M^8 O^4, goth.
Paris BN Rés. Y^2 2126 (-A 1).
References: *NRB* 19.

R 15. **[Rabelais, François].**

Gargantua. La vie inestimable du grand Gargantua, pere de Pantagruel. — Lyon, François Juste, 1535.
16°: A-N^8, goth.
Paris BN Rés. Y^2 2130. Chantilly Condé III.c.49. Berne StU.
References: *NRB* 20.

R 16. **[Rabelais, François].**

Gargantua. — [Lyon], [Denis de Harsy], 1537.
16°: a-q^8, rom.
Paris BN Rés. Y^2 2131. Paris BEBA Les 695. Besançon BM Rés. 245.206. Munich BSB Rar 54 acc.
References: *NRB* 21.

R 17. **[Rabelais, François].**

La vie inestimable du grand Gargantua, pere de Pantagruel. — Lyon, François Juste, 1537.
16°: a-p^8, goth.
Paris BN Rés. Y^2 2133. London BL C.57.a.2. Geneva Bodmer.
References: *NRB* 22.

R 18.   **[Rabelais, François].**

La vie treshorrificque du grand Gargantua, pere de Pantagruel. — Lyon, François Juste, 1542.
16°: A-T^8 V^4, goth. V 3v: Impr. à Lyon par Francoys Juste.
Paris BN Rés. Y^2 2134. Chantilly Condé XI.D.91. Montpellier BM C 828(1). London BL G 10322(3). Glasgow UL Hunt Cm.3.19 (+).
References: *NRB* 23.

R 19.   **[Rabelais, François].**

La Plaisante, et joyeuse histoyre du grand Geant Gargantua. Prochainement reveue, et de beaucoup augmentée par l'Autheur mesme. — Lyon, Estienne Dolet, 1542.
16°: a-s^8, rom.
Paris BN Rés. Y^2 2144. Paris BA 8° BL 19585 Rés. Grenoble BM F 25732 Rés. Lyon BV Rés. 389861. Versailles BM Goujet 12° 259 (+).
References: *NRB* 24.

R 20.   **[Rabelais, François].**

Grands Annales ou croniques Tresveritables des Gestes merveilleux du grand Gargantua et Pantagruel son filz. Roy des Dipsodes. — ?, ?, 1542.
8°: A-P AA-NN^8 AAA-CCC^4, goth.
Paris BN Rés. Y^2 2137-2138. London BL G 17652. Geneva Bodmer.
References: *NRB* 26.

R 21.   **[Rabelais, François].**

La vie treshorrifique du grand Gargantua, pere de Pantagruel. — Lyon, Pierre de Tours, ?
16°: a-p aa-pp^8, rom.
Paris BN Rés. Y^2 2140. Paris BN Rothschild VI.2.13. London BL C.97.a.7(2) (aa-pp only). Geneva Bodmer. Chicago Newberry (+).
References: *NRB* 27.
Notes: Gatherings aa-pp: *Pantagruel* and *Pantagrueline Prognostication*.

R 22.   **Rabelais, François.**

Tiers livre des faictz et dictz Heroïques du noble Pantagruel. — Paris, Chrestien Wechel, 1546.
8°: a^4 A-Y^8 Z^4, ital. Z 4r: Impr. à Paris par Chrestien Wechel... pour et au nom de M. Franc. Rabelais, docteur en Me[de]cine.

Paris BN Rothschild II.7.40. Metz BM Clm F 11. Tours BM Marcel
Rés. 3537. Harvard CL.
References: *NRB* 28.

R 23. **Rabelais, François.**
Tiers livre des faictz et dictz Heroiques du noble Pantagruel. — Lyon, ?, 1546.
8°: πa^4 a-p^8, rom.
Paris BN Rothschild IV.9.58. London BL G 10418. Yale UL.
References: *NRB* 29.

R 24. **Rabelais, François.**
Tiers livre des faictz et dictz Heroiques du noble Pantagruel. — Paris, ?, 1546.
16°: a-t^8 Aa^2, rom.
Troyes BM Rés. Éd.préc. F 31.
References: *NRB* 30.

R 25. **Rabelais, François.**
Tiers livre des faictz et dictz Heroiques du noble Pantagruel. — Paris, ?, pr. Jacques Fournier (Toulouse), 1546.
16°: a-t^8 Aa^2, rom.
Paris BN Rothschild VI.2.52 (s.n.). Lyon BV 389863.
References: *NRB* 31.

R 26. **Rabelais, François.**
Le Tiers livre des faictz et dictz Heroiques du noble Pantagruel... Reveu et corrigé diligemment depuis les autres impressions. — Lyon, [Pierre de Tours?], 1547.
16°: A-T^8, rom.
Paris BN Rés. Y^2 2161. Paris BA 8° BL 19592. Chantilly Condé XI.D.89. Tours BM Marcel Rés. 3583. Chicago Newberry.
References: *NRB* 32.

R 27. **Rabelais, François.**
Le tiers livre des faictz et Dictz Heroiques du noble Pantagruel. — Lyon, Pierre de Tours, ?
16°: A-Q^8 R^4, rom.
Paris BN Rés. Y^2 2141 (-R 1-4) and Rés. Y^2 2158.
References: *NRB* 33.

R 28.   Rabelais, François.

Tiers livre des faictz et dictz heroiques du noble Pantagruel. — Paris, ?, 1547.
16°: 293 pp.
References: *NRB* 34.

R 29.   Rabelais, François.

La Plaisante, et joyeuse histoyre du grand Geant Gargantua. Prochainement reveue, et de beaucoup augmentée par l'Autheur mesme. — Valence, Claude La Ville, 1547.
16°: a-p⁸ q⁴, rom.
Paris BN Rothschild V.7.73. Paris BEBA Masson 1144 (-a 1-8, b 1,2, h 4,5).
References: *NRB* 38.1.
Notes: This and the following two numbers were printed together, but constitute discrete bibliographical entities.

R 30.   Rabelais, François.

Second Livre de Pantagruel, Roy Des Dipsodes, Restitué á son naturel: avec ses faictz, et prouesses espouventables. — Valence, Claude La Ville, 1547.
16°: A-T⁸, rom.
Paris BN Rothschild V.7.74. Paris BEBA Masson 1144.
References: *NRB* 38.2.

R 31.   Rabelais, François.

Tiers Livre Des Faictz, et Dictz Heroiques du noble Pantagruel. — Valence, Claude La Ville, 1547.
16°: a-r⁸, rom.
Paris BN Rothschild V.7.75. Paris BEBA Masson 1144. Paris BN Rés. Y² 2160.
References: *NRB* 38.3.

R 32.   Rabelais, François.

Le quart livre des faictz et dictz Heroiques du noble Pantagruel. — Lyon, [Pierre de Tours], 1548.
16°: A-G⁸, rom.
Paris BN Rés. Y² 2160 bis. Paris BN Rothschild VI.2.52. Paris BA 8° BL 19593 Rés. Chantilly Condé XI.D.89.
References: *NRB* 41.
Notes: Shorter version, in 11 chaps.

R 33.   **Rabelais, François.**

Le quart livre des faictz et dictz Heroiques du noble Pantagruel. — Lyon, [Pierre de Tours], 1548.
16°: A-F^8, rom.
Paris BN Rothschild V.7.78. Chicago Newberry.
References: *NRB* 42.
Notes: Shorter version, in 11 chaps.

R 34.   **Rabelais, François.**

Quart livre des faictz et dictz Heroiques du noble Pantagruel. — Lyon, Pierre de Tours, ?
16°: A-F^8 G^4, rom.
Paris BN Rés. Y^2 2141.
References: *NRB* 43.
Notes: Shorter version, in 11 chaps.

R 35.   **Rabelais, François.**

Quart livre des faictz et dictz heroiques du noble Pantagruel. — Rouen, Vincent Coffin, 1548.
16°.
References: *NRB* 44.
Notes: Known only from a 17th-cent. MS bibliography of Rabelais's works. The complete *Quart livre* (in 67 chaps) appeared in 1552.

R 36.   **[Rabelais, François: pseud.].**

Le cinquiesme livre des faictz et dictz du noble Pantagruel. Auquelz sont comprins, les grans Abus, et d'esordonnêe vie de, Plusieurs Estatz, de ce monde. — ?, ?, 1549.
16°: A-H^8, rom.
Chicago Newberry.
References: *NRB* 111.
Notes: Reprints without acknowledgement extracts from Jean Bouchet.

R 37.   **[Rabelais, François: pseud.].**

[Le Cinquiesme Livre]. — ?, ?, 1551?
16°: A-H^8, rom.
Paris BSG Rés. D 9983(2) (-A 1-8, H 8).

References: *NRB* 112.

Notes: Closely copied from previous number.

R 38.   Recueil.

Brief recueil de la substance et principal fondement de la doctrine Evangelique. — [Paris], [Simon Du Bois], 1526?

8°: A-B^8 C^4, goth. a 3v: 'Au fidele liseur' dated Sept. 1525.

*Paris SHP R.15940.

References: Clutton #46. Tricard *APR* pp. 12-17. Moreau III #775. *Index* I #479. Higman *Censorship*, p. 84.

Notes: In a letter of Dec. 1525 (Herminjard, *Correspondance* I, 414, n. 16), from Gérard Roussel to Nicolas Le Sueur of Meaux, Roussel mentions 'compendium tuum in rem Christianam': same text? On 2 March 1531 the Faculty of Theology condemned ten propositions from this text.

R 39.   Redon, Gilles de.

La Musique Angelique toute nouvelle De Salve regina. — Paris, Denis Janot, 1535.

8°: F^8 G^4, rom. G 4r: Impr. à Paris par Denys Janot.

*Versailles BM Goujet 8° 33.

References: Peach/Brunel #271. Moreau IV #1329. Rawles #39.

Notes: The Versailles copy bound with Gringore, *Chantz royaulx*, 1535 (A-E^8), but with independent t.p. The author is described as a 'ung frere mineur et cordelier ... docteur en theologie'.

R 40.   Réfection spirituelle.

La reffection spirituelle de lame devote avec la profession de religion contenant en soy xx petites parties. — Paris, Vve Jean Trepperel, 1515?

8°: 64 ff., A-H^8, goth. Impr. à Paris par la veufve Jehan trepperel.

Chantilly Condé XII B 71.

R 41.   Réfection spirituelle.

La refection spirituelle de lame devote contenant en soy .xx. petites parties. — Paris, Vve Jean Trepperel, Jean Jehannot, 1516?

8°: A-H^8, goth. H 7v: Impr. à Paris par la veufve feu Jehan Trepperel et Jehan jehannot.

*London BL 1360.1.6(3).

Notes: Composed, according to the t.p., by 'ung devot religieux de lave maria'. Instructions for preparing to receive the Eucharist.

R 42.   Refuge des Chrestiens.

Le Refuge des Chrestiens compose sur les dix commandemens de Dieu. — Lyon, Jean Mosnier, 1540.
References: Frankfurt cat. 1610. Du Verdier.

R 43.   Remède pour bien vivre.

Remede convenable Pour si bien vivre en ce monde que nous puissions acquerir le royaulme des cieulx. — Paris, [Jean Marchant], pr. Jean Petit, 1512?
4°: 4 ff., goth./rom.
*Paris BN Rés. D 5692(5).
References: Moreau II #443.
Notes: B. Moreau suggests the date. The titles are in goth., but the text is in rom.

R 44.   Remède pour bien vivre.

Remede convenable Pour si bien vivre en ce monde que nous puissions acquerir le royaulme des cieulx. — Antwerp, Guillaume Vorsterman, 1527?
8°: 4 ff., goth. fol. 4v: Impr. en Anvers par Guillame Vorsterman.
Séville Colomb.
References: Dagens. Babelon 199. NK #3793.

R 45.   [Rhegius, Urbanus].

La Doctrine Nouvelle et Ancienne: Lesquelles arguent ensemble, pour donner a congnoistre par la verite Evangelicque les abuz qui sont advenuz au monde. Nouvellement corrigee et augmentee. selon la verite de la saincte Escripture, et des droictz canons. — [Geneva], [Jean Michel], 1542.
8°: A-H⁸ I⁴, goth. I 4v: ach. d'impr. 25.05.1542.
*Vienna ÖNB 79.H.46.
References: Berthoud 'Michel' #17. *BG* 42/21. *Index* I #398 and 387.
Notes: A certain Jean de Bourges was imprisoned in Rouen in 1534 for having sold this text: no known copy of an ed. of this date. Censured by the Sorbonne in 1543 (Higman *Censorship*

A13). Trans. of *Novae Doctrinae ad veterem Collatio* (Augsburg, *c*. 1526). Urbanus Rhegius (1489-1541) was a Lutheran pastor in Augsburg, later Celle, Luneburg and Hanover.

R 46.   [Rhegius, Urbanus].

La Doctrine Nouvelle et Ancienne: lesquelles arguent ensemble, pour donner a congnoistre par la verite Evangelicque les abuz qui sont advenuz au monde. Nouvellement reveue et augmentee, selon la verite de la saincte Escripture, et des droictz canons. — [Geneva], [Jean Michel], 1544.

8°: A-I^8, goth.

*Geneva MHR D 10. *Paris BN Rés. D^2 7154. *London BL 702.a.14.

References: Moore #123. Berthoud 'Michel' #21. *BG* 44/31.

R 47.   [Rhegius, Urbanus].

La Doctrine nouvelle et ancienne, Nouvellement reveuë selon la verité de la saincte Escriture, et augmentée oultre les precedentes editions. — [Geneva?], [Jean Crespin?], 1551.

8°: A-G^8 H^4, rom.

*Vienna ÖNB 79.V.89. *Wolfenbüttel HAB 1028.17 Th.

Notes: The attribution to Crespin is based on several printing habits which this text shares with known Crespin eds.

R 48.   [Rhegius, Urbanus].

La Medecine de l'ame. — Geneva, 1542?

References: Franz #3.42.

Notes: Higman *Censorship* A 14 (censure which specifies 'imprimée à Geneve'). The censure may refer to the Lyon ed. of the same year incorporated into *Simulachres et historiées faces...* (see *Images de la mort*), and re-ed. in 1547. Trans. of Rhegius's *Seelenertzney für die gesunden und kranken* (Augsburg, 1519, Latin trans. 1537).

=>   Rochefort, Jean de: see Poullain, Valérand.

R 49.   [Rolewinck, Werner], trans. from Latin by Pierre Sarget, augmented by Pierre Desrey.

Les fleurs et manieres des temps passez et des faitz merveilleux de dieu tant en lancien testament comme ou nouveau. Et des premiers seigneurs princes et gouverneurs temporelz en cestuy monde: de leurs gestes: definement jusques a present. — Paris, Jean de la Roche, Jean Petit and Michel Le Noir, 1513.

2°: A^8 b^8 c-o^6 p-q^4 R^8, goth. q 4v: Impr. à Paris par Jehan de la roche pr. Jehan Petit et Michel Le Noir. 03.12.1513.

*Paris BA fol T 480(3). Paris BN Rés. G 1413.

Notes: Acc. to the colophon, Pierre Sarget, Doctor of Theology and Augustinian, translated the work in 1483. Desrey updated it to 1513. The name of the author given in 15th-cent. eds.

R 50.   Rome, Jean de.

Sensuyt ung petit directoyre pour aprendre es symples gens a reduire a memoyre leurs peches en euls confessant. — Avignon, Jean de Channey, 1532?

8°.

Notes: *NLA* 78, p. 16: a request from Gladys Bouchard, BM Montpellier, for information about this text. Frère Jean de Rome is described on the t.p. as 'de la relygion des presheurs du convent de Borges'.

R 51.   Rosay, G. de.

Le relief de l'ame pecheresse. — Paris, Jean André, 1542.

8°.

References: Renouard MSS.

R 52.   Royer, Colin.

La Nouvelle du reverend pere en Dieu et bon Prelat ... demorant en Avignon, et le moyen comme il ressuscita de mort, à vie. Avec le deschiffrement de ses tendres amourettes. — Troyes, Nicole Paris, 1546.

4°: A-E^4 F^2, rom. F 2r: Impr. à Troyes par Nicole Paris. 1546.

*Paris BN Rés. Y^2 799.

References: Cartier *Arrêts* p. 26. Brunet *Suppl.* II, 531. Re-ed. Paris 1862.

Notes: A lively narrative attacking clerical, and particularly episcopal, debauchery. See Higman, 'Genres', p. 126.

S

=> *Sacrifice Quotidian*: see *Vif Sacrifice*.

=> Sadolet, Jacques: see Calvin, Jean.

S 1.   Salve Regina.
Le salve regina en francoys fait a la louenge de la vierge Marie. — Paris, Alain Lotrian, 1535?
8°: A⁸, goth. A 8v: Impr. à Paris par Alain Lotrien.
*Paris BN Rés. pYe 300.
Notes: Octosyllabic verse in praise of the Virgin Mary. The last stanza gives an acrostic: JAQUINCHIPART.

S 2.   Saulnier, Antoine.
Chanson nouvelle composee sur les dix commandemens de Dieu extraicte de la saincte Escripture. — ?, ?, 1531?
4°.
Paris SHP (missing).
References: Bordier *Ch. Hug.* 1-10.
Notes: The text is reprinted in *Sensuyvent plusieurs belles et bonnes chansons* (see *Chansons*).

S 3.   [Saulnier, Antoine].
Chanson nouvelle. Composee sus les dix commandemens de Dieu extraicte de la saincte escripture. — [Lyon], [Jacques Moderne], 1540?
4°: 4 ff., a⁴, rom.
*Paris BN Rothschild IV.6.64.
References: Rothschild # 3299. Bordier *Ch. hug.* p. xxiv.

S 4.   [Saulnier, Antoine].
L'Ordre et maniere d'enseigner en la ville de Genéve, au College. Description de la ville de Genéve. — Geneva, Jean Girard, 1538.
8°: a⁸ b⁴, ital. b 4r: De l'imprimerie de Jehan Gerard. 12.01.1538.
*Zurich ZB Res. 1336.
References: Moore #190. *BG* 38/8.

S 5.   Sauvage, Jean.

Sensuit leschelle damour divine. — Paris, Vve Jean
Trepperel, Jean Jehannot, 1516?

8°: A-D⁸ E⁴, goth. E 4v: Impr. par la veufve feu jehan trepperel et
Jehan jehannot.

*Paris BN D 17400(2). Nantes Dobrée 126.

Notes: Dedic. (A 1v) to his 'treschere et bien aymee seur' by
'frère Jean Sauvage, vicaire des Cordeliers de l'Observance'
(see Moreau II, p. 60).

S 6.   Savonarola, Jérôme.

Exposition et paraphrase ... Miserere. — Paris,
Godefroy (?), ?

References: Frankfurt cat. 1610.

Notes: The preceding notes taken from the Frankfurt catalogue. No printer or bookseller in Renouard, *Répertoire*, has
the name Godefroy.

S 7.   Savonarola, Jérôme.

*Exposition de l'oraison dominicale... Meditation sur
les psalmes: Miserere mei Deus... In te, Domine,
speravi... Breve interpretation du decalogue.* —
Lyon, Balthazar Arnoullet, 1543.

16°.

References: Baudrier X, 112 < Du Verdier II, 228.

S 8.   Schuch, Wolfgang, [François Lambert].

*Epistre chrestienne envoyee a tresnoble Prince mon-
seigneur le duc de Lorayne.* — [Strasbourg], [Johann
Pruss Jr.], [Johann Knobloch Sen.], 1526?

8°: A-B⁸ C⁴, goth.

*Amsterdam VU XC 05993(3). *London BL C.37.a.22(5). *Vienna
ÖNB 79.M.65.

References: Moore #198. Peter 'Prem.ouvr.' #1. Bodenmann
p. 161.

Notes: François Lambert is probably the 'Theodulus Phila-
delphus' who introduces Schuch's epistle with a narrative of
the latter's death at the stake in Nancy on 21 June 1525.
Schuch's letter is dated (C 1r) 11 Jan. 1525.

S 9.   **[Scrimgeour, Henry], pref. by Jean Calvin.**

*Un Exemple notable et digne de memoire d'un homme
desesperé, pour avoir renoncé la verité de l'Evangile.*
— Geneva, Jean Girard, [René de Bienassis], 1550.
4°: A-F⁴, rom. F 4v: 'Assez tost, si assez bien'.
Vienna ÖNB 72.X.96.
References: CDM p. 16. *Index* I #299.
Notes: Calvin's preface dated from Geneva, 15 Nov. 1549.
The text narrates the tragic case of Francesco Spiera who,
having forsaken his evangelical beliefs, died of despair.

S 10.   **Sebond, Raymond, trans. Jean Martin.**

La Theologie Naturelle <> mise de Latin en François.
— Paris, Michel de Vascosan, 1551.
4°: [6] + 140 ff., *⁶ A-Z Aa-Mm⁴, rom. Mm 4v: 1551.
*Paris BN Rés. Z Payen 608.
Notes: * 2r: Jean Martin explains to the Cardinal de Lenon-
court that he undertook the translation of R. de Sebond at the
request of 'Leonor royne douairiere de France.' It is he that
invented the title *Theologie naturelle*. Dated 20 July 1550.

S 11.   **Sentence de Jean Guibert.**

Sentence de frere Jehan Guibert, hermite de Livry.
— [Paris], [Simon Du Bois], 1527?
8°: A⁸, goth.
*London BL C.37.a.22(6).
References: Moore #199. Clutton #40. Moreau III #1334.
Notes: Jean Guibert, associated with the Meaux group, had
denounced simoniacal practices in the Church, and was con-
demned to six months in prison. This document presents the
annulment of the sentence by a panel of nine judges, including
René Du Bellay and Jean de Selve.

S 12.   **Sentences.**

*Sentences extraites de l'escriture sainte pour
l'instruction des enfans.* — Paris, Louis Grandin,
1548.
8°.
References: Renouard MSS.

S 13.   **Sentier de devotion,** trans. Nicole Caling.

Le Sentier et ladresse de devotion, et contemplation intellectuelle ... a ledification et instruction de tous bons et loyaulx chrestiens. — Toulouse, Jacques Colomies, pr. Jean Richard, 1533?

4°: +⁴ a-c D-V⁴, goth. + 4v: Impr. à Tholose par Jacques Colomies.
*Paris BN Rés. D 64413 (a) and Ld⁴ 69 bis(3) (b). *Paris Univ Rés. XVI 935 (b). Poitiers BM 3810. Toulouse BM Rés. D XVI.344.

References: *Rép.bib.* #200.

Notes: Translation of *Precordialle devotorum*, text already existing in Latin in the 15th cent. (Strasbourg ed., 1489, in Paris BN, London BL). There are two issues, with recomposition of gathering +: (a) says Nicole Caling translated the work 'a linstigation de ... Guillaume de Aresme' for the nuns of Albi, (b) says it was done 'a la requeste des devotes Religieuses...' of Albi, and adds that the printing was subsidized by Guilhaume de Aresmo.

S 14.   **Sermon pour ... la dedicace.**

Sermon notable pour le jour de la Dedicace. — [Geneva], [Jean Michel], 1539.

8°: A⁸, goth.
Nantes Dobrée No. 247. *Paris BN Rothschild IV.9.54. *Vienna ÖNB 2.W.19.

References: Rothschild #3246. Th. Dufour *Not.cat.* pp. 162-3. Moore #200. Mayer *Marot* #83. Berthoud 'Michel' #7. *BG* 39/14. *Index* I #395.

Notes: J. Michel obtained permission to print this title on 5 Sept. 1539. Poem on abuses in the Church, and defending the 'luthériens'. Sometimes attrib. to Marot, but the attribution is doubtful.

S 15.   **Sermons des six paroles,** trans. Jean de Gaigny.

Sermons des six paroles de Jesuchrist en croix. — Lyon, Jean de Tournes, 1543.

16°: a-c⁸ d⁴, rom.
*Coll. privée.

References: Cartier *De Tournes* #14. Sale Lignerolles (1901).

Notes: T.p.: 'Translatez pour le Roy treschrestien par Jean de Gaigny, docteur, et premier aumosnier dudict Seigneur'. See also Brodeau, *Louanges*, 1541.

S 16.   Seuse, Heinrich.

Lorloge de Sapience en laquelle est contenu deux livres. Le premier fait mention de la mort et passion... Le second livre enseigne comment un bon chrestien se doit gouverner en ce monde. — Paris, Alain Lotrian, Denis Janot, 1533?

8°: A⁴ B-X y-z &⁸, goth. & 7v: Impr. à Paris par Alain Lotrian.
London BL 1412.a.24 (Janot). *Paris BN Rés. D 52882 (Lotrian).

References: Rawles #335.

Notes: Trans. of the *Horologium sapientiae*, by the German mystic Heinrich Seuse (*c.* 1295-1366).

S 17.   Significations de la messe.

Les XXXIII. significations et considerations qui sont en la messe lesquelles doyvent estre considerees et rememoreez a tous devotz crestiens et vrays catholicques en la foy de nostre seigneur. — Lyon, Barnabé Chaussard, 1525?

8°: [8] ff., A⁸, goth. Fol. 6r: Impr. à Lyon par Barnabe chassard.
Séville Colombine.

References: Baudrier XI.35. Babelon #228.

=>   *Simulachres de la mort*: see *Images*.

S 18.   [Sleidan, Jean].

Escript adresse aux Electeurs Princes, et aultres Estatz de Lempire. Contenant comme et par quelz moiens sest esleve la Papalite, la decadence dicelle, ses merveilleuses praticques, et en somme ce quon en peult esperer de ce temps. Dung chef nouveau Qui au temps des Empereurs sest esleve a Rome. — Strasbourg, [Johann Knobloch Jr.], 1542.

8°: A-G⁸, rom. G 7v: Impr. à Strasburg. 1542.
Florence BN Guicc. 16.4.32.

References: Peter 'Prem.ouvr.' #9a.

Notes: 'Requisitoire contre Rome avec un vibrant appel aux Princes' (Peter). The German original appeared in 1541. Probably trans. by Sleidan himself.

S 19. **[Sleidan, Jean].**

D'un nouveau chef qui au temps des empereurs s'esleva à Rome. Livre contenant comment et par quelz moyens s'est eslevé la Papaute: La decadence d'icelle, Ses merveilleuses pratiques, et en somme ce qu'on en peut esperer de ce temps. — [Geneva], [Jean Girard], 1543.

8°: a-g⁸, rom.

*Berne StU B 176. *Geneva BPU Rés. Bc 3523. *Rouen BM Montbret p4171. *Stuttgart LB Kirch.G. oct 1340.

References: *Index* I #388.

Notes: Re-ed. of the *Escript adresse aux electeurs* of 1542.

S 20. **[Sleidan, Jean].**

D'un nouveau chef qui au temps des Empereurs s'esleva à Rome. Livre comment et par quelz moyens s'est eslevée la Papauté, la decadence d'icelle, ses merveilleuses pratiques, et en somme ce qu'on peut esperer de ce temps. — Geneva, Adam et Jean Rivery, 1550.

8°: A-I⁸ K⁴, rom.

*Cambridge Emma. 324.7.82(1). *Geneva BPU Rés. Bc 3366. *Paris SHP R 15996 (s.l. s.n.).

References: Adams R 736. CDM p. 16.

S 21. **Sommaires de la Bible.**

Le Sommaire des livres du Vieil, et Nouveau Testament. Les dix parolles, ou Commandements de Dieu. — Lyon, Estienne Dolet, 1542.

16°: A-B⁸, rom.

Toulouse BM Rés. D.XVI.175.

References: Longeon *Dolet* #221. *Index* I #495, 496. Cat. Drilhon #28. Text reprod. by J. Mégret, *BHR* 1944, pp. 129-37.

S 22. **Sommaires de la Bible.**

La doctrine des Chrestiens, extraicte du Vieil et Nouveau testament. Les dix parolles ou commandemens de Dieu. Loraison Dominicalle... Les commandemens de nostre mere Saincte Esglise. Les sept Sacremens. — Paris, Denis Janot, 1543.

16°: A-D⁸, rom.

*Chantilly Condé XI.D.35.

References: Rawles #196.

Notes: Includes the Commandments of the Church, as was demanded of R. Estienne (see next item).

S 23.   Sommaires de la Bible.

Le Sommaire des livres du Vieil et Nouveau testament. Les dix parolles, ou commandemens de Dieu. — [Paris], [Robert Estienne], 1543?
16°: a-b⁸, rom.
*Paris SHP A 1167(1).
References: *Index* I #495, 496.
Notes: R. Estienne's *Sommaires* were censured on 19 Dec. 1542 (Farge, *Registre* n° 252 A-C, pp. 210-12. Higman *Censorship*, pp. 92-3). Estienne says he obtained the King's protection against the theologians, and indeed an order to reprint his 'tables'. The theologians complained again on 19 June 1543 (Farge, *Registre* n° 267 D, p. 234): Estienne was ordered to reprint his 'tables' inserting the Commandments of the Church. In 1544 they were placed on the *Index*. Gilmont 'Sommaire' lists some 200 eds of Estienne's *Sommaires* in various languages, and gives the text in Latin and French.

S 24.   Sommaires de la Bible.

Le sommaire des livres du Vieil et Nouveau testament. Les dix parolles, ou Commandemens de Dieu. — Paris, Robert Estienne, 1547.
16°: a-b⁸, rom.
*Geneva BPU Rés. Bc 3362.

S 25.   Sommaires de la Bible.

La Doctrine des Chrestiens extraicte du vieil et nouveau Testament. Les dix parolles ou commandementz de Dieu. Les commandementz de nostre mere saincte Esglise. Les sept sacremens... — ?, ?, 1547?
8°: Aa-Bb⁸, rom.
*Paris BSG D 8° 6193(3) inv. 7888 Rés.
Notes: A note added (Aa 8r) on idolatry: 'Les Chrestiens eslevent ymages et statues aux sainctz pour reduire en memoire les beaux faictz qu'ilz ont faictz, et souffertz pour l'honneur de Jesus Christ, mais ilz ne mettent point leur fiance en icelles, comme les idolatres ont mis en leurs idoles. La paincture

sert aux gens non sçavans, de ce que sert l'escriture aux gens sçavans.'

S 26.   **Somme de l'écriture,** extract from Luther, *Von weltlicher Obrigkeit.*

La Summe de lescripture saincte, et lordinaire des chrestiens, enseignant la vraye foy Chrestienne: par laquelle nous sommes tous justifiez. Et de la vertu du baptesme, selon la doctrine de Levangile, et des Apostres. Avec une information comment tous estatz doibvent vivre selon Levangile. — 'Basle' [Alençon], 'Thomas Volff' [Simon Du Bois], 1532?

8°: A-Q^8 R^{10}, goth.

*London BL C.37.a.20.

References: Moore #22. Clutton #50. Bietenholz #4014. J. Trapman (1978). *Index* I #487.

Notes: Dated '1523' on t.p., but this cannot be correct (see Higman, 'Dates-clé'). Known in Latin (*Oeconomica christiana*, 1527) and Dutch (1523). See Trapman for the debate on the identity of the author. Probably a French ed. in Antwerp, *c.* 1529 (lost), since an English translation based on the French appeared in Antwerp in 1529 (*STC* 3036), with multiple re-eds.

S 27.   **Somme de l'écriture,** extract from Luther, *Von weltlicher Obrigkeit.*

La Somme de lescripture saincte, enseignant la vraye foy, par laquelle sommes justifiez. Et de la vertu du baptesme, selon la doctrine de Levangile et des Apostres. Avec une information, comme tous estatz doibvent vivre selon Levangile. Nouvellement reveue et corrigee. — [Geneva], [Jean Michel], 1539.

8°: A-Q^8 R^4, goth. R 4r: ach. d'imprimer 05.05.1539.

*Cambridge Emma. 321.7.6(3). *Paris BA 8° T.5341.

References: Adams S 1421. Berthoud 'Michel' #5.

S 28.   **Somme de l'écriture,** extract from Luther, *Von weltlicher Obrigkeit.*

La Somme de lescripture saincte, enseignant la vraye foy, par laquelle sommes justifiez. Et de la vertu du baptesme, selon la doctrine de Levangile et des

Apostres. Avec une information, comme tous estatz doibvent vivre selon Levangile. Nouvellement reveue et corrigee. — [Geneva], [Jean Michel], 1544.
8°: A-S⁸, goth.
Gotha FB Theol. 61/1 Rara. La Rochelle BM 8888C. Lübeck SB Theol. 8° 4263. *Strasbourg BNU R 100600.
References: Th. Dufour Ms.Fr. 3807 #126. N. Weiss, *BSHPF* (1919) p. 64. Berthoud 'Michel' #18. Cat. Drilhon # 24 (this ed).

S 29.   **Spagnuoli, Battista,** trans. François Le Breton.

La Vie d'honneur et de Vertu: Ou est monstré comme ung chascun doibt vivre en tout aage, en tout temps, et en tout lieu: envers Dieu et envers les hommes. Nouvellement corrigé. — Paris, Jean Bignon, Charles Langelier, 1540.
16°: 64 + [1] ff., a-h⁸ + 1 f., rom. h 7v: Impr. à Paris par Jehan Bignon, rue Judas, pres les boucheries ste. Geneviefve du mont.
*Paris BN Rés. (shelfmark not yet allocated).
Notes: After an introduction on the creation of man, the text is mainly based on classical authors for the definition of virtue. 'Vie honneste et vertueuse nest aultre chose sinon que lhomme en vivant doibt user de raison, et ne se assubjectir point a ses affections comme les bestes: et entant que par nature il est possible quil soit de vie tellement quellement semblable a dieu, laquelle ne consiste en aucune autre chose si non en VERTU.'

S 30.   **Spagnuoli, Battista,** trans. François Le Breton.

La Fontaine de tous biens, Vie, d'honneur et de Vertu. — Paris, [Estienne Caveiller], Charles Langelier, 1542.
16°: a-k⁸, rom.
*Paris SHP A 1167(2).
References: Moore #151. Droz *Chemins* I, 295-7.
Notes: Mlle Droz says it is an adaptation of Hermann Schotten, *Vita honesta*, 1530.

S 31.   **Spagnuoli, Battista,** trans. François Le Breton.

La Fontaine d'honneur et de vertu ou est montré comme un chascun doit vivre en tout aage. — Lyon, Jean de Tournes, 1544.
16°.

References: Cartier *De Tournes* #27.

S 32.   **Spagnuoli, Battista,** trans. Jacques de Mortières.

La parthenice Mariane de Baptiste Mantuan poete theologue de lordre de nostre dame des carmes. — Lyon, Claude Nourry, Jean Besson, 1523.

4°: a⁴ b-m⁸, goth. m 6v: Impr. à Lyon pour Claude nourry et Jehan besson. 22.10.1523.

*Paris BEBA Masson 764.

Notes: Dedic. (a 4r) to Marguerite d'Alençon, by Jacques de Mortières. At the end, an acrostic giving Marguerite's name. The text is a 'biography' of the Virgin Mary, in verse, with Latin on the left, and explanatory notes on the right.

S 33.   **[Stumpf, Jean],** [trans. François Bonivard].

Histoire veritable et digne de memoire de quatre Jacopins de Berne, heretiques et sorciers, qui y furent bruslez: ensemble les finesses et meschancetez, desquelles ilz usoyent envers un convers de leur ordre. — [Geneva], [Jean Girard], 1549.

4°: A-C⁴ D⁶, rom.

*Cambridge Emma. 30.6.14(4)(var. t.p.). *Geneva BPU Rés. Ba 3436.

References: Adams B 752. Moore p. 409. *BG* 49/16.

Notes: An extract from Stumpf's *Swiss History*, narrating a lawsuit which created a scandal in 1509 (see Gilmont *Crespin* 66/7).

S 34.   **Sur l'epistre à Philemon.**

Sur l'epistre S. Paul à Philemon petit commentaire. Auquel entre autres choses est declairé comment nous debvons traiter avec toute douceur et humanité les pecheurs qui se recongnoissent. — Agen, Antoine Reboul, 1546.

References: *Index* I #389. *Rép.bib.* #6. Frankfurt cat. 1610.

Notes: The title is taken from the 1547 *Index*. The 1551 and 1556 reprints give the address as 'Geneve, par Antoine Keboul'. No known copy.

T

T 1.   Te Deum des Luthériens.

Le Te Deum pour l'eglise Lutherienne: en françoys et en latin. Avec la Ballade et la chanson d'yceulx Lutheriens. — ?, ?, 1528?
Séville Colombine.
References: Moore #203. Babelon #222.
Notes: See *Balade*.

T 2.   Testaments des patriarches.

Les testamentz des douze patriarches Enfans de Jakob. — Antwerp, 'Martin Lempereur', 1540.
16°: A-G^8 H^2 +^{6}, rom. H 2v: Impr. à Anvers par Martin Lempereur. 1540. + 6v: Impr. à Envers par Martin Lempereur. 1540.
*Cambridge UL CCE.2.3.
References: Adams P 428. NK #4529.
Notes: Martin Lempereur died in 1535. The text may have been printed by his widow. According to a note at the end (H 2r), the Hebrew text was translated into Greek, and thence (by Robert Grosseteste) into Latin (in 1242). It is followed (gathering +) by *Le Testament de Anne, faict a son filz Esaye.*

T 3.   Testaments des patriarches.

Les testamens des douze patriarches enfans de Jacob. — Paris, Jacques Bogard, 1548.
16°: A-I^8, rom. I 7v: Impr. à Paris par Jaques Bogard. 16.04.1548.
Ghent UB Acc.3990. *Paris BN Rés. 8° Z don 594(375.2).
References: Machiels #116.
Notes: Priv. (fol. I 7r) for four years to Jacques Bogard, dated 14 Apr. 1548.

T 4.   Testaments des patriarches.

Les Testamens des douze patriarches, enfans de Jacob. — Paris, François Girault, pr. Martin Le Jeune, 1549.
16°: A-I^8, rom. I 7v: Impr. à Paris par Françoys Girault pr. Martin le Jeune. 1549.
Aix Méj. In 16° 137. *Paris BSG B 8° 1069(8) inv 1517 Rés.
References: Renouard MSS.

T 5.   **Testaments des patriarches.**

Les testaments des douse Patriarches, enfants de Jacob. — Ghent, Josse Lambert, 1551.
8°: A-G^8 H^4.
Ghent BU 198(1) and 198(2).
References: Machiels #117.

T 6.   **Testaments des patriarches.**

Les Testamentz des douze patriarches, enfans de Jacob. — Rouen, [Nicolas Le Roux?], pr. Robert et Jean Du Gort, 1551.
16°: A-K^8, rom.
*Paris BEBA Masson 1099.
Notes: The attribution to Nicolas Le Roux is according to a MS note in the Paris BEBA copy.

T 7.   **[Textor, Benoist].**

Confession vrayement chrestienne, pleine de saine doctrine, de beaux et salutaires advertissemens, de vehementes exhortations, et de consolations singulieres. En laquelle sont brievement comprins les principaux poinctz de la Foy catholique, afin qu'un chascun mette peine de profiter en la vraye cognoissance de Dieu, de le glorifier, et s'adonner à toute bonne oeuvre. — [Geneva], [Jean Girard], 1549.
8°: A-M^8, rom. M 7r: 27 Juin 1548. Recogneu 12 Juin 1549.
*Wolfenbüttel HAB 1218.5 Th(1). *Vienna ÖNB 79.Ee.2.
References: Cartier *Arrêts* 121-42. *BG* 49/18. *Index* I #391.
Notes: Benoist Textor, Calvin's doctor, obtained permission from the Geneva Council on 20 May 1549 to print his 'Confession crestienne avec amplez exortacions'.

T 8.   **Theodoret,** trans. Claude d'Espence.

Sermons de Theodoret, evesque Cyrien, autheur Grec, ancien et catholique: ascavoir, le IX. et X. — Lyon, Jean de Tournes, 1547.
16°: A-G^8 H^6, rom.
*Geneva BPU Rés. Bd 1889. *Paris BN D 88506(2).
References: Cartier *De Tournes* #103.
Notes: Two sermons, one treating of eternal life, the other of the providence of God.

T 9.   **Theodoret,** trans. Claude d'Espence.

Deux Sermons de Theodoret, evesque Cyriem, autheur Grec, ancien et catholique, a sçavoir, le neufiesme et dixiesme. — Paris, Jean Ruelle, 1550?
16°: A-D^8 E^4, rom.
*Paris BSG Rés. D 8° 6502(3).
Notes: Re-ed. of the 1547 De Tournes ed.

T 10.   **Théologie spirituelle.**

La theologie spirituelle extraicte des livres sainct Denis ... tresutile et prouffitable a tout homme et femme tendant a perfection soit seculier ou regulier. — Paris, Vve Jean Trepperel, Jean Jehannot, 1512?
8°: A-D^8, goth. D 8r: Impr. à Paris par la veuve Jehan trepperel, et Jehan Jehannot.
*Paris BEBA Masson 619.
Notes: According to the t.p. and the colophon, the work is translated from Latin by 'ung venerable religieux de lordre des freres mineurs de lobservance'.

T 11.   **Thomas a Kempis.**

Sensuit ung petit traictie de discipline claustralle <> En quoy consiste discipline reguliere. — Paris, Simon Vostre, ?
8°: A-C^8 D^4, goth.
*Paris BN Rés. R 2046.
Notes: Simon Vostre was active 1485-1521.

T 12.   **Tissarrant, Jean.**

Une tresbelle salutation faicte sur les vii festes de Nostre dame, Laquelle salutation lon chante au salut a saint Innocent a Paris. — ?, ?, ?
8°: 4 ff.
*London BL C. 107.a.12(6). Oxford Bodl.

T 13.   **Tissarrant, Jean.**

Sensuyt une tresbelle salutation faicte sur les sept festes de nostre Dame, laquelle lon chante au salut a sainct innocent a Paris <> Avec laleluya du jour de pasques. Et ... les Graces a Dieu. — [Paris], [Julien Hubert], 1529?

8°: A-B⁴, goth.
*Paris BN Rés. Ye 301 (- B4).
References: Moreau III #1927.
Notes: *La Salutation* A 1-4. *Alleluya* B 1-2r. *Graces a Dieu* B 2v-3v (or beyond), with prayers for 'le bon roy Francoys et la royne', 'nostre daulphin et son accordee dame des angloys'.

T 14. Traité de lire l'escriture.

Traicté auquel est deduict s'il est loysible de lire la saincte Escriture en langue Vulgaire, et du fruict qui en peult sortir. — Lyon?, ?, 1544?
16°: 94 pp., a-f⁸, rom.
*Coll. privée.
References: Berthoud *Marcourt. Index* I #503.
Notes: The address to the reader is dated 10 May 1544 (a 3r), and the text 'achevé d'escrire le 12 déc. 1543' (f 7v).

T 15. Traité du souverain bien.

Le traicte du Souverain Bien. Par lequel le vray chrestien pourra apprendre (a layde des sainctes Escriptures) a contemner la Mort: mesmes icelle desirer, pour avoir claire vision de Dieu, par nostre seigneur Jesuchrist. — [Paris], [Simon Du Bois], 1526?
8°: a-f⁸, goth.
*Paris SHP A 1161.
References: Clutton #47. Tricard *APR* 18-21.
Notes: The work is dedic. to Marguerite, 'duchesse d'Alençon et de Berry', which suggests that it antedates her marriage (Jan. 1527) to Henri de Navarre.

T 16. Trépas de Martin Luther, trans. Jacques Estauge.

Le trespas de Martin Luther. — Basle, Jacques Estauge, 1546.
8°: a⁸, rom. a 8v: Impr. à Basle par Jaques Estauge. 20.04.1546.
*Zurich ZB Res. 966.
References: Moore #36. *Index* I #502.
Notes: Luther died on 15 Feb. 1546. Several 'lives' appeared promptly in German, in particular *Doctor Martin Luthers Christlicher Abschid und Sterben*. According to the dedication by the printer to Claude de Tournes (a 2r), dated from Basle, 15 Apr. 1546, Jacques Estauge himself did the translation, or rather adaptation, into French of the German text.

T 17.   **Trésor de dévotion.**

Le Tresor de devotion traictant plusieurs belles vertus par lesquelles on peut apprendre à aymer Dieu. — Lyon, Claude Nourry, ?
16°.
References: Du Verdier p. 1186.

T 18.   **Trésor de dévotion.**

Le Thresor de devotion, traictant de plusieurs belles vertus par lesquelles on peut apprendre a aymer Dieu. — Lyon, Pierre de Sainte-Lucie, ?
8°. Impr. à Lyon chez le Prince.
References: Baudrier XII, 166 < Cat. Danyau #107.

V

V 1.   **Vengeance de Jérusalem.**

La vengeance et destruction de Hierusalem par personnaiges Executee par Vaspasien et son filz Titus. Contenant en soy plusieurs cronicques et hystoires Romaines. — Paris, Alain Lotrian, 1539.
4°: [4] + 209 + [1] ff., ã a-z & # A-X AA-EE^4 FF^6, goth. FF 5r: Impr. par Alain Lotrian, escu de France. 22.10.1539.
*Chantilly Condé X D 53.
Notes: The prologue praises Francis I and makes a comparison with 'le bon roi Vespasien' who punished the Jews by destroying Jerusalem. Octosyllabic verse. Rothschild I.5.37 (#1076): identical title and collation, but dated '1530' (not in Moreau). Same ed.?

V 2.   **Ventes d'amour divin.**

Les ventes Damour Divine. — Paris, [Alain Lotrian], 1530?
8°: A^4, goth. A 4r: Impr. à Paris, rue neufve nostre Dame, enseigne de l'escu de France.
*Paris BA Rés. 8° BL 12077(3).
References: Moreau III #1625.
Notes: Each flower 'vends' (homophone with French for 'praises', *vante*) its particular religious symbolism in a quatrain.

V 3.   **Verger florissant.**

Vergier flourissant pour lame fidele, remply de fleurs Mistiques odoriferantes. — Antwerp, Martin Lempereur, 1534.

8°: A-G⁸, goth.

Antwerp MPM R 51.34.

References: NK #2117.

Notes: My thanks to Mme Francine de Nave, Conservateur des Musées Historiques, Antwerp, for confirming the details.

V 4.   **[Vergerio, Pietro Paulo].**

La Bulle de l'indiction du Concile, avec son comment et exposition. — [Geneva?], Jean Marcorelles, 1551.

16°: A-C⁸, rom./ital.

Vienna ÖNB 80.L.93. Wolfenbüttel HAB 1338.8 Theol(2).

V 5.   **[Vergerio, Pietro Paulo], [trans. Joachim de Coignac?].**

Le Conseil de trois Evesques, sur la determination du Concile general de Trente. — [Geneva?], Jean Marcorelles, 1551.

Vienna ÖNB 80.L.94.

V 6.   **[Vergerio, Pietro Paulo].**

La Declaracion du jubilè qui doit etre a Rome l'an M.D.L. — [Basle], [Jacques Estauge], 1550?

8°: A-B⁸, rom.

*Munich BSB Asc 2/3875. *Vienna ÖNB 79.Ee.175.

References: Trans. of the Latin original, *Declaratio Iubilaei futuri Romae 1550.* At the end of the text (B 6v), the epistle is dated from Basle, 1 Nov. 1549.

V 7.   **[Vergerio, Pietro Paulo], trans. Joachim de Coignac.**

Des Faitz et gestes du Pape Jules III. Et ce qui se peut Esperer de ce Concile, lequel il pretent recommencer à Trente. — [Geneva], [Jean Girard], 1551.

8°: A-F⁸ G⁴, rom.

*Geneva BPU Rés. Bc 3371. *Vienna ÖNB 79.Ee.11. *Wolfenbüttel HAB 1218.5 Theol(3).

References: CDM p. 18.

Notes: Written as a letter to Edward VI of England.

V 8.   Vérité cachée.

La Verite cachee, devant cent ans faicte et composee a six personnages: nouvellement corrigee et augmentee avec les autoritez de la saincte escripture. — [Neuchâtel], [Pierre de Vingle], 1533?
8°: A-E⁸, goth.
*Paris SHP R 1000. *Vienna ÖNB 39.Mm.90.
References: Th.Dufour *Not.cat.* pp. 113-15. *Index* I #507.
Notes: The work has been attributed to Matthieu Malingre, but there is nothing to support the hypothesis.

V 9.   Vérité cachée.

La Verite cachee, devant cent ans faicte et composee a six personnages: nouvellement corrigee et augmentee avec les autoritez de la saincte Escripture. — [Geneva], [Jean Michel], 1544.
8°: A-E⁸, goth.
Florence BN Guicc. 2.3.43bis. *Geneva MHR D Mal 1. *Vienna ÖNB *38.K.138.
References: Moore #206. Berthoud 'Michel' #23. *BG* 44/33. *Index* I #511 (specifying the date 1544).

V 10.   Vie de Jésus-Christ.

La Vie de Jhesucrist. — Lyon, Claude Nourry, 1517.
4°.
London BL 4823.bb.27.

V 11.   Vie de Jésus-Christ.

La vie de Jesuchrist. — Lyon, Barnabé Chaussard, 1520?
8°: a-n⁸ o⁶?, goth.
*Geneva BPU Ba 508.
References: Baudrier XI.41.
Notes: The Geneva BPU copy is incomplete at the end.

V 12.   Vie de Jésus-Christ.

La Vie de Jesus Christ avec sa Mort et sa Passion. La Sentence donnee par Pilate a l'encontre de Jesus Christ. La vie de Judas Scarioth. Le Trespassement de la glorieuse vierge Marie. La vengeance et

destruction de Hierusalem. — Poitiers, Jean et Enguilbert de Marnef, 1530?
References: *Index aurel.*

V 13.   Vie de Jésus-Christ.

La vie de Jesuchrist, La mort et passion de Jesuchrist ... le trespassement de nostre dame ... La destruction de Hierusalem et Vengeance de nostre saulveur. — Lyon, Jean Cantarel, 1551.

8°: A-N⁸, goth. N 8r: Impr. à Lyon par Jehan Canterel en la mayson de feu Barnabe Chaussard. 07.04.1551.
*Paris BEBA Masson 731 (-all before B8).

Notes: The title is reconstructed from the various sections of the text. It is a romanced narrative of the life and death of Christ, based at least in part on apocryphal Gospels. 'La mort et passion de Jesuchrist' begins (E 8v) by saying that the narrative 'fut composé par les bons et expers maistres Gamaliel, Nycodemus, et Joseph dabarimathie disciples secretz de Jesuchrist, lesquelz en ont traicté bien au long: car ilz estoyent tousjours presens mieulx que les evangelistes'.

V 14.   Vie de s. Albin.

Cy ensuyt la vie de Monseigneur Sainct Albain roy de hongrie et martyr. — Paris, Pierre Ratoire, Pierre Sergent, 1530?

4°: A-E⁴, goth. E 4r: Impr. à Paris par Pierre Ratoyre pr. Pierre Sergent.
*Paris BN Rothschild IV.6.54.
References: Rothschild #3098.

V 14a.   Vie de s. André.

Sensuyt la vie Et mistere de Saint Andry Nouvellement composee et Imprimee. — Paris, Pierre Sergent, 1533?

4°: A-O⁴ P⁶, goth. P 6v: Impr. à Paris pour Pierre sergent, ens. sainct Nicolas.
*Paris BN Rés. Yf 121.
Notes: Play in verse, with 86 characters.

V 15.   Vie de s. Barbe.

La vie et lystore de ma dame saincte barbe par personnages, avec plusieurs des miracles dicelle. Et si est a xxxviii. personnages. dont les noms sensuyvent. — Rouen, Jean Burges, 1530?

4°: [28] ff., A⁶ B-C⁴ D⁶ E-F⁴, goth. F 4v: Impr. pr. Jehan burges le jeune, Rouen.
*Paris BN Rothschild IV.6.78.
References: Rothschild #3012.
Notes: The colophon states the work has been 'corrigee a la verite du texte de la vie contenue en la legende doree'.

V 16.   Vie de s. Barbe.

La vie ma Dame saincte Barbe par personnaiges. Avec plusieurs des miracles dicelle. Et est a trente et huict personnaiges: dont les noms sensuyvent. — Paris, Jean Saint Denys, pr. Pierre Sergent, 1531?
4°: [28] ff., A⁴ B⁸ C-F⁴, goth. F 4v: Impr. à Paris pr. Pierre sergent.
*Paris BN Rothschild IV.4.178.
References: Rothschild #1078.
Notes: The colophon, F 4v, is followed by the mark of Jean Saint Denys, who died in Dec. 1531.

V 17.   Vie de s. Catherine.

Cy commence la vie de ma dame saincte katherine de seine vierge de lordre sainct dominique. Et plusieurs miracles faitz a son intercession et requeste avec plusieurs approbacions de nostre seigneur. — Lyon, Pierre Mareschal, 1520.
4°: A-D⁸ E⁴ F⁶, goth. F 6v: Impr. à Lyon par Pierre Marechal. 15.01.1519.
*Paris BN Rothschild II.4.13.
References: Rothschild #2025.
Notes: The Rothschild catalogue indicates 'in-fol', but it is a large quarto.

V 17a.   Vie de s. Catherine.

La vie saincte Katherine de Seine. — Lyon, Vve Barnabé Chaussard, 1532.
4°: [76] ff., A-T⁴, goth.
Chantilly Condé III.F.87.
References: Baudrier XI.49-50.

V 17b.   Vie de s. Christophe.

Sensuit le mistere du Tresglorieux martir Monsieur sainct christofle Par personnages. — Paris, Vve Jean Trepperel, Jean Jehannot, 1518?

4°: [20] ff., A⁸ B-D⁴, goth. D 4r: Impr. à Paris par la veufve feu Jehan trepperel Jehan Jehonnot.
*Paris BN Rés. Yf 1606.
Notes: Play in verse, with 34 characters.

V 17c. Vie de s. Christophe.

Sensuyt le Mystere du tresglorieux Martyr Monsieur sainct Christofle Par personnaiges. — Paris, Pierre Sergent, 1533?
4°: [20] ff., A⁸ B-D⁴, goth..
*Paris BN Rés. Yf 123 (-A 3-6, D 1-4).
Notes: The address is 'rue neufve nostre dame, ens. s. Nicolas.' Line-for-line copy of the 1518 ed., hence the suggested collation despite the incompleteness of the only known copy.

V 17d. Vie de s. Jean Baptiste.

La vie sainct Jehan baptiste. — [Troyes], [Jean Le Coq], 1527?
8°: 4 ff., goth.
Notes: Narration of the life of St John Baptist in verse; re-edition of a 15th-century publication. Information from Stuttgarter Antiquariat catalogue 164 (1996) #81, on an apparently unique copy.

V 18. Vie de s. Laurens.

Sensuyt la vie de monseigneur sainct Laurens par personnaiges. Avec le martire de sainct ypolite. — Paris, Alain Lotrian, Denis Janot, 1534?
4°: A-Q⁴ R⁶, goth. R 6r: Impr. à Paris par Alain lotrian et Denys janot.
*Paris BN Rés. Yf 122.
References: Moreau IV #1168.
Notes: The colophon describes the work as the 'mistere de Mgr sainct Laurens'.

V 19. Vie de s. Marguerite.

La vie ma dame saincte Marguerite vierge et martire. Avec son oraison. — Paris, Alain Lotrian, Denis Janot, 1532?
8°: A⁸ B⁴, goth. B 4r: Impr. à Paris par Alain Lotrian et Denis Janot, ens. escu de France.
*Chantilly Condé IV. D. 77.

References: Moreau IV #547.
Notes: Life of St Marguerite in octosyllabics.

V 20.   Vie de s. Marguerite.

La Vie et Passion de Ma Dame saincte Marguerite Vierge et Martyre. — Troyes, Jean Le Coq II, 1541?
8°: A⁸ B⁴, goth. B 4v: Impr. à Troyes chez Jean Lecoq.
*Paris BEBA Masson 1136(2). Paris BN Rothschild IV.3.109.
References: Rothschild #593.
Notes: Jean Le Coq II was active 1541-89.

V 21.   Vie de s. Nicolas.

La vie de sainct Nicolas. — Lyon, Barnabé Chaussard, 1520?
8°: [8] ff., A⁸, goth. A 8r: Impr. à Lyon par Barnabe chaussard.
*Paris BN Rothschild VI.3(bis).39(2).
References: Rothschild #2542.
Notes: Extract in prose from the *Legende dorée*.

V 22.   Viexmont, Claude de.

Le Pain de vie, pour les filz de Dieu, Demonstrant la verité du corps de nostre seigneur Jesus Christ, au venerable sacrement de l'autel: et la foy que l'hom y doibt havoir: Avec la maniere comment les fils de Dieu en peuvent deuëment manger: et quel fruict spirituel ils en remportent. — Paris, Regnault and Claude Chaudiere, 1548.
16°: a-n⁸, rom.
*Paris BN Rés. 8° Z Don 594(375.1).
Notes: On the t.p. Claude de Viexmont is described as a 'religieux des Filles Dieu..., de l'ordre de Fontevrauld'.

V 23.   Vif sacrifice.

Un Vif Sacrifice Quotidian, une saincte enflambée oraison, un doulx sacrifice. — Antwerp?, Vve Martin Lempereur?, 1540?
16°: A-B + §⁸, goth.
*Cambridge UL CCC.2.3.
References: NK #4529. Adams T 428.
Notes: Bound in Cambridge UL with the *Testamentz des douze patriarches*, but the printing material is not the same. Contains some elements of the *Introduction pour les enfans*.

V 24.   Vincent, Saint, de Léris.

Verité de la foi catholique. — Paris, Michel de Vascosan, 1541.
Coutances.
References: Renouard MSS.

V 25.   Viret, Pierre.

Admonition et consolation aux fideles, qui deliberent de sortir d'entre les Papistes, pour eviter idolatrie, contre les tentations qui leur peuvent advenir, et les dangiers ausquelz ilz peuvent tomber, en leur yssue. — [Geneva], [Jean Girard], 1547.
8°: A-G^8, rom.
*Lausanne BCU AZ 4217. *London BL 3901.a.47. *Paris SHP A 493 and 15858(3). *Munich BSB Asc 4945(2). *Vienna ÖNB 79.W.41.
References: *BG* 47/10. Barnaud #10. *Index* I #353.

V 26.   Viret, Pierre.

De la communication des fideles qui cognoissent la verité de l'Evangile, aux ceremonies des Papistes, et principalement à leurs Baptesmes, Mariages, Messes, Funerailles, et Obseques pour les trespassez. — [Geneva], [Jean Girard], 1547.
8°: A-N^8, rom.
*Geneva BPU Bd 1467. *Lausanne BCU AA 199 and AZ 4217. *Paris SHP A 494. *Wolfenbüttel HAB 1241.52 Theol(2). *Vienna ÖNB 79.W.43.
References: Barnaud #9. *BG* 47/11.

V 27.   [Viret, Pierre].

De la difference qui est entre les superstitions et idolatries des anciens gentilz et payens, et les erreurs et abuz qui sont entre ceux qui s'appellent Chrestiens: et de la vraye maniere d'honnorer Dieu, la Vierge Marie, et les Sainctz. — [Geneva], [Jean Girard], 1542.
8°: A-Z AA-FF^8, rom.
*Zurich ZB D 356.
References: *BG* 42/22. *Index* I #436.
Notes: First important work by Viret. He subsequently developed the text into several different treatises: see S. E. Mason, *BHR* 1988.

V 28.   Viret, Pierre.

*De la source et de la difference et convenance de la
vieille et nouvelle idolatrie, et des vrayes et fausses
images et reliques, et du seul et vray Mediateur.* —
Geneva, Jean Girard, 1551.
8°: a-p^8 q^4, rom.
*Cambridge Emma. MSS.4.4.12(1). Lausanne BCU AZ 4278.
*London BL 3901.a.48 (t.p. dated '1548'). *Paris SHP A 497.
*Zurich ZB III.N.156.
References: Barnaud #13. CDM p. 18.
Notes: The t.p. of the London BL copy has been restored with
an erroneous date. An important preface in which Viret lists
all his publications up to 1551.

V 29.   Viret, Pierre.

*Du Devoir et du besoing qu'ont les hommes à
s'enquerir de la volonté de Dieu par sa Parolle, et
de l'attente et finale resolution du vray concile.* —
[Geneva], [Jean Girard], 1551.
8°: A-B^8 C^2 a-n^8, rom.
*Geneva BPU Bc 658. Paris BM. Wolfenbüttel HAB 1204.7 Theol.
*Aix Méj. Rés. S. 62 (fragment).
References: Barnaud #14. CDM p. 18.
Notes: Viret dedicates his work to the 'Nobles et bourgeois
d'Orbe', dated from Lausanne, 11 May 1551 (C 1r). The Aix
copy contains only fols. A 1,8, B 1-8, C 1-2, a-b 1-8.

V 30.   Viret, Pierre.

*Dialogues du desordre qui est a present au monde, et
des causes d'iceluy, et du moyen pour y remedier:
desquelz l'ordre et le tiltre sensuyt. 1 Le monde à
l'empire. 2 L'homme difformé. 3 La metamorphose.
4 La Reformation.* — Geneva, [Jean Girard], 1545.
8°: a-z A-Z aa-rr^8 ss^2, rom.
*Geneva BPU Rés. Bc 3411. Paris BA 8° T 9506. *Paris SHP A
492. *Wolfenbüttel HAB 1166 Th. *Vienna ÖNB 71.Z.82 (+).
References: Barnaud #7. *BG* 45/28. *Index* I #349.

V 31.   Viret, Pierre, pref. by Jean Calvin.

*Disputations chrestiennes en maniere de deviz,
divisées par dialogues.* — Geneva, Jean Girard, 1544.
8°: π^8 a-z^8 A^{10}, rom.

Geneva BPU Rés. Bc 850. *London BL 3901.b.38. *Paris SHP A 491. *Wrocław BU 331646. *Zurich ZB D 215 (s.l.n.d.) (+).

References: Barnaud #6. *BG* 44/34. *Index* I #346. Cat. Drilhon #25.

Notes: π 2r: note from the printer: 'j'ay esté adverty par plusieurs, que ceux qui se delectoyent à lire ces livres Chrestiens que nous imprimons, prenoyent plus grand plaisir de les avoir de nous, par petis traictés et volumes, que grans et mal-portatifz.' He has therefore divided the *Disputations* into three volumes.

V 32.   Viret, Pierre.

La seconde partie des Disputati... [Geneva], [Jean Girard], 1544.

8°: a-q⁸ r⁴ s¹⁰, rom.

Geneva BPU Rés. Bc 850. Paris BSG... A 491(2). *Wrocław BU 331646. *Neu...

References: *Index* I #347. Cat. Drilh...

V 33.   Viret, Pierre.

La troisiesme partie des Disputations Chrestiennes. — [Geneva], [Jean Girard], 1544.

8°: a-t⁸, rom.

Geneva BPU Rés. Bc 850. *Neuchâtel BV ZQ 619. Paris BSG Rés. D 8° 7047. *Wrocław BU 331646. *Zurich ZB D 215 (+).

References: *BG* 44/36. *Index* I #348. Cat. Drilhon #30.

V 34.   [Viret, Pierre].

Epistre consolatoire, envoyée aux fideles qui souffrent persecution pour le Nom de Jesus et Verité evangelique. — [Geneva], [Jean Girard], 1541.

8°: a-b⁸, rom.

*Lausanne BCU AZ 4207.

References: Barnaud #1. *BG* 41/15.

V 35.   Viret, Pierre.

Epistre envoyee aux fideles conversans entre les Chrestiens Papistiques, pour leur remonstrer comment ilz se doyvent garder d'estres souillez et polluz par leurs superstitions et idolatries et de deshonnorer Jesus Christ par icelles. — [Geneva], [Jean Girard], 1543.

8°: A-I⁸, rom.
*Lausanne BCU IU 451 and AZ 4207. *Paris SHP A 490. *Vienna ÖNB 80.W.98. *Zurich ZB XVIII.2002.5.
References: Barnaud #2. *BG* 43/34. *Index* I #409.
Notes: Viret recognizes (A 2r) that he is going over the ground of Calvin's *Petit Traité monstrant...*, but his text was already written before the other treatise was printed.

V 36.   Viret, Pierre.

Epistre envoyee aux fideles qui conversent entre les Papistes, pour leur remonstrer comment ilz se doyvent garder d'estre souillez et polluz par les superstitions et idolatries d'iceux et de deshonnorer Jesus Christ par icelles. Reveuë et augmentée. — [Geneva], [Jean Girard], 1547.
8°: A-K⁸, rom.
*Lausanne BCU AA 199 and AZ 4217. *Wolfenbüttel HAB 1241.52 Theol (1). *Vienna ÖNB 36.M.46. Aix Méj. Rés. S. 85.
References: Barnaud #2b. *BG* 47/12. *Index* I #354.
Notes: Revised ed. of the 1543 *Epistre envoyée...* Viret published at the same time his *Admonition et consolation, De la communication des fideles...*, and his *Remonstrances aux fideles...*, all dealing with the question of 'nicodemism'.

=>   Viret, Pierre: see Calvin, *Deux Epistres.*

V 37.   Viret, Pierre.

Exposition familiere de l'Oraison de nostre Seigneur Jesus Christ, et des choses dignes de consyderer sur icelle, faite en forme de dialogue. — Geneva, Jean Girard, 1548.
8°: 615 pp., a-z A-P⁸ Q⁴, rom.
*Geneva BPU Rés. Bc 3412. *Paris BN D² 12104. *Paris BA 8° T 9507. *Munich BSB Catech 641(1). Lausanne BCU AZ 2667 (+).
References: Barnaud #12. *BG* 48/18. *Index* I #351.
Notes: a 2r: Viret dedicated his work to the 'Burgmeister et Conseil de Lausanne', dated (a 7r) 22 Aug. 1547. He had not yet composed his exposition of the Ten Commandments.

V 38.   Viret, Pierre.

Exposition familiere de l'oraison de nostre Seigneur Jesus Christ, et des choses dignes de consyderer sur icelle, faite en forme de Dialogue. — Geneva, Jean Girard, 1551.

8°: 316 ff., A-Z Aa-Qq⁸ Rr⁴, rom.

*Geneva BPU Bc 3446 (- A 2, 7). *Paris SHP A 498 and 15845. Vienna ÖNB 80.V.93.

References: Barnaud # 12b. CDM p. 18. *Index* I #356.

V 39.   Viret, Pierre.

Exposition familiere sur le Symbole des Apostres, contenant les articles de la foy, et Religion chrestienne, faicte par dialogues. — Geneva, Jean Girard, 1544.

8°: a-o⁸ p⁴, rom.

Freiburg im Breisgau N 2911. *Lausanne BCU U 454 (- h 1-3).

References: Barnaud #3. *BG* 44/37.

Notes: a 2r: Viret to the faithful reader: 'Il y a trois ou quatre ans passez que par la solicitation d'aucuns bons personnages, j'avoye entreprins d'escrire quelque exposition bien familiere sur la Symbole des Apostres... et sur l'orayson de nostre Seigneur... et pareillement sur le decalogue... [Ce traité] a longtemps demouré entre mes papiers, à cause que j'attendoye que j'eusse le loisir de parachever le reste.'

V 40.   Viret, Pierre.

Exposition familiere faict par dialogues sur Le Symbole des Apostres, contenant les articles de la Foy, et de la Religion Chrestienne, Reveue et augmentée. — Geneva, Jean Girard, 1546.

8°: a-r⁸, rom.

*Zurich ZB D 216.

References: Barnaud #3. *BG* 46/11. *Index* I #350.

Notes: Second ed. of Viret's commentary on the Creed. According to *Index* I #350 there was a third ed. in 1550 by Jean Girard, but no copy of it is known.

V 41.   Viret, Pierre.

Exposition familiere sur les dix commandements de la loy, faicte en forme de dialogue. — 1549?

References: Barnaud #5.

Notes: In *De la source*, 1551, Viret lists his publications and mentions this treatise. No known copy. The title is given as in the 1554 ed. (Paris BA).

V 42.   Viret, Pierre.

*De la nature et diversité des voeuz, et des loix qui en
ont esté baillées de Dieu. Premiere partie.* — [Geneva],
[Jean Girard], 1551.
8°: 193 pp., a-m^8 n^4, rom.
Vienna ÖNB 80.H.90 (described from microfilm). *Aix Méj. 8° 8658.
References: Barnaud #15. CDM p. 18.
Notes: The 'Seconde Partie' begins on e 7r, with a running
title: 'Seconde partie des voeuz de Jacob et de David, et des
sacrifices pacifiques, et de la conference et difference d'iceux,
avec ceux des vrays fidelles et des idolatres'.

V 43.   Viret, Pierre.

*Remonstrances aux fideles, qui conversent entre les
Papistes: et principalement à ceux qui sont en court,
et qui ont offices publiques, touchant les moyens
qu'ilz doivent tenir en leur vocation, à l'exemple des
anciens serviteurs de Dieu, sans contrevenir à leur
devoir, ny envers Dieu, ny envers leur prochain: et
sans se mettre temerairement en dangier, et donner
par leur temerité et par leur coulpe, juste occasion à
leurs adversaires de les mal traitter.* — Geneva, Jean
Girard, 1547.
8°: A-Y^8, rom.
*Geneva BPU Rés. Bd 1466. *Neuchâtel BV Rés. C 35. *Vienna
ÖNB 79.H.48. *Wolfenbüttel HAB 1241.52 Theol(4).
References: Barnaud #8. *BG* 47/13. *Index* I #355.

V 44.   Viret, Pierre.

*Petit traicte de l'usage de la salutation angelique, et
de l'origine des chapeletz, et l'abuz d'iceux.* —
[Geneva], [Jean Girard], 1544.
8°: A-E^8 F^4, rom.
*Munich BSB Liturg. 1314. *Vienna ÖNB 39.Mm.86. *Zurich ZB
Gall XVIII.2002.1.
References: Barnaud #4. *BG* 44/38. *Index* I #501.
Notes: Violent condemnation of mariolatry.

V 45.   Viret, Pierre.

*Petit traicte de l'usage de la salutation angelique, et de
l'origine des chapeletz, et l'abuz d'iceux.* — [Geneva],
[Jean Girard], 1545.

8°: 76 pp.+ [2 ff.], A-E⁸, rom.
*London BL 3833.aaa.1. *Vienna ÖNB 17.G.60. *Aix Méj. Rés. S. 70.
References: *BG* 45/29.

V 46.   Viret, Pierre.

De la vertu, et usage du ministere de la parolle de Dieu, et des Sacremens, dependans d'icelle: et des differens qui sont en la chrestienté, à cause d'iceux. — [Geneva], [Jean Girard], 1548.

8°: a-c⁸ d⁴ a-z A-Z aa⁸ bb⁴, rom.
*Geneva BPU Bc 2415. *Paris BSG Rés. D 8°7044. *Vienna ÖNB 79.M.39. *Lausanne BCU U 455 (- a-c⁸ d⁴). *Zurich ZB D 170 (- a-c⁸ d⁴) (+).
References: Barnaud #11. *BG* 48/17. *Index* I #352.

V 47.   [Vitrier, Jean].

Lexposition sur le sermon que nostre seigneur fit en la montaigne contenant les huyt beatitudes. — Paris, François Regnault, 1511?

8°: A-K⁸ L⁴, goth. L 4r: Impr. à Paris pour Francoys regnault, ens. S. Claude.
*London BL 3832.aaa.20(1).
Notes: Massaut, 'Théologie universitaire': Josse Clichtove examined this text in 1515 and condemned certain propositions. The pagination which he gives corresponds to this ed. Attributed to Jean Vitrier by Massaut. Bound in London BL with a treatise by St Ambrose also printed by Fr. Regnault and dated 1511, hence the suggested date for this ed.

V 48.   [Vitrier, Jean].

Lexposition sur le sermon que nostre seigneur fist en la montaigne contenant viii beatitudes. — Paris, Pierre Vidoue, François Regnault et Jean de la Porte, 1518?

8°: A-L⁸, goth. L 8r: Impr. à Paris par Pierre Vidoue pour Fr. Regnault/Jehan de la Porte.
Séville Colombine. Coll privée.
Notes: Information kindly provided by D.J. Shaw.

V 49.   **[Vitrier, Jean].**

*Lexposition sur le sermon que nostre seigneur fist a
la montaigne contenant les viii beatitudes.* — Paris,
Nicolas Higman, Simon Vostre, 1520?
8°: A-H⁸, goth. H 8v: Impr. à Paris par Nycolas Hygman pour
Symon Vostre libr.
*Paris BN Rés. D 16040(3).

V 50.   **[Vitrier, Jean].**

*Le Sermon que nostre Seigneur feist en la montaigne
avecques L'exposition contenant les huit beatitudes.*
— Paris, Nicolas Gilles, Jean Foucher, Antoine
Bonnemere, 1540.
16°: A-K⁸, rom.
*Vienna ÖNB *38.K.181 (Gilles). *Paris BSG D 8° 6479 inv 8208 bis
Rés. (J.Foucher). Poitiers BU XVI.199(2) (Bonnemere).

V 51.   **[Vitrier, Jean].**

*Le Sermon que nostre Seigneur feist en la montaigne,
avec lexposition contenant les huyt beatitudes.* —
Paris, [Gilles Corrozet], 1540.
8°: A-K⁸, rom.
*Cambridge Emma. 321.6.3(2).
References: Adams O 228.
Notes: The Cambridge copy bound with the *Livre de vraye et
parfaicte oraison* signed by Corrozet, and printed with the
same characters.

V 52.   **[Vitrier, Jean].**

*Le Sermon que nostre Seigneur Jesuchrist feit en la
montaigne, avec lexposition contenant les huyt beatitudes.* — Paris, Vve Jean de Brie, 1541.
16°: a-k⁸, rom.
*Paris BN Rés. D² 35026.
References: Moore #201.
Notes: K 2v sqq: an extra text: 'aucuns extraictz tant du viel
que nouveau testament lesquelz monstrent et enseignent tous
fideles la confidence et esperance qu'ilz doibvent avoir en
Dieu'.

V 53.   [Vitrier, Jean].

*Le Sermon que nostre Seigneur feist en la montaigne,
avec Lexposition contenant les huyt beatitudes.* —
Paris, [Nicolas Buffet], [Jacques Regnault], [Antoine
Foucault], 1544.

8°: A-K⁸, rom.
*Geneva MHR D 3. *Paris SHP A 1211(2). *Troyes BM H.12.4705(2).
References: Moore #201.
Notes: The Paris and Troyes copies bound with the *Livre de
vraye et parfaicte oraison* printed by Buffet for Regnault and
Foucault, 1543. Same typographical material. See also [Luther
and Farel], *Livre de vraye et parfaicte oraison*, 1545.

V 54.   Vivès, Juan Luis, trans. Pierre de Changy.

*Institution de la femme Chrestienne. Tant en son
Enfance, que Mariage et Viduité. Aussi, de l'office
du Mary.* — Lyon, Sulpice Sabon, pr. Antoine
Constantin, 1541?

8°: 270 pp., a-r⁸, rom. r 7v: Impr. à Lyon, par Sulpice Sabon.
*Paris BN Rés. D 54643 (- r8).
Notes: a 3v: Pierre de Changy sends this translation to his
daughter: 'Car je trouvois indecent telz et si bons enseignemens pour Filles, Femmes et Vefves y contenus leur estre occultez
et mussez par tel et si hault Latin a elles non entendible.'

V 55.   Vivès, Juan Luis, trans. Pierre de Changy.

Livre de l'institution de la femme chrestienne. —
Paris, Jacques Kerver, 1542.

12°.
References: Dagens. Facs. reprod. 1891.

V 56.   Vivès, Juan Luis, trans. Pierre de Changy.

*L'institution de la femme chrestienne, Tant en son
Enfance, que Mariage, et Viduité. Avec l'office du
Mary.* — Lyon, Jean de Tournes, 1543.

16°: a-v⁸ x⁴, rom.
*Geneva BPU Rés. Se 6323.
References: Cartier *De Tournes* #15.

V 57.   **Vivès, Juan Luis,** trans. Pierre de Changy.

Livre tresbon plaisant et salutaire de Linstitution de la femme chrestienne, tant en son enfance, que mariage et viduite. Aussi de loffice du mary <> Auquel est adjoustee de nouveau une tresbriefve et fructueuse instruction de la vertu Dhumilite. Avec une epistre de sainct Bernard touchant le negoce et gouvernement dune maison. Le tout reveu et corrige. — Paris, Jacques Fezendat, Jacques Kerver, 1543.

8°: A-T^8 V^4, rom. V 3v: Impr. à Paris par Jaques Faezandat pour Jaques Kerver. 25.06.1543.
*Paris BN Rés. D 61286.
Notes: The priv., to Jacques Kerver, dated 7 Nov. 1541.

V 58.   **Vivès, Juan Luis,** trans. Pierre de Changy.

L'Institution de la femme chrestienne, tant en son enfance que mariage et viduité. Avec l'office du Mary. — Lyon, Jean de Tournes, 1545.
16°.
References: Cartier *De Tournes* #45 <sale cat.

V 59.   **Vivès, Juan Luis,** trans. Pierre de Changy.

L'institution de la femme chrestienne. Tant en son Enfance, que Mariaige, et Viduité. Avec l'office du Mary. — Paris, Denis Janot, Galliot Du Pré, 1545.
16°: a-y^8, rom.
London BL 08416.de.15. *Wolfenbüttel HAB 0.58 Helmst. 12°.
References: Rawles #225. Cat. Rosenthal 258 #96 notes a third copy.

V 60.   **Vivès, Juan Luis,** trans. Pierre de Changy.

Institution de la femme chrestienne. Tant en son enfance, que mariage, et viduité. Avec l'office du mary... Auquel a esté adjousté de nouveau une tresbriefve et fructueuse instruction de la vertu D'humilité. Ensemble l'epistre Sainct Bernard, touchant le negoce et gouvernement d'une maison. — Paris, Ponce Roffet, 1546.
16°: 384 pp., a-z &^{8}, rom. & 8v: Impr. à Paris. 1546.
Besançon BM 229 409.
References: Renouard MSS.

Notes: My thanks to Mme H. Richard of the Bibliothèques municipales de Besançon for the details above.

V 61. **Vivès, Juan Luis,** trans. Pierre de Changy.

L'Institution de la femme chrestienne, tant en son enfance que mariage et viduité. Avec l'office du mary. — Lyon, Jean de Tournes, 1547.
16°.
References: Cartier *De Tournes* #106.

V 62. **Vivès, Juan Luis,** trans. Pierre de Changy.

Institution de la femme chrestienne. — Paris, Guillaume Le Bret, 1548.
16°.
References: Renouard MSS.

V 63. **Vivès, Juan Luis,** trans. Pierre de Changy.

L'institution de la femme chrestienne, Tant en son Enfance, que Mariage, et Viduité. Avec loffice du mary. — Lyon, Jean de Tournes, 1549.
16°: a-t⁸ v⁶, rom.
*Paris SHP A 1210(1). Aix Méj. 16° 343.

V 64. **Vivès, Juan Luis,** trans. Pierre de Changy.

L'Institution de la femme chrestienne. — Paris, 1549.
8°.
References: Renouard MSS < Brunet.

V 65. **Vivès, Juan Luis,** trans. Jean Colin.

Introduction à la vraye sapience. — Paris, Langelier, 1548.
8°.
References: Renouard MSS < Du Verdier, Brunet.

V 66. **Voie de Paradis.**

La voye de paradis. — Paris, [Julien Hubert], Jean Saint Denys, 1529?
8°: 4 ff., A⁴, goth. A 4v: Impr. à Paris pr. Jehan sainct denys.
*Paris BN Rés. pYe 330.
References: Moreau III #1952.

Notes: Poem in octosyllabics on good morals, the Virgin Mary and the saints: 'Pitye avoir, paix et concorde,/ Charité et misericorde,/ Ce sont les traictz et la voye/ Qui l'homme en paradis envoye.' The text featured in Jean Bouchet, *Regnars traversant*, 1504, 1522... (Moreau).

V 67.   Voie de Paradis.

La Voye de Paradis. — Paris, [Alain Lotrian], 1530?
8°: A⁴, goth. A 4r: Impr. à Paris.
*Paris BA Rés. 8° BL 12077(2).
References: Moreau III #1112.

=>   *Voies spirituelles*: see *Quatre voies*.

V 68.   Volcyr de Sérouville, Nicolas, sermon by fr. Jean Glapion du Maine.

Collectaneorum Libellus. Le petit Recueil du Poligraphe instructif: et moral: faict en latin et françoys sur les elementz des lettres: commandemens de la loy: oraison dominicale: et sermon des cendres. — [Paris], [Didier Maheu], 1523?
4°: A-L⁴, goth.
*Paris BN Rés. D 67938.
References: Moreau III #587.
Notes: A series of letters to François marquis de Pont-à-Mousson, all dated March-April 1523. The preface (A 2r) to the son of Francis I dated 20 July 1523. Priv. (K 4r) dated 2 August 1523. A note dated 4 Sept. 1523 on I 2r underlines the anti-Lutheran intention of the entire text.

V 69.   Volcyr de Sérouville, Nicolas.

Lhistoire et Recueil de la triumphante et glorieuse victoire obtenue contre les seduyctz et abusez Lutheriens mescreans du pays Daulsays et autres, par treshault et trespuissant prince et seigneur Anthoine par la grace de Dieu duc de Calabre, de Lorraine et de Bar. etc. en deffendant la foy catholicque, nostre mere leglise, et vraye noblesse. — [Paris], [Antoine Couteau], [Galliot Du Pré, Didier Maheu], 1526?
2°: §⁶ ã⁴ A-P⁶ Q⁸, goth.
Harvard CL. Paris BN Rés. Fol. Lk² 960. Paris BA. *Paris BSG H Fol 413 inv 467 rés. Strasbourg BNU R 10656.

References: Moore #207. Mortimer #553. Moreau III #1114.
Notes: The priv. is dated (§ 1v) 12 Jan. 1526 (a.s.). Celebration of the victory of Antoine duc de Lorraine over the peasants of Saverne in May 1525.

V 70.   **Volcyr de Sérouville, Nicolas.**

Traicté nouveau de la desecration et execution actuelle de Jehan Castellan heretique faicte à Vic en Austrasie le XI janvier, avec une oraison de la foi. — 1534.

References: Moore p. 249.
Notes: Moore dates the publication to 1525. But the Paris Theology Faculty discussed the work on 12 September 1534, and the execution of Castellan seems to date from that year. See J.K. Farge, *Registre des conclusions* II, p. 28, n. 49.

V 71.   **Voragine, Jacques de,** trans. Jean de Vignay.

La legende doree et vie des Saincts et Sainctes. — Paris, Jean de La Roche, 1513.
2°: 255 + [1] ff., A-Z & § a-g⁸, goth. g 7r: Impr. à Paris par Jehan de la roche. 03.08.1513.
*London BL 4826.f.2.
References: Moreau II #631.
Notes: Prologue by Jean de Vignay, A 1v. The text begins A 2r.

V 72.   **Voragine, Jacques de,** trans. Jean de Vignay.

La Legende doree. — Paris, Nicolas de La Barre, Hémon Le Fèvre, 1516.
4°.
References: Moreau II #1405. Sales Piat, Nourry.

V 73.   **Voragine, Jacques de,** trans. Jean de Vignay.

La legende doree et vie des Sainctz et Sainctes. — Paris, [Bernard Aubry], Michel Lesclencher, Pierre Viart, 1521.
2°: 255 + [1] ff., A-V x-z & 9 AA-GG⁸.
*Paris BN Rés. H 1111.
References: Moreau III #145.

V 74.   **Voragine, Jacques de,** trans. Jean de Vignay.

La grant et vraye Legende doree. et la vie des sainctz et Sainctes de paradis... corrigee des erreurs et choses apochrifes... Et y sont adjoustees plusieurs nouvelles Legendes. — Paris, [J. Cornillau], Jean Petit, 1526.

2°: 255+[1] ff., A-Z & § AA-GG⁸, goth. GG 8r: Impr. à Paris. 15.10.1526.

*London BL 4805.h.29. Edinburgh NLS. Paris BU.

References: Moreau III #1037.

Notes: The printer identified by Moreau. T.p. gives the date 12.10.1526.

V 75.   **Voragine, Jacques de,** trans. Jean de Vignay.

La grant et vraye Legende doree: et la vie des sainctz et des sainctes de Paradis... corrigee des erreurs et choses apocrifes... y sont adjoustees plusieurs nouvelles Legendes. — Lyon, Jean Lambany, 1529.

4°: 324 ff. Fol. 324 r: Impr. a Lyon par Jehan Lambany. 08.07.1529.
Besançon. Dôle.

References: Baudrier XI.46-48.

V 76.   **Voragine, Jacques de,** trans. Jean de Vignay.

La Legende Doree et vie des Sainctz et Sainctes, qui Jesuchrist aymerent de pensees non fainctes... Avec la Legende des nouveaulx sainctz additionnez. — Paris, Nicolas Couteau, [Guillaume Le Bret], 1540.

2°: [4]+232 ff., *⁴ A-X AA-RR⁶ SS⁴, goth. SS 4r: Impr. à Paris par Nicolas couteau. 28.08.1540.

*London BL 204.e.13.

Notes: Guillaume Le Bret identified by the address 'au clos Bruneau à l'enseigne de la corne de Cerf' on the t.p.

X

X 1.   **Ximenis, Francesc.**

Le livre des sainctz anges. — Paris, Michel Le Noir, 1518.

4°: A-Z & § AA⁶, goth. AA 5v: Impr. à Paris par Michel le noir. 05.01.1518.

*Aix Méj. Rés. O. 37. *Paris BM Rés. 35867. *London BL C.107.d.16.
*Paris BN Rés. D 80006.

References: Moreau II #1966.

Notes: Translation of the *Libre dels angels* by the Franciscan
and Bishop of Elne Francesc Ximenis. There was already an
ed. of the French translation in 1478 (Geneva, A. Steinschaber),
and other eds in Lyon and Paris in 1486 and 1505. The text
contains five treatises on the nature of angels, their ranking,
their service, their victory, and their 'honnorable president
monseigneur sainct Michel'. The text is dated (AA 5v) 1392.

Z

Z 1.   **Zwingli, Ulrich.**

*Brieve et claire exposition de la Foy Chrestienne <>
escripte Au Roy Chrestien.* — [Geneva], [Jean Michel],
1539.

8°: A-H⁸, goth.
*Bruxelles BR LP VH 2021(1). *Geneva BPU Rés. Bc 3333. La
Rochelle BM 8887C (variant t.p.). Grenoble BM F 15739 Rés.

References: Berthoud 'Michel' #8. *BG* 39/16. *Index* I #360.

Notes: Translation of *Christianae fidei a Huldricho Zwinglio
praedicatae brevis et clara expositio...*, published in Latin in
1536. The La Rochelle copy has variants on the t.p., and the date
'1540' on fol. H 8v. It could be a second ed.

2 Finding List of Anonymous Titles

Les Actes de la journee imperiale, tenue en la cité de Regespourg: see Calvin, Jean.

Advertissement sur la censure qu'ont faicte les Bestes de Sorbonne: see Calvin, Jean.

Articles veritables sur les horribles, grandz et importables abuz de la Messe papalle: see Marcourt, Antoine.

Les Articles de la sacree Faculté de Theologie de Paris. Avec le Remede contre la Poison: see Calvin, Jean.

Du Benefice de Jesuchrist crucifié: see Benedetto da Mantova.

La Bergerie du bon pasteur: see Marot, Clément?

Le Bouclier de la foy, en forme de Dialogue: see Grenier, Nicole.

La Bulle de l'indiction du Concile: see Vergerio, Pietro Paulo.

De La Tressaincte Cene de nostre Seigneur Jesus: see Farel, Guillaume?

Chanson nouvelle. Composee sus les dix commandemens: see Saulnier, Antoine.

D'un nouveau chef qui au temps des empereurs s'esleva à Rome: see Sleidan, Jean.

Confession de la Foy ... de Geneve: see Farel, Guillaume.

Confession vrayement chrestienne: see Textor, Benoist.

Le Conseil de trois Evesques: see Vergerio, Pietro Paulo.

La consolation des desolez: see Aumen, Gervais.

Consolation chrestienne: see Luther, Martin.

Consolation en adversité: see Luther, Martin.

Declamation contenant la maniere de bien instruire les enfans: see Erasme, Desiderius.

La declaration De la Foy chrestienne, faicte par ung bachelier en theologie: see Landry, François.

Declaration d'aucuns motz desquelz use souvent sainct Pol: see Luther, Martin.

Declaration de la Messe: see Marcourt, Antoine.

Declaration de la reigle et estat des Cordeliers: see Menard, Jean.

La Declaracion du jubilè qui doit etre a Rome l'an M.D.L.: see Vergerio, Pietro Paulo.

Le Dialogue de consolation entre lame et raison: see Le Roy, François.

De la difference qui est entre les superstitions et idolatries: see Viret, Pierre.

La Doctrine Nouvelle et Ancienne: see Rhegius, Urbanus.

Enchyridion ou Manuel contenant plusieurs matieres traictees es livres de Lancien Testament: see Branteghem, Guillaume de.

Epistre chrestienne: see Farel, Guillaume?

Epistre Chrestienne, aux Freres Mineurs, de lordre de S. Françoys: see Menard, Jean.

Epistre Chrestienne tresutile a ceulx qui commencent lire la saincte escripture: see Farel, Guillaume?

Epistre consolatoire, envoyée aux fideles qui souffrent persecution: see Viret, Pierre.

Epistres et Evangiles pour les cinquante et deux sepmaines de lan: see Lefèvre d'Étaples, Jacques.

Escript adresse aux Electeurs Princes ... Dung chef nouveau: see Sleidan, Jean.

Excuse de noble seigneur Jaques de Bourgoigne: see Calvin, Jean.

Un Exemple notable et digne de memoire d'un homme desesperé: see Scrimgeour, Henry.

Familiere et briefve exposition sur l'apocalypse De Sainct Jehan: see Du Pinet, Antoine.

Exposition sur l'Apocalypse de Sainct Jehan l'Apostre: see Du Pinet, Antoine.

Exposition sur le cantique virginal, Magnificat: see Luther, Martin.

Exposition chrestienne Dés dix commandemens: see Megander, Gaspard.

Exposition des dix commandemens du Seigneur: see Calvin, Jean.

Exposition sur les dix commandemens de la loy: see Luther, Martin.

Exposition sur les deux epistres de Sainct Paul, envoiées aux Thessaloniciens: see Bullinger, Heinrich.

Exposition sur les deux Epistres de S. Pierre, et sur celle de S. Jude: see Luther, Martin.

Exposition sur la premiere Epistre de S. Jehan Apostre: see Oecolampadius, Johann.

Exposition de Levangile de nostre seigneur Jesus Christ, selon S. Matthieu: see Bucer, Martin.

Exposition de l'histoire des dix Lepreux, prinse du dixseptiesme de Sainct Luc: see Luther, Martin.

Une exposition sur le Magnificat: see Luther, Martin.

Devote exposition sur le cinquantiesme pseaulme: see Gaigny, Jean de.

Lexposition sur le sermon que nostre seigneur fit en la montaigne: see Vitrier, Jean.

Les faictz de Jesus Christ et du Pape: see Luther, Martin.

Des Faitz et gestes du Pape Jules III: see Vergerio, Pietro Paulo.

Des faicts et gestes du Roy Françoys: see Dolet, Estienne.

La farce des theologastres: see Berquin, Louis de?

La Fleur des Commandementz, et declaration des Bonnes Oeuvres: see Luther, Martin.

Les fleurs et manieres des temps passez et des faitz merveilleux de dieu: see Rolewinck, Werner.

La Forme des prieres et chantz ecclesiastiques: see Calvin, Jean.

Gargantua: see Rabelais, François.

La Guerre et deslivrance de la ville de Geneve: see Dentière, Marie.

Histoire veritable et digne de memoire de quatre Jacopins de Berne: see Stumpf, Jean.

Histoire d'un meurtre execrable: see Calvin, Jean.

Hystoire evangelique des quatre evangelistes en ung: see Nachtigall, Ottomarus.

Instruction et confession de Foy, dont on use en Leglise de Geneve: see Calvin, Jean.

Linstruction des enfans, contenant la maniere de prononcer et escrire en françoys: see Olivétan, Pierre Robert.

Breve Instruction pour deuement lire lescripture saincte: see Luther, Martin.

Instruction observée par la ville, baillage et pais de Berne: see Megander, Gaspard.

Quatre instructions fideles pour les simples, et les rudes: see Luther, Martin.

Le jardin amoureux de lame devote: see Bougain, Michel.

Le Jardin de paradis: see Bougain, Michel.

Letres certaines daucuns grandz troubles et tumultes advenuz a Geneve, avec la disputation faicte lan 1534: see Farel, Guillaume.

Le cinquesme livre des faictz et dictz du noble Pantagruel: see Rabelais, François: pseudonym.

Le livre des marchans: see Marcourt, Antoine.

Le livre faisant mention des sept parolles que nostre benoist saulveur .. dit en larbre de la croix: see Gaigny, Jean de.

Le livre de vraye et parfaicte oraison: see Luther, Martin.

Le livre de la toute belle sans pair qui est la vierge Marie: see Henry, Jean.

Livre tresutile de la vraye et parfaite subjection des chrestiens: see Luther, Martin.

Mandat et advertissement a ses Ecclesiastiques de recepvoir la parolle de Dieu: see Osiander, Andreas.

La Maniere de lire levangile et quel profit on en doibt attendre: see Luther, Martin.

La Maniere de mediter et penser a la passion de nostre sauveur Jesuchrist: see Luther, Martin.

La maniere et fasson quon tient en baillant le sainct baptesme: see Farel, Guillaume.

La Manyere de faire prieres aux eglises Françoyses: see Calvin, Jean.

La Medecine de l'ame: see Rhegius, Urbanus.

Dung seul mediateur entre dieu et les hommes: see Heyden, Sebald.

Le miroir de lame pecheresse: see Marguerite de Navarre.

Lardant miroir de grace: see Le Moyne, Pasquier.

Les quatorze miroirs pour consoler la creature en Dieu: see Luther, Martin.

Moralite de la maladie de Chrestiente: see Malingre, Matthieu.

Noelz nouveaulx: see Malingre, Matthieu.

Des bonnes oeuvres sus les commandemens de Dieu: see Luther, Martin.

Oraison Chrestienne au Seigneur Dieu: see Poullain, Valérand.

Loraison de Jesuchrist, qui est le Pater noster, et le Credo: see Farel, Guillaume.

La tressainte oraison que Jesus Christ a baillé à ses Apostres: see Farel, Guillaume.

Les Oraisons de la Bible: see Brunfels, Otto.

L'Ordre et maniere d'enseigner en la ville de Genéve: see Saulnier, Antoine.

Lordre et maniere quon tient en administrant les sainctz sacremens: see Farel, Guillaume.

Pantagruel: see Rabelais, François.

Paraphrase sur les Heures de nostre Dame: see Cailleau, Gilles.

Le Pater noster, et le Credo en francoys: see Farel, Guillaume.

Les Prieres et oraisons de la Bible: see Brunfels, Otto.

Prophetie de Iesaie de lenfant nouveau ne Jesuchrist: see Luther, Martin.

Brief racueil des oeuvres des dix commandemens: see Luther, Martin.

La Responce donnee par les princes d'Allemaigne: see Melanchthon, Philippe.

Sermon au jour de l'ascension: see Luther, Martin.

Ung sermon de mammone iniquitatis: see Luther, Martin.

Sermon de la maniere de prier Dieu: see Luther, Martin.

Le Sermon que nostre Seigneur feist en la montaigne: see Vitrier, Jean.

Summaire, et brieve declaration: see Farel, Guillaume.

Supplication et remonstrance, sur le faict de la Chrestienté: see Calvin, Jean.

La Tapisserie de l'église chrestienne et catholique: see Corrozet, Gilles.

Le Temporiseur: see Musculus, Wolfgang.

Petit traicte tres utile, et salutaire de la saincte eucharistie: see Marcourt, Antoine.

Le traicte de lutilite et honneste de mariage: see Dumolin, Guillaume.

La vie de nostre Seigneur, selon les quattres Evangelistes: see Branteghem,
    Guillaume de.
Les Visions de Pasquille: see Curione, Celio Secondo.
Vocabulaire du pseautier exposé en François: see Lefèvre d'Étaples, Jacques.

3 Chronological List

1511

Ambroise, Saint: *Le traicte <> du bien de la mort* .... A 6

Béda, Noël: *La doctrine et instruction necessaire aux crestiens et crestiennes* .... B 7

Bernard, Saint (pseud.): *Le traitie ... contenant la maniere de vivre en la religion chrestienne* .... B 21

Desmoulins, Laurent: *Le cymetiere des Malheureux* .... D 21

Guillaume d'Auvergne: *Traite touchant la doctrine et enseignement de prier Dieu* .... G 61

Jérôme, Saint: *Les Epistres* .... J 2

Lemaire de Belges, Jean: *Le traictie ... de la difference des scismes* .... L 28

Lemaire de Belges, Jean: *Le traictie ... de la difference des scismes* .... L 29

Le premier (-Second) volume des exposicions des Epistres et Evangilles de Karesme .... P 25

Le Tiers volume des exposicions des Epistres et Evangiles de Toute lannee .... P 26

Le Psaultier nostre dame .... P 50

Vitrier, Jean: *Lexposition sur le sermon que nostre seigneur fit en la montaigne* .... V 47

1512

Béda, Noël: *La petite Dyablerie dont lucifer est le chef* .... B 9

Bouchet, Jean: *La deploration de leglise militante* .... B 220

Concile. Pise: *Censuivent Les faitz institutions et ordonnances ... faitz dedans la ville de Pise, pour commencer le concile* ... C 125

Desmoulins, Laurent: *Le cymetiere Des Malheureux* .... D 22

La fleur des commandemens de dieu .... F 35

Jérôme, Saint: *La Vie des peres* .... J 6

Lemaire de Belges, Jean: *Le traictie ... de la difference des scismes* .... L 30

Lemaire de Belges, Jean: *Le traictie ... de la difference des scismes* .... L 31

Le Roy, François: *Le Mirouer de penitence* .... L 58

Le mistere de la Passion de nostre saulveur et redempteur jesu-christ .... M 92

Le quart (-Ve) volume des exposicions des Epistres et Evangilles de Toute lannee .... P 27

Remede convenable Pour si bien vivre en ce monde que nous puissions acquerir le royaulme des cieulx .... R 43

La theologie spirituelle extraicte des livres sainct Denis .... T 10

1513

Le Psaultier de David contenant cent et cinquante pseaulmes avecq leurs titres .... B 70

Desmoulins, Laurent: *Le catholicon des mal advisez autrement dit le Cymetiere des malheureux* .... D 23

Rolewinck, Werner: *Les fleurs et manieres des temps passez* ...... R 49

Voragine, Jacques de: *La legende doree et vie des Saincts et Sainctes* .... V 71

1514

Le premier/second volume de la bible en francoiz .... B 25

Bonaventure, Saint (attrib.): *Le Mirouer de discipline* .... B 219

Fabri, Pierre: *Le defensoir de la conception* .... F 2

Guillaume d'Auvergne: *La rethorique divine* .... G 59

Lemaire de Belges, Jean: *Le traictie intitule de la difference des scismes* .... L 32

Le grant Ordinaire des chrestiens .... O 9

Lordinaire des crestiens .... O 10

1515

Le defensoire de la conception de la glorieuse vierge Marie ...... D 1

Linstruction des curez pour instruire le simple peuple ... par tout levesche de Sainct Malo .... I 40

Maurice de Sully: *Les expositions des evangiles en francoys* ...... M 47

Le mistere de la conception Nativite Mariage Et annonciation de la benoiste vierge marie .... M 85

Le mistere de la passion nostre seigneur jhesucrist .... M 93

La Resurrection de nostre seigneur jhesuchrist Par personnages ... M 102

La reffection spirituelle de lame devote .... R 40

1516

La bible en francois .... B 26

La bible en francoys .... B 27

Bougain, Michel: *Le Jardin spirituel de lame devote* .... B 233

Columbi, Jean: *Confession generale... Et une oraison tresdevote a dire devant que on recepve le corps de nostre seigneur* .... C 120

Les commandemens de saincte eglise et la confession generale du jour de pasques .... C 124a

La complainte de nostre mere sainte eglise .... C 124b

La fleur des commandemens de dieu .... F 36

Henry, Jean: *Le Jardin de contemplation* .... H 3

Henry, Jean: *Le livre de la toute belle sans pair qui est la vierge Marie* .... H 4

Henry, Jean: *Le livre de meditation sur la reparation de nature humaine* .... H 5

Henry, Jean: *Le livre de reformation utile et profitable pour toutes religieuses* .... H 6

Henry, Jean: *Le livre dinstruction pour religieuses novices et professes* .... H 7

Linstruction des curez pour instruire le simple peuple, cest assavoir le livre des troys parties .... I 41

Petite instruction et maniere de vivre pour une femme seculiere I 55

Loys, Jean: *Le ravisement du pelerin de verite nomme Jehan Loys* L 70

Lucidaire ... diverses matieres subtilles et merveilleuses en maniere dinterrogation .... L 71

Meditation tresdevotte pour chascune heure du jour sur la passion M 51

Michel, Guillaume: *La forest de conscience contenant la chasse des princes spirituelle* .... M 72

Le mistere du viel Testament .... M 108c

La refection spirituelle de lame devote .... R 41

Sauvage, Jean: *Sensuit leschelle damour divine* .... S 5

Voragine, Jacques de: *La Legende doree* .... V 72

1517

Ambroise, Saint: *Le Traicte du bien et de la mort* .... A 8

Augustin, Saint: *Trois opuscules <> de lestat de veuvage, de la maniere de prier Dieu, et de la vie de saincte Monique* ...... A 32

Le premier/second volume de la bible en francoiz .... B 28

Columbi, Jean: *Confession generale. Et une oraison tresdevote a dire devant que on recepve le corps d'nostre seigneur et une apres* .... C 119

Jérôme, Saint: *La vie des peres* .... J 7

Lemaire de Belges, Jean: *Le traictie de la difference des scismes* L 33

Le Roy, François: *Le livre de la femme forte Et vertueuse* .... L 57

Le mirouer de contemplation fait sur la tressaincte vie, mort et passion de nostre seigneur JesuChrist .... M 77

La Vie de Jhesucrist .... V 10

1518

Le premier/second volume de la bible en francoys .... B 29

Devote contemplation: sur le mistere de nostre redemption .... C 132

Eusèbe de Césarée (pseud.): *Le testament du tresglorieux sainct et amy de dieu Eusebe* .... E 67

Linstruction des curez pour instruire le simple peuple ... par tout levesche De Sainct Malo .... I 42

Michel, Guillaume: *Le Penser de royal memoire ... et aultres choses convenables a lexortation du soulievement et entretiennement de la saincte foy catholicque* .... M 74

Le mistere de monseigneur sainct pierre et sainct paul .... M 108a

Le mistere du Tresglorieux martir Monsieur sainct christofle ..... V 17b

Vitrier, Jean: *Lexposition sur le sermon que nostre seigneur fist en la montaigne* .... V 48

Ximenis, Francesc: *Le livre des sainctz anges* .... X 1

1519

Augustin, Saint: *Sensuyt la saincte et sacree exposition <> sur le psaultier de David* .... A 29

Le livre de la discipline damour divine .... D 29

Les Fleurs de la somme angelique des branches des sept pechez mortelz .... F 41

Gerson, Jean: *La mendicité spirituelle. Les meditacions de lame: le consolatif de tristesse* .... G 20

Jérôme, Saint: *Les Epistres* .... J 3

Le Grand, Jacques: *Le livre de bonnes mœurs* .... L 26a

Lemaire de Belges, Jean: *Le Traictie de la difference des scismes*   L 34

Le premier (-Second) volume des exposicions des Epistres et Evangilles de Karesme .... P 29

Le Tiers (-Ve) volume des exposicions des Epistres et Evangilles de Toute lannee .... P 28

Les prieres et commandemens de saincte eglise ... Et Le petit traicte maistre Jehan gerson qui aprent a bien mourir .... P 40

Quatre voyes spirituelles pour aller à Dieu .... Q 2

1520

Le premier/second volume de la bible en francoiz .... B 30

Sensuyt la Bible en francoys .... B 31

Bougain, Michel: *Le jardin amoureux de lame devote compose par ... maistre Pierre dally* .... B 232

Bougain, Michel: *Le Jardin de paradis* .... B 236

Columbi, Jean: *Confession generale ... Et une oraison tresdevote a dire devant que on recepve le corps de nostre seigneur* .... C 121

La declaration de lestat et ordonnance de la ... confrarie du psaultier, rosier et chappelet .... C 129

Le dialogue spirituel de la Passion .... D 25

Erasme, Desiderius: *De la declamation des louenges de follie*.... E 26

Guillaume d'Auvergne: *La Rhetorique divine* .... G 60

Le livre intitule Internelle consolacion .... I 9

Jérôme, Saint: *La vie des peres* .... J 8

Le Moyne, Pasquier: *Lardant miroir de grace* .... L 55

Michel, Guillaume: *La forest de conscience contenant la chasse des princes spirituelle* .... M 73

Mistere de la saincte hostie .... M 106a

Parfaite foy pour estre sauve cest croire tout ce que saincte eglise croit .... P 5

Les Postilles et expositions Des epistres Et evangilles dominicalles .... P 29a

Le proufit quon a douyr messe .... P 46

La vie de Jesuchrist .... V 11

La vie de ma dame saincte katherine de seine .... V 17

La vie de sainct Nicolas .... V 21

Vitrier, Jean: *Lexposition sur le sermon que nostre seigneur fist a la montaigne* .... V 49

1521

Bellemere, François: *Directoire de la vie humaine* .... B 13

Le premier/second volume de la bible en francoys .... B 32

Charles Quint: *Edit et mandement ... Lan de grace Mil cinq cens.xxi. Contre Frere Martin luther* .... C 104

Les Epistres sainct Pol glosees .... E 13

Linstruction des curez pour instruire le simple peuple .... I 43

Jérôme, Saint: *Les epistres* .... J 4

Lemaire de Belges, Jean: *Le traictie de la difference des scismes* L 35

Ludolphus de Saxe: *Le premier (-second) volume du grant vita Christi en françois* .... L 74

Tresdevote meditation de la ... passion de nostre benoist sauveur et redempteur Jesuchrist .... M 55

Michel, Guillaume: *Le siecle dore: contenant le temps de Paix, Amour, et Concorde* .... M 75

Voragine, Jacques de: *La Legende doree* .... V 73

1522

Augustin, Saint: *Le Mirouer des vanitez et pompes du monde*..... A 30

Le Baston pour chasser les loups .... B 2

Dyalogue et ung merveilleux parlement ... d'ung Abbe, Curtisan et du Dyable, allencontre le bon pape Adrian .... D 27

Le livre intitule Internelle consolation nouvellement corrige ...... I 10

Jordan, Raymond, dit Idiota: *Les Contemplations faites à l'honneur et louange de la Tres sacree Vierge Marie* .... J 11

Lambert, François: *Traictie dévot et tresutile a ceulx qui desirent a avoir en practique la vie de nostre seigneur* .... L 12

Le mistere de la conception Nativite Mariage Et annonciation de la benoiste vierge marie .... M 86

1523

Le tressainct et sacres texte du nouniaulx testament translates du latin en franhois .... B 151

Les choses contenues en ce present livre. La S. Evangile selon S. Matthieu/Marc/Luc/Jehan. [II]: ... *Epistres/Actes/Lapocalypse S. Jehan* .... B 152

Lemaire de Belges, Jean: *Le traicte de la difference des Scismes* .. L 36

Lesnauderie, Pierre de: *La Louenge de mariage et recueil des hystoires de bonnes, vertueuses et illustres femmes* .... L 61

Le mistere de la passion de nostre seigneur jhesucrist .... M 94

Le proufit quon a d'ouyr messe .... P 47

Spagnuoli, Battista: *La parthenice Mariane de Baptiste Mantuan* .... S 32

Volcyr de Sérouville, Nicolas: *Collectaneorum Libellus* ... *sur les elementz des lettres: commandemens de la loy: oraison dominicale: et sermon des cendres* .... V 68

1524

Le psaultier de David ... *Argument brief sur chascun Pseaulme* ..... B 71

Les choses contenues en ce present livre. La S. Evangile selon S. Matthieu/Marc/Luc/Jehan. [II]: *Epistres/Actes/Apocalypse* ..... B 153

Les choses contenues en ce present livre. La S. Evangile selon S. Matthieu/Marc/Luc/Jehan. [II]: *Epistres/Actes/Apocalypse* ..... B 154

Les choses contenues en ce present livre. La S. Evangile selon S. Matthieu/Marc/Luc/Jehan. [II]: *Epistres/Actes/Apocalypse* ..... B 155

Erasme, Desiderius: *Maniere de se confesser* .... E 36

Farel, Guillaume?: *Epistre chrestienne* .... F 7

Farel, Guillaume: *Le Pater noster, et le Credo en françoys* .... F 24

Gacy, Jean: *Trialogue nouveau contenant lexpression des erreurs de Martin Luther. Les doleances de Ierarchie ecclesiastique Et les triumphes de verite invincible* .... G 2

Gringore, Pierre: *Le Blazon des heretiques* .... G 38

Gringore, Pierre: *Le Blazon des heretiques* .... G 39

Le Conte, Jean: *Les miracles de la benoite et glorieuse vierge marie* .... L 17

Lemaire de Belges, Jean: *Le traicte de la difference des Scismes* ...... L 37

Lemaire de Belges, Jean: *Le traictie de la difference des scismes* ...... L 38

Maillard, Olivier: *Lexemplaire de confession ... avecques la confession de frere Olivier Maillart* .... M 1

Devote meditation sur la mort et passion de nostre saulveur et redempteur .... M 52

Le mistere de la passion nostre seigneur Jhesucrist .... M 95

Picard, Jean, O.F.M.: *Les trois mirouers du monde* .... P 21

Le profit quon a douyr messe .... P 48

1525

La Balade des leutheriens avec la chanson .... B 1

Béda, Noël: *La doctrine et instruction necessaire aux crestiens et crestiennes* .... B 8

Bellemere, François: *Directoire de la vie humaine Contenant quatre traictez* .... B 14

Le psaultier de David. Argument brief sur chascun Pseaulme ..... B 72

Les sept pseaulmes du royal prophete David, exposees: puis nagueres divulguees .... B 73

Le nouveau testament .... B 159

Les choses contenues en ce present Livre. La S. Evangile selon S. Matthieu/Marc/Luc/Jehan. [II]: *Epistres/Actes /Apocalypse* .... B 156

Les choses contenues en ce present Livre. La S. Evangile selon S. Matthieu/Marc/Luc/Jehan. [II]: *Epistres/Actes /Apocalypse* .... B 158

Les choses contenues en ceste partie du nouveau testament .... B 157

Caupain, Henri: *Le sepulchre spirituel pour donner a congnoistre comment on doibt dignement recepvoir et garder le precieulx corps de nostre seigneur au sainct sacrement de Lautel* .... C 94

Erasme, Desiderius: *Brefve admonition de la maniere de prier ... avec une brefve explanation du Pater noster* .... E 15

Erasme, Desiderius: *Declamation des louenges de mariage* .... E 27

Erasme, Desiderius: *Exhortation au peuple* .... E 35

Erasme, Desiderius: *Le symbole des apostres ... par maniere de dialogue: par demande et par response* .... E 57

Exhortation sur ces sainctes parolles de nostre Segneur Jesus. Retournes vous, et croyes a Levangile .... E 71

Le Fagot de myerre, presche en ... la cite Dangiers. 1525 .... F 3

Farel, Guillaume?: *Epistre Chrestienne tresutile a ceulx qui commencent lire la saincte escripture* .... F 8

Farel, Guillaume: *Loraison de Jesuchrist, qui est le Pater noster, et le Credo, avec la declaration diceulx. La salutation angelique. Les dix commandemens. Les sept pseaulmes: et autres choses tresutiles* .... F 25

La fleur des Commandemens de Dieu .... F 37

Gringore, Pierre: *Heures de nostre dame translatees en Françoys et mises en rithme* .... G 48
Illyricus, Thomas: *Le Sermon de Charité, avec les probations des erreurs de Luther* .... I 3
Illyricus, Thomas: *Le Sermon de Charité, avec les probations des erreurs de Luther* .... I 4
Linstruction des curez Et vicaires pour instruire le simple peuple avec la maniere de faire le prosne .... I 44
Lefèvre d'Étaples, Jacques: *Epistres et Evangiles pour les cinquante et deux sepmaines de lan* .... L 19
Lesnauderie, Pierre de: *La Louenge de mariage et recueil des hystoires des bonnes, vertueuses et illustres femmes* .... L 62
Luther, Martin: *Des bonnes oeuvres sus les commandemens de Dieu* .... L 86
Luther, Martin: *Une exposition sur le Magnificat* .... L 88
Luther, Martin: *Une exposition sur le Magnificat* .... L 89
Luther, Martin: *Exposition sur les dix commandemens de la loy* .... L 91
Luther, Martin: *Livre tresutile de la vraye et parfaite subjection des chrestiens* .... L 113
Luther, Martin: *Brief racueil des oeuvres des dix commandemens* ... L 81
Mauburne, Jean: *Une petite eschelle pour faire bonne et entiere confession* .... M 46
La Resurrection de nostre Seigneur Jesuchrist par personnaiges ... M 103
Le proufit quon a de ouyr messe .... P 49
Les XXXIII. significations et considerations qui sont en la messe .... S 17

1526

Les Arrestz et ordonnances de la court contre Luther: les lutheriens et leurs livres: et aultres livres deffendus .... A 19
Sensuit la bible en francois .... B 33
Le psaultier de David. Argument brief sur chascun pseaulme ..... B 74
Le directoire de la salut des Ames: tant pour les Pasteurs d'icelles que aussi pour le commun peuple .... D 28
Heyden, Sebald: *Dung seul mediateur entre dieu et les hommes, Jesuchrist... Ung sermon de mammona iniquitatis* .... H 12
Lemaire de Belges, Jean: *Le traicte de la difference des Scismes* ..... L 39
Maillard, Olivier: *La confession generale de frere Olivier maillard* M 3
Nachtigall, Ottomarus: *Hystoire evangelique des quatre evangelistes en ung* .... N 1
Petit, Guillaume: *Le viat de salut tresnecessaire et utile a tous chrestiens pour parvenir a la gloire eternelle* .... P 13
Brief recueil de la substance et principal fondement de la doctrine Evangelique .... R 38

Schuch, Wolfgang: *Epistre chrestienne envoyee a tresnoble Prince monseigneur le duc de Lorayne* .... S 8

Le traicte du Souverain Bien. Par lequel le vray chrestien pourra apprendre (a layde des sainctes Escriptures) a contemner la Mort .... T 15

Volcyr de Sérouville, Nicolas: *Lhistoire et Recueil de la triumphante et glorieuse victoire obtenue contre les seduyctz et abusez Lutheriens mescreans.* .... V 69

Voragine, Jacques de: *La grant et vraye Legende doree* .... V 74

1527

Bodius, Hermann: *L'Union de toutes discordes* .... B 209

Conrard, Olivier: *Le mirouer des pecheurs* .... C 130

Dumolin, Guillaume: *Le traicte de lutilite et honneste de mariage* D 97

Dumolin, Guillaume: *Tresutile traicte, du vray regne de antechrist* D 98

Dumolin, Guillaume: *Notable et utile traicte Du zele et grant desir que doibt avoit ung vray christien pour garder a Jesuchrist son honneur entier* .... D 99

Les Hymnes communes de lannee .... H 16

Luther, Martin: *Prophetie de Iesaie de lenfant nouveau ne Jesuchrist* .... L 118

Luther, Martin: *Sermon au jour de l'ascension* .... L 120

Luther, Martin: *Sermon de la maniere de prier Dieu et comment on doibt faire processions et rogations* .... L 122

Lorayson de nostre seigneur Jesuchrist appellee le Paternoster Avec lave maria. Le credo contenant les articles de la foy. Les dix commandemens de la loy Avec les cinq de leglise .... O 7

Petit, Guillaume: *Le viat de salut necessaire et utile a tous chrestiens* .... P 14

Petit, Guillaume: *Le Viat de Salut tresnecessaire et utile a tous chrestiens* .... P 15

Remede convenable Pour si bien vivre en ce monde que nous puissions acquerir le royaulme des cieulx .... R 44

Sentence de frere Jehan Guibert, hermite de Livry .... S 11

La vie sainct Jehan baptiste .... V 17d

1528

Béda, Noël: *La petite diablerie dont lucifer est le chef* .... B 10

Le premier volume de lanchien testament contenant les chinq livres de Moyse .... B 62

Le dernier volume de lanchien testament contenant les prophetes.. B 66

Bodius, Hermann: *La seconde partie de Lunion de toutes discordes* B 210

Bougain, Michel: *Le Jardin spirituel de lame devote* .... B 234

Caupain, Henri: *Le desert de devotion* .... C 93

Gaigny, Jean de: *Le livre faisant mention des sept parolles que nostre benoist saulveur ... dit en larbre de la croix* .... G 6

Gringore, Pierre: *Chantz Royaulx, figurez morallement sur les misteres miraculeux de Nostre saulveur* .... G 41

Illyricus, Thomas: *Devotes oraisons en françois avec une chanson d'amour divin* .... I 1

La grande Irrision des Lutheriens de Meaulx .... I 59

Lemaire de Belges, Jean: *Le traicte de la difference des Scismes* ..... L 40

Lemaire de Belges, Jean: *Le traictie de la difference des scismes*... L 41

Le Livret des consolations contre toutes tribulations .... L 64

Luther, Martin: *Le livre de vraye et parfaicte oraison* .... L 97

Petit, Guillaume: *Le viat de salut necessaire et utile a tous chrestiens* .... P 16

Le Te Deum pour l'eglise Lutherienne: en françoys et en latin. Avec la Ballade et la chanson d'yceulx Lutheriens .... T 1

1529

Le premier/second volume de la bible en francoiz .... B 34

Le troisiesme volume de lancien testament contenant le livre de Tobie, de Judith, de Hester, de Job: et les trois livres de Salomon .... B 65

La premiere/seconde partie du nouveau testament .... B 162

Le nouveau Testament, contenant les quattre Evangelistes... avec les faitz des Apostres et les Epistres de Saint Paul, de Saint Jaques... et avec Lapocalipse.. .... B 161

Les choses contenues en ce present livre... Une breve instruction, poür deuement lire lescripture saincte .... B 160

Bonaventure, Saint (attrib.): *Laguillon damour divine* .... B 217

Bonaventure, Saint (attrib.), *Lesguillon damour divin* .... B 217a

Brunfels, Otto: *Les Prieres et oraisons de la Bible* .... B 271

Erasme, Desiderius: *Enchidirion (ou Manuel) du chevalier Chrestien* .... E 28

Farel, Guillaume: *Summaire, et brieve declaration daucuns lieux fort necessaires a un chascun Chrestien* .... F 26

Gouda, Gerard van der: *Linterpretation et signification de la Messe* .... G 21

Internelle consolation nouvellement corrige .... I 11

Lambert, François: *Somme Chrestienne a tresvictorieux empereur Charles* .... L 11

Lasseré, Louis: *La Vie de monseigneur sainct Hierosme* .... L 14

Lefèvre d'Étaples, Jacques: *Vocabulaire du pseautier exposé en François* .... L 26

Lemaire de Belges, Jean: *Le traictie de la difference des scismes*.... L 42

Luther, Martin: *Breve Instruction pour deuement lire lescripture saincte* .... L 115

Luther, Martin: *La Maniere de lire levangile et quel profit on en doibt attendre* .... L 114

Luther, Martin: *Le livre de vraye et parfaicte oraison* .... L 98

La Marchandise spirituelle laquelle est tresutille et necessaire a tous marchans et marchandes. Et generallement a tous bons crestiens et crestiennes .... M 14

Mauburne, Jean: *Le Beneficiaire divin* .... M 45

Une devote meditation sur la mort et passion de nostre saulveur et redempteur jesuchrist .... M 53

La pacience de job selon lhystoire de la bible .... P 8a

Tissarrant, Jean: *Sensuyt une tresbelle salutation faicte sur les sept festes de nostre Dame* .... T 13

La voye de paradis .... V 66

Voragine, Jacques de: *La grant et vraye Legende doree* .... V 75

1530

Almanach spirituel et perpetuel... A 5

L'armure de patience en adversite tresconsolatif pour ceulx qui sont en tribulation .... A 14

Lassumption de la glorieuse vierge Marie. A xxxviij. personnages... A 25

La saincte Bible. en Francoys, translatee selon la pure et entiere traduction de sainct Hierome .... B 35

Sensuyt la bible translatee de Latin en francoys....................... B 36

Les Sentences de Solomon ... selon la verite Hebraique.............. B 145

La premiere /seconde partie du nouveau Testament................... B 163

Bouchet, Jean: *Les Triumphes de la noble et amoureuse dame*.... B 221

Brunfels, Otto: *Les Oraisons de la Bible*............................. B 272

Brunfels, Otto: *Les Prieres et Oraisons de la Bible* .... B 273

Le Chappeau des lutheriens Avec la revocation de Luther.......... C 103

Chevalet: *La vie de sainct Christofle ... par personnages* .... C 105

Le combat chrestien... C 124

Eschelles de la passion: par le moyen desquelles on pourra a chascun jour de la sepmaine soy spirituellement occuper a penser a la douloureuse mort et passion de Jesucrist .... E 1

Lenfant Prodigue par personnaiges............................... E 5

Erasme, Desiderius: *Maniere de se confesser*........................... E 37

Brefve et devote exposition par maniere dexhortation et doraison, faicte sur le Pater noster: et autres parolles de nostre Seigneur Jesuchrist recitees au .vi. chapitre de sainct Matthieu............... E 75

416 PIETY AND THE PEOPLE

*Brefve exposition sur la treschrestienne et tresparfaicte orai-
son du Pater noster*... E 74

Gringore, Pierre: *Le Blazon des heretiques*............................... G 40

Gringore, Pierre: *La complaincte de la cite crestienne faicte
sur les lamentations Hieremie*... G 47

Gringore, Pierre: *Heures de nostre dame, translatees de latin
en françoys et mises en ryme*... G 49

Illyricus, Thomas: *Copie de la prophetie faicte par le pauvre
frere thomas*.. I 2

Le livre intitule Internelle consolation nouvellement corrige...... I 12

Livre intitule Internelle consolation nouvellement corrige.......... I 13

Breve Instruction pour soy confesser en verite........................... I 57

Lasseré, Louis: *La Vie de monseigneur sainct Hierosme*........... L 15

Lefèvre d'Étaples, Jacques: *Epistres et evangiles des cinquante
et deux dimenches de lan*... L 20

Le Grand, Jacques: *Le Tresor de Sapience*................................ L 26b

Luther, Martin: *La Fleur des Commandementz, et declaration
des Bonnes Oeuvres*.. L 96

Luther, Martin: *Le livre de vraye et parfaicte oraison*............... L 99

Luther, Martin: *La Maniere de lire levangile et quel proffit on
en doibt attendre ... et aussi la maniere de mediter et penser
a la passion de nostre saulveur Jesuchrist*.................................. L 116

*La Marchandise spirituelle ordonnee et distinguee en sept
regions spirituelles, selon les sept jours de la sepmaine*............ M 15

*Le mistere de la conception Nativite Mariage. Et annonciation
de la benoiste vierge marie*.. M 87

*Sensuit la Resurrection de nostre seigneur jesucrist par per-
sonnages*.. M 104

Picard, Jean, O.F.M.: *Les trois Mirouers du monde*.................. P 22

*Sensuyvent les Postilles et expositions des Epistres et Evan-
giles dominicales*.. P 30

*Sensuyvent aucunes belles Preparations pour devotement rece-
voir le Sainct Sacrement de lautel*... P 38

Les ventes Damour Divine.. V 2

*La Vie de Jesus Christ avec sa Mort et sa Passion. La Sentence
donnee par Pilate a l'encontre de Jesus Christ. La vie de
Judas Scarioth. Le Trespassement de la glorieuse vierge
Marie. La vengeance et destruction de Hierusalem*.................... V 12

*Cy ensuyt la vie de Monseigneur Sainct Albain roy de hongrie
et martyr*.. V 14

La vie et lystore de ma dame saincte barbe par personnages...... V 15

La Voye de Paradis... V 67

1531

Augustin, Saint: *Le premier Volume <> de la Cite de Dieu*........ A 26

Augustin, Saint: *Le second volume et acomplissement des .xxii.
livres <> de la Cite de Dieu* .... A 27

Aumen, Gervais: *La consolation des desolez, et les douze utilitez
qui sont es tribulations paciemment pour lamour de dieu porteez* A 36

La Bible en Francoys............................ B 38

Le premier/second volume de la Bible en francoys.................... B 37

Lecclesiaste Preschant que toutes choses sans dieu sont vanite .. B 68

*Le .VI. Pseaulme de David qui est le premier Pseaulme des
sept Pseaulmes translate en françoys*............................. B 77

*Le livre des Pseaulmes de David, ... ensuyvant linterpretation
de Felix*................................ B 75

Les sept pseaulmes en francoys........................... B 76

*Le nouveau Testament, auquel est demonstre Jesu Christ sau-
veur du monde estre venu*............................ B 164

Bougain, Michel: *Le Jardin spirituel de lame devote*................. B 235

Brigitta, Sainte (pseud): *Les Quinze oraisons ... Avec les sept
principalles peines des dampnez. Et les sept joyes des Saulvez* .... B 263

Clerici, Jean: *Sensuit ung traicte des fondemens du temple
spirituel de dieu* .... C 111

Erasme, Desiderius: *La complainte de la Paix* .... E 24

*Le livre intitule Internelle consolation, tresutile et proffitable a
tous Chrestiens*............................ I 14

*Limitation de nostre seigneur Jesuchrist: Et du parfaict con-
tempnement de ce miserable monde*........................... I 15

*Linstruction des Curez pour instruyre le simple peuple ... appelle
en latin Opus tripartitum* .... I 45

Le Grand, Jacques: *Le Tresor de sapience* .... L 26c

Ludolphus de Saxe: *Le grant Vita Christi ... en francoys*............ L 75

Marguerite de Navarre: *Le miroir de lame pecheresse. ouquel
elle recongnoist ses faultes et pechez*........................ M 34

*Miroir de lhumaine redemption contenant plusieurs belles
matieres de lAncien Testament*........................ M 78

Missus est translate de latin en francois........................... M 80

*Cy ensuyt loraison de Missus est, translate en francoys selon le
latin Avec loraison de nostre dame de recouvrance. Et le
testament de nostre sauveur jesuchrist*........................ M 81

Le mistere de la saincte hostie .... M 107

Petit, Pierre: *La chanson de frere Pierre petit Religieux de lave
Maria*........................ P 20

Le Premier (-second) volume des grandes Postilles et exposi-
tions des Epistres et Evangilles pour toute lannee..................   P 31

Saulnier, Antoine: *Chanson nouvelle composee sur les dix*
commandemens de Dieu..   S 2

La vie ma Dame saincte Barbe par personnaiges......................   V 16

1532

Apolologie pour la foy chrestienne contre les erreurs de ...
George Halevin...   A 10

Bellemere, François: *Directoire de la vie humaine contenant*
quatre traictez...   B 15

Le second volume de lanchien Testament contenant pour sa
premiere partie le Livre de Josue, le Livre des Juges, et le
Livre de Ruth..   B 63

Le second volume de lancien Testament, contenant pour sa
seconde partie les quattre livres des Roix, les deux livres de
Paralipomenon, et les quattre livres de Esdras......................   B 64

Le Livre des Psalmes..   B 78

Le nouveau Testament de nostre saulveur Jesu Christ translate
selon le vray text en franchois...   B 165

Le nouveau Testament, contenant les quattre Evangelistes... avec
les faictz des Apostres: et les Epistres sainct Paul, les
Epistres Canoniques, et Lapocalipse....................................   B 166

Bodius, Hermann: *La Premiere (-seconde) partie de Lunion de*
toute discorde...   B 211

Bouchet, Jean: *Les Triumphes de la noble et amoureuse dame*....   B 222

Clerici, Jean: *Le manuel des chrestiens, traictant, de foy de*
esperance et de charite...   C 112

Erasme, Desiderius: *Enchiridion (ou Manuel) du Chevalier*
Chrestien ....   E 29

Farel, Guillaume?: *De La Tressaincte Cene de nostre Seigneur*
Jesus: Et De la Messe quon chante communement...................   F 5

Farel, Guillaume: *Summaire et briefve declaration daulcuns*
lieux fort necessaires a ung chascun chrestien, pour mettre
sa confiance en Dieu, et ayder son prochain.........................   F 27

Fossetier, Julien: *Conseil de volentier morir*..............................   F 50

Gringore, Pierre: *Chantz royaulx figurez morallement*................   G 42

Gringore, Pierre: *Heures de nostre dame* ....   G 50

Le livre intitule Internelle consolation.......................................   I 16

Jordan, Raymond, dit Idiota: *Les contemplations du simple devot...*
En la fin est adjoinct ung sermon preparatoire a recepvoir le
Sainct sacrement de lautel ....   J 12

La Boulaye, Guillaume de: *La pronostication du Ciecle advenir, contenant troys petis traictez* .... L 1

Lefèvre d'Étaples, Jacques: *Epistres et evangiles pour les cinquante et deux sepmaines de lan* .... L 21

Lemaire de Belges, Jean: *Le Promptuaire des Conciles de Leglise Catholique, avec les Scismes* .... L 47

Lesnauderie, Pierre de: *La Louange de mariage et recueil des hystoyres des bonnes, vertueuses et illustres femmes* .... L 63

Le livre de consolations contre toutes tribulations .... L 65

Le livre de paix en Jesuchrist. .... L 68

Luther, Martin: *Consolation chrestienne, contre les afflictions de ce monde* .... L 82

Luther, Martin: *Quatre instructions fideles pour les simples, et les rudes.* .... L 119

Le Mirouer dor de lame pecheresse .... M 76

Sensuit le mistere de la Passion de nostre seigneur Jesuchrist.... M 96

Sensuyt le mistere de la Passion notre seigneur Jesuscrist......... M 97

Sensuyt le grand ordinaire des chrestiens: qui enseigne a chascun bon chrestien et crestiene la voye et le chemin de aller en paradis .... O 11

Les paroles memorables entre Jesus Christ et le pecheur .... P 6

Rabelais, François: *Pantagruel* .... R 1

Rome, Jean de: *Petit directoyre pour aprendre es symples gens a reduire a memoyre leurs peches en euls confessant* .... R 50

La Summe de lescripture saincte, et lordinaire des chrestiens, enseignant la vraye foy Chrestienne .... S 26

La vie saincte Katherine de Seine. .... V 17a

La vie ma dame saincte Marguerite. .... V 19

1533

Berquin, Louis de?: *La farce des theologastres a six personnages....* B 22

Bodius, Hermann: *La premiere partie de lunion de plusieurs passaiges de lescripture saincte* .... B 212

Bodius, Hermann: *La seconde partie de Lunion de plusieurs passages de lescripture saincte* .... B 213

Bouchet, Jean: *Les Triumphes de la noble et amoureuse dame....* B 223

Brunfels, Otto: *Les Oraisons de la Bible* .... B 274

Sensuivent plusieurs belles et bonnes chansons, que les chrestiens peuvent chanter en grande affection de cueur .... C 101

Clément VII: *La translation en francoys de la bulle ... pour extirper lheresie Lutherienne et autres sectes pullulans en ce royaulme* .... C 110

Clerici, Jean: *Le Manuel des chrestiens traictant de Foy, de Esperance et de Charite*... C 113

Clerici, Jean: *Le Traicte de Exemplaire penitence*..................... C 115

La confession et raison de la foy de maistre Noel Beda.............. C 126

Ung breif enseignement tire hors de la saincte escripture Pour amener la personne a volentier morir et point craindre la mort E 6

Ung devot et nouveau Traicte contenant plusieurs expositions utilles sur l'oraison dominicale, aultrement dicte la Patinostre E 78

Brefve et salutaire exposition sur la salutation angelique........... E 82

Farel, Guillaume: *La maniere et fasson quon tient ... es lieux lesquelz dieu de sa grace a visite* .... F 19

Florimond: *Epistre familiere de prier Dieu*.............................. F 42

Florimond: *Epistre familiere de prier Dieu. Aultre Epistre familiere d'aymer chrestiennement* ....:................................. F 43

Florimond: *Epistre familiere de prier Dieu. Aultre Epistre familiere d'aimer chrestiennement* .... F 44

Gaigny, Jean de: *Le Livre contenant devote exposition sur le cinquantiesme pseaulme*... G 3

Gaigny, Jean de: *Le livre faisant mention des sept parolles*........ G 7

Hugues de Saint-Victor: *Larre de lame... Ensemble le Cueur navre de amour divin*.. H 15

Le livre intitule Internelle consolation...................................... I 17

Linstruction des curez pour instruire le simple peuple................ I 46

Lemaire de Belges, Jean: *Le Promptuaire des Conciles de Leglise Catholique, avec les Scismes*....................................... L 48

Lemaire de Belges, Jean: *Le traicte de la difference des Scismes* ..... L 43

Malingre, Matthieu: *Moralite de la maladie de Chrestiente*........ M 8

Malingre, Matthieu: *Noelz nouveaulx*..................................... M 10

Marcourt, Antoine: *Le livre des marchans*.............................. M 23

Marguerite de Navarre: *Dialogue en forme de vision nocturne* ... M 31

Marguerite de Navarre: *Le miroir de lame pecheresse*............... M 35

Marguerite de Navarre: *Le miroir de lame pecheresse*............... M 36

Marguerite de Navarre: *Le miroir de treschrestienne princesse Marguerite de France*... M 37

Marguerite de Navarre: *Le miroir de treschrestienne princesse Marguerite de France*... M 38

Olivétan, Pierre Robert: *Linstruction des enfans, contenant la maniere de prononcer et escrire en françoys*............................ O 5

Les grans pardons et indulgences, le tresgrand Jubile de plainiere remission.. P 3

Les .xv. joyes de nostre dame .... Q 5

Rabelais, François: *Pantagruel*... R 2

Rabelais, François: *Pantagruel*... R 3

Rabelais, François: *Pantagruel*.. R 4
Rabelais, François: *Pantagruel*.. R 7
Le Sentier et ladresse de devotion, et contemplation intellectuelle S 13
Seuse, Heinrich: *Lorloge de Sapience*....................................... S 16
La Verite cachee, devant cent ans .... V 8
La vie Et mistere de Saint Andry .... V 14a
Le Mystere du tresglorieux Martyr Monsieur sainct Christofle ... V 17c

1534

Béda, Noël: *La petite Dyablerie. Aultrement apellee Lesglise*
    des mauvais... B 11
La saincte Bible en Francoys, translatee selon la pure et entiere
    traduction de Sainct Hierome... B 39
Texte de Hiob, translate selon la verite hebraique .... B 69
Le nouveau testament de nostre seigneur et seul sauveur Jesus
    Christ... B 167
Campen, Jean van: *Paraphrase ... sur tous les Psalmes, selon*
    la verité Hebraique.. C 83
Chansons nouvelles demonstrantz plusieurs erreurs et faulsetez .... C 98
Desmoulins, Laurent: *Le cymetiere des malheureux*.................. D 24
Exhortation sur ces sainctes parolles de nostre Seigneur Jesu.
    Retournez vous et croyez a levangile .... E 72
Farel, Guillaume: *Summaire, et briefve declaration ... Item,*
    ung traicte du Purgatoire... F 28
Gringore, Pierre: *Heures de nostre dame, translatees de latin*
    en francoys et mises en ryme, additionnees de plusieurs
    chantz Royaulx figurez et moralisez.................................. G 51
Le livre intitule internelle consolation nouvellement corrige...... I 18
Introduction pour les enfans .... I 48
Jérôme, Saint: *La Vie des Peres* .... J 9
Ludolphus de Saxe: *Le premier (-second) volume du grant vita*
    Christi translaté de latin en francoys.................................. L 76
Luther, Martin: *Les faictz de Jesus Christ et du Pape*................ L 94
Luther, Martin: *Le livre de vraye et parfaicte oraison*............... L 100
Marcourt, Antoine: *Articles veritables sur les horribles, grandz*
    et importables abuz de la Messe papalle............................. M 18
Marcourt, Antoine: *Declaration de la Messe, Le fruict dicelle,*
    La cause, et le moyen, pourquoy et comment on la doibt
    maintenir .... M 19
Marcourt, Antoine: *Le livre des marchans, fort utile a toutes gens* M 24
Marcourt, Antoine: *Petit traicte tres utile, et salutaire de la*
    saincte eucharistie de nostre Seigneur Jesuchrist................ M 29

Petit, Guillaume: *Tres devotes oraisons a lhonneur de la tres-sacree et glorieuse Vierge Marie*.. P 12

Rabelais, François: *Pantagruel*.. R 5

Rabelais, François: *Pantagruel*.. R 6

Rabelais, François: *Pantagruel*.. R 8

Vergier flourissant pour lame fidele, remply de fleurs Mistiques odoriferantes... V 3

La vie de monseigneur sainct Laurens par personnaiges............ V 18

Volcyr de Sérouville, Nicolas: *Traicté nouveau de la desecration et execution actuelle de Jehan Castellan heretique*......... V 70

1535

Augustin, Saint: *La Seule parole de Lame a Dieu*...................... A 31

La Bible Qui est toute la Saincte escripture............................ B 40

La Bible translatee de latin en francoys au vroy sens pour les simples gens... B 41

Le nouveau Testament, auquel est demonstre Jesu Christ sauveur du monde, estre venu... B 168

Bouchet, Jean: *Les Triumphes de la noble et amoureuse dame*.... B 224

Branteghem, Guillaume de: *Enchyridion ou Manuel contenant plusieurs matieres traictees es livres de Lancien Testament*.... B 237

Branteghem, Guillaume de: *Vergier spirituel et mistique*........... B 240

Chansons Nouvelles demonstrantz plusieurs erreurs et faulsetez.... C 99

Clerici, Jean: *Le Manuel des chrestiens*................................ C 114

Briefve et salutaire exposition sur la salutation angelique. vulgairement dicte Lave Maria... E 83

Farel, Guillaume: *Letres certaines daucuns grandz troubles et tumultes advenuz a Geneve*... F 17

La fleur de devotion.. F 34

Gacy, Jean: *La deploration de la Cite de Genesve*.................... G 1

Gaigny, Jean de: *Le livre de nouvel reimprime faisant mention des sept parolles que nostre saulveur ... dit en larbre de la croix*....... G 8

Grégoire, Jean: *Devote exposition sus le Pater noster*............... G 27

Gringore, Pierre: *Chantz Royaulx, Figurez morallement sur les misteres miraculeux de Nostre saulveur et redempteur Jesuchrist .*,... G 43

Hangest, Jérôme de: *Contre les tenebrions lumiere evangelicque*..... H 1

Henry, Jean: *Le pelerinage de nostre dame, et de joseph*........... H 8

Le livre intitule Internelle consolation nouvellement corrige...... I 19

Marguerite de Navarre: *Le miroir de treschrestienne princesse Marguerite*... M 39

Maurice de Sully: *Sensuyvent Les expositions des evangiles. Avec les cinq festes nostre Dame*...................................... M 48

Le mistere de la conception, Nativite, mariage, et annonciation de la benoiste vierge Marie.. M 88

Le mistere de la Passion de nostre seigneur Jesuchrist.............. M 98

Ordonnances nouvelles nagueres faictes ... contre les imitateurs de la secte lutherienne.. O 12

Petit, Guillaume: *Le viat de salut*...................................... P 17

L'Ordre de la procession generalle celebree a Paris, le .xxj. jour de Janvier Mil cincq cens trentequatre................................ P 44

Procession generale faicte a Paris, Le Roy estant en personne. Le xxij. jourt de janvier. Mille. cinq centz, trente et cinq....... P 43

Rabelais, François: *Pantagruel*.. R 9

Rabelais, François: *[Gargantua]*.. R 14

Rabelais, François: *Gargantua*.. R 15

Redon, Gilles de: *La Musique Angelique toute nouvelle De Salve regina*... R 39

Le salve regina en francoys... S 1

1536

Le nouveau Testament, de nostre Seigneur et seul sauveur Jesus Christ... B 169

Bouchet, Jean: *Les Triumphes de la noble et amoureuse dame*.... B 225

Bouchet, Jean: *Les Triumphes de la noble et amoureuse dame*.... B 226

Branteghem, Guillaume de: *Enchyridion ou Manuel contenant plusieurs matieres traictees es livres de Lancien testament*..... B 238

Dentière, Marie: *La Guerre et deslivrance de la ville de Geneve*.... D 5

Farel, Guillaume: *Confession de la Foy, laquelle tous Bourgeois et habitans de Geneve et subjectz du pays doivent jurer*........... F 6

La fleur des commandemens de Dieu.................................. F 38

Hervet, Gentian: *Oraison ou Sermon de l'Ascension*................. H 10

Internelle consolation... I 20

Les Postilles et expositions des epistres et evangiles dominicalles.... P 32

1537

Petit traicte appelle Larmeure de pacience en adversite............. A 15

Bellemere, François: *Instruction salutaire a toute personne de lestat seculier*... B 17

Le premier / second volume de la bible en francoiz.................... B 42

Les Psalmes de David. Translatez d'Ebrieu en Françoys............ B 79

Les sept pseaulmes penitenciaulx et la letanie en françoys......... B 80

Bouchet, Jean: *Les Triumphes de la noble et amoureuse dame*.... B 227

Brigitta, Sainte (pseud): *Les oraisons <> en francoys*............... B 264

Calvin, Jean: *Instruction et confession de Foy, dont on use en Leglise de Geneve*.. C 63

Campen, Jean van: *Paraphrase ... sur tous les Psalmes, selon la verite Hebraique... Traicte du sainct Athanase* .... C 84

Le Livre de la Discipline d'amour divine: contenant La repeticion de la disciple .... D 30

Doré, Pierre: *Les Voyes du Paradis* .... D 91

Erasme, Desiderius: *La maniere de bien instruire les enfans... avec ung petit traicté de la civilité puerile* .... E 25

Erasme, Desiderius: *Le Preparatif à la mort* .... E 42

Erasme, Desiderius: *Preparation a la Mort* .... E 41

Gerson, Jean: *Le Confessional, aultrement appelle le Directoire des confesseurs* .... G 14

Gerson, Jean: *Le doctrinal de la foy catholique* .... G 19

Hangest, Jérôme de: *En controversie voye seure* .... H 2

Internelle consolation nouvellement corrige .... I 21

Linstruction des curez pour instruire le simple peuple .... I 47

Le Roy, François: *Le Dialogue de consolation entre lame et raison* .. L 56

Olivétan, Pierre Robert: *L'Instruction dés enfants* .... O 6

Rabelais, François: *Pantagruel* .... R 10

Rabelais, François: *Pantagruel* .... R 11

Rabelais, François: *Gargantua* .... R 16

Rabelais, François: *Gargantua* .... R 17

1538

L'Abouchement de nostre sainct pere le Pape, Lempereur et le Roy .... A 4

Les Livres de Salomoh .... B 146

Le Nouveau testament de nostre Seigneur Jesuchrist .... B 171

Le nouveau Testament, auquel est demonstre Jesu Christ sauveur du monde .... B 173

Le Nouveau Testament, Cest a dire, La nouvelle Alliance. De nostre Seigneur et seul sauveur Jesus Christ .... B 174

Le nouveau Testament, de nostre Seigneur Jesu Christ .... B 170

Le Nouveau Testament. de nostre Seigneur Jesu Christ seul sauveur du monde .... B 172

La conversion et revocation des Lutheriens faicte en Alemaigne .... C 133

Cymbalum mundi en françoys contenant quatre Dialogues Poetiques .... C 137

Cymbalum mundi en françoys, contenant quatre Dialogues Poetiques .... C 138

Le livre de la Discipline Damour divine .... D 32

Le livre de la Discipline et amour divin .... D 31

Doré, Pierre: *Les Allumettes du feu divin... Avec les Voyes de Paradis* .... D 41

Doré, Pierre: *Les Allumettes du feu divin... Avec les Voyes de Paradis* .... D 42

Doré, Pierre: *Les Allumettes du feu divin... Avec les Voyes de paradis* .... D 43

Doré, Pierre: *Dialogue instructoire, des Chrestiens en la foy, esperance, et amour de Dieu* .... D 66

Doré, Pierre: *Dyalogue Instructoire des Chrestiens en la Foy, esperance, et amour en Dieu* .... D 67

Doré, Pierre: *Les Voyes de Paradis* .... D 92

Erasme, Desiderius: *Preparation à la mort* .... E 43

Farel, Guillaume: *Lordre et maniere quon tient en administrant les sainctz sacremens* .... F 20

Gaigny, Jean de: *Le Livre contenant devote exposition sur le cinquantiesme pseaulme* .... G 4

Gaigny, Jean de: *Le livre de nouvel imprime faisant mention des sept parolles que nostre benoist saulveur ... dist en larbre de la croix* .... G 9

Gerson, Jean: *Le Directoire des confesseurs* .... G 15

Gouda, Gerard van der: *Linterpretation et signification de la Messe* .... G 22

Greban, Simon: *Le premier (-second) volume du triumphant mystere des actes des Apostres* .... G 23

Heyden, Sebald: *D'ung seul mediateur et advocat entre Dieu et les hommes nostre Seigneur Jesus Christ* .... H 13

Les simulachres et faces hystoriées de la Mort .... I 6

Les simulachres et historiees faces de la mort, autant elegamment pourtraictes, que artificiellement imaginées .... I 5

Le livre de L'Internelle consolation, nouvellement reveu, et diligemment corrige .... I 22

Introduction pour les enfans. Recogneue et corrigee a Lovain .... I 49

Jérôme, Saint: *Les Epistres de s. Jérôme et de s. Basile* .... J 5

Jordan, Raymond, dit Idiota: *Les Contemplations du Simple devot ... En la fin est adjoinct ung sermon preparatoire a recepvoir le sainct sacrement de lautel* .... J 13

Luther, Martin: *Le livre de vraye et parfaicte oraison* .... L 101

Marguerite de Navarre: *Le miroir de treschrestienne princesse Marguerite de France* .... M 40

Megander, Gaspard: *Instruction observée par la ville, baillage et pais de Berne* .... M 56

Petit, Guillaume: *La formation de lhomme et son excellence* ...... P 10

Saulnier, Antoine: *L'Ordre et maniere d'enseigner en la ville de Genéve, au College. Description de la ville de Genéve* ...... S 4

1539

Aneau, Barthélemy: *Chant natal contenant sept noelz, ung chant Pastoural, et ung chant Royal, avec ung Mystere de la Nativité* .... A 9

Arétin, Pierre: *Trois livres De l'Humanite de Jesuchrist* .... A 12

Arétin, Pierre: *La Passion de Jesus Christ* .... A 13

Ung petit traicte appelle larmeure de patience .... A 16

Aulcuns pseaulmes et cantiques mys en chant .... B 82

Les Psalmes de David translatez d'Ebrieu en langue françoyse ..... B 81

Les sentences de Solomon .... B 147

Le nouveau Testament auquel est demonstre Jhesu Christ nostre Sauveur .... B 175

Le Nouveau Testament, C'est à dire, La Nouvelle Alliance, de nostre Seigneur et seul Sauveur Jesus Christ .... B 176

Le Nouveau Testament, C'est à dire, La nouvelle Alliance, de nostre Seigneur et seul Sauveur Jesus Christ .... B 177

Bodius, Hermann: *La premiere Partie de Lunion de plusieurs passaiges de lescripture saincte* .... B 214

Bodius, Hermann: *La seconde partie de Lunion de plusieurs passaiges de lescripture saincte* .... B 215

Bouchet, Jean: *Les Triumphes de la noble et amoureuse dame*.... B 228

Branteghem, Guillaume de: *Enchyridion, ou Manuel contenant plusieurs matieres*... B 239

Branteghem, Guillaume de: *La Vie de Nostre Seigneur Jesu-Christ par figures, selon le Texte des quattre Evangelistes*..... B 243

La confession de Foy faicte par le Chrestien joyeux en Christ.... C 128

Dentière, Marie: *Epistre tresutile <> Envoyée à la Royne de Navarre seur du Roy de France. Contre les Turcz, Juifz, Infideles, Faulx chrestiens, Anabaptistes, et Lutheriens*.............. D 4

Doré, Pierre: *Les Allumettes du feu divin ... Avec les Voyes de paradis*... D 44

Doré, Pierre: *Le College de sapience, fondé en Luniversité de Vertu ... Avec le Dialogue de la Foy*..................................... D 57

Doré, Pierre: *Dialogue. Instructoire, des Chrestiens en la foy, Esperance, et Amour en Dieu*... D 68

Du Pinet, Antoine: *Familiere et briefve exposition sur l'apocalypse De Sainct Jehan l'apostre* .... D 100

Erasme, Desiderius: *Les Apophthegmes*................................. E 16

Erasme, Desiderius: *Le Preparatif à la mort... Adjoustee une instruction chrestienne pour bien vivre, et soy preparer a mourir*... E 44

Erasme, Desiderius: *Le Preparatif à la mort... Adjoustée une instruction chrestienne pour bien vivre, et soy preparer à mourir*... E 45

Breve exposition faicte par maniere d'exhortation et d'oraison prinse sur le Pater noster.. E 76

Exposition sur le Salve Regina.. E 84

La fleur des commandemens de Dieu.................................. F 39

Gaigny, Jean de: *Le livre de nouvel reimprime Faisant mention des Sept parolles que nostre benoist Saulveur ... dist en larbre de la croix*... G 10

Gerson, Jean: *Le Directoire des confesseurs*............................ G 16

Grégoire de Nazianze, Saint: *De la cure, et nourrissement des Pauvres. Sermon*... G 26

Gringore, Pierre: *Heures de nostre Dame*................................ G 52

Internelle consolation.. I 23

Le livre intitule Internelle consolation nouvellement corrige...... I 24

Le livre intitule Internelle consolation Nouvellement corrige..... I 25

Breve instruction faicte par maniere de Lettre missive: pour se confesser en verité... I 58

Lefèvre d'Étaples, Jacques: *Contemplations salutaires d'Innocence perdue... avec une oraison à Dieu pour la paix et union de nostre Mere l'Eglise*....................................... L 18

Le Grand, Jacques: *Le Tresor de sapience*............................... L 26d

Luther, Martin: *Exposition de l'histoire des dix Lepreux, prinse du dixseptiesme de Sainct Luc*.. L 87

Luther, Martin: *Le livre de vraye et parfaicte oraison*............... L 102

Marguerite de Navarre: *Le miroir de treschrestienne princesse Marguerite de France*... M 41

Marot, Clément?: *La Bergerie du bon pasteur*......................... M 43

Merlin, Jacques: *Lexposition de levangille Missus est*............... M 71

Sensuit le mistere de la Passion de nostre seigneur Jesuchrist.... M 99

Sensuit le mistere de la Passion de nostre seigneur Jesuchrist.... M 100

Sensuit la Resurrection de nostre seigneur Jesuchrist: Par personnages.. M 105

Parenti, Ch. de: *Instructions et oraisons tres salutaires*............. P 4

Petit, Guillaume: *Le viat de salut ... instruction pour soy confesser et plusieurs devotes chansons*................................ P 18

Sensuyvent aucunes belles preparations pour devotement recevoir le sainct sacrement de lautel.. P 39

Sermon notable pour le jour de la Dedicace............................ S 14

La Somme de lescripture saincte, enseignant la vraye foy, par laquelle sommes justifiez.. S 27

La vengeance et destruction de Hierusalem par personnaiges ....   V 1

Zwingli, Ulrich: *Brieve et claire exposition de la Foy Chrestienne* ..   Z 1

1540

La Bible en laquelle sont contenus tous les livres canoniques, de la saincte escriture..   B 43

Les sept Pseaulmes de la penitence de David............................   B 83

La premiere/seconde partie du Nouveau Testament ....   B 179

Le nouveau Testament de nostre Seigneur Jesu Christ, seul sauveur du monde..   B 178

Branteghem, Guillaume de: *La Vie de Jesus Christ*...................   B 245

Branteghem, Guillaume de: *La Vie de nostre Seigneur Jesu Christ par figures, selon le Texte des quattre Evangelistes*.....   B 244

Branteghem, Guillaume de: *La Vie de Nostre Seigneur Jesus Christ par figures selon le texte des quatre Evangelistes*........   B 246

Branteghem, Guillaume de: *La Vie de Nostre Seigneur Jesus Christ par figures selon le texte des quatre Evangelistes*........   B 247

Branteghem, Guillaume de: *La Vie de Nostre Seigneur Jesus Christ par figures, selon le texte des quatre Evangelistes*.......   B 248

Branteghem, Guillaume de: *La Vie de Nostre Seigneur Jesus Christ par figures, selon le texte des quatre Evangelistes*.......   B 249

Branteghem, Guillaume de: *La Vie de Nostre Seigneur Jesus Christ par figures, selon le texte des quatre Evangelistes*.......   B 250

Brodeau, Victor: *Les Louanges de JesuChrist nostre Saulveur*....   B 267

Brodeau, Victor: *Les Louanges De Jesus Nostre Saulveur ... Avecques Les Louenges de la glorieuse Vierge Marie*.............   B 266

Bucer, Martin: *Exposition de Levangile de nostre seigneur Jesus Christ, selon S. Matthieu*...   B 278

Bullinger, Heinrich: *Exposition sur les deux epistres de Sainct Paul, envoiées aux Thessaloniciens*......................................   B 280

Calvin, Jean: *Epistre de Jaques Sadolet Cardinal envoyée au Senat et Peuple de Geneve:... Avec la Response de Jehan Calvin*..   C 42

La confession et raison de la foy de Maistre Noel Beda.............   C 127

Dolet, Estienne: *Les Gestes de Françoys de Valois Roy de France* ...   D 33

Doré, Pierre: *Les Allumettes du feu divin ... Avec les Voyes de paradis*...   D 45

Doré, Pierre: *L'arbre de vie, appuyant les beaux lys de France* ......   D 50

Doré, Pierre: *Limage de vertu demonstrant la perfection et saincte vie de la bienheuree vierge Marie*.............................   D 73

Doré, Pierre: *L'image de vertu demonstrant la perfection et saincte vie de la bienheuree vierge Marie*.............................   D 74

Doré, Pierre: *Les Voyes de Paradis*...   D 94

Doré, Pierre: *Les Voyes du Paradis* .... D 93

Le livre intitule le Fagot de Myerre.. F 4

Farel, Guillaume: *Letres certaines daucuns grandz troubles et tumultes advenuz a Geneve* .... F 18

Gaigny, Jean de: *Le livre de nouvel reimprime Faisant mention des Sept parolles que nostre benoist Saulveur ... dist en larbre de la croix.*... G 11

Greban, Simon: *Le premier (-second) volume du triumphant mystere des actes des Apostres*... G 24

Gringore, Pierre: *Chantz Royaulx ... avec plusieurs devotes Oraisons et Rondeaulx contemplatifz*.................................... G 44

Gringore, Pierre: *Chantz Royaulx, ... avec plusieurs devotes Oraisons et Rondeaulx contemplatifz*.................................... G 45

Gringore, Pierre: *Heures de nostre dame ... Additionnees de plusieurs chantz royaulx figurez et moralisez*........................ G 53

Gringore, Pierre: *Heures de nostre dame ... Additionnées de plusieurs chantz royaulx figurez et moralisez*........................ G 54

Gringore, Pierre: *Heures de nostre dame ... Additionnées de plusieurs chantz royaulx figurez et moralisez*........................ G 55

Guerric: *Sermons*.. G 58

Le livre de l'internelle consolation nouvellement reveu et diligemment corrige... I 26

Le livre de l'Internelle consolation nouvellement reveu, et diligemment corrigé.. I 27

Le livre de l'Internelle consolation, nouvellement reveu et diligemment corrigé.. I 28

Instruction pour les Chrestiens... I 51

Introduction pour les enfans ... Ou sont adjoustees de nouveau, une tresutile maniere de scavoir bien lire, et orthographier, par Alde. Et la doctrine pour bien et deuement escripre selon la propriete du language francois, par Clement Marot.............. I 50

Jérôme, Saint: *La vie des Peres*... J 10

Lemaire de Belges, Jean: *Le traicte de la difference des Scismes*.. L 44

Lescagne, Tristan de: *Le Lys treschrestian florissant en la foy chrestiane* .... L 59

Lucidaire en françoys... L 72

Luther, Martin: *Exposition sur les deux Epistres de S. Pierre, et sur celle de S. Jude ... Avec un Sermon du vray usage de la loy*... L 92

Luther, Martin: *Les faitz de Jesus Christ et du Pape* .... L 95

Luther, Martin: *Le livre de vraye et parfaicte oraison*................ L 103

Luther, Martin: *Le livre de vraye et parfaicte oraison*................ L 104

Luther, Martin: *Le livre de vraye et parfaicte oraison*................ L 105

Malingre, Matthieu: *Moralite de la maladie de Chrestiente, a .xiij. personnages* .... M 9

Devote meditation sur la mort et passion de nostre saulveur et redempteur... Une meditation pour lespasse dune basse messe ... M 54

Megander, Gaspard: *Exposition chrestienne Dés dix commande-mens, Dés articles de la Foy, De l'oraison de nostre Seigneur* ... M 57

Menard, Jean: *Epistre Chrestienne, aux Freres Mineurs, de lordre de S. Françoys* .... M 69

Le mistere de la conception: nativite: mariage: et annonciation de la benoiste vierge Marie.. M 89

Oecolampadius, Johann: *Exposition sur la premiere Epistre de S. Jehan Apostre, divisee par Sermons*........................... O 4

Petit, Guillaume: *La formation de l'homme et son excellence et ce qu'il doibt accomplir pour avoir Paradis* .... P 11

Petit, Guillaume: *Le Viat de salut*.. P 19

Pinet, Guillaume: *Le Contemnement du monde ... la conversion de l'ame*.. P 23

Primasius: *Briefve et fructueuse exposition sus les Epistres Sainct Paul aux Romains et Hebreux*........................... P 41

Le Refuge des Chrestiens compose sur les dix commandemens de Dieu.. R 42

Saulnier, Antoine: *Chanson nouvelle. Composee sus les dix commandemens de Dieu*.. S 3

Spagnuoli, Battista: *La Vie d'honneur et de Vertu*........................ S 29

Les testamentz des douze patriarches Enfans de Jakob.............. T 2

Un Vif Sacrifice Quotidian, une saincte enflambée oraison, un doulx sacrifice.. V 23

Vitrier, Jean: *Le Sermon que nostre Seigneur feist en la mon-taigne*.. V 50

Vitrier, Jean: *Le Sermon que nostre Seigneur feist en la mon-taigne*.. V 51

Voragine, Jacques de: *La Legende Doree et vie des Sainctz et Sainctes* .... V 76

1541

Larmeure de patience en adversité... A 17

Béda, Noël: *La petite dyablerie dont Lucifer est le chef*............. B 12

La saincte Bible en Francois.. B 44

Le premier/second Volume de la Bible en francois .... B 45

Le livre des Pseaulmes de David, traduictes selon la pure verite Hebraique: ensuyvant ... linterpretation de Felix.................. B 84

Les sept psalmes du pecheur converty à Dieu .... B 89

Les sept pseaulmes de la penitence de David .... B 88
Paraphrase et devote exposition sur les sept tresprecieux et notables Pseaulmes. .... B 87
Psalmes de David, Translatez de plusieurs Autheurs et principallement de Cle. Marot. Veu ... et corrigé par les théologiens. ...... B 85
Psalmes de David, Translatez de plusieurs Autheurs et principallement de Cle. Marot... Sermon du bon et mauvais pasteur ..... B 86
Trente Pseaulmes de David mis en françoys par Clement Marot ...... B 90
Les Livres de Salomon .... B 148
La Premiere/seconde partie du Nouveau Testament .... B 182
La premiere / seconde partie du Nouveau Testament de Jesu Christ B 180
La premiere/seconde partie du Nouveau Testament de Jesu Christ... B 181
Bonaventure, Saint (attrib.): *Le libvre tressalutaire nomme Lesguillon damour divin* .... B 218
Bouchet, Jean: *Les triumphes de la noble et amoureuse dame* ..... B 229
Bouchet, Jean: *Les triumphes de la Noble et amoureuse Dame* ... B 230
Branteghem, Guillaume de: *La vie de nostre Seigneur Jesuchrist, selon le texte des quatre Evangelistes* .... B 252
Branteghem, Guillaume de: *La Vie de Nostre Seigneur Jesus Christ par figures, selon le texte des quatre Evangelistes*. ...... B 253
Branteghem, Guillaume de: *La vie de nostre Seigneur, selon les quattres Evangelistes*. .... B 251
Cabosse, Jean: *Le mirouer de prudence* .... C 1
Cabosse, Jean: *Traicte du treshault et excellent mistere de l'incarnation du verbe divin*. .... C 2
Calvin, Jean: *Les Actes de la journee imperiale, tenue en la cité de Regespourg* .... C 7
Calvin, Jean: *Epistre au treschrestien roy de France Françoys premier de ce nom*. .... C 41
Calvin, Jean: *Institution de la religion chrestienne* .... C 58
Calvin, Jean: *Petit Traicté de la saincte cene de nostre Seigneur Jesus Christ*. .... C 73
Chocquet, Louis: *Lapocalypse Sainct Jehan Zebedee ... ensemble les cruaultez de Domicien Cesar* .... C 106
Doré, Pierre: *La Deploration de la vie humaine, avec la disposition a dignement recepvoir le Sainct Sacrement* .... D 63
L'Epistre Catholique de Sainct Jaques Apostre. Avec une exposition breve, et bien facile. .... E 12
Erasme, Desiderius: *Comedie ou dialogue matrimonial ... Uxor memphigamos, C'est à dire: La femme mary plaignant*. .... E 23
Erasme, Desiderius: *Le Preparatif à la mort* .... E 46
Exhortation tresutile sur les sainctes parolles de nostre Seigneur Jesus, Retournez vous et croyez à l'Evangile. .... E 73

Exposition Sur les Articles de la Foy et Religion chrestienne, qu'on appelle communement le Symbole des Apostres .... E 80

Farel, Guillaume: *La tressainte oraison que Jesus Christ a baillé à ses Apostres* .... F 21

Gaigny, Jean de: *Le livre contenant devote exposition sur le cinquantiesme Pseaulme* .... G 5

Greban, Simon: *Les Catholiques oeuvres et Actes des Apostres redigez en escript par sainct Luc Evangeliste* .... G 25

Le livre de l'Internelle consolation, nouvellement reveu, et diligemment corrigé. .... I 29

Linstruction des curez .... I 47a

Petite instruction et maniere de vivre pour une Femme seculiere: et comme elle se doibt conduire en pensees, en parolles, et en oeuvres .... I 56

Lasseré, Louis: *La Vie de monseigneur sainct Hierosme. Recongneue et augmentee du tiers, pour la troisiesme fois* .... L 16

Mailly, Nicolas de: *La divine cognoissance ... ensemble les cantiques divins de l'ame regrettant, joinct l'exposition de l'oraison dominicalle* .... M 4

La marchandise spirituelle ordonnee et distinguee en sept regions spirituelles, selon les sept jours de la sepmaine .... M 16

Marcourt, Antoine: *Le livre des marchans, fort utile a toutes gens...* M 25

Melanchthon, Philippe: *La Responce donnee par les princes d'Allemaigne ... en matiere de la Religion Chrestienne* .... M 66

Le mistere de la Passion de nostre seigneur Jesuchrist .... M 101

La Resurrection de nostre seigneur Jesuchrist: par personnages... M 106

Les Parolles memorables de Jesuchrist au pecheur pour le attirer a son amour ... Avec la maniere de se scavoir bien confesser ...... P 7

Quentin, Jean: *Lorloge de devotion* .... Q 3

Les quinze effusions du sang de nostre Sauveur Jesuchrist .... Q 4

La Vie et Passion de Ma Dame saincte Marguerite Vierge et Martyre .... V 20

Vincent, Saint, de Léris: *Verité de la foi catholique* .... V 24

Viret, Pierre: *Epistre consolatoire, envoyée aux fideles qui souffrent persecution* .... V 34

Vitrier, Jean: *Le Sermon que nostre Seigneur Jesuchrist feit en la montaigne* .... V 52

Vivès, Juan Luis: *Institution de la femme Chrestienne... Aussi, de l'office du Mary* .... V 54

1542

Arétin, Pierre: *La Genese de M. Pierre Aretin, avec la vision de Noë* .... A 11

Augustin, Saint: *De la Vanité de ce siecle et monde inferieur*..... A 33

Augustin, Saint: *De la vie Chrestienne, avec les Traictez de Charite, de la Vanite de ce Siecle et monde inferieur, Dobedience et Humilite, et Leschelle de Paradis*.......................... A 34

Bernard, Saint: *De la maniere d'aimer Dieu*............................ B 20

[*Psaumes de Clément Marot. Sermon du bon et mauvais pasteur*].... B 92

Psalmes du royal Prophete David. Fidelement traduicts de Latin en Françoys... B 93

Traité tres utile des sept degres de l'echelle de penitence, figurez au vray sur les sept Pseaumes penitentiels .... B 91

Les Livres de Salomon .... B 149

La Premiere/seconde partie du Nouveau Testament .... B 186

Le Nouveau Testament.. B 185

Le Nouveau Testament de nostre seigneur Jesus Christ.............. B 183

Le Nouveau Testament de nostre seigneur Jesus Christ.............. B 184

Branteghem, Guillaume de: *Le vergier spirituel et mystique*....... B 241

Branteghem, Guillaume de: *Vergier Spirituel et mystique*........... B 242

Branteghem, Guillaume de: *La Vie de nostre Seigneur Jesus Christ par figures, selon le texte des quatre Evangelistes*....... B 254

Branteghem, Guillaume de: *La Vie de nostre Seigneur Jesus Christ, selon le texte des quatre Evangelistes* .... B 255

Brief Discours de la Republique françoyse desirant la lecture des livres de la saincte Escripture luy estre loisible en sa langue vulgaire .... B 261

Bris, Nicolas de: *Institution a porter les adversitez du monde patiemment*.. B 265

Brodeau, Victor: *Les Louanges Du sainct nom de Jesus ... Six sermons des six parolles de nostre Seigneur en croix* .... B 268

Brunfels, Otto: *Les Prieres et oraisons de la Bible*..................... B 275

Calvin, Jean: *Les Actes de la journee imperiale, tenue en la cité de Reguespourg* .... C 8

Calvin, Jean: *Le catechisme de l'Eglise de Geneve* .... C 20

Calvin, Jean: *Exposition sur l'epistre de sainct Judas apostre*.... C 47

Calvin, Jean: *La Forme des prieres et chantz ecclesiastiques* ..... C 49

Calvin, Jean: *La Manyere de faire prieres aux eglises Françoyses. tant devant la predication comme apres*...................... C 65

Calvin, Jean: *Petit Traicté de la saincte cene de nostre Seigneur Jesus Christ*.. C 74

Campen, Jean van: *Paraphrase, c'est adire, claire, et briefve interpretation sur les Psalmes ... et sur l'Ecclesiaste de Salomon*... C 85

Campen, Jean van: *Paraphrase. C'est à dire, claire, et briefve interpretation sur les Psalmes ... sur l'Ecclesiaste de Salomon*.... C 86

Campen, Jean van: *Paraphrase, c'est à dire claire et briefve interpretation sur les psalmes ... sur l'Ecclesiaste* .... C 87

Chansons demonstrant les erreurs et abuz du temps present .... C 100

Diffinition et perfection d'amour. Sophologe d'amour .... D 2

Doré, Pierre: *L'arbre de vie, appuyant les beaux lys de France* .... D 51

Doré, Pierre: *Dyalogue Instructoire des Chrestiens, en la Foy, Esperance, et Amour en Dieu* .... D 69

Erasme, Desiderius: *Le Chevalier Chrestien* .... E 30

Erasme, Desiderius: *Le Chevalier Chrestien..* .... E 31

Erasme, Desiderius: *Le Chevalier Chrestien..* .... E 32

Erasme, Desiderius: *Le vray moyen de bien et catholiquement se confesser* .... E 38

Erasme, Desiderius: *Preparation à la mort* .... E 47

Erasme, Desiderius: *Le sermon de Jesus enfant* .... E 54

Exhortation à la lecture des sainctes lettres .... E 69

Traicte contenant plusieurs expositions utiles et salutaires sur loraison dominicale aultrement dicte la Patinostre .... E 79

Farel, Guillaume: *Summaire, et briefve declaration daucuns lieux fort necessaires a ung chascun Chrestien ... Item, ung traicte du Purgatoire* .... F 29

Farel, Guillaume: *Summaire. C'est, une brieve declaration d'aucuns lieux fort necessaires à un chascun Chrestien... corrigé, reveu, et augmenté* .... F 30

La Fontaine de vie .... F 45

La Fontaine de Vie. De laquelle resourdent tresdoulces consolations ... Plus y est adjouste linstruction pour les enfans .... F 46

Gringore, Pierre: *Chantz Royaulx ... avec plusieurs devotes Oraisons et Rondeaulx contemplatifz* .... G 46

Les Heures de la compagnie des penitents .... H 11

Les Simulachres et historiees faces de la mort, contenant La medecine de l'ame .... I 7

L'Internelle consolation. oeuvre divisée en trois parties .... I 31

Le livre de Linternelle Consolation ... Larmeure de Patience... Devote contemplation ... sur le Salve regina .... I 30

Le livre intitule Internelle consolation Nouvellement corrige ..... I 32

Lefèvre d'Étaples, Jacques: *Les Epistres, et Evangiles des cinquante, et deux Dimenches de l'An* .... L 22

Le Grand, Jacques: *Le Tresor de Sapience et fleur de toute bonte...* L 27

Livre de la compagnie des Penitens contenant l'ordre de recepvoir un Novice .... L 66

Luther, Martin: *Le livre de vraye et parfaicte oraison* .... L 106

Marcourt, Antoine: *Declaration de la Messe, Le fruict dicelle, La cause, et le moyen, pour quoy et comment on la doibt maintenir* M 20

Marcourt, Antoine: *Petit traicte tres utile, et salutaire de la saincte eucharistie de nostre Seigneur Jesuchrist*.................. M 30

Melanchthon, Philippe: *De l'authorité de l'Eglise, des docteurs d'icelle, et de l'authorité de la Parolle de Dieu*..................... M 59

Menard, Jean: *Declaration de la reigle et estat des Cordeliers*... M 70

Mystere du vieil testament par personnages............................ M 109

Osiander, Andreas: *Mandat et advertissement a ses Ecclesiastiques de recepvoir la parolle de Dieu*.............................. O 13

Rabelais, François: *Gargantua et Pantagruel*........................... R 20

Rabelais, François: *Gargantua. Prochainement reveue, et de beaucoup augmentée*.. R 19

Rabelais, François: *Gargantua* .... R 18

Rabelais, François: *Pantagruel*... R 12

Rabelais, François: *Pantagruel*... R 13

Rhegius, Urbanus: *La Doctrine Nouvelle et Ancienne* .... R 45

Rhegius, Urbanus: *La Medecine de l'ame* .... R 48

Rosay, G. de: *Le relief de l'ame pecheresse*............................ R 51

Sleidan, Jean: *Escript adresse aux Electeurs Princes, et aultres Estatz de Lempire... Dung chef nouveau*............................ S 18

Le Sommaire des livres du Vieil, et Nouveau Testament. Les dix parolles, ou Commandements de Dieu.............................. S 21

Spagnuoli, Battista: *La Fontaine de tous biens, Vie, d'honneur et de Vertu*... S 30

Viret, Pierre: *De la difference qui est entre les superstitions et idolatries des anciens gentilz et payens, et les erreurs et abuz qui sont entre ceux qui s'appellent Chrestiens*.............. V 27

Vivès, Juan Luis: *Livre de l'institution de la femme chrestienne*..... V 55

1543

L'armeure de patience en adversité... A 18

Les Articles de la faculté de Theologie de Paris, touchant et concernant nostre Foy et Religion Chrestienne..................... A 22

La Bible translatee de latin en francois au vray sens pour les simples gens... B 46

Le premier/second Volume de la Bible en francois.................... B 47

Trente-deux Pseaulmes de David [par Marot]... Plus vingt autres Pseaumes.. B 97

Cinquante Pseaumes de Marot.. B 96

Cinquante Pseaumes en françois par Clem. Marot. Item une Epistre par luy.. B 95

Les Psalmes de David, Fidelement traduicts de Latin en Françoys. Avec argument et sommaire à chascun Psalme............ B 94

Le Nouveau Testament de nostre Seigneur Jesu Christ, seul sauveur du monde .... B 187

Le Nouveau Testament de nostre Seigneur Jesu Christ, seul sauveur du monde .... B 188

Le Nouveau Testament de nostre Seigneur Jesu Christ, seul sauveur du monde .... B 189

Le Nouveau Testament, C'est à dire, La nouvelle Alliance de nostre Seigneur et seul Sauveur Jesus Christ .... B 190

La premiere/seconde Partie du Nouveau Testament .... B 191

La Premiere/seconde Partie du Nouveau Testament .... B 192

Branteghem, Guillaume de: *La Vie de Jesus Christ* .... B 258

Branteghem, Guillaume de: *La vie de nostre seigneur Jesu Christ selon le texte des quatre Evangelistes* .... B 256

Branteghem, Guillaume de: *La Vie de Nostre Seigneur Jesus Christ, Selon le texte des quatre Evangelistes* .... B 257

Brodeau, Victor: *Les Louanges du sainct nom de Jesus... Plus une Epistre dung pecheur a Jesus Christ* .... B 270

Brodeau, Victor: *Les Louanges du sainct nom de Jesus... plus Une epistre d'ung pecheur à JesuChrist* .... B 269

Brunfels, Otto: *Les Prieres et oraisons de la Bible* .... B 276

Cailleau, Gilles: *Paraphrase sur les Heures de nostre Dame* ...... C 4

Calvin, Jean: *Advertissement tresutile ... s'il se faisoit inventoire de tous les corps sainctz, et reliques* .... C 13

Calvin, Jean, et Viret, Pierre: *Deux Epistres, l'une demonstre comment nostre Seigneur Jesus Christ est la fin de la Loy... L'autre pour consoler les fideles qui souffrent pour le Nom de Jesus* ..... C 39

Calvin, Jean: *Exposition sur l'epistre de sainct Paul aux Romains* ... C 46

Calvin, Jean: *La Forme des prieres et chantz ecclesiastiques* ..... C 50

Calvin, Jean: *Petit traicté, monstrant que c'est que doit faire un homme fidele ... quand il est entre les papistes* .... C 77

Campen, Jean van: *Paraphrase sur les Psalmes* .... C 88

Castellion, Sébastien: *Dialogi sacri, latino-gallici, ad linguas, morésque puerorum formandos* .... C 92

Chrysostome, S. Jean: *Traicté <> Que nul n'est offensé sinon par soymesme* .... C 108

Chrysostome, S. Jean: *Traicté <> que nul n'est offensé, sinon par soymesmes* .... C 109

Dolet, Estienne: *Les faictz et gestes du Roy Françoys premier de ce nom* .... D 35

Dolet, Estienne: *Les Gestes de Françoys de Valois Roy de France* ... D 34

Dolet, Estienne: *Sommaire et recueil des faictz et gestes, du Roy Françoys premier de ce nom* .... D 38

Dolet, Estienne: *Sommaire et recueil des faictz et gestes, du Roy Françoys premier de ce non* .... D 39

Doré, Pierre: *La deploration de la vie humaine, avec la disposition a dignement recepvoir le Sainct Sacrement* .... D 64

Doré, Pierre: *La caeleste pensée de graces divines arrousée* .... D 86

Doré, Pierre: *La celeste pensée, des graces divines arrousée* ...... D 85

Du Pinet, Antoine: *Exposition sur l'Apocalypse de Sainct Jehan l'Apostre* .... D 101

Edict du Roy Sur les articles faictz par la faculte de Theologie de luniversite de Paris concernans nostre foy .... E 4

Edict sur les articles faictz par la faculte de theologie .... E 3

Erasme, Desiderius: *Enchiridion, ou manuel du chevalier chrestien* .... E 33

Erasme, Desiderius: *Paraphrase sur le troisieme pseaulme de David, faicte en maniere d'oraison* .... E 40

Erasme, Desiderius: *Paraphrase, ou briefve exposition sur toutes les Epistres Canoniques* .... E 39

Erasme, Desiderius: *La Preparation à la mort* .... E 48

Erasme, Desiderius: *Preparation à la mort ... Avecques aulcunes Prieres et Pseaulmes* .... E 49

Erasme, Desiderius: *Le sermon de Jesus enfant* .... E 56

Erasme, Desiderius: *Le Sermon de Jesus enfant... Avec le songe du combat entre le corps et l'esprit* .... E 55

Lexcercice pour jeunes gens lesquelz veullent parvenir en bien et perfection de leur estat .... E 68

Exposition des articles de la Foy et Religion Chrestienne, qu'on appelle communement le Symbole des Apostres .... E 81

Farel, Guillaume: *Epistre envoyee au duc de Lorraine* .... F 12

Farel, Guillaume: *Une Epistre de Maistre Pierre Caroly docteur de la Sorbone de Paris ... envoiée à Maistre Guillaume Farel ... avec la response* .... F 9

Farel, Guillaume: *La Seconde Epistre envoyée au Docteur Pierre Caroly* .... F 10

Farel, Guillaume: *La tres sainte oraison que nostre Seigneur Jesus Christ a baillé à ses Apostres* .... F 22

Farel, Guillaume: *Oraison tresdevote en laquelle est faicte la confession des pechez* .... F 23

La Fontaine de vie .... F 47

Le livre de l'Internelle consolation... Et y sont adjouxtées les Tentations du Diable, avec la defense du bon Ange .... I 33

An Instruction for chyldren/Linstruction des enfans .... I 52

Jérôme, Saint: *Epistre à Paulin, l'induisant à l'estude des lettres* .... J 1

Lactantius Firmianus: *Des Divines institutions, contre les Gentilz et Idolatres* .... L 2

Lemaire de Belges, Jean: *Le Promptuaire des Conciles de l'Eglise catholique, avec les schismes et la difference d'iceulx* .... L 49

Livre merveilleux, contenant en brief la fleur et substance de plusieurs traictiez .... L 69

Luther, Martin: *Le livre de vraye et parfaicte oraison* .... L 107

Luther, Martin: *Le livre de vraye et parfaicte oraison* .... L 108

Luther, Martin: *Le livre de vraye et parfaicte oraison* .... L 109

Luther, Martin: *Les quatorze miroirs pour consoler la creature en Dieu* .... L 83

Malingre, Matthieu: *Indice des principales matieres contenues en la Bible* .... M 6

Melanchthon, Philippe: *Confession de la foy presentee a Tres-invictissime Empereur Charles V. a la journee d'Auspurg* ...... M 62

Melanchthon, Philippe: *De la puissance et authorité de la saincte Eglise chrestienne* .... M 60

Ung beau mystere de nostre Dame ... dune jeune Fille laquelle se voulut habandonner a peche .... M 108b

Traicté de purgatoire .... P 51

Savonarola, Jérôme: *Exposition de l'oraison dominicale... Meditation sur les psalmes: Miserere mei Deus... In te, Domine, speravi... Breve interpretation du decalogue* .... S 7

Sermons des six paroles de Jesuchrist en croix .... S 15

Sleidan, Jean: *D'un nouveau chef qui au temps des empereurs s'esleva à Rome* .... S 19

La doctrine des Chrestiens, extraicte du Vieil et Nouveau testament. Les dix parolles ou commandemens de Dieu. Loraison Dominicalle... Les commandemens de nostre mere Saincte Esglise. Les sept Sacremens .... S 22

Le Sommaire des livres du Vieil et Nouveau testament. Les dix parolles, ou commandemens de Dieu .... S 23

Viret, Pierre: *Epistre envoyee aux fideles conversans entre les Chrestiens Papistiques* .... V 35

Vivès, Juan Luis: *L'institution de la femme chrestienne ... Avec l'office du Mary* .... V 56

Vivès, Juan Luis: *Livre tresbon plaisant et salutaire de Linstitution de la femme chrestienne ... Aussi de loffice du mary... Instruction de la vertu Dhumilite. Avec une epistre de sainct Bernard* .... V 57

1544

La Bible en Francoys.. B 49

Le premier/second Volume de la Bible en francois.................... B 48

Le Premier/Second Volume de la Bible en Francoys .... B 50

Les Oeuvres de Clement Marot .... B 99

Les psalmes du royal prophete David, traduictz par Clement Marot. Avec autres petits Ouvrages par luy mesme .... B 98

Salomon. Les Proverbes. Ecclesiastes. Les Cantiques. Sapience. Ecclesiastique.. .... B 150

La Premiere/seconde partie du Nouveau Testament.................. B 195

Le nouveau Testament auquel est demonstre Jesu Crist nostre Sauveur.. B 193

Le Nouveau Testament, Cest a dire: La nouvelle Alliance De nostre Seigneur et seul Sauveur Jesus Christ .... B 194

Branteghem, Guillaume de: *La Vie de nostre Seigneur Jesus Christ par figures, selon le texte des quatre Evangelistes*....... B 259

Brunfels, Otto: *Les Prieres et oraisons de la Bible*.................... B 277

Bucer, Martin: *Exposition sur l'evangile selon sainct Matthieu* ... B 279

Calvin, Jean: *Advertissement sur la censure qu'ont faicte les Bestes de Sorbonne, touchant les livres qu'ilz appellent heretiques*... C 11

Calvin, Jean: *Advertissement tresutile ... sil se faisoit inventoire de tous les corps sainctz, et reliques*............................ C 14

Calvin, Jean: *Les Articles de la sacree faculte de theologie de Paris ... Avec le remede contre la poison*............................ C 19

Calvin, Jean: *Les Articles de la sacree Faculté de Theologie de Paris ... Avec le Remede contre la Poison*............................ C 18

Calvin, Jean: *Excuse <> à Messieurs les Nicodemites, sur la complaincte qu'ilz font de sa trop grand'rigueur* .... C 43

Calvin, Jean: *Brieve Instruction, pour armer tous bons fideles contre les erreurs de la secte commune des Anabaptistes*....... C 61

Calvin, Jean: *Supplication et remonstrance, sur le faict de la Chrestienté*... C 71

Calvin, Jean: *Supplication et remonstrance, sur le faict de la Chrestienté*... C 72

Calvin, Jean: *Petit traicté, monstrant que c'est que doit faire un homme fidele ... quand il est entre les papistes*................. C 78

Caracciolo, Antoine: *Le mirouer de vraye religion*.................... C 90

Caracciolo, Antoine: *Le mirouer de vraye religion*.................... C 91

Dolet, Estienne: *Les Faitz et gestes du Roy Françoys: premier de ce nom*... D 36

Doré, Pierre: *Le cerf spirituel ... Avec L'adresse de l'esgaré pecheur*... D 53

Doré, Pierre: *Dialogue Instructoire, des Chrestiens en la foy, Esperance, et Amour en dieu* .... D 71

Doré, Pierre: *Dyalogue instructoire* .... D 70

Doré, Pierre: *Le Livre des divins benefices* .... D 78

Doré, Pierre: *La meditation devote du bon Chrestien sus le sainct sacrifice de la Messe* .... D 80

Epistre consolatoire à une soeur soufrant persecution .... E 9

Les Epistres de monseigneur Sainct Paul glosées .... E 14

Erasme, Desiderius: *La Civilité puerile* .... E 19

Erasme, Desiderius: *Le Chevalier Chrestien* .... E 34

Erasme, Desiderius: *Preparation à la mort* .... E 51

Erasme, Desiderius: *De la preparation à la mort* .... E 50

Exhortation à la lecture des Sainctes Lettres .... E 70

Farel, Guillaume: *Epistre envoyee aux reliques de la dissipation horrible de l'Antechrist* .... F 14

Farel, Guillaume: *Epistre exhortatoire, à tous ceux qui ont congnoissance de l'Evangile* .... F 11

Gringore, Pierre: *Heures de Nostre Dame* .... G 56

Heyden, Sebald: *D'un seul mediateur, advocat, et intercesseur entre Dieu et les hommes, nostre Seigneur Jesus Christ* .... H 14

De limitation de Jesu Christ selon la saincte Evangile .... I 34

De limitation de Jesu Christ selon la saincte Evangile .... I 35

Internelle consolation .... I 37

L'Internelle Consolation .... I 36

Lalande, Matthieu de: *Manuel des abus de lhomme ingrat <> Avec la copie des lettres de Martin Bucere* .... L 10

Landry, François: *La declaration De la Foy chrestienne, faicte par ung bachelier en theologie* .... L 13

Lefèvre d'Étaples, Jacques: *Epistres et Evangiles des cinquante et deux Dimenches de l'An* .... L 23

Lefèvre d'Étaples, Jacques: *Epistres et evangiles des cinquantes et deux dimenches de L'An* .... L 24

Ludolphus de Saxe: *Le grand vita Christi* .... L 77

Luther, Martin: *Le livre de la vraye et parfaite Oraison avec le Sermon que nostre Seigneur feist en la montagne* .... L 110

Le Mandement de Jesus Christ a tous les Chrestiens et fideles ... M 11

Marcourt, Antoine: *Declaration de la Messe, Le fruict dicelle, La cause, et le moyen, pour quoy et comment on la doibt maintenir* .... M 21

Marcourt, Antoine: *Le livre des marchans, fort utile a toutes gens...* M 26

Melanchthon, Philippe: *De l'office des princes que Dieu leur commande touchant d'oster les abuz qui sont en l'Eglise* .... M 64

Ochino, Bernardino: *Epistre aux magnifiques Seigneurs de Siene ... Avec une Epistre à Mutio Justinopolitain* .... O 1

Ochino, Bernardino: *L'Image de l'Antechrist* .... O 2

Quatre homelies de trois antiques et excellens Theologiens ... S. Gregoire Nazianzene, S. Jean Chrysostome, S. Basile .... Q 1

Rhegius, Urbanus: *La Doctrine Nouvelle et Ancienne* .... R 46

La Somme de lescripture saincte, enseignant la vraye foy, par laquelle sommes justifiez .... S 28

Spagnuoli, Battista: *La Fontaine d'honneur et de vertu* .... S 31

Traicté auquel est deduict s'il est loysible de lire la saincte Escriture en langue Vulgaire .... T 14

La Verite cachee, devant cent ans faicte et composee a six personnages .... V 9

Viret, Pierre: *Disputations chrestiennes en maniere de deviz, divisées par dialogues* .... V 31

Viret, Pierre: *La seconde partie des Disputations Chrestiennes ...* V 32

Viret, Pierre: *La troisiesme partie des Disputations Chrestiennes ....* V 33

Viret, Pierre: *Exposition familiere sur le Symbole des Apostres .... faicte par dialogues* .... V 39

Viret, Pierre: *Petit traicte de l'usage de la salutation angelique...* V 44

Vitrier, Jean: *Le Sermon que nostre Seigneur feist en la montaigne* .... V 53

1545

Articles concernans la vraye religion et saincte foy catholicque... de Louvain .... A 24

Articles tres utiles et necessaires ... de Louvain .... A 23

Benedetto da Mantova: *Traité du benefice de Jesus Christ crucifié envers les chrestiens* .... B 18

La Bible en francois, En laquelle sont contenus tous les Livres Canoniques, de la saincte Escriture .... B 51

La Bible translatee de Latin en Francoys, au vray sens, pour les simples gens .... B 52

Le premier/second volume de la bible en francoiz .... B 53

Cinquante deux Pseaumes de David, Traduictz ... par Clement Marot .... B 102

Cinquante Pseaumes .... B 101

Cinquante Pseaumes .... B 103

Cinquante Pseaumes de David .... B 104

Cinquante Pseaumes en Françoys .... B 100

Le Nouveau Testament de nostre seigneur Jesus Christ .... B 196

Le Nouveau Testament de nostre Seigneur Jesus Christ .... B 197

Bouchet, Jean: *Les Triumphes de la noble et amoureuse dame ....* B 231

Bullinger, Heinrich: *Exposition sur les deux epistres de Sainct Paul aux Thessaloniciens* .... B 281

Calvin, Jean: *Advertissement tresutile ... sil se faisoit inventoire de tous les corps sainctz, et reliques* .... C 15

Calvin, Jean: *Argument et sommaire de l'epistre sainct Paul aux Romains* .... C 17

Calvin, Jean: *Le catechisme de l'Eglise de Geneve* .... C 21

Calvin, Jean et Viret, Pierre: *Deux Epistres. L'une demonstre comment nostre Seigneur Jesus Christ est la fin de la Loy... L'autre, pour consoler les fideles* .... C 40

Calvin, Jean: *La Forme des Prieres et Chants ecclesiastiques* .... C 51

Calvin, Jean: *Institution de la religion chrestienne* .... C 59

Calvin, Jean: *Brieve Instruction, pour armer tous bons fideles contre les erreurs de la secte commune des Anabaptistes* .... C 62

Calvin, Jean: *Contre la secte phantastique et furieuse des Libertins* .... C 68

Calvin, Jean: *Petit Traicté de la saincte cene* .... C 75

Calvin, Jean: *Petit traicté monstrant que doit faire un homme fidele ... Ensemble l'Excuse aux Nicodemites* .... C 79

Campen, Jean van: *Paraphrase ou briefve interpretation sur les Psalmes de David ... et sur l'Ecclesiaste* .... C 89

Chanson nouvelle contre la secte Lutheriane .... C 97

Chanson spirituelle sur la saincte Cene de nostre Seigneur .... C 95

Chansons spirituelles, pleines de louenges à Dieu .... C 102

Demonstrance des abuz de l'eglise .... D 3

Désiré, Artus: *Lamentation de nostre mere saincte Eglise* .... D 16

Doré, Pierre: *La croix de penitence* .... D 61

Doré, Pierre: *Dialogue Instructoire, des chrestiens en la foy, esperance, et Amour en Dieu* .... D 72

Du Pinet, Antoine: *Exposition sur l'apocalypse de sainct Jehan l'apostre* .... D 102

Enseignement tresutile ... pour fortifier la personne à voulentiers mourir, et ne craindre point la mort .... E 7

Farel, Guillaume: *Epistre envoyee au duc de Lorraine* .... F 13

Farel, Guillaume: *Forme d'oraison pour demander à Dieu la saincte predication de l'Evangile* .... F 15

Gaigny, Jean de: *Le livre de nouvel reimprime faisant mention de sept parolles que nostre benoist saulveur ... dit en larbre de la croix* .... G 12

Lemaire de Belges, Jean: *Le Promptuaire des conciles de l'Eglise Catholicque, avec les Scismes* .... L 51

Lemaire de Belges, Jean: *Le Promptuaire des conciles de l'Eglise catholique, avec les Scismes* .... L 50

Luther, Martin: *Antithese de la vraye et faulse Eglise* .... L 79
Luther, Martin: *Exposition sur les deux Epistres de S. Pierre,
  et sur celle de S. Jude* .... L 93
Luther, Martin: *Le livre de vraye et parfaicte oraison* .... L 111
Luther, Martin: *Le livre de vraye et parfaicte oraison. Avec le
  Sermon que nostre Seigneur feist en la montaigne* .... L 112
Le mandement de Jesus Christ a tous les Chrestiens et fideles .... M 12
Marot, Clément?: *Bergerie. Du bon pasteur et du mauvais* .... M 44
Melanchthon, Philippe: *De l'office des princes* .... M 65
Montfiquet, Raoul de: *Exposition de l'oraison dominicale* .... M 82
Ochino, Bernardino: *L'image de l'Antechrist* .... O 3
Ponisson, François: *Le miroir du pauvre pecheur penitent sur
  le pseaume de David L* .... P 24
Poullain, Valérand: *Oraison Chrestienne au Seigneur Dieu* .... P 35
Brief Traicté de Purgatoire .... P 52
Viret, Pierre: *Dialogues du desordre qui est a present au monde* ..... V 30
Viret, Pierre: *Petit traicte de l'usage de la salutation angelique* ...... V 45
Vivès, Juan Luis: *L'Institution de la femme chrestienne ... Avec
  l'office du Mary* .... V 58
Vivès, Juan Luis: *L'institution de la femme chrestienne ... Avec
  l'office du Mary* .... V 59

1546

*Arrest notable donné le 4e jour d'Octobre, l'an 1546 ... contre
  grand nombre d'Heretiques et blasphemateurs, du grand
  marché de Meaulx* .... A 20
Augustin, Saint: *Les livres <> de la vie chrestienne, de Charite,
  de la Vanite de ce Siecle et monde inferieur, Dobedience et
  Humilite, et Leschelle de Paradis* .... A 35
Beaulieu, Eustorg de: *Chrestienne resjouyssance* .... B 3
La Bible, Qui est toute la saincte escriture .... B 54
Cinquante deux Pseaumes .... B 111
Cinquante deux Pseaumes de David .... B 105
Cinquante deux Pseaumes de David .... B 106
Cinquante Deux Pseaumes de David .... B 107
Cinquante deux Pseaumes de David .... B 110
Livre premier/second contenant XVII. pseaulmes de David .... B 108
Recueil de trente et un Psaumes à quatre voix .... B 109
Le Nouveau Testament de nostre Seigneur Jesus Christ .... B 199
Le Nouveau Testament, C'est à dire, La nouvelle Alliance .... B 198
Calvin, Jean: *Histoire d'un meurtre execrable: commis par un
  Hespagnol, nommé Alphonse Dias* .... C 57

Calvin, Jean: *Deux Sermons* <> ... *l'un le mercredy 4e de Novembre 1545.. le second, le mercredy prochainement suyvant* .... C 70

Chansons spirituelles sur la saincte Cene de nostre Seigneur Jesus Christ .... C 96

Conrard, Olivier: *La Vie, faictz et louanges de sainct Paul* .... C 131

Désiré, Artus: *Le Miroer des Francs Taulpins* .... D 18

Désiré, Artus: *Le Miroer des francz Taulpins* .... D 17

Dolet, Estienne: *Des faictz et gestes du Roy Françoys premier de ce nom* .... D 37

Doré, Pierre: *La premiere partie des Collations royales* .... D 55

Doré, Pierre: *La seconde partie, des collations royalles* .... D 56

Doré, Pierre: *Le College de sapience* .... D 58

Doré, Pierre: *Le College de sapience* .... D 59

Doré, Pierre: *Le Pasturage de la brebis humaine ... Avec lanatomie et mystique description des membres et parties du nostre Saulveur Jesus Christ* .... D 84

Doré, Pierre: *La celeste pensée, des graces divines arrousée* ...... D 87

Epistre d'un gentilhomme à un sien ami contenant la perfection Chrestienne .... E 10

L'Instruction et creance des Chrestiens .... I 54

Lactantius Firmianus: *Des Divines institutions* .... L 3

Lactantius Firmianus: *Des Divines institutions* .... L 4

Lemaire de Belges, Jean: *Le Promptuaire des conciles de Leglise catholique, avec les scismes* .... L 52

Luther, Martin: *Antithese de la vraye et faulse Eglise* .... L 80

Luther, Martin: *Exposition sur le cantique virginal, Magnificat* .... L 90

Malingre, Matthieu: *L'Epistre* <> *envoyee à Clement Marot... Avec la responce dudit Marot* .... M 5

Malingre, Matthieu: *Indice des principales matieres contenues en la Bible* .... M 7

Melanchthon, Philippe: *La Somme de theologie, ou lieux communs* .... M 67

Le Jeu, et Mystere de la Saincte Hostie, par personnages .... M 108

Le Pasquille Dallemaigne. Auquel l'histoire de levangile de nouveau retourne en lumiere, et la cause de la guerre presente sont touchees .... P 8

Sensuyvent les Postilles et expositions des Epistres et Evangilles dominicalles .... P 33

Rabelais, François: *Tiers livre des faictz et dictz Heroiques du noble Pantagruel* .... R 23

Rabelais, François: *Tiers livre des faictz et dictz Heroiques du noble Pantagruel* .... R 24

Rabelais, François: *Tiers livre des faictz et dictz Heroïques du noble Pantagruel* .... R 22

Rabelais, François: *Tiers livre des faictz et dictz Heroiques du noble Pantagruel* .... R 25

Royer, Colin: *La Nouvelle du reverend pere en Dieu ... Avec le deschiffrement de ses tendres amourettes* .... R 52

Sur l'epistre S. Paul à Philemon petit commentaire .... S 34

Le trespas de Martin Luther .... T 16

Viret, Pierre: *Exposition familiere faict par dialogues sur Le Symbole des Apostres* .... V 40

Vivès, Juan Luis: *Institution de la femme chrestienne ... Avec l'office du mary... Une tresbriefve et fructueuse instruction de la vertu D'humilité* .... V 60

1547

Aurigny, Gilles d': *Contemplation sur la mort de Jesus-Christ* ... A 37

La Bible en Francoys, Qui est toute la saincte Escriture .... B 55

Cinquante deux Pseaumes .... B 116

Cinquante deux Pseaumes de David ... Avec plusieurs autres compositions .... B 117

Cinquante deux Pseaumes de David .... B 115

Le Premier Livre des Pseaulmes de David contenant xxiiii pseaulmes .... B 113

Les Pseaumes de David, mis en rithme Françoyse par Clement Marot .... B 112

Pseaulmes cinquante de David ... mis en Musique .... B 114

Cailleau, Gilles: *Paraphrase sur les Heures de nostre Dame* ...... C 5

Calvin, Jean: *Advertissement sur la censure qu'ont faicte les Bestes de Sorbonne* .... C 12

Calvin, Jean: *Commentaire <> sur la premiere epistre aux Corinthiens* .... C 30

Calvin, Jean: *Commentaire <> sur la seconde Epistre aux Corinthiens* .... C 31

Calvin, Jean: *Excuse de noble seigneur Jaques de Bourgoigne* ... C 44

Calvin, Jean: *La Forme des prieres Ecclesiastiques* .... C 52

Calvin, Jean: *Contre la secte phantastique et furieuse des Libertins ... Avec une epistre de la mesme matiere* .... C 69

Chrysostome, S. Jean: *Exhortation à prier Dieu* .... C 107

Cordier, Mathurin: *Quatre epistres chrestiennes* .... C 134

Curione, Celio Secondo: *Les Visions de Pasquille* .... C 136

Désiré, Artus: *Le deffensoire de la foi Chrestienne* .... D 10

Désiré, Artus: *Le Miroer des Francs Taulpins* .... D 19

Doré, Pierre: *L'image de vertu, demonstrant la perfection et saincte vie de la bien heuree vierge Marie* .... D 75

Doré, Pierre: *La Passe-solitaire à tous amateurs de Dieu* .... D 82

Erasme, Desiderius: *Les Apophthegmes* .... E 17

Espence, Claude d': *Homelies sur la Parabole de l'enfant prodigue* .... E 58

Espence, Claude d': *Paraphrase, ou Meditation, sur l'oraison dominicale* .... E 62

Les Figures de l'Apocalipse .... F 31

La Fontaine de vie, de laquelle resourdent tresdoulces consolations .... F 48

Gerson, Jean: *Sensuyt le Confessional, aultrement appelle le Directoire des confesseurs* .... G 17

Grenier, Nicole: *Le Bouclier de la foy, en forme de Dialogue* ..... G 28

Les Images de la mort, auxquelles sont adjoustées douze figures. Davantage, La Medecine de l'Ame .... I 8

Lactantius Firmianus: *Des divines Institutions* .... L 5

Lemaire de Belges, Jean: *Le Promptuaire des conciles de l'Eglise Catholique, avec les Scismes* .... L 54

Lemaire de Belges, Jean: *Le Promptuaire des conciles de Leglise catholique, avec les Scismes* .... L 53

Luther, Martin: *Consolation en adversité* .... L 84

Marcourt, Antoine: *Le livre des marchans* .... M 27

Marguerite de Navarre: *Marguerites de la Marguerite des princesses* .... M 32

Poullain, Valérand: *Traicte tresutile du S. Sacrement de la Cene* .... P 36

Rabelais, François: *Pantagruel* .... R 30

Rabelais, François: *Gargantua* .... R 29

Rabelais, François: *Le Tiers livre des faictz et dictz Heroioques du noble Pantagruel* .... R 26

Rabelais, François: *Tiers livre des faictz et Dictz heroiques du noble Pantagruel* .... R 28

Rabelais, François: *Tiers Livre Des Faictz, et Dictz Heroiques du noble Pantagruel* .... R 31

La Doctrine des Chrestiens extraicte du vieil et nouveau Testament. Les dix parolles ou commandementz de Dieu. Les commandementz de nostre mere saincte Esglise. Les sept sacremens.... .... S 25

Le sommaire des livres du Vieil et Nouveau testament. Les dix parolles, ou Commandemens de Dieu .... S 24

Theodoret: *Sermons de Theodoret* .... T 8

Viret, Pierre: *Admonition et consolation aux fideles* .... V 25

Viret, Pierre: *De la communication des fideles ... aux ceremonies des Papistes* .... V 26

Viret, Pierre: *Epistre envoyee aux fideles qui conversent entre les Papistes* .... V 36

Viret, Pierre: *Remonstrances aux fideles, qui conversent entre les Papistes* .... V 43

Vivès, Juan Luis: *L'Institution de la femme chrestienne ... Avec l'office du mary* .... V 61

1548

Beaulieu, Eustorg de: *Le souverain Blason dhonneur* .... B 6

Beaulieu, Eustorg de: *L'Espinglier des filles* .... B 4

Benedetto da Mantova: *Du Benefice de Jesuchrist crucifié, envers les Chrestiens* .... B 19

La saincte Bible en Francoys .... B 56

Cinquante deux Pseaumes .... B 118

Cinquante deux Pseaumes de David .... B 120

Pseaulmes cinquante de David mis en vers françois .... B 119

Pseaumes de David traduictz en rithme françoise .... B 121

Le Nouveau Testament de nostre Seigneur Jesus Christ .... B 200

Le Nouveau Testament de nostre Seigneur Jesus Christ .... B 201

Calvin, Jean: *Les Actes du Concile de Trente, avec le remede contre la poison* .... C 9

Calvin, Jean: *Le Catechisme De Geneve* .... C 22

Calvin, Jean: *Commentaire <> sur les deux Epistres de sainct Paul à Timothée* .... C 37

Calvin, Jean: *Commentaire <> sur quatre Epistres de sainct Paul* .... C 32

Calvin, Jean: *La forme des Prieres Ecclesiastiques* .... C 53

Columbi, Jean: *Confession generale* .... C 123

Désiré, Artus: *Le deffensoire de la foy Chrestiene* .... D 11

Doré, Pierre: *Les Allumettes du feu divin* .... D 47

Doré, Pierre: *Les Allumettes du feu divin ... Avecques les Voyes de Paradis* .... D 46

Doré, Pierre: *La Conserve de grace* .... D 60

Doré, Pierre: *La croix de penitence* .... D 62

Doré, Pierre: *La deploration de la vie humaine* .... D 65

Doré, Pierre: *Les Triomphes du Roy sans pair* .... D 90

Dupuyherbault, Gabriel: *Regle et maniere de prier Dieu purement, deuement et avec efficace* .... D 103

Erasme, Desiderius: *Colloque d'Erasme ... intitulé Abbatis et Eruditae* .... E 20

Espence, Claude d': *Institution d'un Prince chrestien* .... E 60

Espence, Claude d': *Institution d'un Prince chrestien* ....   E 61
Espence, Claude d': *Paraphrase, ou meditation, sur l'oraison Dominicale. Et autres opuscules* ....   E 63
Espence, Claude d': *Paraphrase, ou, Meditation, sur l'oraison Dominicale. Et autres opuscules* ....   E 64
Espence, Claude d': *Traicté Contre l'erreur vieil et renouvellé des predestinez* ....   E 66
Les Figures et Visions de L'apocalypse ....   F 33
La fleur des commandemens de Dieu ....   F 40
Grenier, Nicole: *Le Bouclier de la foy, en forme de Dialogue* .....   G 29
Grenier, Nicole: *Le Bouclier de la foy, en forme de Dialogue* .....   G 30
Grenier, Nicole: *Le Bouclier de la foy, en forme de Dialogue* .....   G 31
Grenier, Nicole: *Le Bouclier de la foy, en forme de Dialogue* .....   G 32
Gueroult, Guillaume: *Premier Livre de chansons spirituelles* .....   G 57
Lactantius Firmianus: *Des Divines Institutions* ....   L 6
Lemaire de Belges, Jean: *Le traicte de la difference des scismes*   L 45
Lescagne, Tristan de: *Livret intitule C'est Nostre Dame <> En l'honneur de la tressacrée vierge Marie* ....   L 60
Marcourt, Antoine: *Le livre des Marchans, fort utile a toutes gens...*   M 28
Marguerite de Navarre: *Le Triumphe de l'agneau de tresillustre Princesse Marguerite de France* ....   M 42
Rabelais, François: *Le quart livre des faictz et dictz Heroiques du noble Pantagruel* ....   R 33
Rabelais, François: *Le quart livre des faictz et dictz Heroiques du noble Pantagruel* ....   R 32
Rabelais, François: *Quart livre des faictz et dictz heroiques du noble Pantagruel* ....   R 35
Sentences extraites de l'escriture sainte pour l'instruction des enfans ....   S 12
Les testamens des douze patriarches enfans de Jacob ....   T 3
Viexmont, Claude de: *Le Pain de vie, pour les filz de Dieu, Demonstrant la verité du corps de nostre seigneur Jesus Christ, au venerable sacrement de l'autel* ....   V 22
Viret, Pierre: *Exposition familiere de l'Oraison de nostre Seigneur Jesus Christ* ....   V 37
Viret, Pierre: *De la vertu, et usage du ministere de la parolle de Dieu* ....   V 46
Vivès, Juan Luis: *Institution de la femme chrestienne* ....   V 62
Vivès, Juan Luis: *Introduction à la vraye sapience* ....   V 65

1549

Cinquante deux Psalmes de David ....   B 125
Cinquante Pseaumes de David ... Avec le latin en marge ....   B 124

Premier livre contenant xxviii Pseaulmes de David...................... B 127

Psalmes trente du royal Prophete David................................. B 123

Pseaulmes cinquante de David... B 122

Trente Psalmes du royal Prophete David............................... B 126

Bullinger, Heinrich: *La Source d'erreur*.............................. B 282

Calvin, Jean: *Advertissement contre l'astrologie, qu'on appelle judiciaire*.. C 10

Calvin, Jean: *Le Catechisme de Geneve*............................... C 23

Calvin, Jean: *Commentaire <> sur l'epistre aux Ebrieux*............. C 33

Calvin, Jean: *La forme des Prieres Ecclesiastiques*.................. C 54

Calvin, Jean: *L'Interim... Avec la vraye façon de reformer l'Eglise Chrestienne*.. C 64

Calvin, Jean: *Petit Traicté de la saincte cene de nostre Seigneur Jesus Christ*.. C 76

Corrozet, Gilles: *La Tapisserie de l'église chrestienne et catholique*.. C 135

Doré, Pierre: *L'adresse du pecheur*.................................. D 40

Doré, Pierre: *L'arche de l'alliance nouvelle ... contre tous sacramentaires heretiques*... D 52

Doré, Pierre: *L'image de Vertu, demonstrant la perfection et saincte vie de la bienheurée vierge Marie*............................. D 76

Doré, Pierre: *La Passe-solitaire*.................................... D 83

Du Boullay, Emond: *Le combat de la chair, et l'esprit*.............. D 95

Epistre d'un gentilhomme à un sien ami contenant la perfection Chrestienne.. E 11

Erasme, Desiderius: *Les Apophthegmes*............................... E 18

Erasme, Desiderius: *Deux colloques d'Erasme ... Abbatis et Eruditae, l'autre Virgo Misogamos*................................... E 21

Erasme, Desiderius: *Deux colloques d'Erasme plus le Balladin de Marot*... E 22

Erasme, Desiderius: *Brief recueil du livre <> de l'enseignement du prince Chrestien*.. E 53

Erasme, Desiderius: *Brief recueil du livre de l'enseignement du prince Chrestien*.. E 52

Exposition De l'Oraison de nostre Seigneur Jesus,.. Avec l'exposition du Symbole Apostolique ... et aussi une exposition sur les dix Commandemens.. E 77

La Fontaine de vie ... L'instruction pour les enfans................ F 49

Grenier, Nicole: *Le Bouclier de la foy*............................. G 34

Grenier, Nicole: *Le Bouclier de la foy, en forme de dialogue*...... G 33

Grenier, Nicole: *Tome second du Bouclier de la foy*................. G 36

Herp, Henry de: *Premiere partie du Directoire des contemplatifz*.... H 9

Lefèvre d'Étaples, Jacques: *Les Epistres et evangiles des cinquante, et deux Dimenches de L'an* .... L 25

Lemaire de Belges, Jean: *Le Traité de la difference des Schismes et la Legende des Venitiens* .... L 46

Marguerite de Navarre: *Marguerites de la Marguerite des Princesses* .... M 33

Melanchthon, Philippe: *Histoire de la vie et faitz de venerable homme M. Martin Luther* .... M 63

Le Miroir du penitent .... M 79

Primasius: *Exposition sur les Epistres S. Poul aux Romains et Hebrieux* .... P 42

Rabelais, François (pseudonym): *Le cinquiesme livre des faictz et dictz du noble Pantagruel* .... R 36

Stumpf, Jean: *Histoire veritable et digne de memoire de quatre Jacopins de Berne* .... S 33

Les Testamens des douze patriarches, enfans de Jacob .... T 4

Textor, Benoist: *Confession vrayement chrestienne* .... T 7

Viret, Pierre: *Exposition familiere sur les dix commandemens de la loy, faicte en forme de dialogue* .... V 41

Vivès, Juan Luis: *L'Institution de la femme chrestienne* .... V 64

Vivès, Juan Luis: *L'institution de la femme chrestienne ... Avec loffice du mary* .... V 63

1550

Le ABC des Chrestiens .... A 1

Arrestz et ordonnances royaux de la supreme, tres-haute et souveraine Court du Royaume des Cieux .... A 21

Beaulieu, Eustorg de: *L'Espinglier des filles* .... B 5

Bèze, Théodore de: *Abraham sacrifiant. Tragedie françoise* .... B 23

La Saincte Bible ... à Louvain .... B 57

La Sainte Bible. Contenant les Saintes escritures .... B 58

Cinquante Psalmes de David .... B 137

Les cinquante pseaulmes de David ... Le tout mis en Musique .... B 132

Cinquante deux Psalmes .... B 134

Cinquante deux Pseaumes .... B 131

Cinquante deux Pseaumes de David .... B 130

Cinquante deux Pseaumes de david .... B 133

Cent Psalmes de David .... B 136

Les Cent Psalmes de David, qui restoient à traduire .... B 135

Les Pseaumes de David .... B 128

Pseaumes de David ... avec le latin qui est en marge .... B 129

Le Nouveau Testament De nostre Seigneur Jesus Christ .... B 202

Le Nouveau Testament de nostre Seigneur Jesus Christ .... B 203

Calvin, Jean: *Commentaire <> sur l'epistre aux Romains* .... C 35
Calvin, Jean: *Commentaire <> sur l'epistre à Tite* .... C 38
Calvin, Jean: *Commentaire <> sur l'epistre de sainct Jaques* ..... C 25
Calvin, Jean: *La forme des prieres ecclesiastiques* .... C 56
Calvin, Jean: *La forme des Prieres Ecclesiastiques* .... C 55
Calvin, Jean: *Des scandales* .... C 66
Calvin, Jean: *Traicté tresexcellent de la vie Chrestienne* .... C 81
Coignac, Joachim de: *Huict Satyres de l'estat et vie des moines* ... C 117
Désiré, Artus: *Les combatz du fidelle Papiste pelerin Romain* .... D 7
Désiré, Artus: *Les combatz du fidelle papiste pelerin Romain* ...
  Ensemble la description de la cité de Dieu .... D 8
Désiré, Artus: *Le Deffensoire de la foi chrestienne, contenant*
  le Miroer des Francs Taupins .... D 12
Désiré, Artus: *La Description de la cité de Dieu... ensemble*
  aussi la Complaincte .... D 14
Désiré, Artus: *Le Miroir Des francs taupins* .... D 20
Doré, Pierre: *Les allumettes du feu divin* .... D 48
Doré, Pierre: *Oraison Panegyrique ... pour ... Claude de Lor-*
  raine... Avec la doulce Musique Davidique .... D 81
Doré, Pierre: *La Piscine de patience ... avec le Miroir de Patience* .. D 88
Doré, Pierre: *Le Nouveau Testament d'amour, de nostre Pere*
  Jesus Christ .... D 89
Espence, Claude d': *Paraphrase, ou Meditation, sur l'oraison*
  dominicale, Avec autres opuscules .... E 65
Farel, Guillaume: *Le Glaive de la parolle veritable, tiré contre*
  le Bouclier de defense .... F 16
Grenier, Nicole: *Le Bouclier de la foy, en forme de Dialogue* ..... G 35
Le livre de l'Internelle Consolation ... Avec l'Armeure de patience
  en adversité .... I 38
Mazurier, Martial: *Instruction et doctrine a se bien confesser* .... M 50
Melanchthon, Philippe: *De la puissance et authorité de*
  l'Eglise .... M 61
Musculus, Wolfgang: *Le Temporiseur* .... M 84
Devotes oraisons de nostre dame .... O 8
Le grand pardon de pleniere remission, pour toutes personnes,
  durant à tousjours .... P 2
Scrimgeour, Henry: *Un Exemple notable et digne de memoire*
  d'un homme desesperé .... S 9
Sleidan, Jean: *D'un nouveau chef qui au temps des Empereurs*
  s'esleva à Rome .... S 20
Theodoret: *Deux Sermons* .... T 9
Vergerio, Pietro Paulo: *La Declaracion du jubilè qui doit etre a*
  Rome l'an M.D.L .... V 6

1551

L'ABC françois .... A 3

Augustin, Saint: *De l'Esprit et de la lettre* .... A 28

Bèze, Théodore de: *Abraham sacrifiant. Tragedie françoise* .... B 24

La Bible en Francoys, Qui est toute la saincte Escriture .... B 60

La Bible, Qui est toute la saincte Escriture .... B 59

La Sainte Bible. Avec les figures et Pourtraits du Tabernacle
    de Moyse, et du Temple de Salomon, et maison du Liban .... B 61

Trente Psalmes du royal Prophete David .... B 141

Trente-quatre psaumes .... B 139

Cinquante deux Pseaumes de David .... B 143

Pseaumes octantetrois de David, mis en rime Françoise .... B 138

Les Cent cinquante Psalmes du Prophete Royal David .... B 142

Les Pseaumes de David ... avec annotations tresutiles .... B 140

Le Nouveau Testament de nostre Seigneur Jesu Christ .... B 208

Le Nouveau Testament, C'est à dire, La Nouvelle Alliance .... B 204

Le Nouveau Testament, C'est à dire, La Nouvelle Alliance .... B 205

Le Nouveau Testament, c'est à dire, La nouvelle Alliance .... B 207

Le Nouveau Testament: C'est à dire, La Nouvelle Alliance .... B 206

Bodius, Hermann: *La premiere (-seconde) partie de l'Union de*
    plusieurs passages de l'Escriture sainte .... B 216

Brief Discours de la Republique Francoyse .... B 262

Calvin, Jean: *L'Accord passé et conclud touchant la matiere*
    des sacremens .... C 6

Calvin, Jean: *Advertissement tresutile ... s'il se faisoit inven-*
    toire de tous les corps sainctz, et reliques .... C 16

Calvin, Jean: *Commentaires <> sur les Canoniques* .... C 24

Calvin, Jean: *Commentaire <> sur l'epistre de S. Jaques* .... C 26

Calvin, Jean: *Commentaire sur la premiere et seconde Epistre*
    de sainct Pierre Apostre .... C 27

Calvin, Jean: *Commentaire <> sur l'Epistre Canonique de*
    sainct Jude .... C 28

Calvin, Jean: *Commentaire <> sur l'Epistre Canonique de*
    sainct Jean .... C 29

Calvin, Jean: *Commentaire sur l'epistre de sainct Paul a Phi-*
    lemon .... C 34

Calvin, Jean: *Commentaire sur les deux epistres de sainct Paul*
    aux Thessaloniciens .... C 36

Calvin, Jean: *Exposition des dix commandemens du Seigneur* ..... C 45

Calvin, Jean: *Exposition sur l'oraison de nostre Seigneur Jesus*
    Christ .... C 48

Calvin, Jean: *Institution de la religion Chrestienne* .... C 60

Calvin, Jean: *Des scandales* .... C 67

Calvin, Jean: *Petit Traicté mostrant que doit faire un homme fidele ... Ensemble l'Excuse aux Nicodemites* .... C 80

Calvin, Jean: *Traicté tresexcellent de la vie Chrestienne* .... C 82

Coignac, Joachim de: *Deux Satyres, l'une du Pape, l'autre de la Papauté* .... C 116

Coignac, Joachim de: *La desconfiture de Goliath, Tragedie* .... C 118

Désiré, Artus: *Les Combatz du Fidelle Chrestien... Ensemble la description de la Cité de Dieu* .... D 9

Désiré, Artus: *Le Defensoire de la foy chrestienne, contenant en soy le Miroër des Francs Taulpins* .... D 13

Désiré, Artus: *Les grands jours du Parlement de Dieu* .... D 15

Doré, Pierre: *Anti-Calvin, contenant deux defenses catholiques de la verité du sainct Sacrement* .... D 49

Eck, Johann: *Les Lieux communs de Jean Ekius, contre Luther* ... E 2

Enseignement tresutile ... pour fortifier la personne à volontiers mourir, et ne craindre point la mort .... E 8

Fabri, Christophe: *Familiere instruction des petis enfans selon la forme qu'on tient en l'Eglise de Neufchastel* .... F 1

Les Figures de l'Apocalypse .... F 32

Garnier, Jean: *Briefve et claire confession de la foy Chrestienne, Contenant Cent articles* .... G 13

Grenier, Nicole: *L'espee de la foy, pour la defense de l'eglise chrestienne* .... G 37

Lactantius Firmianus: *Des Divines Institutions* .... L 7

Lactantius Firmianus: *Des Divines Institutions* .... L 8

Marcourt, Antoine: *Declaration de la Messe, Le fruict d'icelle, La cause, et le moyen, pourquoy et comment on la doit maintenir* .... M 22

Melanchthon, Philippe: *La Somme de theologie, ou lieux communs* .... M 68

Brief Traité de Purgatoire .... P 53

Rabelais, François: pseudonym: [*Le Cinquiesme Livre*] .... R 37

Rhegius, Urbanus: *La Doctrine nouvelle et ancienne* .... R 47

Sebond, Raymond: *La Theologie Naturelle* .... S 10

Les testaments des douse Patriarches, enfants de Jacob .... T 5

Les Testamentz des douze patriarches, enfans de Jacob .... T 6

Vergerio, Pietro Paulo: *La Bulle de l'indiction du Concile* .... V 4

Vergerio, Pietro Paulo: *Le Conseil de trois Evesques* .... V 5

Vergerio, Pietro Paulo: *Des Faitz et gestes du Pape Jules III* ...... V 7

La vie de Jesuchrist, La mort et passion de Jesuchrist ... et Vengeance de nostre saulveur .... V 13

Viret, Pierre: *Du Devoir et du besoing qu'ont les hommes à s'enquerir de la volonté de Dieu par sa Parolle*...................... V 29

Viret, Pierre: *Exposition familiere de l'oraison de nostre Seigneur Jesus Christ*.. V 38

Viret, Pierre: *De la nature et diversité des voeuz* .... V 42

Viret, Pierre: *De la source et de la difference et convenance de la vieille et nouvelle idolatrie*... V 28

1553

Les Cent Psalmes de David qui restoient à traduire en rithme Françoyse .... B 144

Undatable

Abc des chrestiens et chrestiennes... A 2

Ambroise, Saint: *Traictie <> du bien de la mort*........................ A 7

Bellemere, François: *Examen de conscience* .... B 16

Les cantiques salomon .... B 67

Branteghem, Guillaume de: *La Vie de Jesuchrist* .... B 260

Cabosse, Jean: *Traité ... du treshault et tresexcellent mystere de l'Incarnation*... C 3

Columbi, Jean: *Confession generale... Et une oraison tresdevote a dire devant que on recoyve le corps de nostre seigneur* .... C 122

Denys, Saint: *La contemplation spirituelle* .... D 6

Dialogue spirituel de la passion.. D 26

Doré, Pierre: *Le Cerf Spirituel* .... D 54

Doré, Pierre: *L'image de vertu* .... D 77

Doré, Pierre: *Le livre des divins benefices. Avec l'information de bien vivre* .... D 79

Du Buc, Richard: *Devot Traité de la genese* .... D 96

Espence, Claude d': *Homelies sur la parabole de l'enfant prodigue*... E 59

Extraict de plusieurs sainctz Docteurs ... contenans les graces ... du sainct et digne Sacrement de Lautel............................. E 86

Extraits de plusieurs saincts Docteurs ... contenans les graces ... du tressacre et digne sacrement de lautel .... E 85

Gerson, Jean: *Le confessional appelle le directoire des confesseurs*.. G 18

Limitation de Nostre Seigneur Jesuchrist................................. I 39

Instruction et salutaire admonition pour parfaictement vivre en ce monde.. I 53

Lacu, Jean: *La quenouille spirituelle*....................................... L 9

Le livre de la loy et de l'Evangile avec la force d'iceux............. L 67

Lucidiaire en françoys.. L 73

La Lunette des Chrestiens .... L 78

Maillard, Olivier: *La confession generalle de frere Olivier Maillard* .... M 2

Le manuel des Christians: avecq plusieurs psalmes et cantiques et oraisons .... M 13

Marchepallu, Jacques: *Les vertus et excellences des pseaulmes du roy David* .... M 17

Maurice de Sully: *Sensuyt les expositions des evangiles en françoys* .... M 49

Meigret, Aimé: *Epistre en latin ... Plus un sermon en françois ...* M 58

Le Moyen de parvenir à la congnoissance de Dieu, et consequemment à salut .... M 83

Le mistere de la conception, Nativite, mariage, et annonciation de la benoiste vierge Marie .... M 90

Le mistere de la conception, Nativite, mariage, et annonciation de la benoiste vierge Marie .... M 91

Parceval, Jean: *Brieve Doctrine de l'amour divine* .... P 1

Penser a la Mort cest chose proffitable .... P 9

Postilles et expositions des epistres: et evangilles dominicalles .. P 34

Poyvreault, Simon: *Douze devotes Contemplations* .... P 37

Profession de foy accoustumee d'estre juree Par les Bourgeois et subjects de Messeigneurs de Frybourg .... P 45

Rabelais, François: *La vie treshorrifique du grand Gargantua, pere de Pantagruel* .... R 21

Rabelais, François: *Le tiers livre des faictz et Dictz Heroiques du noble Pantagruel* .... R 27

Rabelais, François: *Quart livre des faictz et dictz Heroiques du noble Pantagruel* .... R 34

Savonarola, Jérôme: *Exposition et paraphrase ... Miserere* .... S 6

Thomas a Kempis: *Petit traictie de discipline claustralle* .... T 11

Tissarrant, Jean: *Une tresbelle salutation faicte sur les vii festes de Nostre dame* .... T 12

Le Thresor de devotion .... T 18

Le Tresor de devotion .... T 17

4 List of Printers by City

Agen

Antoine Reboul

1526: *Le directoire de la salut des Ames*..................... D 28
1546: *Sur l'epistre S. Paul à Philemon petit commentaire* .... S 34

A. Villotte

1546: Luther, Martin, *Exposition sur le cantique virginal,
      Magnificat* .... L 90

Alençon

Simon Du Bois

1529: *Les choses contenues ... [Le nouveau testament]*............... B 160
     Luther, Martin, *Breve Instruction pour deuement lire
      lescripture* .... L 115
1530: *Almanach spirituel et perpetuel* .... A 5
     Le combat chrestien .... C 124
     Brefve exposition sur ... le Pater noster................ E 74
     Breve Instruction pour soy confesser............... I 57
     Luther, Martin, *La Fleur des Commandementz* .... L 96
1531: *Lecclesiaste Preschant* .... B 68
     Marguerite de Navarre, *Le miroir de lame pecheresse*....... M 34
1532: *Le livre des Psalmes*..................... B 78
     ('Turin'): Farel, Guillaume, *Summaire et briefve decla-
      ration* .... F 27
     Lefèvre d'Étaples, Jacques, *Epistres et evangiles*............. L 21
     Luther, Martin, *Consolation chrestienne*......... L 82
     Luther, Martin, *Quatre instructions fideles* .... L 119
     ('Basle, Thomas Volff'): *La Summe de lescripture saincte*..... S 26
1533: Marguerite de Navarre, *Dialogue en forme de vision
      nocturne*............... M 31
     Marguerite de Navarre, *Le miroir de lame pecheresse*....... M 35

Angers

No name

1548: *Cinquante deux Pseaumes* .... B 118

Antwerp

Simon Coc

1535: (with Martin Lempereur): Branteghem, Guillaume de,
      Enchyridion ou Manuel contenant plusieurs matieres ...... B 237

Matthieu Crom

1533: *Ung brief enseignement ... a volentier morir* .... E 6
1538: *Le nouveau Testament* .... B 170

1539: (with Adrien Kempe): Branteghem, Guillaume de, *La Vie de Nostre Seigneur JesuChrist* .... B 243
1540: Branteghem, Guillaume de, *La vie de nostre Seigneur Jesu Christ* .... B 244
1541: Branteghem, Guillaume de, *La vie de nostre Seigneur* ...... B 251

Antoine Des Gois

1540: *Introduction pour les enfans* .... I 50
1541: (with Antoine de la Haye): *La saincte Bible* .... B 44
      Le livre des Pseaulmes de David .... B 84
      Psalmes de David .... B 85
      Psalmes de Davis ... Sermon .... B 86
1543: Erasme, Desiderius, *Enchiridion, ou manuel du chevalier chrestien* .... E 33

Guillaume Du Mont

1538: *Le Nouveau Testament* .... B 172
1540: *Le nouveau Testament* .... B 178
1543: *Le Nouveau Testament* .... B 187

Jean Graphaeus (de Grave)

1532: Bible. N.T., *Le nouveau Testament* .... B 165
1544: (with Jean Richard): Branteghem, Guillaume de, *La Vie de nostre Seigneur Jesus Christ* .... B 259
      De limitation de Jesu Christ .... I 34
      De limitation de Jesu Christ .... I 35
1545: (with Guillaume Vissenaken): Luther, Martin, *Le livre de vraye et parfaicte oraison* .... L 111

Adrien Kempe

1539: (with Matthieu Crom): Branteghem, Guillaume de, *La Vie de Nostre Seigneur JesuChrist* .... B 243

Antoine de la Haye

1541: (with Antoine Des Gois): *La saincte Bible* .... B 44

Martin Lempereur

1525: *Le psaultier de David* .... B 72
      Erasme, Desiderius, *Exhortation au peuple* .... E 35
      Luther, Martin, *Brief racueil des oeuvres des dix commandemens* .... L 81
      Luther, Martin, *Des bonnes oeuvres sus les commandemens de Dieu* .... L 86
      Luther, Martin, *Une exposition sur le Magnificat* .... L 88
1527: Bodius, Hermann, *L'Union de toutes discordes* .... B 209
      Luther, Martin, *Sermon au jour de l'ascension* .... L 120
      Luther, Martin, *Sermon de la maniere de prier Dieu* .... L 122
1528: *Le premier volume de lanchien testament* .... B 62
      Le dernier volume de lanchien testament .... B 66

Bodius, Hermann, *La seconde partie de Lunion de toutes*
discordes .... B 210
1529: *Le troisiesme volume de lancien testament* .... B 65
(with Guillaume Vorsterman): *Le nouveau Testament* .... B 161
(with Guillaume Vorsterman): Brunfels, Otto, *Les Prieres*
et oraisons de la Bible .... B 271
Erasme, Desiderius, *Enchiridion (ou Manuel) du cheva-*
lier Chrestien .... E 28
(with Guillaume Vorsterman): Luther, Martin, *La Maniere*
de lire levangile .... L 114
1530: *La saincte Bible. en Francoys* .... B 35
Les Sentences de Solomon .... B 145
Brunfels, Otto, *Les oracions de la Bible* .... B 272
1531: *Le livre des Pseaulmes de David* .... B 75
Le nouveau Testament .... B 164
1532: *Le second volume de lanchien Testament (I)* .... B 63
Le second volume de lancien Testament (II) .... B 64
Le nouveau Testament .... B 166
Bodius, Hermann, *Lunion de toute discorde* .... B 211
Fossetier, Julien, *Conseil de volentier morir* .... F 50
1533: Brunfels, Otto, *Les Oraisons de la Bible* .... B 274
1534: *La saincte Bible en Francoys* .... B 39
Introduction pour les enfans .... I 48
Luther, Martin, *Le livre de vraye et parfaicte oraison* ...... L 100
Vergier flourissant pour lame fidele .... V 3
1535: *Le nouveau Testament* .... B 168
(with Simon Coc): Branteghem, Guillaume de, *Enchyri-*
dion ou Manuel contenant plusieurs matieres .... B 237

'Martin Lempereur'
1539: see Geneva, Jean Girard, 1539: Dentière, Marie
1540: *Les testamentz des douze patriarches* .... T 2

Vve Martin Lempereur
1537: Campen, Jean van, *Paraphrase ... sur tous les Psalmes* ..... C 84
1538: *Le Nouveau testament* .... B 171
Introduction pour les enfans .... I 49
1539: *Les sentences de Solomon* .... B 147
1540: *Un Vif Sacrifice Quotidian* .... V 23
1541: *Le Nouveau Testament* .... B 180
Le Nouveau Testament .... B 181

Jacques de Liesvelt
1539: Branteghem, Guillaume de, *Enchyridion, ou Manuel*
contenant plusieurs matieres .... B 239
1544: *Le nouveau Testament* .... B 193

Jean de Liesvelt
1539: *Le nouveau Testament* .... B 175

Jean Loe
1544: *Salomon. Les Proverbes. Ecclesiastes* .... B 150
1548: Bible, *La saincte Bible en Francoys* .... B 56
Martin Nuyts
1549: (with Jehan Rijckaerts): Grenier, Nicole, *Le Bouclier de
la foy* .... G 33
Henry Pierre
1536: Branteghem, Guillaume de, *Enchyridion ou Manuel contenant plusieurs matieres* .... B 238
1543: *Le Nouveau Testament* .... B 188
Jehan Rijckaerts (Jean Richard)
1542: Branteghem, Guillaume de, *La Vie de nostre Seigneur
Jesus Christ* .... B 254
1543: *Le Nouveau Testament* .... B 189
1544: (with Jean de Grave): Branteghem, Guillaume de, *La Vie
de nostre Seigneur Jesus Christ* .... B 259
1549: (with Martin Nuyts): Grenier, Nicole, *Le Bouclier de la
foy* .... G 33
Jean Steelsius
1538: *Le nouveau Testament* .... B 173
Luther, Martin, *Le livre de vraye et parfaicte oraison* ...... L 101
1543: Campen, Jean van, *Paraphrase sur les Psalmes* .... C 88
Adriaen van Berghen
1523: (with Jean Brocquart, Tournai): *Le tressainct et sacres
texte du nouniaulx testament* .... B 151
Guillaume Vissenaken
1545: (with Jean de Grave): Luther, Martin, *Le livre de vraye
et parfaicte oraison* .... L 111
Guillaume Vorsterman
1524: *Devote meditation sur la mort et passion* .... M 52
1525: *La S. Evangile ... Epistres* .... B 156
1527: *Remede convenable Pour si bien vivre en ce monde* .... R 44
1529: (with Martin Lempereur): *Le nouveau Testament* .... B 161
(with Martin Lempereur): Brunfels, Otto, *Les Prieres et
oraisons de la Bible* .... B 271
Gouda, Gerard van der, *Linterpretation et signification
de la Messe* .... G 21
(with Martin Lempereur): Luther, Martin, *La Maniere
de lire levangile* .... L 114
1535: Branteghem, Guillaume de, *Vergier spirituel et mistique* .. B 240
1538: Gouda, Gerard van der, *Linterpretation et signification
de la Messe* .... G 22

No name
1543: Erasme, Desiderius, *Preparation à la mort* .... E 49

Armentières

Jaspard Bernard
1521: (with Jean Du Pré, Paris): *Tresdevote meditation de la ...*
   passion .... M 55

Arras

Baudouin Dacquin
1545: (with Bonaventure Brassart, Cambrai): *Articles tres*
   utiles ... de la faculte de theologie de Louvain .... A 23

Avignon

'Avignon, Honorat d'Arles': see Geneva, Jean Girard, 1539:
Marguerite de Navarre

Jean de Channey
1517: Columbi, Jean, *Confession generale avec certaines rigles* ..... C 119
1520: Columbi, Jean, *Confession generale avec certaines reigles* .... C 121
1532: Rome, Jean de, *Petit directoyre pour aprendre es*
   symples gens ... leurs peches .... R 50
1535: Grégoire, Jean, *Devote exposition sus le Pater noster* .... G 27

'Avignon, Jean Daniel': see Geneva, Jean Crespin, 1551

Imbert Parmentier
1548: Grenier, Nicole, *Le Bouclier de la foy* .... G 29

Basle

Andreas Cratander
1524: Erasme, Desiderius, *Maniere de se confesser* .... E 36
   Farel, Guillaume, *Le Pater noster, et le Credo en francoys* .... F 24
1525: (with Johann Schabler): *Le nouveau testament* .... B 157
   Exhortation sur ces sainctes parolles... Retournes vous ... E 71

Jacques Estauge
1546: Malingre, Matthieu, *L'Epistre ... envoyee à Clement Marot...* M 5
   Le Pasquille Dallemaigne .... P 8
   Le trespas de Martin Luther .... T 16
1548: Beaulieu, Eustorg de, *Le souverain Blason dhonneur* .... B 6
1550: Vergerio, Pietro Paulo, *La Declaracion du jubilè* .... V 6
1551: Garnier, Jean, *Briefve et claire confession de la foy* .... G 13

Johann Schabler
1525: (with Andreas Cratander): *Le nouveau testament* .... B 157

J. Walder
1539: *Le Nouveau Testament* .... B 176

Robert Winter
1547: Poullain, Valérand, *Traicte tresutile du S. Sacrement de
       la Cene* .... P 36
1550: Beaulieu, Eustorg de, *L'Espinglier des filles* .... B 5

Thomas Wolff
1532: Farel, Guillaume, *De La Tressaincte Cene de nostre
       Seigneur Jesus* .... F 5

'Thomas Wolff': see Alençon, Simon Du Bois, 1532.

No name
1524: Farel, Guillaume, *Epistre chrestienne* .... F 7
1544: Calvin, Jean, *Les Articles de la sacree Faculté de
       Theologie de Paris* .... C 18
1548: Beaulieu, Eustorg de, *L'Espinglier des filles* .... B 4

Bordeaux

Jean Guyant
1521-42: Bellemere, François, *Directoire de la vie humaine* .... B 13

Bourges

Guillaume Alabat
1538: (with Nicolas Couteau, Paris): Greban, Simon, *Le
       triumphant mystere des Actes des Apostres* .... G 23
1540: (with Nicolas Couteau, A. et C. Langelier, Paris): Greban,
       Simon, *Le triumphant mystere des actes des Apostres* ...... G 24
1541: (with Nicolas Couteau, A. et C. Angelier, Paris): Greban,
       Simon, *Les Catholiques oeuvres et Actes des Apostres* ..... G 25

Caen

Michel Angier
1516: (with hér. Richard Auzoult, Rouen): *La bible en francoys* ...... B 27

Hér. Laurent Hostingue
1535: *La Bible* .... B 41

Martin & Pierre Philippe
1550+: *Brief Discours de la Republique Francoyse* .... B 262

Cambrai

Bonaventure Brassart
1545: (with Baudouin Dacquin, Arras): *Articles tres utiles ... de
       la faculte de theologie de Louvain* .... A 23

Geneva

Conrad Badius
1550: (with Jean Crespin): Bèze, Théodore de, *Abraham sacri-
       fiant* .... B 23

(with Jean Crespin): Calvin, Jean, *Traicté tresexcellent de la vie Chrestienne* .... C 81

Jean Crespin

1550: (with Conrad Badius): Bèze, Théodore de, *Abraham sacrifiant* .... B 23

Calvin, Jean, *Des scandales* .... C 66

(with Conrad Badius): Calvin, Jean, *Traicté tresexcellent de la vie Chrestienne* .... C 81

1551: *L'ABC françois* .... A 3

Bèze, Théodore de, *Abraham sacrifiant* .... B 24

La Bible .... B 59

Pseaumes octantetrois de David .... B 138

Trente-quatre psaumes .... B 139

Les Pseaumes de David traduicts .... B 140

Calvin, Jean, *L'Accord passé et conclud* .... C 6

Calvin, Jean, *Exposition des dix commandemens du Seigneur* .... C 45

Calvin, Jean, *Exposition sur l'oraison de nostre Seigneur Jesus Christ* .... C 48

Calvin, Jean, *Des scandales* .... C 67

Fabri, Christophe, *Familiere instruction des petis enfans* ... F 1

Melanchthon, Philippe, *La Somme de theologie* .... M 68

Rhegius, Urbanus, *La Doctrine nouvelle et ancienne* .... R 47

1552: Calvin, Jean, *Traicté tresexcellent de la vie Chrestienne* ... C 82

Michel Du Bois

1540: Bullinger, Heinrich, *Exposition sur les deux epistres ... aux Thessaloniciens* .... B 280

Calvin, Jean, *Epistre de Jacques Sadolet ... Avec la Response* .... C 42

1541: Calvin, Jean, *Epistre au ... roy de France Françoys premier* C 41

Calvin, Jean, *Institution de la religion chrestienne* .... C 58

Calvin, Jean, *Petit Traicté de la saincte cene* .... C 73

Melanchthon, Philippe, *La Response donnee par les princes d'Allemaigne* .... M 66

Jean Girard

1536: *Le nouveau Testament* .... B 169

1537: *Les Psalmes de David* .... B 79

Olivétan, Pierre Robert, *Linstruction dés enfans* .... O 6

1538: *Les Livres de Salomoh* .... B 146

Heyden, Sebald, *D'ung seul mediateur et advocat* .... H 13

Megander, Gaspard, *Instruction observée par la ville ... de Berne* .... M 56

Saulnier, Antoine, *L'Ordre et maniere d'enseigner en la ville de Genéve* .... S 4

1539: *Les Psalmes de David* .... B 81

Le Nouveau Testament.. B 177

Dentière, Marie, *Epistre tresutile envoyée à la Royne de Navarre* .... D 4

Du Pinet, Antoine, *Familiere et briefve exposition sur l'apocalypse*.. D 100

Breve exposition faicte ... sur le Pater noster .... E 76

Breve Instruction faicte ... pour se confesser en verité ...... I 58

Luther, Martin, *Exposition de l'histoire des dix Lepreux*... L 87

Marguerite de Navarre, *Le miroir de ... Marguerite* .... M 41

1540: *La Bible*.. B 43

Megander, Gaspard, *Exposition chrestienne Dés dix commandemens* .... M 57

1541: *Les sept psalmes du pecheur converty* .... B 89

Calvin, Jean, *Les Actes de ... Regespourg*....................... C 7

L'Epistre Catholique de Sainct Jaques............................ E 12

Exhortation tresutile sur les sainctes parolles ... Retournez vous.. E 73

Exposition Sur les Articles de la Foy............................. E 80

Farel, Guillaume, *La tressaincte oraison que Jesus Christ a baillé à ses Apostres*... F 21

Viret, Pierre, *Epistre consolatoire, envoyée aux fideles* .... V 34

1542: Calvin, Jean, *Les Actes de ... Reguespourg*.................. C 8

Calvin, Jean, *Le catechisme de l'Eglise de Geneve*........... C 20

Calvin, Jean, *Exposition sur l'epistre de sainct Judas*....... C 47

Calvin, Jean, *La Forme des prieres et chantz ecclesiastiques* C 49

Calvin, Jean, *Petit Traicté de la saincte cene* .... C 74

Campen, Jean van, *Paraphrase ... sur les psalmes* .... C 87

Chansons demonstrant les erreurs et abuz....................... C 100

Farel, Guillaume, *Summaire. C'est, une brieve declaration* ... F 30

Melanchthon, Philippe, *De l'authorité de l'Eglise*............ M 59

Viret, Pierre, *De la difference qui est entre les superstitions* V 27

1543: *Cinquante Pseaumes en françois*................................. B 95

Cinquante Pseaumes .... B 96

Le Nouveau Testament.. B 190

Calvin, Jean, *Advertissement tresutile ... s'il se faisoit inventoire de ... reliques*.. C 13

Calvin, Jean, and Viret, Pierre, *Deux Epistres*................. C 39

Calvin, Jean, *Exposition sur l'epistre ... aux Romains*....... C 46

Calvin, Jean, *Petit traicté, monstrant que c'est que doit faire un homme fidele*... C 77

Castellion, Sébastien, *Dialogi sacri*............................... C 92

Du Pinet, Antoine, *Exposition sur l'Apocalypse* .... D 101

Exposition des articles de la Foy................................. E 81

Farel, Guillaume, *Epistre de Maistre Pierre Caroly ... avec la response*.. F 9

Farel, Guillaume, *La Seconde Epistre envoyée à ... Caroly*.... F 10

Farel, Guillaume, *Epistre envoyee au duc de Lorraine*...... F 12

Malingre, Matthieu, *Indice des principales matieres contenues en la Bible* .... M 6

Melanchthon, Philippe, *De la puissance et authorité de la saincte Eglise* .... M 60

Traicté de purgatoire .... P 51

Sleidan, Jean, *D'un nouveau chef qui au temps des empereurs s'esleva à Rome* .... S 19

Viret, Pierre, *Epistre envoyee aux fideles conversans entre les Chrestiens Papistiques* .... V 35

1544: Bucer, Martin, *Exposition sur l'evangile selon sainct Matthieu* .... B 279

Calvin, Jean, *Advertissement sur la censure ... de Sorbonne, touchant les livres* .... C 11

Calvin, Jean, *Advertissement tresutile ... sil se faisoit inventoire de ... reliques* .... C 14

Calvin, Jean, *Les Articles de la sacree faculte de theologie de Paris* .... C 19

Calvin, Jean, *Excuse ... à Messieurs les Nicodemites* .... C 43

Calvin, Jean, *Brieve Instruction ... contre les Anabaptistes* .... C 61

Calvin, Jean, *Supplication et remonstrance, sur le faict de la Chrestienté* .... C 71

Calvin, Jean, *Supplication et remonstrance, sur le faict de la Chrestienté* .... C 72

Calvin, Jean, *Petit traicté, monstrant que c'est que doit faire un homme fidele* .... C 78

Farel, Guillaume, *Epistre exhortatoire, à tous ceux qui ont congnoissance de l'Evangile* .... F 11

Farel, Guillaume, *Epistre envoyée aux reliques de la dissipation* .... F 14

Heyden, Sebald, *D'un seul mediateur, advocat, et intercesseur* .... H 14

Le Mandement de Jesus Christ .... M 11

Melanchthon, Philippe, *De l'office des princes ... d'oster les abuz qui sont en l'Eglise* .... M 64

Ochino, Bernardino, *Epistre aux magnifiques Seigneurs de Siene* .... O 1

Ochino, Bernardino, *L'Image de l'Antechrist* .... O 2

Viret, Pierre, *Disputations chrestiennes* .... V 31

Viret, Pierre, *La seconde partie des Disputations Chrestiennes* .... V 32

Viret, Pierre, *La troisiesme partie des Disputations Chrestiennes* .... V 33

Viret, Pierre, *Exposition familiere sur le Symbole des Apostres* .... V 39

Viret, Pierre, *Petit traicte de l'usage de la salutation angelique* .... V 44

1545: Bullinger, Heinrich, *Exposition sur les deux epistres ... aux Thessaloniciens* .... B 281

Calvin, Jean, *Advertissement tresutile ... sil se faisoit inventoire de ... reliques* .... C 15

Calvin, Jean, *Argument et sommaire de l'epistre ... aux Romains* .... C 17

Calvin, Jean, *Le catechisme de l'Eglise de Geneve* .... C 21

Calvin, Jean, and Viret, Pierre, *Deux Epistres* .... C 40

Calvin, Jean, *Institution de la religion chrestienne* .... C 59

Calvin, Jean, *Brieve Instruction ... contre les Anabaptistes* .... C 62

Calvin, Jean, *Contre la secte ... des Libertins* .... C 68

Calvin, Jean, *Petit Traicté de la saincte cene* .... C 75

(with René de Bienassis): Calvin, Jean, *Petit traicté monstrant que doit faire un homme fidele* .... C 79

Chansons spirituelles, pleines de louenges à Dieu .... C 102

Demonstrance des abuz de l'eglise .... D 3

Du Pinet, Antoine, *Exposition sur l'apolcalypse* .... D 102

Enseignement tresutile ... à voulentiers mourir .... E 7

Farel, Guillaume, *Epistre envoyee au duc de Lorraine* ...... F 13

Farel, Guillaume, *Forme d'oraison pour demander à Dieu la saincte predication de l'Evangile* .... F 15

Luther, Martin, *Antithese de la vraye et fausse Eglise* .... L 79

Luther, Martin, *Exposition sur les deux Epistres de S. Pierre* .... L 93

Le mandement de Jesus Christ .... M 12

Melanchthon, Philippe, *De l'office des princes* .... M 65

Ochino, Bernardino, *L'image de l'Antechrist* .... O 3

Brief Traicté de Purgatoire .... P 52

Viret, Pierre, *Dialogues du desordre qui est a present au monde* .... V 30

Viret, Pierre, *Petit traicte de l'usage de la salutation angelique* .... V 45

1546: Beaulieu, Eustorg de, *Chrestienne resjouyssance* .... B 3

La Bible .... B 54

Le Nouveau Testament .... B 198

Calvin, Jean, *Histoire d'un meurtre execrable* .... C 57

Calvin, Jean, *Deux sermons* .... C 70

Luther, Martin, *Antithese de la vraye et fausse Eglise* .... L 80

Malingre, Matthieu, *Indice des principales matieres contenues en la Bible* .... M 7

Melanchthon, Philippe, *La Somme de theologie* .... M 67

Viret, Pierre, *Exposition familiere ... sur Le Symbole des Apostres* .... V 40

1547: *Les Pseaumes de David mis en rithme Françoyse* .... B 112

Calvin, Jean, *Advertissement sur la censure ... de Sorbonne* .... C 12

(with René de Bienassis): Calvin, Jean, *Commentaire sur la premiere epistre aux Corinthiens* .... C 30 (with René de Bienassis): Calvin, Jean, *Commentaire sur la seconde Epistre aux Corinthiens* .... C 31

Calvin, Jean, *Excuse de noble seigneur Jaques de Bourgoigne* .... C 44

Calvin, Jean, *La Forme des prieres Ecclesiastiques* .... C 52

Calvin, Jean, *Contre la secte ... des Libertins* .... C 69

(with René de Bienassis): Curione, Celio Secondo, *Les Visions de Pasquille* .... C 136

Viret, Pierre, *Admonition et consolation aux fideles* .... V 25

Viret, Pierre, *De la communication des fideles ... aux ceremonies des Papistes* .... V 26

Viret, Pierre, *Epistre envoyee aux fideles qui conversent entre les Papistes* .... V 36

Viret, Pierre, *Remonstrances aux fideles, qui conversent entre les Papistes* .... V 43

1548: Calvin, Jean, *Les Actes du Concile de Trente* .... C 9

Calvin, Jean, *Le Catechisme De Geneve* .... C 22

(with René de Bienassis): Calvin, Jean, *Commentaire ... sur quatre Epistres de sainct Paul* .... C 32

(with René de Bienassis): Calvin, Jean, *Commentaire sur les deux Epistres ... à Timothée* .... C 37

Calvin, Jean, *La Forme des Prieres Ecclesiastiques* .... C 53

Marcourt, Antoine, *Le livre des Marchans* .... M 28

Viret, Pierre, *Exposition familiere de l'Oraison de nostre Seigneur* .... V 37

Viret, Pierre, *De la vertu, et usage du ministere de la parolle de Dieu* .... V 46

1549: Bullinger, Heinrich, *La Source d'erreur* .... B 282

Calvin, Jean, *Advertissement contre l'astrologie qu'on appelle judiciaire* .... C 10

Calvin, Jean, *Le Catechisme de Geneve* .... C 23

(with René de Bienassis): Calvin, Jean, *Commentaire ... sur l'epistre aux Ebrieux* .... C 33

Calvin, Jean, *La forme des Prieres Ecclesiastiques* .... C 54

Calvin, Jean, *L'Interim... Avec la vraye façon de reformer l'Eglise* .... C 64

Calvin, Jean, *Petit Traicté de la saincte cene* .... C 76

(with René de Bienassis): Melanchthon, Philippe, *Histoire de la vie et faitz de ... Martin Luther* .... M 63

Stumpf, Jean, *Histoire veritable ... de quatre Jacopins de Berne* .... S 33

Textor, Benoist, *Confession vrayement chrestienne* .... T 7

1550: *Arrestz et ordonnances royaux ... des Cieux* .... A 21

Les Pseaumes de David .... B 128

(with René de Bienassis): Calvin, Jean, *Commentaire ... sur l'epistre de sainct Jaques* .... C 25 (with René de Bienassis): Calvin, Jean, *Commentaire ... sur l'epistre aux Romains* .... C 35

(with René de Bienassis): Calvin, Jean, *Commentaire ... sur l'epistre à Tite* .... C 38

Calvin, Jean, *La forme des Prieres Ecclesiastiques* .... C 55

Farel, Guillaume, *Le Glaive de la parolle* .... F 16

Melanchthon, Philippe, *De la puissance et authorité de l'Eglise* .... M 61

(with René de Bienassis): Scrimgeour, Henry, *Un Exemple notable ... d'un homme desesperé* .... S 9

1551: *Le Nouveau Testament* .... B 204

Le Nouveau Testament .... B 205

Calvin, Jean, *Advertisssement tresutile ... s'il se faisoit inventoire de ... reliques* .... C 16

(with René de Bienassis): Calvin, Jean, *Commentaires ... sur les Canoniques* .... C 24

(with René de Bienassis): Calvin, Jean, *Commentaire ... sur l'epistre de S. Jaques* .... C 26

(with René de Bienassis): Calvin, Jean, *Commentaire sur la premiere et seconde Epistre de sainct Pierre* .... C 27

(with René de Bienassis): Calvin, Jean, *Commentaire ... sur l'Epistre Canonique de sainct Jude* .... C 28

(with René de Bienassis): Calvin, Jean, *Commentaire ... sur l'Epistre Canonique de sainct Jean* .... C 29

(with René de Bienassis): Calvin, Jean, *Commentaire sur l'epistre ... a Philemon* .... C 34

(with René de Bienassis): Calvin, Jean, *Commentaire sur les deux epistres ... aux Thessaloniciens* .... C 36

(with Laurent de Normandie): Calvin, Jean, *Institution de la religion Chrestienne* .... C 60

(with René de Bienassis): Calvin, Jean, *Petit Traicté mostrant que doit faire un homme fidele ... Excuse aux Nicodemites* .... C 80

Enseignement tresutile ... à volontiers mourir .... E 8

Marcourt, Antoine, *Declaration de la Messe* .... M 22

Brief Traité de Purgatoire .... P 53

Vergerio, Pietro Paulo, *Des Faitz et gestes du Pape Jules III* V 7

Viret, Pierre, *De la source et de la difference ... de la vieille et nouvelle idolatrie* .... V 28

Viret, Pierre, *Du Devoir et du besoing ... de la volonté de Dieu* .... V 29

Viret, Pierre, *Exposition familiere de l'oraison de nostre Seigneur* .... V 38

Viret, Pierre, *De la nature et diversité des voeuz* .... V 42

Philibert Hamelin

1551: Bodius, Hermann, *L'Union de plusieurs passages de l'Escriture* .... B 216

Wigand Koeln

1522: *Dyalogue et ung merveilleux parlement* .... D 27

1524: Gacy, Jean, *Trialogue nouveau contenant lexpression des erreurs de Martin Luther* .... G 2

1535: *Chansons Nouvelles demonstrantz plusieurs erreurs et faulsetez* .... C 99

1536: Dentière, Marie, *La Guerre et deslivrance de la ville de Geneve* .... D 5

Farel, Guillaume, *Confession de la Foy, laquelle tous Bourgeois ... doivent jurer* .... F 6

1537: Calvin, Jean, *Instruction et confession de Foy, dont on use en Leglise de Geneve* .... C 63

1542: Osiander, Andreas, *Mandat et advertissement a ses Ecclesiastiques* .... O 13

Jean Marcorelles

1551: Vergerio, Pietro Paulo, *La Bulle de l'indiction du Concile* .... V 4

Vergerio, Pietro Paulo, *Le Conseil de trois Evesques* .... V 5

Jean Michel

1538: *Le Nouveau Testament* .... B 174

Farel, Guillaume, *Lordre et maniere quon tient en administrant les sainctz sacremens* .... F 20

1539: Bodius, Hermann, *La premiere Partie de Lunion de plusieurs passaiges* .... B 214

Bodius, Hermann, *La seconde partie de Lunion de plusieurs passaiges* .... B 215

La confession de Foy faicte par le Chrestien joyeux en Christ .... C 128

Marot, Clément, *La Bergerie du bon pasteur* .... M 43

Sermon notable pour le jour de la Dedicace .... S 14

La Somme de lescripture saincte .... S 27

Zwingli, Ulrich, *Brieve et claire exposition de la Foy Chrestienne* .... Z 1

1540: Bucer, Martin, *Exposition de Levangile ... selon S. Matthieu* B 278

La confession et raison de la foy de Maistre Noel Beda .... C 127

Farel, Guillaume, *Letres certaines daucuns grandz troubles* F 18

Luther, Martin, *Exposition sur les deux Epistres de S. Pierre* .... L 92

Luther, Martin, *Les faitz de Jesus Christ et du Pape* .... L 95

Malingre, Matthieu, *Moralite de la maladie de Chrestiente* ... M 9

Menard, Jean, *Epistre Chrestienne, aux Freres Mineurs* ... M 69

Oecolampadius, Johann, *Exposition sur la premiere Epistre de S. Jehan Apostre* .... O 4
1541: Marcourt, Antoine, *Le livre des marchans* .... M 25
1542: Farel, Guillaume, *Summaire, et briefve declaration* .... F 29
Marcourt, Antoine, *Declaration de la Messe* .... M 20
Marcourt, Antoine, *Petit traicte ... de la saincte eucharistie* M 30
Menard, Jean, *Declaration de la reigle et estat des Cordeliers* .... M 70
Rhegius, Urbanus, *La Doctrine Nouvelle et Ancienne* .... R 45
1544: *Le Nouveau Testament* .... B 194
Marcourt, Antoine, *Declaration de la Messe* .... M 21
Marcourt, Antoine, *Le livre des marchans* .... M 26
Rhegius, Urbanus, *La Doctrine Nouvelle et Ancienne* .... R 46
La Somme de lescripture saincte .... S 28
La Verite cachee, devant cent ans .... V 9

Adam et Jean Rivery
1550: Coignac, Joachim de, *Huict Satyres de l'estat et vie des moines* .... C 117
Le grand pardon de pleniere remission .... P 2
Sleidan, Jean, *D'un nouveau chef qui au temps des Empereurs s'esleva à Rome* .... S 20
1551: *Le Nouveau Testament* .... B 206
Coignac, Joachim de, *Deux Satyres, l'une du Pape, l'autre de la Papauté* .... C 116
Coignac, Joachim de, *La desconfiture de Goliath* .... C 118

Pierre de Vingle
1533: Bodius, Hermann, *La premiere partie de lunion de plusieurs passaiges* .... B 212
Bodius, Hermann, *La seconde partie de Lunion de plusieurs passages* .... B 213
Olivétan, Pierre Robert, *Linstruction des enfans* .... O 5
Les grans pardons et indulgences .... P 3

Jacques Vivian
1522: *Le Baston pour chasser les loups* .... B 2

No name
1542: Rhegius, Urbanus, *La Medecine de l'ame* .... R 48
1543: Calvin, Jean, *La Forme des prieres et chantz ecclesiastiques* C 50
Farel, Guillaume, *La tres sainte oraison que ... Jesus Christ a baillé à ses Apostres* .... F 22
Luther, Martin, *Les quatorze miroirs pour consoler la creature en Dieu* .... L 83
1544: *Epistre consolatoire à une soeur soufrant persecution* ...... E 9

Ghent

Josse Lambert
1551: *Les testaments des douse Patriarches*............................. T 5

Godefroy de Rode
1535: Augustin, Saint, *La Seule parole de Lame a Dieu*.............. A 31

Grenoble

Anemond Amalberti
1530: Chevalet, *La vie de sainct Christofle*................................ C 105

Hesdin

Vauldrain Jacquin
1518: *Devote contemplation: sur le mistere de nostre redemption* .... C 132

Limoges

Claude Garnier
No date: *Extraits de plusieurs saincts Docteurs*......................... E 85

Lille

Bertram Boulet
No date: *L'abc des chrestiens et chrestiennes*........................... A 2

Jean Mullet
1519: (with Jean de La Porte, Gilles Couteau, Paris): Augustin,
     Saint, *La saincte et sacree exposition sur le psaultier
     de David*... A 29

London

Thomas Gaultier
1551: (with Edward Whitchurch): *Le Nouveau Testament* .... B 207

Stephen Mierdman
1550: Musculus, Wolfgang, *Le Temporiseur* .... M 84

John Roux
1543: *Instruction for chyldren/Linstruction des enfans* .... I 52

Edward Whitchurch
1551: (with Thomas Gaultier): *Le Nouveau Testament* .... B 207

Longeville

Martin Mourot
1527: Petit, Guillaume, *Le viat de salut*................................. P 14

Louvain

**Bartholomy de Grave, Anthoine Marie Bergagne and Jean
de Waen**
1550: *La Saincte Bible*.. B 57

Lyon

Balthazar Arnoullet

1542: *Le Nouveau Testament*...................................... B 184
1543: Branteghem, Guillaume de, *La Vie de Nostre Seigneur Jesus Christ* .... B 257
Savonarola, Jérôme, *Exposition de l'oraison dominicale*... S 7
1544: *Exhortation à la lecture des Sainctes Lettres*................... E 70
Lefèvre d'Étaples, Jacques, *Epistres et Evangiles des cinquante et deux Dimenches de l'An*........................ L 23
1545: *Cinquante Pseaumes en Françoys*............................... B 100
(with Guillaume Rouillé): *Le Nouveau Testament*............ B 196
Campen, Jean van, *Paraphrase ... sur les Psalmes ... sur l'Ecclesiaste* .... C 89
1549: (with Thibaud Payen): Erasme, Desiderius, *Les Apophthegmes* .... E 18
1550: *La Sainte Bible* .... B 58

Olivier Arnoullet

1524: Maillard, Olivier, *Lexemplaire de confession* .... M 1
1525: *Linstruction des curez pour instruire le simple peuple* ...... I 44
1530: *Les Postilles et expositions des Epistres et Evangiles dominicales*.. P 30
1531: *La Bible en Francoys* .... B 38
1534: Desmoulins, Laurent, *Le cymetiere des malheureux*.......... D 24
1535: *Briefve et salutaire exposition sur la salutation angelique* .... E 83
1539: Petit, Guillaume, *Le viat de salut*................................ P 18
1541: Béda, Noël, *La petite dyablerie dont Lucifer est le chef*.... B 12
Les Parolles memorables de Jesuchrist au pecheur.......... P 7
1542: *Plusieurs expositions ... sur loraison dominicale aultrement dicte la Patinostre*.. E 79
1543: Brodeau, Victor, *Les Louanges du sainct nom de Jesus*..... B 270
Luther, Martin, *Le livre de vraye et parfaicte oraison* ...... L 109
Ung beau mystere de nostre Dame ... dune jeune Fille laquelle se voulut habandonner a peche...................... M 108b
1546: *Les Postilles et expositions des Epistres et Evangilles dominicalles*.. P 33
No date: Maurice de Sully, *Les expositions des evangiles en françoys*.. M 49

Nicolas Bacquenois

1547: (with Jean Pidier, Guillaume Rouillé, Thibaud Payen): *La Bible en Francoys* .... B 55

Pierre Bailly

1521: (with Jacques Sacon): *La bible en francoys* .... B 32
1531: *La Bible en francoys* .... B 37

Estienne Baland
1511: Lemaire de Belges, Jean, *Le traictie Intitule, de la diffe-rence des scismes* .... L 28
Lemaire de Belges, Jean, *Le traictie Intitule, de la diffe-rence des scismes* .... L 29

Jean Barbou
1538: (with Guillaume de Guelques): Erasme, Desiderius, *Pre-paration à la mort* .... E 43
(with Guillaume de Guelques): *L'internelle consolation*.... I 22
1542: *Le Nouveau Testament* .... B 183

Godefroy et Marcelin Beringen
1545: *La Bible en francois* .... B 51
1547: *Le Premier Livre des Pseaulmes de David* .... B 113
Pseaulmes cinquante de David .... B 114
1548: *Pseaulmes cinquante de David* .... B 119
Gueroult, Guillaume, *Premier Livre de chansons spirituelles* G 57
1549: *Pseaulmes cinquante de David* .... B 122
Psalmes trente du royal Prophete David .... B 123

Jacques Berion
1549: *La Fontaine de vie... l'instruction pour les enfans* .... F 49

Jean Besson
1523: (with Claude Nourry): Spagnuoli, Battista, *La parthenice Mariane* .... S 32

Antoine Blanchard
1527: (with Claude Veycellier): Petit, Guillaume, *Le Viat de Salut* P 15
1528: (with Gilbert de Villiers): Petit, Guillaume, *Le viat de salut*... P 16

Benoist Bonnyn
1538: *Cymbalum mundi en françoys* .... C 137

Jean Cantarel
1533: (with Vve Barnabé Chaussard): Berquin, Louis de, *La farce des theologastres* .... B 22
1551: *La vie de Jesuchrist* .... V 13

François Carcan
1525: (with Claude Nourry): 'Turin, François Cavillon': *Le nouveau testament* .... B 159

Barnabé Chaussard
1520: Bougain, Michel, *Le jardin amoureux de lame devote* .... B 232
Bougain, Michel, *Le Jardin de paradis* .... B 236
Le proufit quon a douyr messe .... P 46
La vie de Jesuchrist .... V 11
La vie de sainct Nicolas .... V 21
1523: *Le proufit quon a d'ouyr messe* .... P 47
1524: *Le profit quon a douyr messe* .... P 48

1525: *Le proufit quon a de ouyr messe* .... P 49

Les XXXIII. significations et considerations qui sont en la messe .... S 17

Vve Barnabé Chaussard

1532: *Le livre de consolations* .... L 65

Le livre de paix en Jesuchrist .... L 68

La vie saincte Katherine de Seine .... V 17a

1533: (with Jean Cantarel): Berquin, Louis de, *La farce des theologastres* .... B 22

Les .xv. joyes de nostre dame .... Q 5

1540: *Lucidaire en françoys* .... L 72

Heirs of Barnabé Chaussard

1537: Brigitta, Sainte (pseud), *Les oraisons en francoys* .... B 264

1548: Columbi, Jean, *Confession generale, avec certainez reigles* .... C 123

Antoine Constantin

1540: (with Sulpice Sabon): Brodeau, Victor, *Les Louanges de JesuChrist* .... B 267

1541: (with Sulpice Sabon): Vivès, Juan Luis, *Institution de la femme Chrestienne* .... V 54

1544: (with Sulpice Sabon): *La Bible* .... B 49

(with Sulpice Sabon): *Les Oeuvres de Clement Marot* .... B 99

Jacques Crozet

1543: *Le Nouveau Testament* .... B 191

Estienne Dolet

1540: Dolet, Estienne, *Les Gestes de Françoys de Valois* .... D 33

1542: *Psaumes de Clement Marot* .... B 92

Psalmes du royal Prophete David .... B 93

Les Livres de Salomon .... B 149

Le Nouveau Testament .... B 185

Brief Discours de la Republique françoyse .... B 261

Brunfels, Otto, *Les Prieres et oraisons de la Bible* .... B 275

Campen, Jean van, *Paraphrase ... sur les Psalmes* .... C 85

Campen, Jean van, *Paraphrase ... sur les Psalmes ... sur l'Ecclesiaste* .... C 86

Erasme, Desiderius, *Le Chevalier Chrestien* .... E 30

Erasme, Desiderius, *Le Chevalier Chrestien* .... E 31

Erasme, Desiderius, *Le vray moyen de bien et catholiquement se confesser* .... E 38

Erasme, Desiderius, *Preparation à la mort* .... E 47

Exhortation à la lecture des sainctes lettres .... E 69

La Fontaine de vie .... F 45

Les Heures de la compagnie des penitents .... H 11

L'Internelle consolation .... I 31

Lefèvre d'Étaples, Jacques, *Les Epistres, et Evangiles des cinquante, et deux Dimenches de l'An* .... L 22
Livre de la compagnie des Penitens .... L 66
Rabelais, François, *Pantagruel* .... R 13
Rabelais, François, *Gargantua* .... R 19
Le Sommaire des livres du Vieil, et Nouveau Testament .... S 21
1543: Brodeau, Victor, *Les Louanges du sainct nom de Jesus* ..... B 269
Dolet, Estienne, *Les Gestes de Françoys de Valois* .... D 34
1544: *Les psalmes du royal prophete David* .... B 98

Simon Du Bois dit de la Haye

1549: (with Guillaume Rouillé, Pierre de Tours, Thibaud Payen): Marguerite de Navarre, *Marguerites de la Marguerite des Princesses* .... M 33

Antoine Du Ry

1528: Lemaire de Belges, Jean, *Le traictie de la difference des scismes* .... L 40

Barthelemy Frein

1548: (with Philibert Rollet, Thibaud Payen, Guillaume Rouillé): *Le Nouveau Testament* .... B 201

Jean et François Frellon

1538: (with Melchior et Gaspar Trechsel): *Les simulachres et historiees faces de la mort* .... I 5
1542: Branteghem, Guillaume de, *Le vergier spirituel et mystique* B 241
Les Simulachres et historiees faces de la mort, contenant La medecine de l'ame .... I 7
1545: Marot, Clément, *Bergerie. Du bon pasteur et du mauvais* M 44
1546: *Cinquante deux Pseaumes* .... B 111
1547: *Les Images de la mort ... La medecine de l'Ame* .... I 8
1548: *Le Nouveau Testament* .... B 200
1550: *Le Nouveau Testament* .... B 202

Sebastien Gryphe

1539: Aneau, Barthélemy, *Chant natal contenant sept noelz* .... A 9
Grégoire de Nazianze, Saint, *De la cure, et nourrissement des Pauvres* .... G 26
1540: *Les sept Pseaulmes de la penitence de David* .... B 83
1542: Arétin, Pierre, *La Genese ... avec la vision de Noë* .... A 11

Guillaume de Guelques

1538: (with Jean Barbou): Erasme, Desiderius, *Preparation à la mort* .... E 43
(with Jean Barbou): *L'internelle consolation* .... I 22

Denis de Harsy

1530: (with Romain Morin): Le Grand, Jacques, *Le Tresor de Sapience* .... L 26b

1532: (with Romain Morin): Lemaire de Belges, Jean, *Le Promptuaire des Conciles de Leglise Catholique* .... L 47
1533: (with Romain Morin): Lemaire de Belges, Jean, *Le Promptuaire des Conciles de Leglise Catholique* .... L 48
1537: Rabelais, François, *Pantagruel* .... R 10
      Rabelais, François, *Gargantua* .... R 16
1542: *Sept degres de l'echelle de penitence* .... B 91
      Linternelle Consolation .... I 30
      Le Grand, Jacques, *Le Tresor de Sapience* .... L 27

M. Harvard
1515: Maurice de Sully, *Les expositions des evangiles en francoys*   M 47

François Juste
1533: Rabelais, François, *Pantagruel* .... R 7
1534: Rabelais, François, *Pantagruel* .... R 8
1535: Rabelais, François, *Gargantua* .... R 14
      Rabelais, François, *Gargantua* .... R 15
1537: Doré, Pierre, *Les Voyes du Paradis* .... D 91
      Erasme, Desiderius, *Preparation a la Mort* .... E 41
      Rabelais, François, *Pantagruel* .... R 11
      Rabelais, François, *Gargantua* .... R 17
1538: *L'Abouchement de nostre sainct pere le Pape, Lempereur et le Roy* .... A 4
1539: Lefèvre d'Étaples, Jacques, *Contemplations salutaires d'Innocence perdue* .... L 18
1540: Branteghem, Guillaume de, *La Vie de Jesus Christ* .... B 245
      L'internelle consolation .... I 26
      Pinet, Guillaume, *Le Contemnement du monde* .... P 23
1541: Branteghem, Guillaume de, *La vie de nostre Seigneur Jesuchrist* .... B 252
1542: Rabelais, François, *Pantagruel* .... R 12
      Rabelais, François, *Gargantua* .... R 18
1544: Erasme, Desiderius, *De la preparation à la mort* .... E 50
      (with Pierre de Tours): *L'Internelle Consolation* .... I 36

Jean Lambany
1529: Voragine, Jacques de, *Legende doree* .... V 75
      La pacience de job selon lhystoire de la bible .... P 8a

Jean de La Place
1522: Lambert, François, *La Corone de nostre saulveur jesus-christ* .... L 12

Claude La Ville
1543: Erasme, Desiderius, *Paraphrase, ou briefve exposition sur toutes les Epistres Canoniques* .... E 39

Jean Le Converd
1549: Erasme, Desiderius, *Deux colloques d'Erasme* .... E 21

Claude Marchant
1550: *Pseaumes de David. Avec le latin* .... B 129

Jacques Mareschal
1524: Lemaire de Belges, Jean, *Le traictie de la difference des
    scismes* .... L 38

Pierre Mareschal
1520: *La vie de ma dame saincte katherine de seine*.................. V 17

Jean Marnax
1551: Eck, Johann, *Les Lieux communs* .... E 2

Jacques Moderne
1525: *La Balade des leutheriens avec la chanson*....................... B 1
1540: Saulnier, Antoine, *Chanson nouvelle. Composee sus les
    dix commandemens de Dieu*...................................... S 3
No date: Columbi, Jean, *Confession generale avec certaines
    reigles* .... C 122
No date: Maillard, Olivier, *La confession generalle de frere
    Olivier Maillard*.. M 2
No date: Marchepallu, Jacques, *Les vertus et excellences des
    pseaulmes*.. M 17

Romain Morin
1530: (with Denis de Harsy): Le Grand, Jacques, *Le Tresor de
    Sapience*.. L 26b
1532: (with Denis de Harsy): Lemaire de Belges, Jean, *Le
    Promptuaire des Conciles de Leglise Catholique*......... L 47
    Les paroles memorables entre Jesus Christ et le pecheur....... P 6
1533: (with Denis de Harsy): Lemaire de Belges, Jean, *Le
    Promptuaire des Conciles de Leglise Catholique*......... L 48

Jean Mosnier
1540: *Le Refuge des Chrestiens*... R 42

Claude Nourry
1516: Columbi, Jean, *Confession generale avec certaines regles*..... C 120
    Lucidaire ... diverses matieres subtilles........................... L 71
1517: *La Vie de Jhesucrist* .... V 10
1523: (with Jean Besson): Spagnuoli, Battista, *La parthenice
    Mariane*.. S 32
1524: Le Conte, Jean, *Les miracles de la benoite et glorieuse
    vierge marie*.. L 17
1525: (with François Carcan): 'Turin, François Cavillon': *Le
    nouveau testament*.. B 159
1526: Maillard, Olivier, *La confession generale de frere
    Olivier maillard*... M 3
1532: Rabelais, François, *Pantagruel*..................................... R 1
No date: *Le Tresor de devotion*.. T 17

Thibaud Payen

1541: *Le Nouveau Testament*.....................	B 182
1542: *Le Nouveau Testament*.....................	B 186
1543: *Le Nouveau Testament*.....................	B 192
Erasme, Desiderius, *Le sermon de Jesus enfant*	E 56
1544: *Le Nouveau Testament*.....................	B 195
1547: (with Nicolas Bacquenois, Jean Pidier, Guillaume Rouillé): *La Bible en Francoys*	B 55
1548: (with Barthelemy Frein, Philibert Rollet, Guillaume Rouillé): *Le Nouveau Testament*....................	B 201
1549: *Epistre d'un gentilhomme à un sien ami*......................	E 11
(with Balthazar Arnoullet): Erasme, Desiderius, *Les Apophthegmes*.........................	E 18
(with Simon Du Bois dit de la Haye, Guillaume Rouillé, Pierre de Tours): Marguerite de Navarre, *Marguerites de la Marguerite des Princesses*..................	M 33

Nicolas Petit

1540: *Le Nouveau Testament*.....................	B 179

Jean Pidier

1547: (with Nicolas Bacquenois, Guillaume Rouillé, Thibaud Payen): *La Bible en Francoys*	B 55

Jean Pullon

1551: Désiré, Artus, *Les Combatz du Fidelle Chrestien*.............	D 9

Philibert Rollet

1548: (with Barthelemy Frein, Thibaud Payen, Guillaume Rouillé): *Le Nouveau Testament*....................	B 201
1551: *La Bible en Francoys*	B 60

Guillaume Rouillé

1545: (with Balthazar Arnoullet): *Le Nouveau Testament*...........	B 196
1547: (with Thibaud Payen, Nicolas Bacquenois, Jean Pidier): *La Bible en Francoys*	B 55
1548: (with Thibaud Payen, Barthelemy Frein, Philibert Rollet): *Le Nouveau Testament*	B 201
1549: (with Simon Du Bois dit de la Haye, Pierre de Tours, Thibaud Payen): Marguerite de Navarre, *Marguerites de la Marguerite des Princesses*..................	M 33
1550: *Le Nouveau Testament*.....................	B 203

Sulpice Sabon

1540: (with Antoine Constantin): Brodeau, Victor, *Les Louanges de JesuChrist*.........................	B 267
1541: (with Antoine Constantin): Vivès, Juan Luis, *Institution de la femme Chrestienne*.....................	V 54
1544: (with Antoine Constantin): *La Bible*	B 49
(with Antoine Constantin): *Les Oeuvres de Clement Marot* ...	B 99

Jacques Sacon

1518: *La bible en francoys*.. B 29
1521: (with Pierre Bailly): *La bible en francoys*........................ B 32

Pierre de Sainte-Lucie

1535: Gacy, Jean, *La deploration de la Cite de Genesve*............. G 1
    Rabelais, François, *Pantagruel*... R 9
1538: Doré, Pierre, *Dialogue instructoire, des Chrestiens en la foy* D 66
    Marguerite de Navarre, *Le miroir de treschrestienne
      princesse Marguerite*.. M 40
No date: *Le Thresor de devotion*... T 18

Jean de Tournes

1538: *La Discipline et amour divin*.. D 31
1542: Erasme, Desiderius, *Le Chevalier Chrestien*...................... E 32
1543: *L'armeure de patience*.. A 18
    Les Psalmes de David.. B 94
    Brunfels, Otto, *Les Prieres et oraisons de la Bible*............ B 276
    Chrysostome, St Jean, *Traicté que nul n'est offensé
      sinon par soymesme*... C 108
    Erasme, Desiderius, *La Preparation à la mort*.................. E 48
    Erasme, Desiderius, *Le Sermon de Jesus enfant*............... E 55
    La Fontaine de vie... F 47
    Le livre de l'Internelle consolation................................. I 33
    Jérôme, Saint, *Epistre à Paulin*....................................... J 1
    Luther, Martin, *Le livre de vraye et parfaicte oraison*...... L 107
    Sermons des six paroles de Jesuchrist en croix................ S 15
    Vivès, Juan Luis, *L'institution de la femme chrestienne*.... V 56
1544: Brunfels, Otto, *Les Prieres et oraisons de la Bible*............ B 277
    Erasme, Desiderius, *La Civilité puerile*............................ E 19
    Erasme, Desiderius, *Le Chevalier Chrestien*...................... E 34
    Lefèvre d'Étaples, Jacques, *Epistres et evangiles des
      cinquantes et deux dimenches de L'An*........................ L 24
    Quatre homelies de trois ... Theologiens......................... Q 1
    Spagnuoli, Battista, *La Fontaine d'honneur et de vertu*..... S 31
1545: Benedetto da Mantova, *Traité du benefice de Jesus
      Christ crucifié*.. B 18
    Le Nouveau Testament.. B 197
    Vivès, Juan Luis, *L'Institution de la femme chrestienne*.... V 58
1546: Lemaire de Belges, Jean, *Le Promptuaire des conciles de
      Leglise catholique*.. L 52
1547: Espence, Claude d', *Homelies de la Parabole de l'enfant
      prodigue*... E 58
    Espence, Claude d', *Paraphrase, ou Meditation, sur
      l'oraison dominicale*... E 62
    Lemaire de Belges, Jean, *Le Promptuaire des conciles de
      Leglise catholique*.. L 53

Luther, Martin, *Consolation en adversité* .... L 84
Marguerite de Navarre, *Marguerites de la Marguerite
    des princesses* .... M 32
Theodoret, *Sermons de Theodoret* .... T 8
Vivès, Juan Luis, *L'Institution de la femme chrestienne* .... V 61
1548: Espence, Claude d', *Institution d'un Prince chrestien* .... E 60
Espence, Claude d', *Traicté Contre l'erreur vieil et
    renouvellé des predestinez* .... E 66
1549: Lemaire de Belges, Jean, *Le Traicté de la difference des
    Schismes* .... L 46
Le Miroir du penitent .... M 79
Vivès, Juan Luis, *L'institution de la femme chrestienne* .... V 63
1550: Espence, Claude d', *Paraphrase, ou Meditation, sur
    l'oraison dominicale* .... E 65
1551: *La Sainte Bible* .... B 61
Le Nouveau Testament .... B 208

Pierre de Tours
1544: (with François Juste): *L'Internelle Consolation* .... I 36
1547: Rabelais, François, *Tiers livre* .... R 26
1548: Rabelais, François, *Quart livre* .... R 32
Rabelais, François, *Quart livre* .... R 33
1549: (with Simon Du Bois dit de la Haye, Guillaume Rouillé,
    Thibaud Payen): Marguerite de Navarre, *Marguerites
    de la Marguerite des Princesses* .... M 33
No date: Rabelais, François, *Gargantua et Pantagruel* .... R 21
Rabelais, François, *Tiers livre* .... R 27
Rabelais, François, *Quart livre* .... R 34

Melchior et Gaspar Trechsel
1538: (with Jean et François Frellon): *Les simulachres et
    historiees faces de la mort* .... I 5
1539: Arétin, Pierre, *Trois livres De l'Humanite de Jesuchrist* ... A 12
Arétin, Pierre, *La Passion de Jesus Christ* .... A 13

Claude Veycellier
1527: (with Antoine Blanchard): Petit, Guillaume, *Le Viat de
    Salut* .... P 15

Gilbert de Villiers
1526: Nachtigall, Ottomarus, *Hystoire evangelique des quatre
    evangelistes* .... N 1
1528: (with Antoine Blanchard): Petit, Guillaume, *Le viat de
    salut* .... P 16

Pierre de Vingle
1529: *Le nouveau testament* .... B 162
Farel, Guillaume, *Summaire, et brieve declaration* .... F 26
1530: *Le nouveau Testament* .... B 163
Brunfels, Otto, *Les Prieres et Oraisons de la Bible* .... B 273

*Brefve et devote exposition par maniere dexhortation et
doraison, faicte sur le Pater noster* .... E 75
Lefèvre d'Étaples, Jacques, *Epistres et evangiles des
cinquante et deux dimenches* .... L 20
Luther, Martin, *La Maniere de lire levangile et quel
proffit on en doibt attendre* .... L 116
1531: Erasme, Desiderius, *La complainte de la Paix* .... E 24
1532: Erasme, Desiderius, *Enchiridion (ou Manuel) du Chevalier Chrestien* .... E 29

No name
1531: *Le .VI. Pseaulme de David* .... B 77
1540: Doré, Pierre, *Les Voyes du Paradis* .... D 93
1541: *Les Livres de Salomon* .... B 148
1543: *Edict du Roy Sur les articles faictz par la faculte de
Theologie de ... Paris* .... E 4
1544: *Traicté ... s'il est loysible de lire la saincte Escriture en
langue Vulgaire* .... T 14
1545: *Chanson spirituelle sur la saincte Cene* .... C 95
1546: *Le Nouveau Testament* .... B 199
        Rabelais, François, *Tiers livre* .... R 23
1549: 'Rouen, Claude Treszet': Lefèvre d'Étaples, Jacques, *Les
Epistres et evangiles des cinquante, et deux
Dimenches de L'an* .... L 25
1550: Doré, Pierre, *Les allumettes du feu divin* .... D 48

Marburg

Franciscus Rhode
1529: Lambert, François, *Somme Chrestienne* .... L 11

Metz

Jean Pallier
1544: Lalande, Matthieu de, *Manuel des abus de lhomme ingrat* ..... L 10

Nantes

Jean Baudouin
1518: *Linstruction des curez pour instruire le simple peuple* ...... I 42

Neuchâtel

Pierre de Vingle
1533: *Sensuivent plusieurs belles et bonnes chansons* .... C 101
        La confession et raison de la foy de maistre Noel Beda ..... C 126
        Farel, Guillaume, *La maniere et fasson quon tient en
baillant le sainct baptesme* .... F 19
        Malingre, Matthieu, *Moralite de la maladie de Chrestiente* ... M 8
        Malingre, Matthieu, *Noelz nouveaulx* .... M 10
        Marcourt, Antoine, *Le livre des marchans* .... M 23
        La Verite cachee, devant cent ans .... V 8

1534: *Le nouveau testament* .... B 167
Chansons nouvelles demonstrantz plusieurs erreurs et faulsetez .... C 98
Exhortation sur ces sainctes parolles ... Retournez vous ... E 72
Farel, Guillaume, *Summaire, et briefve declaration* .... F 28
Luther, Martin, *Les faictz de Jesus Christ et du Pape* .... L 94
Marcourt, Antoine, *Articles veritables sur ... la Messe*...... M 18
Marcourt, Antoine, *Declaration de la Messe* .... M 19
Marcourt, Antoine, *Le livre des marchans*...................... M 24
Marcourt, Antoine, *Petit traicte ... de la saincte eucharistie* M 29
1535: *La Bible*... B 40
Farel, Guillaume, *Letres certaines daucuns grandz troubles et tumultes advenuz a Geneve* .... F 17

Nevers

Jean Barbaram
1521: (with Nicolas de La Barre, Nicolas Higman, Paris): *Linstruction des curez pour instruire le simple peuple* ...... I 43

Orléans

Éloi Gibier
1536: Hervet, Gentian, *Oraison ou Sermon de l'Ascension* .... H 10

Paris

Jean Amazeur
1550: (with Jean Ruelle): *L'Internelle Consolation* .... I 38
Jean André
1535: (with Nicolas Couteau): *Ordonnances ... contre ... la secte lutherienne*.. O 12
1539: (with Estienne Caveiller, Guillaume Le Bret, Henry Paquot, Simon de Colines): Bouchet, Jean, *Les triumphes de la Noble et amoureuse Dame* .... B 228
1542: (with Nicolas Barbou): Bernard, Saint, *De la maniere d'aimer Dieu*.. B 20
Rosay, G. de, *Le relief de l'ame pecheresse*...................... R 51
1543: *Les Articles de la faculté de Theologie de Paris* .... A 22
(with Adam Saulnier): Doré, Pierre, *La caeleste pensée de graces divines arrousée*.................................... D 86
1545: (with Galliot Du Pré, Jacques Tyson, Nicolas Du Chemin): Bouchet, Jean, *Les Triumphes de la noble et amoureuse dame*.. B 231
Chanson nouvelle contre la secte Lutheriane................... C 97
1546: *Arrest notable ... contre grand nombre d'Heretiques* .... A 20
Désiré, Artus, *Le Miroer des francz Taulpins* .... D 17
Désiré, Artus, *Le Miroer des Francs Taulpins* .... D 18

(with Jean Ruelle, René Avril): Doré, Pierre, *La premiere partie des Collations royales* .... D 55

(with Jean Ruelle, René Avril): Doré, Pierre, *La seconde partie, des collations royalles* .... D 56

(with Adam Saulnier): Doré, Pierre, *La celeste pensée, des graces divines arrousée* .... D 87

1547: (with René Avril): Désiré, Artus, *Le deffensoire de la foi Chrestienne* .... D 10

Désiré, Artus, *Le Miroer des Francs Taulpins* .... D 19

1548: Désiré, Artus, *Le deffensoire de la foy Chrestiene* .... D 11

(with Jean David, Vivant Gaultherot): Grenier, Nicole, *Le Bouclier de la foy* .... G 31

(with Michel Fezandat, Vivant Gaultherot): Grenier, Nicole, *Le Bouclier de la foy* .... G 32

Lescagne, Tristan de, *C'est Nostre Dame ... à la confusion des ... lutheriens* .... L 60

Pierre Attaignant

1546: *XVII. pseaulmes de David* .... B 108

Recueil de trente et un Psaumes .... B 109

Bernard Aubry

1521: (with Michel Lesclencher, Pierre Viart): Voragine, Jacques de, *La legende doree* .... V 73

1525: (with Antoine Bonnemere, Philippe Le Noir): *La fleur des Commandemens de Dieu* .... F 37

Antoine Augereau

1533: Florimond, *Epistre familiere de prier Dieu* .... F 42

Florimond, *Epistre familiere de prier Dieu* .... F 43

Florimond, *Epistre familiere de prier Dieu* .... F 44

Marguerite de Navarre, *Le miroir de lame pecheresse* .... M 36

Marguerite de Navarre, *Le miroir de treschrestienne princesse Marguerite* .... M 37

Marguerite de Navarre, *Le miroir de treschrestienne princesse Marguerite* .... M 38

René Avril

1544: (with Jean Ruelle): Doré, Pierre, *Dialogue Instructoire des Chrestiens* .... D 71

1546: (with Jean Ruelle): Conrard, Olivier, *La Vie, faictz et louanges de sainct Paul* .... C 131

(with Jean André, Jean Ruelle): Doré, Pierre, *La premiere partie des Collations royales* .... D 55

(with Jean André, Jean Ruelle): Doré, Pierre, *La seconde partie, des collations royalles* .... D 56

1547: (with Jean André): Désiré, Artus, *Le deffensoire de la foi Chrestienne* .... D 10

1548: Espence, Claude d', *Paraphrase, ou meditation, sur l'oraison Dominicale* .... E 63

1549: (with Jean de Brouilly): Doré, Pierre, *L'image de Vertu*.... D 76

Josse Badius

1529: (with Jean Petit): Lasseré, Louis, *La Vie de monseigneur sainct Hierosme* .... L 14

1530: Lasseré, Louis, *La Vie de monseigneur sainct Hierosme*.... L 15

1531: Aumen, Gervais, *La consolation des desolez* .... A 36

Nicolas Barbou

1541: (with Jean de Brouilly): Doré, Pierre, *La Deploration de la vie humaine*.. D 63

Gaigny, Jean de, *Devote exposition sur le cinquantiesme Pseaulme* .... G 5

1542: (with J. André): Bernard, Saint, *De la maniere d'aimer Dieu* .... B 20

Pierre Bige

1530: (with Jacques Ferrebouc): Gringore, Pierre, *La complaincte de la cite crestienne* .... G 47

Jean Bignon

1540: (with Charles Langelier): Spagnuoli, Battista, *La Vie d'honneur et de Vertu* .... S 29

1543: (with Pierre Regnault): *La Bible en francois* .... B 47

No date (with Pierre Sergent): Du Buc, Richard, *Devot Traité de la genese* .... D 96

Guillaume Bineaulx

1533: Rabelais, François, *Pantagruel* .... R 2

Jacques Bogard

1545: (with Jean Ruelle): *Cinquante deux Pseaumes de David*.... B 102

(with Jean Ruelle, Nicolas Du Chemin): *Cinquante Pseaumes*... B 103

1546: (with Nicolas Du Chemin): *Cinquante Deux Pseaumes de David*... B 107

1547: Aurigny, Gilles d', *Contemplation sur la mort de Jesus-Christ* .... A 37

1548: *Les testamens des douze patriarches* .... T 3

Jean Bonfons

1543: *Lexcercice pour jeunes gens* .... E 68

1546: *Le Jeu, et Mystere de la Saincte Hostie* .... M 108

1548: (with Jean Réal, Guillaume Le Bret, Vivant Gaultherot): Lemaire de Belges, Jean, *Le traicte de la difference des scismes* .... L 45

1551: (with Guillaume Thibout): *Cinquante deux Pseaumes* .... B 143

No date: Denys, Saint, *La contemplation spirituelle* .... D 6

Nicolas Bonfons

1540: (with Jérôme de Gourmont, Jean de Brouilly): Doré,
Pierre, *L'image de vertu* .... D 74
1547: Doré, Pierre, *L'image de vertu* .... D 75

Yolande Bonhomme

1525: (with Guillaume de Bossozel): *Le Fagot de myerre* .... F 3
1530: *L'armeure de patience* .... A 14
Internelle consolation .... I 13
*Aucunes belles Preparations pour devotement recevoir
le Sainct Sacrement* .... P 38
1539: *Larmeure de patience* .... A 16
Exposition sur le Salve Regina .... E 84
Internelle consolation .... I 24
(with Jean Petit): Merlin, Jacques, *Lexposition de
levangille Missus est* .... M 71
*Aucunes belles preparations pour devotement recepvoir
le sainct sacrement* .... P 39

Antoine Bonnemere

1525: (with Bernard Aubry, Philippe Le Noir): *La fleur des
Commandemens de Dieu* .... F 37
1531: (with Nicolas Savetier, Jean Le Bailli): Clerici, Jean,
Ung traicte des fondemens du temple spirituel .... C 111
1537: *La bible en francoiz* .... B 42
1539: Doré, Pierre, *Le College de sapience* .... D 57
Doré, Pierre, *Dialogue. Instructoire, des Chrestiens* .... D 68
1540: (with Guillaume Le Bret): Doré, Pierre, *Les Allumettes
du feu divin* .... D 45
Doré, Pierre, *Les Voyes de Paradis* .... D 94
(with Jean Foucher, Nicolas Gilles): Vitrier, Jean, *Le
Sermon que nostre Seigneur feist en la montaigne* .... V 50
1541: (with Charles Dudé): *Linstruction des curez* .... I 47a
1544: Gringore, Pierre, *Heures de Nostre Dame* .... G 56

Guillaume de Bossozel

1525: (with Yolande Bonhomme): *Le Fagot de myerre* .... F 3
(with Pierre Ricouart): Mauburne, Jean, *Une petite
eschelle pour faire bonne et entiere confession* .... M 46
1531: (with Jean Saint Denys): *Les sept pseaulmes en francoys* .... B 76
Brigitta, Sainte (pseud), *Les Quinze oraisons ... en
Francoys* .... B 263
Linstruction des Curez pour instruyre le simple peuple ..... I 45
(with Ambroise Girault): Ludolphus de Saxe, *Le grant
Vita Christi ... en francoys* .... L 75
(with Pierre Gaudoul, Ambroise Girault, François
Regnault): *Le premier (-second) volume des grandes
Postilles et expositions* .... P 31

1532: (with Jean Petit): Gringore, Pierre, *Chantz royaulx figurez morallement*...................................... G 42

(with Jean Petit): Gringore, Pierre, *Heures de nostre dame*... G 50

1533: (with Pierre Sergent): *Brefve et salutaire exposition sur la salutation angelique*.................................. E 82

1534: (with Jean Petit): Gringore, Pierre, *Heures de nostre dame*.... G 51

(with Didier Maheu): Ludolphus de Saxe, *Le grant vita Christi translaté de latin en francoys*........................ L 76

1535: (with Jean Petit): Hangest, Jérôme de, *Contre les tenebrions lumiere evangelicque*............................... H 1

1536: (with Pierre Sergent): Bouchet, Jean, *Les Triumphes De la Noble et amoureuse dame*......................... B 226

1541: (with Galliot Du Pré): Mailly, Nicolas de, *La divine cognoissance*.. M 4

1542: (with Vivant Gaultherot, Jean Foucher): Doré, Pierre, *L'arbre de vie, appuyant les beaux lys de France*........ D 51

Rémy Boyset

1545: (with Thielman Kerver, Guillaume Le Bret, Oudin Petit, Nicolas Couteau, Pierre Sergent): *La bible en francoiz*..... B 53

Vve Jean de Brie

1540: Luther, Martin, *Le livre de vraye et parfaicte oraison*...... L 105

1541: Vitrier, Jean, *Le Sermon que nostre Seigneur Jesuchrist feit en la montaigne*.. V 52

Jean de Brouilly

1540: (with Nicolas Bonfons, Jérôme de Gourmont): Doré, Pierre, *L'image de vertu*...................................... D 74

1541: (with Nicolas Barbou): Doré, Pierre, *La Deploration de la vie humaine*... D 63

1543: Doré, Pierre, *La deploration de la vie humaine*............... D 64

1545: (with Guillaume Thibout): Doré, Pierre, *Dialogue Instructoire, des chrestiens en la foy*........................ D 72

1546: Doré, Pierre, *Le College de sapience*........................ D 58

Doré, Pierre, *Le Pasturage de la brebis humaine*.......... D 84

1547: Doré, Pierre, *La Passe-solitaire à tous amateurs de Dieu*... D 82

1548: Doré, Pierre, *Les Triomphes du Roy sans pair*............... D 90

1549: (with René Avril): Doré, Pierre, *L'image de Vertu*.......... D 76

1550: Doré, Pierre, *Oraison Panegyrique ... pour ... Claude de Lorraine*... D 81

Nicolas Buffet

1535: Marguerite de Navarre, *Le miroir de treschrestienne princesse Marguerite*..................................... M 39

1543: *Livre merveilleux, contenant en brief la fleur et substance de plusieurs traictiez*........................... L 69 (with Jacques Regnault, Antoine Foucault): Luther, Martin, *Le livre de vraye et parfaicte oraison*.................... L 108

1544: (with Jacques Regnault, Antoine Foucault): Vitrier, Jean, *Le Sermon que nostre Seigneur feist en la montaigne*... V 53

1545 (with Pierre Regnault): *La Bible translatee de Latin en Francoys ... pour les simples gens*.............................. B 52

1548: *Les Figures et Visions de L'apocalypse*.......................... F 33

Estienne Caveiller

1533 (with Jean Macé): Gaigny, Jean de, *Le livre faisant mention des sept parolles*...................... G 7

1537 (with Denis Janot, Pierre Sergent): Le Roy, François, *Le Dialogue de consolation entre lame et raison*.............. L 56

1538 (with Henry Paquot, Jean Longis): *Le livre de la Discipline Damour*...................... D 32

(with François Regnault, Jean Ruelle): Doré, Pierre, *Les Allumettes du feu divin*...................... D 41

(with Alain Lotrian): Doré, Pierre, *Les Allumettes du feu divin*...................... D 43

(with François Regnault, Alain Lotrian): Doré, Pierre, *Les Voyes de Paradis*...................... D 92

(with Henri Paquot, Les Angeliers): Gaigny, Jean de, *Le livre ... des sept parolles*...................... G 9

(with Les Angeliers, Vivant Gaultherot): Jordan, Raymond, dit Idiota, *Les Contemplations du Simple devot*............ J 13

1539: (with Guillaume Le Bret, Henry Paquot, Jean André, Simon de Colines): Bouchet, Jean, *Les triumphes de la Noble et amoureuse Dame*...................... B 228

(with Jean Ruelle): Doré, Pierre, *Les Allumettes du feu divin*...................... D 44

(with Maurice de La Porte, François Regnault): Gaigny, Jean de, *Le livre ... des Sept parolles*...................... G 10

1542: (with Arnoul Langelier): *La Fontaine de Vie... Linstruction pour les enfans*...................... F 46

(with Charles Langelier): Spagnuoli, Battista, *La Fontaine de tous biens*...................... S 30

1543: (with Arnoul et Charles Langelier): Branteghem, Guillaume de, *La Vie de Jesus Christ*.............................. B 258

Guillaume Cavellat

1547 (with Mathurin Du Puys, Benoist Prevost): Lactantius Firmianus, *Des divines Institutions*............................. L 5

1548: Doré, Pierre, *La Conserve de grace*...................... D 60

1551 (with Benoist Prevost): Grenier, Nicole, *L'espee de la foy*..... G 37

Regnault Chaudiere

1519 (with Pierre Vidoue): *La discipline damour divine*............ D 29

(with Pierre Vidoue): *Quatre voyes spirituelles* .... Q 2

1520 (with Jean Du Pré): *Le dialogue spirituel de la Passion* ....   D 25
1537: *Le Livre de la Discipline d'amour divine* ....   D 30
1544 (with Simon de Colines): Caracciolo, Antoine, *Le mirouer
       de vraye religion*..   C 90
       (with Simon de Colines): Caracciolo, Antoine, *Le mirouer
       de vraye religion*..   C 91
1548: Viexmont, Claude de, *Le Pain de vie* ....   V 22

Simon de Colines
1522: Jordan, Raymond, dit Idiota, *Les Contemplations faites à
       l'honneur de la Tres sacree Vierge Marie*....................   J 11
1523: *La S. Evangile... Epistres* ....   B 152
1524: *Le psaultier de David*..   B 71
       La S. Evangile... Epistres ....   B 153
       (with Antoine Couteau): *La S. Evangile ... Epistres*..........   B 155
1525: Farel, Guillaume, *Loraison de Jesuchrist, qui est le
       Pater noster*..   F 25
       Luther, Martin, *Exposition sur les dix commandemens de
       la loy*..   L 91
1526: *Le psaultier de David*..   B 74
1529: Lefèvre d'Étaples, Jacques, *Vocabulaire du pseautier
       exposé en François*...   L 26
1534: Petit, Guillaume, *Tres devotes oraisons a lhonneur de ...
       Marie*..   P 12
1537: Erasme, Desiderius, *La maniere de bien instruire les
       enfans ... la civilité puerile*...............................   E 25
1539: (with Jean André, Estienne Caveiller, Guillaume Le Bret,
       Henry Paquot,): Bouchet, Jean, *Les triumphes de la
       Noble et amoureuse Dame* ....   B 228
1540 (with Estienne Roffet): Guerric, *Sermons* ....   G 58
       (with Guillaume Merlin): *Devote meditation sur la mort
       et passion de nostre saulveur et redempteur* ....   M 54
1544 (with Regnault Chaudiere): Caracciolo, Antoine, *Le
       mirouer de vraye religion*....................................   C 90
       (with Regnault Chaudiere): Caracciolo, Antoine, *Le
       mirouer de vraye religion*....................................   C 91

Jean Cornillau
1526 (with Jean Petit): Voragine, Jacques de, *La grant et
       vraye Legende doree* ....   V 74

Gilles Corrozet
1540: Luther, Martin, *Le livre de vraye et parfaicte oraison* ......   L 103
       Vitrier, Jean, *Le Sermon que nostre Seigneur feist en la
       montaigne*..   V 51
1542: *Diffinition et perfection d'amour* ....   D 2
       (with Jean Réal, Vincent Sertenas): *Le ...mystere du vieil
       testament* ....   M 109

1549: *Cinquante Pseaumes de David... avec le latin en marge....*   B 124

Raoul Cousturier

1512 (with Guillaume Eustace): Bouchet, Jean, *La deploration
      de leglise militante*..   B 220

Antoine Couteau

1524: *La S. Evangile... Epistres* ....   B 154

       (with Simon de Colines): *La S. Evangile ... Epistres*.........   B 155

1525 (with François Regnault): Lesnauderie, Pierre de, *La
      Louenge de mariage*......................................   L 62

1526 (with Galliot Du Pré, Didier Maheu): Volcyr de
      Sérouville, Nicolas, *Lhistoire et Recueil de la
      triumphante et glorieuse victoire* ....   V 69

1530 (with Nicolas Couteau, Jean Saint Denys): *La
      Marchandise spirituelle*.....................................   M 15

       (with Jean Longis): Picard, Jean, O.F.M., *Les trois
      Mirouers du monde* ....   P 22

1533 (with Vve Pierre Roffet, André Roffet): Clément VII, *La
      translation en francoys de la bulle*............................   C 110

Gilles Couteau

1519 (with Jean de la Porte, Jean Mullet of Lille): Augustin,
      Saint, *La saincte et sacree exposition sur le psaultier
      de David*..   A 29

1520: Le Moyne, Pasquier, *Lardant miroir de grace*..................   L 55

1521 (with Jean Petit, François Regnault): Ludolphus de Saxe,
      La grant vita Christi......................................   L 74

1523 (with François Regnault): Lesnauderie, Pierre de, *La
      Louenge de mariage*...   L 61

Nicolas Couteau

1533 (with Pierre Roffet): Hugues de Saint-Victor, *Larre de
      lame* ....   H 15

       (with Jean Longis): Rabelais, François, *Pantagruel*...........   R 4

1535 (with Galliot Du Pré, Jacques Kerver): Bouchet, Jean,
      Les Triumphes de La Noble et amoureuse Dame ....   B 224

       (with Jean André): *Ordonnances ... contre ... la secte
      lutherienne*..   O 12

1536: *La fleur des commandemens de Dieu*..............................   F 38

1537: *Larmeure de pacience* ....   A 15

1538 (with Guillaume Alabat, Bourges): Greban, Simon, *Le
      triumphant mystere des Actes des Apostres*..................   G 23

1539: *La fleur des commandemens de Dieu*..............................   F 39

1540 (with A. et C. Angelier, Guillaume Alabat of Bourges):
      Greban, Simon, *Le triumphant mystere des actes des
      Apostres*..   G 24

       Jérôme, Saint, *La vie des Peres*.............................   J 10

(with Guillaume Le Bret): Voragine, Jacques de, *La Legende Doree*	V 76
1541 (with A. et C. Langelier): Chocquet, Louis, *Lapocalypse Sainct Jehan Zebedee*	C 106
(with A. et C. Angelier, Guillaume Alabat of Bourges): Greban, Simon, *Les Catholiques oeuvres et Actes des Apostres*	G 25
(with Oudin Petit, Vve François Regnault, Ambroise Girault): *La Bible en francois*	B 45
1545 (with Oudin Petit, Guillaume Le Bret, Thielman Kerver, Rémy Boyset, Pierre Sergent): *La bible en francoiz*	B 53

Jean David

1548 (with Jean André, Vivant Gaultherot): Grenier, Nicole, *Le Bouclier de la foy*	G 31

Simon Du Bois

1525: *Les sept pseaulmes du royal prophete David*	B 73
La S. Evangile... Epistres	B 158
Erasme, Desiderius, *Brefve admonition de la maniere de prier*	E 15
Erasme, Desiderius, *Declamation des louenges de mariage*	E 27
Erasme, Desiderius, *Le symbole des apostres ... par maniere de dialogue*	E 57
Farel, Guillaume, *Epistre Chrestienne tresutile a ceulx qui commencent lire la saincte escripture*	F 8
Lefèvre d'Étaples, Jacques, *Epistres et Evangiles pour les cinquante et deux sepmaines de lan*	L 19
Luther, Martin, *Une exposition sur le Magnificat*	L 89
1526: Heyden, Sebald, *Dung seul mediateur entre dieu et les hommes*	H 12
Brief recueil de la substance ... de la doctrine Evangelique	R 38
Le traicte du Souverain Bien	T 15
1527: *Sentence de frere Jehan Guibert*	S 11
1528: (with Chrestien Wechel): Gaigny, Jean de, *Le livre faisant mention des sept parolles*	G 6
(with Chrestien Wechel): Luther, Martin, *Le livre de vraye et parfaicte oraison*	L 97
1529: (with Chrestien Wechel): Luther, Martin, *Le livre de vraye et parfaicte oraison*	L 98
1534: *Texte de Hiob*	B 69
Campen, Jean van, *Paraphrase ... sur tous les Psalmes*	C 83

Nicolas Du Chemin

1545 (with Jacques Bogard, Jean Ruelle): *Cinquante Pseaumes*	B 103

(with Jean André, Galliot Du Pré, Jacques Tyson): Bouchet, Jean, *Les Triumphes de la noble et amoureuse dame*.... B 231
1546 (with Jacques Bogard): *Cinquante Deux Pseaumes de David* B 107
1549: *XXVIII Pseaulmes de David*.............. B 127
1550: *Les cinquante pseaulmes de David*.............. B 132

Charles Dudé
1541: (with Antoine Bonnemere): *Linstruction des curez*.......... I 47a

Galliot Du Pré
1520: (with Pierre Vidoue): Erasme, Desiderius, *De la declamation des louenges de follie*.............. E 26
1522 (with Pierre Vidoue): Augustin, Saint, *Le Mirouer des vanitez et pompes du monde*.............. A 30
1526 (with Antoine Couteau, Didier Maheu): Volcyr de Sérouville, Nicolas, *Lhistoire et Recueil de la triumphante et glorieuse victoire*.............. V 69
1527 (with with François Regnault): Conrard, Olivier, *Le mirouer des pecheurs*.............. C 130
1531 (with Nicolas Savetier, Poncet Le Preux): Augustin, Saint, *Le premier Volume ... de la Cite de Dieu*.......... A 26
(with Nicolas Savetier, Jean Petit, Poncet Le Preux): Augustin, Saint, *Le second volume ... de la Cite de Dieu*.............. A 27
1535: (with Nicolas Couteau, Jacques Kerver): Bouchet, Jean, *Les Triumphes de La Noble et amoureuse Dame*.......... B 224
1537: (with Olivier Mallard): Erasme, Desiderius, *Le preparatif à la mort*.............. E 42
1538: (with Olivier Mallard): Petit, Guillaume, *La formation de lhomme et son excellence*.............. P 10
1539: Erasme, Desiderius, *Le Preparatif à la mort*.............. E 44
1541: (with Guillaume de Bossozel): Mailly, Nicolas de, *La divine cognoissance*.............. M 4
1542: Erasme, Desiderius, *Le sermon de Jesus enfant*.............. E 54
1543: (with Estienne Roffet): Lactantius Firmianus, *Des Divines institutions*.............. L 2
1545: (with Nicolas Du Chemin, Jean André, Jacques Tyson): Bouchet, Jean, *Les Triumphes de la noble et amoureuse dame*.............. B 231
(with Denis Janot): Lemaire de Belges, Jean, *Le Promptuaire des conciles de l'Eglise catholique*.......... L 50
(with Denis Janot): Vivès, Juan Luis, *L'institution de la femme chrestienne*.............. V 59
1546: (with Pasquier Le Tellier): Lactantius Firmianus, *Des Divines institutions*.............. L 4

Jean Du Pré
1520: (with Pierre Viart): *Internelle consolacion*.............. I 9

(with Regnault Chaudiere): *Le dialogue spirituel de la Passion* .... D 25

1521: (with Jaspard Bernard, Armentières): *Tresdevote meditation de la ... passion* .... M 55

1522: (with Pierre Viart): *Internelle consolation* .... I 10

Mathurin Du Puys

1545: Doré, Pierre, *La croix de penitence* .... D 61

1547: (with Benoist Prevost, Guillaume Cavellat): Lactantius Firmianus, *Des divines Institutions* .... L 5

Robert Estienne

1543: *Le Sommaire des livres du Vieil et Nouveau testament* ...... S 23

1547: *Le sommaire des livres du Vieil et Nouveau testament* ...... S 24

Guillaume Eustace

1512: (with Raoul Cousturier): Bouchet, Jean, *La deploration de leglise militante* .... B 220

1517: *Le mirouer de contemplation* .... M 77

1521: (with Hémon Le Fèvre): Jérôme, Saint, *Les epistres* .... J 4

Jacques Ferrebouc

1530: (with Pierre Bige): Gringore, Pierre, *La complaincte de la cite crestienne* .... G 47

Guillaume Fezendat

1521: (with Hémon Le Fèvre): Michel, Guillaume, *Le siecle dore* ... M 75

Jacques Fezendat

1543: (with Jacques Kerver): Vivès, Juan Luis, *Linstitution de la femme chrestienne* .... V 57

Michel Fezandat

1548: (with Jean André, Vivant Gaultherot): Grenier, Nicole, *Le Bouclier de la foy* .... G 32

Antoine Foucault

1543: (with Nicolas Buffet, Jacques Regnault): Luther, Martin, *Le livre de vraye et parfaicte oraison* .... L 108

1544: (with Nicolas Buffet, Jacques Regnault): Vitrier, Jean, *Le Sermon que nostre Seigneur feist en la montaigne* ... V 53

Jean Foucher

1539: (with Vivant Gaultherot, Nicolas Gilles): Luther, Martin, *Le livre de vraye et parfaicte oraison* .... L 102

1540: (with Ambroise Girault, Charles Langelier, Pierre Vidoue): Lemaire de Belges, Jean, *Le traicte de la difference des Scismes* .... L 44

Luther, Martin, *Le livre de vraye et parfaicte oraison* ...... L 104

(with Nicolas Gilles, Antoine Bonnemere): Vitrier, Jean, *Le Sermon que nostre Seigneur feist en la montaigne* ... V 50

1542: (with Vivant Gaultherot, Guillaume de Bossozel): Doré, Pierre, *L'arbre de vie, appuyant les beaux lys de France*   D 51

Jean Garnier

1519: *Les prieres et commandemens de saincte eglise*................   P 40

Pierre Gaudoul

1531: (with Ambroise Girault, Guillaume de Bossozel, François Regnault): *Le premier (-second) volume des grandes Postilles et expositions*................................   P 31

Vivant Gaultherot

1538: (with Les Angeliers, Estienne Caveiller): Jordan, Raymond, dit Idiota, *Les Contemplations du Simple devot*...........   J 13

1539: (with Jean Foucher, Nicolas Gilles): Luther, Martin, *Le livre de vraye et parfaicte oraison*............................   L 102

Parenti, Ch. de, *Instructions et oraisons tres salutaires*.....   P 4

1540: Doré, Pierre, *L'arbre de vie*..............................   D 50

1542: Augustin, Saint, *De la Vanité de ce siecle*.......................   A 33

Augustin, Saint, *De la vie Chrestienne*...................   A 34

(with Guillaume de Bossozel, Jean Foucher): Doré, Pierre, *L'arbre de vie, appuyant les beaux lys de France*........   D 51

1546: Augustin, Saint, *Les livres ... de la vie chrestienne*...........   A 35

1547: Grenier, Nicole, *Le Bouclier de la foy*............................   G 28

1548: (with Jean André, Jean David): Grenier, Nicole, *Le Bouclier de la foy*................................   G 31

(with Jean André, Michel Fezandat): Grenier, Nicole, *Le Bouclier de la foy*...........................   G 32

(with Jean Bonfons, Jean Réal, Guillaume Le Bret): Lemaire de Belges, Jean, *Le traicte de la difference des scismes*....   L 45

1549: Grenier, Nicole, *Le Bouclier de la foy*............................   G 34

Grenier, Nicole, *Tome second du Bouclier de la foy*..........   G 36

1550: Grenier, Nicole, *Le Bouclier de la foy*............................   G 35

Pierre Gaultier

1545: Montfiquet, Raoul de, *Exposition de l'oraison dominicale*.....   M 82

1547: *Cinquante deux Pseaumes de David*................................   B 117

Gaultier

No date: Parceval, Jean, *Doctrine d'amour*..............................   P 1

Nicolas Gilles

1539: (with Vivant Gaultherot, Jean Foucher): Luther, Martin, *Le livre de vraye et parfaicte oraison*.......................   L 102

1540: (with Jean Foucher, Antoine Bonnemere): Vitrier, Jean, *Le Sermon que nostre Seigneur feist en la montaigne*...   V 50

Ambroise Girault

1529: (with Pierre Leber): *Internelle consolation*......................   I 11

(with Julien Hubert): Lemaire de Belges, Jean, *Le traictie de la difference des scismes*......................................   L 42

1531: (with Guillaume de Bossozel): Ludolphus de Saxe, *Le grant Vita Christi ... en francoys*.............................. L 75

(with Guillaume de Bossozel, Pierre Gaudoul, François Regnault): *Le premier (-second) volume des grandes Postilles et expositions*............................. P 31

1532: (with Gérard Morrhy): Clerici, Jean, *Le manuel des chrestiens*............................. C 112

1533: (with Nicolas Savetier): Clerici, Jean, *Le Traicte de Exemplaire penitence*............................. C 115

(with Nicolas Higman): Lemaire de Belges, Jean, *Le traicte de la difference des Scismes*............................. L 43

1534: (with Nicolas Higman): *Internelle consolation*................ I 18

1535+: Clerici, Jean, *Le Manuel des chrestiens*.................... C 114

1536: Bouchet, Jean, *Les Triumphes de La Noble et amoureuse Dame*............................. B 225

1537: *Internelle consolation*............................. I 21

1540: (with Jean Réal): *Le Fagot de Myerre* .... F 4

(with Charles Langelier, Pierre Vidoue, Jean Foucher): Lemaire de Belges, Jean, *Le traicte de la difference des Scismes*............................. L 44

1541: (with Nicolas Couteau, Oudin Petit, Vve François Regnault): *La Bible en francois* .... B 45

1545: *Cinquante Pseaumes* .... B 101

François Girault

1549: (with Martin Le Jeune): *Les Testamens des douze patriarches*............................. T 4

Godefroy

No date: Savonarola, Jérôme, *Exposition et paraphrase ... Miserere*............................. S 6

Jérôme de Gourmont

1540: (with Pierre Vidoue): Doré, Pierre, *Limage de vertu* .... D 73

(with Jean de Brouilly, Nicolas Bonfons): Doré, Pierre, *L'image de vertu*............................. D 74

Louis Grandin

1548: *Sentences extraites de l'escriture saincte pour l'instruction des enfans*............................. S 12

Pierre Gromors

1521: Charles Quint, *Edit et mandement ... contre Frere Martin luther*............................. C 104

Estienne Groulleau

1547: Chrysostome, St Jean, *Exhortation à prier Dieu* .... C 107

Les Figures de l'Apocalipse............................. F 31

1548: Espence, Claude d', *Institution d'un Prince chrestien*....... E 61

Espence, Claude d', *Paraphrase, ou, Meditation, sur
l'oraison Dominicale*... E 64
1549: *Cinquante deux Psalmes de David* .... B 125
Corrozet, Gilles, *La Tapisserie de l'église chrestienne et
catholique*.. C 135
1550: *Cinquante deux Pseaumes de David*.............................. B 130
1551: (with Jean Ruelle): Désiré, Artus, *Le Defensoire de la
foy chrestienne*.. D 13
Les Figures de l'Apocalypse .... F 32
Lactantius Firmianus, *Des Divines Institutions*................ L 8

Charlotte Guillard

1539: Erasme, Desiderius, *Les Apophthegmes*........................... E 16
1541: Lasseré, Louis, *La Vie de monseigneur sainct Hierosme*.... L 16

Nicolas Higman

1517: (with Enguilbert and Jean de Marnef, Pierre Viart): Lemaire
de Belges, Jean, *Le traictie de la difference des
scismes*.. L 33
1520: (with Simon Vostre): Vitrier, Jean, *Lexposition sur le
sermon que nostre seigneur fist a la montaigne* .... V 49
1521: (with Nicolas de La Barre, Jean Barbaram of Nevers):
Linstruction des curez pour instruire le simple peuple..... I 43
1525: (with Jean Petit): Gringore, Pierre, *Heures de nostre dame* .... G 48
1528: (with Jean Petit): Gringore, Pierre, *Chantz Royaulx,
figurez morallement*... G 41
1533: (with Ambroise Girault): Lemaire de Belges, Jean, *Le
traicte de la difference des Scismes*......................... L 43
1534: (with Ambroise Girault): *Internelle consolation* .... I 18
1537: (with Simon Vostre): *Linstruction des curez pour instruire le simple peuple*....................................... I 47

Julien Hubert

1529: (with Ambroise Girault): Lemaire de Belges, Jean, *Le
traictie de la difference des scismes*......................... L 42
(with Jean Saint Denys): *La Marchandise spirituelle* .... M 14
(with Jean Saint Denys): Mauburne, Jean, *Le Beneficiaire divin* .... M 45
(with Jean Saint Denys): *Une devote meditation sur la
mort et passion de nostre saulveur* .... M 53
Tissarrant, Jean, *Une tresbelle salutation faicte sur les
sept festes de nostre Dame*.................................... T 13
(with Jean Saint Denys): *La voye de paradis* .... V 66

Denis Janot

1529: (with Philippe le Noir, Alain Lotrian): Bonaventure,
Saint (attrib.), *Laguillon damour divine* .... B 217
(with Philippe Le Noir, Alain Lotrian): Bonaventure,
Saint (attrib.), *Lesguillon damour divin*..................... B 217a

1530: (with Alain Lotrian): *La Resurrection de nostre seigneur jesucrist par personnages* .... M 104
1531: (with Alain Lotrian): Bougain, Michel, *Le Jardin spiri-tuel de lame devote* .... B 235
1532: (with Alain Lotrian): Lesnauderie, Pierre de, *La Lou-ange de mariage* .... L 63
(with Alain Lotrian): *Le Mirouer dor de lame pecheresse*.... M 76
(with Alain Lotrian): *Le mistere de la Passion de nostre seigneur Jesuchrist* .... M 96
(with Alain Lotrian): *La vie ma dame saincte Marguerite* ...... V 19
1533: (with Jean Longis): Gaigny, Jean de, *Devote exposition sur le cinquantiesme pseaulme* .... G 3
(with Alain Lotrian): Seuse, Heinrich, *Lorloge de Sapience*... S 16
1534: (with Alain Lotrian): Béda, Noël, *La petite dyablerie* .... B 11
(with Alain Lotrian): *La vie de monseigneur sainct Laurens* .... V 18
1535: (with Alain Lotrian): *La fleur de devotion* .... F 34
Gringore, Pierre, *Chantz royaulx, Figurez morallement* .... G 43
(with Alain Lotrian): Maurice de Sully, *Les expositions des evangiles* .... M 48
(with Pierre Sergent, Jean Longis): Petit, Guillaume, *Le viat de salut* .... P 17
Redon, Gilles de, *La Musique Angelique* .... R 39
1537: (with Estienne Caveiller, Pierre Sergent): Le Roy, François, *Le Dialogue de consolation entre lame et raison* .... L 56
1538: (with Jean Longis): Gaigny, Jean de, *Devote exposition sur le cinquantiesme pseaulme* .... G 4
Les simulachres et faces hystoriées de la Mort .... I 6
1539: *Internelle consolation* .... I 23
1540: *L'Internelle consolation* .... I 27
Lescagne, Tristan de, *Le Lys treschrestian florissant en la foy chrestiane* .... L 59
1541: *Larmeure de patience* .... A 17
Les sept pseaulmes de la penitence de David .... B 88
Cabosse, Jean, *Le mirouer de prudence* .... C 1
Cabosse, Jean, *Traicte du treshault et excellent mistere de l'incarnation du verbe divin* .... C 2
(with Jean Longis et Vincent Sertenas): Erasme, Desiderius, *Comedie ou dialogue matrimonial* .... E 23
Erasme, Desiderius, *Le Preparatif à la mort* .... E 46
L'Internelle consolation .... I 29
1542: Doré, Pierre, *Dyalogue Instructoire des Chrestiens* .... D 69
1543: (with Ponce Roffet): *Edict sur les articles faictz par la faculte de theologie* .... E 3
La doctrine des Chrestiens, extraicte du Vieil et Nouveau testament .... S 22
1544: Doré, Pierre, *Dyalogue instructoire* .... D 70

1545: (with Galliot Du Pré): Lemaire de Belges, Jean, *Le Promptuaire des conciles de l'Eglise catholique*.......... L 50

(with Galliot Du Pré): Vivès, Juan Luis, *L'institution de la femme chrestienne*............. V 59

No date (with Alain Lotrian): *Les cantiques salomon* .... B 67

Limitation de Nostre Seigneur Jesuchrist .... I 39

Jean Jehannot

1511: (with Vve Jean Trepperel): *Le Psaultier nostre dame*........ P 50

1512: (with Vve Jean Trepperel): Béda, Noël, *La petite Dyablerie dont lucifer est le chef*............................. B 9

(with Vve Jean Trepperel): Desmoulins, Laurent, *La cymetiere Des Malheureux*.................................... D 22

(with Vve Jean Trepperel): *La theologie spirituelle* .... T 10

1514: (with Vve Jean Trepperel): *Le grant Ordinaire des chrestiens* .... O 9

1515: (with Vve Jean Trepperel): *Le mistere de la conception ... de la benoiste vierge marie*.................................. M 85

(with Vve Jean Trepperel): *Le mistere de la passion nostre seigneur jhesucrist*.. M 93

(with Vve Jean Trepperel): *La Resurrection de nostre seigneur jhesuchrist* .... M 102

1516: Bougain, Michel, *Le Jardin spirituel de lame devote* .... B 233

(with Vve Jean Trepperel): *Les commandemens de saincte eglise et la confession generale du jour de pasques*... C 124a

(with Vve Jean Trepperel): *Une petite instruction ... pour une femme seculiere*.. I 55

(with Vve Jean Trepperel): *Meditation tresdevotte ... sur la passion douloureuse de nostre doulx saulveur* .... M 51

(with Vve Jean Trepperel): *Le mistere du viel Testament*...... M 108c

(with Vve Jean Trepperel): *La refection spirituelle de lame devote*.................................... R 41

(with Vve Jean Trepperel): Sauvage, Jean, *Leschelle damour divine*.................................. S 5

1518: (with Vve Jean Trepperel): *Le mistere de monseigneur sainct pierre et sainct paul* .... M 108a

(with Vve Jean Trepperel): *Le mistere du Tresglorieux martir Monsieur sainct christofle*.............................. V 17b

1520: (with Vve Jean Trepperel): *Les Postilles et expositions Des epistres Et evangilles dominicalles*...................... P 29a

Antoine Jurie

1548: Benedetto da Mantova, *Du Benefice de Jesuchrist crucifié*... B 19

Thomas Kees

1513: *Le Psaultier de David*.................................... B 70

Jean Kerbriant
1530: (with Chrestien Wechel): Luther, Martin, *Le livre de vraye et parfaicte oraison* .... L 99

Jacques Kerver
1535: (with Galliot Du Pré, Nicolas Couteau): Bouchet, Jean,
    Les Triumphes de La Noble et amoureuse Dame .... B 224
    (with Antoine de La Barre): *Internelle consolation* .... I 19
1542: Vivès, Juan Luis, *L'institution de la femme chrestienne* .... V 55
1543: (with Jacques Fezendat): Vivès, Juan Luis, *Linstitution de la femme chrestienne* .... V 57

Thielman Kerver
1545: (with Guillaume Le Bret, Oudin Petit, Nicolas Couteau,
    Rémy Boyset, Pierre Sergent): *La bible en francoiz* ...... B 53

Antoine de La Barre
1534: (with Jean Petit): Jérôme, Saint, *La Vie des Peres* .... J 9
1535: (with Jacques Kerver): *Internelle consolation* .... I 19

Nicolas de La Barre
1516: (with Hémon Le Fèvre): Voragine, Jacques de, *La Legende doree* .... V 72
1521: (with Nicolas Higman, Jean Barbaram of Nevers): *Linstruction des curez pour instruire le simple peuple* .... I 43

Jean de La Garde
1518: (with Pierre Le Brodeur): Michel, Guillaume, *Le Penser de royal memoire* .... M 74
1519: (with Guillaume Le Rouge): Jérôme, Saint, *Les Epistres* ... J 3

Frères Langelier
    (N.B.:the brothers Arnoul and Charles Langelier are
    treated in a single chronological sequence)
1537: Les Langeliers (with Jean Longis, Jean Macé): Bouchet,
    Jean, *Les triumphes de la Noble et amoureuse Dame* ... B 227
1538: Les Langeliers (with Henri Paquot, Estienne Caveiller):
    Gaigny, Jean de, *Le livre ... des sept parolles* .... G 9
    (with Estienne Caveiller, Vivant Gaultherot): Jordan,
    Raymond, dit Idiota, *Les Contemplations du Simple devot* .... J 13
1540: A. et C. Langelier (with Nicolas Couteau, Guillaume
    Alabat of Bourges): Greban, Simon, *Le triumphant mystere des actes des Apostres* .... G 24
    Charles Langelier (with Pierre Vidoue, Jean Foucher,
    Ambroise Girault): Lemaire de Belges, Jean, *Le traicte de la difference des Scismes* .... L 44
    Charles Langelier (with Jean Bignon): Spagnuoli,
    Battista, *La Vie d'honneur et de Vertu* .... S 29

1541: Charles Langelier: *Paraphrase ... sur les sept tresprecieux et notables Pseaulmes* .... B 87

A. et C. Langelier (with Nicolas Couteau): Chocquet, Louis, *Lapocalypse Sainct Jehan Zebedee* .... C 106

A. et C. Angelier (with Nicolas Couteau, Guillaume Alabat of Bourges): Greban, Simon, *Les Catholiques oeuvres et Actes des Apostres* .... G 25

1542: Arnoul Langelier: Branteghem, Guillaume de, *Vergier Spirituel et mystique* .... B 242

Arnoul Langelier (with Estienne Caveiller): *La Fontaine de Vie... Linstruction pour les enfans* .... F 46

Arnoul Langelier: *Internelle consolation* .... I 32

Charles Langelier (with Estienne Caveiller): Spagnuoli, Battista, *La Fontaine de tous biens* .... S 30

1543: Arnoul et Charles Langelier (with Estienne Caveiller): Branteghem, Guillaume de, *La Vie de Jesus Christ* ...... B 258

1544: Charles Langelier: *Les Epistres de monseigneur Sainct Paul glosées* .... E 14

Charles et Arnoul Langelier: Ludolphus de Saxe, *Le grand vita Christi* .... L 77

Charles Langelier: Luther, Martin, *Le livre de vraye et parfaicte oraison* .... L 110

1545: Charles Langelier: Luther, Martin, *Le livre de vraye et parfaicte oraison* .... L 112

1546: Charles Langelier: Dolet, Estienne, *Des faictz et gestes du Roy Françoys* .... D 37

1547: Charles Langelier: *Cinquante deux Pseaumes de David* .... B 115

Charles Langelier: Erasme, Desiderius, *Les Apophthegmes* .... E 17

1548: Les Langeliers: Vivès, Juan Luis, *Introduction à la vraye sapience* .... V 65

1549: Charles Langelier: Erasme, Desiderius, *Brief recueil ... de l'enseignement du prince Chrestien* .... E 53

No date: Charles Langelier: Cabosse, Jean, *Traité et dialogue ... du treshault et tresexcellent mystere de l'Incarnation* .... C 3

Jean de La Porte

1517: (with François Regnault, Pierre Vidoue): Ambroise, Saint, *Le Traicte du bien et de la mort* .... A 8

1518: (with Guichard Soquand): Eusèbe de Césarée (pseud.), *Le testament du tresglorieux sainct* .... E 67

(with François Regnault, Pierre Vidoue): Vitrier, Jean, *Lexposition sur le sermon que nostre seigneur fist en la montaigne* .... V 48

1519: (with Gilles Couteau, Jean Mullet of Lille): Augustin, Saint, *La saincte et sacree exposition sur le psaultier de David* .... A 29

Maurice de La Porte

1539: (with Estienne Caveiller, François Regnault): Gaigny, Jean de, *Le livre ... des Sept parolles* .... G 10

Vve Maurice de La Porte

1550: *Cinquante deux Psalmes*................................. B 134

Jean de La Roche

1513: (with Jean Petit and Michel Le Noir): Rolewinck, Werner, *Les fleurs et manieres des temps passez*.......... R 49
Voragine, Jacques de, *La legende doree* .... V 71

Jean Le Bailli

1531: (with Antoine Bonnemere, Nicolas Savetier): Clerici, Jean, *Ung traicte des fondemens du temple spirituel* .... C 111

Pierre Leber

1529: (with Ambroise Girault): *Internelle consolation* .... I 11
1532: (with Vve Jean de Saint Denys): La Boulaye, Guillaume de, *La pronostication du Ciecle advenir*...................... L 1
1533: *Internelle consolation*...................................... I 17
1534: Rabelais, François, *Pantagruel*............................. R 6

Guillaume Le Bret

1539: (with Henry Paquot, Jean André, Estienne Caveiller, Simon de Colines): Bouchet, Jean, *Les triumphes de la Noble et amoureuse Dame* .... B 228
1540: (with Antoine Bonnemere): Doré, Pierre, *Les Allumettes du feu divin*... D 45
(with Nicolas Couteau): Voragine, Jacques de, *La Legende Doree*... V 76
1542: (with Jean Ruelle): Branteghem, Guillaume de, *La Vie de nostre Seigneur Jesus Christ* .... B 255
1543: Lemaire de Belges, Jean, *Le Promptuaire des Conciles de l'Eglise catholique*...................................... L 49
1545: (with Oudin Petit, Nicolas Couteau, Thielman Kerver, Rémy Boyset, Pierre Sergent): *La bible en francoiz*...... B 53
1546: *Cinquante deux Pseaumes de David*............................ B 105
1547: (with Guillaume Thibout): *Cinquante deux Pseaumes*....... B 116
(with Jean Ruelle, Guillaume Thibout): Lemaire de Belges, Jean, *Le Promptuaire des conciles de l'Eglise Catholique* .... L 54
1548: *Cinquante deux Pseaumes de David*............................ B 120
(with Poncet Le Preux, Jean Réal): *La fleur des commandemens de Dieu*.. F 40
(with Vivant Gaultherot, Jean Bonfons, Jean Réal): Lemaire de Belges, Jean, *Le traicte de la difference des scismes* .... L 45
Vivès, Juan Luis, *Institution de la femme chrestienne* .... V 62

Pierre Le Brodeur

1518: (with Jean de La Garde): Michel, Guillaume, *Le Penser de royal memoire* .... M 74

Hémon Le Fèvre

1516: (with Guillaume Nyverd): *La fleur des commandemens de dieu*.. F 36

(with Nicolas de La Barre): Voragine, Jacques de, *La Legende doree*.. V 72

1517: Jérôme, Saint, *La vie des peres* .... J 7

1521: (with Guillaume Eustace): Jérôme, Saint, *Les epistres* ...... J 4

1521: (with Guillaume Fezendat): Michel, Guillaume, *Le siecle dore*.. M 75

Martin Le Jeune

1549: (with François Girault): *Les Testamens des douze patriarches* .... T 4

Michel Le Noir

1511: (with Jean Petit): Desmoulins, Laurent, *Le cymetiere des Malheureux*... D 21

1512: *Le mistere de la Passion de nostre saulveur* .... M 92

1513: (with Jean Petit): Desmoulins, Laurent, *Le catholicon des mal advisez ... Cymetiere des malheureux*............... D 23

(with Jean de La Roche, Jean Petit): Rolewinck, Werner, *Les fleurs et manieres des temps passez*...................... R 49

1514: *Lordinaire des crestiens* .... O 10

1516: (with Guillaume Michel): Michel, Guillaume, *La forest de conscience*... M 72

1518: Ximenis, Francesc, *Le livre des sainctz anges* .... X 1

1519: *Les Fleurs de la somme angelique*................................... F 41

Gerson, Jean, *La mendicite spirituelle*.......................... G 20

1520: Guillaume d'Auvergne, *La Rhetorique divine*................. G 60

(with Guillaume Michel): Michel, Guillaume, *La forest de conscience*... M 73

1521: *Les Epistres sainct Pol glosees* .... E 13

Philippe Le Noir

1523: *Le mistere de la passion de nostre seigneur jhesucrist* ...... M 94

1524: Gringore, Pierre, *Le Blazon des heretiques*.................... G 38

Lemaire de Belges, Jean, *Le traicte de la difference des Scismes*.. L 37

1525: (with Antoine Bonnemere, Bernard Aubry): *La fleur des Commandemens de Dieu*.. F 37

1526: *La bible en francois* .... B 33

(with François Regnault): Lemaire de Belges, Jean, *Le traicte de la difference des Scismes*............................ L 39

1529: (with Denis Janot, Alain Lotrian): Bonaventure, Saint (attrib.), *Laguillon damour divine* .... B 217

(with Denis Janot, Alain Lotrian): Bonaventure, Saint
(attrib.), *Lesguillon damour divin*............................. B 217a
1531: *Limitation de nostre seigneur Jesuchrist* .... I 15
Miroir de lhumaine redemption..................................... M 78
1532: *Internelle consolation*... I 16
Le mistere de la Passion notre seigneur Jesuscrist............ M 97
1541: (with Jean Réal, François Regnault, Oudin Petit): Bouchet,
Jean, *Les triumphes de la Noble et amoureuse Dame* ... B 230

Poncet Le Preux
1531: (with Galliot Du Pré, Nicolas Savetier): Augustin, Saint,
Le premier Volume ... de la Cite de Dieu..................... A 26
(with Galliot Du Pré, Nicolas Savetier, Jean Petit):
Augustin, Saint, *Le second volume ... de la Cite de
Dieu* .... A 27
1532: (with Nicolas Savetier): Bellemere, François, *Directoire
de la vie humaine*.. B 15
1537: Bellemere, François, *Instruction salutaire a toute personne de lestat seculier* .... B 17
Gerson, Jean, *Le Confessional, aultrement appelle le
Directoire des confesseurs*... G 14
Gerson, Jean, *Le doctrinal de la foy catholique* .... G 19
1538: Gerson, Jean, *Le Directoire des confesseurs*..................... G 15
1539: Gerson, Jean, *Le Directoire des confesseurs*..................... G 16
1547: Gerson, Jean, *Le Confessional, aultrement appelle le
Directoire des confesseurs*... G 17
1548: (with Jean Réal, Guillaume Le Bret): *La fleur des commandemens de Dieu*.. F 40
1549: (with Jean Réal): Herp, Henry de, *Directoire des contem-
platifz* .... H 9
No date: Gerson, Jean, *Le confessional appelle le directoire
des confesseurs* .... G 18

Guillaume Le Rouge
1511: (with Antoine Verard): *Le Premier/Second volume des
exposicions des Epistres et Evangilles de Karesme* ...... P 25
(with Antoine Verard): *Le Tiers volume des exposicions
des Epistres et Evangiles de Toute lannee* .... P 26
1512: (with Antoine Verard): *Le Quart/Ve volume des exposicions
des Epistres et Evangilles de Toute lannee* .... P 27
1519: (with Jean de La Garde): Jérôme, Saint, *Les Epistres*........ J 3

Michel Lesclencher
1521: (with Bernard Aubry, Pierre Viart): Voragine, Jacques de,
La legende doree... V 73

Pasquier Le Tellier
1546: (with Galliot Du Pré): Lactantius Firmianus, *Des Divines
institutions*... L 4

Jean Longis

1524: Picard, Jean, O.F.M., *Les trois mirouers du monde* .... P 21

1530: (with Antoine Couteau): Picard, Jean, O.F.M., *Les trois
Mirouers du monde* .... P 22

1531: (with Pierre Vidoue): Le Grand, Jacques, *Le Tresor de sapience* L 26c

1533: (with Denis Janot): Gaigny, Jean de, *Devote exposition
sur le cinquantiesme pseaulme* .... G 3

(with Nicolas Couteau): Rabelais, François, *Pantagruel*.... R 4

1534: Rabelais, François, *Pantagruel*. .... R 5

1535: (with Denis Janot, Pierre Sergent): Petit, Guillaume, *Le
viat de salut* .... P 17

1537: (with Jean Macé, Les Langeliers): Bouchet, Jean, *Les
triumphes de la Noble et amoureuse Dame* .... B 227

1538: (with Denis Janot): Gaigny, Jean de, *Devote exposition
sur le cinquantiesme pseaulme* .... G 4

(with Henry Paquot, Estienne Caveiller): *Le livre de la
Discipline Damour* .... D 32

1539: (with Vincent Sertenas): Erasme, Desiderius, *Le Prepa-
ratif à la mort* .... E 45

1541: (with Denis Janot, Vincent Sertenas): Erasme, Desiderius, *Comedie ou dialogue matrimonial* .... E 23

1545: (with Vincent Sertenas): Lemaire de Belges, Jean, *Le
Promptuaire des conciles de l'Eglise Catholicque* .... L 51

1549: Du Boullay, Emond, *Le combat de la chair, et l'esprit* ...... D 95

Alain Lotrian

1525: Béda, Noël, *La doctrine et instruction necessaire aux
crestiens et crestiennes* .... B 8

1528: Béda, Noël, *La petite diablerie dont lucifer est le chef* ..... B 10

Bougain, Michel, *Le Jardin spirituel de lame devote* .... B 234

Caupain, Henri, *Le desert de devotion* .... C 93

Le Livret des consolations contre toutes tribulations .... L 64

1529: (with Denis Janot, Philippe Le Noir): Bonaventure, Saint
(attrib.), *Laguillon damour divine* .... B 217

(with Denis Janot, Philippe Le Noir): Bonaventure,
Saint (attrib.), *Lesguillon damour divin* .... B 217a

1530: *Lassumption de la glorieuse vierge Marie* .... A 25

Lenfant Prodigue par personnaiges .... E 5

Le mistere de la conception ... de la benoiste vierge marie .... M 87

(with Denis Janot): *La Resurrection de nostre seigneur
jesucrist par personnages* .... M 104

Les ventes Damour Divine .... V 2

La Voye de Paradis .... V 67

1531: (with Denis Janot): Bougain, Michel, *Le Jardin spirituel
de lame devote* .... B 235

Missus est translate de latin en francois .... M 80

Le mistere de la saincte hostie .... M 107

Petit, Pierre, *La chanson de frere Pierre petit*................... P 20

1532: (with Denis Janot): Lesnauderie, Pierre de, *La Louange de mariage*........................ L 63

(with Denis Janot): *Le Mirouer dor de lame pecheresse*.... M 76

(with Denis Janot): *La vie ma dame saincte Marguerite*.... V 19

(with Denis Janot): *Le mistere de la Passion de nostre seigneur Jesuchrist*........................ M 96

1533: (with Denis Janot): Seuse, Heinrich, *Lorloge de Sapience*..... S 16

1534: (with Denis Janot): Béda, Noël, *La petite Dyablerie*......... B 11

(with Denis Janot): *La vie de monseigneur sainct Laurens*..... V 18

1535: (with Denis Janot): *La fleur de devotion*........................ F 34

(with Denis Janot): Maurice de Sully, *Les expositions des evangiles*........................ M 48

Le mistere de la conception ... de la benoiste vierte Marie......................... M 88

Le mistere de la Passion de nostre seigneur Jesuchrist ..... M 98

Le salve regina en francoys........................ S 1

1538: (with Estienne Caveiller): Doré, Pierre, *Les Allumettes du feu divin*........................ D 43

(with François Regnault, Estienne Caveiller): Doré, Pierre, *Les Voyes de Paradis.*........................ D 92

1539: Le Grand, Jacques, *Le Tresor de sapience*........................ L 26d

Le mistere de la Passion de nostre seigneur Jesuchrist ..... M 99

Le mistere de la Passion de nostre seigneur Jesuchrist ..... M 100

La Resurrection de nostre seigneur Jesuchrist: Par personnages......................... M 105

La vengeance et destruction de Hierusalem par personnaiges......................... V 1

1540: *Le mistere de la conception ... de la benoiste vierge Marie.*........................ M 89

1541: *Le mistere de la Passion de nostre seigneur Jesuchrist* ..... M 101

La Resurrection de nostre seigneur Jesuchrist: Par personnages......................... M 106

1543: Dolet, Estienne, *Les faictz et gestes du Roy Françoys*....... D 35

Dolet, Estienne, *Sommaire et recueil des faictz et gestes, du Roy Françoys*........................ D 38

1544: Dolet, Estienne, *Les Faitz et gestes du Roy Françoys*........ D 36

No date: (with Denis Janot): *Les cantiques salomon*................... B 67

Le mistere de la conception ... de la benoiste vierge Marie.... M 90

Le mistere de la conception ... de la benoiste vierge Marie.... M 91

Jean Loys

1542: Bris, Nicolas de, *Institution a porter les adversitez du monde patiemment.*........................ B 265

Jean Macé

1533: (with Estienne Caveiller): Gaigny, Jean de, *Le livre faisant mention des sept parolles*........................ G 7

1537: (with Les Langeliers, Jean Longis): Bouchet, Jean, *Les triumphes de la Noble et amoureuse Dame*.................. B 227

Didier Maheu

1523: Volcyr de Sérouville, Nicolas, *Collectaneorum Libellus*.... V 68

1526: (with Galliot Du Pré, Antoine Couteau): Volcyr de Sérouville, Nicolas, *Lhistoire et Recueil de la triumphante et glorieuse victoire* .... V 69

1534: (with Guillaume de Bossozel): Ludolphus de Saxe, *Le grant vita Christi translaté de latin en francoys*........... L 76

Olivier Mallard

1537: (with Galliot Du Pré): Erasme, Desiderius, *Le Preparatif à la mort*.. E 42

1538: (with Galliot Du Pré): Petit, Guillaume, *La formation de lhomme et son excellence* .... P 10

Jean Marchant

1512: (with Jean Petit): *Remede convenable Pour si bien vivre en ce monde que nous puissions acquerir le royaulme des cieulx*.. R 43

Geoffroy de Marnef

1512: Lemaire de Belges, Jean, *Le traictie Intitule, de la difference des scismes* .... L 30

Lemaire de Belges, Jean, *Le traictie Intitule de la difference des scismes* .... L 31

1514: Lemaire de Belges, Jean, *Le traictie intitule de la difference des scismes* .... L 32

Enguilbert et Jean de Marnef

1517: (with Nicolas Higman, Pierre Viart): Lemaire de Belges, Jean, *Le traictie de la difference des scismes*.............. L 33

1519: (with Pierre Viart): Lemaire de Belges, Jean, *Le Traictie de la difference des scismes*.................................... L 34

1520: Jérôme, Saint, *La vie des peres* .... J 8

1521: (with Pierre Viart): Lemaire de Belges, Jean, *Le traictie de la difference des scismes*.................................... L 35

1523: (with Pierre Viart, Jean Petit, François Regnault): Lemaire de Belges, Jean, *Le traicte de la difference des Scismes*.. L 36

1533: Rabelais, François, *Pantagruel*.. R 3

Jeanne de Marnef

1545: *Cinquante Pseaumes de David*.. B 104

Guillaume Merlin

1540: (with Simon de Colines): *Devote meditation sur la mort et passion de nostre saulveur et redempteur* .... M 54

1550: *Cinquante deux Pseaumes de david*.................................... B 133

Estienne Mesviere
1551: *Les Cent cinquante Psalmes du Prophete Royal David*...... B 142

Guillaume Michel
1516: (with Michel Le Noir): Michel, Guillaume, *La forest de conscience* .... M 72
1520: (with Michel Le Noir): Michel, Guillaume, *La forest de conscience* .... M 73

Jean Morin
1538: Cymbalum mundi, *Cymbalum mundi en françoys*.............. C 138

Gérard Morrhy
1532: (with Ambroise Girault): Clerici, Jean, *Le manuel des chrestiens* .... C 112

Conrad Neobar
1540: Branteghem, Guillaume de, *La Vie de Nostre Seigneur Jesus Christ* .... B 246
Branteghem, Guillaume de, *La Vie de Nostre Seigneur Jesus Christ* .... B 247
Branteghem, Guillaume de, *La Vie de Nostre Seigneur Jesus Christ* .... B 248
Branteghem, Guillaume de, *La Vie de Nostre Seigneur Jesus Christ* .... B 249

Guillaume Nyverd
1512: *Les faitz institutions et ordonnances ... Pise, pour commencer le concille*................................. C 125
1516: (with Hémon Le Fèvre): *La fleur des commandemens de dieu* .... F 36

Henri Paquot
1538: (with Estienne Caveiller, Les Langeliers): Gaigny, Jean de, *Le livre ... des sept parolles* .... G 9
(with Estienne Caveiller, Jean Longis): *Le livre de la Discipline Damour* .... D 32
1539: (with Jean André, Estienne Caveiller, Guillaume Le Bret, Simon de Colines): Bouchet, Jean, *Les triumphes de la Noble et amoureuse Dame* .... B 228

Jean Petit
1511: Bernard, Saint (pseud.), *Le traitie ... contenant la maniere de vivre en la religion chrestienne*................. B 21
(with Michel Le Noir): Desmoulins, Laurent, *Le cymetiere des Malheureux*.................................... D 21
1512: (with Jean Marchant): *Remede convenable Pour si bien vivre en ce monde que nous puissions acquerir le royaulme des cieulx*.. R 43
1513: (with Michel Le Noir): Desmoulins, Laurent, *Le catholicon des mal advisez ... Cymetiere des malheureux* .... D 23

(with Michel Le Noir, Jean de La Roche): Rolewinck,
Werner, *Les fleurs et manieres des temps passez*.......... R 49
1514: Bonaventure, Saint (attrib.), *Le Mirouer de discipline* ...... B 219
Guillaume d'Auvergne, *La rethorique divine*.................. G 59
1516: Henry, Jean, *Le Jardin de contemplation*.......................... H 3
Henry, Jean, *Le livre de la toute belle ... Marie*.............. H 4
Henry, Jean, *Le livre de meditation sur la reparation de
nature humaine*.. H 5
Henry, Jean, *Le livre de reformation ... pour toutes
religieuses*... H 6
Henry, Jean, *Le livre dinstruction pour religieuses
novices*... H 7
1517: Augustin, Saint, *Trois opuscules*................................... A 32
Le Roy, François, *Le livre de la femme forte Et
vertueuse*.. L 57
1519: (with Antoine Verard): *Le Tiers/Ve volume des exposicions
des Epistres et Evangilles de Toute lannee*................. P 28
*Le premier/second volume des exposicions des Epistres
et Evangilles de Karesme*....................................... P 29
1520: (with François Regnault): *La bible en francoiz*.............. B 30
*La declaration de lestat ... de la confrarie du psaultier:
rosier: et chappelet*.. C 129
1521: (with Gilles Couteau, François Regnault): Ludolphus de
Saxe, *La grant vita Christi*..................................... L 74
1523: (with Enguilbert de Marnef, Pierre Viart, François
Regnault): Lemaire de Belges, Jean, *Le traicte de la
difference des Scismes*... L 36
1525: (with Nicolas Higman): Gringore, Pierre, *Heures de
nostre dame*... G 48
1526: (with Jean Cornillau): Voragine, Jacques de, *La grant et
vraye Legende doree*.. V 74
1528: (with Nicolas Higman): Gringore, Pierre, *Chantz Royaulx,
figurez morallement*.. G 41
1529: (with François Regnault): *La bible en francoiz*.............. B 34
(with Josse Badius): Lasseré, Louis, *La Vie de monseigneur sainct Hierosme*... L 14
1530: Gringore, Pierre, *Heures de nostre dame*...................... G 49
1531: (with Poncet Le Preux, Galliot Du Pré, Nicolas Savetier):
Augustin, Saint, *Le second volume ... de la Cite de
Dieu*.. A 27
1532: (with Guillaume de Bossozel): Gringore, Pierre, *Chantz
royaulx figurez morallement*.................................... G 42
(with Guillaume de Bossozel): Gringore, Pierre, *Heures
de nostre dame*... G 50
1534: (with Guillaume de Bossozel): Gringore, Pierre, *Heures
de nostre dame*... G 51

(with Antoine de La Barre): Jérôme, Saint, *La Vie des Peres*.. J 9

1535: (with Guillaume de Bossozel): Hangest, Jérôme de, *Contre les tenebrions lumiere evangelicque*......................... H 1

1537: Hangest, Jérôme de, *En controversie voye seure*............... H 2

1538: (with François Regnault): Doré, Pierre, *Les Allumettes du feu divin*.. D 42

1539: (with Yolande Bonhomme): Merlin, Jacques, *Lexposition de levangille Missus est*... M 71

1540: Gringore, Pierre, *Heures de nostre dame*........................ G 53

Oudin Petit

1540: Gringore, Pierre, *Chantz Royaulx, Figurez morallement* ... G 45

1541: (with Ambroise Girault, Nicolas Couteau, Vve François Regnault): *La Bible en francois*.................................. B 45

(with Philippe Le Noir, Jean Réal, François Regnault): Bouchet, Jean, *Les triumphes de la Noble et amoureuse Dame*.. B 230

1545: (with Nicolas Couteau, Guillaume Le Bret, Thielman Kerver, Rémy Boyset, Pierre Sergent): *La bible en francoiz*... B 53

1549: Erasme, Desiderius, *Brief recueil du livre de l'enseignement du prince Chrestien* .... E 52

1551: *Trente Psalmes du royal Prophete David*...................... B 141

Benoist Prevost

1544: (with Jean Ruelle): Doré, Pierre, *Le Livre des divins benefices*... D 78

1547: (with Mathurin Du Puys, Guillaume Cavellat): Lactantius Firmianus, *Des divines Institutions* .... L 5

1549: (with Jean Ruelle): Doré, Pierre, *L'arche de l'alliance nouvelle*... D 52

1550: (with Jean Ruelle): Doré, Pierre, *La Piscine de patience* ... D 88

(with Jean Ruelle): Doré, Pierre, *Le Nouveau Testament d'amour*... D 89

1551: (with Guillaume Cavellat): Grenier, Nicole, *L'espee de la foy*.. G 37

Pierre Ratoire

1530: (with Pierre Sergent): *La vie de Monseigneur Sainct Albain*.. V 14

1541: (with Pierre Sergent): Bonaventure, Saint (attrib.), *Lesguillon damour divine* .... B 218

(with Pierre Sergent): *La marchandise spirituelle*........... M 16

(with Pierre Sergent): Quentin, Jean, *Lorloge de devotion* ..... Q 3

Jean Réal

1538: (with Vincent Sertenas): Doré, Pierre, *Dyalogue Instructoire des Chrestiens en la Foy*................................ D 67

1540: (with Ambroise Girault): *Le Fagot de Myerre*.................. F 4
Petit, Guillaume, *Le Viat de salut* .... P 19
1541: (with Philippe Le Noir, François Regnault, Oudin Petit): Bouchet, Jean, *Les triumphes de la Noble et amoureuse Dame*.. B 230
1542: (with Vincent Sertenas, Gilles Corrozet): *Le ...mystere du vieil testament*.. M 109
1548: (with Guillaume Le Bret, Poncet Le Preux): *La fleur des commandemens de Dieu*........................... F 40
(with Guillaume Le Bret, Jean Bonfons, Vivant Gaultherot): Lemaire de Belges, Jean, *Le traicte de la difference des scismes* .... L 45
1549: (with Poncet Le Preux): Herp, Henry de, *Directoire des contemplatifz* .... H 9

François Regnault

1511: Ambroise, Saint, *Le traicte du bien de la mort* .... A 6
Vitrier, Jean, *Lexposition sur le sermon que nostre seigneur fit en la montaigne*................................. V 47
1512: (with Michel Travers): *La fleur des commandemens de dieu*... F 35
Jérôme, Saint, *La Vie des peres*................................. J 6
1516: (with hér. Richard Auzoult of Rouen): *La bible en francois* .... B 26
1517: (with Jean de La Porte, Pierre Vidoue): Ambroise, Saint, *Le Traicte du bien et de la mort*........................ A 8
(with Barthelemy Verard): *La bible en francoiz*.............. B 28
1518: (with Pierre Vidoue, Jean de La Porte): Vitrier, Jean, *Lexposition sur le sermon que nostre seigneur fist en la montaigne* .... V 48
1520: (with Jean Petit): *La bible en francoiz*............................ B 30
1521: (with Jean Petit, Gilles Couteau): Ludolphus de Saxe, *La grant vita Christi*... L 74
1523: (with Jean Petit, Enguilbert de Marnef, Pierre Viart): Lemaire de Belges, Jean, *Le traicte de la difference des Scismes*... L 36
(with Gilles Couteau): Lesnauderie, Pierre de, *La Louenge de mariage*... L 61
1525: (with Antoine Couteau): Lesnauderie, Pierre de, *La Louenge de mariage*... L 62
1526: (with Philippe Le Noir): Lemaire de Belges, Jean, *Le traicte de la difference des Scismes*........................ L 39
1527: (with Galliot Du Pré): Conrard, Olivier, *Le mirouer des pecheurs*... C 130
1528: Lemaire de Belges, Jean, *Le traicte de la difference des Scismes*... L 41
1529: (with Jean Petit): *La bible en francoiz*............................ B 34

1531: (with Guillaume de Bossozel, Pierre Gaudoul, Ambroise
      Girault): *Le premier (-second) volume des grandes*
      Postilles et expositions .... P 31
1538: (with Estienne Caveiller, Jean Ruelle): Doré, Pierre, *Les*
      Allumettes du feu divin .... D 41
      (with Jean Petit): Doré, Pierre, *Les Allumettes du feu divin* ... D 42
      (with Estienne Caveiller, Alain Lotrian): Doré, Pierre,
      Les Voyes de Paradis .... D 92
1539: (with Maurice de La Porte, Estienne Caveiller): Gaigny,
      Jean de, *Le livre ... des Sept parolles* .... G 10
1541: (with Oudin Petit, Philippe Le Noir, Jean Réal): Bouchet,
      Jean, *Les triumphes de la Noble et amoureuse Dame* .... B 230

Vve François Regnault

1541: (with Oudin Petit, Ambroise Girault, Nicolas Couteau):
      La Bible en francois .... B 45
1544: *La Bible en Francoys* .... B 48

Jacques Regnault

1543: (with Antoine Foucault, Nicolas Buffet): Luther, Martin,
      Le livre de vraye et parfaicte oraison .... L 108
1544: (with Antoine Foucault, Nicolas Buffet): Vitrier, Jean,
      Le Sermon que nostre Seigneur feist en la montaigne ... V 53

Pierre Regnault

1540: Branteghem, Guillaume de, *La Vie de Nostre Seigneur*
      Jesus Christ .... B 250
      Gaigny, Jean de, *Le livre ... Faisant mention des Sept*
      parolles .... G 11
      Gringore, Pierre, *Chantz Royaulx figurez sur les mysteres* ..... G 44
      Gringore, Pierre, *Heures de nostre dame* .... G 54
      Gringore, Pierre, *Heures de nostre dame* .... G 55
      Petit, Guillaume, *La formation de l'homme et son*
      excellence .... P 11
1541: Branteghem, Guillaume de, *La Vie de Nostre Seigneur*
      Jesus Christ .... B 253
1542: Gringore, Pierre, *Chantz Royaulx figurez moralement* .... G 46
1543: *La Bible translateee de latin en francois ... pour les*
      simples gens .... B 46
      (with Jean Bignon): *La Bible en francois* .... B 47
1544: *La Bible en francois* .... B 50
1545: (with Nicolas Buffet): *La Bible translatée de Latin en*
      Francoys ... pour les simples gens .... B 52

Pierre Ricouart

1525: (with Guillaume de Bossozel): Mauburne, Jean, *Une petite*
      eschelle pour faire bonne et entiere confession .... M 46

Estienne Roffet

1540: (with Simon de Colines): Guerric, *Sermons* .... G 58

Primasius, *Briefve et fructueuse exposition sus les Epistres Sainct Paul* .... P 41
1541: *Trente Pseaulmes de David* .... B 90
1542: Brodeau, Victor, *Les Louanges Du sainct nom de Jesus* .... B 268
1543: *Trente-deux Pseaulmes de David ... vingt autres Pseaumes* .... B 97
(with Galliot Du Pré): Lactantius Firmianus, *Des Divines institutions* .... L 2
1546: Lactantius Firmianus, *Des Divines institutions* .... L 3
1549: Primasius, *Exposition sur les Epistres S. Poul* .... P 42

Pierre Roffet
1533: (with Nicolas Couteau): Hugues de Saint-Victor, *Larre de lame* .... H 15

Vve Pierre Roffet
1533: (with André Roffet, Antoine Couteau): Clément VII, *La translation en francoys de la bulle* .... C 110
1535: *L'Ordre de la procession generalle ... le .xxj. jour de Janvier* .... P 44

Ponce Roffet
1543: (with Denis Janot): *Edict sur les articles faictz par la faculte de theologie* .... E 3
1546: Vivès, Juan Luis, *Institution de la femme chrestienne* .... V 60

Jean de Roigny
1548: Dupuyherbault, Gabriel, *Regle et maniere de prier Dieu purement* .... D 103

Jean Ruelle
1538: (with François Regnault, Estienne Caveiller): Doré, Pierre, *Les Allumettes du feu divin* .... D 41
1539: (with Estienne Caveiller): Doré, Pierre, *Les Allumettes du feu divin* .... D 44
1540: *L'Internelle consolation* .... I 28
1542: (with Guillaume Le Bret): Branteghem, Guillaume de, *La Vie de nostre Seigneur Jesus Christ* .... B 255
1543: Doré, Pierre, *La celeste pensée* .... D 85
1544: Doré, Pierre, *Le cerf spirituel* .... D 53
(with René Avril): Doré, Pierre, *Dialogue Instructoire des Chrestiens* .... D 71
(with Benoist Prevost): Doré, Pierre, *Le Livre des divins benefices* .... D 78
Doré, Pierre, *La meditation devote ... sus le sainct sacrifice de la Messe* .... D 80
Internelle consolation .... I 37
1545: (with Jacques Bogard): *Cinquante deux Pseaumes de David* .... B 102

(with Jacques Bogard, Nicolas Du Chemin): *Cinquante Pseaumes* .... B 103
1546: (with René Avril): Conrard, Olivier, *La Vie, faictz et louanges de sainct Paul* .... C 131
(with René Avril, Jean André): Doré, Pierre, *La premiere partie des Collations royales* .... D 55
(with René Avril, Jean André): Doré, Pierre, *La seconde partie, des collations royalles* .... D 56
1547: *La Fontaine de vie* .... F 48
(with Guillaume Thibout, Guillaume Le Bret): Lemaire de Belges, Jean, *Le Promptuaire des conciles de l'Eglise Catholique* .... L 54
1548: Doré, Pierre, *Les Allumettes du feu divin* .... D 47
Doré, Pierre, *La croix de penitence* .... D 62
Lactantius Firmianus, *Des Divines Institutions* .... L 6
1549: Doré, Pierre, *L'adresse du pecheur* .... D 40
(with Benoist Prevost): Doré, Pierre, *L'arche de l'alliance nouvelle* .... D 52
1550: (with Benoist Prevost): Doré, Pierre, *La Piscine de patience* .... D 88
(with Benoist Prevost): Doré, Pierre, *Le Nouveau Testament d'amour* .... D 89
(with Jean Amazeur): *L'Internelle Consolation* .... I 38
Theodoret, *Deux Sermons* .... T 9
1551: (with Estienne Groulleau): Désiré, Artus, *Le Defensoire de la foy chrestienne* .... D 13
Lactantius Firmianus, *Des Divines Institutions* .... L 7
No date: Doré, Pierre, *Le Cerf Spirituel* .... D 54
Doré, Pierre, *L'image de vertu* .... D 77
Doré, Pierre, *Le livre des divins benefices* .... D 79
Espence, Claude d', *Homelies sur la parabole de l'enfant prodigue* .... E 59

Jean Saint Denys
1529: (with Julien Hubert): *La Marchandise spirituelle* .... M 14
(with Julien Hubert): Mauburne, Jean, *Le Beneficiaire divin* .... M 45
(with Julien Hubert): *Une devote meditation sur la mort et passion de nostre saulveur* .... M 53
(with Julien Hubert): *La voye de paradis* .... V 66
1530: *Les Eschelles de la passion* .... E 1
(with Antoine and Nicolas Couteau): *La Marchandise spirituelle* .... M 15
1531: (with Guillaume de Bossozel): *Les sept pseaulmes en francoys* .... B 76
(with Pierre Sergent): *La vie ma Dame saincte Barbe* .... V 16

Vve Jean Saint Denys

1532: (with Pierre Leber): La Boulaye, Guillaume de, *La pronostication du Ciecle advenir* .... L 1

1533: *Plusieurs expositions utilles sur l'oraison dominicale* .... E 78

Adam Saulnier

1543: Chrysostome, St Jean, *Traicté que nul n'est offensé,
sinon par soymesmes* .... C 109

(with Jean André): Doré, Pierre, *La caeleste pensée de
graces divines arrousée* .... D 86

1546: (with Jean André): Doré, Pierre, *La celeste pensée, des
graces divines arrousée* .... D 87

Nicolas Savetier

1530: *Internelle consolation* .... I 12

1531: (with Galliot Du Pré, Poncet Le Preux): Augustin, Saint,
Le premier Volume ... de la Cite de Dieu .... A 26

(with Galliot Du Pré, Jean Petit, Poncet Le Preux):
Augustin, Saint, *Le second volume ... de la Cite de
Dieu* .... A 27

(with Antoine Bonnemere, Jean Le Bailli): Clerici, Jean,
Ung traicte des fondemens du temple spirituel .... C 111

Internelle consolation .... I 14

1532: (with Poncet Le Preux): Bellemere, François, *Directoire
de la vie humaine* .... B 15

1533: Clerici, Jean, *Le Manuel des chrestiens* .... C 113

(with Ambroise Girault): Clerici, Jean, *Le Traicte de
Exemplaire penitence* .... C 115

Olivier Senant

1515: *Linstruction des curez pour instruire le simple peuple* ...... I 40

1533: *Linstruction des curez pour instruire le simple peuple* ...... I 46

Pierre Sergent

1530: (with Pierre Ratoire): *La vie de Monseigneur Sainct
Albain* .... V 14

1531: (with Jean Saint Denys): *La vie ma Dame saincte Barbe*... V 16

1533: (with Guillaume de Bossozel): *Brefve et salutaire
exposition sur la salutation angelique* .... E 82

La vie Et mistere de Saint Andry .... V 14a

*Le Mystere du tresglorieux Martyr Monsieur sainct
Christofle* .... V 17c

1535: Henry, Jean, *Le pelerinage de nostre dame* .... H 8

(with Jean Longis, Denis Janot): Petit, Guillaume, *Le
viat de salut* .... P 17

1536: (with Guillaume de Bossozel): Bouchet, Jean, *Les
Triumphes De la Noble et amoureuse dame* .... B 226

1537: (with Denis Janot, Estienne Caveiller): Le Roy, François,
Le Dialogue de consolation entre lame et raison .... L 56

1539: *Internelle consolation*.. I 25
1541: (with Pierre Ratoire): Bonaventure, Saint (attrib.),
    Lesguillon damour divine .... B 218
    (with Pierre Ratoire): *La marchandise spirituelle* .... M 16
    (with Pierre Ratoire): Quentin, Jean, *Lorloge de devotion*...... Q 3
1545: (with Rémy Boyset, Thielman Kerver, Guillaume Le Bret,
    Oudin Petit, Nicolas Couteau): *La bible en francoiz*......... B 53
1546: *Cinquante deux Pseaumes de David*.............................. B 110
    Doré, Pierre, *Le College de sapience*............................. D 59
No date: (with Jean Bignon): Du Buc, Richard, *Devot Traité de
    la genese*... D 96

Vincent Sertenas
1538: (with Jean Réal): Doré, Pierre, *Dyalogue Instructoire des
    Chrestiens en la Foy*... D 67
    Jérôme, Saint, *Les Epistres* .... J 5
1539: (with Jean Longis): Erasme, Desiderius, *Le Preparatif à
    la mort*... E 45
1541: (with Jean Longis, Denis Janot): Erasme, Desiderius,
    Comedie ou dialogue matrimonial............................... E 23
1542: (with Gilles Corrozet, Jean Réal): *Le ...mystere du vieil
    testament* .... M 109
1545: (with Jean Longis): Lemaire de Belges, Jean, *Le
    Promptuaire des conciles de l'Eglise Catholicque* .... L 51

Guichard Soquand
1518: (with Jean de La Porte): Eusèbe de Césarée (pseud.), *Le
    testament du tresglorieux sainct*............................... E 67

Guillaume Thibout
1545: (with Jean de Brouilly): Doré, Pierre, *Dialogue
    Instructoire, des chrestiens en la foy*........................ D 72
1546: *Cinquante deux Pseaumes de David*.............................. B 106
1547: (with Guillaume Le Bret): *Cinquante deux Pseaumes*........ B 116
    (with Guillaume Le Bret, Jean Ruelle): Lemaire de
    Belges, Jean, *Le Promptuaire des conciles de l'Eglise
    Catholique* .... L 54
1548: Doré, Pierre, *Les Allumettes du feu divin*...................... D 46
    Doré, Pierre, *La deploration de la vie humaine*................ D 65
1549: *Trente Psalmes du royal Prophete David*........................ B 126
    Erasme, Desiderius, *Deux colloques*............................ E 22
1550: *Cinquante deux Pseaumes* .... B 131
1551: (with Jean Bonfons): *Cinquante deux Pseaumes* .... B 143

Geoffroy Tory
1532: *Apolologie pour la foy chrestienne*............................... A 10

Michel Travers
1512: (with François Regnault): *La fleur des commandemens
    de dieu*... F 35

Jean Trepperel

1511: Béda, Noël, *La doctrine et instruction necessaire aux crestiens* .... B 7

Jérôme, Saint, *Les Epistres* .... J 2

Vve Jean Trepperel

1511: (with Jean Jehannot): *Le Psaultier nostre dame* .... P 50

1512: (with Jean Jehannot): Béda, Noël, *La petite Dyablerie dont lucifer est le chef* .... B 9

(with Jean Jehannot): Desmoulins, Laurent, *La cymetiere Des Malheureux* .... D 22

(with Jean Jehannot): *La theologie spirituelle.* .... T 10

1514: (with Jean Jehannot): *Le grant Ordinaire des chrestiens* ... O 9

1515: (with Jean Jehannot): *Le mistere de la conception ... de la benoiste vierge marie* .... M 85

(with Jean Jehannot): *Le mistere de la passion nostre seigneur jhesucrist* .... M 93

(with Jean Jehannot): *La Resurrection de nostre seigneur jhesuchrist* .... M 102

La reffection spirituelle de lame devote .... R 40

1516: (with Jean Jehannot): *Les commandemens de saincte eglise et la confession generale du jour de pasques* ..... C 124a

(with Jean Jehannot): *Une petite instruction ... pour une femme seculiere* .... I 55

(with Jean Jehannot): *Meditation tresdevotte ... sur la passion douloureuse de nostre doulx saulveur* .... M 51

(with Jean Jehannot): *Le mistere du viel Testament* .... M 108c

(with Jean Jehannot): *La refection spirituelle de lame devote* .... R 41

(with Jean Jehannot): Sauvage, Jean, *Leschelle damour divine* .... S 5

1518: (with Jean Jehannot): *Le mistere de monseigneur sainct pierre et sainct paul* .... M 108a

(with Jean Jehannot): *Le mistere du Tresglorieux martir Monsieur sainct christofle* .... V 17b

1519: Le Grand, Jacques, *Le Livre de bonnes mœurs* .... L 26a

1520: *La Bible en francoys* .... B 31

Mistere de la saincte hostie .... M 106a

(with Jean Jehannot): *Les Postilles et expositions Des epistres Et evangilles dominicalles* .... P 29a

1522: *Le mistere de la conception ... de la benoiste vierge marie* .... M 86

1524: *Le mistere de la passion nostre seigneur Jhesucrist* .... M 95

1525: *La Resurrection de nostre Seigneur Jesuchrist* .... M 103

Jean Trepperel II

1532: *Le grand ordinaire des chrestiens* .... O 11

Jacques Tyson

1545: (with Galliot Du Pré, Nicolas Du Chemin, Jean André):
Bouchet, Jean, *Les Triumphes de la noble et
amoureuse dame*... B 231

Michel de Vascosan

1541: Vincent, Saint, de Léris, *Verité de la foi catholique*.......... V 24
1551: Augustin, Saint, *Opuscule ... de l'Esprit et de la lettre* ..... A 28
Sebond, Raymond, *La Theologie Naturelle*....................... S 10

Antoine Verard

1511: Guillaume d'Auvergne, *Traite touchant la doctrine et
enseignement de prier Dieu* .... G 61
(with Guillaume Le Rouge): *Le Premier/Second volume
des exposicions des Epistres et Evangilles de
Karesme*.. P 25
(with Guillaume Le Rouge): *Le Tiers volume des
exposicions des Epistres et Evangiles de Toute
lannee*... P 26
1512: (with Guillaume Le Rouge): *Le Quart/Ve volume des
exposicions des Epistres et Evangilles de Toute
lannee*... P 27
1519: (with Jean Petit): *Le Tiers/Ve volume des exposicions
des Epistres et Evangilles de Toute lannee* .... P 28

Barthelemy Verard

1514: *La bible en francoiz* .... B 25
1517: (with François Regnault): *La bible en francoiz* .... B 28

Pierre Viart

1517: (with Enguilbert and Jean de Marnef, Nicolas Higman):
Lemaire de Belges, Jean, *Le traictie de la difference
des scismes* .... L 33
1519: (with Enguilbert and Jean de Marnef): Lemaire de Belges,
Jean, *Le Traictie de la difference des scismes*.............. L 34
1520: (with Jean Du Pré): *Internelle consolacion*...................... I 9
1521: (with Enguilbert and Jean de Marnef): Lemaire de Belges,
Jean, *Le traictie de la difference des scismes*.............. L 35
(with Michel Lesclencher, Bernard Aubry): Voragine,
Jacques de, *La legende doree*.................................... V 73
1522: (with Jean Du Pré): *Internelle consolation* .... I 10
1523: (with François Regnault, Jean Petit, Enguilbert de Marnef):
Lemaire de Belges, Jean, *Le traicte de la difference
des Scismes*... L 36

Pierre Vidoue

1517: (with François Regnault, Jean de La Porte): Ambroise,
Saint, *Le Traicte du bien et de la mort* .... A 8

1518: (with François Regnault, Jean de La Porte): Vitrier, Jean, *Lexposition sur le sermon que nostre seigneur fist en la montaigne* .... V 48
1519: (with Regnault Chaudiere): *La discipline damour divine* ... D 29
(with Regnault Chaudiere): *Quatre voyes spirituelles* .... Q 2
1520: (with Galliot Du Pré): Erasme, Desiderius, *De la declamation des louenges de follie* .... E 26
1522: (with Galliot Du Pré): Augustin, Saint, *Le Mirouer des vanitez et pompes du monde* .... A 30
1531: (with Jean Longis): Le Grand, Jacques, *Le Tresor de sapience* .... L 26c
1540: (with Jérôme de Gourmont): Doré, Pierre, *Limage de vertu* .... D 73
(with Jean Foucher, Charles Langelier, Ambroise Girault): Lemaire de Belges, Jean, *Le traicte de la difference des Scismes* .... L 44

Vve Pierre Vidoue
1545: Désiré, Artus, *Lamentation de nostre mere saincte Eglise* ...... D 16

Simon Vostre
1512: Le Roy, François, *Le Mirouer de penitence* .... L 58
1516: Loys, Jean, *Le ravisement du pelerin de verite* .... L 70
1520: (with Nicolas Higman): Vitrier, Jean, *Lexposition sur le sermon que nostre seigneur fist a la montaigne* .... V 49
1537: (with Nicolas Higman): *Linstruction des curez pour instruire le simple peuple* .... I 47
No date: Ambroise, Saint, *Le traictie ... du bien de la mort* .... A 7
Thomas a Kempis, *Traictie de discipline claustralle* .... T 11

Chrestien Wechel
1528: (with Simon Du Bois): Gaigny, Jean de, *Le livre faisant mention des sept parolles* .... G 6
(with Simon Du Bois): Luther, Martin, *Le livre de vraye et parfaicte oraison* .... L 97
1529: (with Simon Du Bois): Luther, Martin, *Le livre de vraye et parfaicte oraison* .... L 98
1530: (with Jean Kerbriant): Luther, Martin, *Le livre de vraye et parfaicte oraison* .... L 99
1535: Gaigny, Jean de, *Le livre ... faisant mention des sept parolles* .... G 8
1545: *Articles concernans la vraye religion ... de Louvain* .... A 24
Gaigny, Jean de, *Le livre ... faisant mention de sept parolles* .... G 12
1546: Rabelais, François, *Tiers livre* .... R 22

No name
1516: *La complainte de nostre mere sainte eglise* .... C 124b
1520: *Parfaite foy pour estre sauve* .... P 5
1525: Caupain, Henri, *Le sepulchre spirituel* .... C 94
Illyricus, Thomas, *Le Sermon de Charité* .... I 3

1526: *Les Arrestz et ordonnances de la court contre Luther* .... A 19
1528: Illyricus, Thomas, *Devotes oraisons* .... I 1
1530: Illyricus, Thomas, *Copie de la prophetie* .... I 2
1535: *Procession generale faicte a Paris* .... P 43
1536: *Internelle consolation* .... I 20
1539: Gringore, Pierre, *Heures de nostre Dame* .... G 52
1544: Erasme, Desiderius, *Preparation à la mort* .... E 51
1546: Rabelais, François, *Tiers livre* .... R 24
1547: Rabelais, François, *Tiers livre* .... R 28
1548: Grenier, Nicole, *Le Bouclier de la foy* .... G 30
1549: Doré, Pierre, *La Passe-solitaire* .... D 83
       Exposition De l'Oraison de nostre Seigneur Jesus .... E 77
       Vivès, Juan Luis, *L'Institution de la femme chrestienne* .... V 64
1550: *Le ABC des Chrestiens* .... A 1
       Mazurier, Martial, *Instruction et doctrine a se bien
          confesser* .... M 50
1551: Doré, Pierre, *Anti-Calvin, contenant deux defenses
          catholiques* .... D 49
No date: *Dialogue spirituel de la passion* .... D 26
       Lacu, Jean, *La quenouille spirituelle* .... L 9

Poitiers

Jacques Bouchet

1530: Bouchet, Jean, *Les Triumphes de la noble et amoureuse
          dame* .... B 221
1533: (with Jean and Enguilbert de Marnef): Bouchet, Jean,
          Les Triumphes de la Noble et amoureuse dame .... B 223

Enguilbert de Marnef

1516: *Linstruction des curez pour instruire le simple peuple* ...... I 41

Jean et Enguilbert de Marnef

1530: *La Vie de Jesus Christ* .... V 12
1532: Bouchet, Jean, *Les Triumphes de la noble et amoureuse
          dame* .... B 222
1533: (with Jacques Bouchet): Bouchet, Jean, *Les Triumphes
          de la Noble et amoureuse dame* .... B 223
1536: *Les Postilles et expositions des epistres et evangiles
          dominicalles* .... P 32
1542: Luther, Martin, *Le livre de vraye et parfaicte oraison* ...... L 106
1543: Cailleau, Gilles, *Paraphrase sur les Heures de nostre
          Dame* .... C 4
1547: Cailleau, Gilles, *Paraphrase sur les Heures de nostre
          Dame* .... C 5

Nicolas Peletier

1550: *Les Cent Psalmes de David, qui restoient à traduire* .... B 135

Rennes

Jean Georget
1541: Bouchet, Jean, *Les triumphes de la noble et amoureuse*
  dame.. B 229

Rouen

Hér. Richard Auzoult
1516: (with François Regnault, Paris): *La bible en francois*........ B 26
  (with Michel Angier, Caen): *La bible en francoys* .... B 27

Louis Bouvet
1532: Jordan, Raymond, dit Idiota, *Les contemplations du*
  simple devot... J 12

Jean Burges
1530: *La vie et lystore de ma dame saincte barbe* .... V 15

Nicolas de Burges
1543: (with Jean Petit): Dolet, Estienne, *Sommaire et recueil*
  des faictz et gestes, du Roy Françoys .... D 39

Vincent Coffin
1548: Rabelais, François, *Quart livre* .... R 35

Etienne Dasne
1530: (with Raulin Gaultier): *La bible translatee*....................... B 36

Robert et Jean Du Gort
1548: Marguerite de Navarre, *Le Triumphe de l'agneau*.............. M 42
1550: *Cent Psalmes de David*.. B 136
  (with Jean Mallard): *Cinquante Psalmes de David*............. B 137
  Désiré, Artus, *Les combatz du fidelle Papiste ... contre*
  l'apostat Antipapiste .... D 7
  Désiré, Artus, *Les combatz du fidelle papiste* ....
  contre l'apostat Priapiste .... D 8
  Désiré, Artus, *Le Deffensoire de la foi chrestienne*........... D 12
  Désiré, Artus, *La Description de la cité de Dieu*............... D 14
  Désiré, Artus, *Le Miroir Des francs taupins* .... D 20
1551: Désiré, Artus, *Les grands jours du Parlement de Dieu*...... D 15
  (with Nicolas Le Roux): *Les Testamentz des douze*
  patriarches .... T 6
1553: (with Jean Mallard): *Les Cent Psalmes de David*.............. B 144

Raulin Gaultier
1530: (with Etienne Dasne): *La bible translatee* .... B 36

Guillaume de La Motte
1538: *La conversion et revocation des Lutheriens*....................... C 133

Nicolas Le Roux
1551: (with Robert et Jean Du Gort): *Les Testamentz des douze*
  patriarches .... T 6

Jean Lhomme
1544: Landry, François, *La declaration De la Foy chrestienne* ...   L 13
Jean Mallard
1550: (with Robert et Jean Du Gort): *Cinquante Psalmes de
        David* ....   B 137
1553: (with Robert et Jean Du Gort): *Les Cent Psalmes de
        David* ....   B 144
Martin Morin
1514: Fabri, Pierre, *Le defensoir de la conception* ....   F 2
1515: *Le defensoire de la conception* ....   D 1
Jean Petit
1543: (with Nicolas de Burges): Dolet, Estienne, *Sommaire et
        recueil des faictz et gestes, du Roy Françoys* ....   D 39
'Rouen, Claude Treszet' see Lyon, No name, 1549.
No name, no date: *Postilles et expositions* ....   P 34

S. Nicolas du Port

Jérôme Jacobi
1524: Gringore, Pierre, *Le Blazon des heretiques* ....   G 39
1525: Illyricus, Thomas, *Le Sermon de Charité* ....   I 4

Strasbourg

Jacques Froelich
1545: Poullain, Valérand, *Oraison chrestienne au Seigneur Dieu* ....   P 35
Rémy Guédon
1546: *L'Instruction et creance des Chrestiens* ....   I 54
1547: Cordier, Mathurin, *Quatre epistres chrestiennes* ....   C 134
        Marcourt, Antoine, *Le livre des marchans* ....   M 27
1548: *Pseaumes de David* ....   B 121
Wolfgang Köpfel
1525: (with Johann Schott): Luther, Martin, *Livre tresutile de
        la vraye et parfaite subjection des chrestiens* ....   L 113
Johann Knobloch Sen.
1526: (with Johann Pruss Jr.): Schuch, Wolfgang, *Epistre
        chrestienne* ....   S 8
1527: (with Johann Pruss): Dumolin, Guillaume, *Tresutile
        traicte, du vray regne de antechrist* ....   D 98
Johann Knobloch Jr.
1539: *Aulcuns pseaulmes et cantiques* ....   B 82
1542: Calvin, Jean, *La Manyere de faire prieres aux eglises
        Françoyses* ....   C 65
        Sleidan, Jean, *Escript adresse aux Electeurs* ....   S 18
1543: Farel, Guillaume, *Oraison tresdevote* ....   F 23

Melanchthon, Philippe, *Confession de la foy presentee a
... Charles V.* .... M 62
1545: Calvin, Jean, *La Forme des Prieres et Chants
ecclesiastiques* .... C 51

Johann Pruss Jr.
1526: (with Johann Knobloch Sen.): Schuch, Wolfgang,
Epistre chrestienne .... S 8
1527: Dumolin, Guillaume, *Le traicte de lutilite et honneste de
mariage* .... D 97
(with Johann Knobloch Sen.): Dumolin, Guillaume,
Tresutile traicte, du vray regne de antechrist .... D 98
Dumolin, Guillaume, *Notable et utile traicte Du zele et
grant desir* .... D 99
Luther, Martin, *Prophetie de Iesaie de lenfant nouveau
ne Jesuchrist* .... L 118

Johann Schott
1525: (with Wolfgang Köpfel): Luther, Martin, *Livre tresutile
de la vraye et parfaite subjection des chrestiens* .... L 113

Toulouse

Guyon Boudeville
1546: (with Thomas Du Fert): *Epistre d'un gentilhomme à un
sien ami* .... E 10

Jacques Colomies
1533: (with Jean Richard): *Le Sentier et ladresse de devotion* .... S 13

Thomas Du Fert
1546: (with Guyon Boudeville): *Epistre d'un gentilhomme à un
sien ami* .... E 10

Jacques Fournier
1546: Rabelais, François, *Tiers livre* .... R 25

Jean Lemosin
1545: Ponisson, François, *Miroir du pauvre pecheur* .... P 24

Jean Richard
1533: (with Jacques Colomies): *Le Sentier et ladresse de devotion* S 13

Tournai

Jean Brocquart
1523: (with Adriaen van Berghen, Antwerp): *Le tressainct et
sacres texte du nouniaulx testament* .... B 151

Troyes

Jean Le Coq
1525: Bellemere, François, *Directoire de la vie humaine* .... B 14
1526: Petit, Guillaume, *Le viat de salut* .... P 13

1527: *La vie sainct Jehan baptiste*.. V 17d
No date: Bellemere, François, *Examen de conscience* .... B 16
         Lucidiaire en françoys.. L 73

Jean Le Coq II
1541: *Une petite instruction et maniere de vivre*...................... I 56
       Les quinze effusions du sang de nostre Sauveur Jesuchrist..... Q 4
       La Vie et Passion de Ma Dame saincte Marguerite........... V 20
No date: *Extraict de plusieurs sainctz Docteurs*........................ E 86

Nicole Paris
1546: Royer, Colin, *La Nouvelle du reverend pere en Dieu* .... R 52

No name
1527: *Les Hymnes communes de lannee*.................................... H 16

Turin

see Alençon, Simon Du Bois, 1532

see Lyon, François Carcan, 1525

Valence

Claude La Ville
1547: Rabelais, François, *Gargantua*.. R 29
     Rabelais, François, *Pantagruel*...................................... R 30
     Rabelais, François, *Tiers livre*....................................... R 31

No place, no name

1527: *Lorayson de nostre seigneur Jesuchrist*............................ O 7
1528: *La grande Irrision des Lutheriens de Meaulx*.................. I 59
     Le Te Deum pour l'eglise Lutherienne............................ T 1
1530: *Le Chappeau des lutheriens*... C 103
     Erasme, Desiderius, *Maniere de se confesser*.................. E 37
     Gringore, Pierre, *Le Blazon des heretiques*.................... G 40
1531: *Loraison de Missus est* .... M 81
     Saulnier, Antoine, *Chanson nouvelle composee sur les*
        dix commandemens de Dieu.................................... S 2
1534: Volcyr de Sérouville, Nicolas, *Traicté nouveau de la*
        desecration ... de Jehan Castellan............................ V 70
1537: *Les sept pseaulmes penitenciaulx*.................................. B 80
1540: Brodeau, Victor, *Les Louanges De Jesus Nostre Saulveur*...... B 266
     Instruction pour les Chrestiens .... I 51
1542: Rabelais, François, *Gargantua et Pantagruel*.................. R 20
1543: Branteghem, Guillaume de, *La vie de nostre seigneur*
        Jesu Christ.. B 256
     Erasme, Desiderius *Paraphrase sur le troisieme pseaulme*..... E 40
1546: *Chansons spirituelles sur la saincte Cene*...................... C 96
1547: *La Doctrine des Chrestiens extraicte du vieil et nouveau*
        Testament .... S 25

1548: Erasme, Desiderius, *Colloque ... intitulé Abbatis et Eruditae*.. E 20
1549: Rabelais, François (pseud.), *Le cinquiesme livre*.............. R 36
Viret, Pierre, *Exposition familiere sur les dix commandements* .... V 41
1550: Calvin, Jean, *La forme des prieres ecclesiastiques*........... C 56
Devotes oraisons de nostre Dame .... O 8
1551: Rabelais, François (pseud.) *Le Cinquiesme Livre*.............. R 37

No place, no name, no date

Branteghem, Guillaume de, *La Vie de Jesuchrist*........................ B 260
Instruction ... pour parfaictement vivre en ce monde .... I 53
Le livre de la loy et de l'Evangile.. L 67
La Lunette des Chrestiens... L 78
Le manuel des Christians .... M 13
Meigret, Aimé, *Epistre en latin ... Plus un sermon en françois*.... M 58
Le Moyen de parvenir à la congnoissance de Dieu .... M 83
Penser a la Mort cest chose proffitable.................................... P 9
Poyvreault, Simon, *Douze devotes Contemplations*..................... P 37
Profession de foy accoustumee d'estre juree Par les Bourgeois ... de Frybourg... P 45
Tissarrant, Jean, *Une tresbelle salutation faicte sur les vii festes de Nostre dame*... T 12

5 Alphabetical List of Printers

Guillaume Alabat	Bourges	Bertram Boulet	Lille
Anemond Amalberti	Grenoble	Louis Bouvet	Rouen
Jean Amazeur	Paris	Rémy Boyset	Paris
Jean André	Paris	Bonaventure Brassart	Cambrai
Michel Angier	Caen	Vve Jean de Brie	Paris
Honorat d'Arles	Avignon	Jean Brocquart	Tournai
	[Geneva]	Jean de Brouilly	Paris
Balthazar Arnoullet	Lyon	Nicolas Buffet	Paris
Olivier Arnoullet	Lyon	Jean Burges	Rouen
Pierre Attaignant	Paris	Nicolas de Burges	Rouen
Bernard Aubry	Paris		
Antoine Augereau	Paris		
Richard Auzoult (heirs)	Rouen	Jean Cantarel	Lyon
René Avril	Paris	François Carcan	Lyon
		Estienne Caveiller	Paris
		Guillaume Cavellat	Paris
Nicolas Bacquenois	Lyon	François Cavillon	Turin
Conrad Badius	Geneva		[Lyon]
Josse Badius	Paris	Jean de Channey	Avignon
Pierre Bailly	Lyon	Regnault & Claude	
Estienne Baland	Lyon	Chaudiere	Paris
Jean Barbaram	Nevers	Barnabé Chaussard	Lyon
Jean Barbou	Lyon	Vve Barnabé	
Nicolas Barbou	Paris	Chaussard	Lyon
Jean Baudouin	Nantes	Simon Coc	Antwerp
Anthoine Marie		Vincent Coffin	Rouen
Bergagne	Louvain	Simon de Colines	Paris
Godefroy & Marcelin		Jacques Colomies	Toulouse
Beringen	Lyon	Antoine Constantin	Lyon
Jacques Berion	Lyon	Jean Cornillau	Paris
Jaspard Bernard	Armentières	Gilles Corrozet	Paris
Jean Besson	Lyon	Raoul Cousturier	Paris
Pierre Bige	Paris	Antoine Couteau	Paris
Jean Bignon	Paris	Gilles Couteau	Paris
Guillaume Bineaulx	Paris	Nicolas Couteau	Paris
Antoine Blanchard	Lyon	Andreas Cratander	Basle
Jacques Bogard	Paris	Jean Crespin	Geneva
Jean Bonfons	Paris	Matthieu Crom	Antwerp
Nicolas Bonfons	Paris	Jacques Crozet	Lyon
Yolande Bonhomme	Paris		
Antoine Bonnemere	Paris	Baudouin Dacquin	Arras
Benoist Bonnyn	Lyon	Jean Daniel	Avignon
Guillaume de Bossozel	Paris		[Geneva]
Jacques Bouchet	Poitiers	Etienne Dasne	Rouen
Guyon Boudeville	Toulouse		

Jean David	Paris	François Girault	Paris
Antoine Des Gois	Antwerp	? Godefroy	Paris
Estienne Dolet	Lyon	Jérôme de Gourmont	Paris
Michel Du Bois	Geneva	Louis Grandin	Paris
Simon Du Bois	Alençon,	Bartholomy de Grave	Louvain
	Paris	Jean Graphaeus	Antwerp
Simon Du Bois		Jean de Grave	Antwerp
de la Haye	Lyon	Pierre Gromors	Paris
Nicolas Du Chemin	Paris	Estienne Groulleau	Paris
Charles Dudé	Paris	Sebastien Gryphe	Lyon
Thomas Du Fert	Toulouse	Rémy Guédon	Strasbourg
Robert & Jean Du Gort	Rouen	Guillaume de Guelques	Lyon
Guillaume Du Mont		Charlotte Guillard	Paris
(van Berghen)	Antwerp	Jean Guyant	Bordeaux
Galliot Du Pré	Paris		
Jean Du Pré	Paris	Philibert Hamelin	Geneva
Mathurin Du Puys	Paris	Denis de Harsy	Lyon
Antoine Du Ry	Lyon	M. Harvard	Lyon
		Nicolas Higman	Paris
Jacques Estauge	Basle	Laurent Hostingue	
Robert Estienne	Paris	(heirs)	Caen
Guillaume Eustace	Paris	Julien Hubert	Paris
Jacques Ferrebouc	Paris	Jérôme Jacobi	S. Nicolas
Guillaume Fezendat	Paris		du Port
Jacques Fezendat	Paris	Vauldrain Jacquin	Hesdin
Michel Fezendat	Paris	Denis Janot	Paris
Antoine Foucault	Paris	Jean Jehannot	Paris
Jean Foucher	Paris	Antoine Jurie	Paris
Jacques Fournier	Toulouse	François Juste	Lyon
Barthelemy Frein	Lyon		
Jean & François Frellon	Lyon	Thomas Kees	Paris
Jacques Froelich	Strasbourg	Adrien Kempe	Antwerp
		Jean Kerbriant	Paris
Claude Garnier	Limoges	Jacques Kerver	Paris
Jean Garnier	Paris	Thielman Kerver	Paris
Pierre Gaudoul	Paris	Wigand Koeln	Geneva
Vivant Gaultherot	Paris	Wolfgang Köpfel	Strasbourg
Pierre Gaultier	Paris	Johann Knoblauch	
Raulin Gaultier	Rouen	Sen. & Jr.	Strasbourg
Thomas Gaultier	London		
Jean Georget	Rennes	Antoine de La Barre	Paris
Éloi Gibier	Orléans	Nicolas de La Barre	Paris
Nicolas Gilles	Paris	Jean de La Garde	Paris
Jean Girard	Geneva	Antoine de La Haye	Antwerp
Ambroise Girault	Paris	Jean Lambany	Lyon

Josse Lambert	Ghent	Jean Marnax	Lyon
Guillaume de La Motte	Rouen	Geoffroy de Marnef	Paris
Arnoul & Charles		Jean & Enguilbert	
Langelier	Paris	de Marnef	Paris,
Jean de La Place	Lyon		Poitiers
Jean de La Porte	Lille, Paris	Jeanne de Marnef	Paris
Maurice de La Porte	Paris	Guillaume Merlin	Paris
Vve Maurice		Estienne Mesviere	Paris
de La Porte	Paris	Guillaume Michel	Paris
Jean de La Roche	Paris	Jean Michel	Geneva
Claude La Ville	Lyon,	Stephen Mierdman	London
	Valence	Jacques Moderne	Lyon
Jean Le Bailli	Paris	Jean Morin	Paris
Pierre Leber	Paris	Martin Morin	Rouen
Guillaume Le Bret	Paris	Romain Morin	Lyon
Pierre Le Brodeur	Paris	Gérard Morrhy	Paris
Jean Le Converd	Lyon	Jean Mosnier	Lyon
Jean Le Coq I & II	Troyes	Martin Mourot	Longeville
Hémon Le Fèvre	Paris	Jean Mullet	Lille
Martin Le Jeune	Paris		
Jean Lemosin	Toulouse		
Martin Lempereur	Antwerp	Claude Nourry	Lyon
Vve M. Lempereur	Antwerp	Conrad Neobar	Paris
Michel Le Noir	Paris	Martin Nuyts	Antwerp
Philippe Le Noir	Paris	Guillaume Nyverd	Paris
Poncet Le Preux	Paris		
Guillaume Le Rouge	Paris	Jean Pallier	Metz
Nicolas Le Roux	Rouen	Henri Paquot	Paris
Michel Lesclencher	Paris	Nicole Paris	Troyes
Pasquier Le Tellier	Paris	Imbert Parmentier	Avignon
Jean Lhomme	Rouen	Thibaud Payen	Lyon
Jacques de Liesvelt	Antwerp	Nicolas Peletier	Poitiers
Jean de Liesvelt	Antwerp	Jean Petit	Paris
Jean Loe	Antwerp	Jean Petit	Rouen
Jean Longis	Paris	Nicolas Petit	Lyon
Alain Lotrian	Paris	Oudin Petit	Paris
Jean Loys	Paris	Martin & Pierre Philippe	Caen
		Jean Pidier	Lyon
		Henry Pierre	Antwerp
Jean Macé	Paris	Benoist Prevost	Paris
Didier Maheu	Paris	Johann Pruss Sen. & Jr.	Strasbourg
Jean Mallard	Rouen	Jean Pullon	Lyon
Olivier Mallard	Paris		
Claude Marchant	Lyon		
Jean Marchant	Paris	Pierre Ratoire	Paris
Jean Marcorelles	Geneva	Jean Réal	Paris
Jacques Mareschal	Lyon	Antoine Reboul	Agen
Pierre Mareschal	Lyon	François Regnault	Paris

Vve François Regnault	Paris	Claude Treszet	Rouen
Jacques Regnault	Paris		[Lyon]
Pierre Regnault	Paris	Jacques Tyson	Paris
Franciscus Rhode	Marburg		
Jean Richard			
(Rijckaerts)	Antwerp	Adrien van Berghen	
Jean Richard	Toulouse	(Du Mont)	Antwerp
Pierre Ricouart	Paris	Michel de Vascosan	Paris
Adam & Jean Rivery	Geneva	Antoine Verard	Paris
Godefroy de Rode	Ghent	Barthelemy Verard	Paris
Estienne Roffet	Paris	Claude Veycellier	Lyon
Pierre Roffet	Paris	Pierre Viart	Paris
Vve Pierre Roffet	Paris	Pierre Vidoue	Paris
Ponce Roffet	Paris	Vve Pierre Vidoue	Paris
Jean de Roigny	Paris	Gilbert de Villiers	Lyon
Philibert Rollet	Lyon	A. Villotte	Agen
Guillaume Rouillé	Lyon	Pierre de Vingle	Geneva,
John Roux	London		Lyon,
Jean Ruelle	Paris		Neuchâtel
		Guillaume Vissenaken	Antwerp
		Jacques Vivian	Geneva
Sulpice Sabon	Lyon	Guillaume Vorsterman	Antwerp
Jacques Sacon	Lyon	Simon Vostre	Paris
Jean Saint Denys	Paris		
Vve Jean Saint Denys	Paris		
Pierre de Sainte-Lucie	Lyon	Jean de Waen	Louvain
Adam Saulnier	Paris	J. Walder	Basle
Nicolas Savetier	Paris	Chrestien Wechel	Paris
Johann Schabler	Basle	Edward Whitchurch	London
Johann Schott	Strasbourg	Robert Winter	Basle
Olivier Senant	Paris	Thomas Wolff	Basle
Pierre Sergent	Paris		[Alençon]
Vincent Sertenas	Paris		
Guichard Soquand	Paris		
Jean Steelsius	Antwerp		
Guillaume Thibout	Paris		
Geoffroy Tory	Paris		
Jean de Tournes	Lyon		
Pierre de Tours	Lyon		
Michel Travers	Paris		
Melchior & Gaspar			
Trechsel	Lyon		
Jean Trepperel	Paris		
Vve Jean Trepperel	Paris		
Jean Trepperel II	Paris		

Index of Proper Names

Listed are names of sixteenth-century (or earlier) persons, mentioned either as 'secondary author' in the main list or in the 'Notes' to that list, with the reference number where the reference will be found. Primary authors (who will be found alphabetically in the main list) are only mentioned here if they appear as secondary authors or in the notes; names of biblical persons, or names of more recent writers or authorities, are not included.

Abbot of St Victor: A 36
Ailly, Pierre d': B 73, B 91
Alabat, Guillaume: G 24
Alençon, Pierre et Marie d': L 17
Alexander, Pierre: B 85
Ambrose, St: P 26, V 47
André, Jean: D 11, D 17, D 56, L 60
Aneau, Barthelemy: E 23
Antoine, duke of Lorraine: B 1, V 69
Antoinette de Bourbon, duchesse de Guise:
    C 109, D 56, D 88
Aresmes, Guillaume d': S 13
Arétin, Pierre: B 83, B 88
Arles, Honorat d': M 41
Arnoullet, Balthazar: B 184, B 257, L 25
Athanasius, St: B 93, C 84, C 88
Aubert, A.: C 107
Augustine, St: B 8, P 26
Aurigny, Gilles d': B 123, B 126, B 136,
    B 141, B 142, E 52, E 53
Avril, René: E 64

B., Cl.: B 142
B., E.: H 9
Badius, Conrad: C 66
Badius, Josse: L 15
Baillivi, Nicolas: B 123
Barbou, Jean: B 184
Bartou, Jean, Bishop of Lectoure: D 28
Basile, St: J 5, Q 1
Beaulieu, Eustorg de: A 21, B 3
Beaulieu, Magdaleine de: B 5
Béda, Noël: A 2, A 30, B 7, B 11
Belard, A.: B 91
Bellemere, François: B 13, G 14
Beringen, Godefroy & Marcellin: B 126
Bernard, St: A 30, B 9, B 10
Berquin, Louis de: B 22, E 15, E 24, E 27,
    E 28, E 29, E 30, E 31, E 32, E 33,
    E 34, E 57

Bèze, Théodore de: B 24, B 138, B 139
Biel, Gabriel: E 62, E 63, E 64, E 65
Bienassis, René de: C 9, C 25, E 39
Bienvenu, Jaques: C 64
Bogard, Jacques: B 106, T 3
Bolo, de, dr: D 57
Bonaventura, St: B 217, E 85
Bone, gouvernante de Tournai: D 99
Bonfons, Jean: D 6, E 68, M 108
Bonhomme, Yolande: I 24
Bonivard, François: S 33
Bonnemere, Antoine: I 47a
Bossozel, Guillaume de: L 76
Bouchet, Françoyse de, Comtesse de Mont-
    fort: D 44, D 92
Bouchet, Jacques: B 221
Bouchet, Jean: B 221, R 36, V 66
Bougain, Michel: B 233
Bourgeois, Jacques: C 118
Bourgeois, Loys: B 113, B 114
Bourges, Jean de: R 45
Bourgogne, Jacques de: C 117
Branteghem, Guillaume de: B 237, B 243,
    B 251
Brenz, Johannes: B 68, B 274
Briçonnet, Denis: I 40
Briçonnet, Guillaume: J 11
Brigitte, St: B 263, B 264
Brincel, Robert: B 142
Bris, Nicolas de: B 265
Brodeau, Victor: B 267, S 15
Brouilly, Jean de: D 53, D 74, D 76
Brully, Pierre de: C 65, P 35
Bucer, Martin: B 78, B 93, B 209, B 278,
    C 79, C 80, C 83, C 84, L 10, L 26,
    L 87
Budé, Louis: B 140
Buffet, Nicolas: V 53
Bugenhagen, Johann: D 98
Bullinger, Heinrich: B 280, C 6

Cailleau, Jean: J 1, J 5
Caling, Nicole: S 13
Calvin, Jean: B 18, B 40, B 54, B 82, B 96, B 121, B 140, B 185, B 190, B 198, B 204, B 205, C 9, C 19, C 20, C 39, C 45, C 46, C 47, C 63, C 64, C 65, C 68, C 73, C 79, C 95, D 4, D 52, D 100, E 77, F 9, F 16, G 13, G 37, I 53, L 78, M 66, M 67, M 68, M 84, S 9, T 7, V 31, V 35
Campen, Jean van: C 83, C 84
Carcan, François: B 159
Carion, Jean: D 37
Caroli, Pierre: B 73, B 160, F 9
Castellan, Jean: V 70
Castellio, Sebastien: C 92
Catherine de Medicis, Queen of France: D 89
Catherine de Sarrebruche, Comtesse de Roussy: D 76, D 77
Caupain, Henri: C 93, C 94
Caveiller, Estienne: D 32
Cavellat, Guillaume: G 37
Cercia, Antoine: E 9
Certon, Pierre: B 109
Changy, Pierre de: V 54, V 55, V 56, V 57, V 58, V 59, V 60, V 61, V 62, V 63, V 64
Channey, Jean de: C 121
Chansonnette, Claude: E 36, E 37, E 38
Charles V: A 4, A 24, C 64, F 50, M 66
Charles de Lorraine, archb. of Reims: I 47a
Chaudiere, Regnault: C 90, C 91, D 25, D 29
Chaussard, Barnabé: P 49
Chaussard, Vve Barnabé: P 8a
Chevalet, ?: C 105
Chipart, Jaquin: S 1
Chobelet, Leonard: G 25
Choquet, Louis: C 106
Chrestien, Guillaume: Q 1
Claude de Lorraine, duc de Guise: D 55, D 81
Clement VII, Pope: P 3
Clerici, Jean: C 112, C 115
Clichtove, Josse: A 10, C 130, V 47
Coignac, Joachim de: C 116, V 5, V 7
Colin, Jean: V 65
Colin, Pierre: B 132
Colines, Simon de: B 155, B 156, B 160
Columbi, Jean: C 119, C 123
Columbus, Fernand: B 80, G 40

Conrad, Bishop of Kungen: E 2
Conrard, Olivier: C 130
Cordier, Mathurin: B 115, B 133, C 92, C 102
Cornu, Gilles and Alis: H 8
Corrigie, dr: D 57
Corrozet, Gilles: D 95, V 51
Cousin, Jean: C 70
Couteau, Antoine: B 153
Cranach, Lucas: L 94, L 95
Cratander, Andreas: E 36
Crespin, Jean: C 6, C 81, L 83, R 47
Crom, Matthieu: B 243
Cyprian, St: D 82, I 8

Dalichamps, Jean: M 62
Damas, Claude: B 4
Dammartin, Comtesse de: B 233, B 234
Daniel, Jacques: L 58
Daniel, Jean: B 59
Dasne, Etienne: B 36
Deauratus, dr: D 57
Denis the Carthusian: M 76
Dentière, Marie: D 4, D 5
Des Gois, Antoine: M 44
Désiré, Artus: A 20, C 97, D 11
Des Périers, Bonaventure: B 40, B 102, B 115, C 138
Desrey, Pierre: P 25, P 26, P 27, P 28, P 29, P 29a, P 30, P 31, P 32, P 33, P 34, R 49
Destournel, Jean: C 1
Divolle, dr: D 57
Dolet, Estienne: B 93, B 94, B 124, B 185, B 261, B 269, B 275, B 276, C 86, D 33, D 34, D 37, E 28, E 30, E 32, E 38, E 47, E 69, H 11, I 31, I 33, L 23, L 24, M 44, M 56, M 83, O 4
Doré, Pierre: D 32, D 55, D 56, D 75, D 76, D 77, D 81, D 84, D 88, L 84, M 56
Du Bellay, René: S 11
Du Bois, Michel: C 73, C 74, C 75, C 76
Du Bois, Simon: C 86, F 7, F 27, F 28, L 83, L 84, L 114, L 115
Du Bois de La Haye, Simon: D 101, M 32
Du Caurroy, Valentin: A 28
Du Chemin, Nicolas: B 106, B 107
Dudé, Charles: I 47a
Du Four, Antoine: J 2, J 3
Dumolin, Guillaume: D 98

Du Mont, T.: C 107
Du Périer, Jean: M 102
Du Pinet, Antoine: B 280, B 281, D 100, D 101, L 87
Du Pré, Galliot: E 26
Durand à Serta, Me: D 11
Du Val, Nicolas: C 100, C 102

Eck, Johann: E 2
Edward VI, King of England: C 24, C 118, V 7
Eleanor, Queen of France: B 221, D 95, S 10
Erasme, Desiderius: A 10, A 35, B 274, E 15, E 35, E 47, E 75
Erp, Henry de: H 9
Espence, Claude d': E 60, E 62, L 84, T 8, T 9
Estauge, Jacques: M 84, T 16
Estienne, Robert: B 39, S 22, S 23
Eustache, Guillaume: B 220

Fame, René: L 2, L 4, L 5, L 6, L 7, L 8
Farel, Guillaume: B 73, C 61, C 63, D 4, E 15, E 57, F 7, F 9, F 12, F 16, F 17, F 21, F 24, F 25, F 28, F 30, G 1, G 27, I 49, I 50, L 85, L 91, L 97, L 98, L 99, L 100, L 101, L 102, L 103, L 104, L 105, L 106, L 107, L 108, L 109, L 110, L 111, L 112, L 117, P 13, P 51, V 53
Farget, Pierre: B 26, B 27, B 31, B 33, B 36, B 38, B 41, B 46, B 52
Felix de Prato: B 75, B 84
Fezendat, Guillaume: M 75
Ficino, Marsilio: D 2
Fisher, John: C 130
Flaminio, Marcantonio: B 18, B 19
Florimond: M 38
Fossetier, Julien: F 50
Foucault, Antoine: V 53
Francis I, King of France: A 11, D 29, D 51, G 25, G 58, L 2, L 26, L 59, L 84, P 41, S 15, T 13, V 1, V 68
François, Marquis de Pont-à-Mousson: V 68
François, Michel: C 129
Frellon, Jean & François: B 111, M 44
Froben, Johann: E 36
Froment, Antoine: D 4, G 1
Froschauer, Christophe: B 282
Furbiti, Guy: F 17

Gabrielle de Bourbon: H 5
Gacy, Jean: G 1
Gaigny, Jean de: B 268, G 58, P 41, P 42, S 15
Garnier, Jean (pastor): G 13
Garnier, Jean (printer): P 40
Gastard, Marie: H 7
Gauchier, Joseph: A 33, A 34, A 35
Gaultherot, Vivant: D 51
Gaultier, Pierre: B 117
Gémeau, Adrien: A 32, G 59, G 60
Gentils, Etienne, prieur de S. Martin: E 1
Georges, sr. de Hallewijn: A 10, E 26
Gerson, Jean: B 217, B 217a, B 218, B 221, C 122, C 123, C 124a, E 85, H 9, I 41, M 1
Girard, Jean: A 21, B 89, B 93, B 122, B 169, C 56, C 136, D 4, E 14, F 21, L 83, M 7, M 41, M 56, O 1, O 2, V 40
Girault, Ambroise: C 112, F 4, I 18
Glapion du Maine, Jean: V 68
Gourmont, Jérôme de: D 74
Granjon, Robert: E 70, M 83
Greban, Arnoul: M 92, M 93, M 94, M 95, M 96, M 97, M 98, M 99, M 100, M 101
Gregory, St: P 26
Gregory Nazianze, St: Q 1
Grenier, Nicole: G 28, G 36, G 37
Gringore, Pierre: B 87, G 45, G 47, G 48, R 39
Grosseteste, Robert: T 2
Groulleau, Estienne: J 10
Gruytrode, Jacobus de: M 76
Guédon, Rémy: I 54
Guéroult, Guillaume: B 3, B 114, B 121, C 9, C 70
Guerric, abbot of Igny: G 58
Guibert, Jean: S 11
Guillard, Charlotte: L 16
Guillaume d'Auvergne: G 59

Habert, François: C 2
Hadrian VI, Pope: D 27
Hangest, Jérôme de: H 2
Henri II, King of France: D 52, E 60, G 28, L 60
Henri, King of Navarre: T 15
Henry VIII, King of England: C 130
Henry, Duke of Brunswick: C 70
Henry, Jean: H 3, H 6

Hervet, Gentian: H 10
Herwagen, Johann: B 278
Heyden, Sebald: D 99, E 76, H 12, L 121,
    M 34, M 35, M 36, M 37, M 38,
    M 39, M 40, M 41
Holbein, Hans: I 5, I 6, I 7, I 8
Hubmaier, Balthazar: C 61
Hus, Jan: C 130

Illiers, Milles d': D 23
Illyricus, Thomas: I 1

Jacques de Milan: B 217
Jannequin, Clément: B 127
Janot, Denis: M 104
Jean Chrysostome, St: I 7, L 97, Q 1
Jean de Saint Victor: H 15
Jeanne de Hornes, vve de Hugues de
    Melun: C 115
Jehannot, Jean: B 233, C 124b, M 85
Jerome, St: J 2, P 26
John Frederick of Saxony: M 66
Jonas, Justus: F 25, L 85
Jordan, Raymond: J 11
Julius II, Pope: C 125, L 28

Kempe, Adrien: B 243
Kerver, Jacques: V 57
Koeln, Wigand: D 27, O 13

La Boulaye, Guillaume de: L 1
La Charité, Catherine de: A 34
Lacu, Jean: L 9
La Fin, Jeanne de: A 33
La Garde, Jean de: J 3
Lalande, Matthieu de: J 12, J 13, L 10,
    L 102
Lambany, Jean: P 8a
Lambert, François: D 100, D 101, D 102,
    L 12, L 113, L 118, M 70, S 8
Landry, François: L 13
Langelier, Arnoul & Charles: C 2, E 53,
    F 49, J 10
La Porte, Jean de: E 67
L'Archer, Jean de: M 64, M 65
La Roche, Alain de: C 129
La Rouge, Françoise: see Lempereur,
    M., Vve de
Lasseré, Louis: L 15, L 16
La Tremoille, Charlotte de: A 35
Le Bret, Guillaume: D 45, L 45, L 49,
    V 76

Le Breton, François: S 29, S 30, S 31
Le Comte de la Croix, Jean: I 57
Le Conte, Jean: L 17
Le Coq, Antoine: C 106
Le Coq, Jean: I 56, Q 4, V 20
Lefèvre d'Étaples, Jacques: B 35, B 39,
    B 44, B 56, B 62, B 63, B 64, B 65,
    B 66, B 68, B 71, B 72, B 74, B 78,
    B 145, B 147, B 150, B 152, B 153,
    B 154, B 155, B 156, B 157, B 158,
    B 159, B 160, B 161, B 162, B 163,
    B 164, B 165, B 166, B 167, B 168,
    B 170, B 171, B 172, B 173, B 175,
    B 178, B 179, B 180, B 181, B 182,
    B 186, B 187, B 188, B 189, B 191,
    B 192, B 193, I 57, J 11
Le Gouez, Zacharie: L 61
Le Grand, Jacques: L 26b, L 27
Le Maistre, Claude: B 18, B 19, B 102,
    B 115
Le Menand, Guillaume: L 74, L 75, L 76,
    L 77
Lempereur, Martin: B 72, B 209, C 83,
    D 4, I 49, I 51, L 88, T 2
Lempereur, Martin, veuve de: B 180
Le Noir, Michel and Philippe: M 95
Le Preux, Poncet: B 15, G 14, G 18, H 9
Le Roux, Nicolas: T 6
Le Roy, François: L 56, L 58
Lesnauderie, Pierre de: L 61
Le Sueur, Nicolas: R 38
Leuze, Nicolas de: B 57
Liege, Jean: L 18
Longis, Jean: G 3, G 4, L 51
Lotrian, Alain: D 43, M 88, M 92, M 95,
    M 98, M 104, M 105, M 108
Louis XII, King of France: L 28, L 32
Louis, Cardinal de Bourbon: C 107
Louise de Bourbon, abbess of Fonte-
    vrault: D 63, L 16
Louvet, Jean: G 25
Lupi Second, Didier: B 123, G 57
Luther, Martin: A 10, B 73, B 78, B 160,
    B 274, C 104, C 130, D 27, D 88,
    E 15, E 57, E 76, F 24, F 25, G 27,
    G 37, G 38, G 47, H 12, I 49, I 50,
    L 85, L 91, L 119, P 13, P 35, S 26,
    S 27, S 28, T 16, V 53

Macault, Antoine: E 16, E 17, E 18
Macho, Julien: B 26, B 27, B 31, B 33,
    B 36, B 38, B 41, B 46, B 52

Maillard, Olivier: G 14
Malingre, Matthieu: B 43, B 167, C 95, C 98, C 99, C 101, C 102, M 6, M 8, M 10, V 8
Manutius, Aldus: I 50
Marchant, Jean: R 43
Marcourt, Antoine: B 273, C 126, M 22, M 24, M 26
Marie de Luxembourg: G 59
Marguerite d'Alençon, Queen of Navarre: A 12, B 77, B 267, F 44, L 26, M 32, M 38, N 1, S 32, T 15
Marguerite de France: L 84
Marie de Bretagne, abbess of Fontevrault: H 6
Marie de Lorraine, Queen of Scotland: B 265
Marnef, Geoffroy de: L 32
Marot, Clément: A 4, B 77, B 82, B 85, B 86, B 90, B 92, B 95, B 96, B 97, B 98, B 99, B 100, B 101, B 102, B 103, B 104, B 105, B 106, B 107, B 108, B 109, B 110, B 111, B 112, B 113, B 114, B 115, B 116, B 117, B 118, B 119, B 120, B 121, B 122, B 124, B 125, B 127, B 128, B 129, B 130, B 131, B 132, B 133, B 134, B 136, B 137, B 138, B 142, B 143, B 144, C 49, C 50, C 51, C 65, C 95, E 17, E 20, E 21, E 22, F 43, F 44, F 44, I 50, M 5, M 37, M 38, M 39, M 40, M 41, M 43, M 44, S 14
Martin, Jean: S 10
Martyr, Pierre: C 79, C 80
Mauburne, Jean: E 1, M 14, M 45, M 46
Maugin, Jean: F 31, F 32
Maurice de Sully: M 47
Mauroy, N.: H 16
Mazurier, Martial: B 1, M 50
Megander, Gaspard: D 66, M 56, M 57
Meigret, Aimé: M 58
Melanchthon, Philippe: C 45, C 79, C 80, M 66, M 67
Menard, Jean: F 23, M 69, M 70
Merlin, Jacques: M 71
Meyer, Sebastien: D 100, D 101, D 102
Michel, Guillaume: M 72
Michel, Jean (writer): M 92, M 93, M 94, M 95, M 96, M 97, M 98, M 99, M 100, M 101, M 102
Michel, Jean (printer): M 43, S 14
Montbrun, Charles de: G 2

Montmorency, Anne de: G 37
Morin, Guy: E 42, E 44, E 45, E 46, E 51
Morin, Martin: D 1
Mornable, Antoine de: B 108
Mortières, Jacques de: S 32
Mundavilla, Petrus de: D 28
Musculus, Wolfgang: M 84

N.N.: E 1, M 14, M 45
Neobar, Conrad: B 246, B 249
Normandie, Laurent de: C 66
Nourry, Claude: B 159, B 162, C 120, L 71

Ochino, Bernardino: O 2
Oecolampadius, Johann: G 1
Olivétan, Pierre Robert: B 40, B 43, B 51, B 54, B 55, B 58, B 59, B 60, B 61, B 79, B 81, B 93, B 94, B 146, B 149, B 167, B 169, B 174, B 176, B 177, B 183, B 184, B 185, B 190, B 194, B 195, B 196, B 197, B 198, B 199, B 200, B 201, B 202, B 203, B 204, B 205, B 206, B 207, B 208, C 39
Otto Heinrich, Duke of Bavaria: O 13

Papillon, Almanque: M 44
Paquot, Henry: D 32
Pasquier, Estienne: B 102, B 115
Paul III, Pope: D 75, D 77
Pesseliere, Pierre: C 108, C 109
Petit, Guillaume: O 8, P 10
Petit, Jean: G 41
Petit, Oudin: G 45, G 53
Philippe Landgrave of Hesse: C 70, M 66
Philippe, Martin & Pierre: B 262
Picard, Jean: P 21
Pinet, Guillaume: P 23
Pisseleu, Charles de: A 28
Poitevin, Jean: B 135, B 137, B 144
Poncher, Etienne, Bishop of Paris: I 44, I 47
Ponisson, François: M 79, P 24
Potin, Jean: H 15
Poulignac, Anne de, comtesse de La Rochefoucault: C 4
Poullain, Valérand: C 68, M 84
Presles, Raoul de: A 26, A 27
Prevost, Benoist: G 37

R., C: B 142
Rabelais, François: G 2
Réal, Jean: B 230, B 231, F 4
Redon, Gilles de: G 43
Regnault, François: D 41, L 39, V 47
Regnault, Jacques: V 53
Regnault, Pierre: B 246, G 44, G 55
Rély, Jean de: B 25, B 28, B 29, B 30,
   B 32, B 34, B 37, B 42, B 45, B 47,
   B 48, B 50, B 53
Renée de Lorraine, abbess: D 53
Rhegius, Urbanus: I 7, I 8, R 45
Richard (Rijckaerts), Jean: G 33
Ricouard, Pierre: M 46
Rihel, Wendelin: C 17, C 30, C 44
Rivrain, Pierre: C 107
Rochefort, Jean de: P 36
Roffet, Estienne: P 41
Roffet, Pierre, Veuve de: C 110, P 44
Rohault, Pierre: C 119
Rome, Jean de: R 50
Ronsard, Louis de: B 221
Ronsard, Pierre de: D 17
Rouillé, Guillaume: M 33
Roussel, Gérard: L 20, R 38
Ruelle, Jean: C 135, D 13, D 32, D 41,
   D 52, D 53, D 56, D 77, D 78, D 89,
   L 7, L 8

Sacon, Jacques: B 32
Sadolet, Jacobo: C 42, D 100
Sagon, François: E 42
Saint Denys, Jean: E 78, M 108b, V 16
Saliat, Pierre: E 19, E 25
Salomon, Jean: F 42
Sarget, Pierre: R 49
Saunier, Antoine: B 213, B 215, B 216
Sauvage, Jean: I 55, S 5
Savetier, Nicolas: B 15
Scève, Maurice: B 92
Schott, Johann: B 271
Schotten, Hermann: S 30
Schuch, Wolfgang: S 8
Sebond, Raymond: S 10
Sellier, Nicolas: G 61
Selve, Jean de: S 11
Sergent, Pierre: E 82, I 32
Sertenas, Vincent: L 51
Seuse, Heinrich: S 16
Seymour, Edward, Duke of Somerset: C 37

Sleidan, Jean: S 18
Soquand, Guichard: E 67
Spiera, Francesco: S 9
Stampe, Maximian: A 12
Stumpf, Jean: S 33
Sturm, Johann: C 59, C 60

Telesforo di Cosenza: L 69
Textor, Benoist: T 7
Thierry, dr: D 57
Thomas à Kempis: I 9
Tonnerre, Françoise de: L 15
Tournes, Claude de: T 16
Tournes, Jean de: B 268, B 275, B 276,
   D 31, E 32, L 25, P 24, T 9
Tours, Pierre de: M 33
Touszele, Jeanne de, abbess: I 5
Trechsel, Melchior & Gaspar: B 241
Trepperel, Jean, veuve de: C 124b, M 85,
   M 106a
Treszet, Claude: L 25

Valdès, Juan de: B 18
Vauzelles, Jean de: A 11, A 12, A 13,
   B 83, B 88, I 5, I 6, I 7, I 8, N 1
Verard, Antoine: B 20, E 13, F 40
Vienne, Philibert de: E 54, E 55, E 56
Viexmont, Claude de: V 22
Vignay, Jean de: V 71, V 72, V 73, V 74,
   V 75, V 76
Vingle, Pierre de: B 159, B 162, B 163,
   B 275, C 99, C 126, E 76, F 26, L 22,
   M 6
Viret, Pierre: B 204, C 39, C 40, F 5,
   F 17, G 1, M 19, M 20, M 21, M 22
Vitrier, Jean: L 108, L 112, V 47
Voirier, Jean: A 6, A 7, A 8
Volcyr de Serouville, Nicolas: I 3, I 4
Vostre, Simon: A 7, T 11

Warnet, Thomas: A 2, A 30, B 7, B 8,
   B 9, B 10, B 11, B 12
Wycliffe, John: C 130
Wyssenbach, Rudolf: C 6

Ximenis, Francesc, Bishop of Elne: X 1

Zwingli, Ulrich: C 83